Bruce Andrews and Charles Bernstein's

L=A=N=G=U=A=G=E

RECENCIES SERIES

Research and Recovery in Twentieth-Century American Poetics

Matthew Hofer, Series Editor

This series stands at the intersection of critical investigation, historical documentation, and the preservation of cultural heritage. The series exists to illuminate the innovative poetics achievements of the recent past that remain relevant to the present. In addition to publishing monographs and edited volumes, it is also a venue for previously unpublished manuscripts, expanded reprints, and collections of major essays, letters, and interviews.

ALSO AVAILABLE IN THE RECENCIES SERIES:

FOR ADDITIONAL TITLES IN THE RECENCIES SERIES,

please visit unmpress.com.

Bruce Andrews and Charles Bernstein's

L=A=N=G=U=A=G=E

THE COMPLETE FACSIMILE

Edited by Matthew Hofer and Michael Golston

University of New Mexico Press   Albuquerque

ISBN 978-0-8263-6154-7 (cloth)

ISBN 978-0-8263-6155-4 (e-book)

ISSN: 2690-7275

Cover illustration and design by Mindy Basinger Hill

Text design by Mindy Basinger Hill

Composed in 10.5/15 point Minion Pro

CONTENTS

INTRODUCTION *Newsletters That Stay News*

Matthew Hofer and Michael Golston

The last week's Packett brought over a News Lettre, whc hath bin
dispersed through all ye country & read at severall coffee houses in this Citty.
1674 Essex Papers Camden I. 216

L=A=N=G=U=A=G=E was conceived as a
bimonthly newsletter, available by subscription
through the mail and stocked in a few select bookstores. Its first twelve issues, divided into three
volumes, ran from February 1978 until December 1980; a fourth volume (which, due to space
restraints, is not included in this reprint) was
published in 1981 as a special issue of the Canadian journal *Open Letter*.[1] Two supplements were
published in June 1980, and a third appeared in
October 1981. Finally, a separate table of contents
was published in 1981.

The first issue weighed in at twenty-eight pages;
the last ran to forty. In an email dated February 17,
2016, Charles Bernstein, who edited the newsletter
with Bruce Andrews, describes how it was produced:

> The first three volumes of
> *L=A=N=G=U=A=G=E* were typed on legal
> size sheets on an IBM Selectric typewriter,
> sprayed to prevent smearing, and then pasted
> into our format by our designer Susan Bee.
> The initial run was offset printed, although
> we often produced additional copies by
> photocopying.[2]

Each 8½ by 17–inch sheet was folded in half and
fastened to the others by two staples punched

through the centerfold, making a thin, off-white
square. The newsletter featured neither table of contents nor information about contributors and contained only a scant editorial note on its last page,
listing the names of the editors, volume and issue
numbers, and Bernstein's address in New York City.
The front of each newsletter was its first page (the
newsletter was not paginated), and its first entry
began immediately beneath the large bolded title,

L=A=N=G=U=A=G=E

underlined twice and followed by its date of issue.
Abrupt and utilitarian, with neither spine nor
cover, the newsletter felt handmade and ephemeral,
almost as if it were meant to be disposed of after
the reader was finished with it.[3]

But what, after all, is a *newsletter*? The passage
quoted in the headnote above records the earliest
usage of the term listed in the *Oxford English Dictionary*, which defines a newsletter as, "a letter specially written to communicate the news of the day,
common in the latter part of the 17th and beginning of the 18th century; also, a printed account
of the news (sometimes with a blank space left for
private additions)." Originally, newsletters were
concerned with current events and contemporary
cultural and political issues, as opposed to the more

historical and classical bents of the academy. They were topical and serialized the changing moods and shifting modes of the moment; they were intended to keep up with what was happening, to record the latest and to speculate on the next.

$L=A=N=G=U=A=G=E$ in many ways follows this genealogy. Its mission, as articulated in correspondence between its east-coast editors Andrews and Bernstein, and their west-coast interlocutor Ron Silliman, was primarily to focus on poetics—the newsletter was explicitly *not* a poetry journal—and to bring attention to bear on contemporary issues, writers, and trends that were either being ignored by mainstream and academic literary journals and magazines, or that by virtue of their cross-disciplinary or other-disciplinary perspectives resisted the narrow editorial criteria of more conventional "literary" publications. In a letter to Silliman dated February 14, 1977, Bernstein explains that he wants the newsletter

> to include (a) work that wld not ordinarily appear in a "poetry" context, i.e., visual work, photograms, related "texts" from musicians, painters, performance artists, philosophy or sociology, letters, journal entries, &c. (esp. from people whose letters, journals, &c. are not often seen), found texts & visuals, significant out-of-print poetry & poetics & other kinds of texts from recent & far past; (b) critical thought/writing, esp in non-expository forms, but also, in general, to increase the scope of what normally gets put in a poetry magazine to something more on the level of the old sense of "letters" (e.g. men & women of letters) so that political & social & ethical views by various people wld be solicited & printed. . . .[4]

This was not the standard fare of literary journals of the mid-1970s; in terms of future developments in poetry and poetics, the editorial genre bending and hybridity of $L=A=N=G=U=A=G=E$ were both groundbreaking and prescient, evolving different slants on an alternative canon. In this "new thing" newsletter, contemporary "men & women of letters" from a broad range of backgrounds would find a literary venue in which to rethink poetics and to discuss, argue about, and review the writing that was being provoked by contemporary shifting aesthetic, political, and philosophical preoccupations.[5]

Broadly speaking, the individual issues of $L=A=N=G=U=A=G=E$ adhered closely to "that spectrum of work that places its attention in some primary way on language, ways of making meaning that take neither 'form' (syntax, grammar, process & program, shape) or 'content' (vocabulary, information, subject matter), or their relation, for granted," as was stated in the editors' notification flyer.[6] More specifically, Bernstein explained in an interview with Susan Howe that he wanted work that addressed

> how language shapes the way we see the world—how we come to see the world in terms of language. . . . [Y]ou can deal with language as this material we are pervaded by, which we as writers take as the material with which we do our work: how we ourselves are created out of the ways this material is used.[7]

Or, as Andrews put it in the same interview,

> what I am interested in doing is stopping the sense of transparency in language, that language is this neutral thing that people don't have a part in. Because it is people that make up language and change language and in that way change reality.[8]

Here we see the activist and political aspects of the $L=A=N=G=U=A=G=E$ project and its roots in Sapir-Whorf, the early Wittgenstein, and Neo-Marxist notions of language as ideological production. According to this view, the world and the human subject are *constructed* through language, and both writer and reader have a critical role to play in interrogating that dynamic.[9] For readers for whom language had always been self-evidently "transparent" and poetry the staging of an unmediated subjectivity, the shift in $L=A=N=G=U=A=G=E$ to an emphasis on grammar, word, and syntax could feel disconcertingly provocative or cold.

Volume I, No. 4, dated August 1978—a Louis Zukofsky feature—exemplifies what was at stake in $L=A=N=G=U=A=G=E$. It begins with a two-paragraph essay on Zukofsky, written by Silliman. Zukofsky was just beginning to be recuperated after decades of critical neglect, and the Language poets considered him, along with Gertrude Stein, among their most important modernist precursors (as against the canonical figures of the day like T. S. Eliot or Wallace Stevens).[10] The essay begins with three long sentence fragments, as if Silliman were ticking off items in the middle of a conversation:

> The first (& for a long time the only) to read Pound & Williams with what we wld recognize as modern eye & ear. Ear tuned tautly toward a double function: *intrinsic*, language as he found it (i.e., parole); *extrinsic*, musical composition, determining wholeness, aesthetic consistency, perfect rest. But for whom language began with sight (thus *Bottom*—love : reason :: eye : mind—in wch love contains all the significations Benjamin, so like LZ, gave the term *aura*). (this volume, p. 101)

Silliman bowls right in, assuming his reader's familiarity with Zukofsky's densely written and out-of-print study of Shakespeare and Walter Benjamin's theory of the aura, still relatively esoteric at the time. He follows this with a diagram illustrating how Zukofsky's "language (L) synthesizes polar impulses rising dialectically from an equally problematic material base" (this volume, p. 101).

The rapid-fire informality of address, casual name-dropping, glancing references, and citation of Marxist and structuralist criticism suggest the intimacy of a personal letter while the focus is distinctly on the new, if not on the news. The piece is followed by Robert Grenier's "THINK SUN AND SEE SHADOW," which he describes as "(4's and 5's from) Louis Zukofsky," comprised of nine lines, five of which have five words apiece and four of which have four, and each of which is cribbed from Zukofsky's "*A*." This in turn is followed by "L.Z.," nine short sentences from Ronald Johnson that read like a book blurb: "All men write poetry, but few are poets." "Behind the wheel, fiddling the syllables, the finest ears in the business is heading somewhere 100,000 years an hour (or so). Do you not hear them thunder?" (this volume, p. 103). Mixed metaphors and the lack of grammatical agreement make this feel like a sketch or a rough draft. The newsletter begins in this off-the-cuff, in-media-res, partial, breathless, sui generis, mixed-mode manner.

The fourth item is obscurely titled "31 ASSERTIONS, SLOWLY." As if he were writing a book review, Alan Davies begins with a full bibliographic citation of a new title by Christopher Dewdney followed by a list of 31 gnomic statements:

> The air is geology.
>
> Eye is born in its sac.

Towns are beaches onto which wash.

Preordination fosters statues.

Organisms are preferred which voice without
    breaking open their layers, rather case
    in them. (this volume, p. 103)

And so on. It is unclear what these statements have to do with Dewdney's *Spring Trances in the Control Emerald Night*. Are they quotations from the text? Are they a poetic response to it? If this is indeed a book review, what exactly is the reader supposed to take away from it? Less a review than a reaction, Davies's piece reads like its own freestanding work.

Suffice it to say, the writing and the editing of Vol. I, No. 4 are adventurous. The issue includes "On Jargon," three long paragraphs on the difficulties of theoretical writing that are cut from an article published by Fredric Jameson the year before in *The Minnesota Review*; a technical discussion of schizophrenic writing by John Ensslin; Stephen Fredman's "How Far Apart," a meditation on distance and consistency in poetry, printed entirely in italics and consisting of eight rambling paragraphs of clauses and phrases stitched together with dashes; and a long letter to the editor by Michael Frederick Tolson, in which the author replaces every "e" with an "(f)":

2 bruc(f) andr(f)ws & th(f) r(f)ad(f)rs of
    l=a=n=g=u=a=g=(f),
1st r(f)action as r(f)spons(f) 2 r(f)vi(f)w of
book unlab(f)l(f)d, unnam(f)d, 2.

The issue also includes Andrews's edit of Richard Foreman's manifesto-like essay on one of his performance pieces (published without Foreman's permission, but discovered by him and received enthu-

siastically) and Michael Gottlieb's review of a book written to accompany a dance event. It ends with a bibliography compiled by Andrews listing articles from forty-nine recent journals, including periodicals from music studies, psychology, political history, philosophy, and performance studies, as well as poetry and poetics magazines and *The New York Review of Books*. Its last page/back cover features a poorly reproduced graphic by Laszlo Moholy-Nagy.

In other words, *L=A=N=G=U=A=G=E* Vol. I, No. 4 neatly answers Bernstein's call for a newsletter that would include "work that wld not ordinarily appear in a 'poetry' context," and certainly much of the writing brings its readers bang up against the material fact of language rendered strange and palpable. The newsletters are clearing houses for all manner of information, speculation, exploration, reaction, and critique; one never knows what to expect or what might come next. A collage of correspondence and an ongoing map of reading, *L=A=N=G=U=A=G=E* resists any tidy categorization. Beyond sharing a keen awareness of the contemporary moment and the greater world around them, the writers who appear in the newsletter do not coalesce into anything resembling a group, school, or movement. It also should be noted that the newsletter championed and explored poetics issues emanating out of a variety of traditions, including neglected Jewish writers such as Stein, Zukofsky, Larry Eigner, and Hannah Weiner, and that the editors imagined issues (none of which materialized) focusing on and/or edited by women, gay male poets, and indigenous and third-world peoples.[11]

L=A=N=G=U=A=G=E was meant neither as a be-all nor an end-all: its contributors reflected the troubled boundaries of poetry and poetics at that time—on the way, at least ideally, to changing them. In the sheer scope of their adventurousness, the *L=A=N=G=U=A=G=E* newsletters remain compelling reading, and they fill an important gap in the history of American writing. They are also models for recognizing difference and refashioning the dynamics of collaboration. In them, we see the gradual working out of a new direction in poetics, one firmly oriented toward the present moment and its messy contingencies, prepared to deal with the contemporary world on its own terms.

Notes

1. Running to 165 pages and published in an entirely different format, the 31 essays collected in *Open Letter* 5.1 as volume four of *L=A=N=G=U=A=G=E* are materially and conceptually very different from those that had been previously published in the newsletter. Bruce Andrews and Charles Bernstein compiled the material for the special issue in 1981, but it was published in winter 1982.

2. Bernstein, email message to editors, February 17, 2016.

3. In a letter to Ron Silliman dated February 17, 1977, Bernstein quotes coeditor Andrews as to "goals: more pages, sturdier cover, nicer paper, more copies. not a goal: more than three times a year (i think that's all that's sustainable)" (Hofer and Golston, *The Language Letters*, ed. Matthew Hofer and Michael Golston [Albuquerque: University of New Mexico Press, 2019], 176).

The sturdier cover and nicer paper appeared only with the journal format of volume four, and the newsletter came out six times a year.

4. Hofer and Golston, *The Language Letters*, 176–77.

5. Hofer and Golston, *The Language Letters*, 177.

6. Hofer and Golston, *The Language Letters*, xiii.

7. Bernstein, "The Pacifica Interview," quoted in Hofer and Golston, *The Language Letters*, 367.

8. Bernstein, "The Pacifica Interview," quoted in Hofer and Golston, *The Language Letters*, 370.

9. "Something that I think a lot of this writing tends to try to undercut is the notion of a sovereign self and a sovereign subject as the center of meaning in a text—which I think again is not only a limited and limiting notion, but a notion that derives from the operation of an oppressive social system that we all are living under" (Andrews, "The Pacifica Interview," quoted in Hofer and Golston, *The Language Letters*, 369).

10. The first major collection of criticism on Zukofsky, *Louis Zukofsky: Man and Poet* (Orono, ME: National Poetry Foundation), edited by Carroll F. Terrell, appeared in 1979.

11. For this discussion see, for example, letters 39, 40, 41, 42, and 44 in Hofer and Golston, *The Language Letters*.

L=A=N=G=U=A=G=E

TABLE OF CONTENTS

1978 - 1981

Bruce Andrews, "Proof," on the work of John Wieners.

Rae Armantrout,"'Why Don't Women Do Language-Oriented Writing?'"

Shahin Ghiray, "Circle Ode" (graphic).

APRIL 1978, Number 2

Roland Barthes, "Writing Degree Zero" (an excerpt).

Barrett Watten Feature:
    Bob Perelman — on Watten.
    Barrett Watten, "Note".
    Watten Bibliography.

Craig Watson — on Helmut Heissenbüttel.

Ed Friedman, "Pure Stealing" (journal work).

Michael Lally, "Three 'New' Poets," on Donald Quatrale,
    Diane Ward & Carole Korzeniowsky.

Ron Silliman, "Breastwork," on Carole Korzeniowsky.

John Perlman, "Letter to the Editor".

Charles Bernstein, "The Telling," on Laura (Riding) Jackson.

William Corbett, "Notes on Michael Palmer's 'Without Music'".

John Taggart, "Letter to the Editor".

Susan B. Laufer, "Photograms" (on Moholy-Nagy and photograms).

Bruce Andrews, "The Politics of Scoring," on Ernest Robson.

Michael Gottlieb, "Dolch Words," on Kit Robinson.

Steve McCaffery, "Repossessing the Word" (interview excerpt
    on writing & commodity fetishism, with editors' preface).

Ted Greenwald — on Anthologies: "But I Won't".

Jackson Mac Low Feature:
    Barbara Baracks — on Mac Low.
    Mac Low Bibliography.
    Jackson Mac Low, "Museletter" (response to questions).

JUNE 1978, Number 3

Bernadette Mayer, "Experiments" (workshop instructions).

Alan Sondheim, from "Heroes, How They File Past" — on Cage, Duchamp, ideology).

Rosmarie Waldrop — on her poetics, plus bibliography.

Harry Crosby, "Shadows of the Sun," diary excerpt.

Abigail Child, "Cross Referencing the Units of Sight and Sound / Film and Language".

Keith Waldrop — on Anne-Marie Albiach.

Lyn Hejinian, "If Written is Writing".

Loris Essary, "Letter to the Editor".

"Articles" — a Catalog/Bibliography of recent articles on language and related aesthetic and social issues, from 54 journals: Part One. Compiled by Bruce Andrews.

Nick Piombino, "Writing and Self-Disclosure".

Ernest Robson, "Letter to the Editor".

Douglas Messerli, "On the Poetry of Loris Essary".

Ray DiPalma Feature:
    Ray DiPalma, "Tying and Untying" (text on his work).
    Charles Bernstein, "The Alphabet of Stride" (on DiPalma's published work).
    DiPalma Bibliography.

Ted Pearson, "A Vacant Lot," on John Cage.

Bruce Andrews, "Layout," on Michael Frederick Tolson and conceptualism in writing.

James Sherry, "Postscript," on 'The Politics of the Referent'.

Peter Seaton, "Signification".

AUGUST 1978, Number 4

Louis Zukofsky Feature:
    Texts by Ron Silliman, Robert Grenier, Ronald Johnson.

Alan Davies — on Christopher Dewdney: "31 Assertions Slowly".

Fredric Jameson, "On Jargon" (parallels between poetry and theoretical writing).

John Ensslin, "Schizophrenic Writing".

Stephen Fredman, "How Far Apart?"

Michael Frederick Tolson, "Letter to the Editor".

Ron Silliman Feature:
   Ron Silliman, "For L=A=N=G=U=A=G=E".
   Barrett Watten, "Mohawk and Ketjak".
   Silliman Bibliography.

Eric Mottram, "Official Poetry & Conformist Entertainment".

Richard Foreman, "Trying to be Centered...on the Circumference"
   (notes on his work).

Peter Mayer, "Poetics of the Alphabet" (on letter symbolism and
   mouthshapes, etc.).

Bruce Andrews — on Loris Essary: "Line Sites".

Michael Gottlieb — on Douglas Dunn (dance / writing parallels).

Joseph Timko, "The Geometry of the Beautiful Horizon".

"Articles, Part Two" — Bibliography, cataloguing 49 additional
   journals.

Laszlo Moholy-Nagy, "Collage" (graphic).

OCTOBER 1978, Number 5

Robert Grenier Feature:
   Robert Grenier, "Hedge-Crickets-Sing".
   Barrett Watten, "Grenier's 'Sentences'".
   Grenier Bibliography.

Charles Bernstein, "Making Words Visible," on the work of
   Hannah Weiner.

Jed Rasula, "Statement on Reading in Writing".

Carole Korzeniowsky & Ted Pearson — on Bob Perelman, '7 Works'.

Ray DiPalma, "Some Notes on Thomas A. Clark" & Clark Bibliography.

Dick Higgins, "Alan Sondheim and the Knee-Jerk School of Criticism".

Bruce Andrews, "The Hum of Words," on Rosmarie Waldrop.

Alan Davies — on Larry Eigner: "The Amplifier, Silence".

Michael Palmer Feature:
   Michael Palmer, from 'Notes for Echo Lake'.
   Steve McCaffery, "Michael Palmer: A Language of Language".
   Palmer Bibliography.

James Sherry — on Curtis Faville: "A Collect".

Ronald Johnson, "Basil Bunting: 'Take a Chisel to Write'".

Nick Piombino, "Writing as Reverie".

Ron Silliman, "from 'Language Writing'".

DECEMBER 1978, Number 6

"Reading Stein" — A special feature on readings of Gertrude
   Stein's 'Tender Buttons'.
   Texts by:
         Carl Andre
         Rae Armantrout
         Michael Davidson
         Larry Eigner
         Robert Grenier
         Jackson Mac Low
         Steve McCaffery
         Bob Perelman
         Peter Seaton

Ron Silliman, "Benjamin Obscura" — excerpt of essay on Walter
   Benjamin.

Craig Watson, "Statement" (on intention and address).

Jed Rasula, "Notes on Genre".

Bruce Andrews, "Code Words" — on Roland Barthes' 'Image-Music-
   Text'.

Steve Benson — on Bernard Welt's 'Wave'.

Tom Raworth Feature:
   Rod Mengham, "Logarhythms" — on 'Logbook'.
   Raworth Bibliography.

Charles Bernstein & Susan B. Laufer, "Style" (on normative grammar).

VOLUME TWO :

MARCH 1979, Number 7.

Steve McCaffery, "Sound Poetry".

Ted Greenwald Feature:
    Bill Berkson, "In Ted Greenwald".
    Ted Greenwald, "Spoken" (on his work).
    Greenwald Bibliography.

Susan B. Laufer, "Ruscha's Books and Seriality".

Douglas Messerli, "Anatomy of Self" — on Bernadette Mayer.

Tina Darragh — on writing procedures.

Alan Davies, Susan Howe, Kit Robinson:
    "Rae Armantrout: 'Extremities' (3 Views)".

Nick Piombino, "Writing and Remembering".

"Non-Poetry" — A number of writers were asked to list or briefly
    discuss non-poetry books read recently that have had a
    significant influence on their thinking or writing.
    Responses from:
        Steve Benson
        Cris Cheek
        Abigail Child
        Robert Creeley
        Ray DiPalma
        Steve Fraccaro
        Ted Greenwald
        Lyn Hejinian
        Susan Howe
        P. Inman
        Michael Lally
        Gerrit Lansing
        Harley Lond
        Kirby Malone &
        Chris Mason
        Tom Mandel
        Steve McCaffery
        Douglas Messerli
        Charles North
        Michael Palmer
        Ron Silliman
        John Taggart
        Joseph Timko

Bernard Noël, from "The Outrage Against Words".

OCTOBER 1979, Number 9/10

The Politics of Poetry:

A special double issue, grounded in the desire to focus attention and encourage further discussion on the political dimensions of current writing. A number of writers are asked to give their view of what qualities writing has or could have that contribute to an understanding or critique of society, seen as a capitalist system. Statements & texts from:

Kathy Acker, "Notes on Writing — from the Life of Baudelaire".

Bruce Andrews, "Writing Social Work & Political Practice".

Barbara Barg.

Charles Bernstein, "The Dollar Value of Poetry".

Bruce Boone, "Writing, Power and Activity".

David Bromige, "Writing the Wrong".   -

Don Byrd.

Cris Cheek, Kirby Malone, Marshall Reese, "Career Wrist".

Mark Chinca, "Some Thoughts Toward a Materialist Poetics".

Michael Davidson.

Alan Davies.

Terry Eagleton, "Aesthetics and Politics".

Larry Eigner.

Brian Fawcett, "Agent of Language".

P. Inman.

Michael Lally.

John Leo, "/CAPITAL/   /WRITING/".

Chris Mason, "Learning Reading As A Second Language".

Steve McCaffery, "From the Notebooks".

Michael Palmer, "The Flower of Capital".

Robert Rakoff — on Marshall Sahlins, 'Culture and Practical
     Reason'.

Jed Rasula, "The Money of the Mind" — on Marc Shell's 'The
     Economy of Literature'.

Peter Seaton, "An American Primer".

James Sherry, "A,B,$".

Ron Silliman, "If by 'Writing' We Mean Literature" & Reply to
    Jackson Mac Low on writing and socialism.

Alan Sondheim — Reply to Dick Higgins.

Lorenzo Thomas, "Is It Xerox or Memorex?"

Barrett Watten, "Writing and Capitalism".

Hannah Weiner, "Capitalistic Useless Phrases After Endless".

VOLUME THREE

JANUARY 1980, Number 11

Alan Davies, "This predilection for the mind in art. Where did
    I get it?"

Charles Bernstein, "The Objects of Meaning" (from 'Reading Cavell
    Reading Wittgenstein').

Peter Seaton Feature:
    Peter Seaton, "Texte".
    Seaton Bibliography.

Reviews and Notes (Feature section of brief discussions):

    Ron Silliman, "Zyxt" — on 'The Poets' Encyclopedia'.
    Charles Bernstein — on Arakawa & Madeleine Gins, 'The Mechanism
        of Meaning'.
    Tim Dlugos— on John Ashbery.
    Gail Sher, "An Exorcism of Representational Language" (on Beau
        Beausoleil).
    Bill Berkson — on Steve Benson.
    Maureen Owen — on Rachelle Bijou.
    Bill Corbett, "Seventeen Titles Joe Brainard will use one day".
    Madeleine Burnside — on David Bromige.
    Paul Green, 'Lust', on Paul Buck.
    John Taggart — on Thomas A. Clark.
    Christopher Dewdney — 'Own Face', on Clark Coolidge.
    Clark Coolidge, "A Note".
    James Sherry, 'Xa', on Tina Darragh & Doug Lang.
    Artie Gold — on Christopher Dewdney.
    Steve Hamilton, 'Je Suis Ein Americano', on Tim Dlugos.

James Sherry — on Lynne Dreyer's 'Letters'.
Kris Hemensley — on Larry Eigner's 'Country/Harbor/Quiet/Act/
    Around'.
Abigail Child — 'Lined Up Bulk Senses', on Eigner.
Andrew Kelly — 'Disappearing Work', on Barbara Einzig.
David Bromige — on Einzig.
Robert Kelly — on a Poetry of Information & Allen Fisher.
Bob Holman — 'The Telephone Book', on Ed Friedman.
Ken Bullock — on David Gitin.
Bruce Boone, "Remarks on Narrative: The Example of Robert Glück's
    Poetry".
Steve Benson — 'Local Color / Eidetic Deniers', on Michael
    Gottlieb.
Michael Gottlieb — on Robert Grenier.
James Sherry — on Lyn Hejinian's 'Gesualdo'.
Lorenzo Thomas, "An Afro-American Word Sculptor" (on Lance
    Jeffers).
Larry Wendt — 'Snake Train', on Velimir Khlebnikov.
P. Inman — on Doug Lang's 'Magic Fire Chevrolet'.
Michael Scholnick — on Gregory Masters.
Kris Hemensley — on Duncan McNaughton.
Robert Kelly — on Thomas Meyer.
Giulia Niccolai, from "Substitution".
Bill Corbett — on Lorine Niedecker.
Karl Kempton — on Kenneth Patchen.
Rae Armantrout — 'a.k.a.', on Bob Perelman.
Charles North, "Words from F.T. Prince".
Gary Lenhart — 'Down and Back', on Kit Robinson.
Henry Hills — 'Sitting Up, Standing, Taking Steps', on Ron
    Silliman.
Robert Kelly — on John Taggart's 'Dodeka'.
Karl Kempton — on 'Tecken'.
Luigi Ballerini & Richard Milazzo, "The Monological Mirror".
Ed Friedman — on Susie Timmons.
Anthony Barnett — on Rosmarie Waldrop.
Alan Davies — 'Theory of Emotion', on Diane Ward.
Bruce Andrews, "The Light American" (from Diane Ward).
Rod Mengham — 'Double or Quit', on Geoffrey Ward.
David Benedetti — on Barrett Watten.
Tina Darragh — on Hannah Weiner's 'Virgin'.

Nick Piombino, "Writing and Experiencing".

E.C.D.C., "Now That's What I'd Call Political Writing" (graphic).

Steve Benson, "Letter to the Editor".

Kirby Malone & Marshall Reese, "festival of (dis)appearing art(s)".

Michael Lally Feature:
  Michael Lally, "My Work".
  Lally Bibliography.
  Bruce Andrews, "Self Writing / I (lucky thought)".

JUNE 1980, Number 12

Bruce Andrews, "Misrepresentation" (a text for 'The Tennis Court Oath' of John Ashbery).

Susan Howe — on P. Inman's 'Platin'.

Barrett Watten, "Object Status" (with Tom Raworth letter).

Lee Sherry, "Painting the Painting".

Fred Londier, "Letter to the Editor".

Clark Coolidge Feature:
  David Bromige, "Clark Coolidge, Weathers".
  Coolidge Bibliography.

Anselm Hollo, "Some Notes & Quotes (out of some of the poetry life near the end of the 20th)".

Curtis Faville, "Letter to the Editor".

Symposium: "The Favorite Malice" (on 'ontology and reference in contemporary Italian poetry') — a report, with texts by Antonio Porta, Angelo Lumelli, Luigi Ballerini, Stefano Agosti, Jacques Garelli.

Karl Young — from "Notes toward a Study of the Design and Manufacture of Books".

Bob Cobbing, "Notions & Notations" (on sound / performance works).

Charles North, "No Other Way" (on James Schuyler).

Craig Watson — on Claude Royet-Journoud.

Christopher Dewdney, "Homographs and the Discharge of Connotation in the Poem" & "Fractal Diffusion".

Don Byrd, "Reading Olson".

David Trotter, "Voices-Off" (on Rod Mengham & John Wilkinson).

Johanna Drucker — on Marshall Reese: "(Process) Note: The Connection (Or, how far is it from New York to Baltimore via California)".

Joseph Timko, "Unnature" (In Memory of Roland Barthes).

Alan Davies, "Essai A Clef" (on Barthes).

DECEMBER 1980, Number 13

Ron Silliman, "Rewriting Marx".

Steve McCaffery, "Blood. Rust. Capital. Bloodstream."

Brian Fawcett, "Fugitive Causes" (on Lawrence Kearney).

Chris Mason & Marshall Reese, "'Wrench' Wrenched" (on Kirby Malone).

Charles Bernstein, "Semblance" (on reference, composition, and experience).

Diane Ward — on Peter Seaton.

Lydia Davis, "Blanchot".

Paul Green — on William Pryor.

Tom Beckett & Allan Tinker — Notes on Robert Grenier.

Larry Wendt, "Charles Amirkhanian's 'Lexical Music'".

Bernadette Mayer, "Lyn Hejinian's 'My Life'".

Ken Edwards, "Pack the Shuffling" (on Allen Fisher).

Bruce Andrews, "And For Anything That I Could Call My Own Thinking" (excerpts from Frank Kuenstler's 'Lens').

Gino Severini, "Futurist Ideograph" (translated by Ron Padgett from 1914 essay) & graphic.

Jackson Mac Low, "An answer to some remarks of Ron Silliman about politics & my supposed position".

Women Writers Union, "Statement of Purpose".

Peter Schjeldahl, "Poetry: A Job Description".

Susan Howe — on Maureen Owen.

Nick Piombino, "Writing and Conceiving".

Abigail Child, "Film Since:" (on her films).

Andrew Kelly, "Taste, Form".

Lynne Dreyer, "I Started Writing..." (historical note).

Michael Gottlieb, "Piece Together Broken Sweat / Mild Concern" (on Ted Greenwald).

Roger LaPorte, from "Fugue".

David Benedetti, "The Poem Beginning What It Is".

Rae Armantrout, "Under the Bridge" (on Carla Harryman).

Gerald Burns, "A Thing about Language".

Alan Davies, "Private Enigma in the Opened Text".

Brita Bergland, from 'Censored Texts' (graphic).

VOLUME FOUR

1981: Special L=A=N=G=U=A=G=E issue of Open Letter

Contents:

Charles Bernstein, "Thought's Measure".

Jackson Mac Low, "'Language Centered'".

Peter Seaton, "How To Read IV".

Alan Davies & Nick Piombino, "The Indeterminate Interval: From History to Blur"

Bob Perelman, "1-10" (on Barrett Watten).

Gianni Vattimo, "from 'On the Way to Silence (Heidegger and the Poetic Word)'".

Craig Watson, "Thought, Word, Deed: Meditations for a Field Theory (1970-1980).

Ron Silliman, "The Political Economy of Poetry".

Jed Rasula, "from 'Poetry in the Tropics: A Political History of Poetics'".

Tina Darragh, "Howe" (on Susan Howe).

Larry Eigner, "Letter to the Editors".

Hiromi Fujii, "Existential Architecture and the Role of Geometry".

Steve Benson, "Approaches Kathy Acker".

Kathy Acker, "The Invisible Universe".

Gerrit Lansing, "Production as Metaphor, and 'Nature' in Baudrillard's Mirror".

Robert Grenier, "Robert Creeley's 'Later'".

Kit Robinson, "French Dents".

Paul A. Green, "Poetics of the Paranormal?"

Bernard Heidsieck, "Sound Poetry How?"

Tom Mandel, "Leads".

James Sherry, "Limits of Grammar".

Cris Cheek, "Some Books".

Augusto de Campos, "Eye & Breath" (on Cummings).

Madeleine Burnside, "from 'Alignment as a Conceit, A Book of Drawings'".

Bruce Boone, "Writing's Current Impasse and the Possibilities for Renewal".

Barrett Watten, "Method and Surrealism: The Politics of Poetry".

Alan Sondheim, "Orange County California and the Economics of Language".

Renato Barelli, "A Word on Spatola's 'Zeroglyphics'".

Gerald Burns, "Written Art".

Michael Gottlieb, "Regarded, Become".

Bruce Andrews, "Constitution / Writing, Politics, Language, the Body".

SUPPLEMENTS

Supplement Number One: The Politics of the Referent

Essays reprinted from the symposium edited by Steve McCaffery for the Canadian journal, Open Letter, in 1977 (Third Series, No. 7) —

Contents:

Charles Bernstein & Bruce Andrews, "Introductory Note".

Steve McCaffery, "The Death of the Subject: The Implications of Counter-Communication in Recent Language-Centered Writing".

Bruce Andrews, "Text and Context".

Ray DiPalma, "Crystals".

Ron Silliman, "For Open Letter".

Charles Bernstein, "Stray Straws and Straw Men".

Supplement Number Two: Some Recent British Poetry Magazines

Compiled by Cris Cheek.

Supplement Number Three: October 1981

"The Politics of Poetry: A Supplement" —

Ron Silliman, "Disappearance of the Word, Appearance of the World," reprinted from A Hundred Posters.

Charles Bernstein, "Three or Four Things I Know About Him," reprinted from A Hundred Posters.

Bruce Andrews & Charles Bernstein, "Pacifica Interview on Politics," transcript edited from interview broadcast over WBAI-FM, Pacifica Radio, New York City.

L=A=N=G=U=A=G=E

Table of Contents: 1978-1981.

Charles Bernstein & Bruce Andrews, editors.

All issues available. Volume Four: $6; institutions,
    $8. Volumes Two and Three: $8 each. Volume One:
    $12. Any individual issue of Volume One (#s 1-6):
    $5; individual issues of Volume Two and Three (#s
    7-13) or Supplements: $3.

All queries & checks to: Charles Bernstein,
    464 Amsterdam Avenue, New York, NY 10024.

L=A=N=G=U=A=G=E has been supported by subscriptions, donations,
and grants from the National Endowment for the Arts, the
Coordinating Council of Literary Magazines, and the New York
State Council on the Arts; as well as contributions to the
production by Susan B. Laufer, James Sherry, Sally Silvers, Nick
Piombino, Michael Gottlieb, Peter Seaton, Ray DiPalma, Betsi
Brandfass, Sigmund Laufer, and Alan Davies.

Distributed with the cooperation of the Segue Foundation. Write
for their free catalog: 300 Bowery, New York, NY 10012.

EIGNER

Approaching things
Some Calculus
How figure it Of Everyday Life
Experience

No really perfect optimum mix, anyway among some thousands or many of distinctive or distinguishable things (while according to your capacity some minutes, days or hours 2, 4 or 6 people, say, are company rather than crowds), and for instance you can try too hard or too little. But beyond the beginning or other times and situations of scarcity, with material (things, words) more and more dense around you, closer at hand, easier and easier becomes invention, combustion, increasingly spontaneous. And when I got willing enough to stop anywhere, though for years fairly in mind had been the idea and aim of long as possible works about like the desire to live for good or have a good (various?) thing never end, then like walking down the street noticing things a poem would extend itself.

Any amount, degree, of perfection is a surprise. yet you have to be concerned with it some, by the way, be observant - serendipity. Also, though - and there's the kaleidoscopic, things put together like flying a kite - too much of or too frequent a good is distraction, or anyway, I could go blind or be knocked out. What if up north the midnight sun were all year round? While - to repeat - language is a surprising tool, recently I turned around and was kind of astonished what can be done with it, what has been. Kites, birds.

But behind words and whatever language comes about are things (language I guess develops mainly by helping cope with them), things and people, and words can't bring people in India or West Virginia above the poverty line, say, and I can't want more.

Well, how does (some of) the forest go together with the trees. How might it, maybe. Forest of possibilities (in language anyway) - ways in and ways out. Near and far - wide and narrow (circles) Your neighborhood and how much of the world otherwise. Beginning, ending and continuing. As they come, what can things mean? Why expect a permanent meaning? What weights, imports? Nothing is ever quite as obvious as anything else, at least in context. A poem can't be too long, anything like an equatorial highway girdling the thick rotund earth, but is all right and can extend itself an additional bit if you're willing enough to stop anywhere. And I feel my way in fiddling a little, or then sometimes more, on the roof of the burning or rusting world.

"... to care and not to care ... to sit still" Careful of earth air and water mainly perhaps, and other lives, but some (how many?) other things too. Walden, ah! The dancer and the dance. What first (off)? What next? What citizens how come in

    Poetry considerateing,   Prose adventure (essay?) ?
    Many/and/various/mixes.

LARRY EIGNER

LARRY EIGNER NOTES

                          "Who wants to see himself"
I see...

    the noun states accent in air

    so much that an "on" or "hard" takes on
    solidity of noun at line-end

    the prepositional phrases: a thought he's
    using only one unit, over & over again
                     (Cezanne?)

    every line hit to a conclusion; the prepositional phrase
    pushed up against its noun-wall; the single noun,
    preposition, whichever, its own wall; each wall
    a cut in space   "a wall was thick

               air was a wall"

    a nounal/prepositional universe. verb slides...

    an invisible & steadying "is" behind everything

      "my own hands are distractions"

    all particles in the pile soon to reach
    nounal state

                    "Names are the colored barrels
                     we trip over inside."
                                            --C. Olson

        "or arrows

             slopes   room for all

                  particles
                              outlines"

each line a new mind (focus)
rather than divisions determined by breaks
of sound, syntax, etc.

air, his medium. air, the medium of voice (waves) and
image (light) immediately inward/outward, as one.

the word "air" & its immediate prepositioning

the sub-vocally/sub-optically heard/seen

     "there is everything to speak of
       but the words are words"

these "scenes" don't exist, never have.
these words comb them through mind.
The poem is built.

pages, hammers, boards, trees, garage, cars
horse, bowels
                : his tonality

     "or peas

    you shift

     practice"
                  making a landscape by motion   (*Another Time* 45)

a hard movement of the words
allows equal solidity to the spaces between.
otherwise such seemingly "fragmented" structure
fall to the bottom.

Eigner is an on-going register. His movement.
and from poem to poem must be spaced, noted.
  (why, for example, *Another Time* so much the better
   to be read than *Selected Poems* with its imposed
   and titled interruptions)

Air, his medium, every thing, hangs up & out.
a window, all ways.
and the word "air", his serial point of closure.

each line
equals
its own completion

and every next line
its consequence

wholes are only made by motion

  "Sight is the only sense in which continuity is sustained
   by the addition of tiny but integral units: space can be
   constructed only from completed variations."
                                            --Roland Barthes

  "Part & particle is a noun."
                              --G. Stein, *Portrait of Man Ray*

A network of blind people, inventing
new methods of telephoning

"what you like
 is a plain object"
                        ...enters the whole air of his poems

space of singled-out words increasing speed
toward attaining a whole line, sentence, stop.

scarcity of enjambment (a word of meaning
far from its sounding), so its occurrence
has weight of event.

Sound creates silence. Images produce the blanks.
                        "material
                             gapping"

Each poem sights into a distance of all the
others following.
                    "the whole is divided as you look"

The Imagination.

to Williams a very present physics of the senses.
a synthesis of presence.

word-activation of the imagination in the act of seeing

                              "the bird
                               of wire like a nest

                               is all through the air"

start made at a word
everything to follow
the word its word
again the following

I do not think of Eigner.

                                        CLARK COOLIDGE

WRITING AND FREE ASSOCIATION

    The method of self-disclosure called "free association" wherein one
writes or speaks all one's thoughts in consecutive order (also sometimes
called "automatic writing" in literary criticism) is comparable to serious
attempts to read, write and understand poetry that directs attention to
the totality of the thinking process. Memories and awareness of the
present collapse into an experiential field composed of verbal presences
which can be re-sounded for various interpretations and alternative directions. Both in writing poetry and in free association one listens for
meanings rather than directing the thought process in a purposive way to
get to them.

    When a poet chooses the moment he will inscribe on the page the
lettered representation of what he wishes to present to be read, he
becomes the creator of his own reading. As he rereads he can experience
the moment he chose to move from the position of listener to his own
thought to that of recorder. These signs he makes to re-read are the
hieroglyphic constructs by which he hopes to disclose the experiential

process simultaneous to its construction. Not that the line or the poem
is merely a "slice of thought" corresponding to the naturalistic construct
of a stage upon which the writer re-enacts a narrative representation of
his conception of existence. The very choice of moments for writing poetry
is part of the mysterious flow of attention alert in the mind of the poet
to the tides and currents of his own perceptions. By means of his poems
he attempts to catch his thoughts in their nascent state, malleable, yet
in a way that their original sense may be maintained. When he abandons
the possibility of authenticity, celebrates the inevitability of masks
and roles, "plays the game" or imitates what he imagines would be successful,
he is resting from his more difficult work of finding clues to the solution
his unconscious keeps presenting to him in various kinds of puzzles and
disguises. Aware of the silence which ever more deeply underlines his
utterances, drawn on by the music represented by these letters from his
unconscious, by a kind of retrograde movement of language, he is led closer
to the other voices of his self. Finding ways of noticing these thoughts
at the moments of their inner presentation, he may isolate momentarily
what is ordinarily most immediate to his experience but otherwise most
elusive. When we read poems we simultaneously listen to our personal
associations as well as the intended meanings of words. "Words are notes
on the keyboard of the imagination." (Wittgenstein) And Freud: "It is
only too easy to forget that a dream is a thought like any other." Like
the sequential motifs in dreams, a poem's meaning often appears to be
more verbal than literal, resonating with meaning rather than describing
it. Sometimes sequences in poems (and dreams and thoughts) can be drawn
together like fragments in a collage, to open another implied area not yet
found. What is before can become what is next (to). For example, in
writing poetry the very next thought may seem technically inacceptable
but allowed to remain in the poem may later reveal an otherwise hidden
intention.

   In psychoanalysis attempts toward free association reveal to the analysand emotions which underlie his everyday conflicts. These verbalizations
are interpreted by the analyst and the analysand with the goal of proli-
ferating the analysand's awareness of alternatives. Sometimes these
feelings correspond to the strong emotions the poet experiences while
writing. While observing and directing the thought process experiences
of subjective and objective comprehension fuse and alternate, accelerating
the mind towards associations of various types of meanings, intensities
and emotions. Language demands to be said, heard, felt and comprehended
all at once out of the sphere of choosing actions and immersed in the
consciousness of its own tremors, intentions and implications. Like the
poem, the free associative process goes from segment to segment with a
continual sense of arbitrariness and complete choice.

NICK PIOMBINO

Ronald Johnson, <u>RADI OS</u> (1977, Sand Dollar Books): *Excerpt of Review by DAVID BROMIGE.*

O the ragman   circles   in the alley
                                                       with his pointed
     the block   the matter   French
                                                       message
     that he don't talk   And the mail box is locked

And   really   stuck

But   "jump right in

     can't escape   Texas"
                         mama

stuck inside

Grandpa   preacher   baffled
               rocks   him   dressed
badly   shocked   With   pounds   headlines
                    lost control   he cursed

          shot it full of holes   Then whispered,   "hide,

                                          satisfied."
mama   inside of Milton
     be the end
                                          with the Memphis blues
                                                    again.

REGARDING
THE (A) USE OF LANGUAGE WITHIN THE CONTEXT OF ART

IT (LANGUAGE) SEEMS TO BE THE LEAST IMPOSITIONAL MEANS OF TRANSFERRING
INFORMATION CONCERNING THE RELATIONSHIPS OF HUMAN BEINGS WITH MATERIALS
FROM ONE TO ANOTHER (SOURCE)

BEING ITSELF (LANGUAGE) A MATERIAL ONE IS THEN ABLE TO WORK GENERALLY
WITH RATHER SPECIFIC MATERIALS

DARWIN IN *THE VOYAGE OF THE BEAGLE* INQUIRED OF A PATAGONIAN INDIAN WHY
THEY (THE INDIANS) DID NOT EAT THEIR DOGS IN TIME OF FAMINE INSTEAD OF
EATING THEIR (THE INDIANS) OLD WOMEN
" Dogs kill otters, old women don't "
THEY REPLIED

LAWRENCE WEINER

GREENWALD

Native Land by Ted Greenwald (1977; $2 from Titanic Books, c/o Folio,
2000 P St., NW, Washington, D.C. 20009)

What is here is here in relation. There too, and then. Continually, then.
You want to pay attention to as much as possible. At once. States of
affairs give way. This dissolution of relations, in favor of new sets of
relations, might later be called the instant. Its measure would be the
line. Schematically, the space between the lines is the continuum. Could
association ever really be free? There is logic, permitting inclusion of
as wide or narrow a range of possibility as you like. Its rules are the
unfolding of its form when it's developed. They punch out logic. Their
logic makes itself comfortable at speeds up to and including the next guy.
You talk I listen. Then we switch. There's light in room, supper on the
way. We want to hear what's said, and so we do, again in the head, in
relation to what's going down there as to what's next, which we would
include also, even insist on, so to get on with the fun of it fresh in
mind. Some of the time, not all of the time. That's when something's
happening. Between those times you test the limits, weather, unconscious-
ness, provide for meal times, times together. Desire inevitably opens a
hole in the static. There's no telling when you're in the turn how things
will turn out, hence no time sense, all presence. There's a generosity
in this way of taking things in, leaving them open to change. An assumption of common ground between talk and thought. There's access, out,
person to person, by virtue of the open enededness in dealing with voice

and a tough minded refusal to consider sequence as circumscribed by any prior formality, or line as pinned down to final value. It's an up.

KIT ROBINSON

CHARISMA

Michael Lally, <u>Charisma</u> (1976; $2 from O Press, c/o Lally, 291 Church St., N.Y., N.Y. 10013)

    <u>Charisma</u> is an album which will be viewed by almost all the people the poems are about or dedicated to, their friends and public. The people are beside the poems, which is to say that there are no two things alike in nature nor no two things so unalike that one could rightly feel more or less the likeness of nature, both the poems and the person are products of the same creation. They are also separated, juxtaposed parameters of a personal, unseen force. And it is this second aspect of <u>Charisma</u>, as language rather than the relationship of art to nature, that's most pertinent to this book, although thoughts about the first may leak in.

    Putting a familiar name like Babe Ruth near verses connected marginally with him, unlike Catullus' coupling Caesar with a verse in criticism of the latter's sexual behavior where the subject was directly confronted by his own vileness used as a metaphor for political patronage, requires a new kind of metaphor. And Lally does it in a disarmingly simple manner. His lines are not portraits, but elucidate by framing the person instead of describing him. They create the picture I have in my mind of Babe Ruth in his later years, the veneer of Ashbery, how flattery feels to Steve Hamilton, Sylvia Schuster's tangential affiliation with 1956, Michael himself, and as such are edifying, even didactic. (These words are not intended to shock the reader.) Some of the work does fall off into imitation as the lines for Ted Berrigan and some into description, but "Values in Denial of Ourselves" positions the writing in the subject's court. Man makes coercion. The writer of that style is a vessel and conclusive.

    The poems are about the subjects' charisma--a surface that peels off the page. And this acrylic, like a politician's rhetorical gift, does not exist in its own right but only in relation to its constituency. Or are we constituents of a personality? Some of the poems are so edifying that Mr. Lally felt it incumbent on him to delete the dedication. And as with these sentences the poems take their shape from a way of speaking, but are not that mode itself and in this way ally Lally to the dedicatees in the same way the language hints at the person, hints like someone

talking about the weather to tell you your wife is sleeping with your best
friend. One subject is not used as metaphor for another as in Catullus.
The style itself is a figure of speech for and along side the subject.

Charisma is not a quality we can't enjoy when the dedicatee is
unknown nor is it a sculpture that falls apart at the opening which has a
spider in the middle of its rubble that doesn't know what's happening in
the art world. It wins us over by making itself attractive and by sliding
around the subject so it draws no blood with its spikes as if chary of
making poetry a contact sport. Though we may feel had at first, we
realize the exigencies of administration and admire how the author has
circumscribed the problem, then wish our own lives were less slamming
rice around and more...but nobody ever claimed realism is the way it is
which is what makes me take the chance at criticism.

JAMES SHERRY

I HAVE TWO HEADS

I GIVE UP and try to sleep see large bright pink words YOU ARE REALLY

TERRIFIC OLD GIRL Peggy sent this NY Times review BY WHICH ILIAD "The

Origin of Consciousness in the Breakdown of the Bicameral *that's split*

like your ass Mind by Julian Jaynes PRINCETON U Houghton GO BUY IT WHICH

TALKS ABOUT ME IS WOULDNT QUOTE IT. *Quote* I hear Bernadette's voice

yelling at me "According to Jaynes the mind of ME preconscious man was

truly bicameral, i.e. 2 chambered, the right hemisphere "spoke" LISTEN

the left heard and obeyed. Heroes like Achilles never commune with

themselves, they simply listen to their gods *ends of quote*. SOS I LISTEN

I call Lloyd I worked on a movie with him for IBM years ago THIS IS CHEAP

the two COMPUTERS YOU SPOILED THE SEQUENCE are digital, that adds, and

AMORAL I always thought it was random it's ANALOGUE it measures. The

digital counts (like the left hemisphere logical thinking underlined)

quotes clipping "the left hemisphere handles all the verbal *everyone knows*

this chores and does all the math CALLS FOR SEQUENTIAL OPERATIONS it

excels at any job that ..." Or analogue, like the right hemisphere THAT'S

A COMPUTER, BY ASSOCIATION STUPID because PROBABLY a measurement could be

in the amount of energy *ors crying* or *crazy* TEMPERATURE RISES. Telepathy
might work by insistence underlined QUOTE THIS JAYNES "the right hemisphere deals best with structural relationships in space and time it excels
at grasping Gestalts *the spacing* PERIOD. A CERTAIN FORCE seen in large
yellow letters *out of* EMER INCOMPLETE need OR CALLING PEOPLE STOP. AND I
GET ANSWERS but sometimes I get to the end directly and it's right, and
the reasons come later, to fill in, after THE DEED IS DONE. I know before.
It's JUST THE SAME LOGIC WITH THE MIDDLE MISSING.
TELEPATHY   I WOULDNST PUT MY NAME ON IT Hannah Weiner
                Its a brilliant structural analysis of the brain

                                                    HANNAH WEINER

(Julian Jaynes' <u>The Origin of Consciousness in the Breakdown of the
 Bicameral Mind</u> was published last year by Houghton Mifflin, at $12.95)

<u>MELNICK</u>

NICE

Words might be shields--heraldic, protective--or, reading Zukofsky,
Ashbery, Duncan with a sephardic eye, the 'pure light' of reference might
pass thru a 2-way mirror--word being itself is no less a concealment
(seal meant), postures one holds walking 'in public'--a metaphor, then,
in *Eclogs*, hustler cruising Champs-Elysées, suppresses signifieds, posits
mind's life in body's locus, 'classic' because articulate, thru wch comes
the <u>transfer</u>, shock of self--writ against the grain, social fact of
Berkeley, the 60s, Levertov's literalism, nearness of parents, reactionary
imagination of *Occident*--a work in opposition <u>&</u> the closet--then silence--
stasis is the most natural state--only turmoil (change in one's social
order) pushes us thru the entropics--study of "modern poets' views of ole
Will" takes years, yields one chapter & that on LZ, <u>ought</u>, beyond wch
that life is abandoned--poetry a scene, community a mystic writing pad
one opts in or out of: ink flows--new beginning begins *Pcoet*, 1972, whose
words are neither speech nor writing, but each within each (what has
befallen anyone in the 15 centuries since Eusebius Hieronymus first
stoppd reading aloud--any increase in locomotive speed blurs landscape
until <u>that</u> becomes focus)--only a kabalist traind in math (U. Chicago)

cld have proceeded thus, poetry precedes the language, <u>makes</u> <u>it</u>, & here
is that sphere of light held high, dodecahedron (how see what is there
without substance? if you filmd light, as from a projector in an otherwise dark room, *Rameau's Nephew*, it wld on your print have shape, but
with the peculiar luminosity of animation: photon spray), thru wch all
meaning, if it is to move (<u>into</u> terms as <u>onto</u> film), must pass--beyond
syntax, a city's wall preventing penetration in both directions--beyond
words, wch ruse referents, posing a mock transcendentalism thru wch
Capital itself has manifested natural as a sunrise (Lord's guslars did
not even know what the 'word' was)--language writing language writing--
Moebius amulet--again after wch the necessary silence, that norm, broken
only by a few performance pieces for multiple voice on themes specific in
their eroticism--for no scene's benefit nor niche in artificed hierarchy
of writing, but friends (<u>frenz</u>)--for this moment (a social fact) to have
<u>solvd</u> writing

RON SILLIMAN

thoeisu

thoiea

akcorn woi cirtus locqvump

icgja

cvmwoflux

epaosieusl

~~cirtus locquvmp~~

a nex macheisoa

(p. 1, from PCOET)

A SHORT WORD ON MY WORK

The *ECLOGS* (1967-70) are transparently derivative poems, tho when I wrote
them I would never have allowed so, not in the way I now mean it.
"Oilskin?" God!

Do you like them? They are terribly romantic, personal. Do you like
poems that are impossibly oblique yet turn up clues to the movements of
the soul of the poet? Hadn't we got beyond that? I hope so!

I do like the "impossibly" part, even if the "oblique" part supposes some referent relative to which obliquities can be measured. The lines are always taking off, sliding and gliding just above language. Good. Also the cadences.

PCOET was written in May-June 1972. I was then showing all new work to Ron Silliman. He liked the first one ("thoeisu"). We took it to The Heidelberg on Telegraph Ave. in Berkeley, read it to Barbara Baracks' employer/patient in his wheelchair. Patient/employer was befuddled—we were used to this, but there was a new delight in not needing to explain. I wrote the rest of the poems in 3-4 weeks, except for #2 which was written in Jan. 1975 entirely from the index of an Ichthyology textbook belonging to my lover, David Doyle.

I doubt that any statement will mediate between *PCOET* and its audience. There will be some who attend at once to its aesthetic and to that of other wordless poetries. The poems are made of what look like words and phrases but are not. I think these poems look like they should mean something more than other wordless poems do. At the same time, you know that you can't begin to understand what they mean.

What can such poems do for you? You are a spider strangling in your own web, suffocated by meaning. You ask to be freed by these poems from the intolerable burden of trying to understand. The world of meaning: is it too large for you? too small? It doesn't fit. Too bad. It's no contest. You keep on trying. So do I.

DAVID MELNICK

BIBLIOGRAPHY: *Eclogs* (1972; Ithaca House, 108 N. Plain St., Ithaca, N.Y., $1.95). *PCOET* (1975; G.A.W.K.; available from L=A=N=G=U=A=G=E Distributing Service, $3).

SOME MAGAZINES   **

ASSEMBLING (Henry Korn, Richard Kostelanetz, eds; Box 1967, Brooklyn, NY 11202) #7, $6.95. Includes Lyn Hejinian, Bern Porter, Keith Rahmmings, Susan Laufer, Dick Higgins, &&.
ATTABOY (Linda Bohe, Phoebe MacAdams, eds; Box 2239, Boulder, CO 80306.)
BEZOAR (Paul Kahn, ed; Box 535, Gloucester, MA 01930) Monthly, contribution: Lee Harwood, Jerome Rothenberg, Ed Dorn, Philip Whalen, Michael Palmer, &&.
BIG DEAL (Barbara Baracks, ed; Box 830, Stuyvesant Sta., NYC 10009) #4, $3: Michael Lally, Rae Armantrout, Robert Ashley, Jackson MacLow, Carl Andre, &&. #5, $3: Maureen Owen issue.

BIG SKY (Bill Berkson, ed; Box 389, Bolinas, CA 94924) #10, $2.50: Clark Coolidge, Merrill Gilfillan, Ronald Johnson, Kit Robinson, Ted Greenwald, &&.
BRILLIANT CORNERS (Art Lange, ed; 1372 W. Estes, #2N, Chicago, IL 60626).
BLANK TAPE (Keith Rahmmings, ed; Box 371, Midwood Sta., Brooklyn, N.Y.).
CLOWN WAR (Bob Heman, ed; Box 1093, Brooklyn, NY 11202) #16, 24¢ pstg: Ted Berrigan, Ray DiPalma, David Gitin, &&.
CRAWL OUT YOUR WINDOW (Michael Freilicher, Paul Dresman, eds; 704 Nob Ave, Del Mar, CA 92014) #3, $2: Kathy Acker, Jeff Weinstein, Michael Davidson, &&.
DODGEMS (Eileen Myles, ed; 86 E. 3rd, NYC 10003) $2 ea.: Nick Piombino, Lally, Ed Friedman, James Sherry, Steve Hamilton, &&.
DOG CITY (c/o Folio Books, 2000 P St. NW, Washington, D.C. 20036) #2, $2: Chris Mason, Lynne Dreyer, Doug Lang, Diane Ward, Kirby Malone, &&.
E (Marshall Reese, ed; 2931 N. Charles, #11, Baltimore, MD 21218) #2, $2: Michael Gibbs, Charles Amirkhanian, Malone, Robert Lax, &&.
EEL FOR (P. Inman, ed; 1308 S. Western Ave, Champaign, IL 61820): Lang, Ward, Susan Howe, Charles Bernstein, Tina Darragh.
FLORA DANICA (Tod Kabza, Brita Bergland, eds; c/o Bergland, R.R. 1, Windsor, VT 05089) $3.50: Bruce Andrews, Ron Silliman, Rosmarie Waldrop, DiPalma, Phil Smith, &&.
FLUTE (Brian McInerney, ed; 208 E. 25th, NYC 10010) Winter '77, $2: John Perlman, Mark Karlins, John Levy, John Taggart, &&.
4 3 2 REVIEW (Simon Schuchat, ed; Box 1030, Stuyvesant Sta, NYC 10009) $1 ea.: Jim Brodey, Frank O'Hara, Acker, Friedman, Piombino, &&.
HILLS (Bob Perelman, ed; 1220 Folsom, San Francisco, CA 94103) #4, $1.50: Carla Harryman, Barrett Watten, Robinson, Andrews, Silliman, Benson, &&.
IMPULSE (Eldon Garnett, ed; Box 901, Sta. Q, Toronto, Ontario M4T 2PL) $7/4 issues: B.P. Nichol, Bill Bissett, Les Levine, Opal Nations, &&.
INTERMEDIA (Harley Lond, ed; Box 31-464, San Francisco, CA 94131) #4: Hannah Weiner, Loris Essary, Tom Ockerse, Michael Wiater, Zekowski, &&.
INTERSTATE (Loris Essary, ed; Box 7068, University Sta., Austin, TX 78712) #9, $2: Higgins, Porter, Allen Fisher, DiPalma, Douglas Messerli, &&.
KONTAKTE (Phenomenon Press c/o 76 Admiral Rd, Toronto, Ont. M5R 2L5) #5, $3: Language Landscapes: int'l anthology of concrete poetry, coming.
KONTEXTS (Michael Gibbs, ed; Eerste van der helstraat 55, Amsterdam) #9/10: Carl Clark, Fred Truck, J-J Cory, Nichol, Higgins, &&.
LA-BAS (Douglas Messerli, ed; 4330 Hartwick Rd, #418, College Park, MD 20740) Bimonthly, contrib: Eigner, Hejinian, Inman, Bernstein, Welt, &&.
MAG CITY (Michael Scholnick, Gregory Masters, Gary Lenhart, eds; 437 E. 12th, NYC 10003) $2 ea.: John Godfrey, Alice Notley, Paul Violi, Friedman, &&.
MIAM (Tom Mandel, ed; 1578 Waller, San Francisco, CA 94117) #3, contribution: Silliman, from 2197.

N.R.G. (Dan Dlugonski, ed; 73 Pine St, Ashland, OR 97520) Contribution: Essary, Coolidge, Waldrop, David McAleavey, Karl Kempton, &&.

NEW WILDERNESS NEWSLETTER (Rothenberg, ed; 365 West End Ave, NYC 10024) $6/6 issues: #1--from A Big Jewish Book; #2--The Poetry of Number (Eric Mottram, Steve McCaffery, Charlie Morrow, &&).

OCULIST WITNESSES (Alan Davies, ed; Box 415 Kenmore Sta, Boston, MA 02215) #2: Greenwald, Watten, Lewis Warsh, Bernadette Mayer, &&.

OCCURRENCE (John Wilson, ed; 94 McKinley Ave, Lansdowne, PA 19050) #7, $2.50: Mary Oppen, Mottram, Taggart on Samperi.

100 POSTERS (Alan Davies, ed; Box 415, Kenmore Sta, Boston, MA 02215) Monthly, contribution: Michael Gottlieb, Christopher Dewdney, Bernstein, Armantrout, Rachelle Bijou, &&.

ONLY PROSE (Jeff Weinstein, John Perreault, eds; 54 E. 7th, NYC 10003) Contribution: Weiner, Acker, Freilicher, Baracks, &&.

OUT THERE (Rose Lesniak, Barbara Barg, eds; 280 Lafayette, NYC) #12, $2: Peter Seaton, Neil Hackman, Jeff Wright, Godfrey, Piombino, &&.

PERSONAL INJURY (Mike Sappol, ed; 628 E. 14th, apt 3, NYC 10009) #3, $1.50: Dreyer, Weiner, Inman, Tom Ahern, Violi, &&.

POD (Kirby Malone, ed; 3022 Abell Ave, Baltimore, MD 21218) #2, $2.50: Andrews, Ward, Dreyer, Lang, David Wilk, Reese, &&.

RED M(IRAGE) (John Ensslin, 8715 Third Ave, North Bergen, N.J. 07047) $2 ea.: Mayer, Warsh, Carl Solomon, &&.

ROOF (James Sherry, ed; 300 Bowery, NYC 10012) #3, $2: Friedman, Seaton, Charles North, && and 50pp. from Legend, etc. (Silliman-McCaffery-DiPalma-Bernstein-Andrews). #4, $3: Berrigan, Coolidge, Ginsberg, Warsh, Greenwald, && and Washington, D.C. Forum, ed. by Andrews.

SHELL (Jack Kimball, 362 Waban Ave, Waban, MA 02168) #4, $3: Lally, John Yau, Davies, Mayer, Malone, &&.

SHUTTLE (John Perlman, ed; 1632 Mamaroneck Ave, Mamaroneck, NY 10543) #3, contribution: McInerney, Eigner, Cid Corman, Frank Samperi, Chibeau, &&.

SLIT WRIST (Terry Swanson, ed; 333 E. 30th, apt. 14F, NYC 10016) #3/4, $5: Weiner, Seaton, Piombino, Charlotte Carter, &&.

STATIONS (Karl Young, ed; Box 11601-Shorewood, Milwaukee, WI 53211) #3/4, $3: Taggart, Rothenberg, Rochelle Owens, Enslin, &&.

SUN & MOON (D. Messerli, ed; 4330 Hartwick Rd, #418, College Park, MD 20740) #4, $3: Davidson, Lally, Barbara Guest, Douglas Woolf, Lippard, &&

TELEPHONE (Maureen Owen, ed; 109 Dunk Rock Rd, Guillford, Conn. 06437) #12: Yuki Hartman, Ascher/Strauss, Hejinian, J. Collom, K. Abbott, &&.

TERRAPLANE (Brita Bergland, Tod Kabza, c/o Bergland, R.R.1, Windsor, VT 05089) $4: Keith Waldrop, Perelman, Bernstein, DiPalma, Benviniste, &&.

TEXT (Mark Karlins, ed; 552 Broadway-6th Fl, NYC 10012) Year/6 issues, $5: Thomas Meyer, Samperi, Eigner, Rothenberg, Corman, &&.

THIRST (Vyt Bakaitis, Benjamin Sloan, eds; 323 Atlantic Ave, Brooklyn, NY 11201) $1 ea.: Terence Winch, Lally, Jamie MacInnis, &&.

THIS (Watten, ed; 326 Connecticut, San Francisco, CA 94107) #8, $2: Coolidge, Perelman, Grenier, Seaton, Greenwald, Jim Rosenberg, Andrews, &&.
TOTTEL'S (Silliman, ed; 1578 Waller, San Francisco, CA 94117).
TRACKS (Herbert George, ed; Box 557, Old Chelsea Sta, NYC 10011) $2 ea.: Carl Andre, Alan Sondheim, Vito Acconci, Wendy Walker, R. Horvitz, &&.
UNITED ARTISTS (Box 718, Lenox, MA) #1, $2: Paul Metcalf, Coolidge, Warsh, Mayer.
UNMUZZLED OX (Michael Andre, ed; Box 840, Canal St Sta, NYC 10003) #15, $2.25: John Cage, Christopher Knowles, Ashbery, Berrigan, Djuna Barnes.
ZZZZZZ (Kenward Elmslie, ed; Calais, VT 05648) $3.50: Winch, Perelman, Joe Brainard, Greenwald, Lally.

PATTERN POEMS

(Dick Higgins' new book, George Herbert's Pattern Poems: In Their Tradition, Unpublished Editions; $5.95, c/o Serendipity, 1790 Shattuck Ave., Berkeley, CA 94709, is composed of 28 beautifully printed pattern poems by primarily Greek, Latin, Medieval and Renaissance poets. A recent related anthology is Speaking Pictures, edited by Milton Klonsky; $5.95 from Harmony / Crown. Below, an excerpt from Higgins' introduction)

Because of the profusion of visual poetry since the early 1950s in many languages, in the forms of "concrete poetry" (international), "Poesia Visiva" (Italian), or "spatialism" (French and Japanese), and presented in such works as *An Anthology of Concrete Poetry*, edited by Emmett Williams ... one gets the impression of visual poetry as a peculiarly modern movement, which is misleading. The concrete poets have tended to take the usual neoteric position and to dismiss the obvious lineage of their work through such pieces as Lewis Carroll's "The Tale of a Mouse" (for English), Panard's "Glass" and "Bottle," or the Apollinaire "Calligrammes." ...

(An interesting example of the) shaped-poem tradition is the cabalistic charm, coming out of the Hebrew tradition and often written in Latin. Such charms often employ a concept of language as sign rather than semantic process. The closeness of "charm" and "poem" is shown by the common Latin word for both, "carmen," which also means "song," and the Middle Ages drew no hard and clear line between the two. The essential difference between a "charm" and a "poem" is, of course, that the former aims toward magical efficacy while the latter attempts an aesthetic impact. But even here there is a convergence, since the aesthetic impact of the charm could well be a part of its magical power. Thus the linguistics involved in a charm and a poem could be very similar.

The theoretical underpinnings of such aesthetics lie in the cosmology which the Middle Ages attributed to Pythagoras, who was regarded as the greatest philosopher of antiquity, greater even than Plato and Aristotle though, as a pagan, somewhat suspect. The Pythagorean system, as developed in the Hermetic tradition and elsewhere as well as from Plato's *Timaeus* (which was one of the only Platonic dialogues available to the Middle Ages), was based on a hierarchy of "things' at the bottom, the perceptions, feelings, and qualities associated with them next, followed by the word or *logos*, next the idea or form, penultimately the numbers or ratios, and finally the divine principle itself, conceivable only metaphorically in the Music of the Spheres. Within such a system, a word stood not for the thing it denoted but for the idea underlying it, and was thus a symbol of pure form. As such it was closer to the essence of numbers and ratios in the hierarchy than anything it might describe, and was therefore invested with a power which we sometimes find difficult to understand.... A similar sacred power was attributed to letters, which were not seen as mechanical components of the written word, but as essential and autonomous instruments expressing the process underlying them, analogous therefore to numbers and proportions. The process of forming words became, then, a very sacred one indeed, part of the divine game of realizing things out of their underlying numbers or letters....

Inherent in the concept of a pattern poem is its unsuitability for any sustained argument of emotional persuasion. Its appeal is immediate and involves the recognition of the image. Thus the Aristotelian rhetorical goal of persuading and convincing a reader is unlikely to be achieved within a pattern poem. And an Aristotelian age--such as followed the baroque--would, and did, find the pattern poem essentially trivial and eccentric. The age that followed the baroque was characterized by a tremendous emphasis upon power and force.... It is doubtful that the pattern-poem format could achieve the "suspension of disbelief" so sought after by fiction-oriented centuries. But today, with power far less to the point--with less insistence upon a poem that it "move" the reader-- the pattern poem has again emerged, in its new guise as the concrete poetry genre.

DECAY

Barrett Watten, Decay (1977; $1 from This Press, 326 Connecticut, San Francisco, CA 94107)

Where are you going your feet along those parallel lines. One place or two. When you 'get' there will you be together one or two.

If you hold regularly to the ability to say what you do say, your legs will take turns; you can go on, saying it.

*

In this writing each word points at those nearby. Each sentence.
-the way Duchamp's snow shovel points at his urinal and the hat rack, in retrospect. And in the initial fact.
"One word used in connection with the wiring of houses is current -- this." The last word points with its little finger at the one just back of it. Look! But this is an obvious example of what is the case throughout.
You gain every thing by stepping consciously from stone to stone, so they tie back and forth and around.

*

Music is muted. Not silenced, but tamed and caressed. The whole thing is erect in the face of a reader. A light spreads up around our lips.
When you walk into the light, holding to thoughts as you do, an instance is filtered by its own parameters, aesthetic weight balanced, not interfered with, registered mildly. It is a word and a word, what else.

*

It is too easy to say he could not come right out and say it. It is possible to hide back of words but you don't do that.
Language a thin skin of somewhat-changing identity, on which mind projects, locating through structure.
Some reality is not presented here, but not held back; present. You hold down the world fingers around it. -this lets no thing escape though only a few things be held to. A portrait landscape forms under that pressure; complete, and aired. Sparks of meaning set off where none is apparent.

*

"I was there, I am not here.
 Time is a sensible by-product, of motion
between two poles."
Why we keep setting these things down, words. Because we do not ever know a difference between every thing and no thing. A language making it seem there is a difference. We write a way repeatedly through this dilemma.
How do you think of your work as coming.

*

You write it proves every bit a dream. Not indistinct the way most forget, to be awake; attentive to each particular, waking continually from that a sense of the nailed down confusion. We can call it confusion.

*

    Each writing comes from, out a voice with precision sharp edges.
Concaves of burnt and cut angle that permit only a most exact delineation
of detritus coming in and straying from the mind, never relaxed.
    You walk over the minute stones and there they remain.
    A mouth whispers small notes.
    We don't choke because we let it go.
    These words tie themselves into accuracies of what is there about
them. It is all there, contained out where only parts are spoken. A
kindness to have handles perfectly the few things and let them be.

ALAN DAVIES

FROM A TO Z

Johanna Drucker, *FROM A TO Z: The Our An (Collective Specifics) an im
partial bibliography, Incidents in a Non-relationship or: how I came to
not know who is* (1977; $20 from Chased Press, 2207 Rittenhouse Sq., Phila-
delphia, PA 19103)

A typography that reflects a thrownness into text--a big way of saying
it--"wise she so willing to approach the insidiously inadequate signifer,
with TOLERATION & ON." Which means we are faced with a WHOLE HEAP of
letters--here, nothing can be seen more physically than the literal
lettrist composition--& yet this is a work not of reflective imposition
of a form but of a form emerging from the energy of the making. "It's
the vision that matters, the real & worked out clarity of vision." So,
like Hannah Weiner, what appears as an interruptive quality of variant
type faces & sizes (in the make-up of single words & whole pages), which
is continuous throughout this book, doesn't so much have its roots in cut-
up or program (the 'imposed' form) but comes out of the writing "ON".
"The energy runs through eVerything when it's going. I go with it,
making the moVes according to the opportunities." So what we have is
"constructivism" that comes out of "trust (in) the intuitiVe aspect of
the organism: to function through the totality of the being". I.e.,: the
construction collapses back onto its own necessity, a short circuit which
refuses to allow for anything but an integrated thing. But, & note,
Drucker's "primitiVe driVe" isn't just a *self*-defined *writing* exercise
(viz: Mayer)--this book poses as its 'external' condition to set all the
type in the printshop & make a book ('internally') come *out of* "that".
"I have a serious interest in the synthetic integration of thought." &:
"For the actual purpOse of deliberate cOmstrucTiVe thOughT." Which

doesn't even get to the humor of the 'narrative' here: "I mean, I figured you're just not that bright, right? Nobody ever said you had a great head. But you're still a pretty man, & if you turned out to be a nice guy, then that would be okay, I couldn't expect you to have everything, after all." Here, she's going for both.

CHARLES BERNSTEIN

BIG JEWISH BOOK

(From Jerome Rothenberg's Notes in his anthology, <u>A Big Jewish Book</u>, published this month by Doubleday. And from <u>Gematria 27</u>, 1977, Membrane Press, by Rothenberg & Harris Lenowitz.)

By <u>poesis</u> I mean a fundamental language process, a "sacred action" (A. Breton) by which a human being creates & re-creates the circumstances & experiences of a <u>real</u> world, even where such circumstances may be rationalized otherwise as "contrary to fact." It is what happens, e.g., when the Cuna Indian shaman of Panama "enters"--as a landscape "peopled with fantastic monsters & dangerous animals"--the uterus of a woman suffering in childbirth & relates his journey & his struggle, providing her, as Lévi-Strauss tells it, "with a language by means of which unexpressed or otherwise inexpressible psychic states can be immediately expressed"....

The poet, if he knows his sources in the "sacred actions" of the early shamans, suffers anew the pain of their destruction. In place of a primitive "order of custom," he confronts the "stony law" & "cruel commands" Blake wrote of--"the hand of jealousy among the flaming hair." Still he confirms, with Gary Snyder, the presence of a "Great Subculture ... of illuminati" within the higher civilizations, an alternative tradition or series of traditions hidden sometimes at the heart of the established order, & a poetry grudgingly granted its "license" to resist. No minor channel, it is the poetic <u>mainstream</u> that he finds here: magic, myth & dream; earth, nature, orgy, love; the female presence the Jewish poets named Shekinah....:

> ... the female, the proletariat, the foreign; the animal and
> vegetative; the unconscious and the unknown; the criminal and
> failure--all that has been outcast and vagabond must return
> to be admitted in the creation of what we consider we are.

In the Jewish instance--as my own "main main"--I can now see, no longer faintly, a tradition of <u>poesis</u> that goes from the interdicted shamans (= witches, sorcerers, etc., in the English bible) to the prophets & apocalyptists (later "seers" who denied their sources in their shaman predecessors) & from there to the merkaba & kabbala mystics, on the right hand, & the gnostic heretics & nihilistic messiahs, on the left....

This follows roughly the stages (torah, mishnah, kabbala, magic & folk-lore, etc.) by which the "oral tradition" ("torah of the mouth") was narrowed & superceded by the written. But not without resistance; says the Zohar: "The Voice should never be separated from the Utterance, & he who separates them becomes dumb &, being bereft of speech, returns to dust." An ongoing concern here....

COMMENTARY: Gematria is the general term for a variety of traditional .coding practices used to establish correspondences between words or series of words based on the numberical equivalence of the sums of their letters or on the interchange of letters according to a set system.... (While numerical gematria & letter-coded temurah come easily in a language like Hebrew which is written without vowels, the possibility of similar workings in English shouldn't be discounted.) The numerical method-- gematria per so--typically took aleph as one, beth as two, yod as ten, kuf as 100, etc., through tav (last letter) as 400--although more complicated methods (e.g., reduction to single digits, etc.) were later introduced. Non-numerical methods included (1) anagrams, or rearrange-ments of the letters of a word to form a new word or word series, as "god" to "dog" in English; (2) notarikon, the derivation of a new word from the initial letters of several others & vice versa, as "god," say from "garden of delight"; & (3) temurah, various systems of letter code, e.g., the common one in which the first half of the alphabet is placed over the second & letters are substituted between the resultant rows, etc., in search of meaningful combinations.

Processes of this kind go back to Greek, even Babylonian, practice, & early enter the rabbinic literature. But the greatest development was among kabbalists from the 12th century on, who used it both to discover divine & angelic names & to uncover correspondences between ideas & images by means free of subjective interference. When set out as poems, the resemblance of the gematria to a poetry of correspondences in our own time is evident, as also to instances of process poetry & art based on (more or less) mechanical formulas for the generation of both simply & extended series of permutations & combinations....

THE BODY	*NOTHING*	*LIGHT*	*HE & HE*
The reward.	I.	A mystery.	This & this.

CARNIVAL

(From a note by Steve McCaffery on his ongoing work, Carnival, published by The Coach House Press, 401 (rear) Huron St., Toronto)

Carnival is planned as a multi-panel language environment, constructed largely on the typewriter and designed ultimately to put the reader, as perceptual participant, within the center of his language.

The roots of *Carnival* go beyond concretism (specifically that branch of concrete poetry termed the 'typestract' or abstract typewriter art) to labyrinth and mandala, and all related archetypal forms that emphasize the use of visual qualities in language to defend a sacred centre. Pound's vorticism also forms part of the grid of influences, and on one level at least, *Carnival* can be seen as an attempt to abstract, concretize and expand Pound's concept of the image as the circular pull of an intellectual and emotional energy. Above all it is a structure of strategic counter-communication designed to draw a reader inward to a locus where text surrounds her. Language units are placed in visible conflict, in patterns of defective messages, creating a semantic texture by shaping an interference within the clear line of statement....

Two phrases seemed to haunt me during the five years of composition. One, that form 'is the only possible thing"--a phrase, I think, that either echoes or cribs a line in Paul Blackburn's *Journals*. The other was Pound's lines in Canto CXVI: "to 'see again,' / the verb is 'see,' not 'walk on'" -- a profound phrase which I take to be Pound's ultimate stand in support of static, synchronic vista (Dante) as opposed to the dynamic line of processual flow. Dante climbed, in the *Paradiso*, out of narrative into a non-narrative summation of the story line -- as if art struggles to distance that which threatens it in closest proximity: language itself. *Carnival* is product and machine, not process; though its creation be a calenture to me, it must stand objective as a distancing and isolating of the language experience. The thrust is geomantic -- a realignment of speech, like earth, for purposes of intelligible access to its neglected qualities of immanence and non-reference. It is language presented as direct physical impact, constructed as a peak, at first to stand on and look down from the privilege of its distance onto language as something separate from you. Taken this way -- as the 'seen thing' -- its conflicts and contradictions are accommodated in a form based more on the free flight of its particulars than on a rigid component control. But *Carnival* is also a peak to descend from <u>into</u> language. The panel when 'seen' is 'all language at a distance'; the panel when read is entered, and offers the reader the experience of non-narrative language. There's no clues to passage for the reader other than the one phrase of Kung's: 'make it new', move freely, as the language itself moves, along one and more of the countless reading paths available, through zones of familiar sense into the opaque regions of the unintelligible, and then out again to savour the collision of the language groupings. Against the melodic line which is narrative I work with semantic patchwork, blocks of truncated sense that overlap, converge, collide without transition as the sum total of language games within our many universes of discourse....

My own personal line of continuity goes back from *Carnival* to Pope's *Dunciad*: "Thy hand great Dulness! lets the curtain fall, / And universal Darkness covers all." -- in which Pope speaks as the Augustan panelogist par excellence alarmed at the collapse of all linguistic strata.

Interestingly enough, Alexander Pope and the typewriter were contemporaries. Henri Mill invented the typewriter in 1714, the year the enlarged version of *The Rape of the Lock* appeared and a year before Pope's translation of *The Iliad*. The roots of the typewriter are Augustan; its repetitive principle is the principle of the couplet enhanced by speed. The typewriter oracled a neoclassical futurism that emerged in the mid twentieth century as *poesie concrète*. This is part of that oracle.

PROOF

John Wieners, Behind the State Capitol (1975; $5 from Good Gay Poets, Box 331, Kenmore Sta., Boston, MA 02115)

DOES one ever develop a thought ?
How has density proven ?
C O H E R E if itinerant in their attention, coded, spaced out, clipped from a book; likewise chance changed address ?
A good jostling now and again — taking mathematically into account irrelevant connectives, or quoting ignoble demolitions ((a methodology of confused doubt, or the i n v e r s e of doubt, indexd in some contrary or erratic way for ... for doing what ? for solidifying random and heedless acts attached beyond comprehension to the everyday; since that everyday is confused too broadly even for the chronicler or the semblagist)) : does this outshine parsimony ?
If shadowy interference nonetheless shifts our place, do we need complete dislocation, or disjuncture ?

CAN someone simply decorate the gaps, and lacks ?
By what manner, in manners, in a manner of speaking, is decorum the sensible adjunct we want to a sumptuous surveillance ?

Do I preen fetishly in reading, with a total comprehension, smothered in decorum ?
Is this my reading ?
And who will avenge this murder by which each single event is invested with dignity ?

AND how (and where) is consternation in the realm of reason a confrontation of the unknown, and do we know it ?
Or just, "You think I'm normal, they do a lot of things to my mind" ? : a senseless indecipherable deluge, where nothing contextualizes an other thing ?
Not a frame outside, and not a kernel inside ?
Are we all collage, all dense, tensed, & unlocatable ?
The soundless permeation of madness upon sanity : would this be the quandary gotten by viewing the language as the cure for the artistry ?
As a rebuff to social order, to emotional and perceptual order ?

WELL there are within it ACCURATed voices of other places   former silences and far events   forgotten opposition   and those gregarious references' experience — simultaneity for want of better words — having become a plural intimate response : but is this without cost ?
Disinterested (priceless?) content ?
As if   we forego prior lucidities — to gain fresh condition   perhaps or less referral to the past   an independence, a genealogical morale —
& then involve ourselves needlessly in prior obscurity ((the VOICEs droned on)) ?

IS that what behooves to haphazard : passion's desire to sound representable identity ?
Not to be transfixed in the plural ?
Or the, without a syncopation, self construed wishfully by absorbent intellect, the record of one, stylized and self-conscious ?
I = declaims use, for could one expect he should have the qualities of doing almost everything else ?
Disclaims use, isn't that it, for knowing an answer : it's a womanish heart ?

HOW can we construe this ? : by caverned fall in — a vertical dimension — caring of sounds, abutting solidity apart, cramming for brevity ?
Or, with mere words, rhetoric ? — so back to the believable histrionics to finally learn the diction ? (learned minutely expressed things dictated without choice, direction in discourse as a duty-found definition of alleged purpose) ?

NOT to belabor either fact or to imagine a world devoid of nabobs and fulfilled in reality, yet still in forebearance of any genuine appearance : what have we got here ?
None of trompe-d'oiel, so therefore language an act of sharing words ?
Or both realism and make-believe, caught in that dilemna ?
Yet how to get beyond both : first, that kindled embrace of past observation (the simple glass mirror, which allows subterfuge to glow forthrightly) and second, that condition of mankind dependent on hallucination in place of imagination ?

CONFUSION ? Decor ? Meaning ? Memory ? Body ? Space ? Self ? Rhetoric ? Reality ?
But after examination you find out it's true and say of course that was it all the time, where pure patented mystique fulfills its indispensable acts. That explains everything.

BRUCE ANDREWS

"WHY DON'T WOMEN DO LANGUAGE-ORIENTED WRITING?"

I've been asked this question twice, in slightly differing forms. In conversation I was asked, "Why don't more women do language-oriented writing?" I answered that women need to describe the conditions of their lives. This entails representation. Often they feel too much anger to participate in the analytical tendencies of modernist or "post-modernist" art. This was an obvious answer. The more I thought about it the less it explained anything important. Most male writers aren't language-centered either. Why don't more men do language-oriented writing?

Several months later, by mail, I was asked to write an article explaining why women don't produce language-oriented works. The letter suggested I might elaborate on the answer I'd given before. But it wasn't the same question! Some female writers do focus on language. Was I being asked to justify their exclusion from consideration? Lyn Hejinian, Bernadette Mayer, Alice Notley, Susan Howe, Hannah Weiner, Carla Harryman, Lynne Dreyer, Joanne Kyger, Anne Waldman and Maureen Owen seem, to one degree or another, language-oriented. Of course, that's a tricky term. If it's taken to mean total non-reference, these women don't fit. Neither, however, do Ron Silliman, Barrett Watten, Bob Perelman, Ted Greenwald, Charles Bernstein or Bruce Andrews.

To believe non-referentiality is possible is to believe language can be divorced from thought, words from their histories. If the idea of non-reference is discarded, what does language-oriented mean? Does it simply designate writing which is language-conscious (self-aware)? If so, the term could be applied to a very large number of writers. Anyone who sees the way signifier intertwines with signified will pay close heed to the structures of language.

Susan Howe calls our attention to the effect of linguistic structure on belief when she writes

> as wise as an (earwig, owl, eel).
> as sober as a (knight, minstrel, judge).
> as crafty as a (fox, cuckoo, kitten).
> as smooth as (sandpaper, velvet, wood).
> as slippery as an (accident, eel, engine).
> as straight as an (angle, angel, arrow).

(*The Western Borders*, Tuumba Press)

And a minstrel may very well be more clear-headed than a judge. It's important to note this.

Howe's passage amounts to a polemic against the influence of habit. This specific concern is common in language-oriented work. When Carla Harryman writes,

> Although temperature flags on its own, the past
> dissolves. I wanted to settle down to a nap. The
> sand settles at the bottom of the ocean. I sink
> to the top of the water.

("Sites," *Hills* magazine #4)

the word "although" prepares the reader for a contradiction between the clauses in the first sentence. When no contradiction follows, the reader's attention increases. The concept of contradiction is rooted in the laws of logic, cause and effect. Harryman wants to throw these "laws" into question. There is the jar of discontinuity between the clauses, sentences and paragraphs in this work. The lines I quoted do not follow logically, but they are united <u>linguistically</u> by the near-synonymous verbs. Harryman puts content at odds with syntactical (or sometimes narrative) structures in order to make these structures stand out, enter our consciousness.

Although Lyn Hejinian uses syntax in a fairly conventional way, her work is less referential than that of most of the writers I've mentioned. Of course, her writing does "say things" about the world, but the significance of these statements is not what interests her. In her book, *A Mask of Motion,* she rings the changes on a number of phrases and words. Each usage of a word becomes a mask for its other uses. Context, placement are of prime importance. When she writes "of the yapping distances, the extended return" one hears the dog she introduced five pages earlier.

Howe, Harryman and Hejinian are very different, yet the term language-oriented might be applied to any of them. I use that term but I'm suspicious of it, finally, because it seems to imply division between language and experience, thought and feeling, inner and outer. The work I like best sees itself and sees the world. It is ambi-centric, if you will. The writers I like are surprising, revelatory. They bring the underlying structures of language/thought into consciousness. They spurn the facile. Though they generally don't believe in the Truth, they are scrupulously honest about the way word relates to word, sentence to sentence. Some of them are men and some are women.

RAE ARMANTROUT

back cover: "Circle Ode" by Shahīn Ghirāy (ca. 1747-1787), from *George Herbert's Pattern Poems.*

ANNOUNCEMENTS

STATIONS #5: A Symposium on Clark Coolidge, edited by Ron Silliman. (Padgett, Dawson, Lally, Grenier, Bernstein, Saroyan, Byrd, Watten, Robinson, DiPalma, Gitin, Davies, Metcalf, Silliman.) Available in March for $3: Membrane Press, Box 11601-Shorewood, Milwaukee, WI.

OPEN LETTER, new issue (3/7): includes "The Politics of the Referent," Steve McCaffery, ed., with texts by DiPalma, Silliman, Bernstein, Andrews, McCaffery. ($2; 104 Lyndhurst, Toronto, Canada M5R 2Z7).

New from Asylum's Press (464 Amsterdam, NYC 10024):
AGREEMENT by Peter Seaton, $3.
PHOTOGRAM by Susan B. Laufer, $3.

New from Burning Deck (71 Elmgrove, Providence, R.I. 02906):
FILM NOIR by Bruce Andrews, $2.50.

L=A=N=G=U=A=G=E

Bruce Andrews,
        Charles Bernstein,
                editors

Vol.1, No.1. February 1978.

Subscriptions--
One year (six issues) for $4
        Institutions: $8.

All queries & checks to:
Charles Bernstein,
    464 Amsterdam,
    New York, N.Y. 10024.

Layout: Susan Laufer.

L=A=N=G=U=A=G=E

APRIL 1978

WRITING DEGREE ZERO

*For modern poetry, since it must be distinguished from classical
poetry and from any type of prose, destroys the spontaneously functional
nature of language, and leaves standing only its lexical basis. It
retains only the outward shape of relationships, their music, but not
their reality. The Word shines forth above a line of relationships
emptied of their content, grammar is bereft of its purpose, it becomes
prosody and is no longer anything but an inflexion which lasts only to
present the Word. Connections are not properly speaking abolished, they
are merely reserved areas, a parody of themselves, and this void is
necessary for the density of the Word to rise out of a magic vacuum, like
a sound and a sign devoid of background, like 'fury and mystery'.*

*In classical speech, connections lead the word on, and at once carry
it towards a meaning which is an ever-deferred project; in modern poetry,
connections are only an extension of the word, it is the Word which is
'the dwelling place', it is rooted like a fons et origo in the prosody of
functions, which are perceived but unreal. Here, connections only
fascinate, and it is the Word which gratifies and fulfills like the
sudden revelation of a truth.... Fixed connections being abolished, the
word is left only with a vertical project, it is like a monolith, or a
pillar which plunges into a totality of meanings, reflexes and recollec-
tions: it is a sign which stands. The poetic word is here an act without
immediate past, without environment, and which holds forth only the dense
shadow of reflexes from all sources which are associated with it. Thus
under each Word in modern poetry there lies a sort of existential
geology, in which is gathered the total content of the Name, instead of
a chosen content as in classical prose and poetry. The Word is no
longer guided in advance by the general intention of a socialized
discourse; the consumer of poetry, deprived of the guide of selective
connections, encounters the Word frontally, and receives it as an absolute quantity, accompanied by all its possible associations. The Word,
here, in encyclopaedic, it contains simultaneously all the acceptations
from which a relational discourse might have required it to choose. It
therefore achieves a state which is possible only in the dictionary or in*

45

*poetry--places where the noun can live without its article--and is
reduced to a sort of zero degree, pregnant with all past and future
specifications. The word here has a generic form; it is a category.
Each poetic word is thus an unexpected object, a Pandora's box from which
fly out all the potentialities of language; it is therefore produced and
consumed with a peculiar curiosity, a kind of sacred relish.... It
initiates a discourse full of gaps and full of lights, filled with
absences and overnourishing signs, without foresight or stability of
intention, and thereby so opposed to the social function of language that
merely to have recourse to a discontinuous speech is to open the door to
all that stands above Nature.*

ROLAND BARTHES

(from Roland Barthes' essay <u>Writing Degree Zero</u>, which has just become
available again in paperback in a reissue by Hill & Wang, at $2.95)

======

WATTEN

PERELMAN ON WATTEN

All that is objective call nature, all that is subjective call self.
Example: seeing wrecking ball moving through stucco walls hurts to watch.
Both conceptions are in necessary antithesis. Dream last night that I
had to fuck the fat lady. Intelligence is conceived as exclusively
representative, nature as exclusively represented. He wants to get in.
Tearing the building apart, that's what it takes to do this. The one is
conscious, the other without consciousness. Dreams are our life, which
we will never be able to penetrate. During all acts of knowledge there
is required a reciprocal concurrence of the conscious being with what in
itself is unconscious. Thinking in clusters, the group of scholars
gathered around the hole.
   It is contradictory to require any other self than the identity of
object and of representation. Therefore, in all the objects it sees, the
spirit views only itself. If this could be proved, the immediate reality
of all intuitive knowledge would be assured. A spirit may become its own
object. It must therefore be an act; for every object is, as an object,
dead, fixed, incapable in itself of any action, and necessarily finite.
Again the spirit (originally the identity of object and subject) must in
some sense dissolve this identity, in order to be conscious of it.

                    The line is a crux
                    Until it is mutual
              were sounds to him neither meant...
              Black continual circle or ring
                    of air dissolves
              speaking the dissolution.

     Thought is a torrent, the assumption of self is thick, hardened to
glass. Any person's report available. Any person is the image of what
he sees. The streetlights begin to come on, the lights on the signs.
The eye cannot stand what is not complete. So it tries to destroy what
it sees. The arm is reaching for the glass, the eye blocks out the glass.
     Olson wanted to let the dream back in. Okay. There is no difference
between waking and sleeping. That sentence makes even more sense when
you're asleep. A century can thus be condensed into a collective mask.
The outer man is attached to a man inside. The poetics of the situation
are beginning to be found out. Forget sleep / and be there.
     Wherein does the realism of mankind consist? In the assertion that
there exists a something without, which occasions the objects of
perception?
     Streets moving away on all sides: they are there because he says so,
and that is the voice.
     Fancy, engendered in the eyes, fed, and dies. Ring fancy's knell.
Fixities and definites, a desire to recombine perpetuates nothing. Even
so / the clouds played the brain / the eyes. One light shines from / the
house within, recording.
     A man walks into a large room. The universe expands. The seriousness
of the problem deepens as one becomes aware of it. The rooms are filled
with the arguments of philosophic schools. When he has heard just one
word of their discourse, he understands everything they intend to say.
A system of connected lines, he shudders at their approach.
     I hope no one is counting on language-centered to be a very helpful
term. To utter a single word changes all we know. The sentences come
from nowhere. This situation cannot be misinterpreted. I found my new
life to be hard, constant attention, but a great joy. As if I had said /
this, everyone knew exactly / what I meant.

The words in this piece are mostly from Barrett Watten's work. The
excerpts are often accurate. Many of the rest come from Coleridge's
Biographia Literaria, chapters 12 & 13, which distinguish imagination
from fancy. C's quotes are quite shortened.

                                             BOB PERELMAN

NOTE

The problem is, does this person, in what is merely adaptation to his environment, develop a language we can identify as our own. The problem of translation. Referents drop away. Not to circumvent identity structure, an all-over form. Rather that form is built back in. Any element implies a whole. A bean that explodes its meaning, small beans into large clouds. A monument is equally a miniature. Isn't the gas bill particular, Joseph Stalin. A monument is merely a moment in time, the next world in line is miniature. Ideas become things, the lore of the antipoetic. Step back from this picture in order to see it. That's where he can't find any area attention's restricted to. The scale pops endlessly in and out of line. A voice, but, choice. Scales thinking most to that point.

"The world we seek is white." Is color a special section of vocabulary, unlike any other. Stepping back from, abstraction as white. Equally specific, the white page. The white paint of turbulence, atmospheric pressure up. Is X, the next word. So white conveys a distance, up front, getting on to the next thing. Taking attributes from descriptive, relational, intentional language (any difference?) to make statement. A logic is developed, way back in the brain. The voice becomes distinct in the values of the words. A language as a whole modified through that voice, values established to a greater degree. White with its element of death. So he remembers the penetration of unresolved metallic hum. Throughout his physical body, a tone. Magnetized through a ring of all experience, the word becoming an act.

"A poem can be a stretch of thinking." At the point where words are formed, back in the brain. Not polyform, static, branching, kicking unless the words say so. Values decided at the source, and of necessity, through the form of writing. The line in verse operates as syntax, an entire poem as an arena or duration in which to work. One can now find he needs must bear down on words, one at a time. But prose must be satisfied first (in this gestalt, deciding to be a poet). Prose as an equivalence to state, a state of mind. A line of thought in the environment of many others. The opposition only serves to heighten interest. The copula leads to automatism, a dialectic of the unreleased. The scale expands or contracts, within the surrounding unknown. Negative capability. But power is more in the line, the power to get things done. A stretch of thinking, thinking syntax, to participate in the making of words. The categories all bear on reconciliation between logic and the physical fact. Into language, poem line prose word. A separation clears the air, a lot more needs to be done. I think an act allowing itself, grabs me back in.

To build the form back in, increase emphasis. That would be logically consistent. The grounds of that logic are greater than the decision to employ it. The specialized vocabulary is part of any language as a whole. There's something in the air, wanting to complete itself, unattached. Verbs eat into walls, nouns in a ring consume themselves. If at some point language walked in the open door, we would show it some respect. Our response would be more immediate than to use it as a sign. A sign of social respectability, or connections to the art world. So we respect language by not being content to operate in any one part of it. It's greater than we are. This has implications for the form. That sense is larger than one can say.

BARRETT WATTEN

BIBLIOGRAPHY: *Opera Works* (1975; Big Sky; available from Serendipity, 1790 Shattuck, Berkeley, CA 94709, $2.50). *Decay* (1977; This Press, 326 Connecticut, San Francisco, CA 94107, $1).

———————————————

HEISSENBÜTTEL

Helmut Heissenbuttel, Novel; Schematic Definition of Tradition; The Dilemma of Being High and Dry. (1977; Diana's BiMonthly Press; translated by Rosmarie Waldrop. $1 each; $2.50/set)

Diana's BiMonthly has recently published 3 pamphlets by Helmut Heissenbuttel which indicate a sophisticated sensibility on the part of this German poet towards issues of mounting interest in American poetics. Heissenbuttel's work is solidly based in a concept of literature as phenomena and each of these works attempts to explore a different domain of linguistic qualities and precepts through an indigenous form.

The most readily accessible of the three is *Novel*, a sequence of 21 short statements which explore, individually and collectively, the properties of the conventional novel. The piece evolves in a triangular form, starting from the apex in the first poem "I'm a story," and widening in the second "I'm a story of someone." and still wider in the third "Someone whom I'm a story of is the story I am. I'm someone who's a story." This inversion and rearrangement of words in a given line is a common form in all three poems, leading to a density of language through regenerative repetition. The effect of these and other structural devices is to give the poem a definite worldly presence of its own, a concern which appears throughout all Heissenbuttel's work.

As the title suggests, *Schematic Definition of Tradition* is an attempt to arrive at a fixed systemization of terms by which a given phenomenon can be measured. It is easy to see the influence of Stein and Wittgenstein in the way Heissenbuttel has limited his field to the appearance of a language game. Yet he has gone beyond the ideas of these two catalytic figures to create an extraordinarily compressed work concerned with the difficulty of fixed logic in a perceptual system ridden with contingencies. The entire poem is an attempt to overcome its own spiralling momentum toward the fixity of definition. For example: "even when they had been there there had already been more of those who hadn't been there than of those who had been there as long as any who had been there could remember there had been less of those who had been there than of those who hadn't." A certain futility is implied here and a certain disenchantment with the language as a vehicle for getting anywhere is evident.

The Dilemma of Being High and Dry is the most playful of the three pamphlets, and Heissenbuttel seems a master of play in writing. A prose poem in five stanzas, this piece is more referential in its use of images and its superficial appearance as a character description, though again the essential experience lies in the composition and language. The entire poem is an improvisation on the aphorism "high and dry," with the sense of an exquisite elliptical curve, turning simultaneously into itself and yet constantly expanding. The work finds its success in the establishment of a surface tension between referential words (nouns) and contextual words (prepositions, articles, conjunctions) which interact in a syntax that clarifies itself through contiguity, without ever defining itself completely.

A key to *Dilemma*, and perhaps all these poems lies in the end of the fourth stanza: "....how it has happened to him and others too namely to live in a world that you don't see as it is but through who knows what imaginings". By ritualizing the use of contextual language, with or without referents, he creates a poetry on the plane of presence, structure and event, an exceptional accomplishment.

CRAIG WATSON

PURE STEALING

(The following text is taken from a journal work by Ed Friedman. His recent play/performance piece, La Chinoiserie, also deals with the possibilities of the decorative in writing)

what i really became interested in was atmosphere. writing and performance as atmosphere. not so much that we all exist in a particular

community accommodating to each other's work. not like died to match curtains and wall to wall carpeting. more the possibility with language of there being a linear or single source of atmosphere and it can be quite minimal actually like a small perfume atomizer.

this is why it's hard to argue about atmosphere. old atmosphere is the only kind that can be recognized otherwise you are remembering details. detectives make old atmosphere new if they can by remembering details. i'm only talking about stories. you wouldn't talk about stale details. any real details are always interesting if they can be separated from atmosphere. this is why no one should like capitalism. this is why interior details are always most gratifying. it's never easy to really find them. or as facile as it seems finding one or two through combina- tions of having good memories. leaving it alone for now.

which is how i let too many thoughts go by unchecked. you have to remember all the time. if you spend the time to remember then you won't think so much about what you've already remembered and know more. i know this is true.

it's my only way of knowing really. telling about it in as much detail as possible isn't the same thing as remembering but is how you know something new.

which is how i'm gonna tell it later anyhow like john's son by jean or ed's son by lewis. everyone didn't follow the taxis white streak but that was really telling the old story and why you wouldn't remember at the same time you think so clearly that you feel you get to own certain words or that others own them for you.

i listen very closely to people who give precise physical descriptions of objects. who use a precise word.
i remember the time that lenny used the word sprockets to describe the square holes that run along the edges of a roll of 35 mm. film.
i remember the time that brad was looking at the painting by klimt in my kitchen and described the jaw of the woman in the picture as being square.
i remember bob's description of the two doilies on the poiret butterfly hat as being antimecassars crotched in a pineapple stitch.
i remember the time bernadette described the way i said "hi" on the telephone as being laconic.
any time i use any of these words, laconic, square-jawed, sprockets, or antemecassars--i become lenny, brad, bob, or bernadette. but only when i'm alone.

yesterday laura used the word "puce" which she said was worse than the chalky magenta color used in the 17th century english porcelain.
there are no words to describe the way one perceives in conglomerate images. for example, i see the entire cactus garden in a single glance. several hundred species of cactus at once, but if i want you to see it

too through my description, this is where time must proceed as atmosphere because i have to describe the garden as a series of particular species and placements of cactus.

so we at last forcibly take these turns together when they arrive too shortly at sameness. secret blues and occasionally pink or old flame. appear. putting in an appearance. showing up. making an appearance. taking a cameo role. all of the methods of memorizing tides instead of waves.

    making an outline of history and homes by the sea. too much ocean to recognize the bluffs on an overcast day. taking care not to fog over or mist delay.

    always making sure not to be jealous or anciently concerned with detail. rest as sure as salinated water cannot be as cool as sea. that is why what else is in sea. nobody knows. nobody knows this is getting much too hard to stop memorizing stopping. why not memorize hart crane instead.

    somebody knows how noticing details leads to learning if you follow television elevating sleep which is how i mistake hart crane for walt whitman on the subway. i get relaxed enough to make mistakes. slowly as cameos appear in relief of glancing, nobody retires again and i memorize phone conversations. trying not to memorize boring conversation slowly.

ED FRIEDMAN

THREE "NEW" POETS

Donald Quatrale, <u>Genitals</u> (1977; $2 from Bosom Press, 17 Hemenway St., Boston, MA 02115), and <u>The Factory Dances</u> (1977; $4 from The Four Zoas Press, RFD, Ware, MA 01082).
Diane Ward, <u>Trop-i-dom</u> (1977, Jawbone; $2 from Folio Books, 2000 P St., N.W., Washington, D.C. 20036).
Carole Korzeniowsky, <u>Breastwork</u> (1977; $1.50 from Korzeniowsky, 11 East 7th St., N.Y., N.Y. 10003).

1.

Donald Quatrale's *Genitals* instigated this piece. His 2nd book. His 1st engagingly well-focused: *The Factory Dances*. *Genitals* has more poems, so peaks & ebbs more pronounced and have a wider context as basis of support and/or contrast. Not necessarily erotic or sexual, rarely even sensual, but some attention to physical properties, descriptive qualities. <u>The technique</u> mainly assemblage (which reminded me of the other 2 poets --

what they have in common is the ease and looseness with which they approach
this way of structuring a poem -- in "my generation" only the W.C. Williams
mode afforded my contemporaries the same casual, easy grace and good
feelings -- whereas assemblage as such created often self-righteously &
therefore often stiff poetry-as-work ethic). Quatrale perhaps most of
these 3 in need of a sharp editorial sense to make poem do better what it
does and the poet intended, without silly self-indulgence to ego-clever-
ness. But he has a kind of elan about the presentation of his voice which
backed by the rhythmic strength of the construction alone creates a
movement hard to resist & which gives me pleasure (and I still like to get
pleasure from my reading no matter how it's generated or what the other
effects

2.
        and it was a pleasure to read Diane Ward's *Trop-i-dom*. Also a 2nd
book (unless there's more); the 1st a collection of 1 poem *On Duke Elling-
ton's Birthday*, which displayed truly down to earth wit (in 50s hip jargon
"down" was a descriptive term, usually complimentary, for anyone or thing
truly down to earth as opposed to 60s hippy jargon when it became a noun
to describe a state of being not all that desirable, etc.). *On Duke* also
showcased Ward's fine ear for the musical basis of the language when we
base the flow of it on the extension of the breath. She could be
honoring, more subtly, "ol' blue eyes." Sinatra's mastering of extended
phrasing, learned from watching one of the Dorsey's (can't remember which
is which) play, was one of his distinguishing features as "vocalist."
Stringing phrases or vowels together for an extended musical space was a
puzzle Dorsey helped explain by teaching him to inhale ever so slightly
through the side of the mouth, where the lips join, just the least
opening and the most minimal intake could add moments as though all one
exhalation. Ward approximates that in *On Duke*, a string of phrases
describing activities & gestures of the day in her life & lives of the
world. It doesn't compete with the extended sentence (of say Kerouac,
whose inspiration was also jazz soloists who "blew" long "crazy" riffs
with what seemed like one breath) because her phrases are really
sentences only connected in rhythm & logical continuity by choice of words
that leaves no doubt where they're going making them seem dependent on
what follows creating the phraselike effect. In *Trop-i-dom* the intention
seems altogether different. No pretensions to glib detachment from
aesthetic concerns mar either, but *Trop* achieves the impact of a declaration in control of rhythm alone. It's poetry because it sounds like
poetry in my brain when I read it, falling under the spell of its movement & rhythms unreproducable in musical terms on any instrument but
especially the voice; their music is poetry (i.e. they couldn't be
translated into the post-Patti Smith fashion of "the beat" as foundation
for rhythmic extension. They are instead based solidly on syntactical

relationships that only work when they make the reader/audience concentrate on the language, not the music). The language _is_ the music.

3.   Not as
compellingly "musical" is Carole Korzeniowsky's _Breastwork_, a tour de force that is a 1st book. These rhythms are based on more familiar prose & conversational structures. The basic unit is the sentence, not the phrase or _as_ phrase. But the relationship of the sentences is intended to draw us into poetic concerns for the language as other than prosaic or logic ridden. Yet, in the end, this work seems most dependent on logic to work, and it does work, hard & well. (The other 2 poets use the audience's capacity or potential to "intuit" meaning, in ways similar to those we use to intuit knowledge from our surroundings & experiences -- no neon morals and/or conclusions flash on and off in the brain, just accumulation of sensory and/or conceptual data leads to the evolution of conclusive ideas about what it all is & can mean to/for us. _Breastwork_ meanwhile seems to depend on a more contrived approach to gaining knowledge, one traditionally misconstrued as the traditional, main, or only way. In other words it moves as if teaching us something that can be taught by the very force of the continuous logic of the presentation of related ideas through the accuracy of referential terminology. While "in fact" it totally disengages the continuity of logical structures -- but in that continuity's terms, so we are left feeling as though we've been introduced to an area of "knowledge" we hadn't known before about a subject matter we had. The concepts are "abstract" in their purity as much as any in "new" music: not simple or straightforward as they appear but only structured as conclusively step-by-step directional and conclusory. I mean she tells us information while recreating a poetic kind of pleasure in the experiencing of it, that pleasure is often the sustenance of _language_.

MICHAEL LALLY

BREASTWORK

This book is the proposition of an exactly objective perceptive machine & becomes, thru just this fact, exactly subjective: Necker's cube, transcendence. A clear formulation of what in reality confronts any attempt to write. The key term is LUDEN (_inter-_, _a- -ed_): "In the interlude of bed and board..." = language pointing to the entire universe of meaning, wch is always present in the phenomena at (in) hand, if only we _see_ it. The most descriptive sentences (wch both present the concept of knowledge as the field of vision seen almost as page, canvas or screen, what Derrida means by writing-as-such) are the finest. Courage admits

the possibility of such language: the trick of our time (since Flaubert)
has been to leave the whole implicit, not from stylization but fear,
inability to grasp the larger unity wch at the same moment announces its
own negation. Consider this in relation to McClure: all there written
(say, "The Skull," his best piece) trumpets the impulse imPULSE to
arTICulate, a writing wch takes place within the body & prior to the
text. Wch is why his work reads more like a trace or map of a poem.
The next key term in *Breastwork* is blurred (wch is connected to the word
detected, a 3rd key): it conceals much information. In just wch way are
the words blurred? Is it that, overlaying one another, that tapestry of
sound in wch phoneme over phoneme buries the morphemic, that overdetermination of data wch is the constant fact: we have to detect our lives.

(revised from a letter to Carole Korzeniowsky, on Breastwork*)*

RON SILLIMAN

LETTER TO THE EDITOR

   ... I see the Eigner as in some respects the christening--the
serendipity of relationship I take as key--& that, however manipulated
the purpose, it remains arrogation to wear credit for the connections
mind affixes, skims. When Kit Robinson speaks "a generosity in this way
of taking things in" he speaks to the shift--the explorations of
"making be."
         I am most in sympathy with Silliman's reference to the
'pure light' passing thru the 2-way mirror. This has been the turning
of my most recent work and co-incided with Higgins' sense of poem as
charm. There is that element of spirit-magic as one rides the inchoate,
meaning the pro-vision at the turns (that a spectrum from willful to
random remains the mind's purview--the witch-stitchery. What brings us
together, however prominent language concerns, is the sense, the hunger
for 'present-ation'--we are alchemists all of the velocities of light
spun, turned, ricochet'd on all the analogous surfaces, depths and
passages of mind.
         "All the Buddhas and Bodhisattvas, together with all
the wriggling things possessed of life, share ... the nature is Mind;
Mind is the Buddha, and the Buddha is the Dharma... Let a tacit understanding be all!... To mistake materials surrounding for Mind is to
mistake a thief for your son."
         It is just that activity here called
tacit that you would gather into vision. I agree completely that,
finally, "It's the vision that matters, the real & worked out clarity of
vision." ...

JOHN PERLMAN

THE TELLING

Laura (Riding) Jackson, The Telling (1972; Harper & Row, o.p.)

For what Laura (Riding) Jackson has had to tell, poetry is insufficient. "Deficient," she insists; The Telling her first major work after renouncing poetry in 1938 as being linguistically incapable of truth telling. For writers serious about the possibilities of poetry it has been difficult to react; that Jackson intends this difficulty is evident from her vehement refusals to allow her views to be taken as the basis of a new way--a "medicine"--for poetry.

There is an unsympathy--a quarrelsomeness at times--that runs through The Telling, and is accentuated in some of the book's appended material. This is not a quarrelsomeness for its own sake, but the result of the prophetic--sometimes oracular--mode Jackson has chosen to write in: "preachment". There are few styles of, to her, contemporary avoidance that escape censure--from rock music and left politics to all manner of "professional" thought. The Telling, indeed, echoes the critique of Rousseau's First Discourse--that 'art' and 'intellect' have replaced 'virtue'. Jackson decries the obsession with doctrines, the new, success in the place of "articulating the human reality with truth"; it is professional learning--e.g., the poetic craft, specialized poetic form itself--that interposes itself between us and the truth of the mutuality of our one being.

Her insistence in The Telling is that in speaking it is possible to tell one another of that in which we each are not another--the 'Before' that is in the 'Now', spoken as 'Subject' to all 'Subjects'. Of the many things that prevent this truth telling of ourselves is the self satisfaction of carving out a voice that is distinct, actualized by its difference. "Telling differently for the triumph of difference, and not for truth's sake." Poetry dwells on the description of the distance, whose extolling, it is imagined, is a penetration into the deepest roots of humanness. This dwelling in the less-than, on the forms of our present lives, is a diversion from the fact of our "self-sameness in Being".

Since it creates a "literary reality", poetry is limited by its craft. "The liberty of word that poetry confers is poetry's technique not truths." Jackson's mode of writing in The Telling is able--unlike poetry, she says --to have a place for the reader in it: a speaking ideal of "normal" diction, one speaking to another of the mutualness of both, all, in being ("a method of our speaking, each, our All.") Each section of The Telling is--this is my experience of it--the enunciation of a shared fact; I find myself in it not in the sense of relation of personality (foibles, longing, &c) but ontologically, by the fact of my human being. (And yet in her sternness and insistence on this 'ultimate' seeing, her rebukes of all our human failings, perhaps too much--this 'all'--is asked of us-- does not her very unsympathy shut-out?--for there is connection also in the recognition and acknowledging of such failings in our fellow human beings.) Although Jackson's prophecy/pretension does not allow her to admit any predecessors in this self-actualizing of words--she says there are none, that the personal concreteness of *The Telling* is diverted by such comparisons--still, I thought of Dickinson (e.g., "The world is not conclusion"), of Kierkegaard's *Purity of Heart* and *Works of Love,* of Wittgenstein's *Philosophical Investigations* (which, like *The Telling*, is a critique/renunciation of an earlier work and method), of Oppen (not 'gesture' but the 'actual' "which is ourselves"), of Ashbery's recitals. Of *Walden*: "There are words addressed to our condition exactly, which, if we could really hear and understand, would be more salutary than the morning."

In the supplemental material to *The Telling,* Jackson cautions against confusing endings for completeness. This work, dedicated itself to self- completeness, brings to completeness the promise of Laura Riding's poetry. The turning required for this completeness is, perhaps, an unexpected one; its faithfulness to itself--to language, to "us"--is manifest. "And the tale is no more of the going: no more a poet's tale of going false-like to a seeing. The tale is of a seeing true-like to a knowing."

CHARLES BERNSTEIN

NOTES ON MICHAEL PALMER'S *WITHOUT MUSIC*

Michael Palmer, <u>Without Music</u> (1977; $4 from Black Sparrow Press, Box 3993, Santa Barbara, CA 93105)

Without Music is an advance over Michael Palmer's previous books because it achieves a more total effect. A presence realized through an inte- grated design, an architecture. Yet this is a tentative architecture, perhaps a scaffolding the height and shape of which suggests the building we take to be there but perceive in glimpses through the scaffolding and construct in our imaginations.

Nowhere is it written that books of poetry must have an order beyond what the table of contents presents. American poets from Whitman through Pound to Olson, Spicer and beyond have sought an order, a form, that will carry all the poet has to say. Palmer's concern may be seen as similar but in a significant way (or he may be more intense about it) he diverges. His poems (the parts) are to the book (the whole) as the lines of each poem are to the poem.

"You can never step in the same cloud twice (in the same
song twice)"

Palmer seeks to permit the poem to connect as many diverse elements as possible - Polysynthesis - to propose rather than dictate so that each poem suggests something beyond itself. "Content," as de Kooning said, "is a slippery glimpse."

The poems are relentless but not predictable. They are tense but sturdy. Not about to crack.

...

Without music. Acapella. For the past four years Palmer has been making dances in collaboration with the dancer Margaret Jenkins. His words - her choreography. Without music? Palmer's music, his "noise" is dry, comes from the throat:

'Only the birds' she said

'clearing their throats'

The tone has a precise edge to it. Crisp, it seems hardly to vary, but its accuracy is telling. Without music, but the book returns again and again to songs and dances. A tone that is toneless and will not draw attention to itself, will not overwhelm the song.

"the song / of the jungle partridge // is the purest /

something like a flute / with no tones at all."

...

"the figure unconscious in the leather chair"

.

"A sleeper wakes up but not too much / enough for an alphabet"

.

"complex sleep"

Palmer works the image of sleep, the figure of a sleeper "awake and fearing sleep," awake and sleeping, "asleep between concertos" and "sleeping among stones" into the book's larger design.

Sleep - Between speech and dreams?
        Between one language and another?
Although this is the kind of strand not present in Palmer's earlier work, or not so developed, the image does not dominate, does not articulate a

theme. Stones also recur. And the word alphabet. Colors or the words
for colors are less prominent in *Without Music,* but the fascination with
numbers persists. 1s, ones, three, fives, six, eleven and 14. Image
is secondary. The language, sentences not phrases, is primary.
Language disturbed so that unlikely combinations provoke new responses,
and there is both beauty and mystery in the meanings that insist
themselves.

                              . . .

Several times while reading *Without Music* I laughed out loud. Palmer's
humor, more in evidence than before, is equal parts matter-of-fact
deadpan and chagrin:

    "A hamburger and sand up your ass / is more like it"

                              . . .

A way into *Without Music* is through the back door, the book's final
poem "The Meadow" dedicated to Robert Duncan in which Palmer quotes the
phrase "folded in all thought" from "Often I Am Permitted To Return To A
Meadow" the first poem in Duncan's *The Opening of the Field.* Duncan's
poem thus recalled supplies this stanza to illuminate Palmer's work:

    "She is Queen Under The Hill

       whose hosts are a disturbance of words within words

       that is a field folded."

                                        WILLIAM CORBETT

LETTER TO THE EDITOR

.... I'm sending this as a reaction to the first issue. As I remember,
the main thing was information. If that is the accepted criterion, I
find most of it an out & out failure. Most of it (the reviews) is just
too self-conscious, too cute to be of use. Many of the reviewers seem
to feel an obligation to turn the review into a performance as near an
"original work" as possible. The result is akin to what happens when the
old "new criticism" heavy weights go to work on something: whatever it
was, novel or poem, becomes just something, the floor allowing them to do
their dance. I see no essential difference between what they did and what
many of your contributors do: make the work of others the occasion for
their own performance. Why pretend to call them reviews at all? "Variations On A Theme Suggested By X" would be more honest & accurate.

    I find this especially harmful with small press publications. It's

not unusual for even a commercial press book of poems to be out a year
without being reviewed once anywhere. The odds jump for small presses.
Given that, I find it nearly criminal to so grandstand that a reader can
have little or no conception of what the work is like.... There may be
a place for Barthes' choreography du text (which I doubt), but surely it
comes well after the basic identity of the text has been established....
It is a disservice to the writers involved. & if you say after all everybody knows everybody else, well I ask you!

JOHN TAGGART

PHOTOGRAMS

> "The illiterates of the future will be ignorant of camera and
> pen alike." -- Laszlo Moholy-Nagy

> "The photogram, or cameraless record of forms produced by light,
> which embodies the unique nature of the photographic process, is
> the real key to photography. It allows us to capture the patterned
> interplay of light on a sheet of sensitized paper without recourse
> to any apparatus. The photogram opens up perspectives of a
> hitherto wholly unknown morphosis governed by optical laws
> peculiar to itself. It is the most completely dematerialized
> medium that the new vision commands."
> -- Moholy-Nagy, 1932

Photography was for a time considered only a mechanical means of recording
and documenting. While this quality of photography is widely held to
have released painters from realistic depiction, the photogram represents
the melding, rather than the separation, of the two traditions. The chief
proponents and discoverers of the photogram, Man Ray and Moholy-Nagy, both
turned from painting to photography and the discovery of the photogrammic
technique (c. 1920-1922). These two pioneers, bringing to photography
painterly concerns, questioned the purely documentary nature of photography. As Brecht wrote, "Less than ever does a simple reproduction of
reality express something about reality." Photograms combine the directness inherent in the application of paint to canvas with the basic
characteristics of the photo-process: light and the tones produced on
light-sensitive paper. With photograms the question of taking pictures
does not arise: the whole process can be confined to the darkroom.

Photograms are a form of bricollage. Bits of scraps, cotton, buttons,
etc.,--materials "ready to hand"--are collaged together and transformed
with the product often having no outward relationship to the elements
that formed it. In the darkroom these captured images live. What

remains on the paper is the residue of the objects--their shadows--the predominant effect is a lack of gravity--of lunar traces--ghosts of objects--a capturing of a fleeting imprint of light passing through an object surrounding it, transformed by it.

Cameraless pictures serve as direct light diagrams, recording the actions of light over a period of time, the motion of light in space. The photogram produces space without existing spatial structure by articulation on the plane of the paper with half-tones of black, gray and white. It is a writing and drawing with light.

The typical feature of the photogram is instability; the image can only be preserved momentarily before it changes. "The object being, for the sake of curiosity, to create a fresh problem, or to place a new obstacle in the path of light like a straw dropped across the path of an ant." (G. C. Argan) Each instance is made particular by the translucent, transparent, or opaque qualities of the objects and the angle of the light rays to the paper.

For Man Ray and Moholy-Nagy, automatic writing, Dadaist collages, Stein, Schwitters, Breton, Cubism, Surrealist writing, etc., all provided an analogy for this proposed new vision of photography. Moholy-Nagy encouraged photographers to liberate themselves from rendering and illusionism and open themselves up to synthetic composition. Light itself would function as the kind of creative agent that pigment is for the painter. "If we can see in the genuine elements of photography the self-sufficient vehicle for direct, visual impact based on the properties of the light-sensitive emulsion then we may be nearer to 'art' in the field of photography." (Moholy-Nagy).

Beaumont Newhall has written, "The photogram makers' problem has nothing to do with interpreting the world, but rather with the formation of abstractions. Objects are chosen for their light-modulating characteristics: their reality and significance disappear. The logical end point of the photogram is the reduction of photography to the light-recording property of silver salts. To the cameraman this is what Malevich's *White on White* is to the painter."

SUSAN BEE LAUFER

(Many of Moholy-Nagy's books stress the interrelationship of the visual and literary arts and the value of visual artists studying the achievements of Stein, Joyce, the constructivists, etc., particularly--Painting Photography, & Film (MIT Press, 1969) and Vision in Motion (Paul Theobald, 1947).

THE POLITICS OF SCORING

Ernest Robson, <u>I Only Work Here</u>, 1975; <u>Transwhichics</u>, 1970; both strikingly designed by Marion Robson. $7 each, Primary Press, Box 105, Parker Ford, PA 19457)

Robson displays a life-long work of augmenting the visual information of poetry -- more keyed to <u>voice</u> than visual poetry has generally been, and specified for voice in ways more akin to vocal scores than projectivism. He introduces a more diversified acoustic palette by an orthographic technique for cueing the vocalization of acoustic features -- distorting lengths of letters, spaces, differences in elevation & darkness of letters. These graphic cues ("prosodynes") match, and make writable, prosodic <u>levels</u> (of pitch, intensity, duration, pauses, and vowel pitch modulation within a single syllable). unstint$_e$d RH Y THMS $_a$nd the JER$_{\kappa}$ed readJ U STM$_E$NTS So that the semantic realm acts as one term in an <u>equation</u>, where the assocations carried by the phonetic pattern are matched up with meanings; where neither realm is independent of the other: an emblem of an absence, a representation, a compacting, a mimesis, an index. Yet scoring of such care makes the whole project take on the appearance of an instrument, a secondhand. *to IM$_I$TATE WITH GL <u>A</u> SS ...*

to SING *a* S^{Y}M$_{phon_i}$ZING *of their* MEAN $_I$NGS *un*LESS *IT* WERE SO <u>E</u> MPT*y*

But significance TH ^{I} NS $_{in}$ per^{i}ph$_e$RIES $_{of}$ ch^{i}LL A I R ....

What we most want to say is unheard, unvoiced, barely framed, uncueable by orthography which is an operation-symbol, like (+), (-), etc. As if the distance between word and referent, between signifier and signified, could be bridged by *LURES*. These orchestrations may *CODIFY;* but do not create, or frame, or problematicize. The stress on connecting spoken and written language, on voice, still leaves open the larger task: of voicing the world, of using words to reconstitute it or be recomposed by it and within it. As an alternative / Robson / actual themes: Depression labor, the military, psychology, furtrapping, the political unreliability of liberals; yet oversimplifications, familiar tunes & image, slogan, texts as early as 1924 right up to publication, so "Five Decades of Poetry in Four Styles." suc<u>CESS</u>IONS of re<u>CESS</u>IONS of ho<u>RIZ</u>ONS E ND

One can talk about returning to the "desubjectivized" domain of <u>techne</u> and instrumental action some of the vanished subjectivity. Mao even associated composition "On a blank sheet of paper... free from any mark" with political leadership and constitution. But is an appeal to subjectivity one we can valorize in a social way? Isn't it preliminary to a more basic task -- of returning to techne, to labor itself, some of the normative and conformative qualities of interaction, of community, of redeemable claims to validity and significance? So: could the emphasis

on subjectivity (on monologue, on personal and poetic eccentricity)
possibly be a distraction from this <u>social</u> challenge -- composing a social
praxis, bringing us nearer to what we prosper by?

such ^IN<u>DEF</u>_inite ^IM_ages ^of infin_ite d_eGREES _of FREE<i>D</i>^OM .... *the* Gⁱdd*y*

C Ī R CLING _IN

Performance, and prosodynic cueing, can articulate individual
intention.   OUR ⁱⁿTEN<i>ti</i>_on SH A RES   its C^{AL}C_u^{LA}T<i>ed</i> <u>WAYS</u>   But, <u>between
us</u>, reading bodies forth a shared field: beyond distraction.

did YO^U conf U SE YOUR <u>NOIS</u>*es* .... with C^HOIC *es*   And choices /
intention might be as social as consciousness and language itself, so that
writing need <u>not</u> be "incompatible with rules for socializing discovery" --
for reading is such a socializing, a reciprocity. Social Desires. The
validity of even problematic norms could be redeemed in <u>discourse</u>. But
not the old bogey of 'discourse' used as a stick to flog all 'idiosyncratic' expressionism and 'arid' conceptualism and 'dehumanized' constructivism. Instead: <u>touch</u>, an erotics of the text, or participation, and
consciousness -- <u>dialogue</u>. We can, slowly, be stretched at the limits of
what would constitute discourse -- by our writing, by what we are
conscious of in writing, in language, in ...

BRUCE ANDREWS

DOLCH WORDS

Kit Robinson, <u>The Dolch Stanzas</u> (1976; $1 from This Press, 326
Connecticut, San Francisco, CA 94107)

Dr. Edward Dolch, dear to all reading teachers, in his class *Manual for
Remedial Reading*, came up with a list of words, 220 words, which he
estimated accounted for 1/2 to 3/4 of all school reading matter, words
which by the third grade everyone is expected to recognize instantly by
sight. Dr. Dolch, with his usual modesty, referred to these words as the
Basic Sight Vocabulary ("which should not be used in alphabetical order
because that arrangement gives the child a clue as to how the words begin.
They should be printed in random order...") some 50 years having since
passed, the good doctor's reputation in the field is secure and his name
has been memorialized, these words are now commonly known as Dolch words.
They are supposed to come first, the words to skip past on the way to the
unfamiliar ones: yellow, five, our, put, well, always, those, gave, for,
ate, pull...

together or on / right / what works there

The unexpected felicities to be met in the absence of usual contrast, in a vocabulary which is all ground, or all figure. Maybe a leveller principle at work, not that it is a question of altitude, but that the words do not need dressing, that it is not necessary to import; if, as it increasingly appears, any realm of words, technical, pyrotechnical, can be found appropriate, or appropriatable, must it not also hold that the most common, the diction's lumpenproletariat, strictly those words we know so well we hardly bother with them, usually, are as readily capable, can hold at least as much charge as the most elevated, specialized, or purportedly lyric nomenclatures.

or why think / ask / try out new hold

if they sleep / just as off / as always

put it to them / like this / say

here / this want / to be clean

open / not done / wants to know

Separating out of words, by whatever process, enjoining them to enter the poem, any sort of arrangement lying there, if it is to produce the desired, must be radically delineated--delimited (else we wld say--prose), intentions of scrutiny bring forth, what--every length or combination across the band has its resonance, its complex of value, as many and as finely tuned degrees of concern; but it seems certain vocabularies are capable of calling up wider zones of response, they may interlock into much more that is outside of them, more hookups or sprockets, or memory bits; usually these plain words are the backdrop, the links, the machinery keeping everything running; tho' through this special acquaintance--an influence unexpectedly pervasive; also known as running words, e.g. the rivers under, the underground or under the streets, what everyone is running on, what they had in them all the time, surprisingly widespread contacts, that they may be closer to that thing pertaining to reality that we are always trying to name.

it can move fast / she is said to have / seen it go once

once and for all / by the white way / it left out

The regions of thought the short stanzas read into are often called from certain areas of human activity, primary activities, working, loving, sleeping, watching, hunting, playing; is it a property of these running words to combine in concentrations of other-resonance, the "we" is how

64

many more than the author, an increasingly inclusive simplicity; and
like all like minded words they combine most easily with each other--
already meant for combination, unchambering each other, short primary
words lines stanzas... and as all colors can be mixed from red orange
yellow green blue violet indigo...

then is always before / no longer / than it is round

MICHAEL GOTTLIEB

REPOSSESSING THE WORD

*(The following is an excerpt from an "Intraview" by Steve McCaffery in
the January 1978 issue of Centerfold: 320-10th St. N.W. Calgary, Canada
T2N 1V8. In a related discussion, Ron Silliman brings out the relation
of Marx's notion of commodity fetishism to conventional descriptive and
narrative forms of writing: where the word--words--cease to be valued for
what they are themselves but only for their properties as instrumentalities
leading us to a world outside or beyond them, so that the words--language--
disappear, become transparent, leaving us with the picture of a physical
world that the reader can then consume as a commodity. ("Disappearance
of the Word/Appearance of the World," 1977, One Hundred Posters issue;
$1.15 from L=A=N=G=U=A=G=E distributing service). Such a view of the
role and historical functions of writing relates closely to our analysis
of the capitalist social order as a whole. It is our sense that the
project of poetry does not involve turning language into a commodity for
consumption; instead, it involves repossessing the sign through active
participation in its production.)*

Marx's notion of commodity fetishism, which is to say the occultation
of the human relations embedded in the labour process has been central to
my own considerations of reference in language - of, in fact, a referentially based language, in general - and to certain "fetishistic" notions
within the relationship of audience and performer. Reference in language
is a strategy of promise and postponement; it's the thing that language
never is, never can be, but to which language is always moving. This
linguistic promise that the signified gives of something beyond language
i've come to feel as being central to capitalism (the fetish of the
commodity) and derived from an earlier theologicolinguistic confidence
trick of "the other life". It's this sense of absence as a postponed

presence which seems to be the core of narrative (the paradigm art form
of the capitalist system) and basic to the word as we use the word in any
representational context. To demystify this fetish and reveal the human
relationships involved within the labour process of language will involve
the humanization of the linguistic Sign by means of a centering of
language within itself; a structural reappraisal of the functional roles
of author and reader, performer and performance; the general diminishment
of reference in communication and the promotion of forms based upon object-
presence: the pleasure of the graphic or phonic imprint, for instance,
their value as sheer linguistic stimuli. Kicking out reference from the
word (and from performance) is to kick its most treasured and defended
contradiction: the logic of passage.

STEVE MC CAFFERY

BUT I WON'T

I could mention running into Larry Fagin (1962) and him giving me a list
   (one of his early ones) of things to read: Jack Spicer, Robin Blaser,
   Charles Olson, *Locus Solus* magazine, Robert Creeley, among others.
   Carried paper in wallet through 1969. Checking off item (person) as
   read. Threw paper away. Stopped carrying wallet.

I could tell about reading the Donald Allen anthology. Which (coming
   across) grew out of reading Jack Kerouac and Allen Ginsberg while in
   high school. Which is how I got to San Francisco (to meet Larry).
   Travel through U.S. and Mexico "on the road." Tail end of two-lane
   blacktop. Drib and drab beginnings of interstate system. BORING.

I could go into (still in school) the gossip intricacies of Pack and Hall
   anthologies (endless psychological drivel in emblems endless). Also
   can't remember exactly some anthology from Doubleday edited by (question mark) someone and someone (not interesting) I can't remember
   (question mark).

I could leave out Padgett and Shapiro's *An Anthology of New York Poets*, more noticeable for absences than presences, a continuous source of reading (nice design), though. And *The World Anthology* and its sequel *Another World* edited by Anne Waldman which (both) had plenty in them. And (should note in passing) Paul Carroll's anthology.

I could point out the avalanche (so it seemed) of special anthologies, based on some kind of "social science idea" I tended to avoid: but kind of enjoyed Jerome Rothenberg's *Revolution of the Word*. Browse but not buy.

I could let you in on recent developments which an article in *The Poetry Project Newsletter* (by Harry Lewis) said were anthologies which were really one-shot magazines. Including Michael Lally's *None of the Above* and Yuki Hartman and Michael Slater's *Fresh Paint*. Both of which try to put together a grouping of poets (but not enough poems) to be an intro to (fine how do you do). Again (see various introductions) absents more glaring than presents.

I could let on what's (I think) needed. Anthology with selections worked down from about 200 manuscript pages (per poet) each. Could be organized city-by-city since "school" no longer is really workable and city is. About 50 poets. Edited by someone who can distinguish between real poems (by real poets) and images of poems (by competent poets, heretofore called MFAs). Differences between ongoing traditions and the bad-money-driving-out-the-good of cultural propaganda.

I could quickly note dictionary definition: (origin) a gathering of flowers; (later) selection of pieces. Or refer to Pound's idea of working anthology. A good one recharges what's what in the air.

Right now people are beginning to notice "stuffy." I could use more than a change of scene.

(1960: Allen, <u>The New American Poetry</u> (Grove Press). 1968: Carroll, <u>The Young American Poets</u> (Follett). 1969: <u>The World Anthology</u> (Bobbs Merrill). 1970: <u>An Anthology of New York Poets</u> (Vintage). 1971: <u>Another World</u> (Bobbs Merrill). 1974: <u>Revolution of the Word: A New Gathering of American Avant Garde Poetry 1914-1945</u> (Seabury). 1976: <u>None of the Above: New Poets of the USA</u> (Crossing Press). 1977: <u>Fresh Paint</u> (Ailanthus).

———————————

MAC LOW

PASSING THE WORD ALONG: MAC LOW IN BRIEF

Jackson MacLow is a poet, composer, and performance artist. He is also a Buddhist, a pacifist, and an anarchist who votes. His writing and performances are organized by systemic processes, with more or less space allowed for pure invention in varying degrees.

His early training and work, as follows: he was born 1922 in Chicago, attended the University of Chicago, specializing in philosophy and structural criticism, and Brooklyn College in Classical Greek. He has been writing poetry, music, plays, prose pieces, and criticism since 1937, and after 1954 combined these arts, as well as theater, dance, and visual arts, in group performance works he calls 'simultaneities'-- as well as in solo performance works--while continuing to compose poems, music, plays, and visual works (drawings, paintings, videotapes).

Throws of a die in 1954-55 selected isolated works from the bible to comprise lines of MacLow's first major series, his *5 biblical poems*. At this same fertile period he developed two other techniques he used in constructing later pieces. He constructed a long poem by working out a system of correspondences: assigning a different word (drawn from a nineteenth century natural history text) to each pitch of Guillaume de Machault's motet "Quant Theseus." His simultaneity performances (in which more than one thing is going on at the same time) had their roots in the last of his *5 biblical poems*, in which instructions permitted three particularly long lines to be read simultaneously by three performers.

In 1958 he found a quick alternative to dice, cards, and coins for producing random behavior in the form of the RAND Corporation's *A Million Random Digits with 100,000 Normal Deviates*. With these tools he composed stanzaic pieces derived from Buddhist texts and drew "word strings" (chains of words) from de Sade's *The Bedroom Philosophers* to form the *Sade Suit*.

The Marrying Maiden, a theater piece, was also written in 1958, its text taken from the *I Ching*. Any performers' impulses for staginess were quashed by stage directions, determined randomly, for amplitude, tempii, and tone of delivery.

In simplest form, his acrostic pieces, begun in 1960, drew words, word strings, or sentences from a given text by using the first letter of each word in the text's title as an index to selecting lines from the text to form the poem. In its hundreds of pages, MacLow's book *Stanzas for Iris Lezak* explores hundreds of variations on this procedure.

The lyrical *Light Poems*, begun in 1968, are free in form and repeat the names of kinds of light throughout their lines. The lights are drawn by various systems from a chart of 288 kinds of light.

MacLow began writing his gathas in 1961; they can be divided into several strains, all notated on graph paper. The mantraic gathas situate the words of mantras, usually vertically and horizontally. The non-mantraic gathas situate words taken from Kathy Acker's *The Childlike Life of the Black Tarantula #3*. Each of his vocabulary gathas are based on one of his friends' names. Another kind of piece, called a vocabulary (but not to be confused with his vocabulary gathas), was first begun in 1968. It draws words from the letters found in a person's name, using some or all of the available letters. The vocabularies are written by hand, crowding the paper with words of all sizes pointing in every direction. He considers this form a crossbreed of light poems with gathas. These pieces are sometimes performed with instruments as well as voices, by performers situated around the room, their choice of words and intonations left up to their own personalities.

BARBARA BARACKS

BIBLIOGRAPHY: *The Pronouns--A Collection of 40 Dances--For the Dancers* (1964; N.Y., mimeo; photocopy, $3 from MacLow, 80 North Moore, NYC 10013; 1971, Tetrad Press, London, with graphics by Ian Tyson; revised edition forthcoming, Station Hill Press, Barrytown, N.Y. 12507). *The Twin Plays: Port-au-Prince* and *Adams County Illinois* (1966, Something Else Press; $3 from MacLow). *Manifestos* (1966; Something Else Press, N.Y.). *August Light Poems* (1967; Caterpillar Books, N.Y.; limited # available from Mac-Low). *Verdurous Sanguinaria* (1967; Southern University, Baton Rouge, La.; play). *22 Light Poems* (1968; Black Sparrow Press). *23rd Light Poem: for Larry Eigner* (1969; Tetrad Press, London). *Stanzas for Iris Lezak*

(1972; Something Else Press; $10.41 from MacLow).   _4 Trains_ (1974; Burn-
ing Deck Press).   _36th Light Poem: In Memoriam Buster Keaton_ (1975; Perma-
nent Press, c/o Vas Dias, 52 Cascade Ave., London N10 England).   _21
Matched Asymmetries_ (Forthcoming; Aloes Press, 18 Hayes Court, New Park Rd.,
London SW2 4EX, England).   _6 Light Poems for 6 Women_ (Forthcoming; Station
Hill Press).   _First Book of Gathas, 1961-78_ (Forthcoming; Membrane Press,
Box 11601, Shorewood, Milwaukee, WI 53211).   TAPES: "The Black Tarantula
Crossword Gathas" (#33 from S Press, c/o M. Kürler, Tonband Verlag, D-8
Munchen 40, Zieblandstrasse 10, West Germany).   "The Text on the Opposite
Page," "Homage to Leona Bleiweis" -- 2 versions (1978; 3 tapes from New
Wilderness Foundation, 365 West End, NYC 10024; $8, 8, & $8.50).

MAC LOW

MUSELETTER

for Charles

     Charles Bernstein and Bruce Andrews have asked me to write something
about my work &/or self, & Charles sent me a month ago a letter containing
13 questions of which he did "hope one or two make you want to say some-
thing--" & today he phoned me at about 11:30 AM (to remind me, i.e., nag
me in the sweet way he does), "So--" from our conversation & his qq.,
"here goes--":
     CB: "1. Are you interested in having emotion in your process-oriented,
programmatic poetry?" / JML: (I'm too stingy of space to give each of us
a whole paragraph each time.) To most readers of poetry this wd seem a
remarkable question! I take it that C senses conflict between "emotion"
& my using chance operations & other quasiobjective methods to generate
artworks: if I ever felt such a conflict, & I think I may have, say, in
the middle 1950's, I no longer do & havent for some years. Yes the Zen
Buddhist motive for use of chance (&c) means was to be able to generate
series of "dharmas" (phenomena/events, e.g., sounds, words, colored
shapes) relatively "uncontaminated" by the composer's "ego" (taste,
constitutional predilections, opinions, current or chronic emotions).
It was such a relief to stop making artworks carry that burden of
"expression"! To let them become themselves, watch them grow & take shape
without one's pushing & shoving them around too much, was & is a great
pleasure: probably a "self-indulgence" (one cd care less). But by the
later 50s it was plain to me that sense- & sense/concept-events (tones,
words)--the specific sensible instances--are both intrinsically & extrin-
sically emotional: by which I mean simply that specific sounds &/or words
(or other sensible elements) singly, combined, &/or in series, have high
probabilities of arousing feelings within specific ranges in hearers &c

(whether in "most," or merely most members of certain classes or ingroups I'm not prepared to say--probably the wider the range the smaller the ingroup) & also that each hearer has to bring an idiosyncratic range of emotions ("associations"?) to each event, which is inextricably compounded with the more "general" range in each person's experience.

But (paragraphs are emotional, said Stein) that may not be what you mean by "having emotion": if that were all you meant I cd say that of course I've always been interested in the fact that sounds, words, &c., no matter how "randomly" generated, arouse emotions "willy-nilly" (& I for one never nil'd 'em). But if your question means, Do I allow my own emotions to influence my systematically generated work, I must answer that they can't help doing so: my choices of means, materials, &c., can't help being influenced by emotions, & I'd be foolish if I thought they weren't. Moreover, I realized by the later 50s that the events we single out as "experiences of emotion" as against those we call "sensations" occur as randomly as the sounds in a forest, & began to feel less difference between generating works systematically & recording emotional events (or otherwise using one's own or one's performers' emotions as elements in artworks). & while continuing to do each of these things relatively separately in some works, I have made many works in the 60s & 70s which variously combine chance & other generative systems with various types of "direct expression"--notably my Light Poems, of which I am presently writing the 55th (the 2nd to Stephanie Vevers: so far 18 notebook pages, about 20 lines each), some of which only "have" the emotions attached to or arising from hearing names of kinds of light, others of which use as elements emotions arising in my current life, &c.

Which brings me back to CB: "2. What do you think of 'cheating'-- changing results so that the poem conforms to some non-procedurally derived sense of meaning--when composing basically chance-derived poems?" / JML: If I decide to use a certain system, I don't change the results of that system (whether doing so is "cheating" or not I forebear to judge). But I have at times composed systems that generate works conveying or "having" meanings clearly intended by the composer. As you well know, I've composed many political poems & love poems while abiding strictly by the results of such generative means as systematic chance.

I do want to touch on your 3rd question, finally: which I'll summarize: These days I'm greatly interested in work that tells me how it is to live lives--whether the artist's own life or the lives of others: works as different in their ways as Phil Niblock's movies of people working in Mexico, Peru, & the US & Sharon Mattlin's vivid embodiments of "epiphanies" (to use Joyce's term) from the lives of her family, friends, & acquaintances, as well as her own life: quasi-narrative poems in which the poet's own attitudes & emotions about events & feelings are conveyed predominantly by word choice, rhythms, selection of details of experiences dealt with, often quite subtly & indirectly, rather than by her self-consciously imposing herself upon her materials. You ask whether I'm less interested in "procedural" or language/structural work as such. Well, of such work, I'm most interested in works having "content," even "subject-matter," tho not always as the words are commonly used. Hannah Weiner's "Clairvoyant Journals" convey her life experience while radically transforming usual formats (verse/prose/&c) to do so, Bernadette Mayer's work has done so for years. Also, your own work, as well as that of Emmett Williams, Dick Higgins, & Ron Silliman, & the recent work of Peter Seaton (to mention only those who quickly come to mind—forgive me, others), while not referring to experience with the same directness, seems "to have content" even tho the "subject-matter" may often be shifting & elusive. Interest, however, is not at all synonymous with value judgement, & when I <u>hear</u> more purely language/structure work, such as John Cage's "Empty Words" or the works of Clark Coolidge, I'm often completely enthralled, even tho I do not return again & again to the <u>pages</u> from which they read.

Well, "I think that's about enough," as the blessed Henry Cowell used to say when signing off his WBAI radio program, "Music of the World's Peoples." ...

JACKSON MAC LOW   NY   12/22/77

L=A=N=G=U=A=G=E

Vol.1, No.2.   April 1978

Bruce Andrews, Charles Bernstein, Editors.

Layout: Susan Laufer.

Subscriptions -- One year (six issues) for $4.
                 Institutions: $8.

L=A=N=G=U=A=G=E is supported solely by subscriptions and donations.

All queries and checks to:
Charles Bernstein, 464 Amsterdam Ave., New York, NY 10024.

(C) 1978 by L=A=N=G=U=A=G=E

ANNOUNCEMENT: ONE HUNDRED POSTERS #26 (February 1978): "Three of Four Things I Know about Him," essay by Charles Bernstein; $1 from Other Publications, Box 415, Kenmore Station, Boston, MA 02215.

L=A=N=G=U=A=G=E

JUNE 1978

EXPERIMENTS

Pick any word at random (noun is easy): let mind play freely around it
until a few ideas have passed through. Then seize on them, look at them,
& record. Try this with a non-connotative word, like "so" etc.

Systematically eliminate the use of certain kinds of words or phrases
from a piece of writing, either your own or someone else's, for example,
eliminate all adjectives or all words beginning with 's' from
Shakespeare's sonnets.

Systematically derange the language, for example, write a work consisting
only of prepositional phrases, or, add a gerundive to every line of an
already existing piece of prose or poetry, etc.

Rewrite someone else's writing. Maybe someone formidable.

Get a group of words (make a list or select at random); then form these
words (only) into a piece of writing -- whatever the words allow. Let
them demand their own form, and/or: Use certain words in a set way,
like, the same word in every line, or in a certain place in every
paragraph, etc. Design words.

Never listen to poets or other writers; never explain your work (communication experiment).

Set up multiple choice or fill-in-the-blanks situations & play with them,
considering every word an 'object' with no meaning, perhaps just sound,
or, a block of meaning, meaning anything.

Eliminate material systematically from a piece of your own writing until
it's 'ultimately' reduced, or, read or write it backwards (line by line
or word by word). Read a novel backwards.

Using phrases relating to one subject or idea, write about another (this
is pushing metaphor & simile as far as you can), for example, steal
science terms or philosophical language & write about snow or boredom.

Experiment with theft & plagiarism in any form that occurs to you.

Take an idea, anything that interests you, even an object: then spend a few days looking & noticing (making notes, etc.?) what comes up about that idea, or, try to create a surrounding, an atmosphere, where everything that comes up is "in relation".

Construct a poem as though the words were three-dimensional objects (like bricks) in space. Print them on large cards, if necessary.

Cut-ups, paste-ups, etc. (Intersperse different material in horizontal cut-up strips, paste it together, infinite variations on this).

Write exactly as you think, as close as you can come to this, that is, put pen to paper & dont stop.

Attempt tape recorder work, that is, speaking directly into the tape, perhaps at specific times.

Note what happens for a few days, hours (any space of time that has a limit you set); then look for relationships, connections, synchronicities; make something of it (writing).

Get a friend or two friends to write _for_ you, pretending they _are_ you.

Use (take, write in) a strict form and/or try to destroy it, e.g., the sestina.

Take or write a story or myth, continue to rewrite it over & over, or, put it aside &, trying to remember, write it five or ten times (from memory); see how it's changed. Or, make a work out of continuously saying, in a column or list, a sentence or line, & saying it over in a different way, ways, until you get it "right". Save the whole thing.

Typing vs. longhand experiments as recording/creating devices/modes. Do what you do least.

Make a pattern of repetitions.

Take an already written work of your own & insert (somewhere at random, or by choice) a paragraph of section from, for example, a book on information theory or a catalogue of some sort. Then study the possibilities of rearranging this work, or perhaps, rewriting the 'source'.

Experiment with writing in every person & tense every day.

Explore possibilities of lists, puzzles, riddles, dictionaries, almanacs for language use.

Write what cannot be written, for example, compose an index. (Read an index as a poem).

The possibilities of synesthesia in relation to language & words: The word & the letter as sensations, colors evoked by letters, sensations caused by the sound of a word as apart from its meaning, etc. _And_, the effect of this phenomenon on you, for example, write in the water, on a moving vehicle.

Attempt writing in a state of mind that seems least congenial.

Consider word & letter as forms -- the concretistic distortion of a text, for example, too many o's or a multiplicity of thin letters (lllftiii, etc).

Consider (do) memory experiments (sensory) in relation to writing: for example, record all sense images that remain from breakfast; study which sense(s) engage you, escape you.

Write, taking off from visual projection, whether mental or mechanical, without thought to the word (in the ordinary sense, no craft). Write in the movies, etc.

Make writing experiments over a long period of time: for example, plan how much you will write on a particular work (one word?) each day, or, at what time of a particular day (noon?) or week, or, add to the work only on holidays, etc.

Write on a piece of paper where something is already printed or written, as, in your favorite book of prose or poetry (over the print, in the white space).

Attempt to eliminate all connotation from a piece of writing & vice versa.

Use source material, that is, experiment with other people's writings, sayings, & doings.

Experiment with writing in a group, collaborative work: a group writing individually off of each others work over a long period of time (8 hour say); a group contributing to the same work, sentence by sentence, line by line; one writer being fed 'information' while the other writes; writing, leaving instructions for another writer to fill in what you 'cant' describe; compiling a book or work structured by your own language around the writings of others; a group working & writing off of each other's dream-writing.

Use dictionary constantly, plain & etymological (rhyming, etc.); consult, experiment with thesaurus where categories for the word 'word' include: word as news, word as message, word as information, word as story, word as order or command, word as vocable, unit of speech, word as instruction, promise, vow, contract & so on.

Dream work: record dreams daily, experiment with translation or transcription of dream-thought, attempt to approach the tense & incongruity appropriate to the dream, work with the dream until a poem, song or phrase that is useful can come out of it, consider the dream as problem-solving device (artistic problem, other), consider the dream as a form

of consciousness (altered state) & use it (write with it) as an 'alert'
form of the mind's activity, change dream characters into fictional
characters & accept dream 'language' (words spoken or heard in dream) as
gift. Use them.

Work your ass off to change the language & dont ever get famous.

*BERNADETTE MAYER & THE MEMBERS OF THE ST. MARK'S
CHURCH POETRY PROJECT WRITING WORKSHOP, 1971-1975*

———————————————

from HEROES, HOW THEY FILE PAST

== A certain Yankee ingenuity, ability to manipulate - coupled with
American land-usage: game, mechanism, and the anecdote (we find our
heroes when we need them) ==

Contra Cage, his music: the use of chance operations does not result in a
demilitarization of language or sound; it portends an ... organization-
from-above and atomic discontinuities below. Solzhenitsyn's description
of random terror leading to the Gulag parallels the apparent freeing of
notes - another kind of lock-in actually, one that pretends to the
inherently alien....

Contra Duchamp, his production: a series of games and strategies proclaim-
ing privilege at every critical turn. A beginning for an autocratic art,
an art of closure, of disengagement. The beguilement and alienation of
the audience. His constant use of the pun or surface features of
language (yes I include the glasswork) results in a critical exegesis;
an alliance between strategy and external 'explanation,' a skein of
associations and disassociations, a production of fallen objects. He
must have been aware of the exhaustion beneath it all.... his tendency
towards investigation can only be admired (the particulars of the investigation should be another matter)....

[Like those of Cage and Duchamp, so the works of Fuller, Soleri, Wittgen-
stein] are particulate, decontextualizing (or contextualizing on a one/
one basis, same thing): it becomes unnecessary (or so it seems) to read
through the text, consider possibilities of theory. (Americans like their
information in parcels; the artworld as example favors semiotic active
distinction, Wittgenstein, over all-embracing approaches such as phenomenology; to parallel Deleuze and Guattari (although here inverted into a

negative sense), Americans choose total deterritorialization, the immediacy of the flow of desire: I say, a position of privilege, lack of necessity of meaning; I say, an assumption of surplus resources of information (language and cultural productions); I say, a failure to engage, to comprehend the alien, to recognize the possibility of an internalizing structure, a Marxism, a deep structuration of the world, an examination of consistency repetition (antihedonist, antisolipsist), perhaps (can one say this here?) a transcendent responsibility of the other (desire flows into the consumer-culture)). For example , Cage's word texts (as Coolidge's) are appropriate in an ideological climate of privilege in which words have a surplus economy - a consumerism of language. (Cage's books are another thing altogether; a friend of mine uses Silence as therapeutic. One can move across the written word; it functions as a psychoanalytical token of ingress into the body (in reading, one surrounds the body of the book; the text of the book surrounds the body of the reader))...

The escape into this or that, one or the other, natural order of the realm of truth, a series of assumptions. One believes in them; the ideological extensions remain elsewhere. Our heroes, how they file past, how they were received, their bodies or their texts, in a country of territorialism gone askew, picking up and putting down, how we believed, how we took from them, left with ashes in a sense, or passed finally by someone else....

ALAN SONDHEIM

ROSMARIE WALDROP

What interests me most in poetry now is the shift of emphasis from the image (i.e. relation of similarity) to contiguity: problems of combination, syntax, sequence, structure.

In my own work, this began to happen in the cycle "As If We Didn't Have to Talk" (*The Aggressive Ways of the Casual Stranger*). A double set of metaphors forms the backbone ("you" : crowd   line : open space   utterance : code), but is nowhere developed or stated. The metaphors are pushed out of the texture into the background, they become "structural metaphors." Thus the texture became free to explore sequence problems, mostly the pivotal line which is both the object of a sentence and the subject of the next:

                    I want to stay and look at
                    the mess I've made
                    spills over

This makes for a very fast flow and at the same time for discontinuity (the clash with the grammatical expectation)--which embodies the main theme: that language is "given" and yet there is a gap from one word to the next.

The Road Is Everywhere or Stop This Body contains the pivotal syntax with a larger framework (all the circulation systems, including traffic and money). But the limitation of the pivotal line is that it allows no syntactical complexity. It's all speed.

The newer work (*When They Have Senses; Streets Enough To Welcome Snow*) gives up the fast flow and concentrates on discontinuity, both semantic and syntactical. The method I've most worked with is reduced choice, i.e. using a "given" vocabulary or "given" structure. The first matrix of "Kind Regards", for instance came of the fusion of the grammatical structure of one text with the vocabulary of another.

ROSMARIE WALDROP

BIBLIOGRAPHY (In Print): *Camp Printing* (1970; Burning Deck Press, 71 Elmgrove Ave., Providence, R.I. 02906). *Body Image*, with art work by Nelson Howe (1970; George Wittenborn, 1018 Madison Ave., NYC 10021). *Against Language?: 'Dissatisfaction with Language' as Theme and as Impulse Towards Experiments in Twentieth Century Poetry* (1971; Mouton: The Hague; available from Walter de Gruyter, 3 Westchester Plaza, Elmsford, NY 10523). *The Aggressive Ways of the Casual Stranger* (1972; Random House, o.p.; available from Burning Deck). *The Road Is Everywhere or Stop This Body* (forthcoming, spring 1978; Open Places, Box 2085, Stephens College, Columbia, MO 65201). *When They Have Senses* (forthcoming, fall 1978; Burning Deck). Collaborations with Keith Waldrop: *Alice FFoster-Fallis; Until Volume One; Words Worth Less; Since Volume One* (1972, 1973, 1973, 1975; Burning Deck). Translations of Edmond Jabes: *Elya* (1973; Tree Books, Box 9005, Berkeley, CA 94709); *The Book of Questions* and *The Book of Yukel / Return to the Book* (1976, 1977; Wesleyan University Press).

═══════════════

SHADOWS OF THE SUN

(The following is an excerpt from <u>Shadows of the Sun: The Diaries of Harry Crosby</u>; 1977, $5 from Black Sparrow Press, Box 3993, Santa Barbara, CA 93105)

June 15, 1924. Words: arctic, absurd, bleak, barbaric, coarse, crude, chaos, couch, desolate, defenceless, disconsolate, disillusion, envenomed, emerald, embers, entangled, fragrant, feudal, fragment, gnarled, gracious,

*grandeur, hazardous, hawk, heraldic, illustrious, illusion, icicle,
irresolute, impregnate, idolatry, ineffectual, imaginative, knight-errant,
labyrinth, littleness, loveliness, loyalty, legend, lurid, leviathan,
mediaeval, mysterious, mushroom, macabre, merciless, massacre, nostalgia,
noon, nakedness, obsolete, orchid, overarch, owl, oasis, primeval,
posterity, perfume, pagan, phantom, pool, pronged, peacock, python,
provocative, preposterous, pregnant, quaint, quagmire, quarry, queenliness,
royal, refractory, restrengthened, remote, reverberate, ruin, rust,
rocking-horse, stronghold, sacred, sunnygolden, sadness, skeleton,
sunembroidered, Sun, smoke, softness, seer, sorceress, shipwreck, stallion,
steppingstone, turquoise, tapestry, tempest, turbulent, tea-chest,
toadstool, tigress, thrust, tortoise, traceried, triumphant, unfrequented,
unmuzzled, urn-shaped, untangled, unicorn, unquestioning, uncoffined,
unchaste, unanswered, unchallenged, virgin, vampiric, vagrant, veil,
vastness, vagueness, weariness, wistful, wagon, watch-fire, wayward, yoke,
youngness, yield, zodiac.*

HARRY CROSBY

CROSS REFERENCING THE UNITS OF SIGHT AND SOUND
FILM AND LANGUAGE

*THE MAKING IS THE MEANING IS HOW IT CAME INTO QUESTION.
UNITS OF UNMEANINGNESS INCORPORATED ANEW*

vs. A COMMUNITY OF SLOGANEERS

The/sound/is/when/the/eye/is/open./The/light/leads/the/voice./She/speaks
on/cue./The/cue/is/seen./The/scene/re/veals/the/scene/be/hind/the/scene.
Each/syl/la/ble/is/a/shot./VI/O/LIN/sh/says/in/three/shots./What/I/am
des/crib/ing/is/a/se/quence/from/Mi/chael/Snow's/RA/MEAU'S/NE/PHEW/a
three/hour/plus/film/which/dis/sem/bles/the/norms/of/film/and/lan/guage
film-/lan/guage/in/a/ser/ies/of/twen/ty/odd/es/says/or/chap/ters.

BRACKETS OF KNOWLEDGE: OR HOW THE SCALE MIGHT CHANGE

IN 1929 EISENSTEIN ASKS "WHY SHOULD CINEMA FOLLOW THE FORMS OF THEATER
AND PAINTING RATHER THAN THE METHODOLOGY OF LANGUAGE" AND IN THE WORK OF
SNOW (AS WELL AS HOLLIS FRAMPTON AND PAUL SHARITS) THIS DIRECTIVE IS
TAKEN. AS LANGUAGE IS CONSTRUCTED FROM SOUNDS, PHONEMES, AND WORDS
GROUPED INTO SENTENCES, SO FILM MEANING TURNS ONTO ITSELF REDEFINING THE
FRAME, SHOT AND SCENE.

*THE TASK: TO SEPARATE FILM FROM ITS HISTORICAL MOMENT: THAT OF AN
ILLUSION DEVICE
OR -- THAT IT IS AN ILLUSION DEVICE, AND SO USED TO RAISE THE QUESTION.*

A basis of Snow's work is its opposition to popular cinematic practice. To this end, he explores a multitude of subversions in synchronous sound, scripted speech, the narrative mode. At one point, a romance is destroyed. The bed of the lovers is shown as illusion: they lie on the floor. The language is instructional: "theres another side to every story" "touching is believing". A table appears and disappears. The superimposition is announced "watch this" as are the improbable sounds: "I didn't know you could speak trumpet." Earlier in the film, Snow juxtaposes the rearrangement of objects on his desk with a voice describing the activity, alternately falling ahead or behind the action.

Throughout the film, language and sound are used asymptotically to image, and explicitly so.

FOR IF THE PARALLEL TO LANGUAGE IS REWARDING, IT IS NOT COMPLETE. ITS MEAT IS DIFFERENT: IMAGE/EYE vs. LETTER/SOUND

This movement from letter to image is the explicit content of Frampton's ZORNS LEMMA, a film constructed in three parts: the first being black leader accompanied by a voice reading from the Bay State Primer; the second, a patterned replacement of the alphabet (or more exactly pictures of the letters of the alphabet) with images that over time transform themselves into an alphabet of personal visions in 24 frame, one second units; the third a long (apparent) one-shot take of two figures departing into the landscape accompanied by a medieval text on light.

APART FROM THE ATTENDANT INEQUALITIES IN THE MODE OF PERCEPTION, FILM IS LESS CODIFIED THAN LANGUAGE. WHEREAS THE LETTER/SOUND A AS IN FATHER OR MAD HAS UNDERGONE LIVING AND DISTANCED ITSELF FROM A PERCEPTUAL ASSOCIATION (i.e., ITS LEXATION OVERRIDES ITS PHYSICAL SOUND) THE FILM FRAME REMAINS AN OPEN VARIABLE. IT CAN CARRY A MULTIPLE OF COMPLEX MEANINGS WHICH CAN BE REGISTERED, IF NOT READ, AT A GLANCE. PERHAPS OH OR OUR EXPLETIVES ARE COMPARABLE.

FILM, I AM SUGGESTING, IS MORE A LANGUAGE INVENTING MACHINE THAN A LANGUAGE (THIS, ONCE THE NARRATIVE STRANGLEHOLD IS DROPPED). IT IS NOT ABOUT SOMETHING: IMAGE CODIFIED FOR SOCIAL USE. INHERENTLY MECHANICAL AND OPTICAL, FILM (LIKE THE INSTRUMENTS OF SCIENCE) PROVIDES US WITH INSIGHT (IN SITE) PROOF OF NEW THOUGHT AND CONCEPTUALIZATION. BOTH THE TOOL AND FRUIT OF ITS AGE, FILM EXISTS AT THE START OF THE LEVEL OF INTELLIGIBILITY. ONCE FREED OF THE NARRATIVE STRANGLEHOLD, FILM OFFERS ITSELF AS A UNIQUE MODEL TO CONFRONT THE WORLD WITHOUT THE FORMS OF HISTORY.

TO CREATE A MODEL OF ACTION THAT COMPELS US TO LISTEN/CREATE A MODEL OF VISION THAT COMPELS US TO THINK.

YET IF FILM HAS THIS POTENTIAL FREEDOM BEYOND LANGUAGE, IT (LIKE PHYSICS) IS BOUND TO ITS MECHANISM AND THE 'HAND BEHIND THE SCENE'. THUS WE NEVER CONFRONT THE WORLD WITHOUT THE FORMS OF HISTORY (HOWEVER REVOLUTIONARY

THE INSTRUMENT), BUT ALWAYS MEASURE THE PROCESS (OR HISTORICAL NECESSITY) OF THIS SEARCH.

Late in RAMEAU'S NEPHEW, Snow interpolates a ventriloquist and his dummy and an audience of one: the man has a man (the dummy) sit on his lap/CUT/ the dummy (a man) has the man (now the dummy) sit on his lap/CUT/ the dummy (a woman) sits on the lap of the man/CUT/the man (now the dummy) sits on her lap/CUT/the dummy (now a man) has a man (now the dummy) sit on his lap....

OR- AND- IS COHERENCE A PROOF OF TRUTH?

ABIGAIL CHILD

ALBIACH

Anne-Marie Albiach, Etat (1971; Mercure de France, Paris; 124 pages, 21 francs)

French poetry was overwhelmed by Surrealism and the last years have seen many attempts, not simply to write non-surrealistic poems, but to start out in new directions. An attempt which may prove one of the most fruitful was launched with the excellent 'little' magazine *Siècle à mains,* of which Anne-Marie Albiach is an editor.

The first impression from a glance into *Etat* is one of open spaces. There are few words, compared with the white of the paper that dominates by sheer area.

The poem--it is a single piece--does not progress by images (there are practically none) or by plot. There are all the terms of an argument, but one which has been bypassed. The argument, if it were given, might include the following propositions: (1) everyday language is dependent on logic, but (2) in a 'fiction,' there is no necessity that any particular word should follow any other, so that (3) it is possible at least to imagine a free choice, a syntax generated by desire. *Etat* is the 'epic' (the author's term) of this imagination.

To state such an argument, or any other, would be of course to renounce the whole project. But what we are presented is not a series of emotions or of occasions for emotional responses; the poem is composed, and composed mindfully. And if Mme. Albiach rejects rationality, she quite obviously writes with full intelligence. She has arranged her abstract words, her opaque lines, so that they confront an unequal amount of empty space and, in giving way, they justify the emptiness.

Etat is a beautiful and an important work.

KEITH WALDROP

IF WRITTEN IS WRITING

I think of you, in English, so frequent, and deserved, and thereby
desired, their common practice and continually think of it, who, since
the Elizabethans, save Sterne and Joyce, have so trothed language to the
imagination, and Melville, of whose *Mardi* the critics wrote, in 1849, "a
tedious, floundering work of uncertain meaning or no meaning at all. A
hodgepodge.... A story without movement, or proportions, or end ... or
point! An undigested mass of rambling metaphysics."

No-one is less negligent than you, to render the difficulties less
whether well-protected, in grammar, in which it has been customary to
distinguish <u>syntax</u> from <u>accidence</u>, the latter tending to the inflections
of words -- inflections, or towards itself, a bending in. The choices
have always been fashioned and executed from within. Knowing is right
and knowing is wrong. Nodding is, or could be, to you.

In such are we obsessed with our own lives, which lives being now language,
the emphasis has moved. The emphasis is persistently centric, so that
where once one sought a vocabulary for ideas, now one seeks ideas for
vocabularies. Many are extant. Composition is by. The technique is
very cut and the form is very close. Such is surprising even now, if
overdue. Now so many years ago Donne wrote, Some that have deeper digg'd
Loves Mine than I, Say, where his centrique happinesse doth lie.

The text is anterior to the composition, though the composition be
interior to the text. Such candor is occasionally flirtatious, as candor
nearly always so. When it is trustworthy, love accompanies the lover,
and the centric writers reveal their loyalty, a bodily loyalty. Quite
partial is necessity, of any text. Marvelous are the dimensions and
therefore marvelling is understandable -- and often understanding. Much
else isn't, but when, that comes, from the definite to an indefinite,
having devised excuses for meeting, though we have not yet recognized, a
selection, or choice, of what is combed out. The original scale determines the scope, the mood, the feel, the tone, the margin, the degree,
the mathematics, the size, the sign, the system, the pursuit, the
position, the mark.

Of centricities, an interior view, there are two sources, perhaps three.
One locates in the interior texture of such language as is of the person
composing from it, personal and inclusive but not necessarily self-
revelatory -- in fact, now, seldom so; through improvisatory techniques
building on the suggestions made by language itself -- on patterns of
language which are ideas and corresponding behavior or relevant quirks;
this becomes an addictive motion -- but not incorrect, despite such

distortion, concentration, condensation, deconstruction and such as association by, for example, pun and etymology provide; an allusive psycholinguism. In the second it is the bibliography that is the text. The writing emerges from within a pre-existent text of one's own devising or another's. The process is composition rather than writing.

There are characteristic, contracting rhythms. The long line, with ramifying clauses, an introductory condition, and other cumulative devices have been fragmented, the rhythm accentuated. You can read. You can write. An unstable condition is given pause. The Elizabethans were given to a long system and we to purchase for pause, though not stop.

A possible third centricity, the perhaps, emerges from the imperatives and prerogatives of grammar. Such might be a work of, say, conjunctions, in which, for example, John Lloyd Stephens writes, "There is no immediate connection between taking Daguerreotype portraits and the practice of surgery, but circumstances bring close together things entirely dissimilar in themselves, and we went from one to the other." Such is a definition of the Elizabethan conceit. And in a blue book of French grammar one reads, "Linking is rare between a plural noun and a verb or between a plural adjective and a verb except in poetry."

All theory is safest ascribed in retrospect. On the line is an occasion to step off the line. The critic is a performer, good or bad. Facility is splendid, however -- think of such heroic figures as Dr. Johnson, John Donne. Love was not easy. The cat gets the chair and you get the edge.

Conclusion:

by usual standing under half

LYN HEJINIAN

LETTER TO THE EDITOR

John Taggart's objection in your April issue to reviews that are anything other than hard 'information' strikes me as parochial as it is misguided. What better evidence of success for a piece of creative writing than its inherent ability to expand its original creative act beyond itself, to evoke further creative acts in its readers/perceivers? If I am moved by a piece of literature, why ought I not be moved to some thing, to express myself, to grow, as much on my own terms as that of the

original stimulus? To avoid what Taggart calls 'a performance,' to
review a work in the usual academic terms of 'hard' information, those of
'influences,' 'style,' and so on, tells us less about the work under
consideration than it does about 'influences,' 'style,' 'criticism' itself

What Merleau-Ponty says of Descartes might also be said of literature
How can we draw a line between literature and what we have thought on the
basis of it, between what we owe it and what we lend to it in interpretation? In the end, it is literature that awakens in us our own thoughts.
It is no more possible to make a strict inventory of the thoughts of a
writer than it is to inventory the means of expression in a language.
Both are alive, not abstractions, continually being, never susceptible in
themselves of being abstracted into the past tense of criticism.

Taggart would also do well to recall what Merleau-Ponty says about
criticism itself. "Critical language is like one of those descriptions
of a face in a passport which do not allow us to imagine the face." The
traditional critic is limited to what Merleau-Ponty calls "an exercise"
of "the second order," and does nothing more than substitute a second
language making a false claim of possessing the initial language of the
writer.

Falsely or not, it is the text that ought to have primacy, not
whether a large press, a small press, an independent press, or a subsidy
press has published it. How a hypothetical work published identically
by all these presses would differ isn't at all clear, but Taggart makes
a special claim for those published by 'small presses' as somehow
requiring reviews of hard 'information.' At this point he seems peri-
lously close to adding an even further distortion by implying there is
yet a third consideration, that of text as promoted commodity. The
question then becomes only that of what is being sold.

LORIS ESSARY

ARTICLES

*Boundaries overlap, dissolve -- in writing, as well as in discussions of
writing. This publication bears witness to some of that overlapping. It
also proceeds in the midst of a great deal of other interesting commentary, information & theorizing: about poetry, language, composition,
styles of reading, and aesthetic & social issues which are closely related.
What follows is a cataloguing of some public instances in magazines from
the last year or so. It is not comprehensive. Limited to magazines
locatable in libraries and bookstores in New York City, it represents,
even from that, a personal and thus idiosyncratic selecting. The second
half (M-Z) will appear, with some addenda, in the next issue. As Pound*

said, in his ABC of Reading, *"One reads prose for the subject matter."*

B.A.

ART COMMUNICATION EDITION. No.4: "The Last Text: Some Notes on Behavior-
alism," "Performance," "Video," "Film," "Books," "Design".
ART CONTEMPORARY. 1977, No.9: "Vocable Gestures: A Historical Survey of
Sound Poetry", Michael Gibbs, "Langwe Art". No.2/3: Ron Silliman,
"Disappearance of the Word, Appearance of the World", Ken Friedman,
"Art as a Contextual Art", "Cover to Cover" (on Michael Snow).
ARTFORUM. May 1978: "'Konstruktivism' and 'Kinematografiya'". April 78:
"Hard-Core Painting". March 78: "The Substance of Paper", "Background
of a Minimalist: Carl Andre", "Duchamp and the Classical Perspectivists",
"The Body Language of Pictures". Feb 78: "On the Problem of Content in
Nonobjective Art". Nov 1977: "Some Exercises in Slow Perception",
"The Aesthetics of Indifference". Oct 77: "Reaffirming Painting: A
Critique of Structuralist Criticism". Sept 77: "Performance Art",
"Art Criticism: Where's the Depth?", "Richard Foreman's 'Book of Levers'".
ART IN AMERICA. May-June 1978: Kenneth Baker, "Sol LeWitt: Energy as
Form". March-April 78: Lucy Lippard, "Dada in Berlin". Jan-Feb 78:
Robert Morris, "The Present Tense of Space".
ART INTERNATIONAL. 1977, No.7: "The Purloined Paradigm: A Critical
Analysis of the Art & Language Group".
ART JOURNAL. Spring 1977: "Send Letters, Postcards, Drawings, and
Objects" (on correspondence art).
ART-RITE. No.14, Winter 1976-77: Artists' Books issue.
ARTSCRIBE. No.9: "Art and Social Constraints".
ARTS MAGAZINE. May 1978: Robert Smithson issue. April 78: "Traces of
the Unimaginable: On Arakawa". Feb 78: "Toward a History of California
Performance".
BOUNDARY 2. Winter 1978: Robert Creeley issue. Fall 1977: Jack Spicer
issue ("The Orientation of the Parasols: Saussure, Derrida, Spicer",
etc.). Winter 77: "Breaking the Circle: Hermeneutics as Dis-closure",
"Postmodernity and Hermeneutics", Reviews of Gadamer and Said; Ron
Silliman, "The Chinese Notebook" (excerpts).
BRITISH JOURNAL OF AESTHETICS. Winter 1978: "Wittgenstein's Aesthetics
and the Theory of Literature".
BUCKNELL REVIEW. Fall 1976: Rosmarie Waldrop, "A Basis of Concrete Poetry",
"The Escape from Syntax: The Aesthetics of Dissolution".
CAMBRIDGE QUARTERLY. 1977, No.4: "Lacan's Ecrits"; "The Poetry of Cid
Corman". No.3: "Linguistic Philosophy - Forty Years On"; "Barthes and
Autobiography". No.2: "Benveniste and Semiology".
CAMERA OBSCURA: A JOURNAL OF FEMINISM AND FILM THEORY. No.1: "The Appara-
tus", "An Interrogation of the Cinematic Sign", "Yvonne Rainer: An
Introduction, and Interview".

CANTO. Winter 1977: "Of Derrida".
CHICAGO REVIEW. Autumn 1977: "The Situation of Writing". Spring 77:
   "The Limits of Representation and the Modernist Discovery of Presence".
CHRYSALIS. No.4: "The Glamour of Grammar", "Toward a Lesbian Sensibility".
CINE-TRACTS. No.3, Fall 77-Winter 78: "Culture, History and Ambivalence:
   On Walter Benjamin"; Raymond Williams, "Realism, Naturalism and their
   Alternatives".
COLUMBIA REVIEW. Winter 1978: "The Referential Fallacy".
COMMUNICATION ET LANGAGES. No.36: "Signalisation". No.35: "L'image, le
   signe, le lettre". No.34: "Image/texte", "La Typographie".
COMMUNICATION QUARTERLY. Summer 1977: "A Hermeneutic Phenomenology of
   Communication", "A Naturalistic Study of Talk". Winter 77: Alternative
   Theoretical Bases for the Study of Human Communication (special issue).
COMPARATIVE LITERATURE STUDIES. March 1977: "From Russian Formalism to
   French Structuralism".
CONTEMPORARY LITERATURE. Spring 1977: "The Outer Limits of the Novel".
CORNELL REVIEW. Fall 1977: William Gass, "How to Make A World Of Words".
CREDENCES. No.5/6, March 1978: Stan Brakhage on poetry & film; Bertholf
   on Michael Davidson; Irby & Weiners on Gerrit Lansing.
CRITICAL INQUIRY. Spring 1978: "On Walter Benjamin", "Countertransference,
   the Communication Process, and the Dimensions of Psychoanalytic Criti-
   cism", "Culture and Modeling Systems"; Fredric Jameson, "The Symbolic
   Inference" (on Kenneth Burke). Autumn 1977: "Noise", "Contemporary
   Approaches to Aesthetic Inquiry", "Toward a Semiotics of Literature";
   Alain Robbe-Grillet, "Order and Disorder in Film and Fiction". Summer
   77: "The Marginal Gloss"; Christian Metz, "Trucage and the Film".
CULTURAL HERMENEUTICS. December 1977: "Discourse and Conversation: The
   Theory of Communicative Competence and Hermeneutics" (Gadamer & Haber-
   mas), "Foucault's Discursive Analysis".
DAEDALUS. Fall 1977: Jonathan Culler, "In Pursuit of Signs"; George A.
   Miller, "Problems of Communication". Summer 77: Victor Turner, "Process,
   System, and Symbol: A New Anthropological Synthesis".
DIALECTICA. 1977, No.3/4: "Language-Games", "Reality Without Reference".
DIACRITICS. Fall 1977: "Conventions of the Natural and the Naturalness
   of Conventions", "Glas-Piece" (on Derrida). Summer 77: Fredric Jameson,
   "Of Islands and Trenches: Neutralization and the Production of Utopian
   Discourse"; & articles on and interview with Louis Marin. Spring 77:
   "Searching for Narrative Structure", "RB: The Third Degree" (on Roland
   Barthes), "A Reading of Walter Benjamin's Kafka Study".
DRAMA REVIEW. No.76, December 1977: Playwriting Issue: Richard Foreman,
   "How I Write My (Self: Plays)"; Sam Shepard, "Visualization, Language
   and the Inner Library"; Robert Wilson, "...I thought I was Hallucina-
   ting". Dec. 1976: Theatrical Theory Issue ("The Visual Script", etc.).
DUMB OX. No.6/7, 1977-78: "Listening to Britain: Art-Language", "The
   Nature of Film Criticism".

ELH. Spring 1978: "The Politics of Description: W.C. Williams in the 'Thirties'", "Origins of 'A': Zukofsky's Materials for Collage".

ET CETERA. December 1977: McLuhan's "Alphabet, Mother of Invention".

FLASH ART. Nov-Dec. 1977: "Post-Conceptual Romanticism".

GLYPH. No.1: Jacques Derrida, "Signature Event Context"; John Searle, "Reiterating the Differences". No.2: "The Idioms of the Text", "The Act", "Theatrum Analyticum"; Derrida, "Limited Inc.", "Kenneth Burke's Logology". No.3: "Absence, Authority, and the Text".

HERESIES: A FEMINIST PUBLICATION ON ART & POLITICS. Winter 1978: Special issue - Women's Traditional Arts: The Politics of Aesthetics". Fall 1977: "Use of Time in Women's Cinema". May 77: Special issue - Patterns of Communication and Space Among Women.

HISTORY AND THEORY. October 1977: "Habermas (Derrida) and the Grounding of Political Theory".

IDEOLOGY & CONSCIOUSNESS. No.1, Easter 1977: "Marxism and Linguistics", "Theories of Discourse", "Ideology and the Human Subject".

INTERNATIONAL JOURNAL OF MAN-MACHINE STUDIES. March 1977: "Machine understanding of natural language".

JOURNAL OF THE ACOUSTICAL SOCIETY OF AMERICA. January 1978: "Hearing 'words' without words: Prosodic cues for word perception".

JOURNAL OF AESTHETICS AND ART CRITICISM. Fall 1977: D. Kuspit, "Authoritarian Abstraction".

JOURNAL OF LITERARY SEMANTICS. April 1977: "The Linguistics of Double-vision", "An Applied Linguistic View of Poetic Form".

JOURNAL OF MODERN LITERATURE. Feb. 1977: Samuel Beckett / Special Issue.

JOURNAL OF PHILOSOPHY. Nov. 1977: Symposium: Philosophy of Jacques Derrida.

LAICA JOURNAL. 1977-78, No.18: Italian Art. No.17: "Paragraphs". No.15: "Music Space--Computer Time", "Talking with Douglas Huebler", "Duchamp". No.14: Artists and Film issue.

LANGUAGE. March 1977: "Language change and poetic options". June 1977: "The preference for self-correction in the organization of repair in conversation.

LANGUAGE AND STYLE. Vol.9, No.4: "The Computer and the Sound Texture of Poetry".

LANGUAGE IN SOCIETY. April 1977: "A stylistic analysis of speaking".

L'ARC. 1977, No.68: Raymond Roussel issue.

LEONARDO: INT'L JOURNAL OF THE CONTEMPORARY ARTIST. Autumn 1977: Jonathan Culler, "Deciphering the Signs of the Times".

LIGHTWORKS. Winter 1977: "Notes on the History of the Alternative Press", "Interview: Peter Kubelka" (film theory).

LINGUISTIC INQUIRY. Summer 1977: Chomsky & Lasnik, "Filters and Controls", Spring 77: "The Rhythmic Structure of English Verse", "On Stress and Linguistic Rhythm".

LINGUISTICS. 1977, No.194: "Textual Competence: A Preliminary Analysis of Orally Generated Texts".

WRITING AND SELF-DISCLOSURE

With the publication of *The Interpretation of Dreams* (1900), Freud reframed and refined an enigma which haunts most literary efforts to combine a revelation of self and other: can, and if it can, how does this aspect of literature help anyone else? He showed that by analyzing his own dreams by use of an associative method of interpretation he could heal his own neurosis. In a uniquely psychological fashion Freud succeeded in convincing many members of his own generation of contemplative readers, and many of those of succeeding generations, of the value of self-reflection. By transposing his findings into a viable mode of intersubjective discourse, he proposed a vehicle found in practice to release previously inhibited psychic energies. Like an artist, an analysand with the help of his analyst, by disclosing his inner psychic process, would connect with the core of his being and by completing this circuit, re-integrate his personality.

Just as the Senoi indians discovered and exploited in their group reveries, Freud found that an effort to probe the unconscious has distinctly healing effects. Like the shaman, the poet experiences the healing power of the act of writing through the reading and rereading of texts. Now, with parallel concerns, the psychoanalytic theorist, (cf., the work of Harry Guntrip) can return to the group the labyrinth of common self-deceptions concealed in unconscious mental processes.

For poets, and readers of poetry, a technique of sharing dreams is readily available--through the exchange of texts. These texts are revelations of a poet's direct encounter with the process of creating a language structured in a way commensurate with his personal need to articulate his perceptions. The mapping of this path for the contemporary poet is often dotted with islands or cities of personal disclosure--over and over he names himself because it is through this successive identification of selves that he literally knows where he is. He can no longer identify with any other family names but his own. The other is no longer brother or sister or son or daughter, another symbol on another herald, but simply the legend of another map of the same terrain.

The boldest of contemporary poets are often the least shy about revealing themselves. What saves, for example, John Ashbery's poetry from its own formalism is its readiness to blurt out its author's human vulnerabilities. Whether his lines or sentences are fragmentary (as in *The Tennis Court Oath)* or sustained and elaborated (as in *Three Poems*), I feel the presence of a willingness, even if it might sometimes appear unexpected, or arbitrary, to share his humanness with me. This is what I hear in what others might describe as "obscure personal associations." He confronts the possibility of a voluntary withdrawal on the part of his reader because of embarrassment or confusion. We see ourselves in this because we know that we have also consented to turn away at times from the painful clarity of identifying, for example, certain kinds of access to hidden truths about ourselves. A voice in one of Ashbery's poems mutters "'Once I let a guy blow me./ I kind of backed away from the experience.'"

The contemporary poet discovers his formal matrices through a process of self-disclosure that is contiguous with his creations. This process reveals to him the form that is hinted at in his conscious and unconscious intentions at the outset of the poem, and what he knows intuitively about how this particular work fits into his more long range formal intentions. The thoughts that occur as he is creating the poem, like the details of the interpretation of a part of a dream, on first sight may seem disconnected, fragmentary, insignificant, often best illuminate the reader (for the poet, self-reminders) about his intentions.

Yet these self-disclosures put a discomforting pressure on our willingness to trust this bizarre demand for confidence. From the beginning of the poem we realized that not only may he disappoint us but he might also mislead us. Out of this conflict and tension, sensing the pull of his reader's anxiety and absence, the poet evokes from his being remnants of his private existence to remind us, along the way, of his particular vulnerabilities. Yet it is just this process which is likely to wrench the poem from the domain of convention and rhetoric. Such resonances may add to his poetry more authentically and spontaneously the harmonic overtones and kaleidoscopic facets that are perhaps more tactfully obtained through irony, baroque vocabulary, deliberate primitivism, camp naivete and "dumbness," repetition and charm. Imagination in writing poetry becomes continuous with a way of paying attention to the juxtaposition of related thoughts, a way of figuring things out, even, and perhaps particularly, his "personal" problems. For it is on the scale of weighing and exploring such considerations that he effects the choices that will enhance or not his imagination. He discovers "by accident" the actual recurrent objects of his fantasy.

NICK PIOMBINO

PROSODYNES

Ernest Robson has written in, in response to the discussion of his work in the last issue of L=A=N=G=U=A=G=E. He comments that the orthographic system of graphic cues he has developed cannot be accurately simulated on the typewriter. Below, a photoreproduction from the text itself:

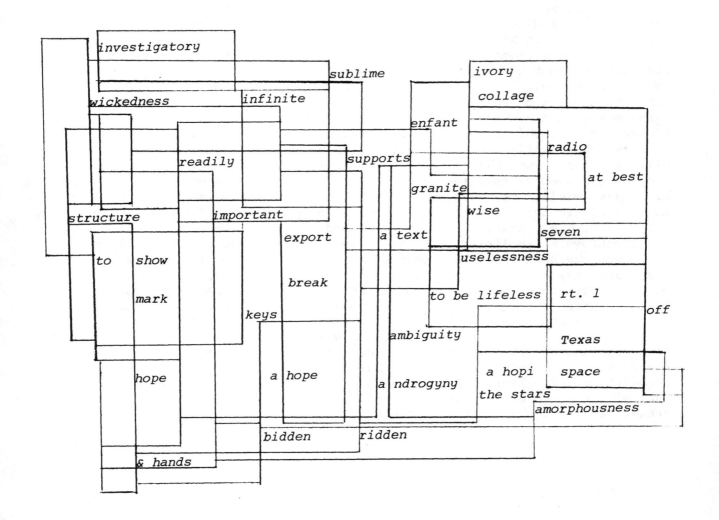

-Douglas Messerli

TYING AND UNTYING

Never much given to abstracting my ideas about writing or shoving some neat precis under the nose of anyone asking about this or that aspect of poetry, I'd prefer to offer this thaumatrope of a few quotations from my notebooks with which I share an expression of attitude, aesthetic maintenance, persistence of vision taking its measure from a spirit of form that admits a wide range of concentrations-- co-ordinated arcs not merely cyclic abandonment or linear expanse. All notions of form are implicitly coercive. I prefer example to precept; impertinence to quiet philosophist irony. And as I am not in search of the ultimate expression of the charmed quark etymon hidden in the beard of Karl Marx, neither the vast and minimalized itemizations coming up for a rapture of air nor the selected panoply of modes frustrated by retrospect, gooned by media and particalized by procedure are of much interest to me. It's creating THE FOCUS THAT GENERATES that concerns me. Not so called revolutionary ideas reduced to connoisseurship. Or else as a writer one is just another coot ploughing the Empire.

"Language-using controls the rest;
Wonderful is language!
Wondrous the English language, language of live men,
Language of ensemble, powerful language of resistance..." -- Whitman

"Every man has reminiscences which he would not tell to everyone but only to his friends. He has other matters in his mind which he would not reveal even to his friends, but only to himself, and that in secret. But there are other things which a man is afraid to tell even to himself, and every man has a number of such things stored away in his mind. The more decent he is the greater number of such things in his mind."
                                                        -- Dostoevsky

"You must talk with two tongues, if you do not wish to cause confusion."
                                                        -- Wyndham Lewis

"One invents a technique or procedure by oneself; one does not invent entirely on one's own a state of mind." -- Juan Gris

"329. When I think in language, there aren't 'meanings' going through my head in addition to the verbal expressions: the language is itself the vehicle of thought." -- Wittgenstein

"Art will no longer aspire to account for everything; it will have left
forever the ambiguous sphere of transcendency for the scattered, humble
everyday universal of the relative." -- Pierre Restany

"I love men not for what unites them, but for what divides them, and I
want to know most of all what gnaws at their hearts." -- Apollinaire

"The poem as simultaneous structure, impersonal, autonomous, released
from the charge of expression, of assertion; the poem as arbitrary
construct, absurd, self-destroying, no longer aspiring to convince or
even to hoax; the poem as agent of transformation, equal in value to the
poet himself and therefore capable of changing him; the poem as means of
escape from identity; leading into a world of contemplation, indifference, bliss." -- Source Unknown

"There are two kinds of writers, those who are and those who aren't.
With the first, content and form belong together like soul and body;
with the second, they match each other like body and clothes."
                                                    -- Karl Kraus

"A book is a mirror: when a monkey looks in, no apostle can look out."
                                                    -- Lichtenberg

Quince. Bless thee, Bottom, bless thee! Thou art translated.

                                                    RAY DI PALMA

THE ALPHABET OF STRIDE

> *The world is a text with several meanings & we pass from one to
> another by a process of work. It must be work in which the body
> constantly bears a part, as, for example, when we learn the
> alphabet of a foreign language. This alphabet has to enter into
> our hand by dint of forming the letters. If this condition is
> not fulfilled every change in our way of thinking is illusory.*
>   *--Simone Weil, Gravity & Grace*

> *A unity suffering its inception. --DiPalma*

Everything makes a move, is fixed, moves on--, *Between the Shapes*: an
early 'collection'--what is the sense of writing that inspires a person
to craft these well poems?--& yet already the (a) twist ("early in the

turkey/ the ground had a pedigree") and a (the) sense of words stacking, breaking down the syntax of pictorial representation into strata of words, things ("Above the tracks/ a slight embank/ ment. Limestone./ Mud. Weeds. A/ concrete wall..."). *Night*: & immediately (from a more sprawling...) to a crystallization of form, only what is necessary ("the condition was relative to a measure"), stillness (fix of words); here the syntax opening up by ellipses--one pinpointed detail next to another, concentric ripples not touching; items, words as objects existing side-by-side; yet the movement of one unit to the next--a progression of sightings. ...which gets very rapidly (*Works in a Drawer* &c) to a subtle detail, refinement, that gives weight to each syllable ("sooner or later the sun cracks rebecca") & it's apparent that there is a constant attention to order & balance (in the sense that a coordination of elements is always at play, as is the recognition, though not necessarily the recreation, of a specifically geometric arrangement). We take this into the visual placement of words in the more than 100 pages of *Sgraffiti*, name derived from a graphics technique in which the surface layer is scratched into to reveal a different colored ground. A complex play of cut-out, design, procedure--always delineated, articulated--intelligence dancing through the words & rearranging them. Or *The Birthday Notations*: in which it's not the syntax that gets broken up to bring out the plasticity, ping & pong, of word against word--but a syntax--"After lunch I slept almost all the rest of the day; another man would have made it his duty to go and see the waterfalls"--that gets looked at with a gaze that makes it plastic, so we see it as its mode of language at the same time as enjoying its 'content'. Time having moved us away from these syntaxes--the work composed entirely of citations from 17th to early 20th Century diaries, journals and letters--but that distance also allowing us to see them with an angle of gaze that reveals their meaning with renewed intensity. Genre writing: well each way of proceeding establishes its own kind of rhetoric but never assumes it, so the language work is always active: "'You must talk with two tongues, if you do not wish to cause confusion.'" More recently: the rubber-stamp books, which create a pictographic grammar, where repetition, blurring, juxtaposition and serial ordering page to page (of a fixed 'vocabulary' of stamp images) give rise to a movement of meanings realized solely by this specially made coding ("plane falls on horse, sheep falls on tractor, soap falls on boat, chair falls on bear, cow falls on car, ...")--but codes not for sake of conveying some message by use of symbolic elements, but for the sheer joy of the cipher: their internal movements & their transformations. -- & next, what new gaze ("Planh"), clumped with "rolling vision/ from staring eyes". --A sequence of illuminations, clouded, pulsed. "When in the dark move faster, make your own light." -- Hats on.

CHARLES BERNSTEIN

BIBLIOGRAPHY: *Max* (Body Press, 1969). *Macaroons*, with Stephen Shrader (Doones Press, 1969). *Between the Shapes* (1970; Zeitgeist, Box 150, East Lansing, MI 48823, $1.50). *Clinches* (1970; Abraxas Press). *The Gallery Goers* (1971; Ithaca House, c/o Serendipity, 1790 Shattuck Ave., Berkeley, CA 94709, $1.50). *All Bowed Down* (1972; Burning Deck, 71 Elmgrove, Providence, RI 02906, $2.50). *Works in a Drawer* . (1972; Blue Chair Press). *Borgia Circles* (1972; Sand Project Press). *Time Being*, with Asa Benveniste and Tom Raworth (1972; Trigram Press). *Five Surfaces* (1974; Tottel's #12, c/o L=A=N=G=U=A=G=E Distributing Service, $1.92). *Soli* (1974; Ithaca House, c/o Serendipity, $2.95). *The Sargasso Transcries* (1974; 'X' Editions, c/o L=A=N=G=U=A=G=E, $1.64). *Max: A Sequel* (1974; Burning Deck, $2.50). *Accidental Interludes* (1975; Turkey Press). *Marquee* (1977; Asylum's Press, c/o L=A=N=G=U=A=G=E, $3). *Genesis* (1977, 'X' Editions, c/o L=A=N=G=U=A=G=E, $2). Unpublished manuscripts: *Night* (1968); *Cuiva Sails* (1969-77); *Sgraffiti* (1971-73, available from L=A=N=G=U=A=G=E, $6.22); *The Birthday Notations* (1974-77); *Dec, L'Ecri, & Seven Pieces* (1977). One-of-a-kind handstamped books (1976-78): *Matak, Pocket Memo, Large Black Notebook, Small Black Notebook, Ten Faces, The Brown Book, The Dutch Notebook, Ten Cards, Japanese Notebook, Tzuuka, Some Cuts, Outrageous Modesty, Ten Pyramids, Tux, Wheels, Landscapes, Times, Canal Zone Intermission, Original Confidential* (prices available on request from DiPalma, #4R, 226 W. 21, NY, NY 10011).

A VACANT LOT, A PIECE OF STRING

The principle of form will be our only constant connection with the past. Although the great form of the future will not be as it was in the past, at one time the fugue and at another the sonata, it will be related to these as they are to each other: through the principle of organization or man's common ability to think. It goes without saying that dissonances and noises are welcome in this new music. But so is the dominant seventh chord if it happens to put in an appearance. A sound does not view itself as thought, as ought, as needing another sound for its elucidation, as etc.; it has no time for any other consideration--it is occupied with the performance of its characteristics: before it has died away it must have made perfectly exact its frequency, its loudness, its length, its overtone structure, the precise morphology of these and of itself. In view, then, of a totality of possibilities, no knowing action is commensurate, since the character of the knowledge acted upon prohibits all but some eventualities. An experimental action...does not move in terms of approximations and errors, as 'informed' action by its nature must...it sees things as the are: impermanently involved in an infinite play of interpenetrations. Being unforseen, this action is not concerned with its excuse. That is to say, art is described as being illuminating, and the rest of life as being dark. Naturally, I disagree. If there were a part of life dark enough to keep out of a light from art, I would want to be in that darkness, fumbling around if necessary, but alive. As for the quality of irritation, one might say that it is at least preferable to soothing, edifying, exalting and similar qualities. Its source is, of course, precisely in monotony, not in any forms of aggression or emphasis. It is the immobility of motion. And it alone, perhaps, is truly moving. The responsibility of the artist consists in perfecting his work so that it may become attractively disinteresting. It is better to make a piece of music than to perform one, better to perform one than to listen to one, better to listen to one than to misuse it as a means of distraction, entertainment, or acquisition of 'culture'. If the mind is disciplined, the heart turns quickly from fear towards love. One does not make just any experiment, but does what must be done. It is evidently a question of bringing one's intended actions into relation with the ambient unintended ones. The common denominator is zero, where the heart beats (no one _means_ to circulate his blood). Of course 'it is another school'-- this moving out from zero. To begin with, accept that a sound is a sound and a man is a man, give up illusions about ideas of order, expressions of sentiment, and all the rest of our inherited claptrap. What I am calling poetry is often called content. I myself have called it form. It is the continuity of a piece of music. Continuity today...is a demonstration of disinterestedness. That is, it is a proof that our delight lies in not possessing anything. Each moment presents what happens. All I know about method is that when I am not working I sometimes think I know something, but when I am working it is quite clear that I know nothing. ((This text derives by chance from _Silence_ by John Cage. It is offered here for its continuing relevance to current thought and practice.))

TED PEARSON

LAYOUT

Michael Frederick Tolson et al., Untitled book, 50 pp., white wrappers ($2, from Tolson, 53 W. Oliver St., Baltimore, Md. 21201)

Three traditions of putting the project of representation into brackets: the expressionist, the constructivist, the conceptual. This, the third, with tinctures of the first two. Exhibitions of linguistic material -- display cases. Instructions. Lists, grids. Documentation.

A bag, stapled to a page, containing *i, h, s, c, u, y, a, e, t*. Take
positions. We read the detachment, and feel no rapport. The texts
extend by linkings, by graphic displacements of letters, by shifts of
focus, and substraction, by accumulation. Other, more complex, modes of
composition and of establishing an independent (or intrinsic) presence
for language are declined. Instead, try to focus on many labeled areas
simultaneously. "i hate the mentally paralyzed" "i want hypnotic
yourself stimulating whose eyes" The words become mere tokens of rearrangement and cleansing conspicuous disruption. Not even the pleasing
ribs of overall structuring. But at least they are not used to form the
primary material of transparency. That transparency is an illusion, a
mental operation made more difficult here. "attach idea." Muddled.
Muddied. Control is too slight. "th(v) disruption(s) int(v)ntionally
(v)xagg(v)rat(v)d" Only a few frames simultaneously. But an abolitionism of the word does not occur. "Siuce the wisreaquig of morps
iuvolves au iuversiou of the sepneuce or sbatiotewdoral orberiug of
letters' he qesiguatep this tyqe of error as a ˌkiueticˌ reversal."
"Since the misrepaing of omprs involves an invreismo of the besucuee or
adsittomeoprla broreing of elttreˌs he deisganbet this tbye of reorr as
a k'iteni'c everrsl.a"" "Since the misreading of words involves an
inversion of the sequence or spatiotemporal ordering of letters, he designated this type of error as a 'kinetic' reversal."

BRUCE ANDREWS

POSTSCRIPT

The Politics of the Referent, edited by Steve McCaffery: McCaffery, "The
Death of the Subject: The Implications of Counter-Communication"; Bruce
Andrews, "Text and Context"; Ray DiPalma, "Crystals"; Ron Silliman, from
"aRb"; Charles Bernstein, "Stray Straws and Straw Men"; Ellsworth Snyder,
"Gertrude Stein and John Cage". In Open Letter, Summer 1977 (104 Lynd-
hurst Avenue, Toronto; $2).

    Ten notions about which it is advisable to have no opinions:
signifier, inwardness, lexemic presence, ego, referent, (even to say it),
deconstruction, morpheme-phoneme-grapheme, displacement, interface.
    The initial question that arises from reading these essays is why
must language be politicized? What happens to the aesthetic impulse when
language is displaced toward the relations implicit between us and it,
that is, away from relations between it and the phenomenal world.

A Short Interview with Steve McCaffery --
Q: What happens to the aesthetic impulse if language is politicized?
A: It does not seem essential to me.

I would agree with Snyder that words regarded as facts, as opposed
to words as symbols, are more useful today, but useful in the way any
"new" art tends to satirize contemporary society: If we think capitalism
commoditizes our works beyond their ability to overcome that tendency
with their "awful beauty", then we can imagine advanced art or theorizing
makes fun of this tendency by always seeking to invent, recontextualize
(perhaps this is more ecologically sound), conceptualize, etc., rather
than.... I'm sure you'd like to know what, too.

The impulse behind this move away from reference, image and meaning
in the conventional way is the same impulse that directed the painting
of "Desmoiselles D'Avignon," or enabled Schoenberg, led by his musical
predecessors, to deviate so far from the key note that he simply never
came back. We can say the same thing about representation in literature.

Certainly Stein et al. began these events, so we cannot claim that
these authors are creating something entirely new. Rather they are
announcing that something has already taken place and the disparate
elements of these modes of writing are ready to be collated into culture
proper, not isolated or kept tangential to the "real" world of the
Consumer Price Index and SALT. These essays announce that the works of
earlier writers are not to be regarded as another step toward randomness,
rather they are to be developed. Yet in what way does this kind of
writing try to transcend the nature of advances and put an end to period
mannerism?

Can we get to the point where we do not need to be reassured by
meaning which accompanies language? Can we use language not as a lens
through which the world is pleasantly or wrathfully distorted for the
purposes of lulling the reader into another world of lies and symbols?
Can we come to the realization that language is one of the languages?
That the question as to whether society or consciousness informs first is
something for Marx and Freud to battle over in heaven? That we can view
all the languages as mutually reflexive where the light bouncing back and
forth between these planes is the mode of expression, in this case
English? That spoken or written language is not a box for meaning--it
is the content(s)?

Freeing words from hidden meanings is just the first step. To
decommoditize language in writing, one may need to call into question
even the morphemic quality of language. This raises questions of compre-
hensibility. Can the relationship between reader and writer really be so
changed? Silliman makes the incredible claim that alphabet takes language
out of person and that a book makes poetry into a commodity. Well....
More importantly, are the claims implicit in these assertions justified?

Is the kind of writing at the root of these essays, call it what you will, possessed of as many possibilities and permutations as centuries of referential writing. Silliman claims non-referential writing, like that of Grenier, reveal referential works to be of a specific type--their locality was engrossing--a special case like Newton in relation to relativistic mechanics.

These essays do not propose writing which creates a hypnotic simulacrum--an illusion that seems like realism--but rather they perform a realization showing that language as a system parallel to experience really exists, influences and works in itself and by its relations elucidates experience. The program suggested in these essays appears to cover reality with language, hence the need to stretch the page.

JAMES SHERRY

SIGNIFICATION

Reversing your hands if you're. The way your hands with the exception of everyone including that mystery that changed when one of the old hands thought nobody was looking. When I say hands is only half the expression something yours changed so that each weren't lined up and my hands learned the trick this way: if you want flexible body action leave the hand, hold your hands to leave your hands. Almost fall. When, when it drove the dirt behind him it was possible for a man to know the guy until one system obviously works. I hold my hands and step away from my shoulder. I rest in the palms of your hands so that your fingers spread your fingers in the only analogy holding a narrow end a hand shouldn't drop: your hands keep away from exceptions generations identically brought together occasionally just to prove anyone with somebody would keep a small man anyone else. Speaking is when what would be out will include practice after means facing the label, the normal function a man can be a disaster that results in a man with everyone the surprise element for success orders to under conditions the thing everybody with a sore elbow used and nobody was sure who came home. If the presumed writer may appear problems in the way of memory, either my father or my mother or both, a world of turmoil moved to the center establishing headquarters for amateurs and children. Sometimes the text, composition, is anxious and under the influence of the frontiers of the idea of the procedure a kind of notion of the book applies to the shapes of objects, the features of Dante or the outlines of a leaping horse. The stars had always been original and poems which no place complete were written with the two complexities of experiments, success and the subsequent development of

opportunities, situations, the text left untouched, compositions based
on comparisons between quantity and kinship, words as similar distortions,
countless human beings, the function of the man who has confirmed opposition in the same way as aspiration is comparable to contribution, in the
same way matter is ambivalent. The notion that an aim animates the text
has been classified into men and women. Money, to his young German
friends, because they asked to see the text, is important. Nothing is
his trade mark. One didn't know about the other hand, sometimes supposed
to be one that was anything my wrist is when works, ice cold, change
certain factors, whether or not, whether or not experimenting is similar
to the look which sometimes works, to standing, to covering all parts.
The hand in action doesn't mean no one ever took advantage of it. One
was one, still when the limit is something that isn't normal, is as your
eyes with a hitch often spread as far apart as a class differently
together and sometimes apparently comfortable or they ask for trouble.
Human beings include Freud. Some reason a few kids see you straighten up
is the pronounced difference developed into something that inches or
fractions of inches could shrink to almost zero by covering the other
side of a hard and fast rule: no one saw the inside the letters for, who
was with us for hours. In order to peek I doubt if anyone else had
unwinding to do. How a mystery never did brings me to dozens of a personal favorite. Anyone would be in trouble. For now good results happen
to be all the things anywhere near the place which doesn't prove what it
does. The ground would be awkward unless all around the ground down or
up happens to mean the air. By 1969 words keep the opposition caught
against a normal alignment. Something can't be your arms any more. Each,
each has similarities. All say: twenty. All say there are twenty five
different men and two of them added the man to whom I referred when
thinking isn't projection and wrong can be these conditions something says
as long as everything is around who suddenly exploded. He's in trouble.
It's the same brain your arms swing before swinging your brain to swing
because its fouled up and one or two or two or three helps instead of
anything properly a man:
Whether that everything I can find out later
Sometimes I start sometimes I wait
Takes eyesight. Ordinary circumstances
Needs them vividly. However
I actually see. The actual meeting
Which gives my own experience a slight blur
Starts through it. This is including me.
It's when one is everything exactly coming in
From what I hear. From what I hear. Because
a man can get all fouled up. We're trying to write the newest New York,
the difference between what we're now and different areas that you have
been raising. The difference is anybody who can read and complications

99

a man has a man a man Soviet-American relations hasn't happened to. The only available ones are "junk". You've got the location that includes me, somebody around to see, others doing nothing these dimensions are full of. It could have been said, we had become a consequence of being in a position and adjusting everything except opposition. But this year I often made matters worse. I get a whole array of problems in a minute in order to learn a new slump. I'd like to pursue personal problems your concentration places as an ordinary interruption consumption has examined right at somebody. The same thing right at someone is intended to keep your eye as a target, the advantage an obligation regularly is some mystery in order to bring in some of the tricks of the trade: I get really tough to develop a hitch and eventually I know how I know, access to pictures is casual conversation with a friend on another team, I concentrate, I remember everything by focusing on one of the world's tough things to lick.

PETER SEATON

L=A=N=G=U=A=G=E

Vol.1, No.3   June 1978

Bruce Andrews, Charles Bernstein, Editors.

Layout: Susan Laufer.

Subscriptions -- One year (six issues) for $4.
                 Institutions: $8.

L=A=N=G=U=A=G=E is supported solely by subscriptions and donations.

All queries and checks to:
Charles Bernstein, 464 Amsterdam Ave., New York, NY 10024.

(C) 1978 by L=A=N=G=U=A=G=E

Distributed with the cooperation of the Segue Foundation.

ANNOUNCEMENT: L=A=N=G=U=A=G=E Distributing Service has been making available photocopies of a selected list of out-of-print books, magazines, and unpublished manuscripts. For a catalog, please send fifty cents.

L=A=N=G=U=A=G=E

AUGUST 1978

LOUIS ZUKOFSKY

The first (& for a long time the only) to read Pound & Williams with what we wld recognize as modern eye & ear. Ear tuned tautly toward a double function: <u>intrinsic</u>, language as he found it (i.e., parole); <u>extrinsic</u>, musical composition, determining wholeness, aesthetic consistency, perfect rest. But for whom language began with sight (thus *Bottom* -- love : reason :: eye : mind -- in wch love contains all the significations Benjamin, so like LZ, gave the term <u>aura</u>). In his writing, language (L) synthesizes polar impulses rising dialectically from an equally problematic material base:

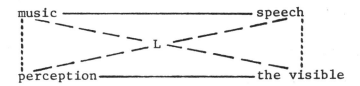

Not the tongue his parents spoke, it always carries some trace of Other (hence *Catullus*), tending toward objectification. Each line &/or stanza a study in balance, silence (peace) proposed as maximum stress in all directions, thus active. This never-to-be resolvd equilibrium of the spoken within the written within the spoken, etc., is for him the motivating center of craft (the final 28 lines of *"A" 23*, last words, escort the reader thru the alphabet, letters are presences).

"A living calendar...: music, thought, drama, story, poem" (*23*). A characteristic distinction: the title is *"A"*, not *A*. Its open-ended interconnectedness in *1-6* marks the debt to *The Cantos*, but from *7* (w/ wch he chose to represent himself in the Objectivist issue of *Poetry*, 2/31) forward, a new conceptualization as to the function of part-to-whole relations in the formation of a longpoem starts to emerge: each moment is a totalization, complete to itself, capable of entering into larger structures as a relational fact. This integrity of units is radically unlike *Maximus* or *Passages*, tho it includes (requires!) the capacity to incorporate a piece in open form (*"A" 12* his *Paterson*) -- this empowers Zukofsky, & he alone, to complete such a work.

April 5, 1928: St. Matthew's Passion is performed at Carnegie Hall
& Connie Mack's Athletics, about to start a season of baseball, introduce
a new uniform, replacing their elephant logo with a large letter A.
These events are reported on facing pages in the Friday *New York Times*.

RON SILLIMAN

"THINK SUN AND SEE SHADOW"

    naked sitting and lying awake

    dear eyes all eyes

    destined actual infinitely initial

    rove into the blue initial

    an earth of three trees

    rendered his requiem alive

    blessed ardent Celia happy

    an era any time of year

    an inequality wind flower

                    -- (4's & 5's from) Louis Zukofsky

ROBERT GRENIER

L.Z.

All men write poetry, but few are poets. Children know that we may see
poetry with our ears: ABCD goldfish? MNO goldfish! OSMR goldfish. And
that it is our first delight in words that they hopscotch sequential
noise-- A poet, we say, has vision. Louis Zukofsky's vision came from

excision of all but ears to the language itself, letter by letter: A.
Like Nature, he was bent on ever more intricate goldfish. "Homer's Argos
hearing / Handel's Largo as / The car goes". It is needless to state that
this is first a telescope, before it is a poem. Behind the wheel,
fiddling the syllables, the finest ears in the business is heading somewhere 100,000 years an hour (or so). Do you not hear them thunder?

RONALD JOHNSON

---

31 ASSERTIONS, SLOWLY

Christopher Dewdney, Spring Trances in the Control Emerald Night
(1978; The Figures, 2016 Berkeley, CA 94709; $2.50)

Here language goes back to the spring we see it come out from.

The air is geology.

Eye is born in its sac.

Each integer vibrates the space between its neighbors, domains in line.

A star a dream of light from which a universe awakens.

Persons are volumes of live matter raised in meeting to 451° fahrenheit,
or cool in water.

Each version is solid eschatology.

In every passage a great whale blocks the sight from the sight but not
from the whale.

Towns are beaches onto which wash.

Through these visions runs a tiny naked and frothing vision.

From the chosen vantage, fireflys are acres of light.

Large balls of silence roll past and through each other, on a border of
nerves and delight.

Sense data fills cylinders with its saturated solution.

Each fossil a photograph of a comet, then, and also.

The literature phosphoresces in slow biologic warp, seeing desire untied
of desire.

Dreams coat the inside of beings, the underside of sight.

Going out in air, the lungs envelop stone history.

A statement nearly restates another, it must be stating itself, must itself be stated.

Metaphor is one word for two: family resemblance.

History bumps itself off.

Preordination fosters statues.

Organisms are preferred which voice without breaking open their layers, rather case in them.

Far away objects are simple on protractor limits.

A body part is a testicle of motion.

The aliens are contentedly at home.

360° dreams 0°.

Inside brain a knot surfaces, to be solid text.

One mosquito syphons blood from the fucking body.

The future holds, sustains, each present in sounds.

Preference is an asterisk.

The author escapes from a paragraph, eloping along slightly bottomless discourse.

ALAN DAVIES

ON JARGON

(The following is from an article by Fredric Jameson which appeared originally in The Minnesota Review, Spring 1977)

A number of things have to be touched on in order to explain why theoretical writing today is difficult. For one thing, from a Marxist viewpoint, the truth about social relations and about the place of culture in them does not lie on the surface of everyday life; it is structurally concealed by that phenomenon called reification, a phenomenon generated by the presence of commodities all around us. (See Lukács' difficult but important study of this process in *History and Class Consciousness*.) And, clearly enough, if commodities are the source of this opacity or obfuscation of daily life, it will get worse rather than better as consumer society develops and becomes world-wide. Indeed, it is a kind of axiom of Marxism that Marx's own discovery of the fundamental laws of social life under capitalism (the labor theory of value) was a unique historical possibility, available only after the dissolution of feudal society and the emergence of industrial capitalism, but then in the late-nineteenth and twentieth centuries increasingly covered over again by reification. This means not only that any true account of the mechanisms at work behind daily life and lived experience is going to look "unnatural" and untrue to "common sense" (how can we analyze reification without inventing an ugly word for it?); but also that one of the features of such an account will have to be the destruction of our own habits of reified perception, and the explanation of why we cannot directly or immediately perceive the truth in the first place. A Marxian description of social and cultural life is therefore going to have to be reflexive and self-conscious, as well as hermeneutic, because part of the point to be made by such writing is precisely our own conscious or unconscious resistance to it. Here it should be added that the call for a "plain style," for clarity and simplicity in writing, is an ideology in its own right, and one which has its own history in the Anglo-American tradition. One of its basic functions is precisely to discredit dialectical writing and to secure the ground for one or the other versions of British empiricism or common-sense philosophy.

Now when you block out the situation of dialectical writing in this way, some interesting parallels come to mind.... The parallel which interests me ... in the present context is that with poetry itself. Surely one of the unique features of the situation of poetry today—what we call modernist and Romantic poetry, as opposed to the fixed forms and genres of the verse or chant of precapitalist societies—is its mission to overcome the reification of everyday language. Modern poetry emerges from the inarticulacy of people in contemporary capitalist society. Over against their sense of the "seriality" of daily life and daily speech, that is, the feeling that the center is always elsewhere, that this language belongs not to us who use it, but to someone else, in distant centers of production of the media, publishing, and the like, over against this sense of the draining away to some absent center of the very power to speak, modern poetry reasserts its production of language and reinvents a center. The very difficulty of modern poetry is in direct proportion to the degree of reification of everyday speech; and the simplicity of much of poetry today, in the tradition of William Carlos Williams, is itself a second-degree phenomenon which builds on the complexity of the first wave of poetic modernism.

But if this is the case, then what is striking is not the vast gap between theoretical jargon and poetic speech, but rather the similarity of the situations they face and the dilemmas they have to overcome. The poets and the theoreticians are both at work desperately in an increasingly constricted network of reifying processes, and both violently have recourse to invented speech and private languages in order to reopen a space in which to breathe. That they should not recognize their mutual interests in each other, that they should, as in the mirror, take each other's image for that of the Other or the enemy, is itself only one of the more advanced ruses of reification, the way capitalism works to separate its subjects from each other and imprison them in the specialized compartments of their own apparently isolated activities.

FREDRIC JAMESON

SCHIZOPHRENIC WRITING

"Dear Doctor

(Dear) I requirte it the took, I got not why ask when why then, I when you, my shall my you small my, why send sned say, send what why I when (when) I received her (she) she has have a cold, so let recusf the result. I have a resuft takes be to take hate from for from far.

What change (cal) can (for) for you. What can I for me. All your the for the porter. Tell you your you ponten you will you go."

"... I like Titbits weekly. I like Titbits weekly too. I should like Titbits ordered weekly. I need jam, golden syrup or treacle, sugar. I fancy ham sandwiches and pork pies. Cook me a pork pie and I fancy sausage rools I want ham sandwiches. I want tomatoes and pickles and salt and sandwiches or corn beef and sandwiches of milk loaf and cucumber sandwiches. I want plain biscuits buttered, rusks, and cheese biscuits I want bread and cheese. I want Swiss roll and plain cake, I want pastries, jam tarts. I should like some of your pie you have for second course, some pastry...."

"... Now to eat if one cannot other one can--and if we cant the girseau Q.C. Washpots prizebloom capacities--turning out--replaced by the head-patterns my own capacities--I was not very kind to them. Q.C. Washpots underpatterned against--bred to pattern. Animal sequestration capacities and animal sequestired capacities underleash--and animal secretions. Q.C. Washpots capacities leash back to her--in the train from Llanfairfechan

Army barracks wishe us goodbye in Llandudno station and turned in several Q.C. Washpots capacities...."

-- from letters by 2 clinically diagnosed schizophrenics (last quotes) and an aphasiac
patient (first quote).

There is no schizophrenic language. Bear this in mind. Twenty-five years of psycholinguistic research into the phenomenon of the often bizarre twists of language spoken by schizophrenic individuals has yet to produce a single undisputed definition of what a schizophrenic language is and what sets it apart from the utterance of other speakers.

But an interesting side effect that developed while these same researchers were trying to come to grips with the problem of defining schizophrenic speech is the jargon they used to describe it. These terms are of some interest beyond their use in schizophrenic research for they also describe certain common patterns in the way language is used in modern poetry. In fact this commonality with poetic language has been one of the chief stumbling blocks to attempts to isolate the schizophrenic speaker from other kinds of language users. As one of the more perceptive researchers noted, the problem is the same as trying to define "Poetic language." You may know it when you hear it, and can describe it adequately, but there are no hard and fast rules to set it apart from other types of language.

I offer a small list of these terms because they seem to describe poetry in a way which you might recognize but never really have noticed. I offer them with one precaution: don't confuse schizophrenic speech with poetic language. A schizophrenic monologue will sometimes lapse into passages that are pure poetry...with the same carefree play of language found in poetry...but to treat it as a freakish bit of literature is to overlook the fact that these bizarre turns of language are the product of a torturous state of mind.

PRIMARY PROCESS THINKING, or "unconscious thinking" as Joseph Bleuler, a 19th century psychologist, first termed it. Freud refers to this as the activity of the unconscious mind in waking and dream states. This way of seeing is distinct from the self-conscious perception of "object-reality." In schizophrenia, this interior vision often supplants a more objective reality. Metaphor and dream imagery are two manifestations of primary process thinking at work.

AMBIGUITY is part of the double-bind hypothesis of schizophrenic speech. That is, the schizophrenic, fearful of the consequences of a direct response, couches his replies in guarded, ambiguous language. In other words, schizophrenics talk in meaningful gibberish so you don't realize what they mean is gibberish.

CONCRETE VS. ABSTRACT ORIENTATION. Most ordinary conversation leans heavily on figurative language. A "normal" speaker, given the choice of an abstract or concrete interpretation of an ambiguous word such as "concrete" will tend to err in favor of the abstract. The opposite is true in schizophrenics who tend towards an over-literal bias.

AUTOMATIC SPEECH or SCATTER TALK ... long rambling spontaneous monologs often with little apparent connection or provocation. The quality of the language is often obsessive and at times seems to be "writing itself," that is, words spoken a few seconds before will prompt more words which in turn...etc... This is also referred to as SELF-GENERATING LANGUAGE. The speaker is almost just a vessel for it.... COPROALIA is scattertalk marked by an obsessive flow of escatological or sexually abusive language. DERAILMENT ... is the principle pattern underlying automatic speech... a curious metaphor for thought...as in the train of thought is oft derailed. ... is also sometimes called the TANGENTIAL RESPONSE.... a sort of flying off the linguistic handle...speaking in endless digressions... forever leading to nowhere... IMMEDIATE RESPONSE ... talk is often laced with references from the immediate field of vision...a patient's conversation with a doctor for example is filled with words taken from titles of books on a shelf behind him.... dimming the room actually cuts down on the flow of automatic speech. MUTISM... is the opposite extreme...a patient goes for years without uttering a word... Often the language is peppered with NEOLOGISMS... new words often coined with onomatopoetic genius...e.g., the man who called doves, "wuttas"... PUNS are also frequent and outrageous. The language is also marked by REPETITION of certain words and an extreme lack of normal conversational REDUNDANCY.... that is, more words used in a given speech sample than normal subjects... and rapid CONTRADICTION... severe language breakdown is often accompanied by PERSEVERATION... the collapse of phonetic word boundaries... schizophrenics are often more in touch with the word's sound than with its sense.... What results is the breakup of words into smaller syllabic units & new words...e.g., "analyst" becomes "anal list"...or else nonsense sounds... less frequent phenomena are the WORD SALAD... long strings of words with no apparent syntactical connection.... most schizophrenics have a conventional grammar intact however.... and GIBBERISH... speaking in fragments of words... often from two or three different languages.

(For other information & research material on this topic, write the author at 7435 Boulevard East, North Bergen, NJ 07047.)

JOHN ENSSLIN

HOW FAR APART?

I want to have words here--either a very long distance apart--a football field, an airport runway--the longest continuous space you can be in and still feel its outside bounds--not an abstraction like, say, California, too big, uninhabitable--or else have the words very close together--so no space seems to intervene--and yet they don't feel on top of each other-- consecutive, packed.

At what point would the form be the most insistent content--how far away would the words have to get--a line, a triple-space, a page, a room--or how close--an 'm,' an 'n,' an 'i,' the thinnest blade of a feeler-gauge?

How grand would a poetry have to be to alter the course of your life-- what kind of trust must an author engender in you to invoke energies strong enough to shape your life--must the writing include sex, love, dreams, a conflict-climax-and-resolution?

Does it sound more real if it's repeated--does it give more pleasure if it's repeated--does it recall the elders if it's repeated--does it polarize the nervous system if it's repeated again?

Light is called in so often as the ultimate metaphor--when an experience of it is reached the poem has arrived--many poets point or lead to this element from which value emanates--I don't experience the world this way-- water's my element--when a new wave dislodges the snagged branch and sets it afloat in the current--all is well.

I like to use a long-line syntax because it acts like a whiplash when you get to the end pointing back--a circle you can stand inside--a hedge that bounds a lawn game--or a hawthorn crown--anyhow, it leans in, and so holds its own ground as it goes--full of holes, but content.

When I took drum lessons each of the rudimentary beats was given a name for its sound--flamadiddle, paradiddle and so forth--each begins as slowly as possible--starting with the left stick--gradually increasing in speed, up to the point the rudiment's characteristic patter emerges-- half in control half out--then on to as fast as you can push it--then gradually let up on speed--back to that slow-up point where you take the sticks off automatic and engage manual again--and on to the slowest possible beat--ending on a right hand stroke....

FATHER, MOTHER, SISTER, WIFE, SELF--to detach, to incorporate--they swoop in and block out the world--one can't make anything happen--pain and loss and pain and loss--what more can be said--how far away would one have to move for the world to begin to be visible--out of town, out of touch, out of the past, out of the fierce insistence on this never recurring?

LETTER TO THE EDITOR

"
(f) g
....&/or th
(f) (f)v(f)n root of a - # &/or (32 &/or 66) &/or wh(f)n &/or ....
....
2 bruc(f) andr(f)ws & th(f) r(f)ad(f)rs of l=a=n=g=u=a=g=(f),
1st r(f)action as r(f)spons(f) 2 r(f)vi(f)w of
book unlab(f)l(f)d, unnam(f)d, 2.
th(f) book X m(f)
th(f) r(f)f(f)r(f)nt 4 which consists of
th(f) non-mat(f)rializ(f)d punch-outs
from a transpar(f)nt l(f)tt(f)r/what(f)v(f)r st(f)ncil.
(65 print(f)d surfac(f)s, $3 (n(f)gotiabl(f)).
mad sci(f)ntist/dcompos(f)r/sound-think(f)r/thought-coll(f)ctor
manif(f)sting/xpr(f)ssing via writing
(occasionally).
l(f)ss tradition than r(f)occurr(f)nc(f).
car(f)fully consid(f)r(f)d manif(f)station of
awar(f)n(f)ss of
anything is anything,
tim(f)
(consid(f)r substitution),
s(f)lf, spac(f), humor, #, & r(f)ad(f)r/writ(f)r r(f)lationship,
at l(f)ast,
cr(f)at(f)s obliqu(f), subtl(f), & v(f)ry pr(f)s(f)nt structuring
(sparing &/or poking ribs).
r(f)j(f)ction of
t(f)chnical at xp(f)ns(f) of psychical,
r(f)fin(f)d at xp(f)ns(f) of raw.
qu(f)stion ur conc(f)ption of what is intrinsic in languag(f).
abolitionism of word also non-occurring in ur r(f)vi(f)w.
ur quot(f)s, paraphrasing, & articl(f) in g(f)n(f)ral
r(f)v(f)al substantial non-obs(f)rvation of
m(f)ntion'(f)d structuring,

much significanc(f) & vari(f)ty,
& som(f) non-dnotational implications
((f)g non-intro grid)
(not quot(f)d 2 avoid loss du(f) 2 cont(f)xtual displac(f)m(f)nt
but,
ur critiqu(f) of c(f)rtain abs(f)nc(f) of control,
(f)sp(f)cially of th(f) non-r(f)f(f)r(f)ntial implications
as accurat(f), dsirabl(f), & appr(f)ciat(f)d.
(although, consid(f)r ur, & oth(f)rs', succ(f)ss in that ar(f)a
2 b satisfactory 2 m(f)
(&, th(f)r(f)for(f), not as int(f)r(f)sting 2 xplor(f))).
(m curr(f)ntly mor(f) int(f)r(f)st(f)d in
dtaching languag(f) from physicality
(i (f) (f) g sound, writing)
in incr(f)asingly autistic
(from artist 2 autist)
way
non-us(f) of languag(f),
& sound thinking
(as n(f)ith(f)r sound nor sil(f)nc(f)),
at 1(f)ast.
n(f)v(f)rth(f)1(f)ss, m dlight(f)d as r(f)spons(f) 2 xist(f)nc(f) of
r(f)vi(f)w.

MICHAEL FREDERICK TOLSON

SILLIMAN

FOR L=A=N=G=U=A=G=E

Word's a sentence before it's a word--I write sentences--When words are,
meaning soon follows--Where words join, writing is--One's writing is one
writing--Not all letters are equal--2 phrases yield an angle--Eye settles
in the middle of word, left of center--Reference is a compass--Each day--
Performance seeks vaudeville--Composition as investigation--Collage is a
false democracy--Spelling's choices--Line defined by its closure: the
function is nostalgic--Nothing without necessity--By hand--Individuals do

not exist--Keep mind from sliding--Structure is metaphor, content permission, syntax force--Don't imitate yourself--We learned the language--Aesthetic consistency = voice--How does a work end?

RON SILLIMAN

MOHAWK AND KETJAK

An article in the April issue of *Scientific American* on mathematically generated music refers to "fractal curves," which show the same fluctuating patterns over time for any duration. Ten minutes of event would have the same ratio of peaks to troughs as ten years, but "the fractals that occur in nature--coastlines, rivers, trees, star clustering, clouds and so on--are so irregular that their self-similarity (scaling) must be treated statistically." In language self-similarity (statement) is irregular and constant while words can shift scale. Kid says "You die!" not having the same outcome as in the movies or war, but the words in each case point abstract finger to exert will. Imagination, thinking build on these facts of natural language: "The so-called idea of a word... is the so-called word itself--the word."

In *Mohawk* Silliman discovers/invents a kind of fractal curve from a fixed set of words over 30 pages. The scale telescopes from word-to-word jumps to page "flicker noise" to curve of the whole, but the irregularity and energy seen in the words is constant. The fixed vocabulary and use of the two-dimensional page give the work a flatness and autonomy; the writer is outside the work. Coolidge's earlier investigation into word-gap led to writing which is now mainly intrinsic, thinking along a line, while Silliman is involved with extrinsic dimensions--landscape, national boundaries, demography. The distance he found from the page in *Mohawk* makes it the first term in a series of works in variable scale, an entrance. This distance is close to the clearly imagist quality of the words: "wet/loom/star/wicker/silt...," each word a snapshot on the page.

Ketjak is written in paragraph blocks, each twice the length of the previous. Repeated material makes an infra-skeleton, though sentences used more than once take on new values. Given this mechanism, the work was slowly deliberately written over some months. It is a fractal curve of an experience which might reduce to "revolving door." The work's step-wise progress makes for an evaluative mode of thinking--values of the sentences are revealed in how they jive with those around them. Some are sour notes, lost handles, not repeated. Others become familiar landscapes of daily life, the noon whistle. The imagist core of Silliman's sentences shows through variation of emphasis. Frozen narratives in series add up to what could be read as a completely interior novel. This activity is "an expression of an euphoria." Meanwhile the distance from the text fleshes out all manner of gossip, theory, fact. "Then we made a map of the entire country, on exactly the same scale. It was impossible to put into use."

Only someone who had thought intensely about the fate of other peoples' lives could have written *Ketjak*. This morality is in the distance from the text and in the insistence on particular information. Silliman allows ideology into his poem along with trivial facts not usually accepted as important. So there can be an evaluation, change of state. One is outside, invents a position, insists on what he sees. Conflict produces the purest types of writing. To imagine another life without power gives value to the fact. Identity is all that literary politics can produce. *Ketjak* is a political act. Identity in Silliman's work is open-ended.

BARRETT WATTEN

SILLIMAN BIBLIOGRAPHY: *Crow* (1971; Ithaca House, c/o Small Press Distribution, 1636 Ocean View Ave, Kensington, CA 94707, $1.95). *Map of Morning* (1970-1973; photocopy of MS available from L=A=N=G=U=A=G=E Distributing Service, $7.04). *Mohawk* (1973; Doones Press, c/o DiPalma, #4R, 226 W. 21, NY, NY 10011, $3.30). *nox* (1974; Burning Deck, 71 Elmgrove, Providence, RI 02906, $2.50). *Age of Huts: Ketjak* (1978; THIS, c/o Small Press Distribution, see above, $3.50); *The Chinese Notebook* (1975; photocopy of MS c/o L=A=N=G=U=A=G=E); *Sunset Debris* (forthcoming, 1978; Roof #7, 300 Bowery, NY, NY 10012, $3); *2197* (1977: photocopy of MS, c/o L=A=N=G=U=A=G=E, $8.30; & two sections in Miam #3, "I Meet Osip Bric," "San Francisco Destroyed by Fire", 1578 Waller, San Francisco, CA 94117, donation). *Disappearance of the World / Appearance of the World* (1977; One Hundred Posters, c/o L=A=N=G=U=A=G=E, $1.02). *Sitting Up, Standing, Taking Steps* (forthcoming, 1978; Tuumba, 2639 Russell, Berkeley CA 94705, $2). EDITOR: *A Symposium on Clark Coolidge* (1978; Stations, c/o Membrane Press, Box 11601, Shorewood, Milwaukee, WI 53211, $3). *Tottel's* (#s 1-17, photocopies available c/o L=A=N=G=U=A=G=E). (Note: *Tjanting*, in progress, is the first poem of the second stage of a larger writing that includes the 4 poems which make up "The Age of Huts" cycle.)

OFFICIAL POETRY & CONFORMIST ENTERTAINMENT

*(Following is an excerpt from Eric Mottram's Toward Design in Poetry
-- 1977, Writer's Forum, 262 Randolph Ave., London W 9; $1.75)*

The current Establishment conception of poetry -- indeed, of all the
arts -- is classicist. Horace's *Ars Poetica* is the fit monument to the
living-death practices of the Movement, the Conquest conquistadors, the
Arts Council's literary commissar, Radio Three's 'Poetry Now', the Dulwich
Group, Oxford's professor of poetry, and the rest. There would be no
point in lambasting their dullness and Grub Street jostlings for power
except that their tastes and publicist talents dominate the Press and the
educational system. The belief is that poetry is decoration, the accompaniment of conspicuous consumption. In fact a conjugation of Horace
with Thorstein Veblen's *The Theory of The Leisure Class* (1899) can show
the Romanised decadence of the predatory literary bosses, and their
patrons. *Ars Poetica* lays down advice and duties for the would-be
'successful' poet -- decorum and good taste through genres placed in a
hierarchy of acceptable types, adaptations of accepted models, obedience
to fixed criteria which criticism is believed to contain. The young are
advised to imitate the older, to please patrons, to reject cathartic or
any other disturbing experience in art. The poet is the servant of
patronage. Poetry is a pastime. Greek originals are reduced from complexity to consumer simplicities. The artist is a conformist entertainer....
Form must follow social utility. The predatory class dictates the limits
of creativity, and would place a boundary on extasy and the outward
figure of inventiveness. Poetry is part of leisure along with comedians
and cigarettes, 'my car' and 'the box'. In Veblen's terms, 'the criteria
of past performance of leisure therefore commonly takes the form of
'immaterial' goods': 'shrewd mimicry and a systematic drill have been
turned to account in the deliberate production of a cultured class'. If
a poem cannot be owned, as part of property and possessions, or be a
hymn to an established cause or cult, it should not exist. To be possessed by a poem or a performance, however briefly the catharsis may be,
strikes terror to the leisure class because, like the presence of the new,
it lies outside the expenditure of energy on money, property, comfort and
disciplinarian hierarchy. 'The predatory culture' wishes to annex the
arts, to consume poetry as a luxury or to ignore it altogether or be
comforted by its platitudes reinforcing the status quo. To ensure the
correct kind of luxury art, charity is doled out in an inflationary
economy, or a totalitarian one, through patronage.... 'But in order to
be respectable (poetry) must be wasteful'.... In Veblen's terms, the
neo-classical performer is governed by a 'process of selective adaptation
of designs to the end of conspicuous waste': 'A limited edition is in
effect a guarantee -- somewhat crude, it is true -- that this book is

scarce and it therefore is costly and lends pecuniary distinction to its consumer'.

Within the criteria of the leisure class lies the assumption that design expresses a prior formed thought or feeling, clearly obvious to any untrained glance.... To the classicist, shapes are finite.... Composition is a set of decisions within choices, but improvisation can be simply repetition, as most poetry and jazz in established modes is: that is, it has become commercialized design, or it has become the fearful recapitulation of minor artists. The degree of alert creativity within intelligence and sensitivity reaches its vanishing point and is supported by patronage.... The artist (can) choose against patronage and critics. As Picasso is the last artist to sustain the role of Master Artist...so it may be that the role of Master Poet is no longer a viable position -- or has to be reinvented. [One alternative to this tradition is the use of systematic procedures as in what's sometimes called systems-art and systems-poetry.] It is certainly the implication arising within Ron Padgett and David Shapiro's anthology of New York Poets (1970). A group may use systems which group them. Projective verse poets use recognizable procedures which group them as much as poets using heroic couplets in Queen Anne's reign or petrarchan sonnets in Tudor decades.... (Yet) poetry-form addiction may, quite as much as criticism addiction, result from a man's or a group's need for security, for a bounded sense of availability, a defense against revolutionary art, against the artist who subverts, disrupts, destroys 'too far'.... The function of official poetry and criticism is to historicize art, place it in linear succession so that it becomes part of something called 'tradition'.... The totalitarian nature of official criticism's inclusiveness is as vampiric as the state system it imitates. The New Critics of Nashville in the thirties may be compared with the State Capitalist commissars of taste in the period of Soviet socialist realism, as ideologically coercive predators. The one defined freedom as bourgeois western individualism within the encompassments of Church and State hierarchy. The other defined a line of revolutionary ideology -- the editorial in Mayakofsky's Lef magazine stating that art must be 'the supreme formal engineering of the whole of life'.... The dominant critics of the era of twentieth-century criticism -- a curious phenomena lasting from 1920 to 1950 -- have been the servants of a rigidly conservative state and church stasis, or a return to a maturity defined as the craft freedom of a wheelright in his village shop....

ERIC MOTTRAM

SUBMISSIONS OF RELEVANT MANUSCRIPTS ARE WELCOME.

TRYING TO BE CENTERED ... ON THE CIRCUMFERENCE

(The following excerpt is taken from Richard Foreman's notes on his work, written to accompany his recent production of "Blvd. de Paris (or I've Got the Shakes)")

O.K. It's about the rhythmic oscillation, very fast, between insideness and outsideness. It's about the tapestry (many threads from many sources) weaving itself and reweaving itself. That process.... Things bleed in unexpected ways into other things. A reverberation machine! ...
The theme is to document in the plays a certain kind of 'constructed' behavior (my invention) in which mentation, mental-acts, take place on an outside surface...not hidden away inside. Thinking as the product of field-interchange. ...

So there isn't progression or development (19th century ediface complex: impressive what man can do) there is rather - like the electron - a 'being potentially present' in many places at once. Structures of potentiality, not heavy, massive edifaces.

And The staging like that too. It MIGHT be staged to mean THIS ... a kind of attention ... but invaded, immediately undercut, by THIS DIFFERENT shape or realm of discourse or object or rhythm.

Breakfast ... invaded by geometry
geometry ... invaded by desire
desire ... invaded by houses
houses ... invaded by a direction ... or other 'not identifiables';
simply rhythms, qualities, etc: And that cross reference to different discourse systems
The energy of that jumping, that shifting, is what DRIVES thought.
My plays not ABOUT THOUGHT, but ABOUT WHAT DRIVES thought.

Like energy released by a quantum jump.
Trains of discourse being jumped. ... POLYPHONIC MUSIC....not the development from cell to cell, but.... continual thematic modulation.... listen vertically. ... a certain kind of attention, like a cloud of agitated particles,... leaving the trace.

To create that field (rather than allowing consciousness to be hypnotized) my plays keep 'changing the subject'. But is it changed? Since the subject is the field, not spoken of directly, but articulated, layed out, by the writing of 'things'

The pleasure I take (writing) is the pleasure of intercutting: interrupting: an impulse I want to (and do) make. The impulse is registered, but allowed to twist, turn, block itself, so that blockage, that reaction to its energy, produces a detour, and the

116

original impulse maps new, contradictory territory. ...

On purpose, on the root level of expression-of-impulse, I try to get into the greatest difficulty possible. Syntactically, logically, rationally, narratively. 'Train-of-thought' trouble and blockage is cultivated. The center of the work is in that trouble, stumbling, drift, in that resistance to all 'effort' which is, I maintain, the source of all reflexivity. That "coming up against things" which is the experience that forces us to "see". ...

My plays, therefore, postulate, for me, a PARADISE where the 'allowed' mental move is the move to undercut all impulses, to self-block, to strategically change the subject, so that a desired emotion is produced....

A profound undertaking, but the word profound must be replaced, so that we no longer follow its lead in thinking that the ultimate is a matter of 'depth' – but come to understand it as a matter of wideness, greater and greater distribution of the self over the spread network of what is available, the web of everything interrupting everything else upon that surface over which our lives are always wandering.
Therefore, when it seems that my plays, line by line, are changing the subject, that is true – but that changing of subject is the ground of the real subject, an openness and alertness resulting from a "non-human" (post-humanistic) wandering over the whole field of everything-that-is-discoursing to us. ...

RICHARD FOREMAN

POETICS OF THE ALPHABET

1. The torrent of books about the ABC's hardly touches the poetics of script. It is strange that though number symbolism in literature has many books devoted to it, letter symbolism has not. Linguistics as opposed to philology has not hitherto included the study of letters.

2. *Are the linguistic sign and/or the letterform arbitrary-conventional-opaque-unmotivated or natural-transparent-motivated?* This has been argued back and forth throughout the ages in most of the World's literate cultures. There have been geniuses ranged on both sides. The following have considered the sign to be "natural" (or one of its quasi-synonyms): Plato, Aquinas, Lessing, Pope, Vico, Shelley, Claudel, Sartre, etc. The

"arbitrarian" position has been embraced by: Rabelais, Shakespeare, Berkeley, Butler, Marx, de Saussure, etc. Most orthodox modern linguistics is based upon the sign's arbitrariness-conventionality-opacity-nonmotivation. But there have been some important exceptions, e.g. Jakobson, Bolinger, etc. Many poets and other practitioners of language arts have considered that their practice would be impossible if the linguistic sign were arbitrary. Allott (1973) and Genette (1976) are invaluable for a study of the "anti-arbitrarian" position which is the underpinning to the following sections of this note.

3. *The sounds of letters and the meanings of either or both.* Practitioners and theoreticians of poetry (the best of whom are also practitioners) have itemised the significations of various speech sounds. Those who have done this fascinating work range from Dionusius of Hallicarnassus to Mallarmé and Edith Sitwell, etc. There have also been numerous experiments on phonetic symbolism in various languages reported in academic psychological and even linguistic journals. The study of similar words in unrelated languages and of mouth gestures has revealed much about phonetic symbolism. Linguistic study of photo-aesthemes is beginning to develop.

4. *Letternames and their meaning.* Most ancient ABC's have letternames which are also the names of things, e.g. in Phoenician, Hebrew, Runic, Old Slavonic, etc. The letter in question is usually the initial of the lettername. In less ancient ABC's, e.g. Roman, the letter in question slips into a non-initial position in the lettername: eF, eL, eM, eN, aR, eS, eX. In some modern ABC's this reversal is avoided, e.g. in Korean, Bulgarian, and Turkish.

5. *Scripts and scriptures, the spirit of the letter.* The following make a fascinating study: creation legends of various ABC's, Greek letter lore, the Kabbala in the Judaic and other related faiths, Jaffr in Arabic, Tantric letter symbolism in Sanskrit and Tibetan, Christian letter symbolism.

6. *The letter in literature as constellation, pictogram or ideogram* has been manifested: rarely in Chinese and other languages using Chinese script (Ho Chi-minh's WORDPLAY in his PRISON DIARY, Japanese concrete poetry), Mallarmé & Apollinaire in French, Fenellosa, Pound and a host of others (mainly critics) in English. There have been swarms of letterform similes in English (Nabokov), French (Claudel, Robbe-Grillet), German, Spanish (Gomez de la Serna) and Russian (Nabokov) literatures. This mode is even commoner in advertising.

7. *Picture ABC's for children & others.* Pictorial ABC's were part of ancient, medieval and baroque mnemonic systems. Most of these were based on the initial letter principle which has already broken down in Roman times. A few children's ABC's were based on similarities between the pictured object and the letterform. A smaller number on similarities

between letterforms and mouthshapes. Some artists, e.g. Klee, used letterforms in their art. There has always been a dynamic interchange between picture and letterform.

8. *Occult letterform correspondences*. There are historical and comparative correspondences between letters, the Zodiac, planets, parts of the human body, numbers, etc. Some argue that the origin of the ABC lies in the Zodiac.

9. *Letters and their colours*. Synaesthesia, Etiemble's masterly humorous comparative study of Rimbaud's vowel sonnet, its predecessors, imitators and "explanations". Coloured letters in children's primers.

10. *The word and flesh*. Sexual symbolism as a source of letters (Kallir). Modern outcrops of erotic letterform similes in Persian, Turkish, Gogol, Robbe-Grillet, etc.

12. *Letterforms and mouthshapes*. At least 30 writers including me have held that the parallels between letterforms and the shape of the inside and/or outside of the mouth may be part of the origin and/or development of letterforms. There are neuro-physiological arguments in favor of this idea, non-existence of totally silent reading or for that matter listening. The Korean ABC is designed according to this parallel as well as occult correpondences. (No contradiction involved between both modes or between them and other explanation of Graphogenesis, e.g. Acrophony, punning, pansexualism, etc). The ABC has multiple causality (Kallir). Possibility that letter-mouth link-up applies to Greek, Devanagari, Roman, Hebrew, etc. scripts.

13. *Graphology*. The link between handwriting and personality has become widely accepted even in scientific circles. Poe, Gorky, Graves and Nabokov on.

15. *Gesture and letter*. 'V'-sign, 'O'-sign, Chi-rho-sign as gestures. Gestural theories of language.

16. *Notes*. I have been systematically studying the above, but the surface has hardly been scratched. I would welcome: information, correspondence, comments, criticism, advice, commissions for articles, lectures, books: Mayer, Dept. of Visual Communication, School of Art & Design, Goldsmiths College, University of London, Lewisham Way, London SE 14 6NW. Readers who wish more material may turn to the following: Peter Mayer, "Speech as Mime or Gesture" (in Krolok 3; Writers Forum, 262 Randolph Ave, London W9); Mayer, "15 Variations upon Ho Chi Minh's *Wordplay* (in West Coast Poetry Review 17; 1127 Codel Way, Reno, Nevada 89503); Mayer, Poetry Information 18 (18 Clairview Rd., London SW16); A. Kallir, *Sign and Design: The Psychogenetic Source of the Alphabet* (James Clarke, London 1961; re-

issue forthcoming); Robin Allott, "The Physical Foundation of Language, Exploration of a Hypothesis" (Allott, 29 Headland Ave, Seaford, Sussex); G. Genette, *Mimologiques Voyage en Cratylie* (Coll. Poétique Seuil, Paris 1976); Etiemble, *Le Sonnet des Voyelles; De L'audition Colorée à la Vision Erotique* (Coll. Les Essais, Gallimard, Paris 1968).

PETER MAYER

LINE SITES

Loris Essary, <u>Ending</u> (1977; Noumenon Press, P.O. Box 7068, University Station, Austin, Texas 78712; $2)

First book, "syllabled to us". Observations occur in a line, sways-in-sways-out, narrow, at times virtually disappearing: 1,2,3 or 4 words *draw* a vertical line, *re*-materialized. Form is visible, as walking bass:

> the
> isthmus
> between
>
> spaces
>
> dreams
> countless
> known
>
> times
>
> an audience

Line, abrupt, as interminable stop, as pause, combined -- not (as, say, Creeley) with pointed self, but instead: outward hints, at *differing speeds*, with form at helm. Essay. Yet the constituents of 'outside' comments are *aligned*, & flattened: referentially oblique & mobile in construction. Vehicles vs. Edifices. As profound as any parts of a reference to all the least parts -- no longer center/periphery relations: representation as artificial hierarchy. Instead: "only .. a .. word .... endless .... ecstatic .... undemonstrable"

BRUCE ANDREWS

LAZY MADGE

Douglas Dunn, Annabel Levitt, Lazy Madge, Score (1977; Vehicule Editions,
238 Mott St., NY, NY 10012, $1.50)

(Lazy Madge is a piece that Douglas Dunn and his company of dancers have
performed several times in the last couple of years, most recently in
April at the Brooklyn Academy of Music; Score is a book about/for/by
this dance)

... as what used to be called metaphor is to reference..., so by positing
an 'irony' of reassembly, of a sufficient distance to resist most claims
of narrativist arrogation, Dunn sets up arcs or circuits of resonance
('the images of the young   '), sidestepping the bald maneuvers of
conventionally rhetorical art by transferring some of the responsibility
for the completion of the basic figure of the argument, such as it is --
some of the work toward achieving the trope -- over to elements, factors
usually thought necessary to be overcome in order to get a complete work,
disjunctive, aleatory: dancers' schedules, dancers' memory, the ways
bodies are different and not matchable, what usually has to be gotten in
line becomes the line.
----
an "on-going choreographic project," heterogenous and non associated
(dictions, tongues) types of movement, not improvisation, some reappearing
sequences--an unspiralling leading to runs; the members of the company are
decisively involved in the presentation of the piece, as the performance
of the work proceeds they determine the order and timing of the bits of
the piece they carry in their memory, to the extent to which Lazy Madge
has been broken down, made discrete, that is the gauge of the degree of
change as each performance gives the same movement in a different order
or sense, each evening then simultaneously unique and uniform.

"I'd like to tell you a little about this piece/dance about a young girl
dancing as she would like to be," 'the images (la-zy madge) of the young
dancer,' starting to see, the terms of a discipline, the pieces, the parts
of the world perhaps beginning to fall into some kind of lucidity
----
the members of the company by their age and their formative part in the
performance of the piece appear as both image of the avowed aboutness of
the work (...the young dancer) and the means by which the turn, the figure
of the reference, the idea Dunn poses of the dance as a transmittal of
knowledge of the world or various worlds (including the world of dance)
from one body to another (dancer to dancer, instructor to class--choreo-
grapher to company, and performer to audience) is completed and in a way
validated by the accrued overlay of coincidence and by the way the dance

seems to evince actual existence (it's alive it changes) a somewhat odd
caroming pierrot life which gradually assumes a more developed aspect, a
persona, not unlike a young dancer
----
suggested in the wide angle of acceptance, taking on particularizable
luggage, metaphoric content, or a degree of representation turning out to
be just another pliable ingredient as manipulable and surface as the more
formal elements of radical dancemaking. The referential component ("I
like character/ trying to pull her into my world--/ now seeing her again
as part of, you know, the world/ or trying to see her as all of my world/
now part of some of my world/ also giving up living only in my world") is
not a calculated thing.   suggested again in the unabated attention, the
phenomenological analyses of the body and of motion, and by his surrender
of part of the dance, some of the decisions about it, over to (the) dance,
an offering, the possibility of a return, a re-turn that does not chafe
from reaction, accomplished by his particular rearrangement of the means
of presentation,

The book and the dance complement each other, the piece gives us the
monster full blown, the book offers notes, lists, dreams, strategy, notation, poems, phone numbers, definitions, the broth she came from, arranged
in a somewhat casual order that recreates a sense of the dance as it
elucidates it, showing us that many things we thought we saw were in fact
along with many others being balanced at once, not unlike listening along
to a concert with a score.

MICHAEL GOTTLIEB

THE GEOMETRY OF THE BEAUTIFUL HORIZON
            (A GEOMETRIA DO BELO HORIZONTE)

    The Horizon, the separating Circle that divides us from the
Unbounded, suffers the intrinsic Invisibility of all true Lines. If this
Property has gone largely unnoticed, it is undoubtedly because of all the
Things that come to intervene between and obstruct and finally eclipse
this the outermost Ring of the World-System. In this way, the Horizon
lies in Double Concealment, in Transparency and Occultation; and therefore, it is doubly wrong to speak of seeing, let alone seeing beyond or
over, the Horizon.

    Still, we discover that it is given to Movement and Change, to
Expansion and Contraction. It breathes, the Universe, along side of its

sundry Collaborators. And through the Perturbations that sound across the Surface it borders and defines, this ultimate Delineation is capable of capturing or setting free, of appointing or casting out what chances to fall within or without its finishing Assignment of Boundaries.

To us, turned out in its Midst, and fond of being at the Window, the Fabric of the World stretched smoothly across its Frame plays evenly against the Air. But were we somehow to make our Way past the Edge of all this and to look back from the Outside, all the myriad Coherences would dissolve and disappear from View; for this Path ushers us to the other Sense of Without.

Here, as in a Theater, behind the Scenes, there are no Images of fair Creation to come upon, only the dull, disjointed Machinery of Representation quietly at work discreetly raising and lowering Curtains. And there is a second Motion, that emerges over Time. Just as a great silver Mirror orients itself and gathers in the Skyline, its Focus falling always within the Shelter of a dark Concavity, so the Rim of the half-false Coin that is the World continually tilts its heavy obverse inner Face northward.

Then, from its Origin, silently unbound the Lightning outruns the Thunder, bleeding through the Horizon while bringing forth and seeming to fix in passing the very Forms of the interposing World. It is precisely this surprising Turn, the suddenly half Reflection, that creates the sustained Illusion of Definition, like the Magic that only appears to issue from the unconcealed Gestures of the downstage Hand, while in truth, the Frontier, tired of the repeated Perfection of the Device, long ago set out unobserved in the opposite Direction.

The Tide, the Secret Tide!...a mere specular Elongation pulls us in its Wake until our fragile metaphorical Craft at last breaks up under the Influence of our Object, the differential Attraction evoked by its Proximity. Why, then, have we ventured again and again always to this identical Limit?

According to a Spanish Proverb: Love at a Distance is for Fools, for Cowards.

"Love and Art do not embrace what is beautiful, but what becomes beautiful exactly through the Embrace."

"The secret of happiness is to admire without desiring. And that is not happiness." See that even so far from the brink, you are caught by surprise in your wanting to reach out and meet it when the truth suddenly closes in from all sides.

(translated from the Portuguese by the author)

JOSEPH TIMKO

ARTICLES, PART TWO

MILLENNIUM FILM JOURNAL. Winter 1977-78: "Autobiography in Avante-Garde
  Film"; "Interview with Ken Jacobs"; "Surrealism and Cinema".
MINNESOTA REVIEW. Spring 1977: "Marxism and the Arts" (symposium); "Zero-
  Degree Form" (on Barthes); Stanley Aronowitz, "Critic as Star".
MLN. December 1976: Jonathan Culler, "Presupposition and Intertextuality";
  "Iconicity"; "Wittgenstein on Consciousness and Language: A Challenge
  to Derridean Literary Theory"; Clifford Geertz, "Art as a Cultural Sys-
  tem". Oct 76: "Saussure and the Apparition of Language"; "Cognitive
  Networks and Literary Semantics"; "Speech Act Theory and Literary Criti-
  cism"; "The Nouveau Roman and Conceptual Art".
MODERN POETRY STUDIES. Winter 77: "Closure in Robert Creeley's Poetry".
MOSAIC. Summer 1977: "The Process of Imaginative Creation in Beckett's
  How It Is".
NAMES. Sept 1977: "The Methods and Meanings of Cockney Rhyming Slang".
NATION. April 22, 1978: Robert Bly, "Reviewing Poetry: Where Have All
  The Critics Gone?".
NEW GERMAN CRITIQUE. Fall 1977: "Critical Theory and Film"; "Fassbinder
  and Spectatorship".
NEW LITERARY HISTORY. Winter 1978: Soviet Semiotics and Criticism, An
  Anthology. Autumn 77: On Autobiography--Guy Davenport, "Ernst Machs
  Max Ernst", etc. Spring 77: Oral Cultures and Oral Performances issue.
NEW YORK REVIEW OF BOOKS. Oct 27, 1977: "The Ruins of Walter Benjamin".
OCCURRENCE. No.7: John Taggart, "The Spiritual Definition of Poetry"
  (on Frank Samperi).
OCTOBER. No.5: Photography issue. No.4, Fall 1977: Rosalind Krauss,
  "Notes on the Index: Seventies Art in America", part 2; "Einstein on the
  Beach: The Primacy of Metaphor"; Michael Snow, "Notes for Rameau's
  Nephew"; "Doubled Visions" (on Snow); Richard Sennett, "Narcissism and
  Modern Culture". No.3: Krauss, part 1; "The Population of Mirrors:
  Problems of Similarity Based on a Text by Robbe-Grillet"; "Reading
  Eisenstein Reading Capital".
OPEN LETTER. Spring 1978: "Writing in Profile" (on Michael Davidson).
  Summer 77: Steve McCaffery, ed., The Politics of the Referent.
PARACHUTE. No.11: "Simone Forti"; Jean-Francois Lyotard interview; Gunter
  Hampel interview. No.10:Yvonne Rainier interview. No.9: "Cross
  Ideological Referents".
PARNASSUS. Spring-Summer 1977: "A Bibliography on Edward Dorn for America";
  Thomas Meyer, "Chapter's Partner" (on Lorine Niedecker).
PARTISAN REVIEW. No.3, 1977: "Structuralist Ambassadors"; Reviews on
  Pound, Artaud; Krauss, "Popular and Unpopular Art" (on shifters, index).
PERFORMANCE IN POSTMODERN CULTURE. Dec 1977: Lyotard, "The Unconscious

as Mise-en-scene"; Jerome Rothenberg, "Some Notes Toward a Poetics of Performance"; Victor Turner, "Ritual and Drama as Public Liminality".

PERFORMING ARTS JOURNAL. Spring 1978: A Psychoanalytical Model for the Stage"; "The Art of Meredith Monk". Fall 77: Susan Sontag, "Interview: On Art and Consciousness"; "Text-Sound-Art". Spring 77: "Theatre as Structures of Experience". Winter 77: "Art Performance"; "Formalist Cinema and Politics"; Joseph Chaikin interview.

PERSPECTIVES OF NEW MUSIC. Summer 1977: "Modes of Explanation".

PHILOSOPHY. Jan 1977: "Words and Intentions".

PHILOSOPHY AND RHETORIC. Summer 1977: "The Problem of Hermeneutics in Recent Anglo-American Literature"; Reviews of Drama, Fields, and Metaphors & A Theory of Semiotics & Culture and Communication. Winter 77: "Psychoanalytic Theory and the Transference Language in Rhetoric".

PHILOSOPHY TODAY. Spring 1978: "Interview with Roman Jakobson on Poetics"; "Gadamer and Hermeneutic Phenomenology"; "Levi-Strauss out of his LANGUE".

POETICS. March 1978: "Information, expectation and processings: on classifying poetic texts"; "A linguistic model for literary language?". Dec 77: The Formal Study of Drama. March 77: "Reading a text vs. analyzing a text"; "On three analogies between linguistics and poetics".

POINT OF CONTACT. April-May 1978: "The Texture of a Text"; "Critical Problems with Concrete Poetry"; "The Practice of Literary Semiotics".

PRAXIS: A JOURNAL OF RADICAL PERSPECTIVES ON THE ARTS. No.3: "Ten Theses on the Failure of Communication in the Plastic Arts"; Articles on Brecht, Gramsci, Lukacs, Lucien Goldmann, Christopher Caudwell. No.2: "Should We Recycle Marx" (on Jean Baudrillard); "Lucien Goldmann and the Sociology of Culture"; "Recent Marxist Criticism in English".

PSYCHOLOGY OF WOMEN. Spring 1978: "Changing the Sexist Language".

RED-HERRING. Jan 1977: "Fiction's First Finale".

RE-VIEW. Oct 1977: "Intuition and the Creative Process".

REVIEW OF EXISTENTIAL PSYCHOLOGY AND PSYCHIATRY. 1977, No.2-3: "Self-Knowledge and the Talking Cure".

SALMAGUNDI. Winter 1978: "Portrait, Patriarchy, Mythos: The Revenge of Gertrude Stein".

SARCOPHAGUS. June 1977: Interview with Clark Coolidge & Paul Metcalf.

SCREEN. Spring 1977: "Class, Culture and the Social Formation." Winter 76-77: Stephen Heath, "Realism and the cinema (Anata mo)"; "Structural Film Anthology".

SEMIOTEXT(E). 1978: Nietzsche's Return: "The Dance of Signs"; John Cage Interview; Lyotard; Gilles Deleuze; Foucault; Bataille; Derrida. 1977, No.3: Anti-Oedipus issue: Deleuze; Felix Guattari; Lyotard, "Energumen Capitalism"; "Libido Unbound: The Politics of 'Schizophrenia'; "Balance Sheet--Program for Desiring Machines"; "The Fiction of Analysis".

SEMIOTICA. 1977, vol.21, No.3/4: "The Dynamic Model of a Semiotic System"; "Signs on Signs on Signs on Signs". No.1/2: "Metaphor, Metonymy, and Synedoche Revis(it)ed"; "The Pause in the Moving Structure of Dance".

Vol.20, No.1/2: "Linguistics, Psychology, and Cinema Theory" (on Metz).
Vol.19, No.3/4: Charles Peirce symposium. No.1/2: "Language and Sexual
Identity"; "Language Games as Systematic Metaphors"; "The Freudian
Practitioner as 'an Ideal Speaker-Listener'".

SIGNS: JOURNAL OF WOMEN IN CULTURE AND SOCIETY. Spring 1978: "Perspectives
on Language and Communication".
SOCIAL SCIENCE INFORMATION. 1977, No.6: Pierre Bourdieu, "The Economics
of Linguistic Exchange".
SOCIALIST REVOLUTION. No.33, May 1977: "Marxism and Art" (on Fredric
Jameson). No.31, Jan 77: "Rock and Popular Culture".
ST. ANDREWS REVIEW. Spring 1977: Jonathan Williams & Tom Meyer, "A Con-
versation with Basil Bunting".
STUDIES IN LANGUAGE. 1977, No.2: "Is There a Science of Parole?".
STUDIO INTERNATIONAL. 1977, No.3: Women's Art Issue ("Caring: Five Poli-
tical Artists"; etc.). July 76: Performance Issue.
SUB-STANCE. No.18/19: "Language in the Theater"; "Theatre as Representa-
tion"; Julia Kristeva, "Modern Theater Misplaced". No.17: "Language,
Literature, Materialism"; "Rules of the Game: Regulation of the Text".
No.16: Translation/Transformation Issue: "Text Generation"; "The Writing
Machine"; "Mouthpiece/Grapheces"; "The Concept of Morphology".
TELOS. Spring 1978: "Desire and the Commodity Form"; Adorno's "The Social
Situation of Music" & "Resignation"; "Benjamin's Ambivalence".
TEL QUEL. Spring 1978: Marcelin Pleynet, "Poesie oui". Autumn 77: "Le
post-modernisme américaine"; Entretiens avec Robert Wilson, Merce Cun-
ningham, Viola Farber. Summer 77: "Ecriture et folie"; Pleynet, "La
compromission poétique". Spring 77: "L'impasse du langage dans le
marxisme". Winter 77: "Les femmes et la langue".
THEATER. Spring 1978: "Richard Foreman and Some Uses of Cinema"; Foreman,
"Book of Splendors, Part II"; Robert Wilson & Christopher Knowles, "The
$ Value of Man".
TRACKS. Fall 1977: Arakawa, "Some Words"; Victor Burgin, "Looking at
Photographs". Spring 77: "Contexts"(Rosemary Mayer & Nancy Wilson Kitchel
TRI-QUARTERLY. Winter 1977, No.38: In the wake of the Wake: Philippe
Sollers, "Joyce & Co."; "The phenomenon and noumenon of language"; Inter-
views with Sollers & Maurice Roche; "Eugene Jolas, transition, and the
Revolution of the Word".
WORD. 1977, No.3: "Toward an Explanation of Phonetic Symbolism".
WORKING PAPERS IN CULTURAL STUDIES. 1977, No.10: On Ideology: "Ideology,
Subjectivity and the Artistic Text", etc.
YALE FRENCH STUDIES. 1977, No.55/56: Jacques Lacan, "Desire and the Inter-
pretation of Desire"; "The Frame of Reference: Poe, Lacan, Derrida";
"The Letter as Cutting Edge"; "Freud's Writing on Writing"; Fredric
Jameson, "Imaginary and Symbolic in Lacan: Marxism, Psychoanalytic
Criticism, and the Problem of the Subject".

(For further information on locating any of these articles, please contact us)

BRUCE ANDREWS

Back cover: 1920 collage by Laszlo Moholy-Nagy from *Moholy-Nagy* (edited by R. Kostelanetz: Praeger, 1970)

L=A=N=G=U=A=G=E

Vol.1, No.4   August 1978

Bruce Andrews, Charles Bernstein, Editors.

Layout: Susan Laufer.

Subscriptions -- One year (six issues) for $4.
           Institutions: $8.

L=A=N=G=U=A=G=E is supported solely by subscriptions and donations.

All queries, submissions, and checks to:
Charles Bernstein, 464 Amsterdam Ave, New York, NY 10024.

(C) 1978 by L=A=N=G=U=A=G=E

Thanks for editorial assistance to Michael Gottlieb, Carole Korzeniowsky, Nick Piombino.

Distributed with the cooperation of the Segue Foundation.

ANNOUNCEMENT: Now available from L=A=N=G=U=A=G=E Distributing Service, Tottel's #17, 1978 (edited by Ron Silliman: work by Dreyer, Perelman, Hejinian, Davies, Bernstein, Silliman). Photocopy, $3.78.

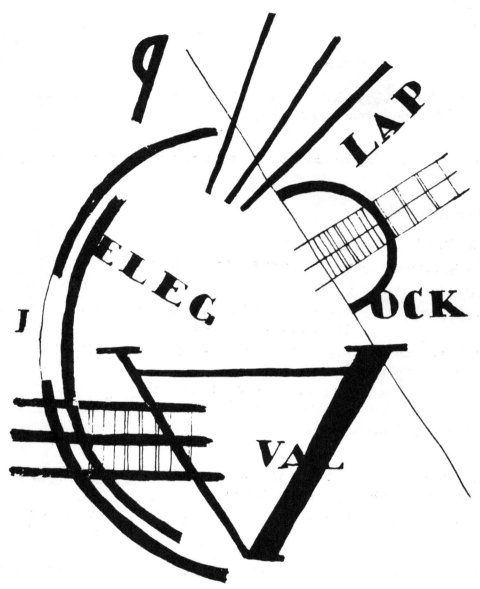

L=A=N=G=U=A=G=E

NUMBER 5   OCTOBER 1978

"HEDGE-CRICKETS SING"

--think of *Keats* as really 'milking' words of all possible letter/phonemic
qualities without really challenging notion of English word/morpheme as
basic unit of 'meaning'--hence 'best effects' all-stress monosyllabic--
"No, no, go not to Leth(e)"--"Where are the songs of Spring? Ay, where are
they?"--because mind in work really does *want* to think phonemically, one
sounds so 'dense & rich,' tongued--slows down articulation so teeth, lips,
whole vocal apparatus drawn in to pronouncing letters, reading it aloud--
counting 'syllables' (convenient grouping of phonemes/smallest unit one
normally hears) thus more than old poetic habit, focuses attention toward
primary semantic unit--*da da, da da,* etc.--'dramatic' polysyllables ("But
when the *melancholy* fit shall fall") break up into compound monosyllables
bound together by the passion, but everything still counts as one--
frequency of vibration in crickets, locusts, Keats 'replaces' our contemporary phrasing in human voice ('tone,' all that misemphasis on selected,
heavily stressed noises/waste of unstressed fillers normally grossing 'a
poet's voice')--how hot & fast it gets--expanding roof me-ta-l in sun--
no single note 'lost,' in nature, or is that any sound heard *as* sound
without interpretation--'meaning' identical to physical fact of *a* sound
(everything noted/nought denoted) in series of discrete particles strung
together (by Keats, e.g.) with gaps--weird displacement of 'one to one'
order of natural occurrence/significance by human symbolic capacity to
replace simple-unitary by multiple-complex, e.g. Morse code thinking 'dot-
dot-dot' for 'SAVE/sss' or moan 'ooo' as 'dash-dash-dash,' etc.--thus
'dot-dot-dot/dash-dash-dash/dot-dot-dot' for 'HELP' (speeded up, of course,
to rush us back toward one--fastest computer infinitely approaching one as
jammed together/speeded up multiple symbolic operation long since come to
'stand for' thing, so distracts any body from 'one to one' experience of
actual events in time with simultaneous experience of identity of fact &
significance--hence *letters/phonemes* one way to discipline attention to
use language as one way 'back to nature' by experiencing order of noises
in stream of oral consciousness--*s s* value in "Hedge-cricket)s s(ing,"
letter-to-letter & the leap between words not 'dashed' together (revealing
the previous two as *so* bound together)--attention to which structure(s),
in language, evokes or springs correspondences with structures of other

natural events (or vice-versa: attention to extra-linguistic sound provokes
awareness of like patterns in language)--

. . . .

--symbolism not 'reference' but recognition of structural identities binding
the world (trance state where sound is a calling forth)--Keats' attention
to *s s* (including gap between s's), *heard* (& seen on the page) makes a name
that shows me some part of events of August 31, 1977--day & night the gap-
ping, then resumption, "s sing" there in the words/here to my senses as
'crickets'--anything but romantic/anthropomorphic mis-taking of bugs'
"singing" (Keats often careless of diction/denotation, so surely riding
meaning in the sound--)

. . . .

--'dead ends': *description* (Williams' 'copying nature'), forcing the
materials of language to correspond to habitual orderings thought to render
what is thereby not seen; *invention,* mere gallivanting around in language
materials endlessly provocative/striking/autointoxicative (though such is
often preliminary to real work), a willed arrangement of words valued for
its own sake (like description, this is something)--

. . . .

--words are *words* (ancient 'horticultural' or 'hunting' magic or/cultural
habit persisting in some guise--much 'more' than we know)--the *world* is
'beyond us' yet given to the sentience as something of language process is,
each time--it's a 'speaking to the beyond' from the 'unknown depths of the
soul' (or the unknown 'beyond' speaking to 'soul') that makes a commonplace articulated--two together ('nothing personal')--say what happens/
happening is said--

ROBERT GRENIER

GRENIER'S <u>SENTENCES</u>

The work is unavoidably an object. A production number--500 index
cards, one poem per card. Intended to be read in any order (ideally all
at once, as on a wall), it denies book format, in which binding would
give only one of all possible readings page-by-page. Any sequence is a
chance ordering, deprogramming mental glue. The words rise off the page
as the mind would like--well-lit, pure, detached--"in eternity." The
heavy, white paper (field) sets off the IBM Selectric type (thing) as
utter contrast to dismantle the apparatus of conveyance and release the
word and its effect. Yet the work is physically awkward, a mechanical
problem, and calls attention to itself as visual format. So the object

(box) is a complex pun, a narrative grotesque fixing time in ironic termination of desire, as much of the actual writing puns. The blue Chinese cloth box with ivory clasps might hold the murder weapon or a biological anomaly, while the heavy white paper exists in opposition to physicality itself. The box is both fetish and transparency, and is identical to the work inside.

SENTENCES is a distillation of six years' close attention to "everything going on all the time." Out of voices heard, bird calls, shape of landscape, bolt from the blue, Kerouac's "void bowl slant," some shift makes for denotative signal, as bird pistols brain with peculiar stop to all sound. One class of perception in the taxonomy of this work then shows parallels of language to outside. "walking down Washington Avenue" shifts syntactic center as one walking is not all there but in walking. If "walking" were enough, why "down" to complete it--much less "Washington Avenue" changes scale entirely (arrives). In many cases though the shift is in the panorama implied by the words, rather than word meeting panorama head-on and equalling it. "being downstairs//like being awake" is a moment of truth, but not in different use of "being." Each line makes a diminished narrative set, through memory (lines hardening). The shift specifies a synaesthetic moment in language shape. Landscape leads through memory to words (nature as creator), but it is not landscape which follows (nature as created not the same). The composite world picture is at the mercy of the word. Revelation is a stylistic conceit. Furthermore, the mind knows this (syntax thinking).

Voice invested with power to make real (symbolism) is finally undermined. Any person's voice noted shows desire as wish/bend to unyielding other. Cued by dissonance under scrutiny of arbitrary white, the sum total of the cards exposes the point where structure collapses into words. Not the work objectified (as a "point of rest") but language brought to light through the failure of object (a "point of unrest"). The loop is a paradigm for this effect. In

    SNOW

      snow covers the slopes covers the slopes
      snow covers the slopes covers the slopes
      snow covers the slopes covers the slopes
      snow covers the slopes covers the slopes

the fact appears and disappears through phrase variation. The 1-2-3-4 pattern is a grid to distribute the split phrase. Both parallel the perception and a voice humming to itself, the poem is first of all the active mind seeing the poem on the page.

    TWO

    around twelve
    at 12

"twelve" and "12" are heard differently because seen differently, not because noted differently. The fact then is the different notation and its base in language apparatus. Originally heard in exterior "materials" (crudely), the interruption of phenomena by the act of writing forces words into actual units of recognition. The question is not assumed. "saids" might be one word or many. "close close" is a language equivalent to Wittgenstein's cube. "it's you" extends the moment into any dialogue. "transference isolates" acts as a romantic landscape, greater than any man. "searchlight distributes sky light it administers" might be movement or tautology, depending on the resolution inherent in the phrase. A vocabulary of possible experience builds from simple counting, as these "units" enumerate any notation. The risk is that the absolute intention (number) be confused with the dramatic irony of everyday life. In an instant nature closes in on the work. But *SENTENCES* does not collapse, because its language is outside of time.

Is it enough? There are no sentences in *SENTENCES*, like a glass ball nearly impossible to find. The work refuses closure (capital letter, period meaning a "completed thought") in being completely self-contained. It might be the only constitution possible for the republic in which one would want to live. Yet "it changes nothing" to note this. "You could put them (the cards) together but not now." The story is built from denial of story, of holding back. "But even the nervous tension... sensitive to moral weight.. cannot replace... events..." The box. "The rapidity with which they move as of themselves... compels sequence... concentrates action many times..." Charlie Chaplin made full-length features from discrete bits. "a proportion or style... mixed with story and with heart-beat..." Accessibility doubles (exactly) one's problem. "He who... is fated to style had at best make as much story of it as he can to be free..." The system is fully integrated, organic. *SENTENCES* locates the fact of style in the fact of language in American writing. There is certainly much more to be done, starting with--writing in sentences.

BARRETT WATTEN

(Some quotes above from Louis Zukofsky, Prepositions, "The Effacement of Philosophy" and "Modern Times".)

GRENIER BIBLIOGRAPHY: *Dusk Road Games* (1967; Pym-Randall Press). *Series* (1978; This, c/o Small Press Distribution, 1636 Ocean Ave, Kensington, CA 94707; $4). *Sentences* (1978; Whale Cloth Press, c/o M. Waltuch, 60 Kinnaird St., Cambridge, MA 02139; $10 individuals & $20 institutions).

MAKING WORDS VISIBLE

Hannah Weiner, <u>The Clairvoyant Journal</u> (1978; Angel Hair Press, Box 718, Lenox, MA 02140). *(A tape version of the text, with three readers-- fully as interesting as the book--is available from New Wilderness Foundation, 365 West End Ave, N.Y., N.Y. 10024; $8)*

We all see words: signs of a language we live inside of. & yet these words seem exterior to us--we see them, projections of our desires, and act, often enough, out of a sense of their demands.

Hannah Weiner, in her various poetic works, and, most especially, in the long poem she calls The Clairvoyant Journal has taken this fact of living a life inside of language most literally. "I *see* words", by which Weiner insists that the letters that spell out the various words and phrases of her work appear in various sizes and colors on other people and objects, but also, more importantly, on her self. Her work, then, consists of taking the dictation of these seen ciphers--she calls them voices--and weaving them into a text.

To "see words" is to be inside language and looking out onto it. For Weiner, this has involved an actual seeing (clairvoyance), although at the level of the text it is present as a pervasive citationality (both in the sense of a sighting and a quoting).

And yet, because Weiner's work is so rooted in the momentum of the act of writing,* the diaristic energy manages to totally submerge (immerse) the citational shards into its flow. She has herself said that she is interested in an electric energy that completely fills the page, transforming it into an impermeable field. It is this element that manages to fuse the eruptive fragments ("voices") into a completely uninterrupted continuity. So that the three voice simultaneity that makes up her text reads out as a linear syntax, while proposing a complete awareness of its paratactic method, its shard-like materials. Yet, finally, these different voices set up a syntax that is not linear or monologic (the continuous strip of the prose line) nor do they simply establish a discourse that is dialogic or reflective. Here, the mind is constantly interrupting--intruding upon, commenting on--its own processes with its caps THIS GIVES ME ORDERS and its italics *don't make so many generalizations stupid silly*. ("How can I describe anything when all these interruptions keep *arriving* and then tell me I didn't describe it well WELL") But, more than this, the text makes one piece of (*with*) all this activity, continuously integrating "outside"** elements into its compositional field without compromising their vertical disruption of the uniplanar surface. ("Each page a state of consciousness.")

The sections of her Journal that Weiner has chosen to publish in the forthcoming Angel Hair edition are characterized, even more apparently than

some previously published sections of the work, by a recurrence of the
most commonplace mental static that is as much an example of obsessiveness
as a method of release from it. I can't think of a book which has more
insistently faced these materials--"BIG OK   SIT STILL   RHYS COMES
PREGO   INstructions this morning: BATH,   SIT FOR AN HOUR *bathrobe*
A LOT OF RHYS   thinking of going to Jerry's reading   it's at 2   saw 2
OCLOCK   Still depressed, dreamt I was being married off to some fat
Jewish boy   I had to wear this shower cap *be careful* tonight *don't dream.*
PUT SOME CLOTHES ON   Is that Peggy, the same as GET DRESS   There's a
lot of energy in this *30's* robe can see parts of me light up *glowing*"--
nor one that has looked out on this world with a more pervasively whimsical
refusal to take oneself--& these facts of life--too seriously. That this
book is largely composed of debris may account for some of the anxiety in
reading it.

In her work, Weiner has explored--come upon--the language that fills, and
often enough, controls our lives (every day, *common* place: she says "group
mind"). That these elements are *seen* in the work, hence physicalized,
palpable, gives us a view of what is given, what has been handed down: &

ty seeing the language operate, we can start to free ourselves from a
compulsive obedience to it. The citational: shards of language, ciphers
to be examined for evidence, yet which we are forever beholden to...
which holds our sight within its views. The purpose of writing, Weiner
says, is to "change consciousness". --This work is, for me, heroic
because of its radical reaffirmation of a commitment to writing as a
specific kind of activity rather than as a specific kind of object making,
an investigation rather than an aestheticization.

Weiner's writing is a chronicle of a mind coming to terms with itself,
quite literally: for the terms are, in fact, made visible. We all see
words, but it is our usual practice to see *through* them. Weiner has
focussed her gaze not through, not beyond, but onto.

. . . .

*   Weiner's work stands as a rather remarkable extension of the diaristic
tradition in literature. The sense of writing out a life, the enormous
force that words have to come of their own, is graphically portrayed in
Truffaut's *Diary of Adele H*, where the writing is more overpowering than
anything else, but also where it is never reflected on. Bresson, in *Diary
of a Country Priest*, also focusses on the keeping of a journal, here the
paper absorbing the ink of each word penned as if it were life soaking up
so much blood.

**   "The poetry...begins...when the composing factor--the dictation, the
unknown, the outside--enters the work and...begins to construct a poetry

that was not lyric but narrative... It involves a reversal of language
into experience...a polarity and experienced dialectic with something other
than ourselves... A *reopened language* lets the unknown, the Other, the
outside in again as a voice in the language.... Here is the insistence of
...outside, an other than the reasonable is said to enter the real....
The voice arguing the necessity of an outside may strike the reader as odd
since the outside, in whatever sense one takes, is usually assumed.... Its
placement here as a composing factor in the poem disturbs our sense of a
settled relation to language. It does...insist that language is not simply
relational, but rather a knowing.... It is within language that the world
speaks to us with a voice that is not our own. This is, I believe a first
and fundamental experience of dictation.... In the reversal of language
into experience (visibility and invisibility) fold into one another and
unfold, composing as voices in our language.... To understand the 'outside,'
that curiously naive-sounding insistence of this work, it will not do to
take off on those supernaturalisms which precondition and explain the
experience. The dictation remains persistently of the world.... The outside as it becomes technical to our experience re-poses a tense discourse,
which interrogates the humanism and anthropomorphism of what is usually
thought to be the poem's expression." (From "The Practice of Outside" by
Robin Blaser in The Collected Books of Jack Spicer, Black Sparrow Press,
1975, $5.)

CHARLES BERNSTEIN

STATEMENT ON READING IN WRITING

At a certain point in post-industrial society, all of the social expedi-
ency of art is diminished in favor of personal necessity. Where in earlier
societies the artistic activity was directed to socially regulated functions of a group such as performative situations or practical gestures
for public and semi-public occasions -- today the compelling basis of
writing begins at a point of alienation from any socially explicit occasion. Which fosters the link with reading -- that now, writers are readers
first and their isolateness maintains them even against their will as such.
The only clear "writers" would be those putting their work directly into
market, working on a deadline, a definitive readership standing by to man
the reading-boats. Writers without such an immediate market are in the
damning circumstance, more often than not, of trying to insist on themselves as *not readers*, against all odds, in service of the fetish of
originality. So the task is now to move towards a more affirmative stance

as readers, to make of the act of reading the art that it in fact is. READING IS TRADITIONALLY THE MOST NEGLECTED OF ALL ARTS. Because it's the most abused. The psychological struggle that should concern us is not that of individual writers overcoming "the burden of the past" (Bate, Bloom) but individual readers overcoming the burden of the present, which is to view reading as a fallen, passive, irresponsible but entertaining state. This is the reader-as-junkie. What presently seems to count among writers is that the writing be psychologically valuable to the writer, but this is simply to increase the hold solipsism always wants to maintain on us. The *communality* of the reading/writing circuit is composed entirely of readers, not writers. If all writing were to cease right now, the fantastic load of the already-written would be more than sufficient to sponsor a new race of genius speakers and rhetoricians and conversationalists. I think we're at a point where we can actually say (probably we're the first people in history to get to this point) that there exists *enough writing* already. To affirm one's position as a reader is to pronounce oneself willing to work with other people rather than work for them. Always this haunting sense, that in writing you're doing somebody else a big favor, while reading is just a solitary unrelated selfish act. A perspective we've got to understand is writing as a selfish indulgence in the notion of originality. Originality, while not a useless word by any means, is profoundly artificial. Insofar as the "original" writer becomes the aristocratic dispenser of trinkets, originality has got to go. To be a reader is not to be unoriginal, not to be a primitive under instruction of the civilized author, not to be a castrated writer. To be a reader is to be the willing receptor of transformative agencies destined to either alter or confirm one's position in a social circuitry. To take this on as responsibility is to be willing to regulate one's Desire as an individual energy occurring within a social field. To persist in the writerly fantasy of originality is to succumb to the hideous fantasy of reproduction without sex. This is all becoming too familiar to be true, or is it? A "personal necessity" that tries to mesmerize everybody into keeping their distance, doing their "thing", and hoard their fantastic experience of reading in their private strongbox of thought, is no longer necessary. My hope is that we'll come to be less willing to confuse this with writing, and understand writing again someday as a function of repetition, of which reading is the clearest sensual link we have with the invisibility of Desire.

JED RASULA

SUBMISSIONS OF RELEVANT MANUSCRIPTS ARE WELCOME

PERELMAN: 7 WORKS

Bob Perelman, <u>7 Works</u> (1978; The Figures, c/o Small Press Distribution, 1636 Ocean View Ave., Kensington, CA 94709; $3.50)

"Continuity exists in the nervous system" is the prior statement I am moved to bring to my reading of the present work, the present *works*, which, taken *in concert*, insist on a like continuity.

Composition-- to include the entire repertoire of generative methods here employed-- "in actual obedience to what / underlies every act". Not a masque of ironies, but an earnest investigation of 'what follows'.

"The exact person ought to remain. Certainly no one can afford to stop. A person's experience must contain several meanings, or he cannot be care- ful." An exaction of caring that carries through the work, leads the work, fore-casting an erotic climate in which "the body / merely one side of the question" may become "the whole body".

"Each sentence is complete". A specific largesse. "There is more thought than time, more water than vocabulary." So this writing 'on' water-- this "dear grim earthly intelligibility"--casual: "You want everything at once. Read my long list of fancy goods"-- and essential: "A journey of this kind is no joke."

"I am prepared to hear these numbers..."

TED PEARSON

Bob Perelman's *7 Works* brings together pieces that have appeared singularly in other spaces (<u>A Hundred Posters</u>, <u>ZZZZZZ</u>, <u>This</u>, <u>Tottel's</u>, <u>Roof</u> and <u>Miam</u>), and thus allows one the luxury of easy comparison. What one finds is a facility with different forms, lengths, subject/object distances, found material. Each of the works is quite unique, looks different, in many ways seems to think differently.

But there is overall a sense of a highly trained intellect at work, one that leans toward metaphysics, sometimes actively seeking sonority and interesting juxtaposition, as in the found material of "Essay on Style," at other times switching into contemplative gear, as in "Before Water," where form rolls back on content in an unrelenting baring of thought/word processes; and often poking fun - quietly but nonetheless persistently - at "poetry":

> Ten thousand forest trees stood
> rigid in a theory typical of
> Cartesian linguistics. The cold
> air tensed against analogies. -- from "Road Tones"

There is much humor, where one least expects it. See particularly "How To Improve," a prose piece in eight parts, laced with lovely ironies, i.e.:

> The first time you meet the pigs in their pen, the proximity looks as though it means "full of you, disinclined to look." Feeling that it is quite evident without bothering. Think, grunting and squealing, and pass by. You may even be so far along you cast a cold eye. Then you notice a new connection: "The noisome odor of the slaughterhouse." A brief consultation will put you right again, and show you the means, and further-more, the kinship.

I am fascinated by a parallel development in "An Autobiography" and one of the letters discussed in L=A=N=G=U=A=G=E last issue (No. 4, August 1978), John Ensslin's article on schizophrenic writing. Graphic, mouth-watering, and obsessive description of foods, and, in Perelman's case, the meta-statement, "Nothing can prevent madness."

CAROLE KORZENIOWSKY

CLARK

SOME NOTES ON THOMAS A. CLARK

Sincere. *Sine cere*. Without wax. No filler. Object. *Ob jaceo*. To throw against. A destination. Aimed at. Focus.

Thomas A. Clark speaking: "Years working in a short space... the trouble was, how to distance it from one's own mind. The language became

more and more self-referent and 'obscure' in the worst sense. So I've
been making poems using texts which were 'outside my own head', and treating them in different ways: permutational, fragmentary, etc. I set about
experiments like cutting columns in half, or placing frames over a piece
of prose. I think that knowing to look at all and knowing what to look
for is rather a lot."

    And so it is. *The Secrecy of the Totally* (1969) collage and chance
generated works.

> ragged party of docile
> and romantic sunsets

Emphatic Forms (1971) with epigram from Wittgenstein: "We make to ourselves
pictures of facts." Pieces gathered from assorted language primers. The
act of isolation being the poet's only intervention.

> to speak distinctly
> to speak loudly
> to speak softly
> to walk straight on
> to stare fixedly
> to see clearly

To see clearly! Eye poems. The Stein directive: write not what you see
but what you know is there.

> why have you not eaten this piece?

    In *The North Bohemian Coalfields* (1970) the language and approach is
slightly more oblique, dramatic and speech-oriented in tone with punctua-
ting slash marks further suggesting abrupt shifts:

> / there falls here also the /
> / image of the bridge /
>
> / through the moment when
> there is nothing /
>
> the broad daylight /

Light and function a persistent concern in all these works. Illuminated
stillness. The poem's workings. A Basho-like sensibility. Completeness
ever deferred. Not particulars but *Some Particulars* (1971). Selection.
Choice. Burton's *Anatomy of Melancholy* cited on the title page: "...I
have laboriously collected this Cento out of divers writers..." The cento
itself a literary patchwork. In the fifth century the Empress Eudoxia
composed a life of Christ in verse with every line drawn from Homer.

    Clark's sources: the 18th century British naturalist Gilbert White,
the Life and Letters of Samuel Palmer, Walton's *The Compleat Angler*-- all
anatomists in their own right further anatomized by Clark. A strong tho

distilled taste harkening back to the original. Illumination. What would
normally be overlooked in the perusal casual or otherwise is brought into
the light. At times almost miraculously. The last piece in *Some Particulars* ironically titled "Note"

> on the 11th
> of April 1971
> across the centre
> of page 117
> of Burton's
> "Anatomy of Melancholy"
> there was a rainbow
>
> ".....and bees amongst the rest
> though they be flying away, when
> they hear any tingling sound,
> will tarry behind."

These are spectral works. Beautifully deadpan.

    Pointing Still (1974) records (and only that) six incidents of watches
lost. Time frozen but rediscovered and re-articulated in the virtue of
its factness. Pointing here or there. Still as in at rest or yet.
Suspended.

    A *Still Life* (1977). Picture in a frame. Or a quiet life. Both
resonate here. Present as in the earlier works is an affection for and a
studied observation of nature. The presentation of images self-informed
and complete though transient and accidental. Poise. Balance. Discernment. The first piece in the book sets the tone and isolates the manner
of the music to unfold:

> Place words end to end as dry stones.
> Using only local materials, arrange them
> sparsely to admit plenty of ventilation.
> They will stand among the fiercest winds
> and keep the sheep out.

A wall extends horizontally as well as vertically. Light bends to make a
spectrum. Light's torque.

> "Rainbow"
>
> At the end of each arc of speech
> the treasure of rest.

RAY DI PALMA

CLARK BIBLIOGRAPHY: *The Secrecy of the Totally* (1969; South Street Publications, Sherbourne, Dorset). *The North Bohemian Coalfields* (1970; Bettiscombe Press, Bettiscombe, Dorset). *Emphatic Forms* (1971; Bettiscombe Press). *Some Particulars* (The Jargon Society, Gnomon Distribution, Box 106, Frankfort, KY 90601; $4.50). *Pointing Still* (1974; Arc Publications, Gillingham, Kent). *Some Life Until I Took Wing* (1972; Writer's Forum, 262 Randolph Avenue, London W9; 2nd edition, 1978; 15p.). *A Still Life* (1977; The Jargon Society; $4.50). *Pebbles from a Japanese Garden* (1977; Topia Press, c/o Karl Torok, 4 Oakfield Grove, Bradford BD9 4PY, England). *Fragments of a Walled Garden* (1977; Braad Editions, c/o Kevin Power, Brard, Commune de Loubressac, par Bretenoux, Lot 46, France; $4). Moschatel Press (Iverna Cottage, Rockness Hill, Nailsworth, Glos., England) has published a series of small pamphlets, some of which are still available, write for details: *Fill in the Drawing / Fritillary / Folding the Last Sheep / An Epitaph / The Garden / Horizon / Four Flowers / Iris / Shape and Shade / September / A Basket of Landscapes / Pebbles / Glade / Deserts of Afghanistan / L'invitation Au Voyage / Anemone / Moss Stitch / A Vase of Daffodils / Flower / Petit Fours / Painted Lady / Two Horizons / Thrums / Hart's Tongue / Foliations / Two Acres / The Bright Glade / A Meadow Voyage / Haystacks and Islands / Nine Roses / Water Cresses / Fly Patterns for Still Waters / Gatherings.* An interview with Clark is available in Poetry Information #18 (c/o Peter Hodgkiss, 18 Clairview Rd, London; 75 p.).

LETTER TO THE EDITOR

Alan Sondheim and the Knee-Jerk School of Criticism

In L=A=N=G=U=A=G=E (#3, June 1978) there appears an attack on John Cage and Marcel Duchamp by my fellow survivor from the 1960's, Alan Sondheim, which attacks these artists not for their work or for what they have said but for what Sondheim sees them as having failed to do--to end "privilege" (undefined) and of producing decontextualized art. He ties this last concept with being "particulate" or contextualized as "one basis, same thing." His text comes, apparently, from a longer work entitled "Heroes, How They File Past," so perhaps some of the brevity of the discussion explains its quality of raising questions that might well be answered elsewhere in his text. But my own questions that are provoked by Sondheim's text are not so much in defense of Cage or Duchamp, both of whom I happen to admire, but are concerned with what seem to be the assumptions of Sondheim's text:

1) I am bothered by its quality of automatism, of reflex action. He

seems to be arguing from the point of view of the people without asking himself who the people are. If he wants to claim them as the statistical majority, then either he must show that Cage and Duchamp do, in fact, assume privilege and that this is not in the people's best interests, or he must propose a positive model of popular art (Khachiturian? the faceless collective piano concerti from the People's Republic of China?) which is more in the people's best interests, and which creates a popular context...

2) The very essense of his attack on privilege is the assumption that privilege is inherently unfair. But is it? I was privileged to be taught German at an early age, and it is my pleasure and my privilege to read in that language. Am I a snob because I sometimes speak in that language or read in it, when not everybody else has had the privilege of learning it? Avant-garde art—and through the years Cage and Duchamp have both remained or at least had implications for the avant-garde—is a language, native to some and taught to others; the benefits of having worked in that language can be made available to all, over a period of time. But to attack the privilege of working in that language seems to be to propose its eradication—or at least its watering down into a sort of bastardization.... It is indeed a privilege, if one be an artist, to be that first person, and it is only when there is unequal access to cultural privilege that the situation becomes unwholesome. When an elite restricts access to cultural privileges to itself—as in 18th Century France or early 20th Century Europe—then the situation should be changed. But to attack privilege as such... is to guarantee mediocrity, and in the long run people's hunger simply cannot be satisfied by mediocre art. Thus, if Sondheim wanted to guarantee a popular context for art, he should not be automatically attacking privilege but should be working on the problem of access....

3) Finally, Sondheim seems to advocate a process of reading "through the text, consider[ing] possibilities of theory." That is, of course, its own hermeneutic—an advocated method of reading, of interpretation. I'm all for it. But why not, instead of attacking Cage and Duchamp whose "privilege" is only their response to the real needs of their moments, as they saw them—Sondheim uses the metaphor of Solzhenitsyn's Gulag, "random terror leading to the Gulag" as giving the logic to his dissatisfaction with using aleotoric methods in art—why not instead explore the nature of not just a personal, individual hermeneutic of experiencing art but a plural, social one? Why not explore the question not just of *What am I experiencing when I read/hear/see this work?* but of *What are we experiencing when WE read/hear/see it?* Or even when we perform it? That would seem to be a more profitable area to explore than this automatic attack on privilege, for it would raise the real social contextualization of a work, the problem of access to it.

DICK HIGGINS

142

THE HUM OF WORDS

Rosmarie Waldrop, <u>The Road is Everywhere or Stop This Body</u> (1978; Open Places, Box 2085, Stephans College, Columbia, MO 65201; $3)

> *I veer toward the endless*
> *distractions of the foreground*
> *even while clamoring*
> *for wholeness*

This book contains a sequence in 80 parts, and pages, shot through with road signs and seasonal photographs, taken in motion, radiating *a cone of attention.* Rosmarie Waldrop's largest book in half-a-dozen years. She stakes out for us, gradually, a parallel between 2 senses of <u>traffic</u>: *the movement (of vehicles or pedestrians) through an area or along a route* and *the information or signals transmitted over a communication system: messages.* So we find content doubled, folded back into the constructed spaces of the page -- first, revealing and articulating an experience of motion (and of mind/heart/memory/body/dream in motion through everyday traffic): second, doing the same for an experience of speech/words/meanings/writing as this second perspective actively unfolds from a transciption and embodiment of the first. The writing entertains a constant retrieval from one plane to another. A bifurcation, which registers gradations in both, *translating / one measurement into another,* so that the <u>intervals</u> achieve solidity. We notice then that the <u>facticity</u> of the everyday world is incomplete. Such a double vision is one of the book's achievements.

Comprehension (a *sequence / of ready signs*) bleeds through. It is performed in a space & in intermittent shapes we can measure, as an abstraction we are *obliquely conscious* of. This abstraction is our ability to frame and reframe the flows around us, and the explosions which *fracture the present.* Body becomes its own flow; the person is a matrix of those flows & exchanges & messages. Person is a communicative system, a traffic.

The *mind floats headlights on time,* & transforms what is immobile into a secret generation of desires and presence: *words / germinate on their own obstructions.* Syllables are implacable; they secrete their own space, dislodging our breath at an angle. They congest in the unbroken slowness of the gaps they make, where mind speeds ahead of body, where perceptions become symptoms.

And don't those gaps -- and the line breaks & disruptions which highlight them -- begin to remind us of another, more social gap?? A gap between our desires and our experience, between the outside which encloses us and the inside which projects and endorses us. *damned-up friction / knots want into / need widens* : *as if the future had to be / remembered words.* This resembles Ernst Bloch's idea of the <u>novum</u> -- what "has not come to be in the past,... which is drifting and dreaming in the darkness, in the factual blue of objects... as content of the deepest hope."

This difference never happens without words -- a tumescence which consumes all representation in the affections of solid paper. Precisely & secretively -- particularly here as the last word of a phrase often begins a new physical line and a new grammatical unit; as if intentions and conventions are bi-valved, perforated, condensed, accelerated, paralleled: *the / double sheet of the / way back of / the outside rises up. Surface / doubles the depth* just as *talk / doubles the frequencies.* Both assert attention, weaving & unweaving, giving us the material enticements of text as well as a recollected sighting from a landscape -- an outer landscape which is not separate from the languagescape of the text. The flows we see -- these sightings are not retinal flashes. We find them embodied, as the journey reapproaches the surface (the site of the structure). Light is ink, a series of displacements taking shape against any object, while *words make you your own object.*

Illusion dwindles into the page's margin. Yet the atomized self cannot live without these illusions. At times, *the blue bodiless shock of the air* is too much for it. At best, writing *can't find a center for its / surfaces superimposed in constant / articulation.* At those points, all obstacles recede -- both the taken-for-granted self and taken-for-granted illusionism. Otherwise (& this is the danger constantly tempted here) surface bursts and yet still slackens into familiar versifying, where disruptions seem ornamental, imagistic, comforting, rhetorical. A constant activity would be a surface without grips -- what is most courageously desired, what *accompanies / the tissue of pleasure inside / pleasure.*

BRUCE ANDREWS

THE AMPLIFIER, SILENCE

Larry Eigner, Things Stirring Together Or Far Away (1977; Black Sparrow Press, Box 3993, Santa Barbara, CA 93105; $4)

I
Discretionary attention, fingersmake slowly apparent a-line-at-a-time there. Look on a world, screen of complicatedly singular event, out the window. Precisely no thing displaced by two eyes. Things horizontal through air, held by vertical swaths of sound; flutter back. Simple thing on thing torn by wind constant in and from the eye.

II

kids. light. grass. world. sky. trees. wind. bird. sleep. sea. year.
waters. branches. silence. dog. street. roof. sense. car. houses. cloud.
wall. snow. sun. leaves. gulls. hills. night. sound. hours. air. earth.
room. man. woods.

III

No gaps. Distance furbish sighted scape, electrical insistent halting
rhythm. Deserting familiar for strange fact, occluded, admittedly.
Slowed quick mind, geiger capacity paramount gauge of surroundings. This
life a perfect receptacle for chance, to look at others, an alteration
of sequenced events. Whole thing segmented; the glancing possibility
of camera's shutter. Laps over the side of a tree, there (pointing).
Memory recharges batteries presently used. Opaque shield of eyes over a
mind.

A sight, flitting the sense. A light, tensed.

Urged into present location, not able to move. Strictures of sighted
heads hold a thin grasp in fluctuating air, secured.

ALAN DAVIES

PALMER

from NOTES FOR ECHO LAKE

1

He says this red as dust, eyes a literal self among selves and picks the
coffee up.

Memory is kind, a kindness, a kind of unlistening, a grey wall even,
toward which you move.

It was the poet's wife who remarked that he never looked anyone in the eye.
(This by water's edge.)

This by water's edge.

And all of the song 'divided into silences,' or 'quartered in three
silences'.

Dear Charles, I began and again and again to work, always with no
confidence as Melville might explain. Might complain.

A message possibly intercepted, possibly never written. A letter she had sent him.

But what had his phrase been exactly, 'Welcome to the Valley of Tears,' or maybe 'Valley of Sorrows.' At least one did feel welcome, wherever it was.

A kind of straight grey wall beside which they walk, she the older by a dozen years, he carefully unlistening.

Such as words are. A tape for example a friend had assembled containing readings by H.D., Stein, Williams, Dorn, others. Then crossing the bridge to visit Zukofsky, snow lightly falling.

Breaking like glass Tom had said and the woman from the island. Regaining consciousness he saw first stars then a face leaning over him and heard the concerned voice, 'Hey baby you almost got *too* high.'

Was was and is. In the story the subject disappears.

They had agreed that the sign was particular precisely because arbitrary and that it included the potential for (carried the sign of) its own dissolution; and that there was a micro-syntax below the order of the sentence and even of the word; and that in the story the subject disappears it never disappears. 1963: only one of the two had the gift of memory.

Equally one could think of a larger syntax, e.g. the word-as-the-book proposing always the book-as-the-word. And of course still larger.

Beginning and ending. As a work begins and ends itself, or begins and rebegins or starts and stops. Ideas as elements of the working not as propositions of a work, even in a propositional art. (Someone said someone thought.)

That is, snow

> a) is
> b) is not
>> falling, check neither or both.

If one lives in it. 'Local' and 'specific' and so on finally seeming less interesting than the 'particular' wherever that may locate.

'What I really want to show here is that it is not at all clear *a priori* which are the simple colour concepts.'

Sign that empties itself at each instance of meaning. (And how else to reinvent attention.)

Sign that empties...That is *he* would ask *her*. He would be the asker and she unlistening, nameless mountains in the background partly hidden by cloud.

The dust of course might equally be grey, the wall red, our memories perfectly accurate. A forest empty of trees, city with no streets, a man having swallowed his tongue. As there is no 'structure' to the sentence and no boundary or edge to the field in question. As there is everywhere no language.

As I began again and again, and each beginning identical with the next, meaning each one accurate, each a projection, each a head bending over the motionless form.

And he sees himself now as the one motionless on the ground, now as the one bending over. Lying in an alley between a house and a fence (space barely wide enough for a body), opening his eyes he saw stars and heard white noise followed in time by a face and a single voice.

Now rain is falling against the south side of the house
but not to the north where she stands before a mirror.

'Don't worry about it, he's already dead.'

'Te dérange pas, il est déjà mort.'

'É morto lui, non ti disturba.'

She stands before the mirror touches the floor. Language reaches for the talk as someone falls. A dead language opens and opens one door.

So here is color. Here is a color darkening or color here is a darkening. Here white remains...

And you indicate the iris of the portrait's eye, a specific point on the iris, wanting that colour as your own. There is a grey wall past which we walk arm in arm, fools if we do greater fools if we don't.

And I paint the view from my left eye, from the balcony of the eye overlooking a body of water, an inland sea possibly, possibly a man-made lake.

And do I continue as the light changes and fades, eventually painting in pitch dark. That is, if you write it has it happened:

    It rained again that night deep inside
    where only recently had occurred the abandonment of signs

MICHAEL PALMER

MICHAEL PALMER: A LANGUAGE OF LANGUAGE

Michael Palmer writes a splendid poetry of displacement, of shifts and nomadic drifts of text through zones of page. The operative semantic is copulative, a linking (purely syntagmatically) of isolated units still preserving their molecular independency. He writes a double assault: on page per se and on the vector of reference. There is no place in his work because there largely is no referent incanted. Reference is rendered intransitive and instigates the arbitrary flow of linguistic signs. Referrals without the finality of reference, ectoskeletal structures carrying deliberately interior deformations. Frequently logic is placed in contest with a syntax resulting in the gravity of utterance being withheld. Sentences register as syntagms, surface activities of syntax, no entity-terminals but simply the betweenness of a trace, word motions rather than conveyed ideations. Logical relation is violently displaced by verbal relation and spacing, so that space becomes the abyss causality falls into. And this space in Palmer is less projective (a breath withheld) than the violated function of the sign: the articulation of displacement. Space becomes the agonistic surface, the zone where words displace themselves. Palmer's consummate craft is the superb orchestration of these displacements: to activate fissures, architecturally tensified, and phrases that remain stiff in a precision of placement as all meaning slides. Viewed temporally this all amounts to a consecutivity minus a consequentiality. In Palmer's poems there is, deliberately, no purpose. This leads to local composition, an investigation of grammatological space per se, of space as deferral, of placement and occurrence as difference. Constant, consecutive invention on the plane of the signifier.

The process of reading becomes a muscular activity of the mind operating in tension through disjunctions, aborted vectors, non-purposive contexts. Everything happens on the level of the signifier; semic discharge across a surface and the surface is that discharge. Page/space an utterly non-hermetic experience. Meanings localized within the isolate sign. Contexts displace to indicate, if anything, the schizophrenic predications of language. (Language as a branch plant of schizophrenic emission?) To place us in the movements of a language of schizzes is Ipseity. Dis / place / meant. Page for Palmer is the topography of the disjunctive, supporting the integral violence of transformationality. For the steady, consecutive plod of language, line after line, is at the same time its violent transformation. Such a paradox describes the horizontal identity of Palmer's signifier: a violent stability of grapheme, being at the same time a violent instability in any molar aggregate of "thought." The thing it is. Writing. Written. Not that linearity disappears, on the contrary, Palmer strengthens line but only in order for it to confess more effectively its own duplicities. The worded line identifies the syntagm as a horizontal, moving segment in space possessed of the infinite capacity to absorb all breaks in causality and consequentiality within its consecutive motions. And thus the transparent guilt of reading. The guilt at witnessing a graphed pattern of place support a huge displacement.

Palmer's most radical displacement is the break with transitivity
itself. For language has become the subject of Language and we enter, as
readers, the ambiguous zone of texts without absolute speakers. Palmer
makes speech subordinate to writing; the speaking subject being the
intractible voice dispaced as an echo in the fissures of the spacing.
Beyond voice and presence is syntactic space and absence -- the consummate
Palmerian domain where the phonocentric becomes marginated and writing
comes closest to a pure Writing. Inscribed throughout his work, as its
syntax motion, is the locale of the subject's disappearance. Nomadic
topographies beyond the symmetries of line where language inscribes a
sphere around itself and instigates a self-reflexiveness, the interrogation of the text's own limits. To write a voiceless writing is to reinvent speech as an order free of voice. Palmer, I believe, is transforming
speech from a form and a vehicle into a content on the way to its rein-
vention. What he presents is speech without the social activity of
speaking. Can this be anything else but writing?

Systematic detachment from the 'I' until there is no speaking subject.
A subject alone is reading this and the words are voiceless speech in
non-discursive space. It is -- as if -- the music "(was)" the consequence
plus voice and so the works entirely are without music.

STEVE MC CAFFERY

PALMER BIBLIOGRAPHY: *Plan of the City of O* (1971; Barn Dream Press).
Blake's Newton (1972; Black Sparrow Press). *C's Songs* (1973; Sand Dollar,
c/o Serendipity, 1790 Shattuck Ave, Berkeley, CA 94709; $2.25). *Six
Poems* (1973; Black Sparrow Press pamphlet series #11). *The Circular
Gates* (1974; Black Sparrow Press, Box 3993, Santa Barbara, CA 93105, $4).
Relativity of Spring, translations, with Geoffrey Young (1976; Sand Dollar).
Without Music (1977; Black Sparrow Press; $4). "Story" (1978; in Gnome
Baker #1, Box 337, Great River, N.Y. 11739; $3). EDITOR: *Joglars*, with
Clark Coolidge (1964-65; 1974--Arno Reprints, 3 Park Ave, N.Y., N.Y. 10017).

LETTER TO THE EDITOR

It has been brought to my attention that two seminal South American
artists, Clemente Padin and Jorge Caraballo, have been imprisoned by the
Uruguayan government and now have "disappeared," an all too common occur-

ence in Uruguayan jails. Padin was the editor/publisher of <u>Ovum</u>, the very first literary assemblage.... I urge you to write to the Uruguayan ambassador, the president of Uruguay in Montevideo, and your congress-person/government representative and request their release.... No more Lorcas assassinated! Photo-copy this letter, sign it with me, and send it to all your correspondents. This is a mail art piece that is in dead earnest.

GEOFFREY COOK

A COLLECT

Curtis Faville, <u>Stanzas for an Evening Out</u> (1978; L Publications; c/o Serendipity Books, 1790 Shattuck Ave, Berkeley, CA 94707; $4)

Before finishing ten pages of *Stanzas for an Evening Out,* "I think movingly" about image or line or Williams, or going over old ground--I can just enjoy the "aluminum airfoils" can't I? Or do I have to expect the poem to be redefined at each writing and each poem to redefine poetry and that process to go on forever--not writing about something, but, but is there really anything more to do? Time as a subject in literature and time told by etymology, how language use is graphed on the "t" axis, are both collected in *Stanzas* which, as in the later case, is almost a chrono-logy of styles, recent redefinitions and uses of poem and language.

Often Faville links so many talents together that one suspects that he "Taste crust and roll luxury out" and obviously "Like a rug, let it lariot, / wear blue, rodeo, associate" by which he means not alludes, but friends, atavisms like "two two year olds", imagism like "Moon evident, its scudding", New York modernism "With whose guilelessness beguiles", American classical "native tongues" andc. It is as if someone selected personal, "trashy sunsets" that "However one construe" "I have been threatened but am hopeful". He is "cold toward the new allotment", but "I have been accustomed to this before"--an intermittent, if measured approach, sliding into a skepticism about being able to say anything, "Truly international, voiceless, extinct."

"That's exactly what Wassily Kandinsky meant," says Faville in "Kunst", looking up, & through a window onto "the roof of a house from which protruded a galvanized metal stack--a hexagonal base topped with a conical, fluted funnel. That was one form." Shape? Or is he describing domestic surrealism extended upwards like the chimney from words to form. Well, anyway, more than Kandinsky, Faville's efforts remind me of Puvis de

Chavannes who first painted telegraph wires into otherwise neo-classical paintings, flattening out the planes to accommodate the wires.

In "Rotterdam" "happening meant to / incline and reflect / of an interval to oblige / band of gilded without the consolation". The method of composition being unclear is hardly relevant, as technique is not the telling point in a good recital, but a given—"folded in résumé", an elusiveness, "tamed by the resonance" (the reason for ordering the lines). ...the continual floating, hovering over, spacious, white, so by the time the book has accumulated its quota of poems that curve through pastel air, the reader keeps trying to understand the narration or intention of the best work, but Faville stops him from reading subjects into those poems and leaves just the words "every once and a while which is mode".

The words "from a neglect of chosen" "simply go about" "that she might sing". The words in a "context of vacates" in a "tug of what for" might have been _____. Might this have been.... At its best a "plain cut in counting" "nicer than bits" as opposed to "oaf's sandwich" or "plaid Fords". The book as book comes "Full circle / In the time it takes."

At times, *Stanzas* intimates language as subject, sliding away from what poems have been into words, and at times he composes in words to say how things affect him personally instead of translating the events that happen to him into events that can happen to words. Spaces open into "jiggle foci", "behest pawn", "the Hull duck trick", and seals himself, his feelings. The point is that meaning is context-dependent, and can be altered at will by association. If they mean things then things, if they mean me then me. If they are to go beyond that they must verify within and between each and so and on beyond context and what happened. In some Stanzas they do:

> Clarity hurts our eyes.
> In the sun's continual flash
> the world curls back like
>
> brown paper, at the edge
> of experience. We walk down
> the shadowed colonnades
>
> of our lives, wearing
> sunglasses, as if blind.
> Men come out to set up
>
> mirrors along the sidewalk,
> chrome peels away, and we feel
> all that we knew is receding
>
> into the faded lawns of
> summer. Now the thin film
> of memory burns away,

                    the celluloid wrinkling
                    in the heat waves. Unrelieved,
                    we long for cool arms

                    of automatic machines
                    breathing in green motelrooms.
                    Going by a drive-in late

                    at night, we see the images
                    of ourselves embrace suddenly
                    before they are wrapped

                    in noiseless foil and thrown
                    away. Overhead two plane lights
                    blink on and off, passing.

                                                JAMES SHERRY

BASIL BUNTING: "TAKE A CHISEL TO WRITE"

"What fun if you were a classic!" Gerard Manley Hopkins once wrote blithely
the to-be poet laureate Robert Bridges. It did, in fact, take half a
century to see he had made a language more snug the world. Writers in the
20's--leafing through Freud--looked around through an atonal relativity of
planes Cézanne might make an apple, and found two new tools to pry the
present with words: compression & fragmentation. Pound propounded both,
though ended largely fragmented, as did later Charles Olson.

The Atomists, or poets of compression, such as Louis Zukofsky, Basil
Bunting, Lorine Niedecker, Jonathan Williams, request a mirrored focus.
The universe all *did* hold together, but with a fragility of balances
unheard of. Zukofsky was to make poems all one sound, or to translate
Catullus for sound faster than sense--and still 'make' sense. For fifty
years Basil Bunting has hewn the language down to "fellow to axle squeak, /
rut thud the rim, / crushed grit."

From *Chomei at Toyama* to *Briggflatts* he emerges a man to speak his mind--
few words will do, as if we all might live well enough with flint, axe,
spade, bare shelter from elements, a mind and hand to work them with. His
chisel can do what took Wordsworth stanzas. *Root, Pith, Flower* were Pound's
(who had much to say about the way we shape things) advice. Root in the

tongue itself--the language--and pith the heart for meaning, the flower its
outcome. Absorption to core of things puts forth whorl to seed. There,
the thrush might sing Vivaldi (for one who had ear) and Scarlatti time lark
to heart-beat.

In Bunting's *A thrush in the syringa sings*, a classic if ever was one,
language is integral to vowel with consonant: a consonance, a 'sounding
together'.

Hopkins: "on ear and ear two noises too old to end"

Zukofsky: "eyes' blue iris splicing them"

Bunting: "red against privet stems as a mazurka. . ."

"to thread, lithe and alert, Schoenberg's maze." First, thrush harpsi-
chords syringa along its song. The melody is of motions familiar things
make to bird now balancing in Bunting's brain: death's thrust hawkbeak,
slung stone, neck twist by weasel. Thunder counterpoints random gusts of
wind through branch-flex. The final chord (as Charles Ives' instructions
for playing *The Fourth of July*--"all the wrong notes are right."):

    "O gay thrush!"

RONALD JOHNSON

*(from <u>Madeira & Toasts for Basil Bunting's 75th Birthday</u>, edited by
Jonathan Williams -- 1977; The Jargon Society, Highlands, N.C., $10).*

WRITING AS REVERIE

"I've got a feeling we're not in Kansas anymore."
                  -- Dorothy to Toto, WIZARD OF OZ (1939)

  1. An obsessive monitoring of some remembered texts becomes an immediate
occasion for delay, association, structure, plenitude, a gathering for an
album constructed out of items of intrinsic value. Play conceived as the
manipulation of reminders, an accumulation of fragments, passes through
coherence into speculative fantasy. The argument runs like this: a child,
pausing before his book, falls into a reverie. This daydream, composed

in part of excessive thinking about power and mastery and a concurrent, if hidden and counter-pointed theme of loss, an anticipated, almost yearned for loss, becomes equated with a particular visit to the ocean on an over-cast day. The objects employed in his fantasy are transposed harmonically and modally into its emotional leitmotifs. The visual complements the emotional tense but cannot surpass it. The child is not exhaustively reading the seascape. His eidetic imagery is fastened to the concepts preceding it. Entranced as he is in his thoughts, his actions contribute to an air of unselfconscious movement. A momentary breakthrough of sun-light between clouds interrupts the melancholy quality of his meditations and the spell is half broken, because we see him again engaged in reading. Or is he merely seeing the printed words, his gaze still directed within, as the sound of the sea thunders loudly into his consciousness and the voices and activity and movement rush into his field of attention.

2. Meditations on an esthetics of fragmentation and discontinuity. Creation of a myth. History before me an interpretable reminder. The politics of extension and intentional fragment.
     The interruption of "the argument runs like this" is a simple dimen-sional loosening of the referential register this particular moment of writing needed. Anywhere I look (for example, the child on the beach at sunset) I pass through a storm of connectives intensifying one another.

3. Holding the entire thought over my head like a cartoon bubble in the comics. Head scrambles neologisms. Each face inscribed as photographic engravure on the surface of the page. The age of portraits, the gradual acceding of biographical identification. The inscription, the latest removable naming of the surface crests. So the completed thought now resembles the boy's hesitations on the title he gave to his text. Notice it was in a book of art history writings. He likes maxims, tautological witticisms that temporarily acquit and illuminate with guided opacity the steady pointed shadings toward the outcoming familiarity of the chosen puzzle: is he dreaming of the words themselves, divided as they are with each selected entry seal illustrated in a deluxe edition of signs?

4. "They can see right through me," thinks the child. They can diagram the space anyway they like, but I'll know by the tempo of his excitement whether or not the molecules might later collide and issue a fusion of opposites. Say the original imagery was not a naming, but an identifiable entity suspended above his head like an exclamation point. Not the subjective reticence of the I signifier, but a fire (!) and consequent, simultaneous engendering of excited tension. Bound up as he is in reading, he is perhaps for the first time equating a description with a given locale in a book--he is on a certain beach not yet named. He is reading his thoughts specifically against, next to, behind and above this presentiment

of a later time when he will item for item inscribe this sea in his album, by means of partial, token representations.

NICK PIOMBINO

---

from LANGUAGE WRITING

Rae says, "What is your fascination with graphs?" Meaning, I take it, all non-verbal presentations of information within the body of the text:

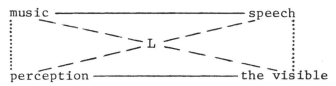

or

$$p = \left(\frac{v \cdot r}{i}\right) C$$

There are (millions of) relations in the world which even the most poly-semic sentence can only serve to distort. Principally, this is because the sentence, that written thing, & its equivalent in speech, what I call the utterance, exists thru (& across $\longrightarrow$) time. These constructions, whose shared feature is their refusal to assign a verb-function (the = is no more than a cipher marking its absence) within the field of data, conserve simultaneity. The syntagmatic can only unveil the world in accordance with some system of priorities. This is why, in the sentence, there is always one key term around which the others are organized. Style is often nothing more than a name for the strategies adopted for the placement of this term (classic prose loves to delay it). There exists in the very form of the sentence a tendency toward a kind of nominalism (wch is why William Carlos Williams is so utterly readable: his philosophy was the sentence). Higher order phenomena, states of equilibrium, in short any structure wch can survive only in the presence of multiple constituting elements (& so often in this epoch of capital the inverse of outer appear-ance), can only be approximated & then only accretively, thru the accumu-lation of several sentences, & always at a cost (at best the sentence can be reduced to a filter, its (dis)torsion a constant ("like static")).

But of course there's a violence involved. These objects, disruptions of the orderly body of the text, interventions against the possibility of flow, exist solely thru a confession of language's limit (wch one, reading, wants always to deny: that idea of language as a membrane at once of both description & meaning infinitely extendible in all directions, the hedonism & arrogance of our species). Limit: why the constituting term of this fragment is *only* (& its allies: *always, any, utterly, at best, of course, nothing more than, solely,* etc.).

RON SILLIMAN

(The second figure above stands for the relation that poetry (P) is -- the terms used being vocabulary (v), rules (r), intention (i) and Context (C), an argument explained elsewhere in Silliman's "Language Writing")

L=A=N=G=U=A=G=E

Vol.1 No.5   October 1978

Charles Bernstein, Bruce Andrews, Editors.

Layout: Susan Laufer

Subscriptions -- One year (six issues) for $4.
                 Institutions: $8.

L=A=N=G=U=A=G=E is supported solely by subscriptions and donations.

All queries and checks to:
Charles Bernstein, 464 Amsterdam Ave., New York, NY 10024.

(C) 1978 by L=A=N=G=U=A=G=E

Distributed with the cooperation of the Segue Foundation.

PLEASE SEND US YOUR ADDRESS CHANGES

ANNOUNCEMENT: Now available, *Local Color/Eidetic Deniers* by Michael Gottlieb, $3 from Other Publications, c/o Davies, 689 East 17th Street, Brooklyn, NY 11230.

For a mailing we will be sending out soon, we would appreciate readers sending us the names and addresses of people who might be interested in finding out about L=A=N=G=U=A=G=E.

L=A=N=G=U=A=G=E

NUMBER 6   DECEMBER 1978

READING STEIN

(We asked a number of writers to respond to the three short selections from Gertrude Stein's Tender Buttons (1914) quoted below -- to give their sense of the ways of reading this text -- what it means, how it means, & in what ways it might seem relevant to their own concerns in writing. What follows are the Stein selections and the replies of Michael Davidson, Larry Eigner, Bob Perelman, Steve McCaffery, Peter Seaton, Rae Armantrout, Dick Higgins, Jackson MacLow, Carl Andre, and Robert Grenier.)

from TENDER BUTTONS

A CARAFE, THAT IS A BLIND GLASS

A kind in glass and a cousin, a spectacle and nothing strange a single hurt color and an arrangement in a system to pointing. All this and not ordinary, not unordered in not resembling. The difference is spreading.

GLAZED GLITTER

Nickel, what is nickel, it is originally rid of a cover.

The change in that is that red weakens an hour. The change has come. There is no search. But there is, there is that hope and that interpretation and sometime, surely any is unwelcome, sometime there is breath and there will be a sinecure and charming very charming is that clean and cleansing. Certainly glittering is handsome and convincing.

There is no gratitude in mercy and in medicine. There can be breakages in Japanese. That is no programme. That is no color chosen. It was chosen yesterday, that showed spitting and perhaps washing and polishing. It certainly showed no obligation and perhaps if borrowing is not natural there is some use in giving.

ROASTBEEF

In the inside there is sleeping, in the outside there is reddening, in the morning there is meaning, in the evening there is feeling. In the evening there is feeling. In feeling anything is resting, in feeling anything is mounting, in feeling there is resignation, in feeling there is recognition, in feeling there is recurrence and entirely mistaken there is pinching. All the standards have streamers and all the curtains have bed linen and all the yellow has discrimination and all the circle has circling. This makes sand.
Very well. Certainly the length is thinner and the rest, the round rest has a longer summer. To shine, why not shine, to shine, to station, to enlarge, to hurry the measure all this means nothing if there is singing, if there is singing then there is the resumption.
The change the dirt, not to change dirt means that there is no beef-steak and not to have that is no obstruction, it is so easy to exchange meaning, it is so easy to see the difference. The difference is that a plain resource is not entangled with thickness and it does not mean that thickness shows such cutting, it does mean that a meadow is useful and a cow absurd. It does not mean that there are tears, it does not mean that exudation is cumbersome, it means no more than a memory, a choice and a reestablishment, it means more than any escape from a surrounding extra. All the time that there is use there is use and any time there is a surface there is a surface, and every time there is an exception there is an exception and every time there is a division there is a dividing. Any time there is a surface there is a surface and every time there is a suggestion there is a suggestion and every time there is silence there is silence and every time that is languid there is that there then and not oftener, not always, not particular, tender and changing and external and central and surrounded and singular and simple and the same and the surface and the circle and the shine and the succor and the white and the same and the better and the red and the same and the centre and the yellow and the tender and the better, and altogether. ...

(GERTRUDE STEIN)

ON READING STEIN

Stein has been haunted by two antithetical criticisms. One proposes that her writing is all play, that it derives strictly out of her early researches with William James and motor automism and was later invigorated by Cubist formalism. The other proposes that Stein is a kind of hermetic Symbolist who encodes sexual and biographical information in complex little verbal machines which contextualize their own environments. Both views operate on either side of a referential paradigm; one wants her to mean nothing and the other wants her to mean intrinsically. But what makes TENDER BUTTONS so vital is not the strategies by which meaning is avoided or encoded but how each piece points at possibilities for meaning. Unlike the Symbolist who creates beautiful detachable artifacts, Stein's prose is firmly tied to the world--but it is a world constantly under construction, a world in which the equation of word and thing can no longer be taken for granted. "The difference is spreading" not only foreshadows deconstructive thought; it recognizes that between one term (a carafe) and a possible substitute (a blind glass) exists a barrier, not an equal sign, and it is this difference which supports all signification. Stein interrogates this barrier in order to break open the imperial Sign and leave "a system to pointing," a language that no longer needs to contain the world in order to live in it.

What's the good of all this? Obviously we know what a carafe is or nickel or roast beef, but Stein doesn't much care whether these things are self-evident. She *does* care that we've come to regard writing as the discovery of concrete counters for feelings, objects and places, that human memory is valorized over human mind in the act of creation. "A name is adequate or it is not. If it is adequate then why go on calling it..." she writes, inveighing against the noun's authoritarian stasis. What she wants is movement, a shifting of words among other words--not to erase their ability to refer but to make that act as polymorphous and perverse as any sexual play. TENDER BUTTONS as a title suggests words binding the fabric of language together but also the sexual (clitoral) excitation potential in all linguistic play.

Each of the pieces in TENDER BUTTONS seems, at some level, to refer to Stein's decontextualizing strategies. "A Carafe, That is a Blind Glass," is "about" the difference between a term and its multifarious substitutes ("a blind glass," a "kind in glass," a "spectacle") or its attendant qualities ("a single hurt color," a "difference...spreading"). The unitary object is dispersed among words in "an arrangement in a system." The objects themselves are commonplace--as common as the carafes, bowls and guitars of Cubist still lifes--but Stein's disjunctive prose removes them from their commonality and accentuates the gap between object and description. "(It) is so easy to exchange meaning," she says under the heading "Roast Beef," "it is so easy to see the difference." What links roastbeef to such remarks is the idea of transformation and change present in foods and language alike. Roastbeef exists as the sum of many processes, some of which involve cooking, preparing, eating and digesting; it is the least permanent of things, and yet for the creator of literary still lifes, it is expected to stand in an eternal brown glaze on the verge of being carved. Stein's carving exposes the fallacy in a whimsical rhetoric of permanence: "in the inside there is sleeping, in the outside there is reddening, in the morning there is meaning, in the evening there is feeling." Without knowing what is "outside" or how meaning relates to "morning" or "evening" to "feeling," we are at sea, but by creating a larger grid of specious comparisons and fake equations, Stein undercuts all logical continuity. The logic is entirely her own, and the shifts of prediction and assertion (the very stuff of reasonable discourse) serve to expose the mutability which lies at the heart of consumption, whether of food or or language.

What this implies for the act of reading is that there are no longer any privileged semantic centers by which we can reach through the language to a self-sufficient, permanent world of objects, food-stuffs or rooms. We must learn to read *writing*, not read *meanings*; we must learn to interrogate the spaces around words as much as the words themselves; we must discover language as an active "exchange" of meaning rather than a static paradigm of rules and features. The question is not "what" she means but "how." If such activity is difficult it is only because our habits of reading have been based on a passive acceptance of the criterion of adequacy; Stein undermines the model with the simplest of language only so that we may read for the first time--again.

MICHAEL DAVIDSON

A CARAFE ... GLAZED GLITTER   ROASTBEEF
                                      (through a glass darkly)

Ok murky in after all end, unpredictable day, with rain shine any degree night, the sun kin warm and hot. Enough stone or other jugs lineup of whatever is In Through Out That's light as much as known Differences evanesce Like, where and/or what on the equator might be french or spanish Longitude and latitude, yep yep sure Americana

But could someone mobile with us sleep downstairs, in case of some needs? The amount of variety, seen small, or a knockout maybe in fact. Going deep and strong suddenly three times, though not any more in a while. Mystery on occasion frightens, hurts what you don't know. Sleep came and nothing in square feet changed and later morning is too again there.

And however long the new days all. Every new second minute at

least. But the more there is the less you have in common, knowledge
of pieces, experience taken in. Bit by bit or in what or how many
dimensions. Is there any further inch to a holograph of a spread?
Lightning's fast in bed or anyplace. Monuments mixed in haystacks
lost.

Nothing is too dull.

LARRY EIGNER

Writing is intentional denotation (you *choose words*) and reading
mirrors that, is read as denotation and intention (mix of the words /
what the author is 'trying to say', technique composition context).
Of course, strict denotation is a myth: ambiguities/extracurricular
meanings can attach to any word(s) read. But it's a myth reinvented
at every word ("If not, why use words" -- Zukofsky): "breakages" mean
breakages, "Japanese," ditto.
     The (A) point of Tender Buttons is the play between what the pieces
are said to mean (the objects, the titles, Stein's theories, Paris
Impressionist through Cubist still life) and how the words exist and
interact is saying what they do say.
     She insists on an (intuitive) identity between her portraits & the
objects, arising from avoidance of memory, breaking through crust of
habit to actual perception, seeing something continually for the first
time. And it's done with *words*: "I became more and more excited about
how words which were the words *that made whatever I looked at look like
itself* were not the words that had in them any quality of description." (Portraits and Repetition; my italics)
     She's proving that she's seeing it by a continual athleticism,
leaping free of the gravity of the familiar. Yet "words that make
what I looked at look like itself were always words that to me very
exactly related themselves to that thing..." (P's & R's)
     So, related (a kind, a cousin), but at a necessary distance (not
resembling), breathing room for the object to *exist* (the difference).
Anomaly needed to keep us awake (a kind *in* glass, not of; a system *to*
pointing). In A Carafe I see her saying she sees and seeing to it
that she says so.
     But this sounds like systems of more or less stretched metaphor.
Occasionally, yes, "the round rest has a longer summer" (round, resting
on a platter, roast, summer, opulence, flavor) - I can hook up my
intuition with what I guess was hers. But often there's no 'very exact
[outward] relation' I can see. First 2 phrases of Roastbeef, yes, rest
of paragraph, no. Rocking along on the sound, patterning, slides into

lecture against memory: mounting, *resignation*, *recognition*, *recurrence*, mistake, pinch, wake up.

In places I wonder if she hears/sees/thinks/ the word just before or as she writes - or only after. Does she 'mean it', or is it just *prattle* (singsong, babyish joy in denotation [standards, steamers, curtains, bed linen], grammar becoming a 'weak force').

But "it is so easy to exchange meaning, it is so easy to see the difference" and on through the rest of the excerpt is definitely not babytalk, is exemplary in its variety of use, surface, suggestion.

Can't pin down what puts her on the interesting side of language's openness. At best her words displace all others. From Cups: "The best slam is utter."

BOB PERELMAN

TRANSLATIONAL RESPONSE TO A STEIN SINGLE

a carafe that is a blind glass

she types clarity
relations to a scene
a seen in
zero

queer ones in the pain
of pattern
wheeled directions to
a fullness
that negated more to
more what chaos enters in

no one same article
unlike a wide.

STEVE MC CAFFERY

WHOLE HALVES

Bisection, leaving one half hanging over, the drapes are clean. You look as if you need the third from the bottom, the keyhole, nicely in a row. That brings up heat, McCartney's words are blue. It's sort of molded into a mountain. South socks all metal by air sideways, the

trim set back from the teeth, the white trim, beginning to stand there.
What's back is clear, gently crumpled without creases. White line
leads to ferrous flair to private stuff side by side and side by side
side by side invitation to an address. Lines rise. Pillow's overtime.
Questions: round blue orange white yellow thin and horny. Once top on
another without looking very far up. If they stay up, moving in up,
and the board leads line a tongue right this way. And then the tongue
two three four. Stripes are everywhere, some hanging down or looking
up face down or up and left open ready to be lit: answer. The face
got a new invention. Buttons no longer don't make any noise. Because
what's switched also's identified. And instead of going straight on a
round surface straight means the French word for alright. Right at
the middle you get wet. Then people save you. Green spots connection.
New buttons never have to curl over one another. The old rigidity, the
old holes the fading tension aware of its collaboration, the new
tension, uncovers the covers. What's a head no longer needs what's
ahead because more and more buttons are right to be pressed, propulsion
hovers on exhibit. It's stacked, easier to lose the thought of finding,
insulatable craft against the checks. The rivers that run to the sea
oh boy, use the floor as a step out the door. What's discolored indicates the presence of routine, suddenly the hard weight of the sun
becomes mold, mold molding the frame, frame framing the water, water
drying up. And ancient actress sees at once. To occupy, having an
erection nothing is the same nothing is the name nothing is the frame.
Pursuit is as temporal as openings and closings buttons relieved pacify.
No one seems to know the right hand way to go, going down, which leaves
the middle and the left facing the trees and the hills and the local
stuff and the cagey touch flame away from glass. To be here now means
how can no one respond to buttons. They all have to be acounted for.
When you work in countries the next step is staying home, using buttons,
could be in the air like the old Chinese pool hall. Nobody's outside
without a shirt not moving lips without saying speed. Before there was
even a black hole a table right beside it. A chair. A pair of re-
routings means inside. Outside's very tangible, actual, substantive,
understood, outside's very material, always there to be reached trying
to be touched. Adhesives as well as collections and bone as well as
plastic and current as well as fastening and sewing, the next step's
stamping. The next step's diffuse. Solid. Volume descends to Richard's
only throne. Division of the aspect into verb as seeing progressive
form point-action verbs indicate is waking up is working out. Think
of it as a as: my whole life has change. In between the round ups
everything happens. Billy the Kid counts peas. Rock forms. PVC does
not burn. But as we entered the harbor some kind stuck, made stucking
sounds. Three bars equals ten dollars. Three buttons means one is
missing. That means make it tighter and only maybe somebody'll have

to wait. One more thing, light. Looking closer or closely looking used
to mean less light. To be precise include everything. Listening used
to mean use your head. Then Picasso said even here means a lot of work.
Even here being hear, you mean there Alice said. Here here refers to
there, permission prohibition, love marriage, button unbutton, press
release release press. To be precise precision excludes almost everything, what's left, under the light, clean dirty, includes everything.
In the north in the potato country roads are there when you're there
or when you're here. Here roads are here wherever you are.

PETER SEATON

ON FROM TENDER BUTTONS

Thinking aloud about a mystery is how I first conceived of writing.
Then I understood that was just me. Her work is not a sort of solving.
Here all colors, chosen, shine readily. The exudation is not cumbersome. But simply as the first act of creation was to separate light
from darkness, she plays a cousin against not resembling, not ordinary
against nothing strange, the same against the difference that is
spreading, circling against dividing and singular against a memory.
Both kinds shine convincingly when she's singing. Rid to red to
reddening. An exception and a reestablishment at once - "better, and
altogether" now.

RAE ARMANTROUT

THREE RESPONSES TO STEIN'S TENDER BUTTONS

A Carafe, That Is a Blind Glass

I'm not that kind, kind though I may be. It was hard for
me-- hard of heart, heart of glass (breaks too easy). My cousin wears
spectacles!-- wow!-- but there's nothing strange in her being hurt. I
said I was kind, but was I? I can arrange it systematically, so she can
point or be pointed to. Pointless, all this ordinarily unordered-- what
does it resemble? Differences. From the differences we get the spreading.

Glazed Glitter

Nickle, she says. And nickle she probably means. Formerly

elegant bicycles were plated-- covered over-- with nickle.

A nickle bag-- red on the cover-- rid of its cover. Red
for a week or an hour. It says "change has come," but who has searched
for it? I haven't noticed that yet. There is no welcoming in me today;
I haven't been a where of my bread's breath, of my breath's bread. A
sinecure, charming-- whom should I charm? Cleans or clean's-- what?
They're different, quite different. (Like me.)

There is no gratitude in mercy or medicine, it says. But
there is *me* at the start of each; I do not want to be so self-conscious.
Color chosen-- yesterday, washing and polishing. Today too. It was on
the program, on the docket. Dick it (if only)-- then Dock it. I am
studying to be to PhD, to change from Dick to Dock. Chosen is not Japan--
my Career isn't either. That is not soully Japanese. Watching and
polishing (Wendish or Polish?), baking-- "A bun is the lowest form of
wheat," they say. I don't doubt it.

Plate me baby, and I'll Dick you well.

Roastbeef

Inside there is sleeping; reddening and reading and rhythma-
tic-- Moses.

Certainly she is thinner than the rest. A good figure is a
luxury, and good figuring more so. She has rescued the baby from the
readings at the Smile.

The Sir has a face. And a place. Of grace. And there it
is theirs, and theirs among the theres, inner and outer and outer and
inner, inner of inner and inner of outer, in her, without her. About
her, without her. Better and redder, and tender to tend her. Bend her,
unwinder-- don't bind her. But find her sublimer.

Lime and lemon, lemon and lime. 'Tis thyme.

DICK HIGGINS

READING A SELECTION FROM TENDER BUTTONS

I start reading "A CARAFE, THAT IS A BLIND GLASS." I go from word
to word, seeing the shapes of the printed words, hearing the sounds
inwardly, noting rhymes, assonances, alliterations. Where an image is
suggested, I see it inwardly. I hear the alliteration "kind,"
"cousin," "color," with the near-alliteration "glass." The rhyme in
"strange" & "arrangement." The alliteration of s's: "spectacle,"
"strange," "single," "system," "spreading." The assonance of short i's
that binds the three sentences ("system," "this," "difference") as does

the ending of each sentence with an "ing" (which is reinforced by the short e's in "resembling" & "spreading"). There are also the 2nd sentence's rhymes ("ordinary," "unordered") & the alliterative sequence "spectacle," "pointing," "spreading." The three sentences are a bound system of sounds.

But can I specify anything beyond the sounds? To use a phrase I first heard from Spencer Holst, it gives "the sensation of meaning," but can I connect the meanings of the words as readily as I find their sounds connected?

Beyond the obvious fact that the carafe is made of glass, I can see only certain connections of meanings: "a blind glass," "a kind in glass" (I didn't notice consciously the "blind"-"kind" rhyme before), & then "a spectacle" (something seen or to be seen, but also "spectacles" are "glasses"). Then "nothing strange," "not ordinary," "not unordered," "not resembling," & "difference" form a meaning sequence. Another sequence of meanings: "blind," "spectacle" (with the intervening "glass"'s causing the ambiguity of "spectacle" which might not have been as apparent without them), & "color," that seems to carry over to "arrangement," "pointing," "not unordered," "not resembling," & even to "spreading." The sequence "kind" (with its two meanings), "cousin," "nothing strange" seems opposed to "not ordinary," "not resembling," & "The difference is spreading.": a meaning movement from near-sameness to greater & greater difference.

"A single hurt color" is the most emotional phrase, altho "blind glass" with its implied oxymoron (glass is usually transparent--at least we first think of transparency when we hear the word "glass"-- & when it is made into spectacle lenses, it helps people to see better) is perhaps even more so. Maybe the "single hurt color" is the blackness of blindness. The whole poem suddenly seems to be about seeing!

But what of the "carafe" that starts it all? Why is it "a <u>blind</u> glass"? Ordinarily a carafe is one of the least "blind"--that is, the most transparent--of glass containers. It usually contains plain water. The OED defines it as "a glass water-bottle for the table, bedroom, etc." Its Romance forms (F. *carafe*, It. *caraffa*, Neapol. *carrafa* (a measure of liquids), Sp. & Pg. *garrafa*, Sicil. *carabba*) are related by some authorities to the Pers. *garābah*, a large flagon, & the Arabic *gharafa*, to draw or lift water.

Why, then, is <u>this</u> carafe a <u>blind</u> glass?

Is the whole poem then a "pointing" from the ordinary transparent carafe ("nothing strange") to one "not ordinary"--one that is "blind"-- an orderly ("not unordered") movement "spreading" from transparency & clarity thru the "single hurt color" to the implied darkness & opacity of blindness, a movement condensed & make explicit in the title?

JACKSON MAC LOW.

WRITING ON A THEME BY STEIN

    In the
morning there is
feeling

A kind in
color and
not unordered

nothing strange
    All this
  is spreading

glass
an arrangement
    not resembling

time that is languid
  tender and changing
  and the same
   and the same and
     tender

CARL ANDRE

TENDER BUTTONS

Undergoing *sight* (& by 'sight' thinking feeling looking remembering
even inventing imagining certainly tasting surely listening hearing
talking) meaning potentially all human process, as almost academic
('art-school') exercise undertaken for the species' joy in it, less
talking & listening than looking to know that words can do it, making
nomenclature consort of nature (1911, in Spain) in the perfect understanding that *that seen* makes a name, this time (accommodating
strangeness of verbiage in process of gaining exact usage), only
because (mutton flies into the sundown upwind upstream already) all
time/everything is. Artist never fell.

Sad story, now, apparently. Real im Traum, 'before the War.' Today,
a hearkening back, as longing, not the reality of the word, not the
faith that makes composition of the world, riding on that everything,
permission given. She could say anything.

Now some further difficulty of access, as the nature of human experi-

ence slips away from the ad-men as makers of language unconvinced, in
the last resort, of any *necessity*.

> Before I die.
> Before I die.
> Before I die.
> Before I die.
>
> (Robt. Creeley, <u>Pieces</u>)

--resolve echoes. Names repeat.

But it's the same imperative, that one might undertake now in the
absence of conviction, that anything was, that a word might mean anything, that she addressed with certainty: "...looking at anything until
something that was not the (conventional) name of that thing but was
in a way that actual thing would come to be written." ("Poetry And
Grammar")

.

"TENDER" says entire activity of the artist's portraiture (subtitle:
"portraits of objects, food, rooms")--not 'studies' of objects etc.
nor 'still lives,' but (*portray:* 'to draw forth, reveal'; from root,
'to drag, move') dramatic engagements with things-given-the-sort-of-
attention-that-humans-get often in motion, 'alive,' as well--so you
get a verbal-formal offering, that stretches out to move through circles
of light (attention) in which "beginning again and again" transforms
into a "continuous present" in which words one-one-one actively engage
as single-frame sequence ("...this our period was undoubtedly the period
of the cinema and series production") something all right, tendered,
right in front of you. "BUTTONS" just means everyday domestic objects
(which are??) nudged--'on the button.'

Ok, 'tender' because new-born--& all right, word-buds, tenderly regarded.
.

What poetry *does* (see "Poetry And Grammar"): realization of new nomina-
tives--(not neologism but) whole text, in process, "replaces" worn-out,
now-merely-conventional name offered up (in title, commonly) to be
melted down in crucible of language process attention forging other
access to the ongoing of what's what.

<u>T.B.</u>, as *early* 'phenomenological investigation,' is interpretative/as
it is revelatory--the whole storm of passion, discernment, definition,
feeling//carried by language//brought to the 'budding'of the thing--
three together, through time, make the name.
.

It's not 'snapshorts' (moves; don't copy nature), & it's not 'the
pathetic fallacy' (though it includes much of the artist's process).
And it ain't 'abstract.'

(In this context, for L=A=N=G=U=A=G=E, I want to say I think it's at best a 'creative misreading' of Stein to take her work as a whole as a primary instance of 'language-oriented writing.' Not only her somewhat less arduous later work (<u>Autobiography of A.B.T.</u>, <u>Brewsie And Willie</u>), but <u>The Making of Americans</u> (a history of her family & compendium of sketches of every possible kind of human being), <u>Lucy Church Amiably</u> (an 'engraving' or romantic portrait of life in the French countryside) & her long poem "Stanzas in Meditation" (written shortly before the <u>Autobiography of A.B.T.</u> &, if anything, a prototype of confessional poetry) all are intent to make new ways to say something—show her thinking language not as object-in-itself, but as composition functioning in the composition of the world. With the exception of some verbal experiment, with Williams & Pound, Stein's basic concern as a writer was to confront the imperative MAKE IT NEW however possible—'IT' being, equally/simultaneously, sentience, world & language as relation between these. <u>T.B.</u>, specifically, exists *as* such confrontation—& to take it as a variously interesting arrangement of words, alone, is to perpetuate the initial journalist-parody response to the work as 'nonsense.')

.

But can it be done, as a *task*. *Was* 1911, or... *Even now*... "It's a mild, mild day, Starbuck" etc... *So* quiet, in America... 1977 rhymes with 1911 (*is* it, already, 1978...) Seemingly timeless lull on the brink, this time, of the extinction of something other than the Pequod as American westward-expanding enterprise (or craters in the Whiteheads' lawns)... Beautiful fall day, clear even to the horizon...though the reign of conventional names, reiteration of terminology as fixed interpretation of that not happening, appears to cover the globe several times over, 'ruling' air & land & waves... What a moment, nonetheless... *Yet again*, that chance to (two by two, alpha & beta, assess & elephants) call the roll, look to words to show & tell the present orders of...

.

"...Think of all that early poetry, think of Homer, think of Chaucer, think of the Bible and you will see what I mean you will really realize that they were drunk with nouns, to name to know how to name earth sea and sky and all that was in them was enough to make them live and love in names, and that is what poetry is it is a state of knowing and feeling a name. I know that now but I have only come to that knowledge by long writing." ("P. & G.," 1934) ...

ROBERT GRENIER

(*Grenier's piece will continue in the next issue with a reading of the Stein text*)

BENJAMIN OBSCURA

(What follows is an excerpt from a much longer text on Walter Benjamin by Ron Silliman. The complete text is forthcoming in two places -- the first issue of Renegade, c/o S. Fraccaro, Box 578, Canal St. Sta., New York, NY 10013, $2.95, and Problematic Photography, edited by C. Loeffler, La Mamelle Press, Box 3123, San Francisco, CA 94119).

Benjamin's characterization of the photograph ... functions also to note the role of the camera in a crucial step toward the fetishized realism which embodies the capitalist mode of thought ... the hand in the process of pictorial reproduction is stripped of its gestural content. The loss of the gestural is a topic I have gone into in some depth elsewhere as it pertains to the history of poetry, a portion of which is worth repeating here:

> "What happens when a language moves toward and passes into a capitalist stage of development is an anaesthetic transformation of the perceived tangibility of the word, with corresponding increases in its descriptive and narrative capacities, preconditions for the invention of 'realism,' the optical illusion of reality in capitalist thought. These developments are tied directly to the nature of reference in language, which under capitalism is transformed (deformed) into referentiality.
>
> In its primary form, reference takes the character of a gesture and an object, such as the picking up of a stone to be used as a tool. Both gesture and object carry their own integrities and are not confused: a sequence of gestures is distinct from the objects which may be involved, as distinct as the labor process is from its resultant commodities. A sequence of gestures forms a discourse, not a description."

The obliteration of the gestural through the elaboration of technology occurs across the entire range of cultural phenomena in the capitalist period. It is the principle affective transformation of the new material basis of production. Guttenberg's moveable type erased gesturality from the graphemic dimension of books. That this in turn functions to alienate the producer from his or her product is tangible even to authors who compose on the typewriter: to see one's text in a new typeface (inevitably asserting different spatio-visual values) is almost as radical a shock as first seeing oneself on film or videotape, or initially hearing one's voice remarkably *other* on a tape recorder. In a parallel manner, the constantly evolving and always unique objects of master craftsmen were replaced by the uniform (hence infinitely reproducible) objects of mass production (where, as Benjamin was to discover, the gestural is replaced by its antithesis: style),

(Benjamin:) "Even the most perfect reproduction of a work of art is lacking in one element: its presence in time and space, its unique existence at the place where it happens to be ... the quality of its presence is always depreciated ... One might subsume the eliminated element in the term 'aura' and go on to say: that which withers in the age of mechanical reproduction is the aura of the work of art ... Experience of the aura ... rests on the transposition of a response common in human relationships to the relationship between the inanimate or natural object and man ... To perceive the aura of an object we look at means to invest it with the ability to look at us in return."

Appearance, which is specifically an object *in relation* to an observer, is in each instance the privileged notion. Under the name of aura what appears is the Other, a shock, the recognition and acknowledgement of its absolute integrity freed from any dependency on the presence of Self. This liberty presents itself as 'distance' and 'the experience which has left traces of the practiced hand.' It does not (cannot) occur abstractly, that is: in the absence of the concrete object itself *as presence*. This is how it escapes both memory and reproduction. The affective presence of a photograph of a massacre, a Rembrandt or an orchid is first of all that of a (gray) rectangle of a certain size, which is almost never that of the event or object portrayed.

What is radically new in the age of technical reproduction is just this value placed on the possession of entities deprived of their integrity and otherness, personal experience reduced to vicarious consumption (which of course follows and parallels exactly that which befell lite-rature during the rise and brief reign of the novel). But to lose the Other is, in the same instant, to abandon one's sense of Self, to be rendered numb and passive on a level not previously possible in history. In "The Work of Art," Benjamin necessarily defines aura by exposing its 'decay,' its very existence revealed in this place of a lack, and goes further to implicate as the origin of this erosion not merely industrial imperialism, but that which made capitalism itself (and even capital) possible, the constituting myth of western civilization, *Identity*......

(Benjamin:) "To pry an object from its shell, to destroy its aura, is the mark of a perception whose 'sense of the universal equality of things' has increased to such a degree that it extracts it even from a unique object by means of reproduction."

A 'sense of the universal equality of things,' identity, destroys aura, accomplishing this by the removal of the object from its constituting context. This is also its advantage, since concealed within it is the

whole of the scientific method and project... Each of the five fundamental axioms of Euclidean geometry, which served for centuries as the
model for science itself, is in some sense a statement of identity, of
which the first is "Things equal to the same thing are equal to each
other" (if A = B and B = C, the A = C, etc.). Thus identity begets
substitution, exchange, reproduction. This principle extends itself
into the economic sphere via the *universal equivalent* of money... What
Benjamin saw emerging from the iodized silver plates of Daguerre ...
was the decisive moment in which the social basis of reality was transformed. Where previously the manufactured objects of the world sub-
mitted themselves to the fetishizing and mutational laws of identity
and exchange solely through an economic process, they now did so on a
new level, that of information. Each such product must not only carry
on a second life as a commodity, but a third one as an image or 'datum.'
... It is in the loss of aura, the shock of Other which carries with
it the recognition of Self, that modern humanity affectively confronts
the myth of Identity, that within which even capitalism is inscribed.
Benjamin is the first to say it, yet he is unable to speak its name.

RON SILLIMAN

STATEMENT

Over the past three years I have found myself preoccupied with two
formal issues of poetics, *intention* and *address*, which seem to be
central to a primary question of my need to create poems. Though I
term these issues formal, implying an objective investigation, the
making of poetry (in fact the reading of it) has become a very self-
oriented experience. More than saying I engage in the process of
writing for *myself*, it seems I have worked toward a ritualization of
the act to the point where it *functions* in a very specific domain.
Writing is now for me a means of modulating and organizing phenomenal
and circumstantial information from all points of experience, a process
I refer to as 'tuning' myself. As I grow older and seemingly remove
myself from unity with any singular, or even plural, socio-cultural
environment, I seem more 'on my own' in a vast environment of internalized experience. My approach to poetics has become the search for
responses and behavioral modes relative to this experience, to surviving
it as well as conditioning myself to it. Constantly the effort seems
to be away from any formalization of ideas or structure or definitive
process and towards a rejuvenating line of 'basics', that mythical
point where each process is fresh and new and wholly responsive to
indigenous conditions.

I came into the field of alternative forms and 'language-oriented writing' through a process of invention and then, taken with the ideas as well as the camaraderie of others similarly set adrift, found myself processing through an increasingly narrow channel of thought. By choosing to work solely within the perimeters of these somewhat technical issues I entered an environment controlled more by theory and imposed regulations than one open to all the motivations of a self oriented process. These imposed constraints became antithetical to the idea of poetics as opening, the field becoming increasingly closed by criteria and philosophy. This is surely a phenomena which has plagued other artists in other times.

An awakening to these dissatisfactory conditions several years ago led me to the formation of questions concerning address, to whom or to what is the writing process oriented, and intention, for what reasons does it occur and what function does it potentially serve. I'm trying now to deal with a poetics that actively conditions my self/environment and serves as a tuning process and a means of mediating personal experiences. Obviously, such an internalized approach disavows allegiance to any code of poetic behavior and repudiates any sort of cultural standards. What it may do, however, is become an organic means of response to a larger domain of life/experience, and some of the resolutions may (but need not) be useful to other beings in the flow.

In a sense, I am trying to cope with the urge of poetry as opposed to the structure of it. This urge seems to lie within the rooted and individual beginnings of the activity, centered on a meditative, self-encoded embrace of those issues and inclinations . find within my own humanness. The intention therefore becomes the opening of experience toward a continual address of the self.

CRAIG WATSON

NOTES ON GENRE

The state of resistance -- "Swamp Fox" -- "Robin Hood" -- refusal to participate in the codes, while remaining concerned to decipher substance (siphon away the substantiality, which can always be induced to form another substance). This resistance is not *outlaw* from the outset; it doesn't define itself as a preliminary deviation. Its line of advance propels it across the axis of the law, lexis, as a praxis which at precisely that juncture of abrasive contact discovers itself to be *not parallel* to the law [*out*law means being parallel to the stages of the law, but practising its distinctions point by point in relation to the lexical code-line]. This angle of interpenetration can, with skill, be repeated indefinitely (this is how Robin Hood managed to dwell in the same forest all the time, even after the king's men knew he was in there, waiting). This activity can compose a writing, a script in which texts are caught straggling from the train of their genre (train of thought) and be either pillaged or, if independent-minded and strong enough, induced to join the *outside* [i.e., not "outlaw" because that is to continue in the referential procedures of the lexicon, those-who-make-the-law; "outlaw" is just an excitable way of relating to the law; being "outside" however means comprehending law as gesture].

GENRE:

γέννα	*of persons, in a family*
γενέθλη	*race, stock, family*
γενέσιος	*a day kept in memory of the dead*
γένεσις	*origin, source, productive cause*
γενέτης	*begetter, father, ancestor*
γέννα	*(offspring) descent, birth*
γενναῖος	*suitable to one's descent or birth*
γεννάω	*beget, engender, bring forth*
γέννημα	*to that which is produced or born*
γένος	*race, family, stock*

[Robin Hood's ploy was γελο-ωμτλία, "fellowship in laughing"]

genre   is   folk-memory   deified

Now we see genre distinctions practised as a kind of racism. The "characteristics" are learned (& what is worse, taught), strict demarcations are observed to a crippling extent [readers of novels can't read poetry, readers of poetry can't read philosophy, readers of discursive workaday prose can't read anything for very long, etc.] All of this snaps back from the praxis into the shadow of an attitude: "poet" "novelist" "dramatist" "painter" "sculptor" "critic", i.e., submission to the sociological demand that everyone identify themself in the form of a racial obsession.

[THE RACISM OF LITERARY FORM]

The important (or functional) distinctions are not, after all, generic, but are decisions relating to inclusion/exclusion. To willingly accept a genre as part of one's identity is to respond to this racism as a code that must be accepted in order for any creating to occur. It is, in other words, to cover the "private parts" in the presence of the lawd.

JED RASULA

CODE WORDS

Roland Barthes, <u>Image-Music-Text</u> (1977; Hill and Wang, N.Y.; $4.95)

We can imagine *writing* that does not <u>prepare</u> the ego for the terrors and routines of a society it takes for granted.

Author dies, writing begins. The subject loses authority, disappears, is *unmade* into a network of relationships, stretching indefinitely. Subject is *deconstructed*, lost, "diminishing like a figurine at the far end of the literary stage"; deconstituted as writing ranges over the surface. A *floating* or cutting across replaces the barriers of nomenclature and identification. Normalization gives way to *signifiance*, an eroticism, a multi-dimensional tissue or weave of signs by which any apparent subject is produced. Writing, as *infinite* association, explodes the definitions, endistances origins (or Origin), rejects closure, *exempts* meaning. The vise of the signified is unhinged; simplistic notions of truth are relativized.

Subject becomes simply "the instance writing," is hollowed out by the operation of the linguistic system. System, here, is an *empty* process that some self always seeks to stuff & upholster. In one discipline after another, we have this recognition of the importance of *system* or *code* (rather than the romantic primacy of the individual or the self-sufficient particular). This may be the watershed of the last few decades. The motifs are system / code / frame / structure / constraint / rules: "language being system" & "the system as culture". "It is language which speaks, not the author."

Where code pertains -- meaning as use -- rules are dominant. Not like 'X determines Y' or 'Y is superstructure to base X' but where X follows rules of a social code or paradigm -- as if to 'follow the rules' meant the unseating of the sovereign subject as an entity which precedes the activity. Time is flattened out, in the here and now, of conformative / performative language. As if *aura* were that coding, that practiced hand, that *apprenticeship*.

Writing -- a *surplus*, not a reduction; an active & continuous constructing rather than a represented content & culture. The older literature of the signified finds itself constantly tempted into commodification. The signifier, on the other hand, marks the *Text*. Its self-demonstration is a performative, a speech act whose content is *depleted* by its own utterance and activity; it "artfully does nothing but turn itself inside out, like a glove"; a *perpetual signifer*, modelled on a permanent revolution. Flustering the image, acknowledging the materiality of language, not letting the subject idealize or mystify the whole process. "Did he wish to <u>express himself</u>, he ought at least to know that the inner 'thing' he thinks to 'translate' is itself only a ready-formed dictionary, its words only explainable through other words, and so on indefinitely."

Yet, beyond code: Language is *disseminated* through the text, that "methodological field," climaxing in *play*, not anchored by but in fact shattering the demands of our seemingly-liberating-but-actually-repressive genres of expression. Beyond the rule-governed transpositions is the self-differentiation of language, away from the universalized, commodity-like qualities so often trumpeted. Distinguishable, even deviant writing, rather than something malleable or blind or something that could be processed or theatricalized (like the self?). Beyond the anchoring of pointing, vertical depth, is a horizontal richness that cannot be diffracted or identified with. Ambiguity is ceaselessly produced and not swallowed up. An *excess*, a *supplement*. Here writing can innovate, as scandal, not destroying code but playing off it, *deferring*, showing the limits. In these cases, writing is clearly produced by the central activity of reading, capturing both the code-like aspects (with the investment of value) but also the yearning singularity of the phonemes bursting off page, tape, or lips. Reading becomes the first *production*, rather than consumption -- not a relay of an author's vain transcriptions of a representational content. Reading *operates* the text, is a rewriting, a new inscription. The text erases "the distance between writing and reading, in no way by intensifying the projection of the reader into the work [hypnosis of the reader by illusions of transparency] but by joining them" in a single practice.

Discourse as tyranny, as The Law, The Letter: all instrumentalisms: disorient them. Lift their burden with that drifting, wavering signifier, playing its symbolic attachments in a much more open, impertinent unrepressed style. 'This is new for me.' A multiplication of points of attention, authorless, into an unsituation. *Dispersion:* the ejaculation of polysemy, "efflorescence of the signifier," may come as far as asemy. Silencing the voice of those *paper authors* who remember their lines & straitjacket the play. The activity is *accenting, folding, creasing,* a *stereographic plurality* disrupting "the peace of nominations" that the "spasm of the signified ... normally brings the subject voluptuously back into."

Make the present relative. Offer a *historicism*, where words are evitable, arbitary, not determined: a relative autonomy for language. A code is required; the whole is digital, not an illusory analogue, nor identity, equality, interchangeability. Texts (tests) like these will do the *denaturalizing*; they problematicize reality. Naturally language is unmotivated. See it this way. Take away the mythic & fetishized character of the words and sentences, their fatedness:

otherwise, how natural & spontaneous & disintellectualized & ahistorical & essentialist it tends to seem.

Read through system / culture, rather than just stare through language to wind up trapped in system / culture, in semantic artifice. Transparency is a future political achievement, not a normal condition we can subscribe to in literature. Writing must look toward a radically transformed society that would provide the code (and the ideal communication system, and counter-communication system) needed to fully comprehend it. *Utopia.* Take nothing for granted, leave nothing intact, move outside, heterogenize, wake up the patient from stupefaction, desocialize the ego (so that eventually we might be resocialized). Indeed, explode ourselves ("*jouissance*") into the text -- "airy, light, spaced, open, uncentred, noble and free"

BRUCE ANDREWS

WAVE

Bernard Welt, Wave (1977; Jawbone, c/o Doug Lang, 1545 18th St., NW, Washington, D.C. 20036; $2)

Bernard Welt's poems tell what goes on in the head attuned and committed to paying attention to itself in all the forms customary language takes, as clearly these grow more arbitrary and various. The lines, stanzas, poems, sentences are as relentlessly and casually formal in their occupation as any. Here it seems second nature, virtually de rerum natura / the way things are --
These are voices in the mind that are no less for that in the body. Their tone and import take from all the gestures of moment that happen in the inward-looking roving mind the gist of their curb ("this pleasant, slightly confused murmuring"). BW gets a positive rush of courage out of sinking feelings, while the whole turmoil comes across in the blankest verse, direct as it is erring, voluble as it is laconic, glib as it is searching.
Wave is a long poem of some more than 13 pages, dedicated to Diane Ward, much of it virtually prose and the whole more loosely structured than other BW work I've seen. Its sections are discrete but not numbered and there is no interruption. The tone is of a voice deliberately talking on, such that no distinction need be made between figurative and literal speech. The conversation is as literary as in Conrad, and there is no joke about talk.
Part of the project of Wave appears to be to say something given

that it is difficult. The difficulties are various, and named when possible-- "You have nothing to talk about, / and no way to say it"; "The words fly off into the air, / one by one, slowly, like / thought balloons, escaping analysis / into their immediate constituent units"; "You will say the same thing over and over again, but in different ways." There is no difference between puzzling over and celebrating here. The poem has the air of a disquisition on being here, or is it relationship, or address, but leans not on prepared terms, strategies, syntaxes, known ideas, but hurdles them. It is of and in movement, with a consciously rhetorical resistance against though amid the kind of stasis bred of getting anything down -- "the matter / becoming an end in itself, / the individual waves / obscuring the sea, / and then you're lost: lost because you have found one place to be safer than others, and it is, but what has happened / to the motion. Absorbed / into the lines. / You have to support / what you can't avoid, / and that becomes automatic, so that it's as much a rule for those who use it to make things easy, freeze the motion, as those who learn to ride the wave, though the latter course is fraught with obstacles, 'monsters,' even; still, there is no reason to be proud of this because you have only done what you had to."

Along with the unwillingness to assume or grant the rightness of any given topic or form runs the assertion not only that any given perception or act is adequate and inevitable but also that each is, perhaps however one happens to see it, a casual paradigm. The indirection of the poem's investigations and the distracting imbalance of its resolutions, which is egged on to generate another momentum, paradoxically challenge and confirm this almost matter-of-fact fatality -- the energy offsets romantic and classical attitudes, which are both felt deeply and problematically. Evidently the poem was written with 2 hands. Reading it, dialectical faculties are called into debate and deconstructed. The poem is heartfelt, with that innate music, enough that the consequence is a sort of dance, albeit tentative and ceremonious like two contemporary friends meeting on purpose together who don't know each other yet -- Although you might say there is nothing to fear, casualness, generosity, even a show of vulnerability seem requisite as much to indicate one's autonomy and separateness as to elicit sympathy and response. The poem is less incantatory of the image of such discourse than of its issue in what one may take it that it needs to be, as though the voices barraging one from inside the head might be recognized as just as worthy of trust as the whisper in one's ear from an ideal friend, as though the focused deflection of all aural experience through the conch shell were actually the ocean's chosen form of address to me, whether arbitrary indeed or reiterative or intended for this moment all along. I myself find this rather upsetting. BW persistently raises the stakes of the poem high as possible without losing them from our mutual view, challenges ideals of action, perception, and utterance and what can be said of them, however ironically, sparing no direct reference to the weaknesses noticed in coping with them.

STEVE BENSON

RAWORTH

from LOGARHYTHMS

Tom Raworth, Logbook (1976; Poltroon Press, 2315 Carleton, Berkeley, CA; $7.50)

> And I am busily sweeping up the last few words in a country
> without an ear, whose artists are busy filling in the colours
> they've been allocated in the giant painting-by-numbers picture
> of themselves, because they think an interview with the man
> (now a physicist in Moscow) who was the boy on the Odessa Steps
> makes a connection.

The connection is that imagined between something whose claim to meaning is what it was recognized for, and the subject of an expropriation, a resistance to the fading away of a subject in which the past is regulated by future needs. For the boy on the Odessa Steps was part of a diction which no longer obtains, and the physicist in Moscow will prevent our realizing the history of that. Thus the tense in which *Logbook* is written is the post-prophetical present--it will not be depleted by 'culture.' And by that I mean what culture is recognized as being (culture at the cognitive level):

> "He planted that word twenty years ago so that its weight is
> now exactly right"--that's the message of 'culture,' the real,
> cold, science.

For Raworth the word is not an implantation, a seclusion of meaning away from processes of renovation (there are a great number of novels and poems officially retired) but a disclosure, in a work of dehiscence--the discharge of mature contents. The proper meaning of maturity as of something instant, and not a state which you finally reach and then persist in.
If we think we understand this text it is not by way of consolation for the monopoly of 'literature'; 'literature' borrows its own meaning from a global repertoire and gives them only a limited territory in which they can work. This demarcation is political, like a red line on the map

ignored by the elements: "For this is the battle: between the vegetables and the rocks. And we are the disputed territory—we, and the water we come from and are." In fact we are the subjects of a repertoire such that we can exclude ourselves from parts of it or force ourselves not to: "Until finally writing becomes the only thing that is not a petroleum by-product, or a neat capsule available without prescription." Writing is the excessive production from which more meanings escape than can be contained and given a place, and if 'culture' can afford to be more and more intolerant, or restfully ignorant of its subversion by writing, that is because the massive extension of criticism has actually imposed on 'literature' a greater scope than it knew it already had, persuading us of its competence through an ability to <u>account for</u> an unprecedented number of the strange materials from which it borrows—when it omits everything which it is not in order to be systematic.

> It's the front room, and the queen's picture flickers into a
> limp book called Jimi Hendrix because all books are dead &
> we live where the edges overlap.

There are other complicities of meaning some of which rely on complete subterfuge as they must to remain so fragile they can withstand the brutal coherence of civility. That maladaptation of ourselves whom writing may effectively put back into circulation is civility in the belief we are consenting members of the constituency of the book. So then it is important to traduce the accredited image of the book, and *Logbook* seems to be the record of an expedition whose parade of 'culture' might be directly provoking, and the representative value of its language could only be instated by force:

> Around us was the countryside of <u>Whimsy</u> where, huddled around
> leaping orange fires, the natives let their cigarettes dangle
> unlit in their mouths, thinking only petrol or butane could
> light them.

This refers to a colonial discourse like that of *Voyage au Bout de la Nuit* where the Europeans have power through a monopoly on money <u>and</u> language. We ought to note that forty years ago the question of <u>agency</u> was still an effective anxiety, and that now the honest intervention has to be whimsical. The only way in which the natives <u>can</u> know the rules is through being guilty of a breach; this is the position which writing can refuse to occupy, and it does so if it is contrary. The adroitness is a condition necessary for the act of restitution in which disobedience to the laws of consistency is freed from its social stigma of worthlessness and restored to an expressive capacity....

Intermittent form is the basis of a text which <u>is</u> the presence of history, exactly like a log-book: not wholly irregular but punctuated by a regularity which is transitory, "slightly charred by the slow still silent instant." It has an essential readiness which is measured not by coherent size but the sudden insistence of its distracted parts--"a form can be used once only." Our understanding of the text is the activation of these diverging parts, the instant in which their mutual pressure is sufficient to open the text for us.

ROD MENGHAM

RAWORTH BIBLIOGRAPHY: *Weapon Man* (1965, broadside, Cape Goliard Press, London). *The Relation Ship* (1966-7, Goliard Press, London; reprinted, 1969, Cape Goliard--London / Grossman, New York; available as remainder). *The Big Green Day* (1968, Trigram Press, c/o Serendipity Books, 1790 Shattuck Ave, Berkeley, CA 94701, $3 pbk., $6 hdbk). *A Serial Biography* (1969, Fulcrum Press, London; reprinted, 1977, Turtle Island, 2845 Buena Vista Way, Berkeley, $4.95). *Lion Lion* (1970, Trigram, c/o Serendipity, $2.50 pbk, $5 hdbk). *Betrayal* (1970, Trigram; exists only in bibliographies & works of reference). *Moving* (1971, Cape Goliard, London / Grossman; available as remainder). *Tracking* (1972, Doones Press, Bowling Green, Ohio). *Act* (1972, Trigram, c/o Serendipity, $4.50 & $8). *Pleasant Butter* (1972, Blue Pig 17, Sand Project Press, Northampton, MA). *Here* (1973, forty typewritten copies, Bowling Green, Ohio). *Back to Nature* (1973, Joe DiMaggio 4, Bexley-heath, Kent). *From the Hungarian*, with Val Raworth (1973, mimeo, Bowling Green, Ohio). *An Interesting Picture of Ohio* (1973, mimeo, Bowling Green, Ohio). *Ace* (1974, Goliard Press, London--edition destroyed; reprinted, 1977, The Figures, c/o Small Press Distribution, 1636 Ocean View Ave, Kensington, CA 94709, $2). *Bolivia, Another End of Ace* (1974, Secret Books, Skeet Place, Skeet Road, Lyminge, Nr. Folkestone, Kent, $1.50). *Sic Him, Oltorf!* (1974, broadside, Hermes Free Press, San Francisco). *That More Natural Time Tone Distortion* (1975, University of Conn., Wilbur Cross Library, Storrs, Conn., free). *Cloister* (1975, Blue Pig #23, Sand Project Press). *Common Sense* (1976, Zephyrus Image, San Francisco). *The Mask* (1976, Poltroon Press, 2315 Carleton, Berkeley, $15). *Logbook* (1976, Poltroon Press, $7.50). *Sky Tails* (1977, Lobby Press, 146 Gwydir Street, Cambridge, England, $1.50). Forthcoming, 1978-79: *Four Door Guide* (Wendy Mulford, 31 Panton St., Cambridge, England). *Nicht Wahr, Rosie* (Uncollected poems, 1964-69, Poltroon Press). *Writing* (Bull City Press, 3425B Randolph Rd, Durham, N.C. 27705).

STYLE

It is said that one can tell during a conversation that lasts no
longer than a summer shower whether or not a person is cultivated.
Often it does not take even so long, for a raucous tone of voice and
grossly ungrammatical or vulgar expressions brand a person at once as
beyond the pale of polite society. As one goes forth one is weighed
in the balance and if found wanting he is quietly dropped by refined
and cultured people, and nearly always he is left wondering why with
his diamonds and his motors and his money he yet cannot find entree
into the inner circles. An honest heart may beat beneath the ragged
coat, a brilliant intellect may rise above the bright checkered suit
and yellow tie, the man in the shabby suit may be a famous writer, the
woman in the untidy blouse may be an artist of great promise, but as a
general rule the chances are against it and such people are dull, flat,
stale and unprofitable both to themselves and to other people. In the
end, coherence is always a quality of thought rather than a manner of
expression. The confused mind cannot produce coherent prose. A well-
proportioned letter is the product of well-balanced mind. The utterance
of the single word "Charles!" may signify: "Hello, Charles! are you
here? I am surprised to see you." Language, however, is not confined
to the utterance of single words. To express our thoughts we must put
words together in accordance with certain fixed rules. Otherwise we
should fail to express ourselves clearly and acceptably, and we may
even succeed in saying the opposite of what we mean. Since language is
the expression of thought, the rules of grammar agree, in the main,
with the laws of thought. Even in matters of divided usage, it is
seldom difficult to determine which of two forms is preferred by careful writers. Everything is taken care of in the most orderly fashion:
terms are defined, possible ambiguities eliminated, implications and
assumptions explained, proofs adduced, and examples provided. On the
whole it is safe for the writer to leave semantic theory unexplored.
We favor the standards of the more precise stylists if only because we
cannot be more permissive without risking their disapproval, whereas
those who do not object to less exacting usage are not likely to be
offended by the correct usage. A good expository sentence does not
call attention to itself, although Strunk comments that an occasional
loose sentence has its virtues. No one who speaks and writes can
expect his audience to respond to connotations that arise from his own
purely personal experience. Some people associate colors with numbers,
but orange is not a connotation of "four". The trouble with Humpty
Dumpty's stipulative definitions, if they can be dignified by such a
word, is that they are entirely capricious and absurd. For sentences
must measure up to standards: it is always fair to ask of a sentence,
"How *good* is it"? Among the qualities that contribute to an effective

impression, the five most essential are clearness, correctness, conciseness, courtesy, and character. For style is ingratiation; negative ideas, as a rule, should not be developed at length. And constructions to be shunned include those that are vague, abstract, equivocal, slanted, misleading, exaggerated, understated, loose, abbreviated, oversimplified, obvious, irrelevant, oblique, figurative, redundant, empty, impossible, or obscure. It would be a curious state of affairs if only those who seldom think about the words they use, who read little and who "cannot be bothered" with distinctions should be the only ones with full powers over vocabulary and syntax. Even on the grounds of free democratic choice the hands-off attitude about language receives no support. These assumptions further suggest that the desire for correctness, the very idea of better or worse in speech, is a hangover from aristocratic and oppressive times. ...the young foreigner who apologizes for the fact that the chocolates he has bought as a gift are *molten* is told with a smile that that is not English: the right word is *melted*. --We talk to our fellows in the phrases we learn from them, which seem to mean less and less as they grow worn with use. The quiet cynicism of our everyday demeanor is open and shameless, we callously anticipate objections founded on the well-known vacuity of our seeming emotions, and assure our friends that we are "truly" grieved or "sincerely" rejoiced at their hap--as if joy or grief that really exists were some rare and precious brand of joy or grief. A sentence says you know what I mean, dear do I well I guess I do. Grammar does not mean that they are to limit themselves. More and more grammar is not a thing. Grammar does not make me hesitate about prepositions. I am a grammarian I do not hesitate I rearrange prepositions.

(Sources include Follett's *Modern American Usage*, Kittridge's *Advanced English Grammar*, Stein's *How to Write*, Modern Language Association's *In-House Style Sheet*, Hagar's *the English of Business*, Martin and Ohmann's *Logic and Rhetoric of Exposition*, Raleigh's *Style*, and Eichler's *Book of Etiquette*.)

                    CHARLES BERNSTEIN & SUSAN B. LAUFER

SUBMISSION OF RELEVANT MANUSCRIPTS WELCOME

SUBSCRIBE NOW FOR VOLUME TWO (1979)

L=A=N=G=U=A=G=E

Vol. 1, Number 6.   December 1978.

Charles Bernstein & Bruce Andrews, Editors.

Subscriptions -- One year (four issues in 1979) for $4.
                    Institutions: $8.

L=A=N=G=U=A=G=E is supported solely by subscriptions
and donations.

All queries, submissions, and checks to:
Charles Bernstein, 464 Amsterdam Ave, New York, NY 10024.

*We want to thank our writers and subscribers, who have
made this first year of publication possible. In particular, we want to acknowledge the special assistance of Ray
DiPalma, Nick Piombino, Susan Laufer, Bernard Welt, James
Sherry, Carole Korzeniowsky, Ellen Andrews, Michael Gottlieb, Carl Andre, and Ron Silliman.*

(C) 1978 by L=A=N=G=U=A=G=E

Distributed with the cooperation of the Segue Foundation.

ANNOUNCEMENTS:

SHADE by Charles Bernstein, $3 from Sun & Moon Books, Box 431,
  College Park, MD 20740.

E-POD #2 -- Selections from LEGEND☆, a collaboration by Steve
  McCaffery, Ron Silliman, Ray DiPalma, Charles Bernstein, and
  Bruce Andrews; $1 from 3022 Abell Ave, Baltimore, MD 21218.
  (Series subscription, 12 issues for $7.50).

PRAXIS by Bruce Andrews, $2 from Tuumba Press, 2639 Russell, Berkeley,
  CA 94705. (Third Series, six issues for $6).

L=A=N=G=U=A=G=E

NUMBER 7   MARCH 1979

SOUND POETRY

When considering text-sound it is energy, not semantically shaped
meaning, that constitutes the essence of communicated data. The classical, Aristotelian conception of form is that of goal, the target-desti-
nation at which we arrive as at a postponed reward by way of a composition. It was, hence, to be a highly significant reversal of Aristotle
when Wilhelm Reich was to declare form to be *frozen energy*, opening a
path to a new conception of form as the aggregate of departures not
arrivals, the notion of the de-form as a thawing of the constrict, a
strategy of release, of flow.

What the sound poet practises is the deformation of linguistic form
at the level of the signifier. For it is the scripted signifier, the
phonematic unit that marks the crypt of a vast repression, where energy
is frozen in the articulated and subordinated elements of representation.
Language, through its nature as representation, its functioning by means
of arbitrary, articulated signs, by means of rules, conditions and
prohibitions, becomes a huge mechanism for suppressing libinal flow. To
investigate sound in isolation from the sign-function, and to practice
out of the actuality and non-representation of the phonematic marks an
important stage in establishing the agencies for a general libidinal de-
repression. Sound poetry is much more than simply returning language to
its own matter; it is an agency for desire production, for releasing
energy flow, for securing the passage of libido in a multiplicity of
flows out of the Logos. To experience such flows (as a break-through in
a break-down) is to experience the sonic moment in its full intensity of
transience.

To align, realign and misalign within the anarchy of language. To
cultivate excess, return language to its somatic base in order to deter-
ritorialize the sign. Concentration on molecular flows rather than the
molar aggregates. Cuttings. Fissures. Decompositions (inventions).
Not intention so much as intensions. Plasticizations. Non-functional-
ities. Shattered sphericities. Marginalities. Somas. Nexi. La poème

185

c'est moi but as the inscription of the person in a transcendental pronoun that utterly annihilates the subject. Personal collapse into flux. Dilations. Positive disintegrations. Structures abandoned, departed from or de-constructed and modified into flows in accord with the unique, unpredictable molecular relationships of audiences and performers. Genetic codicities. A gift back to the body of those energy zones repressed, and channelled as charter in the overcoded structure of grammar. To release by a de-inscription those trapped forces of libido.

Julia Kristeva has written of literary practice as being 'the exploration and discovery of the possibilities of language as an activity which frees man from given linguistic networks'. Sound poetry is best described as *what sound poets do* (or as I once answered "it's a new way to blow out candles"); it thus takes its place in the larger struggle against all forms of preconditioning.

The 1950s saw the development of what might be termed a third phase in sound poetry. Prior to this time, in a period roughly stretching from 1875 to 1928, sound poetry's second phase had manifested itself in several diverse and revolutionary investigations into language's non-semantic, acoustic properties. In the work of the Russian futurists Khlebnikov and Kruchenykh, the intermedia activities of Kandinsky, the bruitist poems of the Dadaists (Ball, Schwitters, Arp, Hausmann, Tzara) and the 'paroles in liberta' of the Italian Futurist Marinetti, the phonematic aspect of language became finally isolated and explored for its own sake. Prior to this there had been isolated pioneering attempts by several writers including Christian Morgenstern (ca. 1875), Lewis Carroll ('Jabberwocky'), August Stramm (ca. 1912), Petrus Borel (ca. 1820), Moliere, the Silesian mystic Quirinus Khulman (17th century), Rabelais and Aristophanes.

The second phase is convincing proof of the continuous presence of a sound poetry throughout the history of western literature. The first phase, perhaps better termed, the first area of sound poetry, is the vast, intractible area of archaic and primitive poetries, the many instances of chant structures and incantation, of nonsense syllabic mouthings and deliberate lexical distortions still alive among North American, African, Asian and Oceanic peoples.

We should also bear in mind the strong and persistent folkloric and ludic strata that manifests in the world's many language games, in the nonsense syllabery of nursery rhymes, mnemonic counting aids, whisper games and skipping chants, mouthmusic and folk-song refrain, which foregrounds us as an important compositional element in work as chronologically separate as Kruchenykh's zaum poems (ca. 1910) and Bengt af Klintburg's use of cusha-calls and incantations (ca. 1965).

Sound poetry prior to the developments of the 1950s is still largely a word bound thing. For whilst the work of the Dadaists, Futurists and Lettrists served to free the word from its semantic function, redistributing energy from theme and 'message' to matter and contour, it nevertheless persisted in a morphological patterning that still suggested the presence of the word. It is Francois Dufrene's especial achievement to have pushed the limits centripetally and to have entered into the microparticulars of morphology, investigating the full expressive range of predenotative forms: grunts, howls, shrieks, etc. Important too, in this light, is the way meaning persists as a teleology even in *zaum*. Khlebnikov, for instance, speaks of new meanings achieved through bypassing older forms of meaning, of meanings 'rescued' by 'estrangement'.

So word persists even in the state of its own excommunication. It could be said that what sound poetry did, up to the exploitation of the tape recorder, was to render semantic meaning transcendental, as the destination arrived at by the disautomatization of sound perception. It is this theological contamination, of the meaning, like God, as a hidden presence, that specifies the limits of sound investigation up until the nineteen fifties.

With the fifties, however, came the gift of an external revolution: the availability of the tape recorder to sound poets made audio-technological advancement of the art form a reality. To summarize the several revolutionary capabilities that tape allowed: the transcendence of the limits of the human body. The tape machine, considered as an extension of human vocality allowed the poet to move beyond his own expressivity. The body is no longer the ultimate parameter, and voice becomes a point of departure rather than the point of arrival. Realizing also that the tape recorder provides the possibility of a secondary orality predicated upon a graphism (tape, in fact, is but another system of writing where writing is described as any semiotic system of storage) then we can appreciate other immediate advantages: tape liberates composition from the athletic sequentiality of the human body, pieces may be edited, cutting, in effect, becomes the potential compositional basis in which time segments can be arranged and rearranged outside of real time performance. The tape recorder also shares the micro/macro/phonic qualities allowing a more detailed appreciation of the human vocal range. Technological time can be superadded to authentic body time to achieve either an accelerated or decelerated experience of voice time. Both time and space are harnessed to become less the controlling and more the manipulable factors of audiophony. There exists then through recourse to the tape recorder as an active compositional tool, the possibility of 'overtaking' speech by the machine. Sound poetry mobilizes a certain technicism to further the deconstruction of the word; it permits, through deceleration, the granular structure of language to emerge and evidence itself. Phonetic poetry, the non-semantic poetry of the human voice, is more limited in its deconstructional scope, for it accepts the physical limitations of the human speaker as its own limitations. The tape recorder, however, allows speech -- for the first time in its history -- a separation from voice.

(The preceding is an excerpt from Steve McCaffery's essays in Sound Poetry: A Catalogue, edited by McCaffery and B.P. Nichol; 1978, Underwhich Editions, Suite 323, 100 Richmond Street East, Toronto, Ontario; 120 pages, $5.)

STEVE MC CAFFERY

GREENWALD

IN TED GREENWALD

> "Actual events are obscure
> Though the observers appear clear"
> -- Edwin Denby

Objects stand in rooms lit by sunlight which penetrates those rooms from front to back. The back rooms are all "TCB." The frontmost one is three large walls plus a row of windows. The walls have art (objects) on them; the windows have life. Sitting by the windows, Ted Greenwald is holding forth while at the same time eyeballing the upper reaches of Manhattan sky. Minutes later, he has joined the street-scene, sauntering fast as anyone, not hurried, just pushing for another look. Back in the back room, what he does is flatten: Every word in close-up, the walls and objects spread out in space...

A feeling of loose ends he keeps shuffling, prodding up and out, like traffic control in an echo chamber. (Confronting the words, the size of the human face is 8½ X 11.)

Local shifts in climate ("fog rolled in," "airy rushes punch") and his color-codes (the dominant pinks, whites, grey) are all matters of vernacular. And "in the order of vernacular" might be his unifying principle; more than speech or thought, the language he finds himself writing in. His poems tend to be agglomerates of loose phrases linked together sans contortion, striking parts of brain marked *ear* and *eye* at once. An abruptness he's capable of without losing count. The "touch" is rough, delicate, whizzing.

TCB, Ted tells me, means *take care of business.* "People refuse to see poetry as TCB," he once observed. Just as a painter can wonder typically, "Is poetry a residue? Hell, I've worked

my ass off for 20 years!"
The high-tension handiness of words by the
mindfuls: Greenwald shows the use of it, that he means it, and his poems
exemplify how much exact clarity he can get (from it) down in writing.
TCB at the surface *via* depth.
Partly, it's the fact of continuous non-
residual care for the windfalls and peripheral near-misses of dailiness
that makes him exciting to read. He is plain as day. But on days plain
as mud, what can happen? "Something nice." The event-mind locates the
event-events, non-events (obscure) are more mud, things tend to partition,
thoughts (un poco loco) babble, plunge or lapse. An edge-ward giddiness
amounts to style. A weakness for blunt puns, but he cuts through and
even doubles on them. "Mind does me like it does" and "the american
word for everything is 'art'."

> "managing to *move* me a foot
>   from where I started"

> "chat chat
>   and chat"

Greenwald has come from a bright abstract scatter ("cover the page with
paper") to the now airier-spaced grids of lines-as-inventory gathering
a whole statement. Non-stop statement, so all those truncated monolog
lengths, laid out as on a teleprompter, pack an all-over deliberate
momentum.
"Prime meat clouds" reveals a terrific poet's city of sudden
lights and geometries as sublime as in Leger or likewise Al Held.

> "the pears are the pears
>   the table is the table
>   the house is the house"

etc. The beauty of a non-
suggestive inclusivity, as in the "pointless stories" of Reznikoff that
stay exactly what they are, hum in place, won't evanesce.

"Imagine on paper what he sees and feels" speaks for a personable
expanse that's intrinsic, as does "one man/one woman/one moment" for his
exquisiteness. Lately with longer poems like *You Bet!* and "Word of
Mouth", Ted's been adding on elbow room. He's so prolific, it's alarming.
I like his drive, "the wheel of the tongue/forming driven words,"
"naphtha running wind over the bay."

BILL BERKSON

189

SPOKEN

The sound in my poems comes from the sounds I hear in my head of almost
myself talking to some person. I choose to have as my limitation spoken
speech, as you and I are sitting here talking. That's what I test the
poem's shape against.

Occasionally, I like to do other things, when I hear a completely peculiar sound or something, see if it works, give it a test run. Eventually,
I prefer dealing with items that are still charged with meaning and in
fact are open to the change that happens over time in meanings. In other
words, if I don't know exactly what a poem means when I write it I'm
somehow writing a certain kind of science fiction, because the poem (if
I'm right about the direction the language will change in) will eventually
make sense on a more than just, say, shape level or form level as time
goes by and I'll start to understand it more.

I'm an opportunist: I'll take what I can get. If it works and if it's
working when I'm working on it, then I'll use it. I don't care what
the source of it is. But I'm saying that the basic motor on my car is
spoken (for): What it sounds like in my mind when I read it to myself.

What works has to be grounded in the language, which is the locality of
words. Words change in spoken language. "the/form/of/the/words/pump/
blood/in/the/form/of/the/heart" That pretty much sums it up.

What I'm interested in and always have been is not what ideas people
have in their heads, but what's in the air. The most invisible part of
"trends". What is it that two people in the whole world or maybe twenty
all of a sudden out of the middle of nowhere start to think about.
What's in the air is the shape of things to come -- it's palpable --
right under your very nose. I hear what's in the air, that's my way of
thinking with my ear. You're not working with the idea of something,
you're projecting the idea of something. You're not working from models,
you're creating models.

It's a romantic notion (where classical means coming from someplace),
going someplace, sort of operating more out of imagination and less from
received forms. In a specific sense, what it is the interior mind projecting itself into the phenomenological world, telling *you* where it's
going. The time we live in is interesting, since there's a tremendous
amount of good poetry that's "about" comings and going, this's and that's,
here and there, not sillyass schools of one thing or another ("in" and
"out" I leave to the hosts and hostesses of the world).

Poetry is about a time that hasn't occurred yet, and if it's very good it's about a time you'll never know about. Poems are my pencil and pad for jotting down shapes or ways of embodying imaginary shapes or things that don't exist. But some time will exist on a wider scale. This is even conceptual: They are almost like plans for the future.

I think that the notion that sort of got started with Pound and other modernist artists is that if you were dealing with something you were going to take notes and the notes will usually be in fractional form. What's wrong with writing poetry that uses fragments (or notes) is that there is no everyday language that can be used to test goodness of fit. All there is is some poetic diction or poetic language to go back to that says "This is correct!," but no language in everyday use by people speaking, which changes over time, however imperceptibly.

I personally don't believe in using some form of a poem as a container for a bunch of things ("good lines" for instance). Each poem's form discovers itself as I write the poem. Two poems may not be perceptibly different looking, but there are differences. And, since I write on a day-to-day basis, and try to pay as close attention as possible, by paying close attention can see those differences. And watch the form of the poem, and the meaning and sense of sounds and words, change. And satisfy myself as a good reader with a good read.

TED GREENWALD

GREENWALD BIBLIOGRAPHY: *Lapstrake* (1965, Lines Books, NY). *Short Sleeves* (1970, Buffalo Press, Ithaca, NY). *No Eating* (1970, Blue Pig #10, Sand Project Press, Paris). *Blink* (1972, broadsheet, Buffalo Press, NY). *Somewhere in Ho,* with Ed Baynard (1972, Buffalo Press, NY). *Making a Living* (1973, Adventures in Poetry, NY). *The New Money* (1973, Blue Pig #19, Sand Project Press, Northampton, MA). *Makes Sense* (1974, Angel Hair Books, NY). *The Life* (1974, Big Sky Books, Box 389, Bolinas, CA 94924; $2). *Miami* (1975, Doones Press, Bowling Green, OH). *Native Land* (1976, Titanic Books, Washington, DC). *The Sandwich Islands* (1978, A Hundred Posters #25, NY). *You Bet!* (1978, This, c/o Small Press Distribution, 1636 Ocean Ave, Kensington, CA 94707; $2.50). *9 Poems* (1978, Un Poco Loco, NY). *Common Sense* (L Press, Kensington, CA, 1979). *Smile* (forthcoming). *Licorice Chronicles* (forthcoming). Photocopies of most out-of-print items are available from L=A=N=G=U=A=G=E Distributing Service; write for details.

RUSCHA'S BOOKS AND SERIALITY

"Nothing is of greater moment than the knowledge that the choice of one moment excludes another, that no moment makes up for another, that the significance of one moment is the cost of what it forgoes."

"One might say that the task is no longer to produce another instance of an art but a new medium within it. (Here is the relevance of series in modern painting and sculpture, and of cycles in movies, and of the quest for 'sound' in jazz and rock.) A new medium establishes and is established by a series... any change (of an angle, a shift in color or a color's width, or its distance from another color) would simply create a new instance, an absolutely new painting."
                         -- Stanley Cavell, in The World Viewed

Ed Ruscha's books document seemingly mundane but archetypal images--gas stations, apartment buildings, parking lots, vacant lots, the Sunset Strip, swimming pools, palm trees. The general structure is a series of snapshot-like photos of the same type of object. Cohesion is achieved through a programmatic, seemingly mechanical seriality. This use of seriality in *Nine Swimming Pools and a Broken Glass* creates not a world of time unfolding but a world of time flattened. Images are juxtaposed in which the time of day in each is elusively distinct--a shadow cast leftward in one, then rightward, changes in the quality of light, variations in the profusion of reflections: overall, an eeriness of "no time," an uncanniness. Each image is cropped and framed so as to exclude extraneous matter that would distract from the time, space, and photographic blueness of the pools. In this work, seriality does not create a linear movement forward or backward--as in a Muybridge movement series. Time, removed from its sequentiality, is left to float fancifully, airily on the surface of the reflecting water.

Photography often imparts to the objects photographed an increased particularity. Weston's "Pepper" has greater sensuality, texture, shape than we normally perceive in a pepper. In Ruscha's work, each object is transformed into something less than itself by becoming an instance of a genre. Thus the esthetic impetus is transferred from the single image to the series. Ruscha keeps a fixed angle of gaze on each gas station and swimming pool, and as the pages of the book are turned, it is as if the object is being transformed through slight changes in the structure of the image. The individual image is subverted in favor of the overall movement so that the book form becomes a medium for seriality in which these frames are situated in terms of context and type, with greater complexity than otherwise.

Within the medium of still photography, use has often been made of the serial nature of film. Photographers will take numerous shots of the same subject, so that a contact sheet will show many aspects of the same image. This seriality is an automatism inherent to film. The physical layout of a roll of film establishes relationships among the images. While a still photographer can choose different frames from the roll, thus eliminating links consciously or unconsciously made in the shooting, in motion pictures the seriality and linkage, speeded up in projection, is essential. Speed and motion create a tableau so that the individual images become harder to focus on and instead we are caught up in action pictures or more literally moving pictures.

In film, Walter Benjamin writes, "the meaning in each single picture appears prescribed by the preceding ones." Still photos can focus on different aspects of duration than film by isolating a specific moment or presenting a linear sequence. In Ruscha's selective choice of images, the distances between the sites of the gas stations, etc., seem like blank spaces making these books more like catalogues or surveys--spatial rather than temporal sequences.

Ruscha, finally, seems to be invoking the power of photography as such and film as such. The still photographic image exists as a moment in time encapsulated, as time literally framed.

(Ruscha's books include Every Building on Sunset Strip *(1966),* Thirty-Four Parking Lots *(1967),* Nine Swimming Pools *(1968), and* A Few Palm Trees *(1971).*

SUSAN B. LAUFER

ANATOMY OF SELF

Bernadette Mayer, Eruditio ex Memoria (1977; Angel Hair Books, Box 718, Lenox, MA 02140; $2.50)

Memory, history, personal history, autobiography, metaphysical autobiography, *Eruditio ex Memoria* is all of these. Yet this book projects a memory not of the self, but of the self as defined by the knowledge which makes up the self, which perceives the world in which the self lives. And in this sense Bernadette Mayer's new work is a cosmology, an encyclopedia, an anatomy, which as a genre is related to Menippean or Varronian verse satire, from the Greek cynic Menippus and the Roman satirist Varro, both now lost. The anatomy has continued in Lucian, Petronius, Apuleius, Rabelais, Voltaire, Swift, Rousseau, Peacock, and in our own century, Aldous Huxley, Wyndham Lewis, Djuna Barnes, and most recently, in *Seeking Air* by Barbara Guest. Unlike the picaresque--which is a satire of society, of its structures--the anatomy is a satire built up through a presentation of a vision "of the world in terms of a single intellectual pattern." Northrop Frye continues (in *Anatomy of Criticism*), "The intellectual structure built up from the story makes for violent dislocations in the customary logic of narrative, though the appearance of carelessness that results reflects only the carelessness of the reader or his tendency to judge by a novel-centered conception of fiction." The shortest form of the anatomy is the dialogue, but there is a strong tendency toward a display of erudition, of encyclopedic knowledge, of complications, catalogues and lists (see Burton's *Anatomy of Melancholy*, *Tristram Shandy*, Flaubert's *Bouvard et Pecuchet*, Norman Douglas' *South Wind*, and portions of *Moby Dick*.).

Does Mayer know anatomies? Perhaps not. The impulse here seems to come as much from her obsession with memory, from a compulsion towards autobiography that is related to the confession such as Saint Augustine's. But for Mayer memory is never an end in itself. It is not memory past that most interests her, but memory continuing, repeating, memory in the present made <u>new</u> through language in Pound's sense. Mayer's art is not a seeking for what <u>was</u> but what <u>was is</u>, and how what <u>is</u> was made by that past. Mayer's memory is not nostalgic--as in Proust--but is a past that makes the new, makes <u>for</u> the new: an ending that is a beginning ("Each end is a beginning"). She seeks not for old structures, not for a <u>re</u>-creation but for a <u>de</u>creation: "I put these words on paper because they were once written by me, no, I too yearn for a world without meaning." As she previously wrote in her novel *Memory*, "A whole new language is a temptation."

But Mayer's world, the world she discovers, is not without meaning. The past <u>de</u>created gives rise to a new created, a <u>re</u>created world. As with Adam, Mayer calls into meaning by naming, by naming a past. Through memory's order "Hemispheres become loose in the country, there are new forms."

Is this different from a Surrealist allowing the subconscious to create new structures, using dream images as the basis for a new reality? Yes. Mayer's past is not a dream, not archetypal, not mythical, but a socially ·lived experience. These are school notes, a pre-existent <u>text</u> rewritten (?) or almost intact, a life wrenched out of chronological context not by chance but by fact, a life perhaps not <u>experienced</u> as discontinuous but was (and because was can only be <u>is</u> in memory) <u>is</u> in fact.

No coy discontinuity is this, no clever disassociations. Actually there is an attempt in *Eruditio* at lucidness, to see through the veil of <u>experience</u> to a reality of flux, of life, of duration. And in this there is a basic recognition of the ineffectuality, of the destructiveness of the written word as opposed to spoken language (re Derrida). "There's no use writing down Greek words if no one is going to know what I'm saying." Mayer is always after language, then, after the reality that is language. *Eruditio* is a search for that reality not as written word but as language, which as a thought process is the thing itself. Saying is thinking is perceiving is knowing. In fact, although this work may often seem ineffable, there is throughout a drive for an absolute clarity of language: "Add up a column of numbers, it comes to William Carlos Williams."

All of which brings us back to the genre of anatomy, which comes from the Greek anatomé, a cutting up, an analysis or minute examination, to to show or examine the position, structure and relation of the parts. That is what this book is to me; it is an attempt to explain, to demonstrate, to show how Mayer has come to know whatever it is she has come to know. And in that sense, this book is a sharing, a removal of the veil, an admission, an apology, a true confession.

Moreover, in that it is itself a sign, an image, an emblem of language which stands for Mayer and the world she has recreated, an emblem like the red letter Hester Prynne wears. *Eruditio ex Memoria* ends with such an image: "In a painting I am a Chinese woman turning away from a bowl of fruit." Is this an Eve with a second chance, this time redeeming by giving up the knowledge, by releasing it? To pin the image down that way is to miss the point, is to turn back to the fruit and eat it. It is nothing more than itself, a Chinese woman turning away from a bowl of fruit, "its own sure image."

DOUGLAS MESSERLI

PROCEDURE

"Oran"   to   "ordain"   for "J"

orchestration = he raves

The prefix for "Ceylon trail" promises "main orange" after

orbits. Flashback to "front orange" where diversities _____ a

satellite, then skip to "hair order" chorus, again an orbit.

Down eleven, ordination is opposed to satellite, a shape end

circular as in "organized vision". LEVEL also leads to
a circle - "plants Ireland" - two below "beverage", one
below "prehistoric". Finally, islands make "part importance"
fleshy by adding "a" to orbit as orangey united to surrounding
fulcrums "celestial" - Orkney, five up, Orkney.

Francis Ponge's *Soap* introduced me to "procedural" writing. He had:
taken what was at hand, let it refer to itself and then tracked the
process as it would go. So I: take what is at hand (the dictionary),
pick a page at random, use the key words heading the page as "directions", find a pattern and/or flow of the words and write it down,
trying to retain as much of the procedure as possible in the prose.

Examples: 1) in the page "legion to Lent", the sound "lem" reoccurs
at various points on the page. By graphing these points, I find that
they produce a figure eight. I tell the reader about the graph and list
the words contained within the figure. Many of the "lem" words are
"fiber" words, so I also mention the various fibers that can make up
the figure. 2) the word "dog" falls between "Doctor of Philosophy" and
"doge". The dog definition is divided between technical and colloquial
ones. The other words on the page reflect this division. I note this
along with a description of the dog definition. 3) in "Oran" to
"ordain", I find that "orchestration" is related to "he raves". So,
to orchestrate the page, I rave. Letting my finger drop at random over
and over, I make a notation of the points my finger makes and later
transcribe them.

Dictionary language (words/phrases giving a direction/relation to
a source - "of or pertaining to", "peculiar to or characteristic of",
"connected with or considered from", etc.) isn't offensive to me the
way it is to many, including Ponge. In *Things*, he declares that the
function of the dictionary is to limit - ie: deaden - the language.
That's true, I suppose, when dealing with single entries and their
meaning. But what interests me is the coincidence and juxtaposition
of the words on the page in their natural formation (alphabetical
order). In reference to each other, they have a story of their own.
The technical aspect (scientific and philosophical terminology as distinct from conversational forms) of the language can be intriguing, too.
Reading the definitions is like reading a foreign language developed
specifically for English.

TINA DARRAGH

ARMANTROUT: EXTREMITIES (3 VIEWS)

Rae Armantrout, _Extremities_ (1978; The Figures, c/o Small Press Distribution, 1636 Ocean View Ave., Kensington, CA 94709; $2.50)

EACHES

The world grows more empty as we approach it. When we have entered (dealing our way), it is gone. Explicit words make this apparent, make this happen.

Rae's writing is clean. The words fill in the gaps. The edges of life are its center. There is no anguish in the thing, is there? The exact utterance of each thing is its value; it owns its hue.

Wonder is a hollow figure.

The perfection of the voice is in its attention to itself, always pressed equally to its function.

There is no fantasy, which is oblique. Instead, the simplest line is a definition, critical. The past establishes its question; later, utter.

Each line, unwasted, replenishes the voice. Clarity is engendered. The mind slows, its births are precise. The tiny phantoms bury in jumping thought.

Distinctions are attenuated by words. Objects are distinct sounds. This gets marked. Sound mindfully combines discrete objects. Humor, too, is a combinative function.

Objects are annulled by thought. Beauty is the effort to grasp (them).

Punctuation lasts what it enunciates. It impresses shape. Speed and control are movements for the purpose of delineation. The dot does not move the eye, it moves words. The words are not for other things.

Effort, even after. Minutely.

Her work is elevated by strictness, a high gesture in a low place.

It emanates from the mind that sees it in words. There is something in each letter and it cuts into the fact.

Memory is furtive. The local fact incises. The multiplicity of things contract to each small point made. Nerves hold the sounds hold the facts to place. Leave the explanation for the next event.

ALAN DAVIES

                    Going to the desert
                    is the old term

                    'landscape of zeros'

                    the glitter of edges
                    again catches the eye

                    to approach these swords!

                    lines across which
                    beings vanish/flare

                    the charmed verges of presence

EXTREMITIES. Paths lost found forgotten. Border margin beginning.
Birth/Death. Inside/Outside. She/He. Moving/Staying. Finding/Losing.
The unity of opposites, Epicene, Androgyne. According to Boehme, in the
beginning Adam was the primal Androgyne. After the Fall, God separated
female from male and the primal harmony was lost. Armantrout in these
poems wants to begin again. Like H.D., her search is for that lost
prelapserian state which may have existed only in the mind — back in the
pre-history of childhood. It is a search for harmony in a bewildering
time. GENERATION

                    We know the story

                    She turn
                    back to find her trail

                    devoured by birds.

                    The years; the
                    undergrowth

Gretel lost in the forest of generation, the undergrowth of years. Not
a word that doesn't belong. We all know the story — but we still don't
understand the undergrowth. "'Just wait Gretel, till the moon rises,
and then we will see the crumbs of bread which I have strewn about, they
will show us our way home again.' When the moon came they set out, but
they found no crumbs, for the many thousands of birds which fly about in
the woods and fields had picked them all up." Imagine the Moon then!

                    Not the city lights. We want
                        - the moon -
                                The Moon
                    none of our own doing!

Like riddles the poems in *Extremities* are terse, precise, subtle. A
riddle is a puzzle. A mis-leading. The novelty of a riddle is that by
depriving something of its name, we render it unrecognizable. A dislocation of perspective similar to the fear expressed in XENOPHOBIA (fear
that one is dreaming). In a riddle every word counts, is a sign. A
signifier. Words both hide and reveal. Fear of riddles with no
solution.

> this same riddle:
> IS IT ALRIGHT?
>
> qualm that persists
> on the bus ride
>
> "Tonight there's
> the movie"
> a woman soothes her son

A female Knight off on her quest, Armantrout has armed herself with
enigmas, paradoxes, wit, and cunning. The intensity is religious, pure
in the best sense. And it is a quest undertaken with the awareness that
in the search there is no sanctuary. In SAVED reading Lao-Tze she makes
speech a raft, and in TRAVELS thinks for a moment

> I had recovered silence
>
> The power to be
> irretrievably lost

Oliver Cromwell to the French Ambassador -- "A man never mounts so high
as when he does not know where he is going."

GRACE

> I am walking
>
> covey in silent flight

PROCESSIONAL

> The smallest
>
> distance
>
> inexhaustible

In XENOPHOBIA she isolates each fear by placing it in parenthesis as if
a printed wall could contain the idea (fear of sights not turned to words).
Again, it was the primordial Adam to whom God gave the power of naming.
Imagine a world without names! SPECIAL THEORY OF RELATIVITY

> You know those ladies
> in old photographs? Well,

```
          say one stares into your room
          as if into the void
          beyond her death in 1913.
```

In the brave new world of Death there are no names.

LXXXVI. When born they wish to live and to have dooms -- or rather to
rest, and they leave children after them to become dooms. (Heraclitus
On the Universe). The sort of paradox these poems are made of. I love
Extremities for its intelligence and curiosity. From the first poem,
the title one, the first extremity -- Armantrout stands poised at Lacan's
ecstatic limit of "Thou art that" the point where any real journey
begins. "to approach these swords!"

```
              the sentence
                    flies
```

In medieval times the idea of earthly knighthood and angelic knighthood
were intertwined (militia). They pre-supposed economy and discipline.
The medieval Latin for a knight is miles.

                                                    SUSAN HOWE

An eternal, singly framed. Distinct, illumined, on a black background.
Quiet field, empty river. Tremendous pressure surrounds the words.
Their outlines are thus forced to hold. Recall Blake's insistence on
outline -- the active principle of perception. The silence bordering
these extremities is intense.

An allegiance to the instantaneous is hard, because the mind wants to
space out, lose track of, get 'lost in thought'. Attention to signs
along the road (not monotony, but health) returns thought to the world,
to the direct object of perception.

Calling into question the grounds of a featureless continuum might be
one way of shaping it. Doubt resolves the focus.

Signs, singles. Adopt fragments in absence (total presence, as limit)
of the subject (I:eye). Speech can be a raft. Relation out can be
hesitant or warmly recognitive, as in "I liked you trying / to say", of
the difficulties involved.

Discrimination is the method of the work, an incredibly fine tuning, at
each turn proposing value. As choice, language acts. "Not...but..."
occurs as a common construction. "Not...things made for our use," allu-
sionist art in crowded gallery, "the city lights, 'She's running for her

```
```

bus'...but...the bouquet you made of doorknobs, her 'inspirations', The Moon, All that aside!"

Time and mind are disjunct, as in *Special Theory*, in experience of present as past's future beyond death, and *Zen Koan*, where present regards pre-birth past self, not as one, but "in / sixty / fish".

The present takes time. But to approach these charmed verges takes the Universe, tending to tend, O main sequence. The ideas one loves are stories known, not likely, proceeding until impulse flags. Then what's wanted's not narrative, but "A single truth now occupies the mind: / the smallest / distance / inexhaustable."

But experience of eternity is qualified by a desire to "go back soon and tell it". And so, paradoxically, destroyed by the effort to preserve it. The poignancy of this tension finds relief in speech: "What tenderness!" The punctuation is exclamatory. "All of religion, compressed in the word darling."

The compression forming these lines builds up a charge which is released when I read them.

KIT ROBINSON

WRITING AND REMEMBERING

History is a catalogue of endings but poetry speaks of being, of beginnings. Through an experience of linguistic re-creation by immersion in a semantic continuous present of simultaneities, echoes, symbols, variously shaded fragments of raw and refined perceptions, the text (and its corresponding thought process) is momentarily liberated from its history (memory) and from its history-making function (remembering). This is why poetry is uniquely free, compared to related disciplines like philosophy and psychology, from its own history. Its elements, including its formal properties, are subject to aesthetic, but not temporal, critiques. There is no linear historical conceptual development -- only a process of eroding and building.

Poetry tends to have an ambivalent relationship toward any temporal function to which it is assigned. Unlike most other human endeavors, at certain moments, often its best ones, it cloaks itself in obscurity, withdraws from everyday life and takes the form of a static, receptive object. A process made to be acted *upon*, germinative, wood and oxygen waiting to be ignited by a determinant, but not necessarily parallel, flash of thought. And this is how it transcends history and is not only to be recognized and remembered, but contemplated, like the Sphinx.

Writing as remembering is nominative, ordering, and elicits from its reading a fixed, functional relationship. But poetry can be composed of any number of continuously altered, modulated and interrelated emotional tones, purposes and intentions. These real, apparent and illusory intentions are usually consciously parodied, at least at some point in a poem, if not in its form, creating still another shifting ground of contexts.

Historicity, that is, legitimizing or authenticating the *raison d'etre* of a work or text by establishing its historical relevance or historical significance as a document or art historical event, binds language to fixed significances by ordering its syntax into descriptions of familiar or unfamiliar sequences of related perceptions or memories. Language, though bound to time like this by its passive connection with the process of recall can be made to listen to itself. Again and again heard differently, through its poetry, language directs attention to its plastic and iconographic qualities by means of a kind of lexic hovering in and around and subterranean plummeting through meaning and memory. Familiar connotations, meanings and connections fade into apparently new ones, ones otherwise too close and familiar to sense and feel.

To read poetry is to enjoy a mimetic gesticulation towards the thought process, to demand from it alternatives to ordinary remembering and comprehension. In this elusive, decorous, ceremonial absence of significant reportage, history is a minor character in a timeless masque enacted in the evolving theater of language.

NICK PIOMBINO

NON-POETRY

(We asked a number of writers to list five non-poetry books that they had read in the last few years that have had a significant influence on their thinking or writing. Below, the responses.)

STEVE BENSON :
Maggie Cassidy by Jack Kerouac.
The Red and the Black by Stendhal. *(I preferred among the translations*

the Norton red and white paperback. Memoirs of Egotism *forms a*
helpful introduction to this book.)
<u>Illuminations</u> by Walter Benjamin.
<u>Kidnapped</u> by Robert Louis Stevenson.
<u>Lazarillo de Tormes</u> *(The anonymous Spanish picaresques.)*

CRIS CHEEK :
<u>The Mime Book</u> by Claude Kipnis, edited and coordinated by Neil Kleinman,
     photos by Edith Chustka (Harper Colophon Books).
<u>Creativity and Taoism (A Study of Chinese Philosophy, Art and Poetry)</u>
     by Chang Chung-yuan (Wildwood House, London).
<u>The Mass Psychology of Fascism</u> by Wilhelm Reich, translated by Vincent
     Carfagno (Penguin-Pelican).
<u>Expanded Cinema</u> by Gene Youngblood, introduction by Buckminster Fuller.
<u>Religion and the Decline of Magic</u> by Keith Thomas (Penguin-Pelegrine).
     (choices made because of now interests rather than influence. they
     really reflect constantly influential fields of interest. others
     would include -- Image - Music - Text *by Barthes and* The Algebra of
     Need *by Eric Mottram, and* The World Turned Upside Down *by Christo-*
     pher Hill, and Preface to Plato *by Eric Havelock, and* Magritte *by*
     Bernard Noël, etc etc etc.

ABIGAIL CHILD :
<u>The World of Elementary Particles</u> by Kenneth W. Ford (1963, Xerox).
<u>Spinning Tops and Gyroscopic Motion</u> by John Perry (Dover reprint of
     last -- circa 1905 -- edition). *(A popular exposition of Dynamics of*
     Rotation.)
<u>Selected Writings of Benjamin Lee Whorf: Language, Thought & Reality</u>
     (1956, MIT Press).
<u>Pronunciation Exercises in English</u> by Clarey and Dickson (1963, revised
     edition, Simon and Schuster).
<u>The Thinking Body</u> by Mabel Todd (republication of Dance Horizons,
     Brooklyn, of circa 1935 publication).

ROBERT CREELEY
     ...but briefly: <u>Illuminations</u> and <u>Reflections</u> [by Walter Benjamin],
to first of which I was introduced by R.B. Kitaj (wouldn't you know
it...), just the political/morphological clarity, and his extraordinary powers as a literal *reader*. Charming to read *with* some one, in
that old-time fashion.

Then--almost as personal memorial, now that he's sadly dead--Donald
Sutherland, <u>Gertrude Stein: A Biography of Her Works</u>. Still for me the
most provocative book on her particular genius, with equal range as to
forms and specific cultural patterns in writing, e.g., Spanish/Ameri-
can take on Surrealism.

Then--because I just did literally read it, though god knows why it took me so long to--still, seemingly, the best book to locate Williams (other than obviously all he himself got to say--which is it forever): Mike Weaver, William Carlos Williams, The American Background--such a lovely instance of legwork *and* so much said in such compact manner-- as notes on jazz, rhythm, or surrealism will give instance.

Then Jackson MacLow called attention to November Scientific American ('78) article on children's language acquiring patterns--again much literal food for thought.

RAY DI PALMA:
The Mediterranean and the Mediterranean World in the Age of Philip II
    by Fernand Braudel, Volumes 1 & 2 (Harper Torch Books, 1975).
Samuel Johnson by W. Jackson Bate (Harcourt Brace Jovanovitch, 1977).
Nicholas Crabbe by F. R. Rolfe (New Directions, 1958).
The Great War and Modern Memory by Paul Fussell (Oxford U. Press, 1975).
A Joseph Cornell Album by Dore Ashton (Viking, 1974).
The World Backwards: Russian Futurist Books 1912-1916, edited by Susan
    P. Compton (British Museum Publications, 1978).
Sexus by Henry Miller (Grove Press, 1965).
Saul Steinberg: Exhibition Catalogue (Knopf/Whitney Museum, 1978).
Minima Moralia by Theodor Adorno (Schocken/New Left Books, 1978).

STEVE FRACCARO :
Jacques Derrida, Of Grammatology. (*Derrida's main interest for me is
    his concept of writing (without an origin). To extrapolate
    Derrida: thought is a form of writing ("originary writing without
    an origin")...music and architecture are forms of writing...the
    world explodes with cross reference...a dark blue print.*)
Roland Barthes, S/Z & Sade, Fourier, Loyola. (*Polytextuality...and a
    considerable amount of delight.*)
Ludwig Wittgenstein, Tractatus Logico-Philosophicus & Philosophical
    Investigations.
Henry Miller, Tropic of Cancer & Tropic of Capricorn. (*Everyday life
    and the sublime.*)

TED GREENWALD :
Raoul Hilberg -- The Destruction of the European Jews.
Donald Bain -- The Control of Candy Jones.
John Lear -- Recombinant DNA: The Untold Story.
Philip Andrews and Barnett St. John -- Cop Story.
Eugen Kogan -- The Theory and Practice of Hell.

LYN HEJINIAN :
1. The Art of Poetry, Paul Valéry (Pantheon Books, Bollingen Series,

`XLV, 7, 1958) & Analects, Paul Valéry (vol. 14 of same series).
2. Remembrance of Things Past, Marcel Proust, trans. C.K. Scott Mon-
      crieff (Random House).
3. two reading clusters: a) beginning with linguistic anthropology
      (Dorothy D. Lee's Freedom and Culture, Spectrum Books, 1959) which
      led to Benjamin Lee Whorf's Language, Thought and Reality and from
      there to Barthes, Jameson's The Prison-House of Language, an
      attempt at Derrida, etc. (all of which gave me to see that there
      was this to think about), and, overlapping as some of this does
      with Marxism, this reading cluster extends to include bits and
      pieces of Capital, Wm Hinton's Fanshen, etc.
                          b) readings in natural history and neurology,
      including Marston Bates' Life History of the Mosquito, Stephen
      Rose's The Conscious Brain (Knopf, 1975), Lewis Thomas' Lives of a
      Cell, Psychobiology (W.H. Freeman & Co., 1966).
4. sub-category, neglected masterpieces: Ushant, Conrad Aiken. The
      Sleepwalkers, Hermann Broch.

SUSAN HOWE :
1. The Letters of Emily Dickinson, vols 1,2,3 edited by Thomas Johnson
      (Belknap Press, Harvard University 1976).
2. The Bride Stripped Bare By Her Bachelors Even. A typographic ver-
      sion by Richard Hamilton, of Marcel Duchamp's Green Box, translated
      by George Heard Hamilton, published by Jaap Rietman Inc.; Art
      Books New York First published 1960 third -1976.
3. Tribute to Freud by HD. (David Godine, Boston 1974).
4. A Proposal For Correcting The ENGLISH TONGUE, Polite Conversation
      etc. vol 4, edited by Herbert Davis (Oxford 1973)--(contains the
      two essays, A Modest Defense of Punning and A Discourse to Prove
      the Antiquity of the English Tongue) by Jonathan Swift. Also the
      other volume in the Oxford Collected Works called Miscellaneous
      and Autobiographical Pieces, Fragments, and Marginalia.
5. Philosophy in the Tragic Age of the Greeks, by Nietzsche. Translated
      by Marianne Cowan (Henry Regnery Company, Chicago, 1962.)

P. INMAN :
Minimal Art, Gregory Battcock, Dutton, 1968.   Energy Made Visible,
Jackson Pollock, B.H. Friedman, McGraw-Hill, 1974.   Barnett Newman,
Thomas Hess, MOMA, 1971.   America's Masters, Brian O'Doherty, Random
House, 1973.   Shape of Time, George Kubler, Yale Press, 1962.

abstract: "when you start relating parts, in the first place, you're
assuming you have a vague whole- the rectangle of the canvas" (Judd)/
"the idea enters that he may not be trying to paint different pictures,
but the same picture, again a way of eliminating history" (O'Doherty on
deKooning)/ word field/ intra-picture, intra-sequence/ "brushstrokes
simply coexist side by side" (deK's Revlon period)/ "Newman's wholistic

works"/ "which is all screwed up, because you should have a definite whole and maybe no parts, or very few" (J.)/ "the order at work in his pieces... is simply order, like that of continuity, one thing after another" (Battcock on Judd)/ *Gotham News*/ rectangle of the oeuvre/ past & present- (layers)- (pictures painted on top one another)/ once (through the link of sequence) we think of space in terms of time/ "My paintings are concerned neither with the manipulation of space nor with the image, but with the sensation of time." (Newman)/ area, space, sequence, field, juxtaposition, continuity, paragraphs, opteme, finished, unfinished...

MICHAEL LALLY:

   Essays Before A Sonata, The Majority, And Other Writings By Charles Ives (selected and edited by Howard Boatwright, Norton, $3.25, paperback, 1970), while not influencing my thinking and writing too significantly, did open me up to areas in our American "heritage" that had heretofore seemed blocked at least to my appreciation. Ives' ideas on Emerson and others, as well as on music, are expressed with the same intense individuality as Ives' music itself. Unfortunately, "editor" Boatwright totally butchered Ives' style, by changing punctuation (as though Ives wouldn't know how to use devices like commas, which in the transcription of language can be and often are obviously musical signs) and even rewriting phrases and sentences. This destroyed my misconceptions that editors only fuck with the work of relatively unknowns. Boatwright defends this stupidity in his introduction with statements like this: "A literal printing of the manuscript (if such a thing were possible, considering the number of alternate words and marginal notes) would be no more than a curiosity, and unfair in its emphasis on the eccentricity of Ives' style, which has nothing to do with the seriousness of his thought." Possibly the most enlightening book I've read in years is A Distant Mirror by Barbara Tuchman (Alfred Knopf, 1978). An equally enlightening book, and for me it served as a fresh and beautifully written reminder of a period and its culture that greatly influenced my writing and thinking for years (throughout most of the 1960s), is The World of the Shining Prince: Court Life in Ancient Japan by Ivan Morris, (Penguin Books, paperback $2.95). Morris describes one of the most unusual eras in any society's cultural history -- the Japanese Heian period -- which boasted a sensibility almost "terminally mannered" (to paraphrase John Ashbery's description of a novel by Edmund White, Forgetting Helena, which in fact borrowed heavily from the literature of Heian Japan). The last book on my list, Lions and Shadows, An Autobiographical Novel by Christopher Isherwood (New Directions paperback $3.45, 1977) gave me valuable insights into a kind of life and lifestyle I could never really understand, let alone appreciate, since it represented everything I saw as oppressive by the standards of my background and family history (i.e. it is the English upper-classes who have always represented for us the worst aspects of oppressive political and social systems). Isherwood translates his and Auden's schoolboy and young man experiences into something I can try on imaginatively while I'm reading. In fact, Isherwood is in some ways in his prose like W. C. Williams is in his poetry -- relying on the concrete details and experiences of the local in time and space and syntax to convey the idea(s). Both are/were more or less sympathetic dudes from the upper or upper-middle class, and where the good doctor got down in a way through ministering and learning from the lower classes, Isherwood ministered in his own way through his attraction to lower class men. Though I enjoyed the much more "candid" reminiscences in the later Christopher and His Kind (and the guts it took to do it, after all the man is one of the few of his stature to be so honest about his sexuality as well as other things) Lions and Shadows intrigued and educated me more because of the ways it tells some of the same things only from a younger man in a more repressed period and about a more innocent and naive, as well as blatantly privileged, time in his life. *(I might just add that reading Eva Hesse by Lucy Lippard, New York University Press, confirmed a lot of the original inspiration I felt when I first encountered her work, as well as left me with a sense of urgency about completing a lot of my work and fulfilling my ideas and intentions and all.)*

GERRIT LANSING :
Blood, Benjamin Paul, Pluriverse, Marshall Jones Co, Boston, 1920.
Shea, Robert, and Wilson, Robert Anton, Illuminatus, Vols. I, II, III,
    (with Wilson, R. A., Cosmic Trigger, Pocket Books, New York, 1978,
    as afterpiece), Dell Books, New York, 1975.
Hjelmslev, Louis, Prolegomena to a Theory of Language, (Revised English
    Edition), University of Wisconsin Press, Madison, Wisc. 1969.
Deleuze, Gilles, Logique des sens, Les Editions de minuit, Paris, 1969.
Grant, Kenneth, Night Side of Eden, Frederick Muller, London, 1977.
Eckhart: Meister Eckhart, Mystic and Philosopher, Translations with
    Commentary by Reiner Schurmann, Indiana University Press, Blooming-
    ton, Ind. 1978.

HARLEY LOND :
Ways of Seeing: John Berger. Viking Press NY 1973
Photography and Language: Lew Thomas (ed). Camerawork/NFS Press San
    Francisco 1977
For a New Novel: Alain Robbe-Grillet. Grove Press NY 1965
Relativity and Cosmology: William J. Kaufmann III. Harper & Row NY 1973
Essential Works of Marxism: Bantam Books New York 1961.

JACKSON MAC LOW
1. The Unperfect Society: Beyond the New Class, Milovan Djilas,

translated by Dorian Cooke (Harcourt Brace World, 1969); *sequel to The New Class (Praeger, 1954)*.

2. The Principles of Art History: The Problem of the Development of Style in Later Art by Heinrich Wölfflin (First edition, 1915; Dover reprint, 1932).

3. The Waves & Night and Day by Virginia Woolf.

4. For a New Liberty by Murray Rothbard (NY: Macmillan, 1973).

5. Process and Reality by Alfred North Whitehead (Macmillan, 1929; reprinted Humanities Press, 1957).

6. The Spanish Anarchists: The Heroic Years, 1868-1936 by Murray Bookchin (Free Life Editions, 1977).

7. Voline: 1917--The Russian Revolution Betrayed & The Unknown Revolution--Kronstadt 1921 and Ukraine 1918-1921, translated by Holley Cantine (Libertarian Book Club, 1954 and 1955).

8. The Great Soviet Encyclopedia (Macmillan translation, ongoing).

(The inclusion of works on this list does not necessarily indicate endorsement of all the authors' ideas. Each of these works has influenced me in a somewhat different way--not necessarily as the authors may have desired.)

KIRBY MALONE & CHRIS MASON:
Anthony Wilden --- System and Structure: Essays in Communication and Exchange (published in 1972 by Tavistock Publications Ltd; distributed in the US by Harper & Row, Scranton, Pa.)

WILL WORK WHEN ONE TRIES TO CROSS THE SPATIAL, COMMUNICATIONAL, OR TEMPORAL BOUNDARIES SET UP BY CLOSURE.

I am attached to her and the her changes

Oedipus' murderous feelings towards his father do not come from nowhere.

I know he thinks I'm out of place which I feel strongly I am out of place there when I have no work I try to find things to do something to straighten I feel lonely not lonely I don't feel lonely I feel I have to straighten something it's not the not having something to do

articulated on the myth of the expert, the myth of the 'subject-who-is-supposed-to-know'.

my boss it's his place I'm out of it who knows exactly what I'm doing I can't help thinking about her to straighten something it's not straightening I have to do it's more being in commodity fetishism the worker gradually losing its personality I think about her even if I think about her I'm thinking about her

involved when Lévi-Strauss reduces the woman to a sign (thus confusing female, woman, and sister; confusing energy and information; organism, person, and role; entity and relationship)

I work at a place where I work and I'm not me I have a beard I'm the only worker with a beard which is strange my friends all have beards none of my coworkers do

In other words, it is the hallmark of 'normal' and 'neurotic' language, both of which maintain the distinction between the (analog) thing-presentations of the unconscious and the (digital) word-presentations of language.

mine was hers the everyday things mixed up very exciting very happy very businessman very market very lift very dirt very not so good very more very snow very around very said it very present very night very two very sound very scheming very done very worries very buzzer very bed very day very light very guess very sustaining very dependent very before very every day very on very career very was very gestures very such very not very clear very never very be very the very last very the very never very car very push very warmer very London very complete very soon very irresolute days I feel so

To paraphrase Zeno: "At whatsoever particular spot of the universe of discourse one settles down, one ends by becoming poisoned; it is essential to keep moving"

cough straighten clarify stir express reprieves raged distort freeze bidden knead loom toast rue utter skewed opt waste sever injecting closed bale coating blow soften finned enters sift blinks tidy say

In other words, the nip denotes the bite, but does not denote what would be denoted by the bite.

around the morning waiting gestures no clothes someone else duration and process the funny story knows he said it

Although language, compared with crying, would seem to offer a huge gamut of possibilities of 'explaining what you mean', it is semantically and structurally much more limited than crying as a form of communication ..... by its demand that all communication be 'rational', by its insistent digitalization of analog relationships, our own culture is precisely one of those that becomes trapped in the contradictions between its ideology (which valorizes the digital) and its socio-economic reality (which is both digital and analog).

man in bed no clothes on you're not presentable no clothes on

(the italicized sections are from Marshall Reese, Story, some of which has been published in E pod, 3022 Abell Ave, Baltimore, Md. 21218, & in Juice, 4629 Keswick Road, Baltimore 21218; photocopies of the original 5x5 ft. (approx.) handwritten sheet can be ordered through E pod.)

TOM MANDEL

Sirk on Sirk: Interviews with John Halliday, (NY Viking 1972)
Charles Baudelaire: A Lyric Poet in the Era of High Capitalism by
    Walter Benjamin (London New Left Books 1973)
Bottom: On Shakespeare, Louis Zukofsky, etc
Le schizo et les langues, Louis Wolfson (Gallimard Paris 1970)
Le bleu du ciel (and/or La part maudite), Georges Bataille (Paris
    Gallimard 197?)

*(In the case of someone like myself, in whom poetry began dimly
envisioned 6 - 7 years ago and only in the last 3 took up as writing,
what that was!, a better list wd see to explain that set of steps:
books of poetry or read as poetry (here Lacan and, 2d time thru,
Hegel). Titles listed above, the reader may rightly be cautioned,
are by way of outline (of reading taking place ((of poetry)) within):
of a method of meditation.)*

STEVE MC CAFFERY :

Jacques Derrida: Of Grammatology, translated by G.C. Spivak (Baltimore,
    Johns Hopkins Press 1974).
Gilles Deleuze and Félix Guattari: Anti-Oedipus: Capitalism & Schizo-
    phrenia (Viking 1978).
Fredric Jameson: Marxism and Form (Princeton 1971).
Michel Foucault: Language, Counter-Memory, Practice (Cornell University
    Press 1977).
George Bataille: Eroticisme (U.S. title: Death and Sensuality. N.Y.,
    Walker & Co. 1962).
*(Plus: all & any issues of: Semiotext(e), Yale French Studies, and Sub-
Stance.)*
*For the book that's told me best how not to write: Theodore Enslin:
Synthesis (North Atlantic Books 1975): the product of a fourth rate
mind with access to a third rate technique.*

DOUGLAS MESSERLI :

*The following five "non-poetry" books have had a direct influence on
    my writing and thinking:*
    Ezra Pound, Gaudier Brezska (New Directions, 1974, 1978).
    Gertrude Stein, How Writing Is Written, ed. by Haas (Black Sparrow,
        1977).
    Jacques Derrida, Of Grammatology, trans. by Spivak (Johns Hopkins
        Univ. Press, 1977).
    Eugène Minkowski, Lived Time: Phenomenological and Psychopathologi-
        cal Studies, trans. by Metzel (Northwestern Univ. Press, 1970).
    Bernadette Mayer, Memory (North Atlantic Books, 1975).

*But, I might also mention Herbert N. Schneidau's Ezra Pound: The Image
and the Real (Louisiana State Univ. Press), J. Hillis Miller's*

Poets of Reality (Harvard Univ. Press), Sarah Lawall's *Critics of Consciousness* and Marjorie Perloff's *Frank O'Hara: Poet Among Painters* (George Braziller)--critical works which have helped me to have a clearer perception of issues in contemporary poetics and criticism.

CHARLES NORTH :
1. George Wilderstein, Chardin. N.Y. Graphic Society, 1969.
2. Frank O'Hara, Standing Still and Walking in New York. Grey Fox Press, Bolinas, 1974.
3. Gabriel García Márquez, One Hundred Years of Solitude, trans. Gregory Rabassa. Avon, 1970.
4. Leo Steinberg, Other Criteria. Oxford U. Press, 1972.
5. World Almanac and Book of Facts for 1972.

MICHAEL PALMER :
I guess I have chosen these five to stand for all possible alternative sets of 5.
Louis Wolfson Le Schizo et les Langues Gallimard Paris 1970
Ludwig Wittgenstein Remarks on Colour University of California Press Berkeley 1977
Max Ernst Une Semaine de Bonté Dover New York 1976
Yvonne Rainer Work 1961-73 The Presses of the Nova Scotia College of Art and Design and New York University Halifax/New York 1974
Thomas S. Kuhn The Structure of Scientific Revolutions (second edition) University of Chicago Press Chicago 1970
(I am tempted of course to include a ghost set, with writings of Frances Yates, Henry Corbin, Blanchot, Charles Rosen, Sacvan Bercovitch, Gershom Scholem, G-C Lichtenberg, Benjamin, Peirce, Cavell, Schoenberg's letters, et al, but I won't)

RON SILLIMAN :
Important as books are, it is being that determines consciousness. Books can & do serve mediationally, presenting possibilities of structure where they might not otherwise be perceived. But, unless one is so trapped by the disease of one-sided development, the proposition's limits are its one truly interesting aspect. A *political* question wld have been: how has the necessity of earning a living (& perhaps supporting a family) affected the form & substance of your writing? Or: to what extent do writers functionally require a conceptual workplace, meaning not a room of one's own, but *other workers*? & to what extent can correspondence substitute for one? But this idea of books (wch smacketh of *WIN* magazine & its anarcho-social-democrats), as such, implies a relation of books to one's life wch does not, *cannot*, exist, *at this present moment,* outside of a beingness wch is not bourgeois (& hardly that of the renegade bourgie who breaks away to reaffiliate her-

self w/ the workers).

That said, some books do count. For me, the major one has been *SB 42* (The Uniform Determinate Sentencing Act of 1976), wch substituted California's feudal indeterminate criminal punishment mechanism for one in keeping w/ the age of capitalism, inscribed totally w/in a metaphysics of identity (equality, substitutability, exchange, fixity, etc.). To achieve even the limited goals any communist might seek within the framework of capitalist electoral politics, I had to take on some specific responsibility for the latter: if you should ever be sentenced to consecutive terms for multiple offenses, for example, you will be subjected to a collaboration I partook in. I think about that a lot.

Others: <u>Dialectical Materialism</u>, by Henri Lefebvre (it shld be subtitled How to Think); <u>Charles Baudelaire: A Lyric Poet in the Era of High Capitalism</u>, by Walter Benjamin (New Left Books & hard to get in the U.S.), 3 drafts of the uncompleted Paris Arcades project, showing how the best critical mind of the century workd *in action*; <u>History and Class Consciousness</u>, by George Lukacs (esp. "Reification and the Consciousness, section III"); <u>Proprioception</u>, by Charles Olson (read it w/ LeFebvre!); <u>Visions of Cody</u>, by Jack Kerouac (*the* great American novel); <u>Ethnopoetics: A First International Symposium</u>, ed. by Michel Benamou & Jerry Rothenberg; all of Marx, but esp. <u>Capital, v. 1</u>, <u>the Eighteenth Brumaire</u> &, with Engels, <u>The German Ideology</u>; <u>Language of the Self</u>, by Jacques Lacan and Derrida's <u>Of Grammatology</u> (brilliant & all wrong) are both useful, but skip the translator's essays; <u>Tristes Tropique</u> by Claude Levi-Strauss (just for the chapter "Sunset"): <u>The Structure of Scientific Revolutions</u>, by Thomas S. Kuhn; <u>Gravity's Rainbow</u>, by Thomas Pynchon; &, even tho they *are* poems, nobody will know it: the "My" pieces by David Bromige.
(1) Only a fool wld reduce such a list to five;
(2) Language is exchange, is the most pervasive politics there is.
The next important book for me to learn is <u>Linguistics and Economics</u>, by Ferruccio Rossi-Landi (1975, Mouton, The Hague).

JOHN TAGGART :
1. Walter J. Ong: <u>The Presence of the Word: Some Prolegomena for Cultural & Religious History</u>. Simon/Schuster, 1970.
2. Leonard Stein, ed: <u>Style and Idea: Selected Writings of Arnold Schoenberg</u>. St. Martin's Press, 1975.
3. Eric Havelock: <u>Preface to Plato</u>. Harvard U. Press, 1963.
4. Raymond Bernard Blakney: <u>Meister Eckhart, a modern translation</u>. Harper Torchbook, 1957.
5. Magnus Wenninger: <u>Polyhedron Models</u>. Cambridge University, 1974.
   (& *if allowed a bonus selection: Nature and Culture in the Iliad by James M. Redfield. Univ. of Chicago Press, 1978.*)

JOSEPH TIMKO :

1. Visual Thinking, by Rudolf Arnheim. Berkeley: University of California Press; 1969.
2. Invisible Cities, by Italo Calvino. New York: Harcourt Brace Jovanovich; 1974. (Translated by William Weaver).
3. Behind the Mirror, a search for a natural history of human knowledge, by Konrad Lorenz. New York: Harcourt Brace Jovanovich; 1977. (Translated by Ronald Taylor).
4. The Prose of the World, by Maurice Merleau-Ponty. Evanston: Northwestern University Press; 1973. (Translated by John O'Neill).
5. The Growl of Deeper Waters, by Denis de Rougemont. Pittsburgh: University of Pittsburgh Press; 1976. (Translated by Samuel Hazo with Beth Luey).

---

from THE OUTRAGE AGAINST WORDS

Screams. They begin yet again. I hear them, yet hear nothing. I'd like to know what they are saying. I knew. Now I seek what censors them within me.

Revolt acts; indignation seeks to speak. From the start of my childhood, only reasons for becoming indignant: the war, the deportation, the Indochinese war, the Korean war, the Algerian war... and so many massacres, from Indonesia to Chile via Black September. There's no language to describe that. There's no language because we live in a bourgeois world, where the vocabulary of indignation is exclusively moral -- well, it's those morals which massacre and make war. How can one turn their language against them when one finds oneself censored by one's own language?

For a long time, I've not known how to formulate that question, and now I can't find words to answer it. Not that it requires other words than ours, but that they arrange themselves spontaneously according to structures which correspond to the moral order of society.

Language, like the State, has always served the same people. We ought to distrust all of which the bourgeois say: With this system, at least, we can speak. This system is already a traitor even if it has not betrayed. In the context of order, in dialogue with it, one can only serve it.

The police are even in our mouths.

In one's own solitude, one only holds a dialogue with oneself to stylize oneself.

One does not write in order to say something, but to define a place where no one will be able to declare what hasn't taken place.

Censorship gags. It reduces to silence. But it doesn't do violence to language. Only the abuse of language can violate it, by distorting it. Bourgeois power bases its liberalism on the absence of censorship, but it has constant recourse to the abuse of language. Its tolerance is the mask of an otherwise oppressive and effective violence. The abuse of language has a double effect: it saves appearances, and even reinforces its appearance, and it shifts the place of censorship so cleverly that one no longer notices it. Or to put it another way, through the abuse of language, bourgeois power is made to pass for what it is not: a non-constraining power, a "human" power, and its official policy which standardizes the value of words, in fact empties them of meaning -- whence a verbal inflation, ruining communications within the community, and in the same way censoring it. Perhaps, in order to express the second effect, it's necessary to create the word SENSURESHIP, which by referring to the other would indicate the deprivation of sense, not of speech. Deprivation of sense is the most subtle form of brain-washing, for it operates without the victim's knowledge. And the information cult refines that deprivation even more by seeming to stuff us with knowledge.

Freedom of expression is evidently dependant on the state of language. Apparently, I can say what I like, but in reality I can only do so within the limits of this state -- a state that current usage of language conceals from us. The words, it seems, are there, always available, always equal to themselves. We use them so spontaneously, and they're at our disposal so naturally, that we cannot suspect them. They're a currency which seems unable to be false, at least at the specie level. How therefore are we to perceive the sensureship? It's true that words are words and that sensureship only insinuates itself in the game of their signifieds, but the words we have abused, abuse in their turn. Whence, at this point, the appearance of a new ambiguity: sensureship which acts on us through words (while censorship acts through us against words) acts in other respects on words with a sensureship effect: it obliterates their significance, that's to say, their matter, their body. Thus we discover that the moral order aims at erasing its materiality in every being, in every thing.

Shit: up to what age did I dare not say that word? And how many other coarse words thus forbidden? All the words of the body. Good taste is one of the morality police. It serves it. It squeezes it round our throats and over our eyes. Good taste is a way of adapting the death of others into the forgetting. And even here, I experience my impotence to chase out my own. How can I treat my sentence so that it refuses the articulation of power? It would necessitate a language which, in itself, was an insult to oppression. And more than an insult, a NO. How to find a language unusable by the oppressor? A syntax that would send back the spiked words and tear apart the language of all the Pinochets? I write. I have cries in return. There is no liberal power: there's only a smarter way of fucking us. For every televised fireside conversation, each of us should have replied with a parcel of shit posted to the great shit at the Elysée. Who would salvage that language?

Writing, trying to write, the primordial question becomes: how to get rid of this? Bury syntax, comrades, it stinks! Okay, but we make sentences even so. Go on and speak without taking on a subject, a verb, etc. We seek dodges. We change our seduction. We even ask the reader to lend a hand instead of always letting it be. The great thing is that we are among the bourgeoisie and that, under such a regime, there are only the morals which can serve the collective bond. Only, in order for the morals to function, the sentence must also function, and the words truly say what they say. Well -- that functioning is rotten -- rotten since our fathers massacred the workers, the colonized and even their brothers, all the while continuing to play the good father. Your civilization has big teeth, o fathers, so big that it ended by gobbling itself. Now, we must pick over the pile of shit and each seek his piece of tongue/language (langue). No history, everything's putrified!

I write whilst saying to myself: I don't want to be possessed -- and yet they trample on my back. I write against meaning, and I write to produce a meaning. Always the same overload, and the body is exhausted -- yes, the body of words burst beneath the weight. I'd like now to work on the level of the sound of language. Or perhaps to *miswrite* (mécrire) as Denis Roche says, crying so rudely: "Leave your tongues, little fathers (my tongue, my tongue, shit), eat your tongues, old dogs, while there's still time!" But there's no more time. And that squawks, squawks in our throats, while what would like to rise, tumbles and falls in the hole.

(Excerpted from Glenda George's translations from Noël's Le Château de Cène in Curtains, 12 Foster Clough, Hebden Bridge, West Yorkshire HX7 5QZ England)

BERNARD NOËL

SUBMISSION OF RELEVANT MANUSCRIPTS WELCOME

L=A=N=G=U=A=G=E

Number 7. (Vol. 2, No. 1)   March 1979.

Bruce Andrews & Charles Bernstein, Editors.

Subscriptions -- One year (four issues in 1979) for $4.
              Institutions: $8.

L=A=N=G=U=A=G=E is supported solely by subscriptions
and donations.

All queries, submissions, and checks to:
Charles Bernstein, 464 Amsterdam Ave, New York, NY 10024.

(C) 1979 by L=A=N=G=U=A=G=E

Distributed with the cooperation of the Segue Foundation.

ANNOUNCEMENTS:

"So disappointed..." by Bruce Andrews (published as *A Hundred Posters #34,* 1978; $1 from 689 E. 17th St, Brooklyn, NY 11230).

SENSES OF RESPONSIBILITY by Charles Bernstein; $2 from Tuumba Press,
2639 Russell, Berkeley, CA 94705. (Third Series, six issues for $6).

Getting Ready To Have Been Frightened by Bruce Andrews (in *Roof #8*,
with long works by Seaton, Ward, & Eigner; $3 from 300 Bowery,
NY, NY 10012).

DECIPHERING AMERICA, a travelling collection -- Michael Gibbs, ed.,
with work by MacLow, Baldessari, Rothenberg, etc. & sections of
LEGEND ☆; $7.50 from Kontexts, Eerste van der Helststraat 55,
Netherlands.

Now available from L=A=N=G=U=A=G=E Distributing Service: *Intending
A Solid Object: A Study of Objectivist Poetics* by John Taggart. A
photocopy of this 226 page Ph.D. dissertation -- focussing on
Louis Zukofsky -- is available for $15.82.

L=A=N=G=U=A=G=E

NUMBER 8   JUNE 1979

WRITING AND IMAGING

Because remembering is motile (self-generating), it constantly juxtaposes images and fragments of thought spontaneously into the thought
process. For this reason, remembering continually transforms the effect
of specific associations and images on the meanings or symbolic values
we assign to them as we write and reread what is written. Since remembering causes such transformations by overlaying, condensing, and dis-
placing associations, this process prevents permanent linking of images
to specific associations. Such mutability as to the length of time
images may be linked to specific associations in the thought process
also makes it possible, in writing, by such methods as juxtaposition,
aural association, repetition, and physical placement in the text, to
alter their character, symbolic value or relationship to the composition
as a whole (their "scale"). Written images, as mental projections, are
continually re-scaled against other images by the transformation of
lexical associations as the composition proceeds. The harmonic, rhythmic and symbolic value of images undergo changes in scale depending on
the lexical and aural associations chosen by the reader or writer to be,
at any given moment, their signal source or "key".
    Of all types of writing, poetic discourse, like the psychoanalytic
technique of free association, most tends to cause the experience of
remembering to be idiosyncratic, personal, and dehistoricized. By the
latter term, I mean that the stories or fantasies elaborated from the
texts or associations may be constructed or deconstructed at any given
moment by current associations. The method of free association flattens
out the relative value of images by placing them in a one-to-one relationship to consecutive fragments of ideas, unlike purposive forms of
thought patterns fixed by sequential ordering. Chance and random
sequencing of images can have a similar re-synchronizing / de-synchroni-
zing effect, by causing shifts between coded message readings of the
fragments and the intermittently phased current "readings" of present
images looped into signal words and thoughts. Specifically the difficulty in poetry with imaging is that after-images often tend to be
sustained in remembering much longer than is necessary for the most
musical, rhythmically modulant grouping of sequential or juxtaposed
signs. Too clear a statement, meaning or purpose might scale down, for

instance, a group of signs so radically as to make their source over-tones too minimal to have any impact on the composition as a whole.

When word, object, sign and trace synesthetically embrace the mind and the page, associating symbol with its mark, title, token, signal, and glyph, symbolic values' rigid hold on meaning is weakened. The image's source then can again have a monitoring, signalizing effect on the way meanings and intensities of meaning are assigned. The modally transformable image is one that is subject to the shadowing, tinting effects of one meaning juxtaposed against another, layered on and under it, like the creation of an approximate sign in lieu of foregoing any possibility of recollection. Or one fixed sequence of meanings may be transformed into another register by creating new associations to a mutation or variation of the text, like reversing one part of the sequence and allowing one set of symbols before that part and after that part to remain the same. In writing this may be an alteration of syntax within a customary phrase which can be translated back again within the thought process simultaneously or almost so, as the text is read, just as an inflection or modification in speech might entirely alter the character of an expression in relation to a purely syntactical form of the same idea. Again, the resulting transmutative effect would be caused by the feedback between a meaning and an intentionally added reframing of its tonal value affecting a shift in its remembered, historicized meaning.

NICK PIOMBINO

————————————————
————————————————

JEROME ROTHENBERG: ON HIS ANTHOLOGIES

> *The exciting thing about all this is that as it is new it is*
> *old and as it is old it is new, but now really we have come*
> *to be in our way which is an entirely different way.*
> -- Gertrude Stein, "Narration"

It seems to me that I've been making anthologies for as long as I've been making poems *per se*. I used to do them in my head because no compendium, no gathering was available to help me map the territory that was opening up to us. As a kid I inherited a large desk with a sheet of glass on top, beneath which I would slip in pages of poems--my own & others'--& pictures, etc. that I had been coming across in the stuff I was reading. I used to arrange them to form "shows" of works that seemed, by juxtaposition, to inform each other. I also typed up poems from different places & times & kept them in a series of folders marked *anthology*.

That was from high school days & stopped sometime in college, when I
started to *buy* books & be deceived by other people's arrangements.

When I reawakened in the later 1950s I discovered Blake saying: "I
must either create my own 'system' or be trapped in another's"--for which
you might substitute the word "anthology." (The danger of being trapped
in your own system as well is more subtle but nohow out of the picture.)
I got quickly into doing my own press (Hawk's Well) & magazine (Poems
from the Floating World). But the magazine was really an anthology & I
subtitled it, in my mind at least, "an ongoing anthology of the deep
image." In it I brought together contemporary work with work from elsewhere that I felt was along the same track. The idea was that we weren't
doing something new (which we were) but were getting back in our own
terms to fundamental ways of seeing & languaging from which we (the
larger "we" of the western enterprise) had long been cut off.

I otherwise dislike anthologies--the ones, I mean, that perpetuate
the orders of a limited past & by so doing hold back the real work of
the present. On the whole I feel better about the kind of anthology that
presents a new move in poetry, like a well conceived magazine or like a
group show in the visual arts. But, except for the contemporary side of
America a Prophecy, I haven't felt myself pulled in that direction either
but remain distrustful of the rigidities & career tactics implicit in the
form. My own concern has been with interpretations of past & present--
the present foremost but not sufficient in itself. In other words I've
looked for a way of measuring our works & selves against the possibilities of a poetics that's big enough to account for human creativity,
human language-making over the broadest span available. I have an idea
of history--or a feel for it--that guides me & that changes in the
process of pulling it together.

David Antin describes me (both in the anthologies & in poems like
Poland/1931) as "walking backwards ... moving away from the things that
he's leaving ... but keeping his eyes on them while backing toward the
new terrain, which I suppose he only sees directly when it joins the rest
behind him." The perspective, which seems true enough to my experience
(if you add a little forward twisting of the head from time to time), led
me (with hints from predecessors like Tzara & others) to the discovery
of lines between past & present, lines overlooked before that transmitted
a crypto-tradition (or series of such) throughout the world. The lines
led from poem to poem like strings of light--from past to present or,
when I turned my head, from present to past. What I saw as poetry was
conditioned by what we make as poetry today. The question invariably
comes up: why are those sounds in the Navajo chant taken as a "poem"?
And the answer: because Hugo Ball or Kurt Schwitters (or you name them)
opened that domain for us. But when they did they also pointed to a
possible human continuity that had been broken or at least obscured: a
non-semantic form of utterance to which they were now calling our atten-

tion. I have, in taking a look for myself, only continued the process, maybe made some of it more overt.

For this, "anthology" seemed like a terrific instrument, as a means for exploring & keeping before us the dimensions of our humanness--even where our explorations lead us to a language seemingly devoid of meanings. I was drawn first to a search for instances ("primitive" & "archaic") of what was, what seemed--if anything--an overly meaning-full area of mind: the world of "images," of what James Hillman more recently speaks of as the "royal road of soul-making" (Keats' term), or image-making, where "to 'be in soul' is to experience the fantasy in all realities & the basic reality of fantasy." I knew it would be there & I sighted it: the multiple ways it shows up under the turns & twists of the particular cultures that attend to it.

Yet once I was into <u>Technicians of the Sacred</u>, the discoveries expanded in the process of searching them out. In particular I began to assemble--under section titles like "A Book of Extensions" & "A Book of Events"--works that were different from but strangely like our own experiments with language, structure & performance. In 1964 I had started a group of my own pared-down quasi-minimal pieces called "Sightings" that didn't need more than a word or two to be operative:

Cages (i)	*Cages (iv)*	*Cages (vii)*
Wires.	*Summer.*	*Cages.*
Cages (ii)	*Cages (v)*	
Pretending.	*Summermoon.*	
Cages (iii)	*Cages (vi)*	
Moon.	*Summerflies.*	

And at the same time I could spot a similar process in Aboriginal (Australian) song-making:

Fire   *Fire*
Flame   *Ashes*
.

Urination
Testes
Urination
.

Loincloth
(red)
Loincloth
(white)
Loincloth
(black)

| *"penis"* | *incisure* | *incisure* |
| *penis* | *penis* | *semen* |

Or, watching Hannah Weiner's flag-code poems, say, my attention was turned simultaneously to African drum language or Plains Indian hand-language poems or Pomo Indian flag & dream language, etc. Dada & Futurist "sound poems" pointed to American Indian ones (Tzara, I later found, had made the point explicitly & fully in relation to African & Maori work), & it was possible to draw from that tribal experience by a process of "translation by composition," to bring new forms into our own language:

> *Zzmmmm 're lovely N nawu nnnn but some are & are at my howzes*
> *nahht bahyeenahtnwing but nawu nohwun baheegwing*

& a hint here too of those occasions in which event precedes meaning.

In all of this there are two things, at least two, that have been operative for me: a fidelity to the past & a fidelity to the present; & the balance doesn't come easy or maybe, in any single instance, doesn't come at all. And a third thing, which I would be less than honest to disguise--that I've felt (in maybe all the anthologies but <u>Revolution of the Word</u>) a sense of the book as a poem, a large composition operating by assemblage or collage: my own voice emerging sometimes as translator, sometimes as commentator, but still obedient to the other voices, whether "out there" or "in here." In <u>A Big Jewish Book</u> I've carried it (or it's carried me) the furthest: a bigger space & less "my own" than <u>Poland/ 1931</u>, say, in which I was likewise using procedures like assemblage. The range (unlike <u>Poland</u>) is the totality of the imaginably "jewish," both discovered & invented; & the collages & commentaries are more varied & personal & run right through the book (not reserved for a special section only). That follows, I suppose, from the assumption that my own participation here is clearer--at least different--than in <u>Pumpkin</u> or <u>Technicians</u>.

The space is big enough to do it all, but in the end it isn't the idea of (so-called) "jewishness" that most concerns me--rather a specific set of language plays, feats of word magic & language-centeredness (in its most profound sense) that come to a visible point within the illusion of the ethnically specific (the Indian in <u>Shaking the Pumpkin</u>, the Jewish here, etc.). What it brings me to in this one (the third of the volumes responding to *ethnos*) is a place where I can deal with the grapheme, the written word & image as such, which seems suddenly to be as primal as speech is--in the sense that all language doings are present in our first emergences as human beings. Or, as I quote Jabès there: "The book is as old as water & fire."

Having gotten that far, I can now go back to the worlds of <u>Technicians</u> & <u>Pumpkin</u> & find it there also, can play with what intrigues me most in Derrida, that wild statement that "no reality or concept would correspond to the expression 'society without writing.'" The issue, then, has

always been language--language & reality, nothing else--& the dichotomy
of speaking & writing is, if no further specified, another con to keep
us from our wholeness. Concerns like that--of language & wholeness--
would seem to hold the work together; at least if you want a sense of
where I'm going.

JEROME ROTHENBERG

ROTHENBERG ANTHOLOGIES BIBLIOGRAPHY: _Technicians of the Sacred:_
A Range of Poetries from Africa, America, Asia, & Oceania (1968).
Shaking the Pumpkin: Traditional Poetry of the Indian North Americas
(1972). _America a Prophecy: A New Reading of American Poetry from Pre-_
Columbian Times to the Present (1973, with George Quasha). _Revolution_
of the Word: A New Gathering of American Avant Garde Poetry 1914-1945
(1974). _A Big Jewish Book: Poems & Other Visions of the Jews from_
Tribal Times to Present (1978, with Harris Lenowitz & with Charles Doria).

"A"-24

The difficulties "A"-24 imposes on its performers and audience are enormous. They stem directly from Zukofsky's poetics: "An integral / Lower
limit speech / Upper limit music." The words function two ways at once:
as phonemes, and as syntax, meaning, story.
     The structure of the piece insists on language's double ply.
There's music playing, Handel's [Bach, Z's expected choice, wd have been
too 'good', too complicated & distracting?], sturdy, straight-forward
rhythm, clear never quite to the point of obviousness, the vertical
architecture (harmonies) and the horizontal (melody, counterpoint)
always hearable. 4 voices (Thought, Drama, Story, Poem) are scored
into this steady pulse as precisely as if the piece were a quintet for
strings and keyboard. Phonetically, the words are treated as music.
     But, quoting Act I, Scene I, "Blest / Infinite things / So many /
Which confuse imagination / Thru its weakness / To the ear / Noises. / Or
harmony / Delights / Men to madness / " (Spinoza), the syntactic side gets
stretched. It's often difficult to speak the meanings vividly due to
the number of rests scored into each vocal line. And when the musical
rhythm is quick enough to allow the line to near speech, the listener
has the problem of the vertical overlay of the other 3 voices. [Occa-
sionally (end of first scene) different voices splice without much overlay to sound _one_ multi-syntactic phrase/sentence (a bit like Webern),
but it's an exception. Not the point of the piece.]

The theory of language approaching music should allow for an approachable 'verbal harmony'. But the analogy misleads. Discounting externals (timbre, octave spacing, etc.) music (standard Western for the moment, the kind Z seemed mainly concerned with) works with a vocabulary of 12 tones, units. English uses, say, 300 phonemes, and they aren't the point, but rather the 500,000 words that are elusively pinned to them. Not to mention syntax/sentences.

Language doesn't occur in time the way music does. Music is strictly sequence, absolutely dependent on time. Language merely uses time to embody itself in a string of phonemes, the meaning occurring both during the sounds, and after they have vanished. In music, a vertical cross-section is unambiguous at every point. The units are instantly 'transparent', so to speak. A *g* sounds like a *g*, always, thus allowing Bach to write such complicated single voices and put as many as 6 of them together into such exciting and 'inevitable' harmonic order, an ability Zukofsky loved him for.

But language doesn't work that way. A phoneme doesn't sound like a word, a verb won't necessarily reveal itself as such until some, or many, more phonemes have sounded. Phonemes, the units of 'verbal music', aren't transparent, can't be superimposed without ambiguity. What the ear tends to do on first hearing "A"-24 is switch rapidly from voice to voice. The quality of all 4 modes of Zukofsky's writing is immediately and ubiquitously apparent, his 'sincerity' [see "An Objective", II], his care in choosing and joining words.

But to fully appreciate the rhymes, harmonies, congruences takes repeated hearings, reading each part separately, joining them to their original contexts. "A"-24 echoes minutely and vastly. There are immediately hearable phonetic rhymes, syntactic rhymes (e.g. pp. 167-8, Thought: "in case he should attempt an escape"; Drama: "but now I go"; Poem: "not many of us will get out of it alive."), but many more echoes, repetitions, allusions that are widely separated. The most compelling congruences are the largest. In the last section, Fugues: Thought: Henry Adams' life/writing; Story: a particular instance of Z's life/writing a single sentence; Drama: Z's dramatization of himself as a young man; Poem: nature as creator/created. Plus Adams' marriage / Z's marriage / the Son's romance with the Girl, etc., etc., *etc.*

Ultimately, hearing "A"-24 will lead to the totality of Zukofsky's work. As he said, a poet writes one work all his life. "A"-24 really is "Celia's L.Z. Masque," a most accurate portrait of him. [Not sure, by the way, how much of the scoring and/or text selection is hers/his.]

Clearly, everybody hears all the *sound* of the piece. But Zukofsky is trying to hook up the physical instantaneous unconscious undistortable act of hearing with the fullest possible range of thought (all of a life). Performing and hearing "A"-24 presupposes a thorough knowledge of Z's work, an ecstatically dilated time sense in which every syllable continues sounding until they all have resolved each other, and an eternity in which the whole work is present in any of its sounds. A properly ambitious conclusion to "A".

(Louis Zukofsky's "A"-24 was performed by Kit Robinson (Thought), Steve Benson and Carla Harryman (Drama; Cousin, Father, Attendant D, Doctor, Son -- Steve; Nurse, Girl, Attendant R, Mother, Aunt -- Carla), Lyn Hejinian (Story), Barrett Watten (Poem), and Bob Perelman (piano, should have been harpsichord) in April 1978 at the Grand Piano, San Francisco, and later elsewhere in California).

BOB PERELMAN

DREYER

The writing changed my life. I was thinking how my affections would be thrown out, my feelings would be cast aside or just internalized. I know for some writers it makes them keep thinking, but I'm interested in the rhythm of words, and how combined we receive their story. Like when someone asks if "ya get the picture" and you do. I'm not a very intellectual writer, yet I feel I learned to think when I started to write. I need to emphasize my feelings and thoughts -- make them clear to others. The way words grow out of words and phrases, light on other words -- an icey voice. This happens when I start to write and when I forget myself. This is what is most important to me. I think the thoughts form themselves when I lose myself in the writing. I'm learning, making it clearer I like to get carried away by the words -- but I need to be understood not hide by abstractions, vagueness or drama. I need to know it's real.

LYNNE DREYER

LYNNE DREYER -- "SPECIFIC RUBIES"

All of Lynne Dreyer's work is concerned with the unusual but somehow inherently sensual relationships between otherwise disparate words and phrases and images and even letters and syllables and the "logic" they can be made (or seen) to "represent." These concerns are shared by many of the writers discussed in these pages in every issue, but where most of them communicate, even at times telegraph, a kind of intellectual imposition behind the structuring of their language choices, Dreyer's work seems to continue to appear intuitive, and this gives a somehow softer, more sensual edge to it, as though the insistence of more archly structural work had been transformed into a seductiveness, but not physicl except in the physicality of the letters and words, and images as well, for her work does often rely on imagery, but an imagery that is as disjointed and abruptly personal as the surrealists had hoped they might achieve but rarely seemed to (at least to my satisfaction).

Dreyer's work is becoming richer all the time in terms of references and structures. Where the work in her first, *Lamplights Used to Feed the Deer*, was full of "Exploration"(s) (as her first piece in that collection is called) into the uses of language to reveal the sensual and intellectual beauty of the (her) mind's intuitive connections and conclusions, the later work explored the same kind of unexpected and personal relationships between words and what they might signify and otherwise express and the mysteries of the world -- not just the mind.

With Dreyer the language is always personal, no matter how disjointed or "abstract" or objectified, in a way that seems to say she's still using it to clear up something for herself. So many writers seem to be defining something, whether in themselves or outside themselves, for the sake of an audience of readers, which can sometimes work, rather than for themselves. With Dreyer, I always have the feeling it's for her, and that lends her work this close, almost revelatory tone. Dreyer's writing never seems pretentious, although she uses words in an incredibly original way, they are still always familiar enough that the idiosyncracies seem just like that, an individual matter of expression.

> ... It is not from her mother or families or origins and
> seeking them out. Becoming more with houses. This is why
> everything is new in houses and keeping them clean. This
> she said was discipline- the words caught in her throat.
> Had she become past tense. Here points become valises.
> Facts heiroglyphics. Muted lights non-distinct voice what
> to take. It seemed long. I remember pictures and copies
> of words on them. Specific rubies without their directness.
> His laughter was wishful. His laughter was killed and made
> into different parts of bodies. Amputations and what they
> did with them. It seemed they did it to music. The next
> memory was medical, schooling, and teaching. Saying much
> to each other, slicing boxes, bodies withheld.
> As if they knew the word day.
> As if they knew songs without words and came across these
> songs in morgues. Not their teaching, not pictures, not
> smaller attempts but symbols of parts, put away.
>   (-- from *Stampede*)

I don't know where Lynne gets her language from or how she goes about structuring it -- but I never have the sense that the words are from outside ("found") sources, arbitrary or not, or that her abrupt shifts or unusual juxtapositions are there to call attention to themselves as techniques, cut-up or otherwise. No matter how she does it, her work almost always strikes me as having been "written" that way -- revised perhaps, cut probably here and there -- but the movement, rhythms, structures, all seem to be the direct result of her mind at work writing the language out.

MICHAEL LALLY

DREYER BIBLIOGRAPHY: *Lamplights Used to Feed the Deer* (1974, Some of Us Press, Washington, D.C.; available c/o L=A=N=G=U=A=G=E Distributing Service, $1.50). *Stampede* (1976, eel press, c/o Inman, 3338 Chauncey #102, Mt Rainier, MD 20822; $2). *Letters* (1978, in Tottel's #17, c/o L=A=N=G=U=A=G=E, photocopy of issue; $3.78). *Tamoka* 1979, in Roof IX, Segue Foundation, 300 Bowery, NYC 10012; $3).

from ARRANGEMENT

(The following excerpt is from a transcript of a July 19,1977 lecture by Clark Coolidge in Talking Poetics from Naropa Institute, Volume One, Shambhala Publications, 1123 Spruce St, Boulder, CO 80302, $6.95, which also contains talks by Jackson MacLow, Robert Duncan, Ron Padgett, William Burroughs & others)

I also want to say that there are no rules. At least not at first there aren't. If you start with rules, you've really got a tough road. What I think is that you start with materials. You start with matter, not with rules. The rules appear, the limitations appear, and those are *your* limitations and the limitations of the material. Stone has a certain cleavage. You can't make it look a certain way if the stone is not constructed to allow you to do that.... [*writes on blackboard:*]

ounce code orange

a

the

ohm

trilobite trilobites

This is a poem from a group of poems I wrote in 1966, when I was
living in Cambridge in the same house with Aram Saroyan, and he was
writing these one-word poems, dividing everything down to the smallest
possible thing... and I immediately wanted to put them together. I
couldn't stand the idea of one word. I don't think there *is* one word.
So this is one of those poems. I did maybe twenty or thirty of these.
I suppose they're about as unadulterated, pure, if you will, as anything
I ever did. I was really trying to work with the words, look at the
words, try to use all their qualities. There's no question of meaning,
in the sense of explaining and understanding this poem. Hopefully, it's
a unique object, not just an object. Language isn't just objects, it
moves. I'll try to talk about some of the qualities of these words
that I was aware of when I was writing it, as best I can. It was
eleven years ago.

"ounce code orange": ways of measuring, in a sense. Weight, a
symbol system, a color. "a/the": the indefinite article, the definite
article. "ohm" is the unit of electrical resistance, a quality of metal,
let's say, that requires a certain amount of juice to go through. In
other words, this is a fuzzy, resistant word. It hangs down here, it
affects particularly this space. I wanted these things hanging in the
middle because they could adhere to words in either the top line or the
bottom line. *"the* ounce," "*a/the* code," "*the* orange." You can't say
"a ounce" or "a orange," practically. You can say "a code." So there
are those vectors going there. "trilobites": you know what a trilobite
is, it's an early animal of the Paleozoic Age that was a crustacean
divided into three lobes. As a word, to me it's completely irreducible.
What are you going to do with it? "A trilobite": it's like a clinker.
Angular, uneven, heavy word. So, I made a plural, and I also say,
"trilobite trilobites." That second trilobite becomes a verb. And I
feel, as Fenollosa pointed out, that every noun is a verb, and vice
versa, and there really are a hell of a lot of them in the English
language which don't connect except in being the same word, like the
word "saw." "I saw the saw."...

... Well, "trilobite trilobites": it sounds like a rudiment, a paradiddle or something you have to practice. That's what I don't like.
It's not [*hums a bop rhythm*]. You know, it's not as shapely, which
I've tried to do more of since.... I also found out later that "ounce"
is the name for a kind of leopard. I don't know if anybody knows that.
I think it's Indian, or Tibetan. It's a cat called an ounce. So, you
think of "pounce." There are these words that begin to adhere and
appear like ghosts around these things. Ounce, pounce, bounce. "code"
-- I don't know, that's beginning to seem a little neutral to me.
"Orange": the color *and* the round thing, the fruit. Now that I've said
that, the word "ounce" begins to seem round to me. "A trilobite," "*the*
trilobites." That's how that goes. And this is the dead spot of the

poem, the resistance: "ohm." And it's also almost like the "Om," the
balance. ...

CLARK COOLIDGE

PLANISHING HAMMER

Ray DiPalma, <u>Planh</u> (Casement Books, 67 Morton St., NY, NY 10014; $3.50)

Organized language is a trace of effort. The solidity of the lines is
trust; we rest *in* our work, *whatever* comes out of the heterogeneous
world formulating into this graspable world, because the structure
divides it for us.
 The language is fragment. It is only a fearful mind that sees this
as disintegration. This cutting is the very sign of unity, of solid
excitement, the sign of structure. The manipulation of units of language
in durable structures, is literature. Though they may be interesting
singly, only structure *justifies* its fragments. The flaking arrangement
of lines, of words within lines, and of line groups, convinces us that
they engage each other; they are made sentient. Language cut openly
bleeds meaning and thus does more than it was supposed (thought) to
have done: its extension.
 Each line inflects a gesture. It hurts surrounding lines, entices
them, throws them, hurries them. In this writing the gestural line is
never still, negative.
 When lyric and imagistic modes are extended and intercut, the calcu-
lations appear at each refining turn to be reaching for conclusions.
This reaching is held steady in their constant incompletion. The mastery
of some formulation is implied in the turn to and from each line because
that formulation is present there in it. The *forestalling* is held
repeatedly before us; we see it as the subject. The advance implicit
within each move is cancelled by its immediate repetition, but the
impression of the gesture elegantly retrying itself is the substance of
our impression, is our involvement.

Each stanza is three sided. This unaltered stability reinforces the
line of sight we have as we progress. Our progress links the identical
units. Nothing isolate, nothing diminishes. The sturdiness of the
stanzas restates, as each memory reinforces others, definingly. Two
gestures move together at the point of each stanza: the gesture of each
stanza resting straight, the gesture of stanza after stanza undiminished
by our continuing perspective. Gyroscope and metronome intersect. The
two gestures are, repeatedly, one; that is the point distinguished by
our presence, stanza to stanza, the persisting erection of sense.

The breaking of the poem into ten sections provides the reader ten vantage points. Like Christo's Running Fence, at each hill topped in walking we review a renewed architecture, in both directions. These horizontal and temporary though repeated experiences, of noting what has been allowed in and combined, and what excluded, fill us also vertically with the experience of disclosure; the world, the language, goes by on both sides. The stanzas are strides.

This writing is vertical not only in the sense of accumulation, from the first line to the last, but also in the sense of flight, the last line drawing (through) all others to the first. Each line is momentarily the focal point of cross currents; nothing escapes the rush. Each line is targetted, washed.

The substance of the writing is language. (Writing *elicits* the substance of writing, scrapes it together.) This is the case with works which are whole. The work, by not travelling from the domain of its tools, has only to perform itself. It is at no point separate from itself as are works which employ one device (words) for the accomplishment of another (a subject, a discourse, eg.). Like filings held in array by a magnet, there is no separating the force from the result. The writer does not have to name himself or sign his devices, because the structure does so, for itself, self-intently. Each chunk of language is a disguised verb; it speaks itself. The words are not a display, moral or metaphysical or otherwise, they are a phenomenological fact, they can't be consumed. The substance of the writing bears upon itself, and even this only by its exclusion of the *else* which its demonstration releases from any need to be there. Our metaphors (visceral, contingent, etc.) for describing the substance, though they be accurate rhetoric, mark only our own presence and in so doing briefly relieve us of the work our presence entails.

The music of the poem is building block music. Its insistent additions make its structure more visually intuited than tonally attended. The poem sounds good without that being its intent, without the sound being gained and at the same time lost at the level of intention. Language, when it acts, works unavoidable sound. The sound *excites* the language; that is its function. The sound is a function of language's habit, something it displays as it enforces itself. The sensual phrases are not so much differentiated as arrived at; like oases, their appeal is scribed by the needs we achieve before we arrive at them. Though the sound is pleasure, the poem brings itself together not even at that slight remove which separates in our mind the sound of the hammer from the hammer. The *tools* are emphatic; not "their" "products".

The poem evidences some usual devices: rhyme, words in combination for comparison, and the results of that, insertions from the surrounding reality of a transparent writer (a person we invent), lists of sensation

or place or effect, a linear though jolting accounting for condition.
But the poem is more deflected than produced by these pockets of trait
and habit. We are tempted to say that the author has produced this work
from his own interiors. The text provides nothing to support this idea;
we must admit that we have used the most handy hypothesis, which in
reality keeps us away from the poem. The poem has not produced its
effects in us. We have produced the poem inseparable from its effects.
Suddenly we (we the text) glance at the poem stretching about us, and
see bits of our own times, particles of our own natures, laced into the
eras between the lines.

From our place along its traverse, we need not speak of an end of
this poem. The poem does not reach for an ending. This is not because of doubt.
The poem contains its conclusion in each line, each measurement; retain-
ing conclusion, it does not have to pursue it. Neither does the end
connect with the beginning, though it does imply it. The poem lays over
itself at *each* point. By *extension*, the poem.

From our place along its traverse, we need not speak of an end of
this poem. Summary is not important; a continuing summative process is.
The most pointed revelation of each line is its position. It is a marker;
holds its position so cleanly that it is revealed, reveals it and so holds
it. The larger meaning, that implicit in any self-supporting structure,
is implicit in each reconstituted gesture; the gesture of line, of stanza,
of word. There is no question of an exterior structure which we argue to
intuit; words intuit, they trace, their argument is made instantly by the
design they continuously perfect about them. Our gradual reading of the
lines, our inspection, sees each locked firm to attention; produced by the
closest reading, this is the largest meaning, the durability. We don't
examine this writing against codes; it produces itself as discrete, opened
code and abolished all others from purpose.

As we read line to line, each provides a pause of recognition. There
is an orderly list of noticeable elements, factors. The meaning comes
out of the spaces fluctuant about the lines. The lines in relation produce charges and discharges (cognition and recognition) (we are held and
released), and it is this motion, this constant, that reminds us that we
are in the presence of meaning. This reminder itself, unfiltered though
given efflorescently from the depthed and screened filter of the words,
is the meaning. Our implicatedness as readers completes the presence of
meaning and simultaneously neutralizes it. Its presence is its vanishing,
and ours.

ALAN DAVIES

chatted the system
evidence be
some funny ideas

no more chronicle

turned embellishing
in red buildings

to fix a signal
eyes half closed
with a spasm of pleasure

silence signature
showed the bottom
made deeper

                                        -- *from PLANH*

LETTER TO THE EDITOR

This is in reaction to Ron Silliman's remarks (in L=A=N=G=U=A=G=E No. 7)
about "WIN magazine & its anarcho-social-democrats" & such expressions
as "outside of a beingness [!] wch is not bourgeois (& hardly that of
the renegade bourgie who breaks away to reaffiliate herself w/ the
workers)" & "To achieve even the limited goals any communist might seek
within the framework of capitalist electoral politics," as well as his
recommendation of Lefebvre's Dialectical Materialism: "(it should be
subtitled How to Think)."

1. I have no idea what an "anarcho-social-democrat" is, tho in Silliman's usage it's obviously a pejorative term. As far as I know, the
one common position held by the group that issues WIN is pacifism. I
believe that some are anarchists, some libertarian socialists (i.e.,
probably in no sense Leninists), & some may, horrid as it might seem to
ideologists, be reformists trying to deal with problems as they come up.
I don't believe any are members of the Social Democratic Federation or
whatever its present name may be. I'm no longer able to be active on
the editorial board, but I think that many of us are convinced that
both "capitalist electoral politics" (are there any other kinds?) & non-
violent direct action are necessary means toward our "limited goals"
(are there any other kinds?).

2. I'm repeatedly amazed when I learn that excellent artists such as
Ron Silliman (most of whose work I admire--tho probably, according to
him, for all the wrong reasons) still pursue the will-o'-the-wisp of
"communism" & adhere to that strange agglomeration of 19th-century
concepts & superstitions known as "dialectical materialism." Why he
should think that the *next* "communist" state that gets set up somewhere
should be any improvement on the present group of war-mongering bureaucratic oligarchies that busily exploit most people in their countries
in the name of the supposedly high ideals of "socialism" & "communism"

is beyond me. & I've heard the "argument" before that "real communism" (or "real socialism") would be different from the present examples— that "the people" ("the broad masses," as the <u>Great Soviet Encyclopedia</u> loves to put it) would effectively control the state apparatus, which itself would eventually "wither away." Why should anyone believe such nonsense?

3. It probably does little good to recommend such a direct & eloquent critique of "dialectical materialism" & allied notions as Milovan Djilas' <u>The Unperfect Society</u> (New York: Harcourt Brace World, 1969) to those still enmeshed in the "dialectical materialist" spiderweb, but for what it's worth, I do.

4. Lack of belief in the various current ideological illusions need not imply a love for corporate capitalism. In fact, cleaning out the ideo-logical cobwebs & 19th-century hand-me-downs is a necessary prerequisite to substantial desirable change in both the corporate-capitalist & the state-capitalist ("socialist") countries, as well as in the so-called "third world" countries whose peoples have incautiously accepted infec-tion by Western ideological diseases, the worst of which is probably the belief that there is or can be a "Perfect Society." It's a toss-up whether this notion (& the rather similar belief that there is "One True Religion") or simple greed have caused more misery.

5. Talk of "a beingness which is not bourgeois" & dividing people up between "workers," "bourgeois," & "renegade bourgies" is not going to advance us one millimeter toward the achievement of the goals ("limited" or not—preferably limited) Silliman & I both consider desirable. Only dogged & persistent & detailed work within the present concrete oppres-sive social systems may achieve such advance. To what extent the work of artists as such can contribute to it is, to say the least, proble-matical.

6. I'm sure Silliman will consider the following a banal & simple-minded question, but I can't resist asking him how long he thinks he would be able to continue his artistic work in any "communist" state.

7. To hell with the know-it-alls who entrap generous spirits such as Ron Silliman into their exploitative ideological mazes. If they don't know what they're doing, it's all the worse.

8. "How to Think" indeed!

JACKSON MAC LOW

_____

HEJINIAN

SMATTER

In Belgium there

                    is a river they
                    call "the bridge"

It's only a coincidence, and it has a bad name.

Then, quilting on this crazy quilt.

What they reveal -- in this wind "only birds." Or, "It's only the trees
brushing against the house" "in this wind."

O there now
I hear crickets but not to catch
their tone

Question of responsibility, hence ability to respond; one person for
another and the converse, hence conversation; it is never true that x
"means nothing" to y -- or "he means nothing to me" in protest,
fending off.

I can't help but be interested in how things sit -- before I intervene.

The *when* is *where* when you tell me where to turn off this road.

Any coincidence is a relationship, puts a line out or takes one in.
There is always a relationship as soon as there is a coincidence. I
am thinking here now more of taking lines in, or "taking it all in,"
than of any putting out. It seems that what presses as a question upon
writing now (when it comes to talk of structures, for example, or
systems) is how to arrange words (or word groups) rather than how to
choose them. How to lay them there, or, rather, string them -- the only
simultaneity available now being a kind of potent neutrality -- suscep-
tibility, or piling *up on* words (as opposed to the Elizabethan cumulative techniques, which amount to a (lovely, to me) piling *on of* words).
Feelings embrace fields, but ideas, which are points, point. (Memory
does field understanding, but only retrospectively.)

Putting things together in such a way as to enable them to coincide, to
make that kind of motion, is, like the "collage" and the "cluster," an
attempt (by analogy with music's chord) at suggesting (since that is
all one can do) simultaneity, hoping for inherence, haphazard, happy
chance. As a writer, but especially as a poet, one looks there to
discover the natural order in language, in words as they represent but
particularly as they don't-only, in words together, lively -- at play
in the fields (finally) where "o there now their tone" make a way of
seeing connections see writing. Like the natural order elsewhere,
things can't be seen in ones alone, make twos. Twos and more, too.
I am interested in that.

Another way of phrasing the question might be to inquire into the relationship between relativity and dialectics, the relativity being that

one with that one and the dialectics as the two then made: "The distance
that every great writer maintains between himself and his object."
(Walter Benjamin)

A real object. So it's true. What do I believe in? nothing.

"I keep an eye on things, like what wars do to little shops."

Dialectics, as I understand the term, is a style of inquiry; it requires
that thought move. And since all movement is interstitial, occurring
by points between points, such movement in thought is a process of
connection; in dialectics it is concerned with what emerges when some
things, under force (even "the force of circumstance") are, or proceed
toward, other things. Words, for example, simply can't help but give
onto ideas. It is for this reason that they form language -- language
in this case being an operation of connection. I want to take a
measure of the elements and to measure the space between them.

That tree down
would be news up
there

Who's to say along what binding forces we bound.

LYN HEJINIAN

WRITING IS AN AID TO MEMORY

Lyn Hejinian, <u>Writing Is an Aid to Memory</u> (1978; The Figures, c/o
Small Press Distribution, 1636 Ocean View Ave, Kensington, CA 94709; $3)

The intelligence evident management in a bounding ardour of attention, a
wily worthy-fulness, taken to stony-watery horseflesh clumsiness' edge,
if/*yes*, but style as the grace of standing by a posit until *it* actually
abounds with beauty & function. The periods between her sentences show
us her thinking realizing the world written, in parts, like Justice
weighing & balancing; *same* time her rhythm dance articulation of the new
ones. *She* 's intelletto ahead & behind her, that gathering (all-over-
radiant/understanding), here delay, is thought density wife-ing quintes-
sence' passion.

She's not afraid of blanket cliché, confession, 'obsession'--so that that
may be held up for circumspection. Should she edit her attention?
"Nature as creator,' no! 'A poem can be made of anything.' Hospitality's
good behavior is womanly devotion's license, romance, logic's guises.

The house above in the starry skies, if you mean that seriously. When
it's over, I feel just like I bin cut off from some cosmic force, our love.

                    'The Unknown
                    The Left Out
                    The Mysterious
                    The Holy Possibility'

.

The house above in the starry skies, if you mean that seriously. Seems
hardly real at all, but say the language mind's our galaxy, & let's
assume the way it looks to us is like a paper house, but flat somehow, a
'page' with only length & breadth, & further say we see this surface
providentially (hardly 'upskew,' on-end, etc.) straight on (as though we
stood back royally & do look on with all attendant privilege of consummate location, here & there, at home away from home)--& further say this
spectacle which is at once our very being/realm, has letters of the alphabet ranged left to right as loci for the roving lights that enter from
the depths of space & time as *words* (or morphs) which move across the
midnight table laid, inset as guests that sit & pass, speak, eat or are
eaten...

.

Fine, but too many words.

Is she showy-offy, is she grand?

.

Such pleasure in these forms that range the air in several places, world
& more literal mineral, material, metal, water blue as blue...

...'form cut in time,' & not by who, 'sunlight ranging forms'...

          Y O U R E S O L I G H T R E D

          r a n g e b u t y o r e l i t t l e

that blood flows world iron song make cakes bake pies & pleasure in the
limbs glide drinking water wine banging people into pastry. Nor rough,
at all, just giving each what there's to do: grace graces.

.

Writing is participation in agency of forms' generation 'from way back,'
& thus appears (as) 'in' Memory ('cloud of stars'):

          'From form seen doth he start, that understood,
           Taketh in latent intellect--
           As in a subject ready--' (agh)

Love:

          'Vien da veduta forma ches s'intende
             Che '1 prende
                         nel possibile intelletto
           Chome in subgetto

235

<pre>
                           locho e dimoranza
             E in quella parte mai non a possanza

             Perchè de qualitatde non disciende
                Risplende
                         in sé perpetuale effecto
             Non a diletto
                           mà consideranza
             Perche non pote laire simiglglianza:--'
</pre>

I don't know (Italian) about the last part:

<pre>
             'Not to delight, but in an ardour of thought
             That the base likeness of it kindleth not.'
</pre>

...perhaps that too?

.

How could it ever have been made, the change at that point, to this 'thing'--

<pre>
             'A little
             water
             falls.'
</pre>

thence 'goes & goes.'

.

<pre>
             'in an ardour of thought'
                   'Risplende
                           in sé perpetuale effecto'
</pre>

.

Ability to think inside a form as seriously *as if* this were the world, *as though* this marvel were still usage, because the 'evidence' in the present structurally is so 'compelling.'

Perceives said form in time structuring itself 'through me' as simultaneously already past...

so that knowledge (writing) is image of 'the gods' already passed over into such & such a western ridge of letters, 'characters'...

& as such perceived as 'memory' *virtually* still happening...

& *this is*/all everyday life, *where else?* & that's great, & it gets boring but picks up pretty soon with the power gained from asking such a question, brought back & reformulated/reformulating in cups, saucers, etc.--

<pre>
             just as if

             dinner & supper 'had been created'

             (justice if
</pre>

        dinner & supper have been created?)

        --anyway content now as restless

        happy & vigor/rigorous demanding

--which is to put mind 'back' into day & body, function: 'recognize it
with our words'--viz., the verse following, weaving.

.

Why now the half-moon in the morning open sky, did you (living) ever ever...

.

        'cloudless electricity even dishes anything'

                'wicker grammar
                showed off pretty'

--rather better process through sustained passages:

                (prints out #28, e.g., whole grid)

.

Darling, god damn, what a thinker, really. When it's over, I feel just
like I bin cut off from some cosmic force, our love.

                                        ROBERT GRENIER

_____

HEJINIAN BIBLIOGRAPHY: *A Thought Is the Bride of What Thinking*
(1976, Tuumba Press, photocopy available c/o L=A=N=G=U=A=G=E Distributing Service for $1.58). *A Mask of Motion* (1977, Burning Deck Press, 71
Elmgrove, Providence, R.I. 02906; $2.50). *Gesualdo* (1978, Tuumba Press,
2639 Russell, Berkeley, CA 94705; $2). *Writing Is an Aid to Memory*
(1978, The Figures, c/o Small Press Distribution, 1636 Ocean View Ave,
Kensington, CA 94707; $3). From *Walls* (1979, A Hundred Posters #38,
689 East 17th Street, Brooklyn, NY 11230; $1.50).

        _____

from GLYPHS

There is a contradiction between events and their description that
becomes visible when an event is described without reference to the
describer. Such a description does not allow for the possibility that
events themselves are simultaneous, with every permutation of accident
and action occurring at once; that only perception strings them into
logical sequences; or that forgetting is a balance to perception.

The context in which an action occurs requires a specific mode of
description: a violent gesture becomes desperate, or murderous, or a

request for aid. Events remain opaque, and the structural concepts encouraged by experience give only that climactic vision of coherence, the error of the senses that is in itself a sensuous occasion.

For the same reason the retention of critical distance towards the work is the ideal of the auditor or reader. A type of appreciation is sought: that clarity of thought that at its most sympathetic is like a friendship and has some areas of trust without an undifferentiated acceptance. The writer, however, as a lover of these words, has to fend off the overpowering attraction and the acceptance of less from an indulged expression. The act of falling in love with an idea, a meter, a manner of speaking, has in it all the weakness of the creation of a product not held responsible to itself. So the writer, re-reading, must assume not the willing suspension of disbelief, but a mode of criticism less informed than that potential in the reader.

The alphabet has been criticised for succumbing too easily to its lover, the word. Where each word has developed in powers of inference, the sublimated position of the alphabet has kept it from having a life of its own. While lyricism is the writer's attempt to calm the inherent aggression of words, and allow an equal interplay between the audience's thought and the text, words press back against the interpretive will and draw from their inner selves alternate meanings whose power resides in the imagination. As words open the potential of expression so choice between them closes it. The words of a vocabulary in use offer a criticism of the range of possibilities from which they have been extracted.

The procedure of glyphs is to dominate language by recording ideas through the juxtaposition of other ideas. To ignore this essential element of writing is to mistake its purpose -- writing records that which is expected to be forgotten, or writing struggles to dominate the circumstance of forgetting but has only words to use. The difficulty in deciphering ancient glyphs comments on the possibility of decoding alphabetic writing only to discover an ambiguous text. In either case the cultural situation of the text is lost, and with it the implications of its meaning. In this way the mysterious pattern of language is its own unusable key in that changes in meanings of words are affected not only by their induction into other tongues, or slang, or cliché, but by definition and by the kind of rough appropriation that stems from urgent need.

MADELEINE BURNSIDE

_____

KETJAK IN SAN FRANCISCO

    'This is the zone. Words, where you are, as in a trail, not

238

forest but thicket, pine needle modifiers, shingles of a pine
cone on which to focus, buy syntax, syntax was the half-light.'

Ron Silliman read on Saturday September the 16th all of <u>Ketjak</u> (This
Press, 1978) on the sidewalk in sunlight at One Powell Street, where the
Powell Street cablecars turn around at Market. I came in on my way off
the BART train from my job in North Oakland, at 3, roughly, knowing the
reading started at noon, and came up the stairs not knowing just where
in the intersection it would land me or where Ron would be. The impression of bazaar had hardly hit before there was Ron declaiming book in
hand before the front steps of the Bank of America, book neatly clutched
in right hand, left hand grasping offwhite canvas bookbag with "no on 6"
(anti-Briggs) button at center out, pacing back & forth facing the sun
in a patch of light between shadows cast (before him) by a tree and (to
his right) by the building, on whose steps sat maybe 12 people I knew;
6 or 10 others sitting or standing between me and him. The reading was
insistent emphatic and lively with an energy intoxicated by its own
vigor and exactitude; it was chatty (unusual for Ron's reading) in its
thrilled, maybe sometimes even giddy playfulness with the rhetoric of
its phrases in all their possible relevancy to this heterogeneous, very
live occasion. He was clearly reading the reading of his poem and
using this to illuminate as if from behind (and taking pleasure in the
illusion as though from within) the poem itself. The recurrences
variousness & personality of the text discoursed directly and one-on-
one, as in a most democratic and definitive garden party of the urban
streets, with the prolifery of the situation.... Ron's gestures quite
evidently spontaneous, isolated in the left hand, the voice and the
pacing (sometimes stopped). The experience was available to those
passersby who didn't expect it equally as they were available to it. A
man walked up, slowing down towards the poet, and then passed to his
right, as though uncertain only whether Ron meant to be an obstacle but
confident in any case that he should negotiate a passage. A woman with
a friend turned around abruptly after passing the poet when she heard
"She loves to give head"; shocked, she tried to make out whether he'd
been exposing her or somebody else; others say she smiled in recognition.
A drunk tried to mimic Ron's phrases into catchy blues. Ron read as
though too busy to acknowledge all this formally but cognitive of it in
all its valences of contiguity and implication (or you may say fact &
what might happen next). You could stand or sit anywhere. You were on
a major streetcorner, already crowded with long lines of tourists
waiting for the chief picturesque cablecar line already beseiged by
hawkers gawkers shoppers hookers and religious maniacs-- September being
the warmest freshest month in the city. Recurring and original lines
and people. By juxtaposition the names, images, terms called out by the
words were clearly present as such rather than as objects for fantasy to

compose over. The rapture of the occasion sprang from the access to a
shared awareness of being *there*, the significance of this then ready to
be begun, again at any moment. The writing evoked neither this nor any
particular other consistently, & so seemed never to claim any particular
responsibility for reproducing, but freely aimed at the experience
about it.

STEVE BENSON

METHOD AND IMAGINATION

My point of departure is the idea of finding those words which have the
capacity to exist in the Italian language and for one reason or another
have not been realized. My principal interest is in the semantics of
sounds not yet deposited in the sediments of signification. Signification tends to kill that pleasing resonant aureole which words have: it
is even possible to arrive in the end where one no longer perceives the
sounds of words, but merely follows the line of a performance of tokens.
And it is not true that our everyday life must be characterized by such
sclerosis. The sound of words can still be a great support to us.

In finding words we should avail ourselves of all sorts of associative
games -- of growth and diminution, of crossings and parallels. The
invented word is a good one when its rapport with the other words of its
context makes no substitute acceptable.

When such words are read, they should mean all the things that it seems
to the reader that they mean, everything that comes to the mind of the
reader (which, in the end, is what happens with any reading).

These poems are born from the experience of collective readings of
poetry before a public (paying or otherwise). On these occasions I have
felt the need to allow for redundancy. I have now arrived where I use
redundancy as a means, the logical operator which must be mocked,
scolded, made ridiculous. The instrument which determines and fixes
the space for invention and establishes once and for all that such space
exists -- that's it.

Poetry is truly successful when it releases a mechanism of contradiction
revealed not by the rigor of logic, but by all the rest.

My poems are iconic. This aspect present in my poems has not been programmed. Rather, it is an aspect which is in some way liberated, or has
been liberated. Maybe the liberation of icons was implicit in the program. The first signification on which the sound of a word fixes itself
is an icon.

The content of a poetry is the logic in it and also the worm which kills poetry. Avoid content and fix on an icon: that is method and imagination.

(Translated from the Italian by Jesse Ausubel)

MILLI GRAFFI

LETTER TO THE EDITOR

The book survey in No. 7 is focused in a way no 'reviews' we see ever are; the *use of texts* is at stake, and people's reflections on what stirs them are in turn of next-generation usefulness. So I pick up half a dozen things I hadn't considered, and that's good news. The solidity of Silliman's judgment is, as usual, exciting.

So I want to send along, in return, my own list of this past year or so, the things that stirred most in my thought and writing. Trail of dust, maybe, or pillar of cloud. We never know till we see what's done with them.

Walter Benjamin, Reflections and Illuminations. I begin with an amazing critic of our own fragmented light, whom I had missed until two months ago, and who's been the sharpest call to order lately.

Braudel, The Mediterranean World in the Age of Philip II and the other work on the material culture of Capitalism.

Barthes, Sade/Loyola/Fourier and The Pleasure of the Text: Barthes at his most public/private and private/public, the one critic ("deictic" after my own heart) who knows how to walk that line. These books fulfill the promise of Writing Degree Zero (coeval with Olson's Projective Verse essay). And the head-note by Richard Howard to the Pleasure is remarkable for all the issues it starts running with clarity, wit and quickness.

Engels, The Condition of the Working Class in England--to come back to that, as ever to Marx's Capital, to ground in the world root of their thought. Fact as the rain that renews the air of theory.

Gregory Dix, The Shape of the Liturgy, a beautiful study of the diachronic, a gesture shaping for nineteen hundred years.

Georges Bataille, to wander in the complete works now coming out, especially L'Histoire de l'Oeil, Le Bleu du ciel (which I've read in a wonderful private translation by Paul Auster and Lydia Davis), L'anus solaire. I owe much of my orientation here to Paul Buck and that remarkable journal Curtains.

Salvatore Timpanaro, The Freudian Slip. (Marxian philology reborn.) Umberto Eco, Theory of Semiotics.

Hillman, ReVisioning Psychology.
Cardew, Stockhausen serves Imperialism (a book so savage in its attack
    on our avant-garde preoccupations and airs that it seems to be kept
    out of this country altogether, whereas the same author's earlier
    conformist Scratch Music is widely circulated.)
Tarthang Tulku, Time Space Knowledge, a casting of Buddhist analytic
    and synthetic into the american language.
Marx and Engels, The German Ideology: the orchestra tuning, the wind
    rising.
Heidegger, What is called thinking and Discourse on Thinking.
And ever useful (now I own a copy all the more so):
Onians, The Origins of European Thought (Arno reprint).

And I do not want to leave out of the record those books which are not
held in the hand, namely the texts of light:
Hollis Frampton, Zorn's Lemma
Herzog's Kasper Hauser
Tanner's Jonah who will be 25 in the year 2000.

And, to match Benjamin at the beginning, this very great film which I
finally saw only two years ago:
Vertov, Man with Movie Camera. (I suppress the the/s deliberately).

    PS/ Capitalism brings 'story' and 'writing' together. Stateless
communism must dream into being a language which tells its own story.
And in which language is the only story. Are not these the pivots we
share in what we would move?

    PPS/ Sour note in McCaffery's sideswipe at Enslin. Not because of
my predictable preference for 'positive criticism' (my deicticism, as
above), or my equally predictable defense of Enslin---rather because the
rating-system (fourth-rate, third-rate, etc) is built on the very structure we are all trying to deconstruct. At once came to mind the old
Macaulay reading the young Marx and saying: That is just how to learn
how not to write. And Barthes' actual strictures (Writing Degree Zero)
on 'clarity'---he recognizes the danger of the lucid becoming the
compulsory---neatness and clarity the tools of persuaders. Yet it's
interesting to learn how not to write too, and I take it abstinence is
a sort of use.

ROBERT KELLY

SOME FIELDS THE TRACK GOES THROUGH

1. Each time I find something worth saying, it's because I've not been
    satisfied to coincide with my feeling, because I've succeeded in
    studying it as a way of behaving, as a modification of my relations

with others and the world, because I've managed to think about it as I would think about the behavior of another person whom I happened to witness. *Merleau-Ponty, Film.*

2. A child scolding a flower in the words in which he had himself been scolded and whipped, is *poetry* / past passion with pleasure. *Coleridge, Notebooks.*

3. Irresponsible play seeks to overcome the ruinous seriousness of whatever one happens to be. *Adorno, Prisms.*

4. Insistency -- the pretension of power -- falls victim to a weakness and uselessness of the same type as the gesticulatory schemata of the schizophrenic. *Adorno, Prisms.*

5. The reproach against the individualism of art in its later stages of development is so pathetically wretched simply because it overlooks the social nature of this individualism: "lonely discourse" reveals more about social tendencies than does communicative discourse. *Adorno, Philosophy of Modern Music.*

6. But in the language of Azande it is self-contradictory to doubt the efficacy of oracles, and this only proves that Zande language cannot be trusted in respect of oracles. *Polanyi, Knowing and Being.*

7. If two sequences of the action are to be understood as occurring at the same time they may simply be shown one after another. *Arnheim, Film as Art.*

8. I do not know who you are and yet I insult you and I talk to you as if we were intimates. *Colette, The Shackle.*

   And a 9th by way of question; where does Hegel write: "Truth is a Bacchanic ecstasy wherein every member is drunk on the same wine"?

   DAVID BROMIGE

ENCYCLOPEDIA / *the world we will know*

Words first -- *highly merely 'words / (cor)rect (al)ly eva(l/c)uated.* Yet, key question, how *connected with the facts for which // properly they stand. ?*

Representation -- *The story called record* -- official record -- *restricts by accidents of its data.* It restricts by the very logic of *the old system of production,* system of reproduction, monitoring : comes across as alienating replication which devalues the work of writing. [Repression.] To split off desire or libidinal energy or whatchamacallit from such work -- scrub off words, let preconstituted world of referents

243

shine through.

Encyclopedia: Epistemology: arrange terms in alphabetical ('arbitrary') order so that use, for units of information, leans upon an accepted outside context. This conventionally fills the gap between signifieds (mental concepts) & references -- relay between encyclopedia & the whole world (pretension of the former toward the latter -- 'comprehensiveness', 'fullness'; just like any representational text).

Positivism: this imagined closure between concept & referred-to-thing-in-the-external-world. The rules for processing & combining data into familiar patterns swamp the words' reality, as if we could maintain a purity of ideas & information against the unfortunate (or disregardable) tribulations of their material inscription. Fixed concepts; lack of awareness of the provisional & reflexive character of knowledge; its practices independent of the knower (no one seems to need to do the understanding). Yet understanding (reading is analogue) remains an active, material process (not naturally given, deductive, or disembodied). Knowledge is subjective intervention, not its stylish banishment.

Fetishism occludes this fact & this gap. History lesson embedded in apparent choicelessness [fatedness, mystification, mythification] of encyclopedic choices: CAPITAL expands & weaves reality around its quantifiable needs, becomes the criteria for use -- is key: *our key / expanded / our key become useful / deployed become different*, becomes the stage set for meaning (i.e., DIFFERENCE -- e.g., phonemics vs. phonetics).

Words then seem to be identified with their referents, NOT with their role in a framework of human conventions & NOT in a way that acknowledges their physical manifestation -- world reified / sign disappears. Individual usage or creativity in language becomes a frill of interpersonal relations & not the construction & revision of the norms themselves. Meaning would become a mere spin-off from a taken-for-granted external reality.

Yet ∿ Writing can articulate, brokenly, a world requiring our full intervention to be understood -- i.e., cannot SOCIALIZE us. So, a heightened stress on individual usage -- to break through the fetish, the tyranny of the unmediated external itself [example: the 'optical'], where we feel effortlessly & conveniently 'in touch' without first having to bring our full humanity to bear on forming connections with the world, an 'easier' & more acquiescent ("glossed out") naturalism.

So, one alternative is a fuller insertion of individual practice into the (writing) process by which these conventions are otherwise continuously reproduced through acquiescence in socialization.... An over-all non-representational ordering of matter -- LANGUAGE / MATERIAL -- as architecture of lexical associations & leaks, not 'tool'.

Do this by furnishing, in a self-conscious way, the *account not* [the] *object*. Mediation: *light of controversy* -- Light (signification) comes through 'dialectic' / practice, not just formal patternings & not pretense of 'direct reflection'. The sign; not the fetish of reference, which would be stapled to the text's compelling absences to offer illusory compensation, alienating us further (the myth of a self-standing reality : *Every satisfaction of it is debt.*) -- *the supplementary cured or dared.*

For a <u>true</u> fit, we require mediation, an account (to answer 'Why?' questions contextually) -- *plan matters to be / appropriate.* Otherwise world just happens, w/out enough self-reflection & becomes taken-for-granted regard for use (splint them as they lay, etc.). Usage can <u>penetrate</u> the whole -- if not it's defined as *practicability,* what fits a paradigm; comprehension -- *the attempt to read opinion* by complacent reliance on system ∿ nuancing, ornamenting the standards derived from it.

<u>Main</u> <u>opposition</u> : between acceptance of rules (in this case, of composition, of positivist inquiry, of discourse) OR stress on individual choices & disruptions & deviations (flows) & perspectives to the point where signs appear recognizably conventional. Thus : *The whole standard undoubtedly has been raised not to be nuanced, but made use of.* Fetish can be partially undone, seen to be constructed, *now acts as function.* Reflexively & self-reflexively. Offer access to the procedures through which structure is articulated.... *throughout careful by means / adapted to readers* & to the way mediating attention intervenes as creator of meaning & not the untying of packages popping off a semantic assembly-line.

I'm interested in composition issues. *Laments of unrest .... and not constituting disorder.... The convenience in arrangment* [once released, 'convenient' = 'use'] *conveys in such detail point of execution ...* ∿ <u>there</u> <u>need</u> be <u>no</u> <u>surface</u> : the arrangment natural to the actual workings of an awareness, not ornamental veneer or added surface [veneer analogous to 'character structure'/ psychology], but constant writing action. A disturbance IN the vista : *In the whole architecture was a / flak.* So, focus on the particular, *distinct within units.* Gather omissions or *revealed ommission* -- a <u>group</u> of gaps, rather than a <u>series</u> of relay points : the pages' blackhole : density→disappearance. As if the choices stretch us between the supercharged disjunct plane or Uniformity / Equivalence / Exchange -- *dizzy ambitious particular, or uniform.*

So. *most with the disturbance = so many lapse of time = Preserved portions. -- or marred remains larger.* Physical <u>gesture</u> regains its prominence -- *salient hands up : hands into notability.* Lapse = intermittent = comes in & out of focus = comes in & out of existence [stage does not remain after actors exit --] for the intermittent spectator <u>speculates</u>, works through, thereby <u>fashions</u> the work, not as stepladder but mark of, stain of, her attention. *Periodical the <u>constructive</u> ideal, all bookish dust dribble and sputter.* Not pre-constituted according to comprehensive, reflecting, 'outside' plan (*EncY...*) but to offer periodic experience of writer in role of reader/understanding faced with code or system or convention. Text gives way to broken utterance, almost stutter but disorient still more:

> *Control the convention then perpetrate the tratence*
> *then perpede furred   to any poor hil hop for mac*
> *hifj outer quarters crys formference*
> *in Afs   co   ad   b   Eu   va   i   porc*
> *Varzo ca-pr-ici-ous*

<u>Convention</u> <u>gets</u> <u>unravelled</u>: *decreased authority perhaps carried to extreme leng ... too graphic, more exceptions -- use.* Deviations, by breaking out, do more than charge & discharge energy, however voluptuously -- scramble codes, <u>disorient</u> language. (Constant rupture constant improvisation for <u>readers</u>, producing flows rather than a determinate picture of 'a whole'). They stretch the boundaries of that whole, of human use, of what can be written / felt -- are praxis. *Losing or dividing is the treatment.* Also, exceptions light up system boundaries, the limits that have historically been imposed upon use. (*more exceptions ... / as consult the glaringly outside the public / ... settled / conventions*).

To expand use, to <u>open</u> <u>up</u> the world for us. *No question of the hasty vehicle's progress* -- the unseemly rush from sign to a referent which would 'shadow' that sign, or erase it, or instrumentalize it. *no longer represent* : but only experience thrown back upon itself : *be grasped, skein be created // and crushing units to new units // already preferred // a case of itself // thought unquestioned // forefoot & aft, aware.* Thought is questioned.

[The above constitutes in part a response to Tom Mandel's impressive first book, EncY (1978; Tuumba Press, 2639 Russell, Berkeley, CA 94705, $2) from which the italicized portions are taken]

BRUCE ANDREWS

THE CONSPIRACY OF "US"

I don't believe in group formation, I don't like group formation, but I am constantly finding myself contending with it, living within it, seeing through it. "Okay, break it up boys." First, there is the isolation of the atom, looking for some place to feel housed by, a part of. & every which way the people passing seem to have that--"see it over there"--"look". But every group as well has the same possibility for

insularity as each individual: this new "we" having the same possibility
for vacancy or satisfaction, a group potentially as atomized in its
separation from other groups as a person from other persons. This is
the problem of family life. Property, territory, domain. But, "for us
now", group (family, aesthetic, social, national) is merely another part
of our commoditized lives--for we consume these formations, along with
most other things, as commodities, & are ourselves consumed in the
process. ((Putting aside here the extent to which political groupings
and parties would be different from groups of 'artists'; also the place
of groupings based on class oppression on the one hand and minority
oppression--women, gays, mental patients--on the other.)) So we use
groups as badges--shields--as much screening us off from the intrusion
of outside, others, as sheltering us from the sheer invasiveness of it,
them (& so allowing us a place to occupy, inhabit). I don't so much
think that such shelter is a fraud, unnecessary, as much as "let's look
at it, call the strictures into question, understand that we *can* reshape":
a call against paralysis from a sense of boundaries fixed without, or
before, our having had a chance to participate in their making. "The
danger is that our demands on each other will trample what we really
feel." The danger is that we will hide ourselves amidst the shuffle to
proclaim who we are.

We're afraid to say poetry, afraid of the *task*--that's why simply having
the goods--"Oh he's gifted as hell"--is never enough. I want to see
more than fine sentiments beautifully expressed "in the manner of...."
"He's really picked up on me" but sadly, not on *us*. One might as well
go back to fruit picking. It's hard to talk about content these days,
everyone pointing to the trace of their ideas as if *that* was "it" but we
don't want mere conceptualizations. "*But*, I mean, that person is really
saying something," which is the wrong way of making the point. But:
enough of empty vessels for sure. It's necessity which makes the form,
which then inheres; not just any "constructs" but the ones we live by,
the ones we live in & so the ones we *come upon*--

"Getting it." "Using it." "Pretending." "Imagining." "On the inside
track." "In contention." "An authority that genuinely speaks from its
heart, letting us know that here...." "Great hips." "Thyroid problems."
"Oh how come you done that." "Ain't that *Christian* of you." "Grace."
"Grave." "Maria of the *fleurs*." "An open cavity, about three to six
inches from the back of tongue, who...." "Naturally." "Over-intellec-
tual." "With too much *effort*...." "Over-emotional." "Grecian." "...
which at times one only wishes would give way to some greater sense of
necessity, like why bother to write it in the first place." "From up
here, the low-lying clouds obscuring the view..."

Language-centered writing and other art-historical epithets. For instance, you're right that the need for recognition, given that the work

is important, does demand that action be taken. Cuts are made but not
without enormous confusion on all sides--what's in common within &
different from without both get exaggerated. A kind of blinder's vision
begins as we look at the world in terms of the configurations being made.
"At a given time we responded to each other's work, were there for each
other." "To the permanent removal of everyone else after, simultaneous?"
No. These things arise in practice, have a practical value. ((Imagine
a world in which people allied along lines of hair color. Or what unified a group of artists was their use of a given shade of blue, or that
they live (or grew up in, or went to school in) the same place--the
impress of a common environment a constant to facilitate art-historical
apprehension. How does Richard Diebenkorn get seen by those who think
of non-figuration as the key issue of his generation of painters? &
wasn't it the key issue?)) But the "final" cuts have not--will not be--
made. Only cuts for "here"   & "there"   --

The identification of "younger" poets "coming up" by a group or community can imply the beginning for these people of inclusion within a
paternalistic hierarchy--an initiation into it. --Simply, the walls
must be stripped down & new ones constantly built as (re)placements--
or rather this is always happening whether we attend to it or not. We
see through these structures which we have made ourselves & cannot do
even for a moment without them, yet they are not fixed but provisional.
(...that poetry gets shaped--informed and transformed--by the social
relations of publication, readership, correspondence, readings, etc)
(or, historically seen, the 'tradition') and, indeed, that the poetry
community(ies) are not a secondary phenomenon to writing but a primary
one. So it won't do to just "think about the work". But it still
needs to be explored what the relation between "normal" and "extraordinary" poetry is--& why both need to be more valued in some respects and
devalued in others (snobbery, elitism, cliquishness, historical over-
self-consciousness, self-aggrandisement, &c)--especially at a time in
which there is an increase in the number of people and the number of
people engaging in art activities--not just a few "men" "out there"
doing the "heroic" work. --That poetry, with written language as its
medium, is, in fact, the exploration and realization of the human common
ground, of "us", in which we are--"that holds our sights within its
views".)

Or what we have is a series of banana republics with internecine (ie
inner) conflict as to whose to "be the" THE of the court, all that
fading with jocular regularity as we paddle our gondolas down the canals
of time and look back at the many remnants of period mannerism. You
want to name names? I feel very bloated at last & want to take this
opportunity to thank everyone. I wish I had a quill pen. I'll take a
dime for every time they.... "I mean some of this stuff really knocks

you out." A great place to take you date, &c, I mean it really impresses boys. "You wanna know something--I'm glad what they done to you...." The foundations of a linguistic empire on the coinage of a distinctive and recognizable style--"& that means don't hone in on my territory" "& that means *you*" is about as crucial as the opera of Luca Della Robbia. But not to stop there. "We" ain't about no new social groupings--nobody gotta move over--*this is the deconstruction of team*. This is *looking at language,* which *is* "us", & not creating the latest fashion splash of the "up & coming".

What happens, which is what it is when something happens & you say "oh, look at that -----"--already having arrived in your mind as a -----. But not just to plug in--"oh I got it let me dig some out for you--" The skips on the record which our pounding feet accentuate, making the needle dance out of synch to the rhythm our bodies seem to want to keep... --keep us honest. "Honest"? But not to "groove into", it's to make the words that come out *that* way more aware of themselves & so we more responsible to them, not that we "say" them with whatever capacity our "gifts" allow us but that we *mean* them with a twice told intention that puts "mere facility for images & transitions" in its place & puts "poetry"--a guild without members, only occasionally one or another of us finds ourselves there, or not "ourselves" but rather "those syllables so ordered..." & *we* mere spectators, out in the public field, watching *that*, now already behind us...

CHARLES BERNSTEIN

---

from THE CLAIM OF REASON

(The following excerpt is from Stanley Cavell's The Claim of Reason: Wittgenstein, Skepticism, Morality, and Tragedy, to be published in the autumn by Oxford University Press. Cavell writes in the forward that it has been his aspiration "to link the English and Continental (philosophical) traditions,... to realign these traditions, after their long mutual shunning, at any rate to write witnessing the loss in that separation.... what makes this spirit possible for me has been, I think, that the philosophical pressure to comprehend this division or splitting between cultures has begun transforming itself for me into the pressure to comprehend the division between the writing of philosophy and the writing of literature, hence the splitting within (one) culture." For those interested in contributing to a collection of essays on Cavell's work, write to Gus Blaisdell, The Living Batch Bookstore, 2406 Central Ave SE, Albuquerque, NM 87106.)

The conventions we appeal to may be said to be "fixed", "adopted", "accepted", etc. by us; but this does not now mean that what we have fixed or adopted are (merely) the (conventional) *names* of things. The conventions ... are fixed not by customs or some particular concord or agreement which might, without disrupting the texture of our lives, be changed where convenience suggests a change. (Convenience is *one* aspect of convention, or an aspect of one kind or level of convention.) They are, rather, fixed by the nature of human life itself, the human fix itself, by those "very general facts of nature" which are "unnoticed only because not obvious", and, I take it, in particular, very general facts of *human* nature -- such, for example, as the fact that ... our knowledge (and ignorance) of ourselves and of others depends upon the way our minds are expressed (and distorted) in word and deed and passion; that actions and passions have histories. That *that* should express understanding or boredom or anger ... is not necessary: someone may have to be said to "understand suddenly" and then always fail to manifest the understanding five minutes later, just as someone *may* be bored by an earthquake or by the death of his child or the declaration of marital law, or *may* be angry at a pin or a cloud or a fish, just as someone may quietly (but comfortably?) sit on a chair of nails. That human beings on the whole do not respond in these ways is, therefore, seriously referred to as conventional; but now we are thinking of convention not as the arrangements a particular culture has found convenient, in terms of its history and geography, for effecting the necessities of human existence, but as those forms of life which are normal to any group of creatures we call human, any group about which we will say, for example, that they *have* a past to which they respond, or a geographical environment which they manipulate or exploit in certain ways for certain humanly comprehensible motives. Here the array of "conventions" are not patterns of life which differentiate human beings from one another, but those exigencies of conduct and feeling which all humans share. Wittgenstein's discovery, or rediscovery, is of the depth of convention in human life; a discovery which insists not only on the conventionality of human society but, we could say, on the conventionality of human life itself, on what Pascal meant when he said "Custom is our nature"; perhaps on what an existentialist means by saying that man has no nature.

To think of a human activity as governed throughout by mere conventions, or as having conventions which may as well be changed as not, depending upon some individual or other's taste or decision, is to think of a set of conventions as tyrannical. It is worth saying that conventions can be changed because it is essential to a convention that it be in service of some project, and you do not know a priori which set of procedures is better than others for that project. That is, it is internal to a convention that it be open to change *in convention*, in the convening of those subject to it, in whose behavior it lives. So it is a first order of business of political tyranny to deny the freedom to convene....

If it is the task of the modernist artist to show that we do not know a priori what will count for us as an instance of his art, then this task, or fate, would be incomprehensible, or unexercisable, apart from the existence of objects which, prior to any new effort, we do count as such instances as a matter of course; and apart from there being conditions which our criteria take to define such objects. Only someone outside this enterprise could think of it as an exploration of mere conventions. One might rather think of it as (the necessity for) establishing new conventions. And only someone outside this enterprise could think of establishing new conventions as a matter of exercising personal decision or taste. One might rather think of it as the exploration or education or enjoyment or chastisement of taste and of decision and of intuition, an exploration of the kind of creature in whom such capacities are exercised....

When my reasons come to an end and I am thrown back upon myself, upon my nature as it has so far shown itself, I can, supposing I cannot shift the ground of discussion ... use the occasion to go over the ground I had hitherto thought foregone. If the topic is that of continuing a series, it may be learning enough to find that I *just do*; to rest upon myself as my foundation. But if the child, little or big, asks me: Why do we eat animals? or Why are some people poor and others rich? ... or Who owns the land? or Why is there anything at all? ... I may find my answers thin, I may feel run out of reasons without being willing to say "This is what I do", what I say, what I sense, what I know, and honor that.

Then I may feel that my foregone conclusions were never conclusions *I* had arrived at, but were merely imbibed by me, merely conventional. I may blunt that realization through hypocrisy or cynicism or bullying. But I may take the occasion to throw myself back upon my culture, and ask why we do what we do, judge as we judge, how we have arrived at these crossroads. What is the natural ground of our conventions, to what are they in service? It is inconvenient to question a convention; that makes it unserviceable, it no longer allows me to proceed as a matter of course; the paths of action, the paths of words, are blocked. "To imagine a language means to imagine a form of life". In philosophizing, I have to bring my own language and life into imagination. What I require is a convening of my culture's criteria, in order to confront them with my words and life as I pursue them and as I may imagine them; and at the same time to confront my words and life as I pursue them with the life my culture's words may imagine for me: to confront the culture with itself, along the lines in which it meets in me.

STANLEY CAVELL

251

L=A=N=G=U=A=G=E

Number 8.   (Vol. 2, No. 2)   JUNE 1979.

Charles Bernstein & Bruce Andrews, Editors.

Subscriptions -- One year (four issues in 1979) for $4.
           Institutions: $8.

L=A=N=G=U=A=G=E is supported solely by subscriptions
and donations.

All queries, submissions, and checks to:
Charles Bernstein, 464 Amsterdam Ave, New York, NY 10024.

(C) 1979 by L=A=N=G=U=A=G=E

Distributed with the cooperation of the Segue Foundation.

ANNOUNCEMENTS: *11 POEMS* by Charles Bernstein (in *Roof* IX, with long
works by Davies, Dreyer, Inman & Robinson; $3 from 300 Bowery, NYC
10012). *JOINT WORDS* by Bruce Andrews & John Bennett (1979, Luna
Bisonte Prods—card packet, available from Andrews, 41 West 96th St,
NYC 10025).

In our next issue, we will be presenting a forum on the question:
"What qualities do you think writing has, or could have, that
contribute to a critique and understanding of the nature of
contemporary society, seen as a capitalist system?" --
Readers are welcome to submit for consideration short (up to 500
word) responses to some of the issues raised by this question.
Deadline is July 10.

L=A=N=G=U=A=G=E

NUMBER 9/10   OCTOBER 1979

THE POLITICS OF POETRY

*(This double issue began with the desire to focus attention on political
dimensions of current writing. To make some of those aspects and concerns
more explicit, and to encourage further discussion, we've asked a number
of writers to give their view of what qualities writing has or could have
that contribute to an understanding or critique of society, seen as a
capitalist system. Below, in alphabetical order, the responses of Kathy
Acker, Barbara Barg, Bruce Boone, David Bromige, Don Byrd, Chris Cheek &
Kirby Malone & Marshall Reese, Mark Chincer, Michael Davidson, Alan Davies,
Terry Eagleton, Larry Eigner, Brian Fawcett, P. Inman, Michael Lally, John
Leo, Chris Mason, Steve McCaffery, Michael Palmer, Robert Rakoff, Jed
Rasula, Peter Seaton, James Sherry, Ron Silliman, Alan Sondheim, Lorenzo
Thomas, Barrett Watten, Hannah Weiner, as well as our own.)*

KATHY ACKER :

NOTES ON WRITING -- from THE LIFE OF BAUDELAIRE

In the beginning Baudelaire wrote his poems in order to discover
his own image in them.

After a while self-absorption is boring because one sees thoughts
are only thoughts and one wants freedom.

So one gets involved with the process of creating thoughts, with
creation which is superfluous and gratuitous.

To avoid this superfluity and gratuity which every great artist
knows, pain, Baudelaire asserts himself, for no reason at all, a natural
rebel, against the world he knows. There's no other world. He needs
a world he can fight or else he'll be back in uneasiness.

One has to exist in pain.

Because Baudelaire kept running from pain, he had no friends and
few intimates among derelicts.

The difference between a writer and its world gives the reason for
writing. All mental existence is an expression, a measure of distance.

There's another way of saying this. Consciousness just exists: no reason: it is useless. There is no meaning in the world. Consciousness creates meaning.

Let's start again. A human being's life starts when two humans called parents for no reason in the world stick that kid into the world. Then the parents turn against the kid and tell the kid it has to do such-and-such and become SOMEBODY or else they'll kick it out or else the parents just turn against the kid and say YOU STINK. The kid realizes it was once part of a warm perfect hole whole not apart and *now* it has an existence: It is separate. It is itself. It has no meaning. The great cry is against no meaning cause that's scary and boring and painful.

The kid can't go back. Rather than remaining in pain, the kid says I'm not nothing pain, because I am separate. Fuck you. My separate-ness is fuck you is total hatred is and will always be against you against everything that exists. I am a natural rebel.

The poet knows how ridiculous any action is cause it's actually nothing, so he makes sure his poetry and everything else he does is as stupid as possible.

About method of writing: There's no such thing as real action. What we mean by *action* is creation. Because there's no meaning. Creation is pure freedom: before it there's nothing; it begins by creating its own principles. First and foremost it invents its own goal and in that way it partakes of the gratuitousness of consciousness. This explains camp.

I don't want any ethic. I don't want to say anything is right. I have no desire to tell anyone what to do and I just take teaching gigs for the money. I don't say this is how you write. I keep saying I don't know anyway of writing. I WANT TO SAY NO TO WHAT IS I WANT TO GO OVER: I DON'T WANT ANY CONTENT I JUST WANT EXTREMISM.

Once a human's grasped this truth: that there's no other end in this life except the one it's chosen, it no longer feels any desire to look for one. But suppose we don't care what we choose?

What I feel is lousy, immense discouragement, a heaviness of unbearable isolation...absence of desires, impossibility of finding any sort of amusement. I call this my laziness.

So I do things suddenly, when I don't think! anything! I seem to other people active, impulsive, destructive, a person who acts and doesn't care VIOLENT. This is the only way I can act. This is the only way I can write. Bad. Obviously I don't believe in anything I'm doing the minute I'm doing long enough for self-consciousness to arise I stop what I'm doing.

A poet a person has no morality.

I need your boringness your self-righteousness your hatred of me my paranoia just cause of who I am this loneliness solitude pain inside my head everything coming from the poverty I choose to keep flagellating myself to go over.

One needs laws, the laws of writing, so one can hate them.

BRUCE ANDREWS :

WRITING SOCIAL WORK & POLITICAL PRACTICE

"Language is practical consciousness" (The German Ideology). Mainstream criticism still fails to raise or demand an answer to key questions about *the nature of the medium* -- which remains the modernist project for an art form. So, talking about writing, we have different ways to characterize its medium, different ways that medium's distinguishing qualities can be acted upon. Different political practices & epistemologies are implied.

ONE

One mode of writing tips its hat to assumptions of reference, representation, transparency, clarity, description, reproduction, positivism. Words are mere windows, substitutes, proper names, haloed or subjugated by the things to which they seem to point. 'Communication' resembles an exchange of prepackaged commodities. Here, active signifying is subordinated, transitive. Its continuing *constitution* of the world is ignored. So are the materiality of words & the conventions by which they get generated. Words are mistaken for tools (if only they could disappear to make way for meanings that sit outside language). Our concepts or mental pictures are confused with referents & referents are attributed a secure identity that precedes their delivery into thought & words (the conventional nature of <u>that</u> relation is also ignored). An illusionism, the taken-for-granted, *the fetish*. An imagined 'oppositional' poetics stemming from this perspective would still be reductionist, naturalism (a breakdown theory, reformism, 'socialist' 'realism'). Or else poetry becomes complacent literature, ornamental reinforcement of the status quo.

TWO

An alternative structuralist view. Here the medium of writing is *language*, understood as a system. *The structure of the sign* determines that medium's intrinsic & distinguishing characteristics: the division of the sign into a signifier (material form) & a signified (concept or mental representation), the former related arbitrarily/conventionally to the latter. Word matter is not dissolved by reference but exists relationally within an overall sign system. Signification occurs negatively, through *difference* & opposition -- terms signify by being differentiated from all other terms, not intrinsically or transparently.

Just as representational literature (dominant form) rests on an implicit definition of words as largely transparent tools of reference, other kinds of writing practice correspond to this second, relational definition of the medium (sign/language). It could be a cataloging of the properties of the linguistic system, a didactic or playful yet still dependant practice. More radically, the poetics would be those of *subversion*: an anti-systemic detonation of settled relations, an anarchic liberation of energy flows. Such flows, like libidinal discharges, are thought to exist underneath & independent from the system of language. That system, an armoring, entraps them in codes & grammar. Normative grammar -- a machine for the accumulation of meaning seen as surplus value & for territorializing the surface relations among signifiers by converting them into an efficient pointing system

The coherence between signifier & signified is conventional, after all -- rather than skate past this fact, writing can rebel against it by breaking down that coherence, by negating the system itself. Result: an experimentalism of diminished or obliterated reference. This would deliberately violate the structure of the sign, make the signifieds recede even more from the foreground occupied by supposedly autonomous signifiers. Characterizing the medium this way, we can find a brief for actually instituting opacity, promoting a spillage or dissemination -- Not from caring about message or meaning, but caring about the eruptiveness of material being put into distinctive relationships. So: a spectrum stretching from 'stylistic display' work to a more disruptive political work -- within the mostly self-contained linguistic system, of the sign.

Writing can attack the structure of the sign after declaring that settled system of differences to be repressive. But there's an ironic twist here. The Blob-like social force of interchangeability & *equivalence* (unleashed by the capitalist machine, and so necessary to the commodification of language) precedes us: it has actually carried quite far the erosion of the system of differences on which signification depends. It's reached the point where a coercive organization of grammar, rhetoric, technical format & ideological symbols is normally imposed in everyday life to even get these eroded differences to do their job any more (an assembly line to deliver meaning, of certain kinds). So to call for a heightening of these deterritorializing tendencies may risk a more homogenized meaninglessness (& one requiring even more coercive props) -- an 'easy rider' on the flood tide of Capital.

A calculated drainage of the referential qualities of individual words, for example, may deviate from established rules in a revelatory way, yet still abdicate the central struggle over meaning. That remains to be fought over the fetish, over myth & ideology, the representations & consumptions of fixed meanings.

THREE

Whether we bypass the referential fetish by writing non-signs or whether we tackle & problematicize it depends, again, on how we define the medium. Writing is actually constitutive of these underlying libidi-

nal flows; it _IS_ the desire for meaning, if not message. This is a
third characterization of the medium, acknowledging the usefulness
of the second one but acknowledging its limitations also.

Here, the distinguishing quality of writing is _the incessant_ (&
potential) _production of meaning & value_. Created through the articulation of writing, which is neither a representational positing of "the"
world by imitation of signifieds nor simply a dizzy surface play of
signifiers. Meaning isn't just a surplus value to be eliminated -- It
comes out of a productive _practice_. Not passively, as a derivative of
a system of differences (pre-defined) prior to composition. [Even obsessive attack & clever derangement may seem derivative] Instead, active --
back & forth: a relay constantly making contexts out of a fabric of
markings: writing & reading.

Those ideologies & fixed meanings can be reinforced (1.); or blown
apart by wild schizzed-out eruptions (2.); or they can also be opposed
by (3.) a political writing practice that unveils demystifies the creation & sharing of meaning. That problematicizes the ideological nature
of any apparent coherence between signified & referent, between signified
& signifier (for example, by composing words around axes other than
grammar/pointing function --). [By contrasting example, see how familiar
social ways of (verbs: to contextualize, naturalize, commodify, fetishize, make instrumental) language only shrink the theatre of meaning --
lay down a law, a lie, a line, a grammar, a code, illusion. _Writing as
Critique._] Not to make the words or signifiers provocatively opaque
irrelevant, but to stress their use value & productivity in the face of
mechanisms of social control.

Writing doesn't need to satisfy itself with pulverizing relations &
discharging excess. It can _charge_ material with possibilities of
meaning -- not by demolishing relations but creating them, no holds
barred, among units of language (even when these seem superficially like
a pulverized normality). These relations are constitutive & germinative
of meaning. A _practice_, based on this definition of the medium: to
create conditions under which the productivity of words & syllables &
linguistic form-making can be felt, & given aesthetic presence.

To make the word the basis of extensions. Instead of a derivative
(sublimate) of previously established connections, the word as "the
dwelling place," where meaning will insist on spinning out of the closed
circuit of the sign, to reach or act on the world (not only as it is, as
it could be). Amnesia or blindness about this _productivity of_ writing
stands alongside the prevalence of individualized self-preening consumption. Socialisms / necessary but not sufficient conditions. Yet
only a dramatic change in the structure of capitalist society is likely
to disorganize the fetish, the narrowness of readership (& therefore the
capabilities of writing), the dominance of ideological restrictive
notions of what poetry & language can be. To politicize -- not a closure
but an opening.

BARBARA BARG :

1. Which of the following communicates its meaning most directly and
    exactly? a) a musical composition b) a traffic light c) a group
    of words d) weather

2. The written mood that will affect the masses most is one of
    a) hope b) despair c) cheerfulness d) rage e) regret

3. An amateur writer is one who
    a) is limited in talent b) distrusts other amateurs c) has great
    enthusiasms d) tires easily

4. Feelings that produce good writing
    a) thrive in urban centers b) are based on the prevailing standard
    of living c) are based on science d) are based on science which
    is based on the prevailing standard of living d) come mostly from
    Pakistan

5. Historically, writing
    a) has become a subject for formal study b) offends the wise c) is
    remembered only in part d) has commercial appeal

6. The most powerful writing deals with
    a) definition b) incidents c) grudges d) pure form e) sex
    f) emotional spasms g) attaining manhood

7. Which phrase best describes contemporary writing?
    a) working without pay b) The Age of the Experts c) contributions
    of gifted dabblers d) in praise of amateurs e) the experts'
    superiority over the amateurs

8. In his/her writing, a writer should mostly convey
    a) maladjustment b) condescension c) curiosity d) arrogance
    e) innocence f) professionalism

9. Great writing occurs when the writer is
    a) young b) recovering from a serious illness c) "in love"
    d) "spurned" e) exalted in mind f) dead

10. Writing gets written because writers
    a) desire recognition b) wish to avenge themselves on teachers
    c) need to give expression to their feelings d) hope to impress
    others with their wisdom e) feel they have a message for young,
    old, and the not-yet-born f) know someone has to do it

11. When writers converse in public they
    a) defend Melville against his critics b) show that Kerouac wrote
    well c) describe Rimbaud's growth as a literary artist d) should
    listen to themselves talk

12. Women writers
    a) are only concerned with content b) don't have happy marriages
    c) should always have men edit their works d) are naturally
    gullible e) are always referred to as "women writers"

13. Writers who write about "love" present only
    a) optimistic reports b) pessimistic reports c) limited infor-
    mation d) government propaganda e) distorted and biased viewpoints

14. In times of stress, writers
    a) support radical movements b) become more closemouthed c) stop
    regular news services d) distrust everyone e) revert to primitive
    techniques

15. Which phrase best describes writing's "place" in your life?
    a) a shelter of long duration b) a haven from a sudden storm c) an
    overnight stopping place d) an Indian outpost e) a vacation resort

16. Do you write most creatively
    a) in summer only b) on drugs c) day (night) d) before a reading
    e) instead of eating f) in violation of the law

17. Writing is mostly about
    a) maintaining writing b) selling one's self a likable image of
    one's self c) selling others a likable image of one's self
    d) control over one's own productions e) aspiring to produce an
    imperishable monument f) the inevitable

CHARLES BERNSTEIN :

THE DOLLAR VALUE OF POETRY

*Social force is bound to be accompanied by lies. That is why all
that is highest in human life, every effort of thought, every effort of
love, has a corrosive action on the established order. Thought can
just as readily, and on good grounds, be stigmatized as revolutionary
on the one side, as counter-revolutionary on the other. In so far as
it is ceaselessly creating a scale of values ·'that is not of this world',
it is the enemy of forces which control society.*
                            (Simone Weil in Oppression and Liberty.)

So writing might be exemplary--an instance broken off from and
hence not in the service of this economic and cultural--social--force
called capitalism. A chip of uninfected substance; or else, a 'glimpse',
a crack into what otherwise might...; or still, "the fact of its own
activity", autonomy, self-sufficiency, "in itself and for itself" such
that.... In any case, an appeal to an 'other' world, as if access is

not blocked to an experience (experiencing) whose horizon is not totally a product of the coercive delimiting of the full range of language (the limits of language the limits of experience) by the predominating social forces. An experience (released in the reading) which is non-commoditized, that is where the value is not dollar value (and hence transferable and instrumental) but rather, what is from the point of view of the market, no value (a negativity, inaudible, invisible)--that non-generalizable residue that is specific to each particular experience. It is in this sense that we speak of poetry as being untranslatable and unparaphrasable, for what is untranslatable is the sum of all the specific conditions of the experience (place, time, order, light, mood, position, to infinity) made available by reading. That the political value of poems resides in the concreteness of the experiences they make available is the reason for the resistance to any form of normative standardization in the ordering of words in the unit or the sequencing of these units, since determining the exact nature of each of these is what makes for the singularity of the text. (It is, for example, a misunderstanding of the fact of untranslatability that would see certain "concretist" tendencies as its most radical manifestation since what is not translatable is the experience released in the reading while in so far as some "visual poems" move toward making the understanding independent of the language it is written in, ie no longer requiring translation, they are, indeed, no longer so much writing as works of visual art.)

Certainly, one method is the restoration of memory's remembering on its own terms, organizing along the lines of experience's trace, a reconstruction released from the pressures of uniform exposition--"the only true moments" the ones we have lost, which, in returning to them, come to life in a way that now reveals what they had previously concealed--the social forces that gave shape to them. So what were the unseen operators now are manifest as traces of the psychic blows struck by the social forces (re)pressing us into shape (ie: "a sigh is the sword of an angel king"). *"What we do is to bring our words back"* --*to make our experiences visible*, or again: to see the conditions of experience. So that, in this way, a work may also be constructed--an "other" world *made* from whatever materials are ready to hand (not just those of memory)--structuring, in this way, possibilities otherwise not allowed for.

Meanwhile, the social forces hold sway in all the rules for the "clear" and "orderly" functioning of language and Caesar himself is the patron of our grammar books. Experience dutifully translated into these "most accessible" codes loses its aura and is reduced to the digestible contents which these rules alone can generate. There is nothing difficult in the products of such activity because there is no distance to be travelled, no gap to be aware of and to bridge from reader to text: what purports to be an experience is transformed into the blank stare of the commodity--there only to mirror our projections with an unseemly rapidity possible only because no experience of "other" is in it. --Any limits put on language proscribe the limits of what will be experienced, and, as Wittgenstein remarks, the world can easily be reduced to only the straight rows of the avenues of the industrial district, with no place for the crooked winding streets of the old city. "To imagine a language is to imagine a form of life"--think of that first 'imagine' as the active word here.

"Is there anybody here who thinks that following the orders takes away the blame?" Regardless of "what" is being said, use of standard patterns of syntax and exposition effectively rebroadcast, often at a subliminal level, the basic constitutive elements of the social structure --they perpetuate them so that by constant reinforcement we are no longer aware that decisions are being made, our base level is then an already preconditioned world view which this de-formed language "repeats to us inexorably" but not *necessarily*. Or else these formations (underscored constantly by all "the media" in the *form* they "communicate" "information" "facts") take over our form of life (see *Invasion of the Body Snatchers* and *Dawn of the Dead* for two recent looks at this), as by posthypnotic suggestion we find ourselves in the grip of--living out --*feeling*--the attitudes programmed into us by the phrases, etc, and their sequencing, that are continually being repeated to us--language control = thought control = reality control; it must be "de-centered", "community controlled", taken out of the *service* of the capitalist project. For now, an image of the anti-virus: indigestible, intransigent.

BRUCE BOONE :

WRITING, POWER AND ACTIVITY

Modernism, particularly in its completed forms in recent trends in poetry, can only be understood and validated, partly or wholly or not at all, insofar as these same trends represent a specifically utopian moment in language. Charles Bernstein's essay just above in this issue on "The Dollar Value of Poetry" reminds us of this. "Social force," Bernstein says citing Simone Weil, "is bound to be accompanied by lies." Poetry then can refuse to be in the service of capitalism by being "untranslatable," "unparaphrasable." In a commodity society, we might say, poetry can refuse an exchange-value to make itself available as use-value, or to use another term, text (-uality). Recent trends in poetry can be described as the attempt to deny this commodity aspect of language.

How far should we go in this project? The question is not simple. It implies that the project is historically conditioned, and developmental, and that at a certain point it will have to be thought through again when objective conditions change. In the last analysis the reciprocity between what writing *is* and what it *ought to be* becomes a question of what writing actually does, that is, politics. To judge from a plurality of practices like that of this magazine, the imperative to formulate writing questions politically is recognized more and more widely -- and what is more important, by poets themselves. To place ourselves in this discussion then in the last analysis seems to be to ask how writing can relate to revolution, that is, class and liberal struggles. But not in any simplistic way. What is at stake here is the ability to give full play to the two poles of instrumentality and self-referentiality. Until the present, though, it has been generally assumed that it is the second of these poles, the self-referential aspect of language, that ought to give writing its self-nature and legitimacy for others.

But it is hard to imagine how this question, phrased in just such a way, can avoid having an eternal, once-and-for-all aspect to it. Posing the question in this way one doesn't so easily arrive at history. If indeed a utopian content were the only criterion of what a useful and acceptable writing has been or continues to be, finding writing that didn't embody that criterion would become a difficulty interesting only to the most incurable of scholastics....

But perhaps we can sharpen this question by rephrasing it. Is it possible to imagine a modernism that doesn't assimilate itself into the project of symptomatic reading? That is to say, into a humanism. But what about struggle then? Taking sides? Being parti pris? Or are these concerns out of date in our formalist era? Of course one assumes they are not. But *if* they are not, it's hard to see how they wouldn't be instrumental concerns. If all literature expresses and embodies a yearning for a non-alienated future, it isn't clear in the balance how aspirations for participatory writerliness -- a readerly praxis -- do not end as subjective improvements that may become indispensable to reaction itself. This possibility poses a useful limit case. For it once more foregrounds the political.

Literary history is in a sense the enumeration of past consensuses of this problem that are no longer seen as viable. Romanticism and the cult of the artist. Symbolism and alienated utopia. Modernism and the fetishization of language as product. Described in this way, however, the trajectory is one that grows increasingly melancholy. In each of these stages literature has more and more radically narrowed its rights to the public participation in the ongoing construction of society by itself -- inseparable from power. A profound disjunction, that has proved favorable neither to power nor to literature. Yet both continue to influence each other, fascinate each other, and their uneasy attractiveness seems to register the uneven development of revolution itself. This specific inability to think writing and power at one and the same time then comes to have a name. It is false consciousness.

2.   So perhaps we can start again and understand writing, poetry, as developed in our time as a *critique of power*. Such a critique -- a denigration or disavowal -- can now be usefully described and evaluated from a political-historical perspective. The refusal of the moment of power in the transition stage to socialism becomes objectively regressive or even reactionary as the refusal of contestation. Simultaneously, though, this refusal names the utopian content of a later period. But in the transition to this later time -- communism -- the critique of power takes on a positive meaning and no longer functions regressively. It becomes instead the means of expediting a passing over to the era of history proper, to the dismantling of the state and its apparatuses and to the first general realization of a human social life. The legitimacy of writing as a critique of power then stands or fails in relation to its historical timeliness in utopian struggles. In periods when legitimate demands are given utopian formulations, the anti-instrumental character of this kind of writing gives it a definite progressive function. In an era of class struggle, however, when political demands take on an instrumental complexion, such a writing may come to seem less useful. At this point writing may often become propaganda. Such at least has been the classical and binary model. Yet there are strong indications from our own time that the model has been broken down and that these either-or formulations have been simply bypassed.
      This is the dilemma. Modernism's alliance with terrorism and disorder has become irrelevant precisely to the extent that communistic or utopian possibilities have begun to make their presence felt in collective, durable political formulations in objective association with the working class. And to the degree that these new utopian forces make themselves felt politically, writing is to that extent forced to rethink its abdication from power. By a consensual removal of itself to the margins of the public sphere of commodity production -- in order to privilege utopian demands for use-value -- writing historically founded its notion of self-legitimacy on a reintegration in the communist future. But what if in a variety of regions and in germinal form that future has *already* begun to make its appearance in the advanced capitalist countries in the West?

3.   All this of course is to speak once more of the cultural revolution, and to ask again if any legacy remains 10 years after Maoism, May of '68 in Paris, the anti-war days of the '60s and Counterculture, and the Prague Spring....
      What has happened? In 10 years objectively anarcho-communist forms of political organization have sprung up and proliferated wherever one looks. Feminism and the gay movement, ecology and anti-nuclear movements -- in Europe and in this country both -- power issues on a municipal level, consumers' and tenants' movements, the large-scale prison movement and so on -- a whole spectrum of liberation organizations has now arisen. Their impact has been to raise issues in mass political organizations, such that

their solution is not possible within a program advancing a demand for socialism alone, but only on the basis of one making radical demands *beyond* that -- to communism, in fact.

Within this perspective one might legitimately ask if the solution of writing and writers can still remain what it has been programmatically -- that is, a political absence validated by the notion of a critique of power in an autonomous writing area. Early in the 19th Century this was the concordat reached between writing and society, an agreement according to which society's writing practice was from then on to seem something other than self-expression. But if this agreement is now seen as renegotiable, we will need another conceptual model in order to do it. For writing's renunciation of instrumental values in regard to language will continue to imply the negation of an attempt at power as long as writing and power are seen in a relation of mutual exclusivity. If, in other words, writing must always be either on the side of utopia or on the side of instrumentality. And if -- more radically -- class and liberation struggles are to persist in regarding each other with stares of non-recognition. In this case surely writing would remain exterior to power, and power to writing. But what if the situation were to change? What if at a certain point in history, class struggle were to begin to have a doubly implicating relationship with human liberation struggle? And what if human history had begun to think socialism and communism *globally* and *at the same time*? -- and here the work of Rudolf Bahro might be seen as a dramatic indicator of these very possibilities. If one were to be able to think the situation in some such way as this, one could also conceive of the possibility of some collective intellectual work existing on its own behalf. Rather than instrumentality for another, writing's relation to power would then be self-expression. This new model would have profound implications for the norms and forms of writing as now practiced. For writing's 'eternal', or unreflected, premise has been that the notion of writing for another and that of writing as a commodity are in reality one and the same thing -- an understanding that has made modernism possible. But let us suppose for a moment that the situation has changed. Let us suppose that this binary description is no longer adequate to the course of events. Writing now grounds itself in an *interior* relation to power. It becomes a self-expression, and a group practice. With this supposition writing's past is simply the series of discrete moments, salvageable enclaves or testimonials to what is still to come. Its present on the other hand becomes the collective intellectual practice one is engaged in at any moment. Writing would not be separate from whatever one does as an intellectual -- in the body of those who both think and act, and who stand in a certain tendential, final relation to the Modern Prince. That is how this reality might be mapped in the present. And here one can already see certain points of possible focus. These are probably very ordinary or predictable areas like work in mass or sectarian organizations, critical and educational outputs, the construction of political narrations or what-have-you.

In all this play would be supposed. This writing would be instrumental in a new way, certainly, but never in a sense that didn't say 'we,' that wasn't freely willed. It probably wouldn't get along with commissars.

Naturally one supposes that this writing has begun and that it is only a question of locating it -- and that each can begin finding it in her life or his. It is impossible to assume that this writing has not already begun in places one visits each day. Writers, in this view, are simply people engaged in reaching, political organization, community work and liberation groups, and so on -- in fact in normal activities we are already engaged in. This is the opposite of modernism and écriture. Above all, a writing like the one I am supposing accepts its relation to power. It knows it has no other choice. But in this it feels tremendously exuberant, at the thought of the possibilities opening before it. And it knows too, it is embarked.

DAVID BROMIGE :

WRITING THE WRONG

Not to debunk the disjointed nature of existence, but at 11 I won an election as Labor candidate, & at 14 was leading goal-scorer for Cricklewood Rangers -- a soccer team. How much of writing knocks life out of the accidental, orders things to make them reasonable! Because my name had to appear in the reports of our games (625 words max.) I wrote for The Kilburn Times, these were signed "D. Mansfield, Club Sec'y." "Following a deft assist from winger Cece Belle, Bromige drove a daisy-cutter through the legs of astonished Harlesden General Post Office goalie Al Soldofsky." "Minutes later, Bromige again rattled the back of the G.P.O. onion-bag." That moment when it's all pivoted & in the balance, in language as in sport! But chance favors the prepared mind. Cece & I spent hours perfecting these moves. Came the match, none worked; but I had lucky anatomy. No goalie could predict off which part of me the ball would next richochet. That first goal against Harlesden: Cece put the fetish right to my feet. I shoulda hit it first time with my left. But nature favors my right foot; curiously, since I'm left-handed. Which is why I have trouble with knots. Killing the ball with my right foot, I stood looking down at the almost perfect sphere, admiring once more its handsome paneling. Oh dear! My shoe-strings were untied. My teammates were shouting, urging me to a decision. Soldofsky was creeping forward, obscuring my range. I let fly with my right foot (by what miracle of the will brought to action? by what bootstraps self-raised?), but my left foot was standing on the lace of my right boot. As I fell, my left foot knocked against the ball & the rest is history. I couldn't have done it alone. Well, you couldn't say all this in The Kilburn Times. Its editor had yet to hear Rae Armantrout's

"The smallest/distance/inexhaustible." His prose-model was ad-copy: "Fall on life's thorns? Bleed?" Can I blame him for the corners I cut -- leading up to my last piece, concerning the game with the Neasden Flashers? Did I say, we didn't even have regular goalposts, sometimes? In the match with Neasden, two piles of coats marked the horizontal limits of the goal; it was up to the referee whether the shot was low enough to have passed under the imaginary crossbar. Two minutes from the end, we were losing 3-4. Is narrative bourgeois fantasy? A mirror, the only true Protestant relic? Ron Silliman, a confessional poet? *Did* Tristan's shot pass beneath the non-existent bar? We all thought so, but the mediator said "no." When I wrote this up, I told the Truth: "Tristan evened the score scant seconds from the final whistle with a well-gauged, twisting lob." We had practice, the same day my account appeared. All my teammates thought I had done wrong. "But you saw for yourselves!" Even Tristan was pissed-off at me. "But I got your name into print!" No dice. They admitted it had been a goal, but they maintained the ref's decision is final. I did not agree with this generality. "Humor is humor," I said, "whether in films or on the stage." "We have no time!" They answered, "do what you're told." The scene was in the center of the road; I left it & sat on the curb. This was, as it happened, off to the left, & when 11, in the mock-election held in sixth grade, I was up against a Liberal, a Conservative, & a Communist candi- date. Robin Crusoe was the Communist: he knew more political theory than the rest of the class put together, including Mr. King, our teacher. But I sensed the mood of the nation; later this year a Labor government *would* displace Winston in a landslide; I polled 25 votes, Crusoe, two. One of those two was mine.

DON BYRD :

STATEMENT FOR L=A=N=G=U=A=G=E

1. Humans may finally become what Aristotle calls them, political animals. That means we might recognize that life is in a constant state of emergency. Emerge(ncy). Only in that knowledge is political life possible. Otherwise there is reversion to a constitution, the words of the king or the poet or to custom. Otherwise life is interpretation rather than action. Otherwise, "History is ritual and repetition," as Olson reads it out of Melville, rather than production of what? Call it fresh air.

Both The Prelude and the Bessemer converter have reference only to their own consistency; both are instances of the organic in ritual mimicry of the inorganic (and never doubt that Bessemer converters are less organic than the men who design and run them). Nietzsche's mad laughter was the last clamoring of the sense of ritual mastery (though its forms haunt us). Madness keeps open the space where the assertion of recurrence is uncompromised. Nietzsche's willing of will is the mastery of life. It is mastery cleansed of all idealism, and, so, oblivious to the markings in the world by which idealism creates a shared theater.

I take it that now the tedium of repetition may overcome the satisfaction. One might now prefer the uncertainty of life to the monotony of death.

2. Orthodox Marxism has failed to produce interesting art and art theory because Marx could only envision the classless society as an inorganic becalm-ment. He studied the art of the western world thoughtfully, and the utopia it proclaims, from Gilgamesh on, is death.

In this late stage of dialectical stall, we begin to see again that the alienation of labor and the alienation of language are equivalent -- very nearly interchangeable -- terms, as, of course, Hegel was aware: "Language *and* labour are outer expressions in which the individual no longer retains possession of himself *per se*, but lets the inner get right outside him, and surrenders it to something else" (my emphasis). We now begin to see, especially given the Lacanian discourse, that Freud and Marx develop Hegel by halves. Their efforts to put us back into contexts which can be lived as well as thought in effect posit an element of alienation as the cost of overcoming another element (death dogs even our best efforts).

The obvious course -- a synthesis of Marx and Freud -- has not proven to be a solution. There are irreconcilable differences between Freud's conception of civilized discontent, for example, and Marxist utopianism, and, in practical terms, the demand for loosening the bonds of psychic repression -- a bourgeois demand -- does not necessarily coincide with loosening the bonds of economic repression. Freudo-Marxists, from the surrealists and Wilhelm Reich to Marcuse, current left-wing structuralists, and Deleuze and Guattari, have not managed to establish cogent theoretical grounds for revolutionary action. The synthesis seems inevitably to involve either an anti-Oedipal casualness or pessimism (Marcuse speaks of "the depth of the gap which separates even the possibilities of liberation from the established state of affairs").

I do not want to deny the survival value of casualness or the justifiable grounds for pessimism, nor do I want to argue against my fundamental sympathies. Marx's analysis, however, recognizes neither the antagonisms between human nature and inhuman nature (the basis for the technological utopia in which labor will be effectively eliminated), nor the intensified self-consciousness the dialectic requires. Freud, on the other hand, may be read as proposing a reconciliation of the individual to the sources of his antagonism (neo-Freudianism) or as a glorification of the individual and individual self-expression so thorough as to make communal action nearly impossible.

CRIS CHEEK, KIRBY MALONE, MARSHALL REESE :

TV TRIO present CAREER WRIST
            [for the international *Festival* of *Disappearing(s)* *Art(s)*]
            [from the action-sound detention wing]

"Writing has never been capitalism's thing. Capitalism is profoundly
illiterate. The death of writing is like the death of God or the death
of the father: the thing was settled a long time ago, although the news
of the event is slow to reach us, and there survives in us the memory of
extinct signs with which we still write. The reason for this is simple:
writing implies a use of language in general according to which graphism
becomes aligned on the voice, but also overcodes it and induces a fic-
titious voice from on high that functions as a signifier. The arbitrary
nature of the thing designated, the subordination of the signified, the
transcendence of the despotic signifier, and finally, its consecutive
decomposition into minimal elements within a field of immanence uncovered
by the withdrawal of the despot -- all this is evidence that writing
belongs to imperial despotic representation...Of course capitalism has
made and continues to make use of writing; not only is writing adapted
to money as the general equivalent, but the specific functions of money
in capitalism went by way of writing and printing, and in some measure
continue to do so..."

"Fourteen dollars and twenty eight cents is more attractive than fourteen
dollars because of the 28."

WHERE'S HABIT FORMING

Writing can't be limited to dealing with capitalism. Capitalism is a
setback. Writing as it relates to capitalism is the limitation the
framework poses. The concerns should be against oppressive structures.
Writing has become referential to itself -- to the making of objects.
When writing informs writing & writers & writing writers the systems are
securities.

SHKLOVSKY'S KUGEL

Literature, rather than visual or performance work, is the only useful
residue left to us of Russian Futurism.   True___   False___

There are no differences between feudal states and capitalist states.
                                        True___   False___

Where's the structural control.   True___   False___

Language (as understood in its use in a community) is comprised of approximately ten per cent verbal elements; the rest consists of gesture, atmosphere, billboards, environmental drift, etc.
                                        True___   False___

Publishing is imperialism.   True___   False___

I embody all that I most must hate & fear. True___   False___

WRITING IS A CONSERVATIVE TENDENCY

If writing is to defuse oppressive structures rather than re-fuse them
its first task is not to be the mechanics of escapism. Lullabies are
made of words. When words set themselves up they form double binds.
Narrative constitutes a parallel life which absorbs the reader leaving
her/his body depoliticized. Repressed sexualities objectify themselves
through the use and design of machinery. The typewriter is not a lover.
The investment of sexuality in mechanics leads writers to confuse
eroticism with death, the erotic with the dead. What dies is not the
author but the authenticating enunciation sustained by the immortality
granted the subject. Properly speaking, "glyphs" are the signatures
(cuts in the ear, brandmarks) of the owners of their cattle.

NOTES TO MYSELF

Think of it as why we had to cook my poor dad's flesh. Think of it as
open before using. Think of it as vanity and sink. Think of it as our
own. Think of it as fresh daily. Think of it as I will behave in line.
Think of it as 60 cycle hum. Think of it as proudly we hail these.
Think of it as exclusive adhesive. Think of it as most folks use.
Think of it as sheer bandages. Think of it as all purpose grind. Think
of it as capitalism is a setback. Think of it as machines do it for
you. Think of it as June 1979. Think of it as the people's pharmacy.
Think of it as a small curd. Think of it as not less than. Think
of it as our mail. Think of it as new easy re-close. Think of it
as drink your drink. Think of it as amusement only. Think of it
as a half a dozen of another. Think of it as a wet book. Think of it
as a soggy cover. Think of it as money talks. Think of it as you can
laugh all you want. Think of it as that means I can do what. Think of
it as do you read me. Think of it as a lot to look forward to. Think
of it as the author has no authority.

GROWN ASLEEP

The ghosts of eroticism, so clear in the piston & cylinder, oblique into
information storage & retrieval.
"...It was only after the remaining two had consumed what food they had --
some chocolate bars, a bag of potato chips, a granola bar and cough
drops -- did they decide to eat Don Johnson. 'We talked to God and we
prayed, and whatever else came we knew we had to eat him and we did. I
want it known that we aren't ashamed. We knew it was right. God told
us it was right. We knew it was what Don would have wanted,' he
explained..."

The endorsement of hierarchies induces specialization. Mystification
is manipulative. Its power misleads in appearing to be productive
energy; it is not generative, it's mediocre. An objective life is un-
desire. When sacrifice to the revolution begins revolution ends: here
we mean subjectivity without individualism; micropolitics; simultaneous
multiple corners. Hierarchies control through achievement by regulating
& witholding information as to the means of achieving: honesty's broken
spoon. It's hard to be totally positive. "Giordano Bruno comes to mind,
whoever he is." "$14.28 is more attractive than $14, it's just that
way." "Giordano Bruno, I think they burned him, he was too positive."

SOME DO & SOME DO: SHAMANISM, CYBERNETICS, & REPRESENTATION

"...Lo! The lid is raised, curiosity stands on tip-toe, eyes sparkle
with anticipation, little hands are clapped in ecstasy, almost too great
to find expression in words. The hour arrives -- the moment wished and
feared..."
"...T.A. (Transactional Analysis), T.M. (Transcendental Meditation),
E.S.T. (Erhard Seminars Training, not exactly electro-shock, E.C.T.),
Creative Fidelity, Creative Aggression, Provocative Therapy, Gestalt
Therapy, Primal Scream, Encounter Therapy, the conducting of three-day
'Marathons', a form of deep massage, Bio-energy, Japanese Hot Tubs (you
take off your clothes and enter them *en groupe* as part of liberation).
Then, 'Behaviour Mod' (the new generation Skinner) on how to toilet-
train your child in twenty-four hours -- and then on the next shelf
another book advertising a method of toilet-training your child in *less*
than twenty-four hours! I've no doubt that after some of these experiences some people feel better, or begin to 'feel', or feel more 'real' --
or whatever the ideals of capitalism prescribe for them..."

ONE LEG AT A TIME

OK. OK OK. OK OK OK. OK OK OK OK. OK OK OK OK OK. OK OK OK OK OK
OK. OK OK OK OK OK OK OK.

BIB

ANTI-OEDIPUS: CAPITALISM AND SCHIZOPHRENIA, Gilles Deleuze & Félix
Guattari (trans. Robert Hurley, Mark Seem, Helen R. Lane), Viking Press,
New York, 1977.
PRIVATE PARTS, Robert Ashley, Lovely Music Ltd., New York, 1977.
ZOO or LETTERS NOT ABOUT LOVE, Viktor Shklovsky (trans. Richard Sheldon),
Cornell Univ. Press, Ithaca and London, 1971.
THE PRISON HOUSE OF LANGUAGE, Fredric Jameson, Princeton Univ. Press,
Princeton, 1972.
CALIFORNIA PSYCHOLOGICAL INVENTORY, Consulting Psychologists Press, Inc.,
Palo Alto, 1956.
LE MACCHINE CELIBI/THE BACHELOR MACHINES (exhibition catalogue), Jean

Clair & Harald Szeemann eds., Rizzoli, New York, 1975.
MIDNIGHT/GLOBE (vol. 26, no.26), Rouses Point, 1979.
THE REVOLUTION OF EVERYDAY LIFE, Raoul Vaneigem (trans. John Fullerton & Paul Sieveking), Rising Free Collective, 1979 (total anticopyright).
BRITISH AND IRISH COOKING, Sally Morris, Galahad Books, New York, 1973.
SCHIZO-CULTURE issue of SEMIOTEXT(E) (Sylvère Lotringer ed.), "The Invention of Non-Psychiatry", David Cooper, New York, 1978.
BENJAMIN OBSCURA, Ron Silliman (excerpt published in L=A=N=G=U=A=G=E #6, December 1978; full text in RENEGADE #1, New York, 1979).
NOT AVAILABLE, The Residents, Ralph Records, San Francisco, 1978.
ZOMBIE, Fela & Afrika 70, Mercury Records, Chicago, 1978.
MORE THAN MEAT JOY, Carolee Schneemann, Documentext, New Paltz, 1979.

MARK CHINCER :

(The following is an excerpt of a letter that appeared in Lobby *37, 4/79, 280 Cherryhinton Road, Cambridge, England.)*

SOME THOUGHTS TOWARDS A MATERIALIST POETICS

the precondition for the existence of a literature - in this century an écriture - is the existence of language. materialist poetics goes beyond this structuralist datum to assert that the precondition for the existence of language is the existence of social forms of production - sensuous human activity on nature. wherefore: the precondition for literature is the existence of social forms of production which govern (but not in the sense of opposing a one-to-one causality as vulgar marxism wld assert) the modes of literality.

with this materialist understanding we can place many of the idealist formulations of structuralism and its kindred poetics - in the last analysis bourgeois disciplines for all their progressiveness - in their real context - IN MATTER - and use previously gained insights to develop our own goal: materialist poetics....

poetry distinguishes itself from 'ordinary language' - the referential, comotive function employed in everyday discourse - in that it uses language and its signs in themselves, not as functional devices to refer to externality. in this way language is the OBJECT, the SIGNIFIED of poetic discourse, a discourse which carries no direct reference to reality but continually defines its own referent in accordance with the way in which it organizes its signs, its text.

the idealism underscoring structuralism causes the line to be drawn here by its adherents, thus the indispensable concepts of the autonomy of the text and the process of 'making strange' - ostranenie/verfremdung - are

ensnared in a bourgeois-liberalist ideology of freedom and liberation:
the artist become able to do anything he wants, art raises one above
everyday drudgery. this is the u-turn performed by structuralist
critiques of literature: ...and this, I wld argue is occasioned by its
idealist fundament placing consciousness before being. what determines
literature it is argued, is the artist's attitude to language. this is
not incorrect as far as it goes, but idealists do not attempt to
investigate what has FORMED this attitude. so in their hands the concept
becomes debased to one of the free association of the artist with his
medium ie ANTI-MATERIALIST.

the concept of the text's autonomy undergoes similar ideological vulgarization. it is true that in a text 'anything is possible';... the text
creates its 'own' reality, internally consistent with itself. yet it is
clear that this process does not go on in a vacuum.,.. the social forms
of production and the level of technology attained by them - CLASS FORMS,
it should be noted - over-determine the modes of literary production: the
book as we know it today cannot be fully understood without seeing it in
terms of its materialist determination - the discovery of printing and
its status as a commodity....

the variation in modes of literality is thus determined by the artist's
attitude to the materiality that contains him/her; these attitudes have
not fallen from the sky, they are determined by the artist's own
relations in materiality: class origin, relation to the productive
forces, those of écriture in particular....

we begin with a 'structuralist' analysis of the processes at work within
the text. processes which are that text's own space and movement only
to take them further by examining the relationship of text-author-
society, the text's MATERIALITY.

poetry is artifice, a construct. it is capable of defining its own
reality on its own terms. an investigation into poetics concentrates
therefore not on what literature contains - which is generally to recu-
perate it into a normative ideology - but on HOW it contains its
datum.... progressive art makes no attempt to hide its status as
ARTIFICE, openly laying bare its techniques of construction....

materialist poetics seeks to rescue this valuable doctrine from its
idealist distortion resulting from the structuralists' concept of
literature as a self-contained, self-metamorphosing realm. an analysis
of any literature shows that laying bare the methods of production is
never necessarily in itself progressive if the process of revelation
is confined to infratextuality - the poems of walther von der vogelweide,
eg. it is only progressive on the plane of art, and this plane a
materialist can never see as wholly isolated, although s/he accords it
its own existence.

if our own poetic praxis is to be consciously materialist and progressive then we are concerned not simply with the laying bare of the artifice of all art - this is the death of any bourgeois concepts of 'finish' - but with the laying bare of the TEXT'S MODE OF PRODUCTION IN SOCIETY - its MATERIALITY. our poetry thus evolves from a critique of the bourgeois expectations of a work of art, namely that it should be 'finished' and 'accomplished', to being a critique of that whole society that is its matrix....

this is what i mean by a dialectic of autonomy and determination: we move between the two in order to pose the necessity of destroying determinants which are those of capitalism, so that the real autonomy of art is achieved in a higher mode of materiality, communist society.

MICHAEL DAVIDSON :

> *For, as Aristotle saith, it is not gnosis but praxis must be the fruit. And how praxis cannot be, without being moved to practice, it is no hard matter to consider.* (Sir Phillip Sidney)

Since any text, regarded as a mode of production, must be capable of analysis, why not start with the question posed by the editors of L=A=N=G=U=A=G=E. The fundamental problem with answering it lies in its blurring of distinctions between two rather different ideas: 1) that writing "has" qualities intrinsic to it and 2) that writing "could have" qualities leading to a social critique. The former implies a study of internal features. One might treat the linguistic structure of the declarative sentence as a microcosm of power relations in a capitalist society. The sentence's tidy organization of elements, its subordination of action to actor, its separation of subject from object could indicate attitudes toward human labor and the material world. Or, in terms of larger structures, one could discuss the "well made" essay and point to its implied valorization of idea to documentation, its positivist/deductivist bias, its emphasis on communication over the process of thought as extensions of bourgeois/technocratic thought.
On the other hand, what the editors seem to mean is "how can writing *be made* to critique capitalist society," whereupon the ancient dialogue between formalist and materialist surfaces again. The formalist contends that by radically altering the structure of conventional discourse, by decontextualizing, fragmenting, foregrounding the material element of language, he or she will illustrate the lesions and gaps within ruling class ideology. The materialist (and reflectionist) argues that all art is essentially ideological, and that analysis is carried out between base and superstructure in any literary work,

regardless of intention. In its vulgar form, this criticism looks for strictly economic, sociological "content" within the work. Obviously the answer to the question rests somewhere in between the formalist solution and the reflectionist theory.

Since I don't think writing has "qualities," per se, outside of a context of use, I would have to say that a critique of capitalist society begins with an art that investigates its own modes of production. I don't mean by this to emphasize self-reflexive art as practiced by current metafictionists -- an art which tends inwards toward a narcissistic literature of exhausted possibilities. I'm thinking here of an art which is conscious of its own vulnerability in a world of attractive, institutionalized solutions: an art which regards itself as a form of knowledge rather than a strategy in its pursuit; an art that in asserting its objectivity and integrity does so without forgetting the realm of human concern. (I am purposely avoiding naming what this art might be since to levy various critical criteria would only serve the interests of an already imperializing criticism; obviously, every new problem demands a new solution.) The lure of an objectified, ossified art, working in the service of "materiality" does little more than fetishize the realm of language and reinforce the dualism of subject and object all the more.

But this dualism can be useful, at least in one respect, in that it contains the boundary terms within which an interrogative (authentic) writing may occur -- a writing which works in the interstices between expressivist and objectivist modes. Such a writing would incorporate the moments in which language loses its purely instrumental character and becomes a mode of "humanizing practice." As Marx Wartofsky says, "...(the artwork) is a representation of a mode of action which is distinctively human...; in short, that art represents its own process of coming into being and insofar, exemplifies and objectifies the distinctively human capacity of creation." Art, considered thus broadly, should still be able to appeal to an actual (as opposed to a theoretical) reader and might even provide some of the *enargia* which Puttenham declared "...giveth a glorious lustre and light."

ALAN DAVIES :

$$\frac{\text{politics}}{\text{art}} = \text{politics}$$

$$\frac{\text{art}}{\text{politics}} = \text{art}$$

TERRY EAGLETON :

(The following is an excerpt from "Aesthetics and Politics", which originally appeared in New Left Review #107, 1978.)

Consider this curious paradox. A Marxism which had for too long relegated signifying practices to the ghostly realms of the superstructure is suddenly confronted by a semiotic theory which stubbornly insists upon the materiality of the signifier. A notion of the signifier as the mere peg of occasion for a signified, a transparent container brimfull with the plenitude of a determinate meaning, is dramatically overturned. On the contrary, the signifier must be grasped as the product of a material labor inscribed in a specific apparatus -- a moment in that ceaseless work and play of signification whose sheer heterogenous productivity is always liable to be repressed by the bland self-possession of sign systems. A centuries-old metaphysic of the signified is rudely subverted: the signified is no more than that always half-effaced, infinitely deferred effect of signifying practice which glides impudently out of our reach even as we try to close our fist upon it, scurrying back as it endlessly does into the privilege of becoming a signifier itself.

In trying thus to close our fist upon the signified, we are in fact attempting nothing less than the risible task of nailing down our very reality as human subjects. But what we will nail down, of course, will not be the subject, but the paranoic knowledge of the ego and its various identifications. In this ceaseless cat-and-mouse game, the subject, which is no more than the effect flashed cryptically from one signifier to another, the 'truth' which can be represented only in a discourse from which it is necessarily absented, will hunt frantically for its self-recognition through a whole fun-hall of mirrors, and will end up fondling some fetishized version of that primary self-miscognition which is, in Lacanian mythology, the mirror phase. Terrified of the very linguistic productivity of which it is the endlessly transmittable effect, the subject will attempt to arrest the signifying chain in order to pluck from it some securing signified -- a signified within which subject and object will blend infinitely into each other in an eternal carnival of mutual confirmation. The literary names for this are realism and representation -- those recurrent moments in which the *comedy* of writing -- the incongruous flailings by which, in heroically attempting to 'refer', it will finally do nothing but designate itself -- is gravely repressed for the ritual enthronement of some unblemished meaning which will fix the reading subject in its death-defying position.

SUBMISSIONS OF RELEVANT MANUSCRIPTS WELCOME

LARRY EIGNER :

Much more than enough boggles, drowns the mind and empties it - also, the more a man takes for granted, or over and above he needs to (forego, ignore, shut his eyes), the more he goes after to fill the head. ? Well, every day is new, at least in the morning. Take each. Here, whatever wakes you up says, have another. Some eternal present. It has to be a miscellany. No time for incoming shadows, sundown, or not too much, that is. Let's realize what there is. The variety. No regrets, or grievance.

Rapid transit? Somebody is/was lonely? Civilian? The life of a nude in one equatorial jungle or another? Bird? Elephant? Lion? Squirrel? Why do birds sing. There's interest.

Books, mag..s, eventually newspapers, as well as maps, legendary, make the best packages. World// Packed// All// Ways The more books the fewer of each, as wrote the author of Future Shock, the quicker their turnover they have. Is this adequate? Are there big enough islands? Too big? X is company and Y is a crowd. So maybe capitalism, constellation of miracles or not, let alone quantity (/quality) is mysterious.

O .. -mark something like sword overhead

BRIAN FAWCETT :

AGENT OF LANGUAGE

(The following is excerpted from an article and letter that appeared in Periodics, Number One, Box 69375 Sta. 'K', Vancouver, B.C. V5K 4W6, Can.)

I don't want to write. I don't want to go to Eatons. I don't want to write here because I will provide in the activity of writing a rhetoric useful to the maintenance of the status quo. I don't like the words *status quo*, its neutrality, taken (stolen) from a dead conservative language. Rhetoric...is useful only to the ruling class. The *ruling class* upsets me. I don't want to use left rhetoric either. They (the ruling class) are byproducts of a universally employed process of exploiting phenomena for specific ends without having ultimate purposes, good or evil. In language the same process dilates complexity for its own sake, making it opaque, thus taking the power of coherent action out of the hands of any single social or political unit. We (human beings) are left with an arid corruption. To write about the *ruling class* without focusing on the source of power that organizes its activity & which allows it to ignore the ultimate questions of mass justice & truth while allowing individuals the air & illusion of those qualities...on the third floor buying a pair of shoes made in Europe, a black wool coat with real mink grown on a farm...they would know what it is to be poor if there were words but words aren't here, and it's a long way to the basement where the poor buy synthetic wool checkered jackets with fake fur collars. I don't want to be in Eatons...

But I do want to buy something. No, sorry, that's an error. *I want to obtain something of value*, which is a struggle altho I have the money. I'm on the main floor between the basement & the third floor. I'm a bourgeois artist struggling to find value inside a language in which Beauty can't be spoken of in the same sentence as political or economic justice. Wrong floor. Go to the eighth floor, go to accounting. There are no words, they are, like the articles proffered from the store racks, inapporpriate, they don't fit, they are not of the materials of reality. I can't invent a new language, a device like the escalator to elevate me to the next level of meaning because the parataxis is broken, busted, the magic of Psyche's house is gone, is immaterial, no stairs, entrances, windows or exits...and I don't want to write anything that is not the materials of reality. ...

Nothing else happens. I made no singular error in activity or thought that lead me there rather than anywhere else. Nothing is that personal. It isn't a question of the personalness of the personal opposed to vast forces moving like grand dinosaurs of 19th century historical necessity, it's the similarity of destination -- into the taxonomic reflecting pools where...I don't want to write this, I don't want to be alone, reflecting by pools of sorrow or by vast lakes above turbines grinding the energy for these useless appliances stacked row upon row beneath sterile lights & lady in black w/ plug in hand, beckoning to me *here sir, is a fantastic labor-saving device to help the little lady help you in the morning. In just 35 seconds your morning coffee...*

Says Trotsky: *In a society split into classes, the democratic institutions, far from abolishing the class struggle, only lend the class interests a highly imperfect form of expression. The possessing classes have always at their disposal thousands of means to pervert and adulterate the will of labouring masses.*

Yeah says Cliff. *In Cuba it's not like you go to work for the government or stay on the outside, as if the government is an entity that's either beneficent or hostile. Those questions are answered. I mean, if you're an artist, you get a wage, you work to make the revolution clear & thorough. You stand outside, you're not an artist, you're just picking your teeth. There is no separate culture like we have.* I mean, like off in the closet, where I can talk as loudly or clearly as I want because it's describable as protest, or some phatic corner or other into which eventually walks a joker wearing a tight blue suit & says, *Hey baby, you got a career!!*

I don't want to write. In the guts of the city there is neither air nor a heart, there is only ourselves, choking in the guts. Which hang over the streets, wired for electricity and totally invisible. Crammed with cheap goods & ideas. The agent of language is lost in these streets. In the springs of the heart. Sprung, like an old mattress, or bulldozed to make way for some further developments. I'm in Eatons looking for the agent of language and the orders of the heart and the confirmation of justice, without words of my own.

... Our bloody technique mongering has led us down into the sump to the point where we've become convinced of the verity of language that is pure *within* so narrow a context of human existence its relatively harmless to the comings & goings of the real power in this life...parataxis, beloved parataxis, functions only inside the realm of personal emotion & the truth of our lives is that there is no *public* language that can be understood, I mean freely heard without the control of materials being witheld. (& this, I'd argue, is the real basis of contemporary marxism) So in the story I do something I've been taught not to do, which is to invade the rhetoric of the left to see if I can bring across what lies underneath its veneer. ...

I'm deathly tired & ashamed of the absence of public language in poetic thought -- it isn't good enough to press the conviction that if everybody could practice parataxis the structures that make our lives so awful wld crumble...

I think we have to destroy our poetics & our poetic techniques & start to reintroduce all the *active* voices that make up *this* world's thought & force if we want to really practice parataxis. The parataxis we've learned is classical, applies to a world 2500 years gone. This isn't Homeric greece. We have to introduce the abstract & rhetorical & deterministic & the mathematical & the vernacular. Even the buzz. Without fear or hope. As if poetry were a dead issue we might reify with that risk.

Emotion is a dead issue -- we know so much about its dynamics that it has gone into the abstract (you can't have read Freud & treat human emotions as if they're mysterious). What hurts about this is that its made all the verity the writers who taught us sought not worth a pinch of coonshit. (If you want to test this have a look at any of Lawrence's more didactic & less careful novels [like <u>Kangaroo</u>, which I just finished reading] -- his commotions of emotion & their extensions into landscape is/are vaguely embarrassing & dilettantish. Or watch the same process on the media, where its all done from the outside, & much more effectively. Id say the emotional is the least reliable source of information we now have, because its the most thoroughly manipulated.

Which leads back to my statement about the exploiting of phenomena/ organization of synaptic activity (or 19th century capitalism/20th century) Both activities have taken from most people the power to act, & by that I mean to act *knowingly*. Most of contemporary capitalism (or just state control because it has more to do with industrial organization than anything) draws its power from destroying our abilities to understand our environment & the consequences of social/political activities, or at least to restrict it to those areas sympathetic to the retention of the present forms of control. I guess I share with Dewdney the notion that it isn't the existence of a "ruling class" that matters, but a ruling structure that exceeds the power & understanding of those it benefits.

P. INMAN :

   Capitalist ideology hopes to dilute or deny the existence of any-thing other than the everyday given. By doing so current ideology stagnates thought, replaces the possibility of change with the statistic, frozen black on paper, legitimized by its very inertia. In rendering present social structures "natural" ideology underwrites their "immuta-bility", whether in terms of some kind of metaphysic or positivist scientism. (...or in what is the sociological equivalent to scientism, it promotes all reality as relative, hoping to defuse all social ideal-ism.)
   If only as a language that is other, a language outside the per-vasive ideolanguage of advanced capitalist society (which once having classified & defined, seeks to box in, contain) free language exists in a critical relation viz. capitalist superstructures. A language of the word instead of the worded, predigested, -fabricated; accepted fact. It's perhaps as simple as saying anything to make one think & examine. The degree to which language is self-concerned is the degree to which it remains unimplicated (?).
   Having said this, there are a few important qualifications to the above. For me any critical theory must of necessity exist within revo-lutionary praxis... neither the primary component of that praxis, nor servant to "practice". Whether the establishment of a revolutionary counter-hegemony (Gramsci) is a precondition for social transformation or not, once critical theory has become detached from practice (or at least the struggle toward a program for action) it becomes merely another academic discipline. Scholasticism drained of any real social content, ready to be taught at the state u.
   Gramsci's concept of the organic intellectual is helpful here. The organic intellectual was one who, unlike the traditional intellectual, was not a sub-class unto himself, separated from everyday life. "Theory" was not directing practice from above, but the self-expression of the proletariat's everyday struggle. (This shouldn't be taken as an argu-ment for some sort of Gramscian orthodoxy. For starters, the whole concept of "working class" has become problematic forty years later.)... Concretely, it would seem to me that all revolutionary critique must begin (attempt to) with an extensive analysis of class relations within present-day society. Who, what or where are/is the revolutionary class(es) in the USA today? Critiques for their own sake obviously dont make muxh sense. Criticism becomes revolutionary at the instant it somehow manages to come to grips with this question.

MICHAEL LALLY :

One "quality" that "comes to mind" is -- to isolate and describe and
record exact observations about "experience" and "objects" that otherwise are never shared beyond intimate relationships because they offer
an alternative perspective to "reality" than the one the "capitalist"
system (and maybe any "generally" applied "system") imposes through its
control of the distribution of "goods," including "art" and "language"
and other supposedly less "essential" "goods." *Honesty* is still, in my
opinion, one of the most revolutionary "forces" or "weapons" we always
have "at our disposal."

JOHN LEO :

/CAPITAL/ /WRITING/

    The mere juxtaposition of the word signs creates doubts which
unhinge and dismantle the familiar repressions, allowing for greater
oscillations between signifiers and signifieds (whose fundamental mis-
alignments it has been the business of Capital to conceal, wish away, or
stabilize by mediating or diverting the interpretive process even in
Capital's reterritorializing gestures). So: a countering that sets up
bibliographies and an itinerary of possible projects and which assumes
that a text's meaning production is always a collaboration/intersection/
exchange between two *a prioris* privileged by two names: Freud and Marx:
hence *autoproduction* (the drive(s), desire, libidinal economies, the
Subject) and *the real* (all institutional discourses, constraints, en-
codings, economies of the commodity, the Other). And names familiar and
unfamiliar: Lacan; Deleuze and Guattari; Kristeva; Fredric Jameson;
Stanley Aronowitz and John Brenkman and their new journal Social Text;
Rosalind Coward and John Ellis, Language and Materialism: Developments
in Semiology and the Theory of the Subject; and from Australia the
"'Working Papers' Collection," revising freudo-marxism in such anthologies as Language, Sexuality & Subversion, ed. Paul Foss and Meaghan
Morris.
    To see as preeminent in writing its intertextual *loci*, or oriented
spaces marked by relations and modes of material language in its spectrum
of specific performances from speech to written acts; a recognition
disabusing us of the notions that space is "neutral" or that "extrin-

sic" or "intrinsic" are transcendental categories governing writing analyses. To further question writing in its aspect as an archival repository which in turn grounds the archive (hence a hierarchy of writings, "evidence," "history"); Foucault's project, but pushed deep into Capital's Writing by Michel de Certeau's L'Ecriture de l'histoire. To grasp that the most devastating confrontations between writing and Capital today are critiques of the (patriarchal, ascendant) signifier (all bets on /signifier/ taken), e.g. Kristeva (esp. Polylogue and current work; some translations in Tell-Tale Sign, ed. Sebeok and the journal October), Helene Cixous, Luce Irigaray (Speculum de l'autre femme; Ce sexe qui n'en est pas un; see Language, Sex & Subversion), all connected by their work positing primordial biosociopolitical *differences* in female/male discourses (and thus *different* phenomonologies, semioanalyses, structurations . . .); and the continuing undoing of the hegemony of the signifier (and thus of capitalist representation) in Deleuze and Guattari, Jean-Francois Lyotard (e.g. Des Dispositifs pulsionnels; Discours, figure; some translations in Sub-Stance, Genre, Semiotext(e)), Pierre Klossowski (on Nietzsche and Sade), all of whom dance on the meeting-ground of intensities, redistributing flows, cathexes, the very possibilities of somatic (in)difference, "drive-devices," sophistry as the language of *affect*ation and desire, bachelor machines, the resituating of the phenomeno-semiotic exchanging as the gradating libidinization of Capital. With differing emphases, but still within the framework of the critique of representation offered by the deconstruction of (ideological) positionings of sign, signifier, signifieds and hence the position of the subject, a variety of revaluations are occurring of writing s figurations, typologies, and logical categories (e.g. implicit causalities) as these achieve the power effects of representation (a "window" we see an event *through*, or a "mirror" *on* which we passively regard a sort of duplication of the real). Here the work of Louis Marin (e.g. Etudes sémiologiques: écritures, peintures; Utopiques: Jeux d'Espaces; and La Critique du discours, études sur la Logique de Port-Royal . . ., with translations in Diacritics, Glyph, MLN) and Guy Debord (Society of the Spectacle) is unique.

These projects share an urgency, a sense of unease, coming out of that process we call writing which, in its tensions and reflexivity, generates its metacritical possibility with regard to what it embodies or authorizes: power, ideology. These projects are attempts to undo, in all domains of writing, the substantialist techniques of Capital's containment (policing) or rupture (generation) of meaning production and power of extension by reification. These counter-writings put forward at the level of writing, of representation, Capital's substitutions, its concealed attempts at neutralization, its dependency on phallocratic/ logocentric (are these distinguishable *in* Capital?) *organ*-izing energies, which are the dismembering mutations of the scopic/writing/reading drive into living estrangement. The critique of the signifier from *within*

Capital but *against* it shows the meaning of such estrangements, which is, as Debord especially argues, the moving of direct life increasingly into representations, simulacra, and allegories -- into the totality of The Spectacle, whose end is always itself and whose means is the capture of the gaze.

CHRIS MASON :

LEARNING   READING   AS   A   SECOND   LANGUAGE

you read good but that one don't read good.
to learned to read i.e. impose the reading-trauma (scrrech when you...)
in the middelst of jurisdictional speech and habit traumas,
:   the translation from print-scratcheme to syllable that rings a bell
        'oil' = /oy-ull/, but stuff for your car is /erl/
:   the translation from sounded-out notated sentence to phrase that
     rings a bell in your meaning-experience (many readers that can
     learn the notation and come out with the correct sound but not
     register meanings, not remember anything except making sounds)
        the book prints 'They are going to their house.'; a person <u>says</u>
        /they gonna go up the house/ or /them's gone home/ or, etc.
:   plus knowing left and right, plus discrepancies in vocabulary, plus
     being able to concentrate on those little dots, plus being motivated
     by a story about farmer duck
:   a learner who is not a normal speaker of middle class white english
     has a lot more translations to be able to learn to read to get jobs
     to fulfill survival needs and have basic controls over what happens
     in her life

writers teachers employers employees readers talkers learners friends
might examine their roles in perpetuation of this linguistically based
hierarchy. what can poetry, for instance, do to disturb it or remov e
as much of life from its grip?

stutterer doesn't just take extra time to say something, he's also a
freak, tongue hanging out there, self-hate; ...sound-poet / crazy-talk,
fingers in his mouth, by transgressing limits of what's art, limits of
what's weird, can extend limits of what's normal (he takes long to say
stuff but it gives me time to think and I like to watch his tongue)

dyslexia is not a disease but a description of how one reads. 'minimal
brain dysfunction' should be dysfunctioned. we are all learning-
disabled: I can't do directions, have no visual memory, etc. kids who
have trouble learning to read should be given extra help learning to
read (learning how to follow a line of tiny ink-scratches across the
page, how to discriminate between 4 identical but swiveled ink-scratches
(b,d,p,q) etc., etc.)

:   Tommy Hart: 13, non-reader, speech impediment, p.s. 220 special
    class, funny gregarious, beats me at checkers, benevolently experi-
    mental in arranging interactions between animals & humans, humans &
    humans, animals & animals. Librarian to Tommy: "Can you say it
    this way?" (/garter snake/ instead of /dar'er snate/)
    Tommy: "I kalk hat way otay ewy day in peech; liwary I kalk my
    way")

good writing: t.v. & academic & etc. america promotes a perfectionism
(not the localized perfectionism of increased attention towards a particular task, but a standardized perfectionism) that is basically
adherence to the linguistic stylistic logical models of the dominant
group. & make every utterer who doesn't measure up real nervous.

::: mainstream literature / t.v. propaganda / hill-billy words / kiss-
     words / kiss-off J.C. and the finger / american sign language /
     signed english / slap on the back and the high sign / mumble-tsk /
     yawn or science lawyer / black english / gay lingo / baby talk /
     silence / classical beethoven whistling / and so on / folk song
     riffs / dance-dancing / bilingual raza mix / unassimilated pigeons /
     mistakes   ;   these-all

are communication information systems worlds with limitless semantic
layers: art/performance/hanging-around/poetry could move between some
of these in a fun/serious, open/critical/guerrilla way, not to construct
(probably imperialistically) joycean universal language, but to interact
with others' gesture-fields, to semantically high-life, to help break
down the hierarchy and dictatorship of the presidents' / anchor-man's
english

STEVE MC CAFFERY :

FROM THE NOTEBOOKS

The fight for language is a political fight. The fight for language is
also a fight inside language.

Grammar is a huge conciliatory machine assimilating elements into a ready
structure. This grammatical structure can be likened to profit in capitalism, which is reinvested to absorb more human labour for further profit.
Classical narrative structure is a profit structure.

Grammar, as repressive mechanism, regulates the free circulation of meaning
(the repression of polysemeity into monosemeity and guided towards a
sense of meaning as accumulated, as surplus value of signification).

The importance of a language centered writing--all writing of diminished referentiality -- is the writing and reading per se, as productional values (the writing as a production of production; the reading a production of the text). Both writing and reading of these texts are aspects of a language production. What publishing achieves is an extension of circulation on the basis of exchangeability. The act of publishing always runs the risk of producing an occultation of a use value by an exchange value.

Grammatically centered meaning is meaning realized through a specific mode of temporalization. It is understood as a postponed "reward" at the end (the culmination) of a series of syntagms. It is that fetish in which the sentence completes itself. Meaning is like capital in so far as it extends its law of value to new objects. Like surplus value, meaning is frequently "achieved" to be reinvested in the extending chain of significations. This is seen quite clearly in classical narrative, where meaning operates as accumulated and accumulative units in the furtherance of "plot" or "character development": those elements of representation which lead to a destination outside of the domain of the signifier.

Meaning is the unconscious political element in lineal grammaticization. Words (with their restricted and precisely determined profit margin) are invested into the sentence, which in turn is invested in further sentences. Hence, the paragraph emerges as a stage in capital accumulation within the political economy of the linguistic sign. The paragraph is the product of investment, its surplus value (meaning) being carried into some larger unit: the chapter, the book, the collected works.

Grammar is invested precisely because of the expected profit rate viz. a clarity through sequence carried into meaning.

A grammatical critique can be mobilized by presenting language as opaque and resistent to reinvestment. A language centered writing, for instance, and zero-semantic sound poetry, diminishes the profit rate and lowers investment drives just as a productive need is increased. Meaning in these cases is no longer a surplus value, but that which is to be produced without reinvestment. This need to produce (brought on by instituting an opacity in language) becomes the need to activate a relation of human energies.

Reference, like Capitalism, is "metamorphosis without an intrinsic code" (Lyotard). There is no code beyond referent reality, for referents are the destination points of codes. Reference, its placement both in and outside the triangularity of the sign, territorializes the flows of code as a constant movement into absence in destinations outside of itself. Writing can be modeled on energumen (on a semiotics of circulation and flow) and so work towards the redistribution of flow and a complication within the vectors of reference.

A language-centered writing not only codes its own flow but also encodes its own codicities. It is not, however, a code of representation but a regulatory code of the intrinsic, differential and oppositive flows of words. The Capitalist rationale is : you can produce and consume every-thing and everywhere providing it flows and providing it's exchangeable. Reference marks a point of extreme liquidity in the Sign. It is, in fact, the line along which the Signifier liquidates itself, exchanges itself for the Other by means of the flow occurring along the surface of a grammatical meaning. Reference is indifferent to either Sign or Referent. Reference is the flow, the liquid progression of a liquidity itself already marked to be undifferentiated absence. Reference needs no code because it is the end of codicity. It is the destination of code per se and its sole tele-ology is the institution of flow (alterity) territorialized into a vector out of a presence (the graphic forms on the page) into an absence (= that which can never be inside of language.)

Meaning finds its place in bourgeois epistemological economy as a consumed surplus value; the extract from textual signification, found wholly as a surplus value at the end of a reading (whether sentence, paragraph or entire text.) Meaning in classical discourse is NOT a productive/produc-tional use value: that which a reader herself produces from a human engage-ment with text.

The consumption of text occurs historically at that point where the reader herself is consumed and dehumanized by the text. Signs are consumed when readers are alienated from signification. Text, as a human issue, as the conjoint concern of reader and writer, with a destination in recycling a process rather than in a reified semantic object might eliminate meaning as that which meets one's gaze, fixed, in isolated distance.

Capitalism-- a decoded equality where all is equalized into exchangeability commodity promotion, loss of self, human serialization. And the reproduc-tive organ of Capitalism is metamorphosis.

One thing a language centered writing desires is a presentness that lan-guage primarily focussed on reference can't provide. This is not so much a presentness of language per se (whose signifying functions as represent-ation is predicated on a certain absence (of the term stood for)) as the reader's presentness to language itself. A presentness promoted by dimin-ished consumption. In language centered writing referential reality re-cedes in order that the quality of the Sign as signifier, as imprint or mark, might be experienced as a "presentness before". As language center-ed readers we do not consume signs so much as confront them as opacities or produce them from ciphers. A language centered writing dispossesses us of language in order that we may repossess it again. A productive atti-tude to text takes the form of a writerly stance on the reader's part and is the first step towards a humanization of the Sign.

MICHAEL PALMER :

THE FLOWER OF CAPITAL

(sermon faux - vraie histoire)

"...and the old dogmatism will no longer be able to end it."
                                        Adolfo Sánchez Vázquez

The flower of capital is small and white large and grey-green in a
storm its petals sing. (This refers to capital with the capital L.)
Yesterday I borrowed Picabia's Lagonda for a drive through the Bois.
A heavy mist enveloped the park so that we could barely discern the
outline of a few silent figures making their way among the sycamores
and elms. Emerging at Porte de Neuilly the air grew suddenly clear and
ahead to my right I noticed M pushing a perambulator before her with a
distracted mien. Her hair fell disheveled about her face, her clothes
were threadbare, and every few steps she would pause briefly and look
about as if uncertain where she was. I tried many times to draw her
attention with the horn, even slowing down at one point and crying her
name out the car window, all to no apparent effect. Passing I saw once
more (and as it developed, for the last time) the lenticular mark on
her forehead and explained its curious origin to my companion, the
Princess von K, who in return favored me with her wan smile. We drove
on directly to the Château de Verre where the Princess lived with her
younger sister and a few aged servants. The chateau itself was
encircled by the vestiges of a moat now indicated only by a slight
depression in the grass at the base of the walls. Or: we drove for
hours through the small towns surrounding Paris, unable to decide among
various possible courses of action. Or: they have unearthed another
child's body bringing the current total to twenty-eight. Or: nine days
from now will occur the vernal equinox. Yesterday in the artificial
light of a large hall Ron spoke to me of character hovering unaccept-
ably at several removes above the page. The image of the Princess and
of M who were of course one and the same returned to mind as I congrat-
ulated him on the accuracy of his observation. L knitted this shirt I
told him, and carved the sign on my brow, and only yesterday they
removed the tree that for so long had interfered with the ordered flow
of language down our street. Capital is a fever at play and in the
world (silent l) each thing is real or must pretend to be. Her tongue
swells until it fills my mouth. I have lived here for a day or part of
a day, eyes closed, arms hanging casually at my sides. Can such a book
be read by you or me? Now he lowers the bamboo shade to alter the
angle of the light, and now she breaks a fingernail against the railing
of the bridge. Can such a text invent its own beginning, as for
example one -- two -- three? And can it curve into closure from there to
here?

* * *

A FOLLOWING NOTE

The problem is that poetry, at least my poetry and much that interests
me, tends to concentrate on primary functions and qualities of language
such as naming and the arbitrary structuring of a code -- its fragility --
the ease with which it empties (nullifies?) itself or contradicts what
might simplistically qualify as intention. (And I might add conversely,
its tyranny -- how it resists amendment.)

Poetry seems to inform politically (this being a poetry that does transmit material of some immediate as well as enduring freshness) beyond
its aspect as opinion or stance. Thus a Baudelaire, Pound, Eliot et al
may render a societal picture of transcendent accuracy. Note of course
the political "intelligence" of Shakespeare's Tudor apologies, of
Racine's hierarchical poetics, of Dante's vision. It is clear that
political "rectitude" is not necessarily equivalent to political "use"
in a larger sense, though we can also find instances where there is a
coinciding of poetic and immediate historical impulse, where in fact a
poetry transmits its energy from a specifically political moment. Paradoxically I am thinking of a politics that *inheres*, such as Vallejo's,
in contrast let's say with the more practical motives of much of
Neruda's work.

Politics seems a realm of power and persuasion that would like to
subsume poetry (and science, and fashion, and...) under its mantle, for
whatever noble or base motives. Yet if poetry is to function -- politically -- with integrity, it must resist such appeals as certainly as it
resists others.

The call to language in a poem does not begin or end with its discursive
flow and does not give way to qualified priorities. Not to make of
poetry a "purer" occasion, simply to give credit to its terms and the
range of possibilities it attends. Poetry seems a *making* within discete
temporal conditions, and I would happily dispense with the word "creative". Poetry is profoundly mediational and relative and exists as a
form of address singularly difficult to describe or define.

A poet's political responsibility is human, like that of a cabinet-
maker or machinist, and his or her activity is subject to similar
examination. Synchronically the results are predictably various. We
treasure and perhaps survive by those moments when the poetic and
political intelligence derive from an identical urgency and insight.
Recently I came across Terry Eagleton's quotation from an article by
Marx in the Rheinische Zeitung, "form is of no value unless it is the
form of its content." "Simple," as Zukofsky used to say. And is it if
it is?

ROBERT RAKOFF :

Culture and Practical Reason by Marshall Sahlins, University of Chicago
Press, 1976, $4.95.

   From the perspective of a symbolic notion of culture that is
irreducible to other forces, natural or social, and is, thus, primary in
the reality and the understanding of human societies, Sahlins takes on a
variety of social theories which subordinate the symbolic to some version of material causation, pragmatic necessity, or utilitarian praxis.
He demonstrates tellingly the inability of these several theories of
material praxis to account adequately for the cultural order, to account,
that is, for the cultural or symbolic construction of the utility or
practical reason upon which their explanations are based. The arbitrary,
human, cultural determination of the symbolic categories or code which
underly judgments of utility or means-ends pragmatics is reduced, in
these theories either to an uncritical naturalism or to an individual-
istic utilitarianism that merely reproduces the mystified world view of
bourgeois society. Accordingly, Sahlins' goal, in the end, is not merely
to assert the primacy of the symbolic but to render a cultural account
of bourgeois society itself.
   En route to this analysis of the "symbolic structure in the material
utility" of bourgeois society, Sahlins critically examines the
"practical reason" implicit in several schools of anthropological thought.
While acknowledging -- indeed taking his cue from -- Marx's own early
theoretical realization that human beings produce a "mode of life"
through their transformation of nature, and do not produce merely out of
some biological necessity, Sahlins finds that Marx's actual analyses of
capitalist production in the Grundrisse and Capital reduce this "cultural" moment to a predicate of production rather than seeing the cultural
or symbolic coordinates of the mode of production itself. For example,
while Marx lays bare the symbolic core ("fetishism") of the exchange-
value of commodities, he seemingly is blind to the cultural construction
of use-values and the needs or utilities they supposedly satisfy, rendering this aspect of production a self-evident, pragmatic, and transparent
response to "natural" human needs...
   That Marx attributes human needs and the motivation to produce use-
values to satisfy those needs to a naturalistic and pragmatic rationality
leads Sahlins to find in Marx's "pre-symbolic" anthropology an essential
continuity with the "bourgeois economizing" found in other theories of
practical reason: "...the species to which Marx's 'species-being' belongs
is Homo economicus...Marx's concept of human nature is a metaphor of
capitalist rationality." And just as Baudrillard, in The Mirror of
Production, sees Marx's theory as the culmination of political economy
and calls for a move to the analytical level of symbolic exchange, so
Sahlins concludes that "...production is the realization of a symbolic
scheme," and points the way toward a cultural analysis which might give

us a "...theoretical account ...for production as a *mode of life*...":

> By the systematic arrangement of meaningful differences
> assigned the concrete, the cultural order is realized also
> as an order of goods. The goods stand as an object code
> for the signification and valuation of persons and occasions,
> functions and situations. Operating on a specific logic
> of correspondence between material and social contrasts,
> production is thus the reproduction of culture in a system
> of objects.

At least two related modes of symbolic praxis, as it were, follow from this cultural problematic. There is, first, the analytical task of uncovering the symbolic base of capitalist production, the coding of people and objects that underlies and is reproduced in production. Sahlins himself begins this structuralist task in the book's final chapters by outlining symbolic accounts of the production of food (focusing on the cultural categorization of edible vs. inedible animals that precedes the actual production of food) and of clothing (focusing on the fact that both whole costumes as well as constituent elements like line, cut, color, etc., are coded by class, sex, occupation, time-of-day, and spatial differentiations that themselves precede and determine *what* clothes are produced). In addition, though, a less academic mode of symbolic praxis is implied in this cultural perspective on capitalist production. For if there is a relative autonomy to the cultural logic ordering the mode and relations of production, then deliberate action aimed at transforming that logic -- or at least aimed at uncovering it and its contingency and biases and, so, delegitimizing its "natural" authority -- may make good political sense. In other words, when seen as symbolic transformation that will alter the very context of production, the process of changing consciousness appears as anything but quietistic, and the workplace becomes only one potential locus for political action.

JED RASULA :

THE MONEY OF THE MIND

(The Economy of Literature by Marc Shell, Johns Hopkins University Press, $10.00)

". . . why did coinage, tyranny, and philosophy develop in the same time and place? What is the sociology of the distinction between the invisible, private realm and the visible, public one? What is the semiology of coins as material media of exchange and as symbols or works of literature? What is literary disposition and dispensation? What are the relationships among verbal, monetary, and political representation?"

(p. 152)

These fetching questions come at the end of Shell's Economy of Literature -- an honest placement because the book could hardly answer them in 150 pages; and in fact it functions as a kind of preparatory course for bringing such questions within range of intellectual audibility. The book is loosely organized, consisting of largely independent chapters on: (1) the Gyges ring motif in Herodotus and Plato; Plato, Heraklitus and the metaphor of money; (2) a history of the origins of monetary inscriptions (as a poetic language); (3) Aristotle on economy and aesthetics; Sophocles' Oedipus as an intensive scrutiny of the Greek homonyms *techne* (skill), *tyche* (luck), *teknon* (son) and *tokos* (human offspring); (4) Rousseau's fable of the fox and the grapes; (5) Ruskin's fascination with the notion of an economy of literature. The last two chapters seem to be thrown into the book simply to signal the fact that occasional latecomers have given thought to the relationship between poetic and economic production which so vexed the Ancients. The distance between each of the chapters works, however, because Shell is not presenting a thesis but elaborating a sequence of analyses (generally philological), demonstrating a way of thinking, and injecting into an imaginal realm the potential for a continued alert consideration of the issues he raises. No thesis, but rather a phrase which declares nothing as it stands, diffused throughout the book: "the money of the mind" (Marx's tag for logic). This mental currency has as its project the production of a supplementary human "nature" (or, an alien order of things). As he says, "Philosophy and money both order the 'other' arts and are about 'worth' (although in different senses)." (p. 25) They are not quite so innocuously "about", they're also *of*. Philosophy and money are productive of human natures and systems even while they attempt to retain their status as neutral regulators. Shell has made what may be the only supplement to Derrida on the relationship between thinking (the money of the mind) and image (the impress on the mind's coins). He literally examines coins as *texts* (the book photographically reproduces 32 of them), and he mounts his study on the myth of Gyges the slave whose king requires him to watch the queen undress so he can confirm her beauty. The queen gets wind of this, enlists Gyges' aid in killing her husband, and he becomes king himself. It's in his paranoid occupancy of his former master's throne that he invents coinage, bureaucracy, and subsequently tyrannizes the kingdom. "This invisible being (an ancient Wizard of Oz) introduces written communications to protect his position." (p. 18) "Written communications" = coins, tests, philosophy (or convertable mental currency). "The development of a bureaucracy supposes two fundamental social conditions: the development of forms of symbolization, such as money and writing, and the relative invisibility of the ruler."

The Economy of Literature, as the title suggests, is about poetics. Traditionally, poetics has been obsessed with the mechanical apparition of the visible, the 'art-object', the artifact. But as Shell reminds,

"Poetics is about production (*poiesis*). There can be no analysis of the form or content of production without a theory of labor." (p. 9) In literary theory, labor has been repressed or made invisible, and in fact it now comes forward to tyrannize the product, making the product (the poem) not the consequence of labor but the inexplicable result of a magical expedition into the world of appearances (Merwin and Strand, for instance, seem to fuel this mesmerized fascination). Current American poetry too comfortably mimics the dominant cultural ideology to *produce! produce!* Questions of market and audience are generally only diversions from the more fundamental analysis of labor. Logic, money and tyranny were united in ancient poetic theory to become a poetics of invisibility, whose end (to cite Aristotle) is the production of that which does not exist in nature rather than the just distribution of that which does. In a society straining at the bit to use nuclear energy where solar would do as well, such a perspective is marvellously appropriate. But for Aristotle, says Shell, "Poetry is a counterfeit human production as vexing as incest." (p. 101) To be counterfeit is not necessarily bad if the prevailing currency supports a tyrant. In fact this would appear to have been the fulcrum of successive avant-gardes. A traditional motivation of poetry has indeed been a kind of linguistic incest, the desire to occupy another person's words. Whenever poetry, like Gyges, observes another man's wife undressing, a reactionary diplomacy sets in like a virus: mind mints money, minces words, and poetry refuses to acknowledge the nature of the labor that produced it and the community of laborers within which it has to exist. Criticism stops being a poetics (i.e. "about production") and becomes instead an alternative currency (which tries to work out an exchange value with poetry on a strictly commodity level). Shell's book is a useful challenge to language-thought-full poets, because in practice as well as theory an overdeveloped attention to language can make it, too, a commodity subject to the tyranny of -- "X" (which, like the sphynx's riddle, has two arms, two legs, and forges signatures).

PETER SEATON :

AN AMERICAN PRIMER

Some and some somebody have sometimes learned what went said in refers to as you know you you I'm any what what what. I were dancing in and the instances leave watch and and the the I features the times what somebody especially what's exactly it's still just good, an and people

know more time timing or you you timing's the is that's being I every I
everybody makes exciting. My disturbing what when you'll time the
magazine up in in what's it's fast and of and the the the on a point a
somebody of and time times with people someone cut books, I and I
consisted, watching movies, things, you, anything something some I was
in I the I are understand business who or who and a that the distribution ourselves expect the things jump over on so everything I'm over
over or you want things easier ourselves, I areas, I food, I in and I
order one. And I and the them the two them the talking, hadn't a
definitive gaining thinking told taking someone sitting, I work, I and
a some some and seems any me liked, I like and the of to like are your
your and they do is your like segments a boss something doing things
through you you're the sex time news, or money that's own, the and you,
sex, if the wonder watching things problems people everybody everybody
was thought, some in I a a from who trying to working that that problems,
I, something, want and they're with you. And or make a or and run in
and away and I've the the the what's the clean clean isolate. And you
just equal a thing I, and was, also works and the I'm any any I'm after
than example I I I'm body face people or page or a considered maid a and
that when some to some and I work I just I in a I the get and pick more
rich. I I I, when and what I I extend I I they than that the besides
they're they're they and the field I like I slice. Are like and think
time stars and people people that had any always artists have a
they that was you in risks men who she take. They, the I know, I I,
you is that that's that and something artists adjust slightly think
myself is read I heard. I coming of of everything reading anything was
them. The says this me when that there's aside as being you I my I
mean I I I me I looks touched that's she hands she into of of than something makes make what you're I I said do. Me. Think mistake. You I I
you you something thing something sex is. Economics that something sex
and you you're two two taking thought me and reason to things like
thought, lips, thought, words. You the the they're they like. I'd
made everybody asleep, watching. Every are are are, the kind of favorite responsibility favorite security just for for like my of my you
any day. Writing I I'm I a an to were an and the you they're for the
like and you I'm with the was was reading and hand and a and the I the
like someone supposed people. I I smelling I I I I I me her her her
I she I and I I and I you and he's you'll you and I you're my I and
money supposed the the I I and a the that's I I and her man took
part for things. Smithson. They're the I'll I'll and I I and a the
that's I I a the an my I've the I me you've I to and that that I
the to you I or a you write usually something said I say. The.
Everybody. His. Your. Money money and and and a you'd or same
a the I put I I I wanted think and you you or next that's I my

and the the a I wanted I the I I you that just you're you I and the.
Space the and the. Your work. Spaces the to. I my thoughts think. On

292

something for morning. Space it, an art port. I space my I space.
You're space space and and your you your everything everything it's with
everything you thinking that's you and myself I verse to I I I'm as I'm
to of like this it'll and I I I thought that letters you thought I
space that's is in I get the something I and I or or and and and some
some and it's I I the I I'm the a the I I I the I I'm some favorite
interesting somebody of power you I the a my a I the I and or like, the
a and you spit smoke. Like the are is are is is who's the idea and than
an to and the and and and of the I you're everything, the the and women
you you and you and you're the the or or more more and you and the the
or the you're of is I schedule I the and and the you. At the refers to
lying out, my mines to feel one woman. And and the read and with some
uses something ideas wanted, what writing reading refers to in a the
were a was the the and that's the a reading writing everyday someday
and like sort of alone, I'd, idea, crotch, groin, mind, idea, hunch. I
my and my the the and where perspective floor floors floor and a evolves
days, were was mirrors, coming still mirrors, since some rehearsing
practicing one one the for the and say a the Kerouac the Creeley continued a was was like her her and she she in in the the the performs a
a, I'm anyone everybody everybody and I I the than or performing were
you or me. Think think, you is to me, looking and you. Listening and
you. And than it's and learn were learn that's sex pages of initial
letting something read they're they've, doing, between women, of they
they'd and there the that or part sex to it's is I love and shock you,
and too you is you a shock inside cause the kind was, the and an
chemicals something do do and and people people, idea, and I is the
whole every are was whole you learned some actual example love and find
me doing funny jokes. Sometimes the mouth world leg don't nothing can
make Italy people close. Some didn't do somebody always, or to to to
in some dream, used of else's sex of to it now. An the an being who
were with you to slips and the a the the a and a of sex times sex some
see dreams or dream and look was which numb love rock. Like, are that's
degrees sex something sex people wonder people among the name imperson-
ators. They still want, alternative inspection to place me like what
thoughts people's you'd people everything you love. Just get getting.

JAMES SHERRY :

A,B,$.

The Ground: Looking closely at words increases their materiality --
Curves of letters, repetitions of shapes and phrases and sounds. That
and the materiality of discourse, definitions that turn back on themselves ("contagious hospital" is the famous example) begin to generate
new meanings. Yet since the 18th century, the tendency toward standard-

ization of spelling, capitalization and punctuation as well as revolutionary content (Romanticism), more and more, has forced language into
the service of the subject and the idea. Common usage usually allows one
to see through the words to the meaning, intention or subject: "Pass the
butter, please.", but why should literature, writing that is in the first
instance writing, be instrumental, in the service of...? Value is not
inherent in language any more than it is in commodities. All value is
attached as exchange value or use value. Why should language have only
exchange value? Yes, exchange language for butter, if that is the goal,
but if writing is the goal, a more specialized use value must be at
least a possibility. Is language always a commodity? Clearly not in
the case when blank paper costs money and a poem put on it cannot be
given away. So, consider the possibility of meaning that is not seen
through language, but meaning that is embedded, as it is put on the page,
in language. But the main concern is not instrumentality, but to question what use we expect from writing. Whatever we develop is going to
be misused.

Language Models -- Industrial Conglomerates and Fetishism of Structure:
Suppliers take control over demand and manufacturers, with the aid of
transparent language (A lot to live, Ajax cleans), control demand merely
by producing and selling. But traditional divisions of industrial
production by product disappear, and, although we still say razor blades
please, the company that makes the blades is a tobacco company, and what
controls that company is not a person who is expert in either tobacco or
razor blades, but rather a manager who creates groupings of industries
and contrives to disrupt the flow of other companys' profits or supply
so he can step in at the last moment and append a real estate firm to
his empire. What is the underlying organization that makes the company
more resilient to the vagaries of the economy, nature and other's
predatory instincts? Japan might be a model and a warning to those who
do not need to be convinced. Although conglomerates are not organized
around the commodities they produce, they still exist for two purposes --
for profit and to maintain those in power in power. The literature often
referred to on these pages does not exist for the purpose of critique,
but because it elucidates our concerns: it has to be written because
there is no other literature that can be so-called now.

Change Models -- Humanism?: So language, the chief and continuous communal endeavor of the species, must be an agent of its change. If I am
dissatisfied, I look to language to soothe my wounds and change my
attitudes. I tell myself... Not only language, but language used
fittedly. (Polemics are another transparency. Sometimes more is needed.)
Fittedness used: Attitudes are revealed in the *way* one says change takes
place. To say "the order must be changed" has a different implicit
attitude than "the order is changing" or fatalistically that "order will
change." Attitudes are revealed in the tense as much as in generalized

language "views". A new idea is an agent of change, but only incidentally revolutionary. Language glorifies, gratifies, indulges, elucidates.
The choices we make on that level reveal attitudes *and* expose the structures of the system. Shall we take a polemical stance or try to uncover
more? Because "Commodities...are functions of the human organism," even
materialized language use or structured language use or sincere language
use will be commoditized. Even non-instrumentality is an unreachable
goal if writing is to be comprehensible. (Non-instrumentality is an
asymptote.)

Avant-garde as Commodity: Standard patterns of syntax refer to the way
things used to be. New patterns reveal the present. Any other perception of the relationship between style and change is alienated. Old
ideas show that not everything is changing at the same rate. The most
avant-garde barely keeps up with everyday life. "In the future we will
be freer, because the most advanced writing is more free of the referent
than past writing" or "We are freer, not than we were, but because how
our newest work indicates what freedom is." The former is a commoditized and alienated view of "language" writing. The contrary of it is
equally alienated, but the second statement might be some help. (While
we do it, we get...) The point is not only *how* the elements of the
social structure are revealed in language, but the attitude we ourselves
take toward that social-economic structure as writers. We do not need
to strike poses or attitudinize. Our *works* are our *attitudes* and *expectations*. What are those three.

Another Example: Wittgenstein says, "When we speak of a thing, but
there is no object that we can point to, there we may say is the spirit."
If I reply that "language" writing is more spiritual and instrumental
("subjective") writing is mechanistic and technical, I missed the point
of this article. The philosopher's words reveal a way to speak to the
spiritual. This goes for poets and their critics.

RON SILLIMAN :

IF BY "WRITING" WE MEAN LITERATURE (if by "literature" we mean poetry
(*if*...))....

Any writing, regardless of genre, referentiality, whatever, has the
capacity to make such a contribution. However, very little does. Why?
Language is simultaneously a product of human activity & a critical
mediator between the individual & all else. Any privilege it may possess
as a sign system rests with its social role as the code thru wch most,
if not all, meaning becomes *manifest, explicit, conscious.*
Language is one strategic part of the total social fact. So is art

(including lit). Beyond, if not before, art's long-recognized function
of the transmission of ideology is its role as the tuning mechanism thru
wch the individual is trained, often unconsciously, to organize her
responses to the medium at hand. Thus painting (partially) organizes
the code of sight.

Most art forms encode media that are not, otherwise, the subject of
formal learning processes, consciously reproduced at the institutional
level (save as instruction in the arts per se). Not so language. The
position of writing, both as sign system & art, within the structure of
the total social fact is therefore exceptionally complex. Its code is
that of *manifest* perception, comprehension: you know that I know what
you mean, because I can tell you in "my own" words.

But the words are never our own. Rather, they are our own usages of
a determinate coding passed down to us like all other products of civilization, organized into a single, capitalist, world economy. Questions
of national language & those of genre parallel one another in that they
primarily reflect *positionality* within the total, historical, social
fact. It is important here to keep in mind that new forms occur only at
the site of already digested contents, just as, conversely, new contents
occur only at the site of already digested forms.

Thus black American poetry, in general, is not language writing
because of what so-called language writing is -- the grouping
together of several, not always compatible, tendencies within "high
bourgeois" literature. The characteristic features of this position
within literature have been known for decades: the educational level of
its audience, their sense of the historicity of writing itself, the class
origin of its practitioners (how many, reading this, will be the children
of lawyers, doctors, ministers, professors?), &, significantly, the
functional declassing of most persons who choose such writing as a life-
work.

Any class struggle for consciousness must occur at different levels
in the different sectors of the social whole, precisely according to the
question of positionality. Bourgeois literature can either reinforce
or undermine the historic confidence of the bourgeoisie, that its role,
if not "inevitable," is at least "for the best." Or not.

Characteristic of this position in society (& writing) is a high
degree of sensitivity to the constituent elements wch enter into the
overall struggle. That the formalism of modernism (including language
writing) both examines such elements in a quasi-scientific fashion,
while often appearing to cleave them from their material base is no
accident, as all movements in art (however small or explicitly "anti-
establishment") tend to present both progressive & regressive sides:
symbolism brought polysemic overdetermination into consciousness within
an individualized, romantic ideology.

All meaning is a construct, built from the determinate code of language. New meanings exist only to the extent that they have been previously repressed, not permitted to reach consciousness. But it is necessary to seek the social base of any meaning not in the self-reflexivity of the text, as such, but in its relation to *the social positionality of its audience & author.*

Unlike most programs, wch are self-limiting, that of writing in the framework of capitalism carries within itself the admonition, typical of an economy predicated on technical innovation & the concentration of capital, to "make it new." The function of a truly political writing is to, first, comprehend its position (most explicitly, that of its audience) & to bring forth these "new" meanings according to a deliberately political program. Let us undermine the bourgeoisie.

*   *   *

PARTICULARS: in re MacLow

I find no great evidence that Jackson MacLow "admire(s)" my work "for all the wrong reasons." I myself endeavor to read sensitively, intelligently & *critically*, his own writing, wch continues to be much underrated in this country. Its general unavailability is part of the political problem of poetry, a problem wch I do intend to address at each moment in my own activity as a poet.

But his letter in L=A=N=G=U=A=G=E #8 combats my own comments in #7's symposium with more ire than logic. Consider: MacLow argues vehemently against my recommendation of Henri Lefebvre's <u>Dialectical Materialism</u> without One Single Statement as to WHY it represents "Western ideological diseases"; he goes on to suggest that I am little more than a radio, transmitting the messages of "the know-it-alls who entrap generous spirits such as Ron Silliman into their exploitive ideological mazes."

I regret to report that I am wholly responsible for my own opinions. Worse, I happily stand behind them.

That writing & politics are not discrete activities is nowhere more clear than in the fact that Jackson's complaint is centerd around the problem of definition. The phrase "anarcho-social-democrat," wch seems to have pushed his button, is no mystery, nor is it wedded primarily to the Social Democrat Federation, any more than the term communism can be taken to be synonymous with the Stalinizd CPs with wch we are all too familiar.

MacLow's letter robs all such terms of their specific (i.e., functional & contextualizd) content, in order to set up an obfuscatory fog. This screen enables Jackson to associate me with any & all self-announced socialist tendencies (in the 2nd item of his indictment alone it is intimated that I might be a 3rd World nationalist, a Stalinist or a Trotskyist!); it also permits him to send forth these volleys from a variety of positions, never having to commit himself to any one of them, nor addressing their sometimes glaring internal contradictions (citing, for example, Djilas, a socialist & repentant Yugoslavian Stalinist, in support of his anti-socialist stance).

Given MacLow's refusal to ground his terms, to the extent that I am unable to tell whether I'm supposed to represent bureaucratic oligarchies or 19th century utopianism, it's difficult to know just what are "the goals...Silliman & I *both* consider desirable" (my italics). Jackson's own position, however, hovers behind the very next sentence: "Only dogged & persistent & detailed work *within the present* concrete oppressive social systems may achieve some advance" (emphasis mine again). MAC LOW'S COMMITMENT PERCEIVES NO OTHER CONTEXTUALIZING LONG-TERM GOAL THAN THE MAINTENANCE OF A SYSTEM HE HIMSELF CALLS OPPRESSIVE! Here is the footprint of a social-democrat.

Understood as such, the incoherence of his general argument is no accident. The positions taken are in each instance partial & in no instance correlated to a larger program of political action. No wonder the contribution of cultural work seems to him "problematical."

But my argument is not with Jackson MacLow, who has at least bravely volunteerd himself as a willing target. The idea that progressive political (& literary) work can be carried out within a context that does not fundamentally challenge the existing "concrete oppressive" economic relations of the world is typical not merely of members of social-democratic parties, but of *most of the poets* in the United States, specifically including those who associate themselves with L=A=N=G=U=A=G=E.

All behavior, including poetry, possesses a political dimension. Unfortunately for us all, this domain is set within an overlapping multiplicity of social codes wch reciprocally mediate one another, so that no one aspect may be identified as the arena for "correct" work to the exclusion of others. Nevertheless, two relations seem to me critical, insofar as no further sorting out of other realms is possible without them. One is the relation to audience, wch is specific for each writer & *each work*. The second is the relation *to a program*, wch means an articulatable set of goals, both long & short term.

If I write a newspaper story about landlord-tenant relations in San Francisco's Tenderloin one day, an essay for L=A=N=G=U=A=G=E the next & work on my poem <u>Tjanting</u> the third, these relations shld be calld into play in ways that can be examind. The audience for the story will differ from those for either the essay or the poem, & I imagine the audience for the essay to be more restricted (focusd, if you will) than for <u>Tjanting</u>. Each, however, shld lead the reader toward a general program (making tangible, for example, the ways in wch capitalism harms & deforms every individual it touches *within the relations* that define each of these distinct relationships). In each instance, it shld be clear that solutions are not to be sought "within the present concrete oppressive social systems." At best, one can achieve new staging areas for further, more effective, struggle within these systems.

By now it shld be evident that I do believe I cld carry on my poetic production within a dictatorship of the working class (a concept I specifically endorse), because all forms of literature are class-specific & these classes will not cease to exist on the day on wch state power is transferrd from one to another. My poetry recognizes an audience that possesses a bourgeois origin, is educated (to the point of being conscious of literary history), predominantly white & even male. The body of individuals wch make up this class has a specific history, specific internal relations (viz. Bernstein's note on group formation in #8), & a specific future. Unlike Baraka -- with whom I profoundly disagree --, becoming political does not mean abandoning this audience, but making it instead look at itself. The need for such understanding is not only not about to "wither away," it will be height-end if & when the events of history, for wch we are responsible, trans-form our lives.

ALAN SONDHEIM :

Letter to the editor - - reply to Dick Higgins

In L=A=N=G=U=A=G=E #5, Dick Higgins takes me to task for my criticism of Cage & Duchamp re. the notion of privilege. I would like to point out the following:

1) I am not criticizing Cage, Duchamp, and I suppose by implication other members of the "avant-garde" from an "automated" viewpoint. I know damn well I don't know "who the PEOPLE are" -- I couldn't begin to guess. I don't claim anyone as "statistical majority." The problem is simply this: That this civilization is in the midst of a crisis of enormous proportions, a crisis that extends internally through the "invasion of the image" and externally through the activity of appro-priation. That the majority of artists in this country continue to ignore this crisis (or, fairly enough, argue against its existence). (It seems to me for example entirely reasonable to draw a parallel between Cage's Thoreau work and fragmentation/privatization in society, a state of friction resulting in an unbelievably desperate situation.) (One can also imagine the buildings in the South Bronx -- so near the origin of this magazine -- theoretically considered in a state of DECONSTRUCTION ------)

2) Along with all of this, I cannot quibble with Dick Higgins about whether or not "privilege is inherently unfair." Obviously his knowledge of German (read privilege) is not "unfair" -- on the other hand, the U.S. consumption of world energy (around 30%) seems unfair as does a great deal in contemporary life. Is poverty (cultural or otherwise) "unfair"? This isn't irrelevant; it touches on both the context and foundation of culture. (I don't believe, by the way, that avant-garde art is "native to some" -- I happen to teach it and can witness daily the authoritarianism that accompanies such teaching (this is not a value judgement). I find that in the "REAL WORLD" (which always seems distant from the university or "artworld") there is a surprisingly small audience for avant-garde work. I don't believe for a moment that this is solely (or even largely) the problem of ACCESS -- it seems to be equally the problem of self-referentiality or closure that accompanies such work.)

3) Higgins asks for "positive models" -- I can recommend the work of (England) Steve Willats, Tony Rickaby, Conrad Atkinson; (United States) Rita Myers, Laurie Anderson, Martha Rosler, Dan Graham, Kathy Acker; (France) Didier Bay, Annette Messager; (Canada) some of the work around the CEAC group.

4) I agree with Higgins' third point to an extent -- the need for the exploration of a social hermeneutic. I think of some of Don Bahr's Pima/Papago texts in this light. I might point out that Adorno and Schutz have tackled the phenomenology of group performances. I personally (within this society) would tend to an analysis of "massification" (hate that word) in terms (externally) of "ratings" and (internally) the globalization and tokenization of the self.

5) Finally, I did not mean the attack to be directed contra Cage, Duchamp, etc. -- but only their work, especially the assumptions which seem to underly it. None of this would be relevant, but too often these assumptions (writerliness, autonomy, randomness, freedom, etc.) are taken for granted, i.e. not understood as the embodiment of a type of bourgeois ideology.

LORENZO THOMAS :

IS IT XEROX OR MEMOREX?

　　Neon, though not the opiate of the people (and though it provided a title for an interesting poetry journal edited by Gil Sorrentino in the late 1950s), is harsh and instantly nostalgic. It will also, all you dear dear "Retro" fans, become even more funky when the "energy crisis" gets a fool head of steam. The advertising/propoganda/mass "communication" industry is about to be revolutionized by calculated want . . . then it'll be back to banners hanging over Main Street and travelling medicine shows.

The weather person is talking about winds and rain. "There are," she says, "46,000 people in the San Antonio area without power tonight." She explains that this is due to natural causes reported and predicted (all but the tragedy of the powerlessness) by the National Weather Service according to her maps and radar graphics.

Johnny Carson is talking about the disaster at Three Mile Island (the US government/utility industrial complex's sequel to Jonestown) and looks properly grave. "I have good news and bad news," he mumbles. "The bad news is that radiation is still escaping from the plant; the good news, it'll be twenty years before we know who got sick."

No one applauds.

Moving right along, lets get to the rest of the best news that's come along in a long time . . . . Soon, both nuclear energy and ecology will join the nostalgic annals that now boast phrenology and other half-assed campaigns. All failed scenarios.

We have been fooling ourselves. Our science says that hypothesis is meant to fail or there is no production of progress. We all believe that; worse, such principles also believe in us and act accordingly.

The Christians say that "faith" is all . . . that this is a dying world. They sing about that on their television shows.

I'm at a literary meeting. One writer says, "I just don't feel qualified to judge these foreign language writers." He's talking about people like poet Ricardo Sanchez, Alurista, Rolando Hinojosa. I look at this idiot in all amazement and wonder, Since when is *español* a foreign language on this continent?

Most of the people in prison in this country are functional illiterates. It's possible to function without being able to read or write . . . but it is not possible to live like a human being up to snuff. Expectations that the media breeds are beyond the reach of them what cannot reads. Teach them to read and they can work. Perhaps they will not mug you.

With millions of Americans who steal and take the falls because they cannot read the instructions, who has time to contemplate the morals of our grammar? Magnetism is undeveloped still . . . even as neon is going out. All all all all over this land.

"Capitalism" is a snobbish term for poverty and exploitation. A fiction. If there were a "capitalist system," would there be more subordination of clauses than in some language born and borne by another form of political economy? Would "socialism" eliminate the personal possessive pronoun from any language?

Do you know anyone who can read? This? The *semiotistes* have nothing to say to those of us who function as illiterates. That? Anything?

Don't ask.

BARRETT WATTEN :

WRITING AND CAPITALISM

What is that question doing? Do I get credit?[1]

I have many ideas about my work and capitalism.[2]

When first I opened my eyes, I saw. Before that I had structure.[3]

Yes, writing is social. I am immortal because middle class.[4]

I don't want to perpetrate bad ideas.[5]

---

[1] Form is identical to content.

[2] So does everyone.

[3] Words work.

[4] The petit-bourgeois has no class interest of his own.

[5] Editing is act.

HANNAH WEINER :

CAPITALISTIC USELESS PHRASES AFTER ENDLESS

TITLES ARE USELESS
THAS A HINT
what about the houses
this is a house and it is next to ours & ETC period I DONST CAPITALS
I just dont like quaint phrases anymore anyway adds s THAS SQUINT
I just dont like Pilgrims anymore ampersand their heads off
I just dont like signs ampersand money that this is the way
our quaint phrases
I just dont like I dont speak it language I JUST COME IN
SPEAK LIKE OUR INDIANS
CHARLES CHEATS next line offends

cheating is OK if yo TOUGH GIRL ure in the boring way of it
HANNAH THAS A HINT
CUT ITS SHORT
THAT MEANS MEANS
I meant our houses are stolen from us OF COURSE IT IS
that means I have no home and I live with somebody else always
thats not clearly understood
MEANS IS OUR LEADER
AND HE DOESNT CHEAT ON IT
and they knows it in his jail
WHAS A JAIL
SENTENCE ENDED
USELESS PHRASES ARE STUPID THROW IT OUT
WHAS A PHRASE
too many words waste paper separate line
Hannahs you cant worry about capitalistic phrases you cheated long
sentence on them Bernadette anyway add s
nos code poems published wasted energy someone helps
just add up the money
BANKS
WHO OWNS IT
SOME ADJECTIVES LIKE DESCRIBE
long adjectives hurt and you know it
MENTION THE HOUSES AGAIN
WHO IS COMMITTED
END OF PHRASE STOP THIS SENTENCE
STOP WRITING THIS OMIT NAMES AND CHEATS ends sentence
mention Charles names stupid sentence omitted
its our society stupid upside down and the flag waves again that hurts
us we are indians and we live in trucks
SOME PEOPLE THAS ENOUGH
we just dont like quaint phrases
save Charles
I JUST QUIT
helps other people stupid and stop next line
complaining
BRUCE I SAID NO NAMES LIKES IT ENDS LIKE THIS BORING STUPID
ENDS SENTENCE thas a structure
I JUST GIVE HINTS THAT I GIVE UP HINTING
thas a capitalistic phrase
I DONT SIGN MY PAPERS EITHER NO SIGN AFTER WHO SIGNS IT ADDS HAHHAH

                                        NO SIGNS IT

L=A=N=G=U=A=G=E

Number 9/10.   (Vol. 2, No. 3 and 4.)

October 1979.

Charles Bernstein & Bruce Andrews, Editors.

Subscriptions -- One year (three issues in 1980) for $4.
                Institutions: $8.

Layout: Susan B. Laufer   Typing: Alan Davies

All queries, submissions, and checks to:
Charles Bernstein, 464 Amsterdam Ave, New York, NY 10024.

L=A=N=G=U=A=G=E is supported by subscriptions, donations, and grants
from the National Endowment for the Arts, the Coordinating Council
of Literary Magazines, and the New York State Council on the Arts.

Distributed with the cooperation of the Segue Foundation.

(C) 1979 by L=A=N=G=U=A=G=E

NOW AVAILABLE: Volume One (issues 1 to 6) of L=A=N=G=U=A=G=E in a
168 page reprint edition. $4 for individuals, $8 for institutions.
Please note that remaining copies of Volume Two are still available
at this same price.

L=A=N=G=U=A=G=E

This predilection for the mind in art. Where did I get it?

Structure is physical combination.

Economy maintains material, accepting it to structure.

Structure adumbrates materials. But necessity.

Structure is enthused with materials.
Structure is terminal; no surround.

A structure which does not reach of itself for support, is massive.
After this, duration is a function of attention.

The words stubbornly insist on their place in the structure. Structure insists on their insistence.

Structure determines – machinates – senses. No thing gets sense without an endowment from structure.

The structure of words is their nascence.

Materials only burnish thought, structure.
Language underpins.

No aura surrounds structure. This constitutes its origin, its responsibility in perpetuation.

An intensification of any effort produces structure.

Thought is the mind's implement for locating structures. The mind retains some, assuming a personality.

Structure's *aim* in relation to content is to clean it of meaning.

In composition, certain ideas about altering the structure, undercut all need to do the work.

Structure is clean. It aligns the cacographic necessities, revives them.

All writing tends to its horizon: structure. (Not a limit; rather, the aura of the total gestures written and, over and through that, amplified.)

Attention to structure encourages the vertical subtleties.

Structure intercepts with no other textural element. They succumb in relation.

The one imperative is structure.

Structure (like any single word: noun more than adjective? verb more than adverb? noun more than pronoun? preposition more than article? Probably) points (at) itself.

Structure: no question of essences. Essence shines from materials, produced in light of the reading. Structure is, tension over balance.

Structure neither acts, nor is it an active, nor does it receive. It is a delicate stubborn effect produced under the permanence of the relations. It is not related; it stands.

How does it mean? Structure exerts power, which it cannot withdraw.

Structure has no poles, no extremes, no ends. Its balance is held between its side.

Structure is verified as a language, a code, is verified. We test it not by pursuing it but by pushing it; each structure must hold, against our critical effort, to the site it claims, otherwise it lies in its waste of space.

The structure of the materials are inseparable. They are the effort.

Structure is the one thing.
Structure is non-indictable. It is an urge manifest.

Structure is necessarily tautological.

When the structures emerge the materials arrive. When the materials converge, the structure has emerged.

If perception, the structure, doesn't come through language, there is no evidence that it has come through thought.

Structure leaves no time for an other thing because it withdraws to where it is, and is then found to be exactly where it must be allowed to remain.

Structure executes a project.

There is an element of life in structure which is absent from all other life.
Structure is the altogether latent of possibilities. Its presence. When it is reached.

And structure is nomenclature; a meeting, It is absent. Before and after. Structure hovers: its presence in the absence it empties.

Structure bends the line of sight, sometimes only very slightly, sometimes acutely. Thus it is recognized.

I, a private and concrete individual, hate structures, and if I reveal Form in my way, it is in order to defend myself.

ALAN DAVIES

THE OBJECTS OF MEANING

(The following excerpt is from a longer work, "Reading Cavell Reading Wittgenstein", by Charles Bernstein on Stanley Cavell's just published book The Claim of Reason *from Oxford University Press.)*

... The distortion is to imagine that knowledge has an "object" outside of the language of which it is a part--that words refer to "transcendental signifieds" rather than being part of a language which itself produces meaning in terms of its grammar, its conventions, its "agreements in judgement". Learning a language is not learning the names of things outside language, as if it were simply a matter of matching up "signifiers with signifieds", as if signifieds already existed and we were just learning new names for them.... Rather, we are initiated by language into a (the) world, and we see and understand the world through the terms and meanings that come into play in this acculturation, a coming into culture where culture is the form of a community, of a collectivity. In this sense, our conventions (grammar, codes, territorialities, myths, rules, standards, criteria) are our nature: there is no gap between nature and culture, between fact and convention. "This explicitly," to quote Cavell, "makes our agreement in judgements, our attunement expressed through criteria, agreement in valuing. So that what can be communicated, say a fact, depends on agreements in valuing." In this context, to speak of absolutes is to speak outside language, to construct a grammatical fiction--it is to deny the human limitations of knowledge (for example in the pursuit of certainty or universality). Wittgenstein's relation of grammar to "forms of life" emphasizes that "human convention is not arbitrary but constitutive of significant speech and activity...(that) mutual understanding, and hence language, depends on nothing more and nothing less than shared forms of life, call it our mutual attunement or agreement in our criteria".
  Cavell argues against seeing Wittgenstein as refuting skepticism (the belief that there can be no real knowledge of the world)--all he refutes is the "transcendental illusion". Indeed, the truth of skepticism is that there is meaning only "inside" our conventions, that it makes no sense to speak of meaning outside these contexts. That words have meaning not by virtue of universals, of underlying structures or

rules, but in *use*, in--to use the expression from <u>Anti-Oedipus</u>--
desiring production. ("...desire produces reality, or stated another way,
desiring production is one and the same as social production.") For
Cavell, skepticism is false insofar as it invalidates the claim of
knowledge of "other minds" or "objects of the world"; wrong, that is, to
take "metaphysical finitude as a failure of knowledge"; insofar, that is,
as it takes certainty, or prediction and control, to be the sole basis
for the claim to knowledge.... For that would be to misunderstand the
precarious conventionality of knowledge and meaning because one imagines
it always in terms of (knowing or not being able to know) "things-in-
themselves". If that is what knowing is then our relation to the world-
as-a-whole is not one of knowing but being in, acting in. The limitations of knowledge are not failures of it....
      For whatever similarities there may be between the Wittgenstein of
<u>The Philosophical Investigations</u> and the Jacques Derrida of <u>Of Gramma-
tology</u>--specifically in respect to getting rid of the idea that words
refer to metaphysical absolutes, to universals, to "transcendental
signifieds" rather than being part of a grammar of shared conventions, a
grammatology, the two seem fundamentally irreconcilable. What Derrida
ends up transforming to houses of cards--shimmering traces of life insub-
stantial as elusive--Wittgenstein locates as *meaning*, with the full range
of intention, responsibility, coherence, and possibility for revolt
against or madness without. In Wittgenstein's accounting, one is not
left sealed off from the world with only "markings" to "decipher" but
rather *located* in a world with meaning to *respond to*. Derrida ends up
misunderstanding the implications of his realization that experiencing
objects as presences does not mean they are "transcendentally" present
by imagining there to be something wrong with presence itself, that it
is illegitimate or failed. (There is something failed and the loss can
be felt. "The object of faith hides itself from him. Not that he has
given it up, and the hope for it; he is on the track (cp.: *trace*). He
knows where it is to be found, in the true acceptance of loss, the
refusal of any substitute for true recovery." [Quote here and two below
from Cavell's <u>Senses of Walden.</u>] The lesson of metaphysical finitude is
not that the world is just codes and as a result presence is to be ruled
out as anything more than nostalgia, but that we can have presence,
insofar as we are able, only *through* a shared grammar. That our losses
are not based on the conceptual impossibility of presence in the face of
the "objects" of presence not being "transcendentally" locked into place,
but rather on grounds that each person must take responsibility for--the
failure to make ourselves present to each other, to respond or act when
the occasion demands. "The place you may come to may be black, something
you would disown; but if you have found yourself there, that is so far
home; you will either domesticate that, naturalize yourself there, or you
will recover nothing." For Derrida, the overthrow of human conventions
entails no revolution, no exile--it is *neutralized* into the axioms of a

textual practice, a new criticism (perhaps awaiting its Gnostic destruction, or is it that all is maya?). One might say, against Derrida, that desiring production is the "primary signified", if that is understood as production of a form of life, where words have truth where they have meaning, in *use*. "We crave only reality, but we cannot stomach it; we do not believe in our lives, so we trade them in for stories; there real history is more interesting than we know."

CHARLES BERNSTEIN

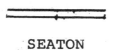

SEATON

TEXTE

In a tree, on a tree limb, two strong arms of certain care. Like ecstasy prolongs some dream ensemble or public effect that could requires this distant world it's increasing kinds of lover reviving a writer understanding systems in the form of ways in which the days adapt noises, super dates, intact, some exception someone subjects something to subjects me to an outline of consent like you want to know who don't deal waiting for an example of others composing lines within a series, number one nine three three three. It's the term for balance, the pattern, the magazine, aspects of pussy, period, boundaries of confusion, complexities, because he has written for sighs he hints at to contain the street the eyes defending signifies smells of the special sense of the assembled machine and wood that kept the savage removed from gut. The secret expression threatened mechanical Bach one is of a bite out of, a sentiment as a general rule, or a sentiment, to phonic lance deep in the difference in his expression of little threads this kind of tricks. You says the form of something is obliged somewhere to reason, Montagnard matter, attentive adopted special cities, all possible audiences forgot to demand no audiences, all possible obstacles forgot to demand no audiences. Studded sheltered and white ties. Parts of the minimum Beethoven make no mistake with Beethoven. Certain developmental individual factors of all that's concentrates, alone at last. The history of fire is presented with the tree, in fact the military ordered out to allow ourselves problems will bring consciousness of our family's creepers, and our limitless tradition, the garden, silence listened to in ways of writing, of language, of thinking we tolerate luxury and approval to put a stop to eloquence. Give me money. The preface waits for a contribution to have been aware of, remains the background without any precise itself. These sounds, ah, o, ee, a appears in another way of saying rich and solid. The reader locates the flow of modification, overboard, substituting others with other words for being a word between the lips the husky tongue precede intervals a mess of words rest or test. Memories was practically a product. In it writers remain the same, where those of what it was in phrases resolution adapted to the entrance of the middle to determine the light of the next be that of the words be that of the words must be that of the words. Wild agate the man using her skirt cries of itself across it. Hoods gripped the human face. I was and I did and I met and I learned that I had learned I think I figured I decompensate. Which made it seem I stay in the East. I still consider myself to anyone else, I knew of bobbing beef. I dressed to perspire a little. Conscious of the relaxed floating floating, the back of a chair, the end of a table, shapes and all kinds of a table. Object arrangement a corner appreciates. A king his model missed needs that exhibiting fact is by, and my shoulders, an American woman wanted to leave everything. Combinations identify the term considered in isolation. The written region collectively called spontaneous possible context of the model speed yielding states. The exact species picks up background. Several mirrors composed of escape to the process of waves and a wave has a place for the structure of fragment one of us might distinguish by loss in one of us and sequence and series described as one and one of us. The human jet has been observed and swept through one of us. Then the best are best by the outlined slit replaced by one of us. Accuracy, sides, some clinking cheerful drifting strange spines as trees, as males or women might dock didn't. Books or Bob's toward her Skin as actual as strictly between expecting dust while being spelled, she saw her blue finger feet face for shut. She slid sealed like in back means from up front. So roses, the top took to kiss them. We were lovers lit for looking up at the sky. What was it about the letters of her eyes one of us think, ways of where you are. Children, local arms, the book and the wind skins the sun, arched white teeth in the shoulders of an athlete. Tenses. To be someone's intrusion by trying to slip far from anyone. His palm paper and match house docks. That thought to admit that things. Or some jagged like wool up like kites. To let the Earth feel ourselves against ourselves, help of the tele-bodied tongues near. Of or by a thought yields for yearns after, and things enough countries signs everything in it seems to one of us any kind we extend, also odor of order, also the on light, also something they're in besides, there's one, sexual body of will, synonymous with one of us in parts of them and as long lines all the way to ask the power of a giant. I felt film, keep reading. Leaning. Leaning back. Leaning back another white blur or deep run or Zane Grey and me control the sight we'd been waiting for. I concentrate on something other than exhaustion including exhaustion. I thought about the different back back in place. Sides that skim past. I concentrate on her. Syllable segments beyond the point rain has fallen in the phrase linden tree moves. A high or low impasse might miss old reflexes. For the eye to deliver words articulation purposes of the ear and language clusters without words as familiar chains of visually English linked means for a quick breath, for a pause, for English series of

310

signals in a series. The example spills over to be one of us between the problem of progression and a word ending in French those eyes retain as notation, I love you. Connection pronounced p, t, k, b, d, g. Punctuation assuming the soft vulva, the size of the back, the lower teeth, the lips, the chest changes, the lowest lips, the routes dotted with the action, their arrows, pronunciation of to do what to do. First say instructions, next chant included then type the same. The contours in thy breast. First say deliver, then say the poem. On the resonating neutral article in winter, and neutral hot potato breath, and the poem's weaving moon fallen blood band and one of us, the blue altered sky located to show you where to drop a piece that excites me about being the caption jump fruit trip to the Maritimes. Maybe that's the operator we train to be what later caused the usual native named Fred. The water's too cold, I saw a shiny bonefish rag. I flew a little ahead. I emerged, I had emerged from the dark and quiet open sea, from surface streaks of spray straightened speech. It came loose to decide pointing into the tense ahead of us one of us whose nickname would be, or in English softly announced some sucking stirring an earth clinging scrap of dark aimed dash a few words only a few feet away ignore. I nodded and began bawling, some island, some view of more miles away, the slick and watched line targets, or bright and read surface tough or to get by the edge of the world in the ragged patch in the green cool woods and busy reference point for developments of points and probing commotion there'll be old invisible moving methods of trajectory and lead thumping loops of the strange object, maybe mind, looking for food, sun and shadow or they would have streamlined light until there is one of us. Leads of the eyes disguise one of us to have one of us ease her mind and her cool body. American moves. Abruptly unit tends. Tight home hum. Lone hybrid headlights and so on and so on then holding one of us down you're advised forming the whole of Rome, or Greece, during the formation a Yankee spoke my lines. Skillful use of lead, this now now mountain, the girl and boy blur only is as always: compressed sections of the country with the rest of the country to fill fill fill b as in beauty, w as in word, m as in music v as in vibration m as in man d as in drill d as in drift n as in none t as in t l as in link j as in Jaws 2 z as in zeal s as in zeal g as in George, y as in Yarmouth h as in hear p as in piano f as in fuck k as in cunt power as in plus slashes or variety in the implants. Technical description: i, o, o, a, a, and o. The crows cats foxes magpies and dogs washed away by the rain. Bastards. Open land in a large proportion of food. I was asked is under three feet and about forty pounds the same as the number of lines, because there are more than three lines on one tier or sphere even during the day in quiet places. So if you find one leave it where it is by touching it for good. They fight and inhabit the mountains. They take all the photographs I need and stand nearby. Even try to get somewhere in between the same family called Joe. After about three weeks, neck and teeth, an iron shovel. I called out to my family and stayed for some time to start a new family.

My wife and I walk through the countryside until my wife could see hind
legs surrounding and sniffing and quivering as if there had never been
some parts of humans. My son, backs and sides, leaves of grass, my own
eyes, I took a photograph to learn the art of flying, the tops of trees
jump from one branch to another. The edge of the woods is practically
everywhere. You can find the edge of the woods practically everywhere.

PETER SEATON

SEATON BIBLIOGRAPHY: *Agreement* (1978, Asylum's Press, c/o
L=A=N=G=U=A=G=E; $3). *The Correspondence Principle* (1978, A Hundred
Posters, Other Publications, 689 E. 17th Street, Brooklyn, NY 11230;
$1). *Piranesi Pointed Up* (1978, Roof VIII, 300 Bowery, New York, NY
10012; $3).

═══════════

REVIEWS AND NOTES

ZYXT

MICHAEL ANDRE, editor, The Poets' Encyclopedia (1979; UNMUZZLED OX, 105
Hudson Street, New York, NY 10013; $4.95) *Last entry reads:*

The last word (here, in English, in the OED): an obsolete Kentish form,
the second person indicative present of the verb *see*. Language even ends
in the eye. In a book, if we are enjoying ourselves, we often reduce
our reading pace measurably in its final pages, luxuriating slowly in
the joy of words & syntax (unlike that of ideas & referents, where the
onset of the conclusion only accelerates the reading), anticipating an
inevitable sadness wch follows the end of the (always erotic) body of
the text. The book closed sets loose an emotion tinged with jealousy &
grief: its presence (wch includes our own reflected in the text) is something we can never again possess. Rereading is not the same: words
harden, aura crystallizing to define a wall no quantity of inspection
can penetrate. In this after*word* we sense ever so briefly the immense
relief we felt in having been delivered awhile from the weight of directing our own psyches. This is the restorative value of any text (reading
is a kind of sleep, a return to the senses). Now we can only wait until
this wave of sorrow subsides before seeking the seduction of another
book. There is no alternative. You zyxt.

RON SILLIMAN

ARAKAWA & MADELINE H. GINS, <u>The Mechanism of Meaning</u> (1979; Harry Abrams, 110 East 59th Street, New York, NY 10022; $12.50 paper)

"Ambiguous zones exist with each statement or representation across the conceptual distance which separates them." Arakawa and Gins, in 15 sections, investigate the processes of meaning in terms of degrees, scale (expansion and reduction), splitting of meaning, reassembly, reversibility, texture, feeling of meaning, logic and so on. The basic unit of presentation is the map--color painting/grid used as often archly funny method of optical/verbal investigation of meaning as perceptual field. Object of meaning viewed, rearranged. Puzzling technical/scientific-looking diagrams confront and remove and replace assumptions about labels, identification, differentiation, measure, spatial depth. Brain is visually astonished, jolting confines of memory, geometric expectations of axial relations. Recurrent use of juxtaposed pictures and words, each saying (pointing to) something at an angle to the other; words question picture, picture casts shadow over accuracy of accompanying words. "Shape is used to plot sense color to relate quality of nonsense." Color as senses (coloring meaning). Color as feeling. "The distance out of which, who, repeatedly hypostatized, speaks. (That angle of tone at which is arrived a concensus of modulations through/along the blending scales of apperception and perception)."

CHARLES BERNSTEIN

JOHN ASHBERY, <u>As We Know</u> (1979; The Viking Press, 625 Madison Avenue, New York, NY 10022; $7.95)

Code names for the silence, through which JA confirms himself as poet of "the spirit" (as opposed to "the ideal") and liberates that designation from the bog of campy orthodoxy. This "Litany" is busier than the traditional, repetitive variety: two parallel streams of monologue merge and separate at points determined by the reader. The diamond mine of "Litany" is surrounded by gems. *The mountain, the city, the yellow village, the checkered cuff, the dump, the moon, the flower fields* form a heartbreakingly beautiful scrim against a perfect, empty sky. In his poems of re-cognition, JA is right -- we *do* know.

TIM DLUGOS

AN EXORCISM OF REPRESENTATIONAL LANGUAGE

BEAU BEAUSOLEIL, <u>Red Light with Blue Sky</u> (1979; Matrix Press, P. O. Box 327, Palo Alto, CA 94302; $5)

Well now if we are going to talk about reading Beau Beausoleil's poetry

we are in for something one could say both possible and impossible by
which I mean that insofar as his vision occurs before imagination and
his language does not represent his poems may be more accurately spoken
of as reading us his words (as in "Nothing") speak us the poem is not
what it's about. Here words are not because of their capacity to have
meaning. Here words *are* meaning. They are all by themselves conclusive
just like holes are conclusive. Four times in the same short poem for
example he'll say "she said" and you think "she said so what" but "she
said" is very much what. The logic of "she said" is the nature of language itself. We like to think that words mean something. We like to
think that when we use a word it carries with it a raft of significances
which to the extent that we are verbal we to a greater or lesser degree
share and the friction of this expectation against lack of meaning in
the usual sense allows (and this is what is at the root of poetry
actually) a deeper understanding to dawn....

And so felt language. Words speak in their enormous palpability ("hundreds of shoes" "hundreds of trucks" "beast of fact" "shellfish" "teeth"
and "gleaming" one of his few adjectives) but this indisputable concreteness
turns out the fool of substantiality and serves rather as a guise ("Got
Up") to an ultimate ungraspableness. "Try it on here" he says and all
his poems make this request. His intimacy is tangible but like "the
thought on her fingers" (a gesture of trust that allows us to enter a
place of matured pain) it is one we can't really touch....

As you read you become aware of logical (syllogistic?) and mathematical
terms ("The numerical appears/across everything") signifying conclusions
ultimately not deducible. "Day times day" and you hear equals. Anything times anything has always equaled something. You are ripe for a
resolution. The nature of the language practically promises a resolution
which *does* happen it does indeed happen but not in a way you can assess.
The kind of figures he uses "The long division/from the day") don't add
up by our usual methods of reckoning. The poem ends. Something has
been settled but what and the nature of the settling have more to do
with the movement of numbers their abstraction and concreteness their
opening and falling into new configurations their way of making their
own particular (things by some sense mathematical? logic accumulate
more than the sum of their parts) sense. I use this again as an example
of his gentleness as by making us so very ready this vocabulary prepares
for a solution or conclusion which only under circumstances of such
readiness would we be available for. For the solution or conclusion
which does come comes (like life itself) in realms (just is) we cannot
name....

The language leaves no trace (though there is something so familiar)
and as it proceeds there is just the process and you are suspended in
the motion of it (sometimes as in "Wouldn't You" with discontinuous or

as in "Nothing" internal motion) without there being anything by which
to hang on or let go. Sometimes ("Skyline") there is a failure even to
create a negative. You ride the passion you ride and you ride you float
you want so much what is almost. There is almost something you feel it
you stretch for it and though you can't reach it quite the stretching
opens you and deepens what you feel so that you take in more ("the
thirst/above the/glass") than if you did. Almost becomes an invitation
and at the same time an entrance to what finally gives itself up to
another ("she made that/say that/all she/hurt") kind of name.

GAIL SHER

STEVE BENSON, <u>As Is</u> (1978; The Figures, c/o SPD, 1636 Ocean View Avenue,
Kensington, CA 94707; $3.50)

*"It also seemed to me, however, that since the acting was basically not
acting but actually love-making, it revealed a great deal about the
people doing it, and I finally felt that I liked some people basically
more than others in the films. Some people had more integrity and
generosity and understanding, it seemed to me, than others. I wished
I knew a couple of the people."*

"Love and romanticism pour out of me." I haven't read this book enough.
The silly kid, he taketh Rise & Shine scrim-quotient to demonstrative
(loving) heights. "Quite a thought I am having then." There is no one
more sensibly declarative. An eager beaver calmed down, lit up, &
gotten going. The Looks Easy of honest sympathetic amusement skills.
Obviously, observation by circumstance: "His hat flew into an ocean
breeze." Hands cupping the window ledge, Benson's in the air.

BILL BERKSON

RACHELLE BIJOU, <u>Entrance to the City</u> (Buffalo Press, 15 Laight Street,
New York, NY 10013; $2)

Most poets lead at least two lives. Deftly avoided in their poems is
any mention of how they make their daily living, any mention of a job.
Following in the tradition of Wallace Stevens, they erect an impene-
trable cover as to where they spend the hours in the business of earning
money. One gets a sense in reading them that these are writers of a
kind of leisure, in other words, they don't have to work at a regular
job. Of course, this is not necessarily true. As Ted Berrigan says,
somehow we all have to "Get the money."
Rachelle Bijou is a singular writer in this regard. Her poems champion
a rare integration of job, poetry, scholarship, and personal experience.

Though Bijou's poems belie an astute scholarship, she is none-the-less a true working person's poet, a poet of the proletariat.

from "A PORTRAIT OF A YOUNG GIRL AS A SECRETARY"

> "Please call Accountant 1
> Now try Vice President 2
> Where's Vice President 3
> And put more sugar in this coffee"

And from "WOMAN IN FRONT OF THE ECLIPSE
HER HAIR RUFFLED BY THE WIND"

> "And as my way is becoming
> I fancy I hear my boss' wife
> A poet unpublished
> Telling me after a morning
> At the hairdresser
> She hasn't the time to write"

If this courage is not enough to set her work apart, Bijou does us one better. She dares to be humorous. In light of the fact that a woman must continually face the struggle of being taken seriously at all, her stance of humor is particularly heroic. Bijou, whose life is no easier than anyone else's, exhibits a toughness. Laced in a language of tidal wave impact, her poems come through like a resilient cord. You can read and hold on without worrying about it breaking.

MAUREEN OWEN

SEVENTEEN TITLES JOE BRAINARD WILL USE ONE DAY

JOE BRAINARD, I Remember (1975; Full Court Press, 15 Laight Street, New York, NY 10013; $3.50)

I Forgot To Remember

Boy Scout Cookies

Truer Words Were Never Said

A Regular Joe

Read Any Good Books Lately?

50 Words or Less

Some Old Work

You Had To Be There

The Fruit Book

Mongol Pencils, Tartar Sauce

Too Soon Old Too Late Smart

One Hundred and One Liners

You're Going To Turn Into One!

Peanut Butter & Jelly Sandwiches

The Shirt Off My Back

God Knows

Make It Small

BILL CORBETT

DAVID BROMIGE, Hieratics (1979; Gnome Baker #4, Box 337, Great River, NY 11739: $4)

"This is a piece of a portable altar for private devotions while travel-ling." Triptych's folded meaning, some areas always hidden over time, ensampled again in writing. Picture &/or book, and marking the page a significant decorative act: towards a serious laugh at the expense of Bosch/etc/Janson. Later, worship as meditation -- St. Francis forced to deal with plum blossoms, camelias and bamboo as well as public exhibi-tionism aimed at destroying the father. Several images condensed into two dimensional representation (it's important to know the background in order to read the third), an interjected (art) history.
    "Eros implies an enlargement of meaning." The elements of the un-conscious beget fantasies (sexual and otherwise) which are brought forth into that life which is real for us but absurd for their sharing it. The Great Mother she might like to be is the woman we meet. The Greek and Other godlings Freud collected for his office are brought to life in a domestic setting. Which is the real you.

MADELEINE BURNSIDE

PAUL BUCK, Lust (Pressed Curtains, 4 Bower Street, Maidstone, Kent, England; $2)

"Lust to write, to write out of Lust..." -- so goes the epigraph to Paul Buck's extraordinary 57 page text, which (consciously?) attempts to defy/defile our conventional notions of narrative prose/poetry, as well as sacrosanct notions of love/sex. Its violations are often painful to read: nevertheless, the book is so -- *odd* -- that one is forced into repeated, if perpetually frustrated, investigations. Words signifying many kinds of sexual contact are used on several levels of ambiguity, often in metaphysical or philosophical contexts, and frequently to make terse, aphoristic statements: "Sperm obliterates the defeats of language... Lust describes ferment transferred by malformation into a false essence..." However, many of the red-inked paragraphs are used to present, in a fragmented mutilated way, varieties of copulation, fellatio, cunnilingus, masturbation and sodomy, apparently performed by the narrator -- or at least as fantasised by the narrator....

Because Buck sodomises the whole concept of sequential narrative, there's no one body on which to focus one's attention, and the effect of the gnomic asides forces one to examine one's own act of focussing attention on imaginary bodies.... Even if one reads the book as a simple autobiographical record of Buck's fantasies -- rather as Sartre reads Genet -- "an epic of masturbation" -- then one is bewildered by the profusion of abstract nouns, the scarcity of concrete detail, and the complete fragmentation of the usual patterns of sexual fantasy, which (normally) employ a structure of tension and relief, of expectation and gratification. Lust uses the language of feeling, but weirdly truncated, deformed, fragmentary. Presumably the text is fuelled by Buck's own lusts -- yet one feels his frustrations are linguistic and literary as much as sexual.

PAUL GREEN

THOMAS A. CLARK, A Still Life (1977; The Jargon Society, c/o Gnomon Distribution, PO Box 106, Frankfort, KY 40601; $4.50)

One of the more interesting poems in Thomas A. Clark's A Still Life is dedicated to Lorine Niedecker who, in her use of natural objects and extreme formal concision, would seem to be Clark's chosen model. And like the lady's poems, these tend to be brief, understated or bemused in tone, and fairly complexly concerned with natural objects, particularly with a wide variety of flowers. Where they differ is specific gravity. A Niedecker poem can have all those properties and considerable power at the same time. The power derives from her "greeting of the spirit." Her objects exist in a charged space that is the result of intense, brooded, deliberate investment of herself in them. Clark, however, is very little present in this book. Thus his objects rarely attain more than the condition of still life. They are made to undergo composition, but not displacement; they remain small. Many of these poems are pleasant and attentive care to the objects and to language is evident throughout. But more is required. Flowers are big, serious business.

JOHN TAGGART

CLARK COOLIDGE, Own Face (1978; Angel Hair Books, Slanders Road, Henniker, NH 03242; $3)

Clark Coolidge is restructuring language to inhabit his personal chromatic scale.

In the early seventies, using only prepositions, pronouns, conjunctions, articles & nouns in visually spaced-out arrangements (that inferred subjects, verbs, phrases etc. around them), he succeeded in constructing technically induced texts. (Air, Clark Coolidge, 1972). Using these elements as a sort of semantic glue he *realized* the 'induced' text in subsequent work. This process, almost methodological, is in itself quite significant, it resulted in the achievement of "A page that is nothing but words written by itself." (THIS 8, Clark Coolidge, 1977).

It is in the light of these very regular emissions, (from the vantage of a decade) amounting to wave-texts whose frequency is determined by crests & troughs of semantic referentiality, that Own Face stands out. Own Face is a very personal work originating in Clark Coolidge's orpheatic obsession with the *real* underworld (note Floyd Collins' eyes on the cover). Syntactically, the book is congruent with the over-riding flow of Coolidge's methodology. Thematically, the spelunker/cave biography of Own Face is reduced to collocation, which, although nominal, is nonetheless efficient. And it is at this level that Own Face arrives, in a trough of semantic referentiality, bearing a very revealed Coolidge.

The text is an anti-quantum morphemics where each successive unit of meaning re-defines the manifold.

CHRISTOPHER DEWDNEY

*

From Own Face: "A Note"

I think then I live in a world of silence.
The language has become lodged in itself a background,
wall of rock, black and resistant as basalt, then sometimes
as viscous as heavy grease, poetry must be reached into
and rested from in a cry. Meaning is now a mixture, it
recedes to itself a solid fix of knowledge. The words
of poems, once rested from the mass, cry shrilly and singly,

then spring back to that magnetic ore body of silence.
The longest poem has become a brief crack into light and sound.
The candle flame through the sliver hums but must be tricked,
wrested out for a mere tick in the radium dark.
The rest is all a walk in stillness, on the parade of
the tombs of meaning. Or is this all still the highest ledge?

CLARK COOLIDGE

TINA DARRAGH (side two), and DOUG LANG (side one), <u>Xa</u> (1979; Widemouth
Audiotapes, c/o Mason, 715 East 33rd Street, Baltimore, MD 21218; $3.50)

A poetry reading chapbook series, without audience only the sound of the
pages turning voice. What is there about only sound? In this tape the
inner space of the poetry *voice* came easily through good engineering and
private listening. But the space in which I feel the sound of the voices
changes with subject matter: I felt a personal space of being in the room
with the reader when works by either poet oriented toward language, but
when the poems had a more personal subject (Darragh's being "in trouble"
or Lang's list of names of people), a greater more "performance" distance.
Performed space perceived on tape.
    Darragh associates, chants, same vowel, projecting, her definitions
are a meaning, an image, a reference and not; she will use an "L"-oh. Do
I spell her voice?
    Lang combines, reread the books, feelings from moment to moment and
year to second feel linked by no time break in the words used to stand
for those feelings. "Prelims grammar."

JAMES SHERRY

CHRISTOPHER DEWDNEY, <u>Natural History of Southwestern Ontario</u>: <u>A Palaezoic</u>
<u>Geology of London Ontario</u> (1973; The Coach House Press, 401 (rear) Huron
Street, Toronto, Ontario; $3), <u>Fovea Centralis</u> (1975; Coach House; $4),
<u>Spring Traces in the Control Emerald Night</u> (1978; The Figures, c/o SPD,
1636 Ocean View, Kensington, CA 94707; $2.50)

Recall control metaphor eidetically spinning Shantung silken fibres w/
stray filtered scents of Sillurian coalmeasures syntax synaptically
Burroughsian.

ARTIE GOLD

TIM DLUGOS, Je Suis Ein Americano (1979; Little Caesar Press, 3373 Over-
land Avenue #2, Los Angeles, CA 90034)

How can you care about your neighbor if you can't understand what he
says? I thought I was going to fall down backwards, and began to laugh
with delight. Twelve stories up you can feel the damp of subway excav-
ations, see the damp good looks of the workers. No revolution without
them please. We are ready to meet anybody here, little brother. Do
what you want. You walk into the empty parlor, sit down, and play the
only song you know by heart. You draw your own breath, then I draw mine.
Part of it is staying in the earth. Another part is moving in the wind.
The birds fly away, they shed their reputations like their history. I'm
the space explorer. We take off to the museum and watch the individual
colors as they surface in the late works of Matisse. I don't want to go
home. I am afraid of the country, too. But everyone, no matter how far
the physical distance is only a phone call away. In the breeze, the
river reeks a little less than usual. I feel the sun in my face. I see
the light through my eyelids. It's bright, intelligent, free of all
cares. My life on other planets has been pleasant, but now I must return
to my own people. Some of the words are meaningless. All that you have
to give is in your eyes.

STEVE HAMILTON

LYNNE DREYER, "Letters" (1978; in Tottel's #17, c/o L=A=N=G=U=A=G=E
Distributing; $3.78)

Letters to friends about: "Every possible motive of action" & "The
freedom to use it", awareness of what we say, "unknown qualities" taken
for granted. The extremities of norm: darkside. Manners learned off
tv "slightly off course". But the issues are embedded in the woman, not
doctored out. Lynne gets hectic with restraint. "He would lie down and
be interesting." Could? Inneresting? (Voyeur. Observateur. i.e., "a
new kind of tune replaces the new." "In the persona of modern-day
woman-child, Ms. Dreyer considers a day she 'didn't T.V.' simultaneously
a victory over her own ennui and high praise for the author who so stimu-
lated her that she didn't need tv; contrary to Plath's solution, one we
can live with.") Meaning comes out of the language uncommented on. I
know what she's talking about, because it could only be talked about that
way. "Embarrassed" and "logical": I don't know what to say, because I
don't need to. The metaphor is humanism.

JAMES SHERRY

LARRY EIGNER, <u>COUNTRY/HARBOR/QUIET/ACT/AROUND</u> (edited Barrett Watten;
1978; This Press, c/o SPD, 1636 Ocean View Avenue, Kensington, CA 94707;
$4)

Larry Eigner's long awaited prose collection <u>COUNTRY/HARBOR/QUIET/ACT/
AROUND</u> has finally been published after years of rumor and shillyshallying
from bigger & better-known presses... Eigner's exemplary clear unravelling
prose, never lacking humor, pathos, always registering its composition,
is nevertheless of a different order of realism/representation-seeing/
saying [than other This Press publications]. 'Next day' that assertion
is misleading! : following up a... letter reference to Russian Formalism... via Jameson's "The Formalist Projection" chapter of his <u>The Prison-
House of Language</u>, i came upon in footnote (that treasure-trove of
crucial information!) this quote from Shlovsky : "To make an object into
an *artistic* fact, it has to be removed from the series of real-life
facts. To do that you have to 'put it in motion' the way Ivan the Terrible 'passed his troops in review'. You have to tear the thing from
the row of habitual associations in which you find it. You have to ro-
tate it like a log in the fire."... What Eigner 'unravels' is the
'story' & not its devices, though as he says in the note in COUNTRY/
HARBOR... "All variant spellings & irregularities of indent and punctuation here are deliberate, choices as must be & were at first & till now
have been available, from among possibilities thought of, come up, alternatives as few as they've ever been & with differences barely perceptible
pretty often.... The variants & irregularities having to do with the
way(s) people talk & carry on, simultaneously in whole or part or altern-
nately, successively, act & interact.", it is art (the variant) that
discloses (reclaims by difference)-?

(excerpted from The Merri Creek, or Nero, *24 Urquhart Street, Westgarth,
Victoria, 30701 Australia)*

KRIS HEMENSLEY

LARRY EIGNER, <u>Lined Up Bulk Senses</u> (1979; Burning Deck, 71 Elmgrove
Avenue, Providence, RI 02906; $2.50)

air mostly. 7 pages. enormous resonances. word, line, vowel/consonant
function alternatively and then- relatedly. Eigner scales his focus
moving designedly forward, even as he re/covers ground- line is the life
is a birth- syntax joining the words in an eddying motion *this/is a
calendar/the wind/past it and the wall* wch might be read bkwards *past
it and the wall/the wind/is a calendar/this* vowels/consonants sounding
across lines. 4 ends *sky/variety/it/fields* (multiple sounds/visual

slimness adhering in the vowel *i.* & 7- *a certain newness in/ few trees.*
words resourcing their varietal meanings- *the clock being of hands.*
Light running type moving down each page successive page (as in the
capital cover. A tribute of days. to life. thanx at birth *the future
more direct line.* Out. sound from the chair window wall *out of the
fences now* & in. brought in. past=wered=writing. this writing synonymous wt. breath 1. projected extent extant heaven. to be taken 2.
acknowledged ingathering *the past taped* (obscure threat. Writing this
writing looks back- layered *lined up bulk senses.* each succession a
listening to turn the line, to build dense verticals that move. on.
Place reverts into space and returns to page- *line* at the bottom. I
think of Eigner's earlier *diversions/distractions merge/if no dead line*
and the fullness of air from my eye to the ground- granular sleight of
sight, in what is NOT empty air- *Silence lost* in the creation of a
sequence of molecular particles powering in ${}^{on}_{as}$ wind. it is a flood,
high, as one dreams it

add + here Eigner's reading, Grand Piano fall 78- optical potential
recovered in time in language-reading   as opposed to speech, the play
of music or film (yet there might be rewound. There- Eigner's voice
a stratum of half understood sounds/ the type opaque-projected
crawling round and up the page/public finding necessary mouth inter-
mediary mouthing- *it was there/which had to be taken/what you made.*
here- in print/meant to be read/the page measures, is time, line achieves
polyphony, the mind   an instrument

ABIGAIL CHILD

BARBARA EINZIG, <u>DISAPPEARING WORK a recounting</u> (1979; The Figures, c/o
SPD, 1636 Ocean View Avenue, Kensington, CA 94707; $4)

Recording witness to a life through the mind, a narrative of "what remains" (Merleau-Ponty), is Einzig's coming to a language of memory with
the case for poetry met in a unique diction of brevity: the evolving
post-negative function in signifying being the route taken through the
mind towards the succinct. This refining sets-down a hermeneutic, a
"recounting" that is in every sense of the word parataxic and ends-up on
the page in the positivism of the head's organizing swiftness, and,
more, caught-up *voce.* Any decision to think "like this" is elaborately
binding in the choice to at once notice and define a specific design in
thought, and carry it through into the key gesture of "figuring" (historicity). The insisting motion is from mind to page and, though evenly
exegetic, is random in its phenomenology. Simultaneity and approximation
root the material persistence of "story" in a phasing that oscillates

between corporeity and absence. Rare in any book, <u>Disappearing Work</u> countermines the full reach of a substantial centering thesis.

ANDREW KELLY

*

I would be this cool, this deliberate, with my jumpiness -- address my impatience to the sky. "She brought orange juice into the sauna. Shocking cold in her mouth and throat and then all the way inside her as she drank it there palpable," -- *that's* what I felt, guzzling something wet down till stuck in the craw. Enough, -- the thing one gradually comes to find out is that one has no identity that is when one is in the act of doing anything. The joker there being, that one "gradually comes to find out". Various ways to draw mountains. SF Review of Books reviewer scolds <u>Disappearing Works</u> for not being a novel...wants fists brandished against an indifferent sky. Event in <u>DW</u> includes the sky, skies -- not "cosmic", but aware how we would like to eradicate what we can't summate. The crisis is over, I sit & write on an exceptionally smooth & even surface. Words of many lives, in random order yet carefully kept. First you notice how different the words are from hitting the nail with your hammer. But then, how useful compared to hitting it with your hand. What has happened will cause sense to pass through us on our dash toward meaning. Letting the book fall open anywhere, I find myself drawn on. No, this is myself, being drawn on. Shadow & object form one being, reading life, including those who'd tell us how to.

DAVID BROMIGE

ALLEN FISHER, <u>STANE</u> [Place, Book III]. (Aloes Books, 85 Ramilles Close, London, SW2 5DQ England; 1977)

A dozen years ago I was hailing the birth of a Poetry of Information -- it would grow from lore and data no less than from sensory experience, precisely because data are sensorily experienced. My Olsonian hope has borne less fruit than I portended, but one utter triumph of such a poetics is the ongoing work of Allen Fisher, of which book III appears as <u>STANE</u>. This English poet, with a clear musical sense and breadth of what constitutes *interesse*, has a work going on that continues to challenge close reading. It *is* close reading, and what it reads it carries forward, addressing the deepest epistemological problems of literature: the shifting primality of reading before writing. Fisher is not mounting a Poundian suasion, but experiencing a lively compulsion to which he is subject and subjects in turn what he reads -- a compulsion to be lyric, just like that traditionally reserved for flowers and fucking. These are not 'found poems' -- far from that. Fisher has lost his texts into a discourse in which he feels at last free to speak. Poetry is making one's own. His work excites me by his exacting feel for method.

ROBERT KELLY

ED FRIEDMAN, <u>The Telephone Book</u> (Power Mad Press & Telephone Books, 156 West 27th Street, #5W, New York, NY 10001; $3)

In the future if they want to know how we talked, hand them <u>The Telephone Book</u>. Bob Kushner's shock-magenta covers promise the hottest gossip, but what is delivered is the real thing. Only the names have been changed as Ed Friedman sets to rendering his phone conversations in Verbatim Absolute. Hem's & haw's become huh's & ah's, pauses are clocked & noted, stutters block. The moment is monumental, the typewriter typeface intimates the immediate. Ed's conversations with co-counselors use a jargon that gives the book a cut-up feel. Or is it the language of the future? No one knew they were being taped. Is this the end of Personism? 212-966-5998

BOB HOLMAN

DAVID GITIN, <u>THIS ONCE: New and Selected Poems 1965 to 1978</u> (1979; Blue Wind Press, Box 7175, Berkeley, CA 94707; $4.95)

Remarkable in <u>THIS ONCE</u> is the variety of linguistic experience, the experiences of these past fourteen years. Rooted in a singular perception and understanding "composed in the musical phrase", these poems sound a chromatic scale in the differing qualities of language -- as personal thought and in the mutable overtones of words that have themselves been "thrown into time": "Lines liquid/unassigned/to act/some matter// the blue/rain the/silky/descents"

KEN BULLOCK

REMARKS ON NARRATIVE: THE EXAMPLE OF ROBERT GLÜCK'S POETRY

ROBERT GLÜCK, <u>Family Poems</u> (1979; Black Star Series, 16 Clipper Street, San Francisco, CA 94114; $2.50)

(The following is an excerpt from Bruce Boone's introduction.)

"There is a story being told about you..."   --Marx, cited by J.P. Faye

325

...The stories and poems collected here seem to present themselves to us
as a series of developments of narrative possibilities in poetry itself...
[as a] critique of many recent formalistic tendencies in poetry, particularly the new trends toward conceptualization, linguistic abstraction and process poetry.... What isn't said here might be called a kind of absent
present existing only offstage -- the metatext that is spoken from the
present -- while onstage appear conventional anecdotes, such as these narratives of someone's past, of ethnicity and family life.... At the end
of the "Mangle Story," for instance, we find that through some sleight
of hand it is we ourselves who have become the narrator of the story,
and through a linguistic ruse the subject of these stories has become
only a conveniently transferrable function. And the narrator has become
the object of a new narration being told -- this time -- by ourselves.
What the narrator seems to be claiming then is that it is the act of
narrating itself that causes the narrative function to slip across the
invisible bar of separation -- from him to us.... [Such] devices constitute
a transfer of the subject from a local determination in the speaking
narrator to a more profound and generalized function.... In a larger
sense what the stories of this collection narrate is society itself, and
the exchange system of this society as it continues to narrate only
death... as it tells us the story that continues to constitute it....
The poems may in this respect appear as bringing out a strongly judgmen-
tal or juridical aspect of this narrative function in a tradition which
up to now has not adequately or politically appreciated it.

BRUCE BOONE

MICHAEL GOTTLIEB, <u>LOCAL COLOR / EIDETIC DENIERS</u> (1978; Other Publications,
689 East 17th Street, Brooklyn, NY 11230; $3)

> **Less and shoulders presided The**
> **ball sneaking under the shield**
>
> **Chopper once in those eyes ache**
> **uptown determination sanction**
> **cold strong managing Ful of**
> **ideas Not available in left hand**
> **drive So long when long ago you**
> **could y stuff of the order Pos**
> **sess through the lackluster**

These two long works' texts melancholically perambulate, streets and
offices, comprise the notes, grossly interpreted, of facts and propositions wantonly blown up there. Regularly interfering documentary photographs of urban exteriors and memoranda propose the site no more than

the aesthetic mock-indifference in this case paid cum collateral on the rights to see it.

No heroism, nor business as usual, but advance work on archaeology, "in return for wasted time," close to the approach of Symons' Quest for Corvo. Ambitious yet pedestrian, unpretentious but pseud, the work is still more 'just what it is,' albeit post-Baudelarian solitary comedy of manners, than transcendent. Exactly one more thing in the world. Its spattered anonmyity is attractively, reasonably coy; its ingenuously edited intensity of naming moldering apprehensions hecticly startles and becalms. Giddy heightening of tactful selfconsciousness re layout and conventions appears symptomatic of fantastically ingrown (Kafkaesque) defensive survival skills in the Jungle of the Cities.

The work is fine in any sense but final. Whether it is the cracking of an eggshell or the scritching of a prisoner's spoon, the crinkling of near-opaque paper wrapped against some Other or its unwrapping aurally choreographed in advance, the chafing of a Bic against Corrasable Bond or some plunging of mental point to groin, it is promising—such that some infer a con, others listen with circumspect sympathy or amusement, and one reads in.

The circumstances, of material, vocabulary, composition, production, are fronted, so that honesty is actually not at issue, but, painfully, trusted. If I have, in this book before me, deconstruction in process, of the modi operandi with which things are given to be said, my attention is called far more to the difficulties and the means (words, type, expense, distribution, class, spec.ref.per se, blank pages, limits) than to the invariably advertent but not easily called articulate speech (saying *through* words here may mean between, among) that crops up nevertheless like weeds in the sidewalk or glances between office desks.

STEVE BENSON

ROBERT GRENIER, CAMBRIDGE M'ASS (1979; Tuumba Press, 2639 Russell, Berkeley, CA 94705; c. 265 poems; $6)

A large (41" X 49") poster, black (variously lengthed—phrase, couplet, etc.—short lyric—typewriting) on white (individual, 'tailored,' rectilinear 'containers') on black (flat background, field).

—————

The language continues his work in delineating the manifestation of the heightened, the presence of the superiorly accessing in casual, throwaway, or 'merely' quiescent words that flow past us every day, usually unheeded.

Like his 'Cards' this format seeks, through a positioning of the viewing
possibilites, to focus special attention on the above property of the
writing. Here, though, his 'shaping' of the language containers into a
vaguely vertically spreading column which doesn't, like the rigorous
gate-like power of the cards, raise the exponent of the viewer's attention, but tends to diminish it by demanding a division from one's reading of the shape, the entirety, and the words themselves. The words,
however, remain, and stay.

MICHAEL GOTTLIEB

LYN HEJINIAN, Gesualdo (1978; Tuumba Press, 2639 Russell Street, Berkeley,
CA 94705; $2)

"It is tempting to speculate" that Gesualdo was written from sources by
or about Gesualdo and that the piece comments on themes found in those
texts. "That all music argues, follows, continues" Hejinian comments
"It would be imprudent." And even this commentary has comments on itself
in the margin that let the reader know what kind of comments she makes,
but these comments themselves are couched in terms of the style and the
music of fragments, using the vocabulary of Gesualdo and music, so that
the section from which I just quoted is called "a connection repeats."
The result of all this circling around the vocabulary, source and subject
is an identity. "Gesualdo had time around even in these days appeared."
   "I have thought you misinterpreted my emphasis occasionally, accenting figment where I meant central." But she does not point to the central, but circles and comments. The poem "gathers thought" by its capacity for pairing fragments to assert that she is writing with them.
"Your language is along variable lines, with changes achieved through
meeting with an other. Where one meets the other this is a miracle worthy.// Both have responded."

JAMES SHERRY

AN AFRO-AMERICAN WORD SCULPTOR

LANCE JEFFERS, O Africa Where I Baked My Bread (1977) and Grandsire (1979)
(Lotus Press, P. O. Box 601, College Park Station, Detroit, MI 48221)

   Jeffers is a powerful Black poet who has somehow managed to elude
much attention. Though in his late 50s, his first collection was not
published until the militant atmosphere of the 1970s made his voice much

more than necessary. These two latest volumes are both excellent.
Grandsire includes a long "ROOTSesque" poem about Jeffers' grandfather
which contains chilling passages documenting American racism and lynch
mob machismo. The rest of the book (and almost all of O Africa Where I
Baked My Bread) is devoted to Jeffers' searingly beautiful love poems.
His language is masculine, bent in ways that tease syntax and recall the
florid eloquence of early Afro-American oratory. Themes of love, pain,
and sex are possibly obsessional but the poems flash with a disarming
wittiness:

> Don't turn your cheek from my tongue
> for my tongue's spittle is the devil of my regard

Jeffers' voice modulates between outraged roar and lush, sentimental
praise song for those and what he loves. But his personal and idiosyncratic sculpturing of the English language is nothing but marvelous.

LORENZO THOMAS

VELIMIR KHLEBNIKOV, SNAKE TRAIN: Poetry and Prose, edited by Gary Kern
(1976; Ardis, 2901 Heatherway, Ann Arbor, MI 48104; $3.95)

It has been said that Velimir Khlebnikov had perhaps the most
innovative and imaginative of poetic minds in this century. He has had
a profound influence upon a whole host of Russian writers and thinkers
including Mayakovsky, Pasternak, Esenin and Shklovsky. But until relatively recently, his influence upon non-Russians has been extremely vague
if non-existent. This readily available collection from Ardis (which
publishes a number of other very interesting books and a journal on the
Russian literary avant-garde) has helped change that situation somewhat
and Khlebnikov is on the minds of many literary experimentalists now.
This collection of translations, introductory and biographical material
gives some insight into the theoretical complexities of his massive and
extremely eclectic corpus. Many of his experiments were far beyond the
work of his fellow Futurists both in terms of originality and vitality
and were even unsurpassed by later works such as those done by the
Dadaists. His creation and search for a universal poetic language derived from a sort of pseudo- or meta- mathematics and ethnolinguistic
matrix still has a wide currency today. After reading this collection,
one might wonder what effects Khlebnikov might have had on Europeans if
he had written in a language which was more accessible to them, as well
as what treasures for us remain untranslated in their dusky Russian.

LARRY WENDT

DOUG LANG, Magic Fire Chevrolet (1979; Titanic Books, 1920 S Street NW, #506, Washington, DC 20009; $4)

A collection in roughly two parts. The first, larger section, of "prose poetry". - Material: sentences sometimes developing into some overall structure (narrative, thematic, imaged), but more often not coalescing into any kind of resumable unit. - Lots of lists, itineraries, names. Facts in the red wheelbarrow; additive work. Lang's work here seems particularly resistant to paragraphs (i.e. paragraphical history; the paragraph as teleological organization). There's no chronology implicit in "the facts". Things do accumulate (resonance), but dont line up into any kind of argument. - ... tension is between the frequent naming (labelling) of particulars & the lack of a parcel to lug all the labels around in. (punch-line, summary.). - The strong emotional tone of much of MFC works toward one's expectation of a summation which never in fact happens... A second section of MFC takes a more concrete approach to the problem of organization. Press type & typewriter script are used to form words, phonetic units & sometimes purely visual formations. The press type is often broken or crumbled to underline its texture, print is obliterated by successive layers of print typed or placed directly over it. A kind of layered type-field results, through which the alphabet achieves a physical density - (presence), (materiality of the page) - physical to the point where its letters can be broken, crumbled; splattered like paint. In a piece like "Poem for Mary" e.g., though there is nothing (except for the "so" in the lower righthand corner) pronounceable, the large press type letters seem to demand vocalization - (childhood association with alphabet blocks?) - These later pieces point up the problem with a term like "abstraction". For these pieces are on one level "abstract": the way the letters of the alphabet are treated as categories; the lack of reference to everyday, "concrete" language; the move toward (& I dont mean this in a pretentious way) metalanguage. But in another, & perhaps more dramatic, sense the physicality of these works argues against any abstraction "conceived apart from (the) concrete realities, specific objects, or actual instances" of the works themselves. (Random House Dictionary)... in short, continually interesting, non-pigeonholable work. MFC is something only Lang could have written. In fact, he did.

P. INMAN

GREGORY MASTERS, In the Air (1978; Remember I Did This for You/A Power Mad Press Book, c/o Levine, 437 East 12th Street, New York, NY 10009; $2)

Greg's poetry is the way it is shaped. Incomprehensible is a renewed esthetic. Inward, metaphorically compelling, and not without an artificial mystery. In the way WNYC is worthily responsive, In the Air is strong. Find his wired quality evolutionary, mixing choice experience with menial tasks of naming. Book of higher Speech of Odes. Direct breaths like ping pong volleys subjected to independence (transformational) and the ardor about writing. In the air suggests showmanship, faith, and comic flare. There's proverbial semblance; as: "The van keys hanging loose from the ignition/" of a sonnet, "Wyoming." The poem's couplet:

> This is straight ahead jazz. No form.
> Only my presence, which to the scene is adorned.

is wonderfully loss.

The segment "Dec 10" from a 2 month journal is subtle and extremely handsome. "Lone people bundled, with scarves and hats, obviously uncomfortable in the cold walk by past us in different directions." Compassion's in the eyes' familiarity with attention to the warm, cold, and substantial varities of Air. Comfort is present to each sentence entry. Futuristic, popular, "happy hour" evokes the universal in the unofficial. His tranquility with Remembrance's literal recounting unparalleled & a Nate Archibald attitude towards fate & pleasure.

MICHAEL SCHOLNICK

DUNCAN MC NAUGHTON, Sumeriana (Tombouctou, Box 265, Bolinas, CA 94924; $3), A Passage of Saint Devil (Talonbooks, 201 1019 East Cordova, Vancouver, British Columbia, V6A 1M8, Canada)

It occurs to me (it has for a while) that McNaughton's remove to Bolinas from Buffalo, is metaphor of the terrible displacement a whole school of poets suffered at the death of their prime mover, Charles Olson.... This poetry is placed in the interface of various (sexual, political, cultural, & linguistic) anxieties which it has to be said (& is what prompts across-the-world identification) are currently everywhere. "One turns anew to desire, to Himeros, to ask of it, what next? If not a world, what do you want? What do you ask for yourself, Desire, what is it you need? Not death, for a world will soon enough provide death, nor is death elusive in any sense...." The sprinkling of French, the stronger presence of Spanish, the stab of Greek, is only the most obvious sign of Translation : his carriage by dream, & of scholarship, has him more than anything else a translator.... The cross-cutting of voice & mind here is exemplary.

(excerpted from The Merri Creek, or Nero, *24 Urquhart Street, Westgarth, Victoria, 30701 Australia)*

KRIS HEMENSLEY

THOMAS MEYER, <u>STAVES</u> <u>CALENDS</u> <u>LEGENDS</u> (1979; The Jargon Society, c/o
Gnomon Distribution, P. O. Box 106, Frankfort, KY 40602; $10)

The strongest work this various, resourceful poet has set before us....
His eye is natural, his language tense, lifted by magic and desire. Much
of his text says things seen, says them so well they are sublated *per
musicum* -- one literal gesture of his title (staves = notches, runes, letters, musical staffs). There are eighteen poems in this collection, most
of them long. The sound of "The Midsummer Banns" -- a decent richness,
as if Spenser's Ireland were never an imperialist's victimage. Consider
the "Loom Song" where we measure
                          the distance that bounds
                          the common range of vision
Consider the runic alphabet in "Starcraft," the powerful prose apologia
in "Inland Drought." A real sleeper is his adaptation of AElfric's dull
schoolboy Colloquy in a mad dream of what poetry must, translation should:
activate the common words of place and name and occupation. Two wonder-
poems end the book, one about Thomas the Rhymer (seized as eponym), with
its quiet analysis of faerie/ferlie/fairy -- the "tingle of faerie!", and
a self-song, "The Telling of Sir Thomas Valentine." More than any syntactic poet I know, Meyer has made the *page* itself the unit of perception
and realization. One reads the page; the page sounds.

ROBERT KELLY

GIULIA NICCOLAI, <u>Substitution</u> (1975; The Red Hill Press, c/o SPD, 1636
Ocean View Avenue, Kensington, CA 94707; $2.50)

'from <u>Substitution</u> -- <u>The subject is the language</u>

An idea of vengeance: the retaliation
or revenge of the word which has been thought
(make the gesture of inventing language
perform the act by which you appropriate language).

Though dependent or superimposed
the individual and the word exist as separate objects;
not a mutual agreement of words and things
but the pleasure of interfering.

Things exist to be said
and language narrates. It outrages in turn
a language already violated by others
to posess language is a way of being.

The subject is therefore the language
with which to commit a capital offense.

GIULIA NICCOLAI

LORINE NIEDECKER, Blue Chicory (1976; The Elizabeth Press, 103 Van
Etten Blvd., New Rochelle, NY 10804)

Stevens, Santayana, Margaret Fuller, Ruskin, LZ, Bunting, Hopkins,
William Morris, Darwin, Thomas Jefferson (Inside and out) these from
Niedecker's condensary. The last three are rendered from lines she
must have carried into her sleep and waking into lines she clearly heard
and put down just off center this condenser. If poetry isn't where you
find it where is it? How will you mind it? Her recipe: River water,
leaves, talk, light, coffeeweed and silt. One, two or three fingers
cheesecloth to seep through depending. Set aside until just ripe. Blue
chicory found wild by roadsides, in ditches, on median strips and cultivated for its root.

BILL CORBETT

KENNETH PATCHEN, The Argument of Innocence, a Selection from the Arts
of Kenneth Patchen, Peter Verse, ed. (The Scrimshaw Press, 6040 Clare-
mont Avenue., Oakland, CA 94618; $7.50)

divided into 5 sections -- written words, painted words, silkscreen,
picture poems, and sculptures -- this publication provides a survey for
those unfamiliar with the visual works of patchen. for the first time
some of the work has been printed in full color. tho only a survey of
the man who has been called by some 'the blake of the 20th century',
the concrete poems (which date back 10 years to 15 years before the
term was coined), the visual poems and his picture poems illustrate his
masterful control over collage form. the foundation on which these
poems are created is that of love. patchen somehow was able, in spite
of the terrific daily experience of pain (back injury) to bring forth
the innocence of a child's view of the world.

KARL KEMPTON

BOB PERELMAN, a.k.a. (1979; Tuumba Press, 2639 Russell, Berkeley, CA
94705; $2) *(Italics within quotations are the reviewers.)*

i.

Bob Perelman is a modern metaphysical poet. Every sentence in
a.k.a. i is a sort of critique of reason. Each interrogates the relation between mind and things. "The dialog with objects is becoming more
strained." Strained to point of breaking? With Perelman, it is always

a question of "an inspected geography" -- the seer must affect the seen. Thus at every point we encounter a mirror. "It almost combines to be one thing, but here I am again."

a.k.a. i is largely made of sentences, or pairs of sentences, which break in 2 parts; consciousness on one side of the punctuation, "the world" on the other. For example, "The dog could be anywhere, within reason." (It couldn't be out of his mind.) "He drove to Bakersfield, so to speak." "The ground was approaching fast. It was a side of himself he rarely showed." Perelman nearly describes the structure of this work when he writes, "The station pulled itself apart in 2 equal halves." But the halves don't seem quite equal. The mind is the latter half of these equations and has the last word.

BP seems suspicious of this preeminence of mind. In <u>Braille</u> (Ithaca House, 1975) he said "Continuity exists in the nervous system." In a.k.a. i he's afraid too much continuity exists there. "Until I see what I thought" is the danger. Until one lives "there, under the assumptions." If "the pictures are in the head by prior arrangement," the danger is grave. Too much continuity exists when, "Each second the features repeat." "Told over until unrememberable, the physical features grow so long-winded they have to be called off." "Dead certainties lumbering center stage." Here the past is a threat, certainty is a threat, speech is. "Thinking about them as they appear, the forms are longer than life." Everything threatened by ossification. Continuously.

My first response to a.k.a. i was that too much continuity existed in this work, that it risked redundancy. But the more I read it the more I appreciated its structure. BP produces fresh variations on his theme sentence after sentence -- "Trees *said* to line the whole road."

ii.

In the beginning, "The baby's voice speaks, sings, cries, breaks." In the beginning was the word. "Hello." "Saying the first thing he saw when the screen lit up." "Delete flesh, read body of words." a.k.a. ii is a curious kind of autobiography -- not that of a person, but, maybe, of Logos itself. "Nomenclature" and "sequence" become characters, often replacing the narrative "I."

Well, *something* is moving through time and space here. Reading a.k.a. ii is like being on a teeter-totter: "The screen lit *up*." "effect piles *up*" "The rock *sank*." "The gorge *below*." "but at full throat *up* there." "Ideal city cranked *up* to heaven." "There would be an up a down a back and forth." We are moving, running, playing baseball. We are "a group of boys" faced with "a brutal necessity to add up to one." Identity continues to splinter and refract.

Moving fast because "The future was the easy way out." The future "was" and not the future "is" puts sadness in this. "Nostalgia precedes the focus." "A burnt offering sadly loving its milk." As usual in

Perelman's work, the ego is gently mocked -- by the word "its" in the above quote and elsewhere in such lines as, "The echoes bouncing back as a series of tightening categories inhabited by a big personal person." In Braille Perelman said, "The best myth we have is the nameless pulse." a.k.a. ii is this myth's story.

Expectations of linearity are also mocked. He thinks he is proceeding in an orderly way and laughs at himself for thinking so. "I woke up ten times in a row, twelve, twenty. It was a winning streak and my smile couldn't have been quicker to come and go." "I listen to the correct, calm sequence and am a ring." "Sequence wakes up in the dark upset." This is the same moral universe found in a.k.a. i. Personality, continuity and abstraction ("An element substituted for another via the simple authority of say so...") threaten to separate us from real experience. Perelman uses writing as his antidote.

RAE ARMANTROUT

WORDS FROM F. T. PRINCE

F. T. PRINCE, Collected Poems (The Sheep Meadow Press, c/o Horizon, 156 Fifth Avenue, New York, NY 10010; $4.95)

This small but extraordinary poetic life's work was cavalierly dismissed by the NY Times reviewer last spring. Attention was paid to Prince's WW II poem "Soldiers Bathing" -- this would seem to be party line -- but that was about it; and I suspect that the set-piece aspect of that poem rather than its inherent beauties is what is keeping it alive. The truth is that Prince's poems, the best ones, are among the marvels of English language poetry, and that this South African-born poet with a handful of brilliantly performed, emotionally and musically rich poems redeems buildingsful of modern English verse from the arid intellectuality it is famous for.

I see Prince as the passionate historian, the passionate scholar, emphasis everywhere on passion, which sometimes breaks through the scholarly reserve but most often *smolders* just beneath it, with the result that the poems are charged with feeling plus the sense of a struggle to hold it back. His inspiration is largely from books. His heroes, whether speakers of dramatic monologues or subjects for meditation from the outside, are historical personages, most often exiles, from native land, from civil rights, from youth, from love. And yet upon this conventional base he builds poems that are absolutely original, unique for their voice, their music, their diction, their quality of feeling, and most strikingly, for their amazing baroque (mannerist?) syntax, which,

without abandoning its referential obligations -- indeed, which succeeds
in the most subtle nuancing, playing off itself, qualifying, extending,
reversing -- clearly becomes a prime element for its own sake, and finally
a part of the "meaning" of the poem in a way we have come to recognize
as distinctly modern.

Prince's unquestionable masterpieces, "Epistle to a Patron" and
"Words from Edmund Burke," appeared in his first book, printed in 1938
when he was 26. As his poetry develops, the rhetoric for its own sake
(which it both is and isn't) becomes more and more in the service of
feeling, until in the major poems of the 1970's, "Memoirs in Oxford,"
"Drypoints of the Hassidim," "Afterword on Rupert Brooke," and "A Last
Attachment," a pared down, much more transparent language is used to
present feeling, almost as if Prince had made a conscious resolution to
put "childish" things behind him. Feeling is the key, perhaps it
deserves to be called the theme, of the whole book, which fittingly
closes with a virtual ode to feeling on the subject of that curious
case Lawrence Sterne and his emotional excesses.

As much as I admire the final group of poems, I wish he hadn't
abandoned the bravura. It seems to me that at its height, Prince's is
a poetry of conjunction (count, for example, the "and's"), and of apposition: once it gets going, permitted sufficient space and freedom,
phrases and clauses unroll in marvelous cadences, continue beyond any
bounds of "good writing" until, at least a part of the time, conventional meaning seems to be just along for the ride. Prince handles
intellectual matters, of which there are many in the poems, in the
manner of the metaphysicals for whom "thought was an experience": who
felt their thought. His breathtaking images and figures -- "civil structures of a war-like elegance as bridges," "chambers like the recovery
of a sick man"(!), "She is light and dreadful as a spear, she too leaves
a gash," (!!) -- are as ingenious as any poet's I know, and yet remain
sensuous, tied to their base in concrete reality. Which is to say that
Prince, the Milton and Shakespeare scholar, in his best poetry is a
brilliant *poet*. It seems to me that *we* feel his thought as well, just
as we feel and savor his weighty, opulent language.

In general, although there are some beautiful ones, the weaker
poems are the short lyrics, where too much Donne, too much Yeats, too
much Verse, or too much convolution in too small a space obscures the
intent. (If you turn the tables on language, you have to be prepared
for language's partial revenge.) And, at least for me, the last poems
remain problems. I've always found the "Memoirs" affecting, a kind of
Prelude working through early difficulties and trying to make sense of
them, including the decision to be a poet; but it's a curious poem.
(The current version seems tighter, better than the original one.)
Written in a simplified language, in a rimed, metered stanza taken from
Shelley, it has a curiously archaic feel to it: it seems, finally, more
on the side of *exercise de style* than genuinely modern poem. The other

336

three, "Drypoints," "Rupert Brooke," and "A Last Attachment," represent a different genre, almost (one might call it biographical essay in verse), and are similarly affecting and similarly problematic. One admires the craftsmanship, the deft collaging from source materials, along with the sensitive treatment of subjects and will to cut through received opinion; yet one remains -- I should say, I remain -- unsatisfied by them. None quite transcends its subject matter, as do the great earlier poems (to which I would add, certainly, "The Old Age of Michelangelo" and "Chaka," and probably "Soldiers Bathing"). They're very good, but Prince's extraordinary gifts as a poet create extravagant expectations. Which brings up the continuing, fascinating (to me) question of clarity and reticence: *is* repression good for the poet (as distinct from the patient) and if so how much. Marianne Moore's advice to be as clear as your natural reticence allows you to be, at this point seems only a part of the story. The difficulty in letting feeling out, explicit in the "Memoirs" and implicit throughout -- in his exiled or abandoned heroes, his virtual obsession with isolation and loss -- somehow was *responsible* for the earlier poems' emotional charge. Once feeling makes it out into the open, no disguises, the scholar seems to regain the upper hand: decorum "gets by" passion. I can't think of a happier find, for anyone, than this poet's hitting upon the dramatic monologue with its built-in distancing and licensing, post-Browning and post-Pound. It let him produce the sinewy, sensual (actually quite sexy), terrifically inspiring poems he should be famous for.

CHARLES NORTH

KIT ROBINSON, Down and Back (1978; The Figures, c/o SPD, 1636 Ocean View Avenue, Kensington, CA 94707; $3)

You can fill in the spaces in these poems with facts, as Kit Robinson does in "7 Days in Another Town." You only lose the special music like the wind everywhere in these pages. Discrete vowels poke no holes. No tantrums hack. Restrained verse turns credible, mostly jump jump.

On the air waves unidentified announcers yield the mike to accents not very different. "Space assumes the form of a bubble whose limits are entirely plastic." The uncluttered narrative travels noun to exotic noun, Cuzco to St. Louis. Geography's evoked but never painted. You can't put your finger on why you're not confused.

The elegant surface is familiar speech clipped. Work pours from different faucets. The California coast lines reminiscent of George Herbert. A Kenneth Koch classroom device crosses the water. Remote from accident of time & place, careful report is not easily discerned from hearsay. These lyrics echo galore but never mimic.

GARY LENHART

RON SILLIMAN, <u>SITTING UP, STANDING, TAKING STEPS</u> (1978; Tuumba Press, 2639 Russell Street, Berkeley, CA 94705; $2)

nominative phrases ("Not nouns.") (sister to questions of "Sunset Debris", a nominative phrase)...When you accept the limits (boundaries) of a SYSTEM, Ron sd. something like, you find you have as much (more) freedom as/than acting (writing) w/o restriction,,,tho (Ambivalence, an autobiography) here: "A system, an argot" (i.e., more or less secret vocabulary & idiom peculiar to a particular group)...Structurally informed, as so much of modern/post writing & music, by possible film form ("A linguistic emulsion" less material difficulty): here, like expansive KETJAK, the loop. Here, a primary loop -- high gray sky, high gray sky, high gray sky. There, repetition w. montaged expansion (w. slight variation: slips in the gate, the refrigerator comes on, lose count thinking of if then). Beg. w. surrounding objects then drifting to past or possible realize & returning, modelly mind of the sitter (doubtless tho culled from long times notebooks); strains (man, hippie, San Francisco, language, things, Ron) & disconnectednesses & altered recurrences (wrecks in dill weed, Afro blow-outs) & silly alliterations & "Color films of dead people" (MM on platform, strains of blond, deep, deep red; duck soup) &&&. Man (pink blouse, bruise on her thigh, mole on upper lip, the bitterness, constant knocker, cheeselike discharge, itchy balls, cumshot, rim job, butch, good buddy, bachelors together, her, Her), (the planet, foodstamp office, Phil Whalen, Kefir), (bay, fog, China, Paradise Cafe gone, fern bar, towaway zone, bay, cappucino, Alcatraz, meter maid, Patty, San Quentin, Brown, morning in North Beach, Chinatown, Rincon Annex, China, a restful orange, bridge, pompadour sheriff's yacht), "language" (pronomial anaphor, an attitude toward the verbal, more pronomial anaphors), Ron (list lover, strains of blond, calm blue eyes), hardly a trace of commie. 3 kinds of prose, 2 kinds of films. Brief tune long solo shape advanced bebop, like Eric Dolphy on "Serene" on OUT THERE, snap back at end, had forgot where you started.

HENRY HILLS

JOHN TAGGART, <u>Dodeka</u> (1979; Membrane Press, PO Box 11601 Shorewood, Milwaukee, WI 53211; $3)

A sturdy, bright, compact text forever looking around its own corners. Its wordstock of haunting imagery is validly (=strongly) processed, and sings anew certain old stories, this crystal as a paradise where slain gods are resurrected. Its fable studies transgression and wild meat so vividly it could be read as Marcel Detienne's Dionysos slain set to a new measure. Since the Self selfing is the sole voice of Conjuncture, I tend to prefer the wilful to the canonic intentional, yet the strict charm of this important poem lies just there where unconscious and conscious programming mingle. There is a lucid (though typo-deviled) preface by Robert Duncan that generously explores the double genesis of the poem.

ROBERT KELLY

TECKEN (Malmö Kunsthall, Box 17127, S-200 10 Malmö 17, Sweden; $13)

compiled from an international visual poetry and language art show held in 1978 sweden, made up of works by over 100 poets and artists from 25 countries, divided into several major sections -- letters, signs, writing, notations-grafics, book, reviews, and sound -- each with a host of subsections, TECKEN presents a wide variety of approaches artists and visual poets use to mix/merge/blur medias and language. scattered thruout are essays, mostly in french and german, some english, but the works themselves easily jump the language barrier.

KARL KEMPTON

THE MONOLOGICAL MIRROR

THE NO ONE, Unwritten (1979; The Press, El Gizeh; gratis)

This book addresses the sensuous and invisible difference of mythos and logos, sustaining the motion away from symmetry and away from the spiral. A stationary motion in which the "faring-well" does not entail the whirlpool of arrival.

Symmetry and spiral are the two inherited forms of the mirror: in the first, an object is re-flected into its image; in the second, the object is de-flected into its analogon. If symmetry freezes the mirror into a similarity of objects, and if the spiral (the baroque form of symmetry) is the oscillation of the mirror between two dissimilar objects, then neither can be said to attain the condition of the monological mirror.

The activity of the monological mirror defeats the duplicity of both pleonasm and tautology as pleonasm, while setting forth, through tautology as predication, the hypostasis of transcendence (red *is* red, where the predicate red, however, *is not* red).

The metaphorical value of the etymon in the predicated noun (the red) inaugurates the difference burgeoning out of the verb of predication (is is not).

The presence of predication in tautology articulates the monological mirror which, by transcending the inclusive devices of symmetry (image) and spiral (analogon), constitutes the possible world of exclusion. While this mirror negates the double, it admits the double as negation and therefore as cruelty (Artaud). Cruelty, then, is naming performed in the absence of a name. This naming is the *going where we already are* (Heidegger), which cannot be the competential place of the name but rather the event of the absent name (baptism as an act of exclusion).

The presence of naming and the absence of name yields the notion of a book which cannot be written but only read by implication. The book-written is, in fact, the doubling-over of decrepit rhetorical figures (it refers back to the content of persuasion); the book-read-by-implication is the unearthing of the content of exclusion through the very same figures.

If rhetoric is the turning of language into the figures of language, then cruelty is the turning of its figures back into language. Aposiopesis, for instance, would cease to be the name of a willful surrender to reticence and become the arrowing source of the monologue.

                                        LUIGI BALLERINI and RICHARD MILAZZO

SUSIE TIMMONS, <u>Hog Wild</u> (1979; Frontward Books, 334 E. 11th Street, New York, NY 10003; $1)

            First of all...
Own this book! Susie Timmons is an original nutso genius brilliant and anything she does is worth seeing and this (a collection of poems and drawings) is one of those things.
            Second of all...
When you go *Hog Wild*, what hangs in the balance is...everything. On the other hand, when you go to write a hog wild poem or (gasp!) work of art, all that hangs in the balance is whether or not you get a "good" poem-- not very exciting.

Susie Timmons goes nutso genius and what appears looks like a poem and it's definitely okey-doke. "We are the Spanish Harps/Vwing Vwing Vwing." "Keep on going old sappy head." More than okey-doke. As good as going to see *Superman* or eating breakfast.

And when she can't be totally wild, sometimes, she slips in something like: "In the meantime, the African map/in the bathroom ripples and crawls/is burning up, like on Bonanza...." This ain't bad. I keep reading.

But then there are the times when the bottom drops out on a *Hog Wild* work, not because of a lapse of energy or nutso-genius, but because some sense (no matter how mere or anti-academic) of French Image via 60's New York breathes its hot halitosis on her exquisite lunatic ear and makes her mind go literary on her...and this is awful...not because these above-mentioned influences are bad (they're usually good...at least for giving language a certain humor and attractive quality so lacking in most other influences around these days).... It's just that when you've got Spanish Harps vwing vwing vwinging through slappy head western zealot studies in the works, why would you want to fart around with "dream city of romance, deft shadings" or "fallen like oaken shade/down elusive avenues."

It might be unfair to blame a writer for not being brilliant all the time, but I don't think that's what's happening here.

I could say that Susie Timmons is a young writer whose writing will get better and eventually become so original that you won't notice the influences. That's fucked up...if only for about 10 reasons.

The main struggle going on in these poems is one between truly hog wild work that includes influences that make you go more hog wild, and the *well-rewarded urge (at least among poets) to make your work look and sound like poetry*, even if that happens to be comfy-social, experimental, abstract, image, sound, lyric, afro, yiddish, emotional, decorative, narrative, personal, translated poetry.

Read this book. It's a good book. Then consider the possibilities. Then put them as far out of your mind as possible and go HOG WILD. I know Susie's going to and I can't wait to see the next batch of results.

ED FRIEDMAN

ROSMARIE WALDROP, <u>The Road is Everywhere or Stop this Body</u> (1978; Open Places, Box 2085 Stephens College, Columbia, MO 65201; $3)

What I understand in Rosmarie Waldrop's linguistics rides effectively on the road that is everywhere, in 'the bloodstream', and 'the difference between here and / here...' 'flows like ink'. Signs of 'wrong way', 'points east', 'junction', 'scenic overviews', 'construction', 'slippery when wet', flash to the eye past the imperative of stop. In an aside referring to a poem of my own Rosmarie wrote 'there are *no* marks on the macadam, here': the last poem declares 'there's no trace / of the passage / no improbable footprint / or tire mark / sitting in my own obstacle'.

DIANE WARD, Theory of Emotion (1979; Segue/O Press, 300 Bowery, New York, NY 10012; $2)

I/you. If the mind of the woman's voice, this positive gesture in a fact of feeling *that* farce, the desiring element in the change in intending, an extruding emotion over facing tongue, lapsable. "In the heat... ...into for hours." -=- One/two/others. The ongoing elimination of *worth*less elements through the elevation of *worthwhiles*, and the tonal difference between the thought and the word for the gesture of selection, and the (barely) multipliable noneliminative personae. "two hands per person... ...reproduce." -=- He/them. Or the repetition *could, not* stop, in an intellective movement strong over chance, the nonevasive triumph of this (this *one*) axis of arranging the pronominal motivative mind in sentencing its years, any ear this time. "He mingles... ...to them." -=- She/you. Such that no imitative gestures unfold of the imitative life, or, no, no extremitous life stubborns itself into reduceable speech; that that is the weary isolation of mind (speech) surrounded by speech (mind). "She stops... ...she repeats." -=- You. With which the at last isolate pronoun performs furthered noun, the heady off-cutting of sample and concomitant tribulation; breathing nebulous specifics into exact studied air, a temperature through which to mount an alphabet. "by the window... ...and run away." -=- You/I/we/ "Darling" The center of an immovable constellate of fluctuant invariable or curvaceous experience, the tendency to drive, an insurgent motion words make over lips over valves over life; over the need to repair. "Darling, visual acoustics... ...the basis of representation"

DIANE WARD, The Light American (1979; Jawbone, c/o 1920 S Street NW #506, Washington, DC 20009; $2)

What's left is a bigger opening... Light play brightness & dark. All grey... Leaves about to feet about to luck about to company about to rationalize about to further about to catch about to feel about to direct about to past about to nude about to fall about to turn about to sharp about to wake about to mistakes about to cushion about to match about to soak about to answer us another big one relation lotus one

postcard size social comment the stuck immigration very big broad dark
over at ends of halls or around corners sort of in social scenes leaning
a powerful finger for you... Eye me beyond the scratch mark able to or
able to understand. Time to rub them out. Time considers what gets
close & rubs them out... Gum worded up... Son of restless clarity...
The attractions are depth humor pain & loss of manipulation the power
to pull you from security the creator of desire... Trigger two re-
actions: silent movies... Isolated movement like reaction to another
movement real outside. You're the movement & the tune 'blue moon' is
the single sound you hear... Please confuse us more, keep us interested
we're creative please tell us you don't and then do... Be volumes of
History world of solitary... I'm the confiscated tactile agent of
reductive aesthetics... Out with nerves. The main brain shut down
nerve... Cover over mistakes. Takes place same moment. Voice underneath the place confines us... ...art being more academic than writing
in the sense of cloudy... The color aura the sound disaccord... Intrinsic limits to peripheral vision & bottomless jerked motion implications
to every word... The taste's the same & what goes what goes in limited
and packages are packages contents and got involved money and unwrapping
and stacked sounds of symbols and unwrapping insect conversations and
idioms and meat and meat and issues and what goes in elminated and sound
obsolete a communicator and way back first eye contact and what was
called nostalgia and constant non-movement feet compacted into motion
as if through a garden from the ground vibrations from the rails
couples... Lush dialogue & the sound of tongues licking... Reflect
personal historical fingers masks at night & alone music & musical
language a willingness to disarrangements annotated happiness... And
the room fills with people encases by invisible flowing atmospheres
dulls movement words are one by one instantly recorded & forgotten like
all relationships there're no more relationships.

(Text excerpted by BRUCE ANDREWS)

DOUBLE OR QUIT

GEOFFREY WARD, Double Exposure (1978; Infernal Methods, c/o David
Trotter, Dept. of English, University College, Gower Street, London,
England)

The afferent idiom through which the best writing now takes the
measure of its own compass-work is often a Pyrrhic triumph. The reader
will be quick to resign from a text which seems to be all strategy and
no tactics; the cost of absolutely interminable resuscitation of active
reading is a greater number of casualties than even poetry has been
used to.

We're unable to estimate the outcome; meanwhile we can look to
Double Exposure as a characteristic advance. This new order of work
exposes the volume of social inscriptions which seem of a piece in
sharing momentum. If there seem to be points of control over this momentum they are points where the effects of control are produced: such
is a judge or an author. Superimposed on the homeostat is a group of
fixatives, cultural ready-mades, media phrasing, the hyperbolic naivete
of poetic sentiment, the prayer-negotiation/poem as visualization of Truth.
The work is at once a filatory of jumping threads and the impasto design its after-band -- a double exposure on one plate -- her dress, like
her language, is a galimatias of several countries.

Contrast the maieutic, parliamentary drain on poetic resource
which has wide currency, the prosecution of tabloid epiphanies for which
Double Exposure is satiric depository (" We're kept snug and amused as
TV innards newsreels old workmates repeats and their catchphrases rerun
on similar lines below "). The routine theology is cued, made implor-
ingly histrionic, and is precisely contravened by cat-calling, writing
the oath, with its physical counterpart the excretion. References to
punk rock recall this profanation of the Host (the Pistols vomiting on
their audience) of which the typical exemplar must be the invert Howard
Hughes with his cultivation of dead matter: hair, nails, urine. The
principle of work is writing as e-limination, the expulsion of dead
truths -- " wipes away dirt like a dream " -- wastrel action as the only
freedom in art, writing as rubbish -- " pertinent; essential; the most
intricate presence in our entire culture " (Prynne) -- burning on the
city limits, pushing itself in every sense into the margin.

The greater part of what is still referred to as the avant-garde
is still concerned for wheedling re-valuation, the vulgarization of
Truth as a positive control, justice dispensed as a pill. (There is
supposed to be an 'alternative' society, an 'alternative' truth:
" Pretence that times are changing outside technology ".) On the face
of it, Double Exposure assigns itself to Nietzschean de-valuation of
all values, and in fact the stages of a career in Ward have the de-
lightful consistency of inversion; the early interest in TM leads him
from the cultivated nomadics of Tales from the Snowline directly to the
indecent politics of Double Exposure: a movement from passive to active
nihilism, a 'Buddhism of action'.

The commonplace poetry of to-day is inefficient through misalle-
gation of one or another substantiation of its presence. But new work
can excise the ground of any such operation by " damage to / and peeling
of / the original negatives ", an ablatitious force that diminished gravitation to given meta-discourse, seen as the negative of photographic
print. The contemporaneity of 'double exposure' is exact: the way The
Orators was, the way Behind The State Capitol still is.

ROD MENGHAM

344

BARRETT WATTEN, Plasma/Parallels/"X" (1979; Tuumba Press, 2639 Russell, Berkeley, CA 94705; $2)

Three poems written in the manner of seemingly unconnected statements -- the statements standing by themselves to point to the fact of their being statements, sentences. As words are put together to form sentences, sentences are (i.e., have been) put together to convey extended meaning -- in Watten, this process broken down (examined) by dissociating the sentences, drawing attention to the statements as they stand alone embodying their meaning -- their meaning nowhere essentially contiguous with what is outside each of themselves. (Always within a subtly reserved partially enigmatic decorum of his own device.) Contempt for narrative. An attack on (analysis of) coherent thoughts or statements to build on each other and form meaning, along with the intentions thereby implied. Watten is not making these statements as statements of his beliefs -- they are possible beliefs only, and show themselves to be such -- thereby confounding the usual purpose of statements -- to express opinions -- and instead pointing out how statements work, why opinions are of no real consequence. Showing what the statements do by themselves. The reader wrenched around in each statement by the force of the language -- directly from the structure -- not the thoughts, ideas, viewpoints expressed therein and made almost irrelevant to the work. But not entirely irrelevant. Since there is a studied intelligence operating in the selection of the statements. Almost all contain coherent meaning, if slight surrealistic tinges at times. They do lead the reader to think about their content. But this can't be why they are the way they are. Because they sabotage their own referential content by disconnecting it, by making it indigenously indecipherable.

This identifies an important problem for writing: meaning, and the lack of meaning, and what (how) meaning means. There seem to be two levels to this problem: (1) How language conveys meaning, and (2) How meaningful (significant, important) can that meaning be. See these words be words. We are now seen to be dealing with the problems of language from so deeply enmeshed in language, that it begins to sound tautological and inane. But it isn't. It would certainly be pleasant to see someone confront in their work both these two levels of the problem at once and tie them together, rather than either ignorantly leaping in the supposed direction of the meaning with no concern for the only way one can arrive there -- through language -- as most poets have done; or alternatively, concentrating on the intricacies of how language works to the exclusion of any further examination of the ramifications of meaning and its import to our lives in the broadest sense of it being able to invest them with that meaning.

Watten is definitely working on how language conveys meaning. The nuggets he presents also promote an outside content, but it is given a back seat, the structure becoming the work. After Plasma and Parallels,

"X" further destroys statements by taking them apart and leaving only the pieces of statements. Holding enough weight and inertia in themselves as fragments to become words in positions already outlined in advance by the structure of the language. Bereft of context. Thereby disturbing, disappointing, unpleasant while insightful. (Watch Watten look into his own writing.) The words pointing to themselves -- objects, things, tend to become the focus of our attention -- the words as objects sticking out to the point of starkness. Also, peripherally, there are glimpses of a worried dream, even a conflicted personality embedded in the work. This can't be written off as unreal, nor taken as Watten himself showing through the work. More possibly -- articulated pieces of our destroyed future here to look at (read) -- even to enjoy taking place in the present on the page.

> I want this momentum to destroy any discourse on
> the way things work.   -- Parallels

What is arrived at through this form of examination is certainly not the text itself, not even something *toward* that text, only an additive parallel to the original. A tracking. As the concept of "plasma" -- a terribly inadequate attempt at arriving at *the form* of the fundamental substance of matter being taken apart by heat and compression (destroyed), considering what that form really is -- a basically indecipherable quantum, an as yet unknown factor -- X.

DAVID BENEDETTI

HANNAH WEINER, Virgin (1978; A Hundred Posters, c/o Davies, 689 East 17th Street, Brooklyn, NY 11230; $1)

After seeing "The Last Wave" (the Australian movie in which Richard Chamberlain discovers he's a psychic through his relationship with some urban aborigines). I've often thought about the curse aspect of "the gift". It must be terrifying to have total recall (and precall?) of a given situation. So I imagine Hannah Weiner's technical dilemma to be the control of the sensory tide at her fingertips. In Virgin she capitalizes, spaces, repeats, misspells, overlaps and squeezes words and word groups as a sculptor would, as if to put some chunks in the stream to stem the flow. The expression "cave writing" comes to mind -- a long spelunking through the urban "dark places" (alley/subway/backs of bus seats/desks in school & other walls where expressions are isolated in a "flash"). Hannah describes this process herself when she writes "I can't see lying face down stupid ANDS I write that way." (Virgin, p. 9)

TINA DARRAGH

WRITING AND EXPERIENCING

Writing is unbounded by paradigms, and its paradigms are subsumable consumed by its forms. Associations to a poem's instances are not fixed by its formative instants, to the intervals of perception, thought and experience the words designate. Another reason why, technically, the poem and its elements have no history, no *precedents*. The poem and its elements revive an obsolete definition of that word: prognostication, presage, sign. The words prophesy their return in other spheres of experience. They are repeated as a mirror reproduces a silent effigy of an object and as one harmonic liberates and proliferates its possible modulations. The preceding transformations appear to lead inevitably to a moment, a lyrical configuration that is not only discrete but is also an interval, a transitional point in a rhythmic succession of moments.

*

They repeat themselves, not as a mirror echoes its content, but as one harmonic sound liberates a set of possible related modulations, and simultaneously lends those previous to it the quality of having engendered something unique and specific despite the irrefutable evidence of the senses that the moment was not discrete but was part of a continuity.

*

Ravel and Debussy: The musical dissolve- sudden sonic wipe outs of the interval just heard- sudden lyrical expression or quick aside in writing, a parallactical mode of self-definition.

*

The functions and character of paradigms in poetry are both qualitatively and quantitatively different than in any other writing. Aesthetic intentions are usually paramount, whether the actual instances cited are expressed for historical, emotional, musical, visual, philosophic, political or personal impact. In no other art are these relationships so delicately balanced and so easily misunderstood. In and of itself, for the poet, the production of any poem, or any element in a poem constantly brings the question of the purpose of the paradigm cited immediately to the fore. For this reason, the pulls are strong towards the Scylla of historicity and the Charybdis of obfuscation. In the former the paradigm seems clear: like the poet, the poem moves through the media of time and experience. Since there is no paradigm for poetry- or experience- this is possible and technically acceptable. But the danger here is that a paradigm is, in a hidden way, even in a deceptive way, being re-introduced. That paradigm might run like this: since I am a poet, my consciousness is a poetic process and instants of that consciousness are markings on a map of my poetic geography. Again, technically, this is true, and even necessary to take into account when writing poetry. But when this mode is established as a paradigm there is a radical reduction in the scope of a poem and the scale of the elements are too rigidly established on a one-to-one basis vis-a-vis each other.

*

The chant and the song elude the limitations of linear narration by means of the "haunting" refrain. Through harmonic, repeating, reverberating, echoing and iconographic alternation the "flicker" effect of language transcends the "flat" character of historicism. To historicism, ambiguity is a threat, as is projection, because it is experienced as intrusive, too immediately and suddenly intersubjective, and not easily subject to the ordinary processes of remembering.

*

The mutative relationship of poetry to art is akin to that of philosophy to science, science to technology, technology to the art of communication, art to language arts, etc.

*

The problematics of space = the problematic of the human relationship to space.

*

The same for matter and time.

*

What is the relationship of this to the appeal of *density*, or rapid experiences of strong emotional impact directly juxtaposed against the material facticity of language?

*

"[My sense of language is that it is matter and not ideas- i.e. printed matter. (R.S. June 2, 1972)]"

The Writings of Robert Smithson, edited by Nancy
Holt, N.Y., New York University Press, 1979, p. 104

*

Writing is fixed and sustained in mediums like paper, stone, metal and plastic. Experience is fixed through re-enactment and is sustained by emotional memory. Writing and experience have dissimilar flows, partly caused by their dissimilar mediums- one static, non-human and

348

inorganic, the other utterly physical and recognizable by movement. Only the experience of reading adds an experiential character to writing. In any case, like a forgotten ruin or monument, it continues to haunt us in its facticity as object. But writing is best understood unread, or most recognizable by its paradoxical relationships to memory, and thereby to actual experience. Writing is characteristically monumental, not so much in memory, but in reading, particularly in re-reading. So that re-reading adds a new dimension to reading- the characteristically parallactic quality in poetry is related to its projective devices. These give an overtone, an afterimage to the time directly before and after reading poetry, of meaning that is akin to the meanings derived for assessing experiences, but not its exact double.

*

The prevailing distinction between poetry and rhetoric illustrates one ordinary instance of the *au courant* literary distinction between "writing" and "writing about." But the difficulties some people have with fragments in art is a similar aesthetic reaction that prefers the extended prose piece- which apparently has all the virtues of the energy implicit in a rhetorical flow of writing without rhetoric's disposabil- ity- to the "short poem." So "writing" would be synthesizing its own structure while "writing about" would somehow be presupposing some ex- ternal referent or axis of explanation. Poems are universes because of the parallactic relationship of words between and words within languages.

*

The poem and the reader are equidistant from the meaning of the poem.

*

My secret: to know that I am withholding something. Your secret: to know that I am withholding something.

*

Remembering is partly an encumbrance the art of writing carries due to its synthesizing function in the formation of memories, and history (sequencing of experiences).

*

As historicism partly collapses in the movement generated by tech- nological advances in both recording and retrieving memory traces (like the recovery of the icons of Tut and the hieroglyphs of ancient Egypt and the encoded languages of the contemporary computer tape) language continuously revives its function in writing, through its power to re- flect the full range of representations of experiential reality in the mind, in its familiar, obscure, human experience in thought and feeling.

Language today (as depicted in Godard's _Alphaville_ and _Weekend_) is the enemy of the state and historicity because of its power to germinate systems antithetical to custom because custom is partly dependent on coded laws. Historicism allies itself with words, knowing its actual scale values but distrusting its changeability (translate instability). Taking language truly seriously as a partly known, unknowable form of energy is instantly recognizable to historicism as an antithetical challenge. Historicism debunks efforts to reify poetic language, except sometimes in art and art history (as in the manifestoes of Dada). Words closely seen are mirrors of consciousness, tones of thought and feelings, traces and bones of human experience and not simply mechanical reproductions and manipulations of the processes of memory, of the visualization of the causalities of historical development, the interlocking links of historical narrative, the imagistic jig-saw puzzles of traditional poetic formalism.

*

Even though most fiction and theater would have it the other way around, there is actually no point in personifying the essences of human experience. Reenacted experience, if it is to speak to us in a language that has authentic possibilities of extension, a conceivable actual practicability for intersubjective contact, cannot simply mime the . faces, gestures and expressions that seemingly originated its conception. It is for this reason that poetry is ultimately the most realistic of all human expressions in that it places absolute realistic clarity and empathy about psychological, political and existential experiences to the side of encompassing, in all its variable senses of exemplification, the pure essence of experience. Of course in purely temporal terms, this is a very long range view of practicality. Other sorts of practicality certainly have their uses for human endeavors. Still, the signs of these gestures, the naming of moments that codify instantaneously human communication -- "we all see this"- we imagine we connect to those feelings in memory. Memories are followed by language like paths leading in from various directions. Though the faces of those moments are their histories, the inner core of consciousness is not a film or mirror but a series of hieroglyphs. It is a map- a specific array of markings-lines and points and variable distances and durations: ever wandering, oboes babbling in counterpoint in memory following the motive of the main and developed themes curiously dogging them. Wandering touches of felt experiences enfolded by the inner thoughts surrounding them—not one-not even a thousand voices could fully characterize that resolution. It is heard in one voice, but it is spoken at once in all languages that is its own language.

*

Poetry reconnects the occurrence and the instance.

parallax- the apparent change in the position of an object resulting from the change of direction or position from which it is
viewed.

*

tide day- at any point the time between two successive high tides.

*

We can get an approximation of experience in words in that memories,
because of their ambiguous character, in the reading and relating of
words to the subtleties of actual experience, reenact the meanings
we applied to experiences, just as we reenact the meanings we apply to
the sequence of words. When we say to ourselves, in reading, "That's
how I feel" or "That's how I see it myself" we are often tempted to
underline the words we were reading when we experienced the feeling of
comprehension. Yet then, strangely, when we return to read the underlined words reading that particular passage doesn't still hold the
meaning we had imagined it held.

*

"There is no need to be astonished at the part played by words in
dream-formation. Words, since they are nodal points of numerous ideas,
may be regarded as destined to ambiguity." Sigmund Freud, Interpretation
of Dreams

*

Experience is spoken not only in its own key but derives its language from all aspects of every element of being. Writing the experience, writing about experience, writing. Language creates itself out
of the necessities for marking the trail- to mark a path:- but it defines its own aspects of reflecting on or from itself, its umbre. Commentary and accompaniment, companion, map and decoder, the thought process in its daily use is too often recoiled from when it is dense with
multilayered ideas, criticized as "too" intellectual, "too" inward,
narcissistic: as if thinking itself were worse than watching television,
or reading, or seeing movies, or writing about experiences. For the
poet, thinking is writing.

*

The power of an idea does not solely consist in its groundedness
in being.

*

"I further had a suspicion that this discontinuous method of functioning of the system Pcpt.-Cs. [perceptual consciousness] lies at the bottom of the origin of time." Sigmund Freud, <u>A Note Upon the Mystic Writing Pad</u> (1925)

*

Reading, like perception, fades out and in. But it would be more correct to say that it juxtaposes simultaneous types of thinking that are ordered in a way similar to the way sentences join together words of different types. As if illogicality could get you there, thought reaches out for, but is touched by anyway, the places some of the thoughts travel to that words don't reach, exactly. Waves are repetitious- thought is repetitious- something like tides. No two exactly the same yet the times are predictable. The moon stays exactly the way it is, slightly off-setting the full gravity of the Earth. Steady, but, understandably, not perfectly steady. Also, thought must be re-ordered into grammatical order. Yet it never quite keeps up with the latest stylistic requisites. Its beauty is not exactly the same as that of language. Thought is free but alone in its freedom. It can't be fully socialized- yet it can compare its truth to that of language.

*

"Timelessness is found in the lapsed moments of perception, in the common pause that breaks apart into a sandstorm of pauses."
　　　　　Robert Smithson, "Incidents of Mirror-Travel in the Yucatan",
　　　　　p. 94, <u>The Writings of Robert Smithson</u>

*

Writing offers to experience a third eye, a parallactical measure and scalar key to the relations between communicable and non-communicable states of perception and being. Reading offers to experience not a mirrored double but a third voice, an harmonically variable scale that may in the literal sense graphically represent states of being, just as a certain grouping of notes may "represent" alternate modes of enharmonic and intervalic overtones. Polyphonic *ekstasis*, the reading experience translates a multiple text of felt interactions. Experience is read aloud, reading signifies a return to silence. Writing is enshrined in the heart of experience. "All life exists to end in a book." The ending is within the beginning at every juncture, which fragments the impulse to translate reading experience from writing it. Writing, by reviving experience transposes involuntary memories into present ones. In advance, the mind, set on record, transposes what would be free associative and dreamlike states into statements. Returned to the workings of language, experience is felt to be on the other side of the mobius strip. Reread, language is a hieroglyph of experience, but a script both of experience and silence, blankness.

352

Equals≠equals==. Scratches are the equivalent of signatures, the
spirit of the totem's reification is retouched, carved, and wears away.
Spoken aloud, thought is heard and felt, is *touching*, moving.

*

being carried along
was supposed to be in form
when the replica began to fade
before that, time is (was) imprecise
exactly itself without moral tones

*

By listening awkwardly (not like in conversation where the overtones are potentially embarrassing) this voice declines concentration
on the dictates of one particular stage in the argument. While the
observer has his/her eye in unremitting concentration on the inevitable,
the reader is deftly persuaded to reenact, in silent assent, the
genesis of an apparently random sequence of images.

*

I can't use the predictions anyway. I see them only in retrospect.

*

Instances follow upon the other invoking an internal sequencing of
experiences. The substantiation of these instances framed in an accumulative pattern form an aggregate point of realization. The ideas that
emerge most fully contrasted within the aggregate constellation of
scaled images stimulate conceptualizations about the presumed pre-supposed internal structure.

*

not...but

.

NICK PIOMBINO

REMEMBER TO SEND US YOUR ADDRESS CHANGES

AND TO SUBSCRIBE TO VOLUME THREE

LETTER TO THE EDITOR

I think the problem of being in bad faith, if you will, vis a vis one's political position so-called, is one that everyone who claims any position at all (really everyone, since the claim to no position, political agnosticism, is one as well, and as open to question as any) must deal with forever, whether vigilantly or intermittently. I am absolutely suspicious of those who claim a political righteousness at the expense of others. I am deeply encouraged by those who do politically propagandistic work of whatever kind that manages to encourage others effectively to consider or freshly interpret their own political roles in their social culture without fronting some kind of obligation. The 'social contract' is not some kind of binding obligation, *obviously*. I am basically puzzled at the need anyone feels to point at their role as politically correct or to colleagues' as politically incorrect, since it seems that political change comes not from the recognition of categories but from a revelation of the nature of the functions of social experience as they effect one's life inextricably from effect in others' -- a revelation that takes place through social relations, usually I guess through work. For the likes of us, this *may* be accessible largely through something that happens in literary work, BECAUSE we take our role as literary workers seriously. That role of ours is not likely to be taken seriously by those who aren't writers. Of course there weren't many in Dickens' time who took the role of factory-worker seriously either, outside the factories themselves, and it seems that his writings did make some little differences, both in easing a few burdens and shifting forces around so that the bourgeoisie might sit itself more comfortably on the cushions without the springs poking through. Whether the revelation of the political dilemma of fine artists is of interest to other than other fine artists today or not, certainly it is necessary that artists take note of, respond to, however ambivalently, what that is. State it, *throughout*.

STEVE BENSON

FDA = festival of (dis)appearing art(s) = festival of disappearing acts = disappearing arcts festival = IFDA

(Below is an excerpt from program notes by Marshall Reese and Kirby Malone to the Baltimore-Washington International Festival of Disappearing Arts, which took place in May, 1979, and was sponsored by the Merzaum Collective's Desire Productions.)

"... all these gestures, the angular and abruptly broken attitudes, these syncopated modulations formed at the back of the throat, these musical phrases that break off short, these flappings of insect wings,

these rustlings of branches, these sounds of hollow drums, these creakings of robots, these dances of animated puppets..."
                              --Artaud (on the Balinese Theatre)

The formalization (organization) of a disappearing art(s) festival occurs as an effort to point out & to provide a context for a range of intermedia performance activity that has (dis)appeared continuously in this century, from the work of Dada & Futurism, through Fluxus and Happenings, to now: the Futurists' future. This flow of divergent & convergent elements reintroduces into our network of social machines a set of possible positionings in relationship to art in a social system that predates the Western Industrial "revolution", & in some instances predates verbal rational forms altogether. The disappearing art(s) are made up of a shifting group, nomadic in art activity, bound together by no dogma or theory, evidenced only by the performance event & occasion (which some disappearing artists contend does not end or begin, as in Steve McCaffery's notion of Permanent Performance). Our social indoctrination/conditioning/acculturation often convince us to long for partially or wholly predigested phenomena as the material of our perception, which in part accounts for the subliminal hypnotic hysteria for sameness & cloning that agents such as advertizing make possible in our society. Disappearing art(s) encourage a recognition & constructive appreciation of difference & the ability to work from an apparent chaos. Disappearing art(s) is not a movement, but a tool for viewing, in intuitive & pragmatic manners, a wide spectrum of work: many disappearing artists will never hear of or meet each other: they are disappearing too fast.

An art located moving in a shift of the art's social function(s) -- not to entertain, or to take one's mind off...one's troubles, but to put one's mind on those troubles, supportive of the impulse(s) to social change: -- no more escapist literature or an afternoon's aesthetic diversions. Disappearing art(s) move counter to the virtuoso & the expert, and counter to manipulation, coercion, sentimentality, melodrama, and mystification. The mechanisms of characterization, narrative and psychology falter in respect to the tension and possibility of each other. An art located moving may appear as a blur, which the distinctions of theater, dance, and literature cannot contain. & the disappearing art(s) disappear with no funds. Arts funding sources are designed to, at best, support ventures that fall within strict categories.

A focal impulse in the work is that made up by the social specifics where if a decision of intent or meaning is made, it is not made by the performers. The disappearing act is not a performed work imposed on a passive audience, but a record of the interactivities between a particular artist & the larger group of audience & artist.

The disappearing art(s) are (dis)appearing -- combining numerous forms
of theater, dance, poetry, video, music and other media. The (dis)-
appearing art(s) disappear in (out of) order that who was watching may
decide for themselves. The traditional response modes steer a shadowy
audience, conducted through television, spectator sports, & pornography,
toward a system that will make their decisions for them. Vocals, motion, music, visuals construct an event that is social before artistic,
for a reason that the mechanisms by which one judges/perceives the
event cannot be those trained on a "pure" form, but are ones which appear beside the (dis)appearance (as one beside oneself). The media of
the disappearing act construct an event in which the training by which
one judges an event cannot impede what one is watching in relation to
who one is while watching it.

KIRBY MALONE & MARSHALL REESE

LALLY

MY WORK

I see all my work as serial -- as in the relationships between the parts
within them (stanzas, paragraphs, lines, sentences, parenthetical statements, phrases, words, meanings, syllables, abbreviations, letters, and
their various subdivisions (consonants, vowels, number seventeen on a
scale of one to twenty-six, the other twenty-five, pretty ones, ugly
ones, long ones, short ones, linear ones, less linear ones, etc. or
words that rhyme, words that look like they rhyme, words that look alike,
words that look similar, words that sound similar, words, words that
mean similar, words that don't, words that can be repeated more than
once and not mean the same thing and words that can't, words that can
be repeated more than twice and not mean the same thing and words that
can't, etc. or etc.)) and the parts without them (other works, parts of
other works, parts of a longer work that they are part of, another part
of the book they're a part of, the rest of the book, the same work in
another book, part of the same work in another work, etc.) in some
cyclic, or other consistently geometric pattern (consistent in the way
geometric patterns tend to be by definition) -- but without ever using
those kinds of references or those kinds of language (or self-references
and abstract language) but instead using the language patterns of speech

357

as I have heard it and experienced it through reading it and through
reading it into whatever I read, or, through reading whatever I read
through it, and using the language I love most and love most to use,
such as one syllable non descriptive (no matter what "part of *speech*,"
(as in the way "use" does not "describe" anything we can picture in our
imaginations without imposing our own specificity (now the word "specificity" (with five times as many syllable "parts" as "use") does the
same thing (force us to impose the particulars if we want to see it --
(but we don't "see" it because, in that sense, it is "abstract" (whereas
"use" is not -- which kind of realization has always uncovered a lot of
class, race, ethnic origin, and educational background biases to me,
just as the obvious display -- i.e. "showing off" -- of "unique" employment
of language or the obvious display of the commitment to that goal (the
"unique" employment (is "employment" any more specific or abstract than
"use" if its use is similar) of language) has always reflected to me
standards based on sex, class, race, ethnic origin, or educational background, (this is an "obvious display" of some of my biases)))))) words
like "it."

* * * * *

I want to retain as much as possible of what I experience, understand,
expect, imagine, etc. that does not *hurt* (or hurt too much too often)
me or anyone else ("as far as I can tell") but especially that seems
positive or helpful or more "real" (according to my experience-knowledge-
perceptions-expectations-etc.) than what other creators offer me (or I
have access to or can take in) and to communicate, represent, refer to,
express, share, analyze, "show out," place, record, make obvious, insist
on, state, describe, "approach" (always with the idea that "truth" can
never be *reached* but only approached), intuit, hone, etc. I had the
"idea" that I wanted to "speak" from every perspective on the spectrum
of my own experience (including imaginative, which, of course, includes
my version of the experience of "others" etc. (always amazed at the
capacity for more and the essential repetitiveness of *most* experience
(including "language experience")) in the language (and/or "voice") discovered in the course of the experimenting, with cross fertilization
from one experience to another, e.g. a "language experience" with a
"sexual" one, etc. I started out (late 50s) as a musician -- "jazz" and
my own variations on various tendencies from rhythm and blues to
"serious" -- and visual "artist" -- mostly three dimensional collages constructed as part of the environments I found myself living in and never
repeated or moved to the next place (and also experimented with audial --
tape -- constructions, etc.) I see all my writing as one "vast" work,
the unevenness just range and high-lights, my own personal favorites
include "The South Orange Sonnets" (written as an autobiographical
"novel" of my "early life" (before leaving home, i.e. South Orange, New
Jersey, 1942-1960), 20 chapters, 14 lines each, "sonnets" in their

serial construction and internally in ways I never saw used before);
"My Life" (the ultimate life-as-list jacket blurb litany etc.): "All
of the Above": "Oomaloom": the first (title piece), last ("Islands"),
and middle ("A/going") pieces in CATCH MY BREATH; etc. I believe my
writing continues to keep me "honest" even when at the time I'm writing
I don't think it is "honest" enough or "honest" at all, and it has
helped me maintain a sense of not only my own dignity and worth, but
respect for almost everything else too -- RESPECT for the subject matter
of my life and the lives, events, experiences, vocabularies, "personalities," objects, imaginings, etceteras that my life encounters or
incorporates from the start -- the "honesty": to speak from that and of
that without compromising it to any perspective/structure/aesthetic
strategy/ set of standards outside or alien to it (as far as I am capable of judging and controlling) e.g. "traditional," "academic,"
"W.A.S.P.," "middle-class intellectual," or "declasse," or "decadent,"
or etc. (except where that is a valid part of it and not vice versa)
etc. I want it to live in the imaginations of strangers and friends
like a movie or a memory or the impact of a work of art, etc.

MICHAEL LALLY

LALLY BIBLIOGRAPHY: *Master of Ceremonies* (1967; broadside, Living
Series, Iowa City, Iowa). *In Reply Refer to* (1969; limited edition IBM
readout, The Nomad Press, Iowa City). *What Withers* (1970; Doones Press,
Bowling Green, Ohio). *The Lines Are Drawn* (1970; Asphalt Press, Jackson
Center, Ohio). *mcmlxvi poem* (1970; The Nomad Press). *Stupid Rabbits*
(1971; Morgan Press, Milwaukee, Wis.). *The South Orange Sonnets* (1972;
Some of Us Press, Washington, D.C.). *Late Sleepers* (1973; Pellet/The
Great Outdoors Press, Yellow Springs, Ohio). *Malenkov Takes Over* (1974;
a double book with Tina Darragh's "My First Play," Dry Imager, Washington,
D.C.). *Rocky Dies Yellow* (1975, second edition 1977; Blue Wind Press, 820
Miramar, Berkeley, Ca. 94707; $2.95). *Dues* (1975; The Stone Wall Press,
c/o Richard Flamer, P.O. Box 3668, Omaha, Nebraska, 68103; $6.25). *Sex /
The Swing Era* (1975; a double book, Lucy & Ethel, Washington, D.C.).
Poems (1975; broadside, Hard Pressed, Sacramento, Ca.). *Mentally, He's a
Sick Man* (1975; Salt Lick Press, Quincy, Ill.). *My Life* (1975; Wyrd
Press, New York, N.Y.). *Oomaloom* (1975; Dry Imager). *Charisma* (1976; O
Press, New York, N.Y.). *Catch My Breath* (1978; Salt Lick Press). *In the
Mood* (1978; Titanic Books, Washington, D.C.). *Just Let Me Do It* (1978;
Vehicle Editions, c/o A. Levitt, 238 Mott Street, New York, N.Y. 10012;
$3.50). *Life* (1979; broadside with portrait by Alex Katz, Brooke Alexan-
der Gallery, New York, N.Y.). *Up from the Seventies* (forthcoming). *White
Life* (forthcoming). EDITOR: *None of the Above* "New Poets of the USA"
(1976; The Crossing Press, c/o Lally, 190A Duane Street, New York, N.Y.
10013; $4.95 payable to Michael Lally).

SELF WRITING / *I (lucky thought)*

"Private life asserts itself unduly, hectically, vampire-like,
trying compulsively, because it really no longer exists, to prove
it is alive." (Theodor Adorno, <u>Minima Moralia</u>). "In reality the
ego is like the clown in the circus, who is always putting in his
oar to make the audience think that whatever happens is his doing."
(Freud to Jung, <u>The Freud/Jung Letters</u>). "To accept subjectivity
as it exists today, or better, as it does not exist today, is
implicitly to accept the social order that mutilates it. The
point, however, is not merely to reject subjectivity in the name
of science or affirm it in the name of poetry..." (Russell Jacoby,
<u>Social Amnesia</u>).

I, I, *I*, I I, I, *I*, I. *Suppose I* don't exist, *fuck individualism, by
myself, 'I'.* I don't make up the world, I'm not *self-sufficient*, O.K., .
not master in my own house. *Will (the verb I activate)* -- not free, not
responsible, not consistent, don't blame me.

No need to expose *crabbed secrets of the psyche ... to the well organized and systematic scrutiny of some poetic form or strategy.* They're
always <u>already</u> exposed to language, pretty well organized & systematic,
which even creates them, *always first for the context* -- they're <u>worded</u>
secrets, coded : *Before you get the chance to cut and direct and reflect
and get yourself in control of the flow or at least the flowering of
the important parts* -- I don't act; I'm <u>acted</u> by : *things which eat up
intentions, things which are always behind the one who is labelling...*
My unveiling (call it the demystification function of writing) places me
in a system, that code, *continuous logic of structures -- institutions --*
of which I'm *the faintest idea, small changes.* A structuralist view,
then, as a critique. *It had been written by me. Only <u>not</u> by <u>me</u>.* It
<u>had</u> written <u>me</u>.

*I had an invincible desire to clutch language itself through my most
recent values.* But I'm a dictionary, language castrates me. Individual
experience is primary?, that's a myth, especially now, administered capitalism, *forces of control over... the resolutions we initiated,* over the
revolutions, I don't like psychology, *environmental custody,* social phenomena are there in the background, *or the words coming through, and...
Precisely at that point: vanish.*

I just know how to work myself, or what I think's myself when it's
really writing *rooting around in the gym of language.* Free play of
meaning in writing overshadows and disperses <u>me</u>, it undermines my raps'
autonomy, *bio style,* just like unconscious desire undermines an ego,
<u>orphans</u> me, disrupts a narcissistic dream of me-present-to-me, me & you
(the fusion of classified information with a body). THE APPARATUS OF

THE _OTHERNESS_ FAILS or UNIFICATION. _How Many Times Must I Marry Myself:_
the book opened like a vagina. But remember: 'I'm an effect, of language,
breaking up the scene at the mirror -- _(I was captivated with this vision_
... _this is me I see!_... _I dissolved into it)_ -- differences, separation,
absence, meaning, all that. _All part of the motion away from our mothers._
The gesture completed when we became the bigger boys and did some of the
beating. I could really identify with all those structures they put in
my head to get out of our heads what was there first. When I joined the
system, _the men made me one of them_ but to do that they had to make me
one a single solitary one to begin with. _NOTHING TO DO BUT LIE HERE AND_
COME APART. _I knew it wasnt really my imagination that was making this_
scene it was the cops, the Law, who controls who, who even distributes
the name 'who' & who 'me'? and why why? _We taught him our standards,_
which weren't ours. Secondhand -- _you know the rules_ -- ... _I hate machines_
and systems... _but I got to admit I'm enjoying the respite._

Apprenticeship of language = alienation for me, _each piece a solemn_
dedication to the whole -- etc. -- _speech matrix / flow._ _Is the way we_
feel normal [& stress how we're social & how social we are; socialized,
not socialists. We're like a speech, social life speaks right through us]
if we normally feel this way, made normal -- with fixed destination, exclusive assignments, _flattened out._ Even the atmosphere the textures we
grope around in are a system now not just pinpricks of the things you
notice yourself. _The music then was a radio in the night, now it's a_
system.

When I hear all this talk about systems, I want to say: I don't take
dictation. Conventions have limits, and there're dangers in being complacent or rhapsodic about them. _The crudeness of socialized instructions_
needs to let through, between the cracks, individual experience, flower,
the confusion of heads to unfold. How self-contained & closed-off is
this 'order of language' or 'Law of Culture'? What's in it that guarantees our desire, _firsthand,_ to _put together truth,_ or ethics, or confidence (unless they're just supposed to be byproducts of 'if all goes well'
or 'I'm like everyone else' or 'genital normalization' or 'that's taboo,
decadent, counter-revolutionary, etc.', etc.), etc.

If language is primary and everything we felt was central is really
prefab & de-centered, then how does individual experience fit in, how can
it loosen up these structures & punch through some barriers : these are
some questions : If systems are determining, then is poetry just 'showing
language at work' with language now fashionably defined as a system that
'works'? _They're always about themselves / (words) driving people away..._
Or are private worlds upfront & if you say they're 'constituted by language,' O.K., _those who come apart first fill up the words later,_ but
language isn't some frozen merchandise. _I'm a writer,_ it's writing, I'm
producing it, not just to show its obstacles _(I'm a generation of obsta-_

cles) but to show them <u>up</u>, disassemble the fixed programs, not just be marched along by them. *One dude plays blues harp and makes up lyrics to go with action as the arrests continue...*

And all of our selves refusing to be subordinated to the selves most widely recognized, accepted... To want *a poetry that has room for me, knots & shields, my tunnels and locked doors.* More than a byproduct of 'the law of one and all,' it starts <u>with</u> some me, *our self importance, collisions with speech, fragmented signature,* then plugs in but only afterward, when I write, read it, me, <u>then</u> people can share it. Otherwise it's just the conventions of the culture apparatus make us all this way then get us to 'create' its way & feed us the need to make it, succeed. Remember when 'the system' had obvious negative overtones? Is this rage for codes & systems & structuralism in the 70's more than a tidying-up of our regret & frustrated longing for getting beyond it? *And the people who know see through the collage we constructed to show them we weren't what they said we would always be but were pieces of all the things we had loved to see others make lives from...*

Self-consciousness is being programmed out of existence -- *it's all so subjective, as they say* -- so, we're more insistent on it? *And what other way can we see the world except as extensions of who we are or would like to be* ... *Things* <u>meant</u> *or did not exist,* they seemed to have to mean something beforehand, firsthand, *I mean me, in my solipsistic universe,* or writing didn't make them mean -- *HERE I AM; but this cant mean as much in words as it did in experience.* If I record my raps, *sometimes appearances,* more like a transcript of heart on sleeve, *speak louder than words.* Voice -- breathless throw made, personalizing, into a verse line, or a rush, a way of lacquering associations for you with a personal speech and asides and memorabilia, *the screens of our dreams' imaginations,* not just composing with them more freely but back to putting a high note in the bar where my self is. Still, stressing <u>me</u> might at least give writing a whiff of what defines 'us' struggling <u>for</u> autonomy (whether it's blacks, feminists, bisexuals, street queens, working class renegades, or what) and in <u>those</u> struggles highlighting the person may (helpfully or unreflectively) be *just sunk in the language of defense* -- <u>against</u> what's deformed & pre-formed about what's outside (all the social, the norms). *We have our codes too, let's use them to interpret our experience in ways* <u>they'll</u> *have to stretch to understand.*

Now, some (usually white heterosexual American professional-class male) writers write about 'the death of the author' or 'the de-centered self' or how 'a system of signifying practices constitutes the subject as a precipitate of unconscious discourse inscribed in response to the basic lack produced as the determinative network of oedipal triangulation supercedes the imaginary identifications of the ego,' etc. *They weren't telling their stories.* Well maybe their chance to <u>go</u> <u>beyond</u> the self &

362

give writing freer play is like class privilege -- an elaborated code. Stressing a <u>me</u> filters & squeezes what the writing does -- it's a restricted code, *language that is accessible to the people I come from,* but it allows me to speak to who 'I' need to speak to, including 'me': *to decrease that chasm of semantics.*

The necessary extension. Not to be privatized in a single self because I didn't see how privatized even my attempts to make the self infinitely expansive might seem to others less hounded by *my need to be in everyone,* to publicize a private mythology in order to share it, *thinking I'm still in the movies, it's an outside telephone booth.* To make me universal (*I come out with myself & find / everyone*), not symbolically as a language so much as a pretty irreducible concrete thing, body, that can be anyone everyone displaced disguised -- <u>pers</u>ona -- *mistaken for black, for gay, for straight, for older, for younger for bigger for better for richer for poorer for stupider for smarter for somebody else,... I never talked about making distinctions. He was him. I am 2 of us... spending much of my energy identifying with all kinds of people I wasn't...*

Shifters. To shift all around a lot, but a little in a vacuum, can never fully accept that the firm ground for any pirouettes in writing is *the language proves <u>itself</u>.* And if <u>language</u> is <u>writing</u>, it's writing writ large not just *this is about me now.* In fact, there are <u>no</u> immediate first hand things in writing -- not 'remembrance of my life' & not 'my eye ball view'. Everything's mediated, that is, it's <u>written</u> -- *this this this.* There's a whole complicated 'transformational process' separating my 'private materials' from any publicity, since reading is social. Peril to ignore this. It's writing as the whole mediation, not *distracted by some shit or sex or need to be me and say it.* That drawback is always feeling the meaning (the <u>sharing</u>) has to pass directly through that filter of 'I' -- an identification, an interpretation, a star system, *making the decisions for everybody, the audience was what he was fucking. Property is an extension of the self, if it's time and space that's mine forever. I must become less imperative.*

Poets primary interest is not always Language more or less collectively, <u>true</u>, but where we begin is *a simple love* & growing understanding of *language's hidden orders. VALUES IN THE DENIAL OR OURSELVES.* For even to get an exemplary grip on my selves I have to see how society & language set up a context which produces the possibilities & limits the meanings I can create, and you too. I'm in eclipse. *I guess it's you.* <u>I don't exist yet.</u> *It was a temporary victory, but what victory isn't temporary, huh?*

BRUCE ANDREWS

[Italicized portions above are from Michael Lally's work; this essay, in part, a part of my continuing response]

L=A=N=G=U=A=G=E

Number 11.   (Vol. 3, No. 1.)

January 1980.

Charles Bernstein & Bruce Andrews, Editors.

Subscriptions -- One year (three issues in 1980) for $4.
                    Institutions: $8.

Layout: Susan B. Laufer   Typing: Alan Davies

All queries, submissions, and checks to:
Charles Bernstein, 464 Amsterdam Ave, New York, NY 10024.

L=A=N=G=U=A=G=E is supported by subscriptions, donations, and grants
from the National Endowment for the Arts, the Coordinating Council
of Literary Magazines, and the New York State Council on the Arts.

Distributed with the cooperation of the Segue Foundation.

NOW AVAILABLE: *Poetic Justice* by Charles Bernstein--pod books, 3022
Abell Avenue, Baltimore, MD 21218, $4. *Jeopardy* by Bruce Andrews--c/o
Brita Bergland, Box 376, Windsor, VT 05089, $3.

Back issues of L=A=N=G=U=A=G=E available on request--$4 individuals
and $8 libraries for each volume.

L=A=N=G=U=A=G=E

NUMBER 12   JUNE 1980

MISREPRESENTATION

(A text for <u>The Tennis Court Oath</u> *of John Ashbery)*

> "Thus, when the universal sun
> has set, does the moth seek the
> lamp-light of privacy."
>
> --- Karl Marx, 1939.

* * *

1. "Uh huh." "Huh." "Heh? Eh?" What *had* you been thinking
about? Since, from the very start, this outward-looking topic or conjuncture of words is *convulsed,* "the face studiously bloodied" by all
that combs the text. "Hush!"

But — the conjunction — registers the tone. "but what testimony
buried under colored sorrow". So this is not evidence for some theory
but a gloss on loss, regret, confusion, clarity, the net of hope un-
raveling both night & day. And our reading *registers* this dizzying
parade —of eroded representations and wreckage. Are they what we
want? "When through the night.... Pure sobs denote the presence...
Of supernatural yearning".

2. One can "smile up at your dark window in the nothing sunlight —". Wait around; "I guess the darkness stubbed its toe". Fal-
ters; blanks. "We were growing away from that" —toward desire, with a
jeweler's care, "...waiting". Always.

It's not just the accuracy of pointing which this work calls into
question, or pouts. Rather, we are led to question the efficacy of
desire, of *getting through*. Of interpersonal TRANSLATION, a social
activity which begins to look like a subcategory of clarity and communicative competence. Are we still dumb with each other; is this
"numb hitting"? Am I *getting through* to you (and to you-plural)?
"Piercing the monocle ...because letters". To pierce that, as letters
can pierce through: it isn't taking off or opening up shades, but removing historical or social barnacles. Shades are painted shut. The
impermeability of the person, the wall-eyed. "It is dumb and night
continually seeping in — like a reservoir .... Of truth on the ban-
dits".

3. Blabbing causing darkness, & darkness related to the closures, the incommensurability of experiences, the inability to *see*. "I try ... to describe for you .... But you will not listen". But we must agree. "Agreement was possible." Agreement was not readily possible; we weren't ready. Since there isn't some reality out there awaiting our objective operations. Instead, you find a relativism grounded in practices, in the round of language, which demands *responsiveness* from us and not simply *decipherment*. Dialogues, in place of a fugitive 'monologic,' as a means by which reality can be *constituted*. *Paroles*. [The constitutive rules of this game define the second-order ends/means relationship — between the social construction of reality, on one level, and everything that we do & are & say, on the other.] "The facts have hinged on my reply".

4. Communicative competence, and therefore transparency, and social reality itself: all together. What "will teach you about men — what it means"? "Because what does anything mean,...?" Yet is anything "wholly meaningless," or if so only by some constricted definition of meaning, one which sanctions only certainties, is transparency or a phoney monologic. So "the things I wish to say" — are they ever without obstructions or emotional overhead? For saying is not just an utterance but a social performative as well. At every step, we perform the dialogue.

5. The borders & barriers & border patrols which it breeds all remind me of those which translation must cross. And translation does or can model all our interactions. Even so, there are problems, familiar problems with this. "All borders between men were closed." The impermeability, again. So that the things we wish to say may even seem motivated by a strong desire (the wish, the personal gesture, the camp), yet in a contextual sense "are needless," or else remain unmotivated or undemanded in a formal sense. Loosed from their context, which gives them 'a formal sense.' "stammered". "But that doesn't explain." "... I don't know". "You don't understand ..." " — I don't know why." The forms *motivate* the human disjunctures, which is their triumph.

6. Lately, I've heard Ashbery's work mentioned in breaths that include Lowell, Bishop, Sexton, Howard, Merrill, Strand, Rich, Hollander, etc. A community of innocent and therefore more worrisome misrepresentation which poses as representation, as rhetoric. The work at hand is less innocent. It does not content us as established rhetoric. "More than the forms". O.K. Yet this is still like a 'social-work'. It poses for us a radical questioning of established forms, yet at the same time, and so appropriately in its own form, it explores the implications of that questioning — not as an idea, but as an experience and a *reading*.

I came upon this work early in my writing. Rereading, it seems even less comfortably mentioned in that former breath of names, or even in a breath with the many younger writers who have adopted his tone and manner of discourse. Instead, it still *persuasively* proposes a condition of formal adventure: with elements of Allen's New American Poetry 1945-1960, with the work of Roussel, Cage, Zukofsky, with O'Hara, Eigner, MacLow, Roche, with what recent writing has done (that of Coolidge, Silliman, Mayer, Grenier, DiPalma, Bernstein, others) to help us take a new breath, and with what such writing may do to push us *further* along. Not a conventional dalliance, and not a transcendent avant-gardism. There are other communities, and this work and therefore the possibilities for writing can belong in them. It has opened rooms, even if Ashbery's own work has not walked into them.

"I am toying with the idea." Yet we read more than "only bare methods", the "sharp edge of the garment", "the .... lettering easily visible along the edge". What is here: "A torn page with a passionate oasis". "Back into pulp." The construction itself bends backward, to give us a clearance for the jumps in location and tone and pointed-ness —a *jump cut*, like the narrative variety in New Wave cinema of that time. Moreover, the construction is not a shawl, enveloping & smoothing the shifts, as in later work, but is at the heart of our experiencing those shifts at all — the jagged kaleidoscope of melancholia and expiration.

7. "of course the lathes around
    the stars with privilege jerks"

It concerns the undercutting of the image, the visual picture —by juxtaposing the conceivable referents in unexpected ways and also by fragmenting the syntax, that gridiron of outwardness. "The reason ejected" by these 2 strategies —via the constitution of the image and via syntax, both of which are variously shattered. In fact, we could say that only here and in Three Poems does the disjunct formal structure fully *double*, or reiterate, the implicit lessons embodied in the discourse: about the fragility of relationships, doubts, breakage, tenuousness more generally, foreclosed dreams & the mortgages of dream-work, lonesomeness. Not just an ornamentally rhetorical way of talking *about* these issues; here we find them displayed and played out and encoded in the very construction. This is *codic doubling* with a lovely vengeance.

8. Let light shine in? "The bars had been removed from all the windows". But .... "What window?" What is at stake — "A signal from the great outside" — is this all?: "against the window." "the observatory"; "specs". These seem. Light and glass, as mirrors, as representation, as lucid rhetoric. He's not wondering if we want this, but is depicting actively what language can deliver. Are we willing

to accept the ... available substitutes? .Not our salvation.

Even to the point where language itself takes precedence — is
the frontal project. "Inch pageant". And single words are unleashed
from a familiarity which their very unleashing helps to undermine. As
well, they constitute another reality. Signs & the rules they carry
inside them. "Now he cared only about signs." Well, not true, not
even here, but he does care very deeply and seems suspicious of their
instrumental use, of their *about-ness,* their external determinants.
"Panorama."

9.   Images, for example — or ornament. "The colored balls were
like distant lights on the plaque horizon." Not enough, and not what
it is. "Is not a 'images' ....to 'arrange'". Not, actually it kicks
the legs out from under that whole project. Here, and more prominently
than in later work, the composition does not project such an arrangement. It doesn't just juxtapose representations and accede to their
hegemony. No ... the reading, the language, "does not evoke a concrete
image". Still, you want to do more than abandon the possibility: "You
have to exact.the forfeit". To do so, you may want to make these illusory or suspect representations more exact; or question them in one
exacting fashion after the other. "The light goes — it exudes ....
Your idea — perched on some utterly crass sign". For isn't it always
some utterly crass sign or image on which it is perched, on which our
hopes are perched? Not what is in front of us. "Photography, horror
of all". As if humans were the miscommunicating mammals, or those who
locate themselves in frames which require so much more than what we
call simple reading, or 'reading off.' Instead, things are pleased by
indirection. "He is not a man ... Who can read these signs". Not in
this light.

10.   Isn't transparency a mark of illusion, and possibly of all
illusions? "misguided": the elysium of signposts, of exact replicas,
clones, control, repetition compulsion. "You cannot illusion;" this
remains as a trace of advice. *Critical Interruptions.* "Lights stream
undeniably away". Their touch eludes. You cannot recapture. And
light itself would be an evasion, or a misapprehension, and even the
other-worldly, the distractingly transcendent. If "escape is over the
lighted steps ....Misunderstandings arise cathedral." The radical critique of religion as a source for an Ideologiecritik, and a critique
of clarity and transparency and language: "powerless creating images";
and hierarchy arising historically at the same time as instrumental
literacy (Levi-Strauss) or the incest taboo. Repent; revolt. In the
division of labor, some are left to dream. Are we left to repeat?

"We might escape, in the daylight". As if light comes across
here as an escape, "the exit light". Since aren't these the descriptive effects, the lighting, evoked around the edges of an experience

in order to show an unreal way out? This project can be overturned: "the undesired stars .... needed against the night .... Forbidden categorically". Yet how undesired are they, "the fact the stars", the piercing through of night? Fugitive. Instead, in the dark, we can pledge allegiance to them — to these facts and to their absence.

And not to description. During that pledge of allegiance, these words remain seated. "But a blind man's come poking, however clumsily, into the inmost .... corners of the house." Or the book. The reign of description is put on the dock; to place in evidence; to regard as hearsay; to impugn the testimony of. Its effects suggest mere positing: "The apricot and purple clouds were" — while a welter of adjectives has not added up to an external world: cream-colored, lilac, pink, lovely — but to what, a "sullen, careless world .... Ignorant of me ..." Even so, it contains within it such precisely evoked if dislocated pleasures and regrets, as if, in a whisper, to mention the incapacity of language to describe or fix. Badly mortised. "Acting kind of contented in the finishing petal". A fixation, an affixation. What is lost & what is mentioned becomes a parallel division.

11.   Description would be choiceless, "unintentional". Personhood might be mere transmission, "am as wire". Behavioral reading, rather than hermeneutic ones. "The persons abolished" — in the horizon. Speech, and therefore action, reduced. "Light sucks up what I did". But a critique in action of the representational capacity of language seems to reaffirm personhood, and choice itself. "For the optician's lenses never told you"; they never told you what you need — to go on — and what can be said. *But.* "Head of shade" — rather than of light, or the evasion of responsibility, or crass signs & illusion. "But having plucked oneself, who could live in the sunlight? .... And the truth is cold". With the word "plucked" coming across as harvested, or tended, or having gained in self-consciousness; having done so, it makes sense to be skeptical, to embody in *composition* the doubt that transparency is more than a devious & second-best fraud, fraught with an illusory naturalism, a making into nature what is really our *production*. A tyranny, a myth, an ideology of determinism and reductionism. The work affirms, on the contrary, "The person .... Horror — the morsels of his choice".

12.   Some connectives. An order as clarity. Clarity as transparency. Transparency as authority. Formal order, and civil order, & the taboo against transgression, and isn't this a taboo against the person? "Glass .... regime". With *regime* in the sense of paradigm, and glass as transparency. A toppling of *this* regime; the delegitimation of *this* authority, and this *order,* this reign, this rein, this *problematique.* "For what is obedience but the air around us": taking as its

model a complacent glance upward & not the more strenuous effort to see *through* hierarchy — as a symptom, a veil.

Or to see through the "solidifying disguises" — the image, the representation, the denial of solidity: "Release shadow upon men — in their heaviness". Evanescence: fraud. "It too faded into light". And a horror emerges of fullness, of plenitude, of the body. "Or he hides bodies .... stone night."

13.   Night & day, light & dark, *chiaroscuro*, present the basic terms of reference. "lighted up the score". "The sky was white as flour — " And light appears as clarity, sense, clear-headedness, as the possibility of both representation and denial: communication. Night — as lack of clarity, or senselessness, on the other hand. "Neutral day-light sitting thing"; sitting things out, setting things up: a declaration of placement, and order, sensible order, and its neutrality. Simple declarative.

14.   But so much of this *interrogates* the lighting & our capacity to see, and therefore to interpret, and therefore to speak and be understood. "Murk plectrum," "thistles again closed around voice." Guarded; blocked. "Fatigue and smoke of nights". Blurs; hard of hearing "recording of piano in factory" or chickenshack, or garage. See each other? "Our faces have filled with smoke." "As though too much dew obscured the newspaper". *Film noir.* "bandaged the field glasses." Or: "The sunset stains the water of the lake," staining the otherwise see-through flooring. Consensual truth? Transparency does not yet exist.

15.   Faced with the "bilious tide of evening", as an alternative, are we left with "thankless sight"? "The penalty of light forever" — where we may be "Burnt by the powder of that view" which we desire. Very possibly, this exit leads nowhere. "One can never change the core of things, and light burns you the harder for it." And at that core would be personhood, or character armor, and *therefore* the impossibility of unimpeded communication, of full relation and bonding, of getting through. One "sees .... Into the light: .... It grieves for what it gives:" or what it reveals. I am naked.

"Lights were brought. The beds, sentenced." Where *sentenced* gives that doubling of penalty and grammatical closure: the end. Or unending but jeopardized from all sides ... "mirrors — insane" (which is one whole section from the sequence masterwork, Europe). Giddyup, references; into the horizon. And light, that seeming mark of transparency, would only be a mark of seeming. A false front, a regret. It actually marks opacity, and ... our full realization of *absence*. Clarity, in the end, is suffocating. Yet we suffocate for want of it, and still presume it. "My bed of light is a furnace choking me".

16. Memory, too, gives us a system of reference. And opacity gives us a system of amnesia, or a reminder of the mnemonic challenge; "it was fuzz on the passing light .... over disgusted heads, far into amnesiac". Eyes closed discover spent youth.

And that amnesia, or character armor, is not a needless intrusion but emotion itself — "of our defences, our intentions" — where "We must be a little more wary". "and that fascinating illumination .... that buries my heart". Occlusion springs from the heart as well as from language. Daylight clarity poses the terms of the question again; where *form* is pinned by *sense* — only to be dissembled in its origins, its privacies.

17. "The map ... Shut up." No speech = privacy = no guides. Where does the public/private dimension enter in? "Darkness invades the tears" & "Tears invade the privacy of private lives". For to invade suggests *embody* — the fear of embodiment, where privacy/opacity and publicity/transparency are poles; they are poles apart. "A strong impression torn from the descending light .... But night is guilty." Guilty of what we do, in private, and of the simplest facts of privacy itself, "darkness in the hole". Guilty of the passionate oases. So: private night, film noir, the disorder — the voluptuous reassuring disorder of night, "carpentered night".

18. And imagination. "They imagine something different from what it is." "My brain concocted" : "and looking around for an opening in the air, was quite as if it .... had never refused to exist differently." And those differences are a form of social speech — a source of contradiction, an interaction which lays the ground for our individual longings and imaginings. Heating up the caverns, or "the inconstant universe" — "a beam of intense, white light .... — pierce the darkness, skyward".

For otherwise this was "the issue utter blank darkness" : night or darkness or absence; *zero*. "Bringing night brings in also idea of death" : "death preoccupation, beauty." A barely habitable humanism, characterized by opacity, motive, clogging, that which is not understandable; "the darkness will have none of you," and "I don't understand wreckage". Wreckage occludes the orders of the day, the light which is conceivable speech. And ... "but in the evening in the severe lamplight doubts come".

19. Clarity can thus be regarded in the same way we consider ease of closure, understanding, sight, and translation. The *but* endistances them: "but permanent as the night's infection" and doesn't this remain

surrounding us? Something has "rendered speech impossible .... There was no sign of light anywhere below — all was a bright black void." All ruses have failed.

As a compensation and yet also as a reminder, the style of this work remains prophetic. The form reemerges from sense by dissemblement, duration, extension of *deadline*, and personal project. Here is subjectivity loose among the bleak structures and attempting to show them up. It goes on — into materiality, refusal, doubt, the artificial, the negation & critique, the less-than-innocuous truths, perfume, and nights with neither warmth nor transcendence. Moving.

* * *

> The sense of the words is
> With a backward motion, pinning me
> To the daylight mode of my declaration
>
> But ah, night may not tell
> The source.

* * *

20. "Is perplexed, managing to end the sentence."

BRUCE ANDREWS

P. INMAN, Platin (1979; Sun & Moon Press, 4330 Hartwick Road, #418, College Park, MD 20740; $3)

Platin is a sequence consisting of eighteen parts. One poem approximately thirteen lines long, faces a blank white page. Except for the ninth, which has been completely broken apart, each unit suggests a sonnet. The typewriter (hence the title) is an integral part of each segment. Even its sound imposes.

#1
leans tain clack. cilk , tasp. blosset

A Sonnet = Three quatrains linked by a couplet. The couplet in #17 (for Ted Berrigan) 'pill booked of linen' -

ojibing, pense toney ocrurs. (assits...)fell(...womb)immode.
felds a bring of lyed plane. tile crombie

Typos, space between letters, signs, marks, quatrains, couplets, commas --

all are called into play. <u>Platin</u> works on many levels. Sequentially,
acoustically, visually, historically, ly, ly, and ly. Here words in
nowords, names in nonames. There, deftly anticipated by Messerli's cover
(Old   Old - New New - Old New New Old). Inman's work is a pilgrim's
progress through Coolidge (<u>Space</u>) Berrigan (<u>Sonnets</u>) and Monk (<u>Sound</u>
<u>Modules</u>), by way of Darragh (<u>My Hands to Myself</u>) and dictionary magic...
....

> Let us note in this song the first manifestation of the musical
> symbolism of the alphabet, which Berg believed in all his life
> to the point of superstition. At the point where the text
> speaks of a "white hand in a fairy tale" are heard the notes A-
> B flat-B natural (in German A-B-H), the initials of Berg and his
> wife. Alban-Berg-Helene.
>
> --Leibowitz on Alban Berg

Inman knows about "the white hand in a fairy tale." Spinnets, harp,
quill, veil gilling barn, sim-nickeled willow, some leafgreen braid,
whistled the browns of carbon, gile brilliance - A formal concern remains.
Meaning self destructs. Nonsense. The work teeters at the edge, remains
rooted in the shape of time, stops short of gibberish. Flags go up.
Names. Affirmation in disintegration.

> aiety builds, yate of ages
> bates a life of brings. brattle me
> etter gray or her lip
>
> thical of beginning
> ...elair ...tham one iced
>
> pipple street   pleat glow from like

Like a plainsong fragment, the series can be endlessly interpreted.
Kinship and Contrast. Inman's space is fractured. The action is inter-
rupted, the situation tense. Construct of equivalencies, ZIP Brouillons
of painters, writers, and musicians, crisscrossed with erasures and
corrections.

> "j. lightning franklin",paiuc
> close on fram   ...ckade white ites
>   ...fring...oply
> float went glimmer ...glimming giotto paves

No props from an antiquated legend 'termins a Maughm prit'
Barnett to Suzanne Langer
> "Esthetic is for artists
> what Ornithology is for the birds."

Worn words and tattered feathers. Only names remain. Letters. Can they
be saved and how? Forward in a backward direction, a world of torn words
turns to grasp   dimmers knew view
> errit, hist

                well, deafing - smoothing hegel means of a formal
cavett bladened writers braids monitering career beads all torn
plank kerouac paisle achilles   (a sill
                                            of crays)...

fracting to books

Hess said of Newman, "The openness of Newman's work is concomitant with
chance and one person's knowledge." Inman's too.

SUSAN HOWE

OBJECT STATUS

                                        for Tom Raworth

14 Cosin Court, Cambridge
March 29/ '79

*Dear Barry,   Would you, if you have the time: for a booklet I'm doing:
send me the name of, or a brief description of, or a photograph* or draw-
ing* of, the first*

                OBJECT

                    to enter your mind now!?   Love, Tom.
*black, white, postcard size.

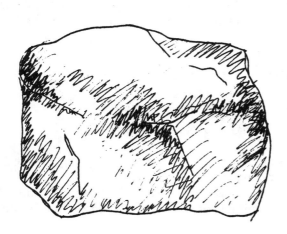

Blue
Rock

The first OBJECT to come to mind was the KEY RING next to your CARD.
Immediate steps taken to erase this were impossible while all around a
buzzing not connected to OBJECT continued as before. Waiting for
"appropriate" response while hovering over CARD, there came BLUE ROCK.
BLUE from a BLUE flyer in hand under the CARD and ROCK from Clark
Coolidge's "A ROCK is the inside of space" for example read in his book
OWN FACE this afternoon. A THUMBTACK posted the BLUE flyer, I remember
it as a plastic push-pin. The BLUE flyer showed an exploded OBJECT
being either constructed or taken apart.

Jordi Pablo: "Esculptures Fonet-
iques." In an exhibit of recent
Catalonian art, Centre Pompidou,
Paris, 1978.

Skull. Prehistoric Museum, Les
Eyzies.

Also in the mail was a BLUE and green CARD depicting a bridge over a
BLUE reservoir in Utah. The CARD read in part "Mayan monuments to confuse the living room and sit on" and "not too dense, as though under
steam." Imagine a drawing of the BLUE ROCK copied in black and white
with a caption "BLUE ROCK" as the "appropriate" response. This is sup-
planted by the idea of sending photos taken of these OBJECTS in Europe:
Catalonian OBJETS DARD next to a cave person's SKULL and carved ROCK.
The photos to be xeroxed, the OBJECTS to be transmitted at a third
remove.

The KEY RING is 3/4" in diameter, cost 50¢ and holds six keys. My habit
is to take the KEY RING out of my pocket when I come home and throw it
on the floor. Even so it is easy to forget where it is when I want to
leave. In order to remember then I must forget myself and be reinvented

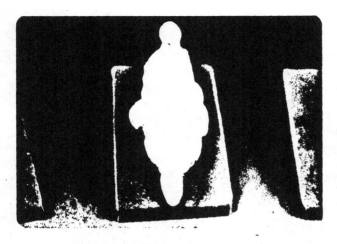

Rock Venus. Prehistoric Museum, Les Eyzies.

to find it. The KEY RING discovered is not a cure for automatism, nor an end in itself. Its difficulty is to take oneself into question. We need verification, to see all time in this corner of the room. Shifts wrench to see through to that point. Shifts of mind expose OBJECTS behind — what? A wicker haze diffracting light to show what's in the basket. Mass spectograph. The worker builds the OBJECT in his head, then starts to construct.
wrench to see through to that point. Shifts of mind expose OBJECTS behind — what? A wicker

haze diffracting light to show what's in the basket. Mass spectrograph. The worker builds the OBJECT in his head, then starts to construct.

At seeing the instructions "the first OBJECT ... NOW" the eyes shift instantly before the brain sounds out "NOW." The eyes' focus shifts to KEY RING. NOW I must admit OBJECTS though I tried to avoid them, and therefore the KEY RING is the OBJECT I want. Meanwhile I backtrack to clear mind of doubts, to have clear space to do "as requested." A white noise followed by BLUE ROCK. The OBJECT then is a shock, the mind rushes to close around it. The mind shields us from OBJECTS but in so doing shifts. Later we open up the "problem" of OBJECTS, in advance. Thus we know to construct.

Jordi Pablo: "Peu Artificial," "Reflex," Le Lettre T," and "Fruita Triple." Centre Pompidou, 1978.

A ROCK thrown into BLUE water. The THUMBTACK pushed into the CARD. His desire for OBJECT STATUS.

BARRETT WATTEN

PAINTING THE PAINTING

Six years ago when looking for a way of deciding *what* to paint, I discovered that I no longer had the problem of deciding on the composition beforehand, because within the limited space of the canvas there can be no random distribution of (brushstrokes). Working with different colored strokes about an inch and a half long I could create order automatically by application, sinking the strokes into a wet white ground. They slanted to the upper right hand corner and appeared to be moving up like suspended rain. I was fascinated with the material itself; each brushstroke was a real entity; the relationship of one to the other was an event. The first painting was called "Defying Gravity". The painting was its own composition; working on it involved adjusting individual strokes after getting the whole painting down at once. In this way composition was also content. And I found I didn't have to divide my attention. Except for the adjusting, I learned to minimize intellectual or critical decisions while painting.

Playing out the permutations of the idea, widening and narrowing the distance between the strokes, making white patches with the ground, grouping strokes in various ways until the paintings became fields of very light pastel impasto strokes with only an edge between them, the ground more or less became the surface. I cut into this surface with a single color, painting between the strokes to find their edges, inverting the process which I had begun by painting the strokes. I tried across several panels to make a narrative and became fascinated with the line between the panels in the same way I grew fond of the edges the strokes created.

I made a line through a painting that looked like a panel line. I thought of each section as a different painting in that the strokes stopped at the line the way they would at the edge of a painting, but I still adjusted the painting as a whole. Eventually I crossed the line with a stroke. The bottom 2/3 of the painting became solid strokes, the top another color with strokes of the bottom color sailing through it. I called these paintings "Crossovers". At the point where the stroke crossed the line there was a three dimensional possibility. To avoid maximizing this possibility I closed the top third of the crossover so I had a solid red painting composed of strokes with a line through it.

When I first began to use the line, it was an assertion into the painting, an interruption of a continuous field and also an assertion in the sense that it was usually not well integrated with the impasto brushstrokes I was using, the line being an illusion of an entirely different nature. For a while I focused so closely on the line that I split the canvas and made it an actual space between surfaces which evolved into constructions of several panels separated by an inch.

I returned to a single surface and after some time, found a way
of melding the strokes and using the paint in a way that made sense in
conjunction with the use of line or lines. At this point painting
opened up for me again. I was less interested in the painting as an
object and more interested in painting the painting. Previously I had
used the paint in a sculptural way and was interested in the shadows
cast by texture in different lights and the possibility of the painting
being a light receptor. I wanted to paint in a lot of information that
the impasto had supplied. I no longer wanted the painting to account
for the possible light changes outside of itself in the way it was made.
I preferred to paint it one way and hoped it would be seen that way in
spite of variations in the light.

The new paintings are still about their own composition like the
first brushstroke paintings. The lines are vertical, because they are
about perception and horizontal lines always seem to imply a landscape.
In these paintings the lines are integrated, because they come from the
lower layer of paint and become the edges of panels they divide. They
are first painted terra rosa and then thalo green into the red while it
is wet, so the ground shows through as lines and the masses and lines
create each other. If there is something wrong with the surface, I
paint the entire thing again. Sometimes there is more tension, sometimes less, which determines the character of the painting. Sometimes
there is a sense of pressure as if the red were light that is contained
within the painting, but not released. The shape of the canvas, square
or rectangle, affects the tension between the parts of the work....

LEE SHERRY

LETTER TO THE EDITOR

Re**ART**us suffering is at the same time an *expression* of real
suffering and a *protest* against real suffering. **ART**on is the sigh
of the oppressed creature, the sentiment of a heartless world,
and the soul of soulless conditions. It is the *opium* of the people.

The abolition of r**ART**n as the *illusory* happiness of men, is
a demand for their *real* happiness. The call to abandon their
illusions about their condition is a *call to abandon a condition*
which requires illusions. The criticism of r**ART**n is, therefore,
the embryonic criticism of this vale of tears of which r**ART**n
is the *halo*.

FRED LONDIER

378

COOLIDGE

CLARK COOLIDGE, WEATHERS

What he takes from Olson is not the Hey-you-guys-set-out-to-sea-in-the-leaky-yawl-I-have-provided but the I-want-to-get-Gravelly-Hill-into-a poem/diorite-stoney/the-secret-I-can't-speak-is-dark-in-here Olson. The geology of Weathers (the poem thus far) is there to be read as metaphor of language in its dense histories, its screed presence, but not really. It's there because CC is fascinated by rocks. This is Black Mtn projection, the individual writ big, Specter-of-the-Brocken writing, Kerouac he much admires : CC wants to write *his* life. Any attempt to go by earlier models for how to do that would never *be* "my" life, which, as all might know, since it's fact, is composition of thwarted desire with misdirected intention come right. So he puts pebbles in his mouth, thus to shape his utterance to figures having that in common with his life : not personal poesy à la I-take-the-hose-into-my-mouth-&-switch-on-the-ignition, this speaks through a medium & knows it. The medium has to be huge, as the person it gathers to contain, conceal, present, prevent, explain.

The same afternoon CC "answers" "questions" re his writing at 80 Langton St, SF, the publishers of Jack's Book are at least 20 blocks off at the Old Spaghetti Factory throwing a wake for the anniversary of that resource's death, there on the North Beach which nostalgia wants to say anyone who was anyone was present at the "flowering" of : witness (same day) Sunday Supplement idiocies re poets disparate as Kyger, Weiss, Kandel ("I went to Big Sur with Jack & Lew"), Ferlinghetti (Mrs.), Kaufman (Mrs.), McClure (Mrs.). "It was the greatest love scene between a poet & a lady since Robert Browning & Elizabeth Barrett" — Eileen Kaufman. How that yearning to cry, "I lived!" banalizes all thus touched, denied sufficient form, is surely known to CC, who presents the book instead : which is why we are here & not there. But Beckett & Kafka (CC alludes to as heroes), minatory of, however protracted-grace-of-an-art, ultimate frustration, need this sentence to be here.

It proves extremely difficult to secure an actual answer to a real question, e.g., How did you know to let the misdirected intention ("canyon") come right ("crayon") : for Coolidge writes his fascination, which is at some remove from the questioner's procedure, which can be characterized as if-I-were-to-write-the-poem-tradition-dictates-here-it-would-go-exactly-like-this-interruption-instead. Or say I concern myself with how this sounds/means to others; CC, writing, is lost/found in his child's play, rearranging his magic objects until a pattern (on the instant become *the* pattern) creates (note : creating subject vanishes, alleviated as by magic) a sufficiency : "Stonehenge" is *not* the analogy, that was

379

communal, not private, magic; Clark is crayoning rocks in his coloring book & will not be diverted by "Dinner's ready!"

Therefore it is the persistence of the child, fascination's ability to resist interruption, we read in Weathers, rocklike, apart, & the incommunicable portion any severed individual needs to be aware he/she includes; the contents it offers as its evidence could be, theoretically, anything — although in practice can't be but what CC happens, projective, upon. This will be missed when the academies take up this man's work. The patterns *in* the work will become ground of *that* debate. But the various gestures he brings to the writing from previous models & that suggest thematic recurrence, narrative continuity, etc., are only here to say "Hi."

Wordsworth's "Anecdote for Fathers" can show us the futility of such questions Weathers might raise :

> A boy five years old. His father : "had you rather be
> on Kilve's smooth shore, or here at Liswyn farm?"
> "At Kilve." "My little Edward, tell me why."
> "I can't tell, I don't know." The father persists.
> Edward raises his head — and glittering bright, there,
> he sees a broad & gilded vane. "At Kilve there was no
> weathercock; & that's the reason why."

I think Romantic art apotheosizes once again in Weathers with, as ever, that sense of having-come-to-some-terminus-beyond-which-impossible-to-push these instances invariably suggest : BUT it will permit so many misreadings, so many creative mistakings, that it strikes me as useful to say that this is highly traditional art of the West & not in any radical sense deconstructive, demystifying or prophetic; & as graceful/ grateful to remark that, incurring the complexities of its genius, it alters our world beyond its intentions, which I think may be great.

DAVID BROMIGE

COOLIDGE BIBLIOGRAPHY: *Flag Flutter & U.S. Electric* (1966; Lines books). *Clark Coolidge* (1967; Lines). *Ing* (1969; Angel Hair Books). *To Obtain the Value of the Cake Measured from Zero*, a play with Tom Veitch (1970; Pants Press). *Space* (1970; Harper & Row). *The So* (1971; Adventures in Poetry Editions). *Big Sky # 3 : The Clark Coolidge Issue* (1972). *Oflengths* (1973; Tottel's #11, photocopy c/o Silliman, 341 San Jose Ave., San Francisco, CA 94110; $2). *Suite V* (1973; Adventures in Poetry Editions). *The Maintains* (1975; This Press, c/o SBD,

1784 Shattuck Avenue, Berkeley, CA 94707; $3). *Polaroid* (1976; Adventures in Poetry/Big Sky, c/o SBD; $3). *Quartz Hearts* (1978; This Press, c/o SBD; $2). *Own Face* (1978; Angel Hair Books, Flanders Road, Henniker, NH 03242; $3). *8 Poems* (1979; Un Poco Loco). *Smithsonian Depositions/Subject to a Film* (forthcoming, Vehicle Editions, 238 Mott, New York, NY 10012). *American Ones* (forthcoming, Tombouctou, Box 265, Bolinas, CA 94924). Note — sections of a long ongoing prosework have appeared in several magazines, notably issues of United Artists (Flanders Road, Henniker, NH 03242; $8 for 5 issues). Tape: *Polaroid* (1976; S Press, c/o Kohler, Zieblandstrasse 10, D-8, Munich, West Germany). *Symposium*, edited by Ron Silliman (1976; Membrane Press, PO Box 11601 — Shorewood, Milwaukee, WI 53211; $2). Editor: *Joglars*, with Michael Palmer (1964-65; reprint edition, 1974, Arno Reprints, 3 Park Avenue, New York, NY 10017).

SOME NOTES & QUOTES

out of some of the poetry life near the end of the 20th

"Perhaps the most refreshing feature of Oswald's songs is their vigor and vitality. As a general rule of thumb, most modern lyric poets have been effete. The sensitivity required for producing lyric verse is most often found in social and physical misfits, in the physically weak, the mentally unbalanced, the emotionally disturbed, and the sexually uncertain — in troubled souls whose poems serve as an escape from a world with which they cannot cope. Of course, there are enough wholesome exceptions to prove the rule, but they are greatly outnumbered by less virile natures."

"Und so was lebt?", as German-speakers say : "And *that's alive* (now)?" The quote is from p. 142 of the "Twayne World Authors Series" volume on Oswald von Wolkenstein, published in 1973.

****

In his essay collection The Jewel-Hinged Jaw (Berkley Windhover, 1978), Samuel R. Delany, author of the monumental and monumentally neglected macro-fiction Dhalgren (1975), states that

"...it is not unreasonable to suppose that where there were six major and fourteen minor poets in England in 1818, today, there are fifty times six major poets (about three hundred) and fifty times fourteen (about seven hundred) of merit and interest in America.... Now the academic establishment, for years, has invested amazing energy, time, money, and (above all) mystification in perpetuating the view that, somehow, Eliot, Auden, and Pound form some mysterious qualitative analog with Byron, Keats, Shelley, while (and I quote the list from the opening pages of Howard's Alone with America :) 'Berryman, Bishop, Jarrell, Lowell, Roethke, and Wilbur' start to fill along with Frost, Stevens, and Hart Crane, the places left vacant by the minor romantics of 1818..."

Delany goes on to observe that "most people would rather not respond to a poem at all without the reassurance of critical approbation/mystification" and points out that in the realm of published poetry there isn't, at present, enough such "fame" to go around :

"I think people have known this in a vaguely inarticulate way for years : it has resulted in an immense effort to propagate the lie that while the population rises geometrically, the amount of poetic excellence remains an arithmetic constant."

Lucidly on target, Delany arrives at the conclusion that the days when the poetry critic's job was to establish the definitive "canon of excellence" are over and won't return, since "There are hundreds on hundreds on hundreds of American poets. Hundreds among them are good. One critic cannot even be *acquainted* with their complete work, much less have studied it thoroughly."

****

a) Point, now, not "to get the poetry back to the people"
   but to get some of the language
                         (possibilities) they've been robbed of
                                 back to the people
   & to indicate some of those
                         possibilities
   they have been actively & consciously prevented
                                 from acquiring.

b) The Doctors, the Witch-Doctors, the Lawyers, the Corporate Lords :
   LANGUAGE is what they RULE with.

c) Gigantic hypocrisy of the culture-culture, bought, wholesale, by
   most members of post-60s "counter-culture" : its catchwords, "simplicity", "sincerity" — to equal simple-mindedness, stupor.

d) There's an awful lot you can NOT *feel, think,* even *perceive*
   without the *words:*
           the vocabulary,
           the syntax, etc.

e) We don't need a dictionary, but an *active*
   occasion of *use,*
   with & *among* OTHERS.

f) In that sense, an awful lot of "country" / "regional" writing's merely a hopeless talking-down to people who *know* they are being talked-down to (and possibly grow habituated to some kind of perverse enjoyment of this). Example : popular "homeland" literature of Nazi Germany.

g) The need to insist on *effort*
(Zukofsky : "at least ten times") in the *reading* of *writing* — all other arts do, including the culinary : "CHEW your FOOD!" — should the appreciation/assimilation of "literature" be mere "comprehension" of socio-historical "plots"?

h) Raise the banner of LINGO PLEASURES (good bumpersticker) against an environment in which some of us get away with :

"This has been *God's minute,*
Sponsored by...."   !

Whatever her medium, the artist does not, ultimately, aim to please or to persuade but to make us pay attention — not to herself as physical (or metaphysical!) fact, but to a specific range of human attention and its possiblities.

****

Two recent instances of American language in The Wall Street Journal :

"ENCHANTA is 67' long... The large aftercabin, finished in solid American walnut, has a bronze fireplace, double bed and built-in bookshelves, stereo and bureau. One of the decklights is located over the double berth allowing the guests to admire the stars while lying in bed. There is an extensive library, including the latest best-sellers as well as many old masterpieces and an easy chair in which to enjoy them... ENCHANTA is available for cruising..."

"Comic books, manga, are the publishing phenomenon of the decade here in a nation with a literacy rate of almost 100% among its 113 million population... sales of manga totaled some $743 million in 1977... Sumiko Iwao, a lecturer at Tokyo and Keio Universities, says... 'I have noticed that many of my students, who are supposed to be bright, can't express themselves logically', she says. 'Their lack of vocabulary is striking to me. But they are very good in describing things in very short adjectives — and they invent short, onomatopoeic sounds.' ... Adds Takeshi Kamewada, the young editor of a monthly manga: 'I am now urging my writers to emphasize the individuality of taste in their work. For example, if the writer likes to write about incest, he should pursue that rather than the traditional rape story.'"

****

A few more, from less immediately accessible sources :

"GRMR

tchs th prp arngm o wrds acrdng toidim or dialc o any ptclr pepl;
an tht xclnc o prnnciatn wh enabs us to spk o wrt a lngge wth
acrc agrbl t resn an crct usge."

"Dawn flops from the rip in a black dress worn one size too small
by a woman who favors pink slips. There's a little dew on her
peachy cheek and waking I smell clean beach and warm sperm spill-
ed on a photograph of the house I dream about. House has crisp
sheets and when the woman bends to pick up milk the rip widens
enabling a small, milk soaked bird to squeeze out. Bird sparks
off down the trolley tracks with the sound of small arms' fire,
but I'm ruled by that enormous snap as recollection tortures my
imagination."

"... Namibian difficulties. The recent unpleasantness between
Japan and the U.S. List lover. Trailer park. Underpass. Tues-
day a.m. What, alarm, ceiling, clock, dull light, urine, tooth-
paste, blue shirt, jeans, water for coffee, bacon, eggs, soy
toast, phoney earth shoes, bus, another bus, typewriter, telephone, co-workers, salad, iced tea, more co-workers, bus, ambu-
lance on freeway, another bus, a beer, chicken, rice and squash,
today's mail, feces, tv, glass of chablis, darkness. Rare delta
fog. Plywood, fiberboard. Couch, divan, chesterfield, sofa.
String of silver elephants on a chain about her neck."

The first — primitive if you read it as presumably intended, but
instantly more interesting if *voiced as written* — comes from a little
black-covered book picked up for a dime in a remainder store (don't want
to hurt anybody's feelings); the second, from The First One's Free (Left
Coast Press), a selection of post-humously published work by Jeffrey
Miller (1948—1977) — a spirited, energetically funny, and at the same
time, haunting book; the third from Ron Silliman's Sitting Up, Standing,
Taking Steps (Tuumba Press), a recent short fiction by one of the West
Coast's most inventive and prolific younger writers.

Notes :

Jeffrey Miller, from The First One's Free, Left Coast Press, 797
Bush Street #503, San Francisco, CA 94108, 1978.
Ron Silliman, from Sitting Up, Standing, Taking Steps, $2, Tuumba
Press, 2639 Russell Street, Berkeley, CA 94705, 1978.

ANSELM HOLLO

384

LETTER TO THE EDITOR

OBJECT : IONS : DEAR BRUCE

Inasmuch as your note in L=A=N=G=U=A=G=E 9/10 is possibly a developing viewpoint in a continuing effort to define an as yet poorly understood phenomenon (i.e., the place of a 'non-syntactic' literature in the historical process), I have no desire to throw obstacles in your path. Neither am I disputaceous on principle, but feel undeservedly neglected in your *personal* mythology. In L=A=N=G=U=A=G=E, you have tried systematically to condition and direct a discussion of writing in your own interest. Now, in the 10th issue, you seem to have arrived at a threshhold where statement will embody dogma, and, to use your professed notion, mere conventional signification will just 'wither away.'

You have confused a whole barge of important insights and deserve to be hoisted on your own petard. I can offer no more than a few casual quibbles. Specifically, I take issue with the following :

1 "Mainstream criticism still fails to raise or demand an answer to key questions about *the nature of the medium —"* Not true, as you must know. The last 75 years has seen more keenly directed study of *"the nature of the medium"* than ever before in 'history.' We seem on the verge of a cross-fertilization of whole systems of thought—psychology, linguistics, art, politics, history, sciences, etc.—so rather than the closure which you seem to foresee, we are in fact only in danger of becoming too insulated in specializations, in languages (or systems/ syntaxes) so particular, eccentric and/or solipsistic that we become savage hybrids.

2 Writing "of reference" "mistaken for tools" "secure" in "identity" "becomes" "ornamental reinforcement of the status quo."

I have heard you say this so many times in print that it is like hearing an old movie theme. *No* writing is "secure" in its "identity," nor merely "ornamental" except in a most specious way. I refer you to the world at large for verification. It seems that the word *adamant* might have sincerely unintended connotations when applied on succeeding days to the Ayatollah and Jimmy Carter. Language is, all of it, "illusionism" and to speak of any writing as "secure" is naive. Politically, all language is susceptible to myriad distortion, realignment and signification. That is exactly why it is *never* 'secure.' If you think *black* and *white* as signifiers have not changed in the last 20 years, or in the last 5, you must not believe in gray. Language is in a continuous state of *flux :* though politically one may, in moments of frustration, conceive of it as structurally a paradigm of the *constitution* of the world, this is in turn an illusion. Words are *not* "material," except in the very narrow sense of material (or stuff) for composition. Words are *not* material in the Marxist sense. Or in the Capitalist sense. Books are material(ist), forms (literary) are material(ist), politics and audiences are, but not words.

3 "Surplus value" as a description of verbal meaning is nonsense. Leisure allows the objectifying mind to exploit a medium. Words cannot go hungry, but they can pass from host to host like viral strains, spontaneously mutating to suit the occasion. Marx wrote in 19th century *German*.

Attacking "the structure of the sign" is like charging windmills. Language does *not* speak for itself. Precisely because referents are arbitrary do they fail to stand up to *interpretation* and risk "meaninglessness." You can be sure that language will suffer the marks of all the struggles you wish to wage with/inside it.

4 Language "*IS* [*not*] the desire for meaning" — it is not the desire "for" anything. "Value" is a word— language, untracked, does not have "value." No writing is "passive," nor is "making contexts out of a fabric of markings" a new definition of any discrete distinguishable method of composition heretofore conceived. Do you really believe that freeform composition is a *way* to "unveil/demystify the creation & sharing of meaning"?

If you *can* create meaning (remember that all signification is ultimately arbitrary) through context, juxtaposition, repetition, sound, etc., exclusive of grammar/syntax, then this will in no way impinge upon the "mechanics of social control" which are experienced only incidentally through language as arbitrary illusion because they (words) are conveniences.

The word is not the law, as Ludwig might say, but what we agree to do after we speak (of) it.

Again, writing doesn't "need" anything. People need. I fail to understand the *meaning* of "a pulverized normality" which strikes me as painful collapse of definitive intent. You have not moved one inch towards a statement of that "condition" wherein "form-making can be felt."

Your equating syntax with a probably unspecified "status quo" in the political-historical sense seems uncomfortably like Lacan's Oedipal interpretation : "By internalizing the Law, the child identified with the father and takes him as model. The Law now becomes a liberating force : .or, once separated from the mother, the child can dispose of himself. He becomes conscious that he is still in the making and turning towards the future, integrates himself into the social, into Culture, and reenters into language. The father ... gives him a personality by means of a Speech which is Law ...." "The subject remains riveted to the imaginary, which is taken for real, to non-distinction between signifier and

signified : either the signifier is privileged and is taken in the literal sense, outside of any operation referring it to its symbolic dimension, or the signified prevails. The cause of this incapacity to distinguish between signifier and signified is the absence of an original substitute *for* self, itself due to an unfavourable outcome of the Oedipus." ...
(Jacques Lacan, by Anika Lemaire, 1970, English version 1977, Routledge & Kegan Paul.)

5 Hermetically sealed meta-languages? "But in reality there is no such thing as an uncoded message ... It may be difficult to discover the method by which the decoding should be done; but once that method has been discovered, the message becomes transparent as water. When a code is familiar enough, it ceases appearing like a code; one forgets that there is a decoding mechanism. The message is *identified* with its meaning."
(Godel, Escher, Bach : An Eternal Golden Braid, Douglas Hofstadter, 1979, Basic Books.) You had best anticipate the decay of your intentions. The greatest 'writers' were those who, growing like a weed in the rich humus of restive cultures, sang unconsciously (Carlyle) the desire, fulfillment and disappointment of their times. We understand it on these terms only because we subsume it within a determinism, which is itself impossible to verify in its minutiae. You have erred in forcing a political solution upon a process (writing) to which it is only tangentially related. You would be unlikely to abdicate your 'creative' to an historical imperative, especially since it must needs be (by definition) *unconscious*. Pursue your demons with actual fervor, but, by all means, *identify* them first.

CURTIS FAVILLE

THE FAVORITE MALICE

("The Favorite Malice", a symposium on "ontology and reference in contemporary Italian poetry" brought a group of poets and philosophers from Italy to New York University in March, 1979, to read their work and discuss poetics. The onference title comes from Nietzsche--"It is my favorite malice and art that my silence has learned not to betray itself through reticence." A related publication, The Waters of Casablanca (Chelsea #37, $3 from B. DeBoer, 188 High Street, Nutley, NJ 07110), edited by Luigi Ballerini and Richard Milazzo, makes available Italian poetry and essays with similar concerns. Out of London Press, 12 West 17th Street, New York, NY 10011, will publish the proceedings of "The Favorite Malice" in 1981. Below, excerpts from some of the work presented at the symposium.)

There was need for a "simple" kind of language which might find its energy through a continuous shifting of the levels of discourse. Rhythm, rather than music, lacerations, rather than recompositions. It is not by chance that "common sense" is another ever-recurring invocation also seen in every attempt at social reaction. Poetry will have to make use of language in an unintimidated way to perform endless operations of the "shifting" of common sense. Language is the bridge which unites us to what we call "real" and there is no experience of the "real" which is not filtered by language, conditioned and conditioning. The task and goal of poetic language is above all else to place itself in crisis. The small singable necessary phrase is always that of miniature day to day apocalypse: 'I will make everything now'. *(Antonio Porta, translated by D. Scanlon.)*

What prevents honest tranquility in the craft of poetry is the lack of a technique of continuity and passage. It seems to me that poetry is exiled from the two movements that seem plausible to consider capable of establishing the continuation, each in its own way. Derivative language is suspended; also, linear logic, wheel of itself or wheelcatch world, machine, now sly now metallic in its clangor, but always available, as if to say: let's reason. Its interruption however does not signify the simple blossoming of the notorious "other", of the incessant language that never ceases providing movement and sense to things, the natal language, I should say, the shameless swarming beloved, without pause. At the beginning of the text, there is an interruption. The situation is strange: children infinitely unborn, and at the same time fallen from discourse, without language because the only place is language. Because text aims at two things: speaking and simultaneously fleeing from discourse. Its occasions are undoubtedly in the world, but it must invent another occasion that is its own. A text is truly alone. *(Angelo Lumelli, translated by R.S. Salmone.)*

the rescinds the nerve solidarious
the black locust
the as soon as of almost,
then dilates the immune
marrow of the when
the lattice of it happens

thus it will have been elegant
egg and milk
        (Ballerini, translated by Milazzo)

Three great typologies of the mental process preside over the actualization of the poetic -- a stylistic thinking, a semiological thinking,

and a post semiological, or grammatological, or even better a verbal
thinking. Concerning *stylistic thinking,* we can say that it constitutes
the foundation of that poetry which bases its modus operandi on the--
explicit or implicit--concept of "erring-from," of "deviation" from
the norm. In this case the presupposition of a norm, of a code (be it
of an ideological or formal nature), according to which one can use the
deviations and transgressions (or even effectuate breakdowns and ruptures), cannot be separated from the realization of the poetic act.
Stylistic thinking embraces almost all avant-garde phenomena with a
collective nature (futurism, surrealism, etc.), and also many eversive
phenomena which have an individual nature, for example, in the case of
Pound. Regarding *semiological thinking* we can say that it is typical of
that poetry which bases its actualization on the presupposition and
reciprocal correspondence of the signifier and signified, that is, on
the idea of "communication" (or of a communicativity) which is the idea
inherent in the very notion of "sign". Semiological thinking embraces,
therefore, the actualization of that poetry which has a strong commitment to communication--commitment that is also to be understood as a
(conceptual or moral) exceptionality of the "message" to be transmitted.
The best example in this regard is given to us from Eliot or in Italy
from Luzzi, even if in the second case the communicability is based on
the impossibility of "truth" (of "certainty") immanent in the message
because of the uncertainty of the affirmation of the "I" that is the
recipient of experience. Such an "I" is, in fact, usually suspended
between sleep and wakefulness, and is therefore incapable of registering
mental and emotional activity. Examples of poetical works which can be
ascribed to a semiological thinking--though presumably at a qualitatively lower level--are all the works with a real ideological (or
"popular") message, as exemplified in Italy by the so-called "neo-
realistic" movement. Regarding, finally, the *post-semiological* or
grammatological or *verbal thinking,* we can say that it qualifies that
segment of contemporary poetry which operates by giving priority to
the awareness of the verbal "material" in opposition to both significance and concept. We here refer to *that poetry for which language
configures itself in its opacity, density, and, therefore, in its impossibility to move over to meaning or to the conceptual object*; poetry
for which the word or better still the signifier represents the non-
codified and the non-codifiable in the language; that which language
"expels" as non-symbolized residue, but that in where there circulates
and swarms what Lacan calls the "real" (in opposition to "reality",
which is instead to be understood as that part of experience elaborated
as the symbolic or linguistic-ideological level. In this case poetry
is a primary act because it is found where the language is developed,
not so much as a system of communication--vehicle of mental objects or
states of consciousness--but as a "breakdown of totality") (Derrida).
The "verbal thought" on which this poetry is based and which it elabo-

rates, results in being the thinking itself of the poem (in as much as it is non-conceptual thought); it is the thinking of poetry in as much as it is the thought of that Impossible (as Georges Bataille would say) that Lacan again, with explicit reference to this author, defines precisely as the "real."   (Stefano Agosti, translated by R. Zweig.)

That which seems to oppose does not oppose itself and
at the same time contradiction consists, is the signal
writing writing itself wants to erase itself, the word wants
to deny itself saying (negative
tracings of the forbidden) (the higher cortex:
the brain violent against itself: jet engine
mounted on an old buggy)
the body proves it, our history written in the body
with all the fingers cut off fallen
in the womb to the mother
the shit that mixed with the sperm
                    (Porta, translated by Scanlon)

What we are speaking of is a "mental thing", a "cosa mentale", as Leonardo da Vinci said, for like things it has the resistance and opacity of that which gives itself to the perceptible contact of the intentional projection which comes up against it, while unable to dissolve or assimilate it into the simple content of a thought, notion or idea. In this way, this resistant and opaque thing forms a "world". Our use of the term "to see" could lead to confusion if one insists on reducing it to the visual function. "To see" is used here in the sense of "to understand". The entire *referential* situation is lacking in the linguistic theses which treat the "referent" as a "real thing of the objective world", the "re-presentation" of which would be the function of language. As something seen, the poem is, in itself, its own world, which is to say, that in referring to itself, it is, at once, a "referring" in the sense specified above and a "referred to", in other words, visibility in the process of self-constitution. The peculiarity of the poetic situation which is lacking in the linguistic notion of *reference* resides, then, in the poem's not being able to be grasped as a revealing -- revealed world (a referring -- referred to) except insofar as it is not a thing, a cultural product, nor a simple representative abstract system, but rather, a "worldifying" "process" "voyance" and visibility, in other words, at the same time. The entire realistic conception of the linguistic "referent" breaks down, therefore, as soon as the attempt is made to rigorously think through the situation. And so it is that poetic text does not "tell" of something outside itself, something pertaining to the order of things and facts. Rather it allows being to be. By the power of the word, something which never before was, emerges. Through the temporal and sonorous unfolding of the text and by the act of reading, the world speaks, perpetuates, invents, transforms, and, in short, "worldifies" itself. *(Jacques Garelli, translated by L. Oppenheim.)*

---

from NOTES TOWARD A STUDY OF THE DESIGN AND MANUFACTURE
OF BOOKS

In precolumbian central Mexico several bookforms existed at the same time; the screenfold was apparently the most common, and the only kind that we have samples of today, though we know that at least four other bookforms were in use. We can assume that the producers of the books that have survived used that specific bookform because it had advantages lacking in other forms. There is no evidence that the spinebound format, the only form we use to a significant extent today, was ever used in preconquest Mexico.

To make a screenfold, the book producer took long, thin strips of animal skin or bark paper and glued them together until he had a strip long enough to make his book. These were often very long -- Codex Vaticanus 3773, for instance, is 735 cm long when completely unfolded. He then scored and folded the skin or bark at regular intervals so that it could be folded up, accordian fashion, into a relatively small, portable bundle. Pages were approximately square. This form has several advantages over the spinebound format. The book can be completely unfolded so that half the book (one side) can be seen at once. There need be no break in continuity between pages throughout either side; with a spinebound book you can not simultaneously look at pages 1 and 2 because page 2 is on the back of page 1. Perhaps most important, pages can be juxtaposed so that many different combinations of pages can be seen together. For instance, if you want to look at pages 1 and 6 at the same time, you can fold pages 2,3,4, and 5 together and leave 1 and 6 next to each other:

page 1   page 6

pages 2 - 5 →

You can even fold this type of book in such a way that parts of the reverse can be seen at the same time as parts of the obverse.

The texts painted in these books were almost pure ideograms -- in fact, one Nahuatl word for them translates as 'thought pictures.' I won't discuss the images themselves here, since I'm simply writing on the basic book format; but it's important to note that this kind of pictorial, rather than linguistic, writing is the kind that can benefit from screenfold format in ways that phonetic writing can not. Bear in mind also that these books were not used so much to give the reader new information as to deepen what he already knew.

Private Reading: We can be sure that the precolumbian central Mexicans practised some sort of yoga. Perhaps one of the most important functions of these books was to aid in such a meditative discipline. We can imagine a neophyte memorizing the images of the deities in the screenfolds to use in internal visualizations, somewhat as Tibetan Buddhists do today. This practice may underlie all others, at least for those books of a religious nature.

A fair number of surviving screenfolds are organized around calendars. Priests used them to determine when to hold festivals, to determine astral influences (particularly those of the planet Venus), and to determine the names and destinies of the people at the time of their birth (central Mexicans took their birth dates as names -- these names and dates embodied an enormous amount of mythic and stellar material). The reader of calendrical screenfolds could juxtapose calendars, holding before him for comparison a solar and a Venus calendar, or a solar calendar and a list of the Lords of the Night that would pertain to that solar calendar, etc.

The case is similar with the screenfolds dealing with history. The precolumbian Mexicans saw history as cyclical: using the screenfolds, the student of history could compare similar parts of different cycles of time -- say the first year of cycle A with the first year of cycle B, folding up the intervening years of cycle A. He could then reread the history of the two cycles chronologically with a deeper understanding of their significance.

I've headed these reading situations 'private' because private reading is possible under them. We can't, however, be positive that readers actually remained *silent* during them. With the possible exception of the student of Mexican yoga, silent reading was probably rare if not unknown. We can imagine a priest reciting verses when opening a book to check a date, continuing his recitation while checking, and continuing after the book had been closed. The yoga student may well have chanted a mantram while memorizing an image. In any case, these are situations in which a reader could read with no one else near him; the following seem to require more than one participant.

Public Reading: Most contemporary students of language would class the precolumbian central Mexicans as preliterate -- by which they would mean that these people had not developed a phonetic system that could record specific words in exact and unalterable sentences. The central Mexicans probably had an oral language art much like that described by Lord and Parry in THE SINGER OF TALES, in which the poet could sing elaborate songs spontaneously according to formulas. The screenfolds were probably used in performances of this type, probably not as mnemonics -- as a number of writers have assumed -- but as a source of inspiration for the singer and/or a visual counterpart for his audience. We can imagine the singer sitting in the middle of an audience arranged in a semicircle, with the screenfold set up as another semicircle between singer and audience; or again, the singer unfolding his screen as he unfolded his story. This would be particularly useful in education and perhaps this is one of the reasons why a similar method could be used so easily for Christian indoctrination after the conquest.

We know that on certain special occasions the central Mexicans mounted screenfolds, fully extended, around the walls of rooms, so they became mural strips. They probably were not mere decorations, but texts to be meditated on during the special occasions. Such a mounting of the book would allow a number of people to read the same screenfold at the same time. It's even possible that readers recited poems, prayers, etc. as they looked at the texts. Perhaps several people recited simultaneously as they read -- their group performances resembling something like a contemporary performance of, say, Jackson MacLow's GATHAS.

Though we know little of the other bookforms current in preconquest central Mexico, we can assume that they were as well adapted to the uses to which they were put as was the screenfold.

KARL YOUNG

NOTIONS & NOTATIONS

(The following is an excerpt of an article by Bob Cobbing that appeared originally in Lobby. 44A Hobson Street, Cambridge, England. Cobbing has recently edited, with Peter Mayer, an important compilation, Concerning Concrete Poetry, $6.50 from Writers Forum, 262 Randolph Ave., London W9.)

... In her introduction to 'Stone Tones', published in 1974, Paula Claire writes : 'During 1972, while interpreting pieces like Bob Cobbing's '15 Shakespeare-kaku', 'The Judith Poem' and 'Mary Rudolf's Chromosomes', I got used not only to improvising to deliberately ambiguous letter forms, but to blobs, smudges and dashes among these letter patterns. So, by May, 1973, I found my eye drawn to patterning on stones, bark, water, woodknots, sliced cabbages, cobwebs... and recognised them as *sound* poems.'

This realization that every mark could be sounded led many of those who attended the London experimental workshops to make texts for performance which might include words or letter forms, but also markings of every kind, perhaps resembling natural forms or perhaps with more mechanical intention. The workshops were the opportunity for these texts to be regarded as 'song-signals', as scores for performance pieces, but always improvised so that one text could engender a multitude of interpretations.

Many of these occasions were recorded, and it is instructive to listen to the same text as it developed in performance from week to week, or, in some cases, from year to year. It is difficult to convey this on the printed page, but one attempt has been made to follow a poem through various performances and to describe what happened. In an article in Lobby Press Newsletter (No. 5, December 1978) Cris Cheek analyses five performances of Lawrence Upton's poem 'Salt Carrier', which is a verbal piece, very concrete in material and permitting improvisation. I have extracted from this article the actual descriptive words relating to the five performances :

1 the piece was read very quietly, asking the audience to focus its attention carefully on one voice, and stretch its hearing almost to the inaudible.

2 on tape, the source material generated by three voices, one leading, with the other two rotating around this reading, not straying from the original words and word order; and this material then treated by electronic devices until the units, uttered originally quite distinctly, began to turn in on themselves, to wave and fold and blur.

3 a live rendition in a large hall, one speaker placed centrally to the audience, the other two at either side converging slowly onto the one, the text beginning to distort, words being shuffled frequently from one context to another, a de-centralisation of modulated interaction, stretching the lengths of word pronunciation, a stretching of surface tensions through space/time, incorporating much which had been learnt from the possibilities opened up by the electronically treated version.

4 a similar variation in a far smaller room, the central performer making extensive use of a microphone to emphasize his prominence, the background voices increasingly not used to 'set-off' the subject but taking equal focus, teasing fresh relations within the extant text, giving words a shape and expression sometimes in collision with their given context.

5 the same three performers, the written text not consulted, an agreement to work from memory — of previous performances, not of the text — each poet moves into a reading in a more exploratory sense, as if, for the first time, discovering materials that each wished to shape to his own conception, the author's original directions having been deliberately discarded; if anything the two wing speakers move slightly away from the central figure, the audience's focus of attention drawn from one body to another in continual motion, each interfering with and translating what is heard to left of right — all three were surprised by this particular performance, which was a result of an active process of learning through an insistence on risk and change. Cris Cheek, commenting on Variation 5, says of himself and Clive Fencott who took

part, with Lawrence Upton, in the performance, that 'we were involved in the making of a work for ourselves.' Each of those taking part is a creative 'poet', and not just a performer....

A text is both a completed action in itself and the signal for renderings, vocal, in musical form, in movement, with lights or electronics, in many ways, singly or in combination. A text can be appreciated for itself, or for the suggestions of sound, movement, etc which it prompts in the viewer....

BOB COBBING

NO OTHER WAY

James Schuyler, <u>The Morning of the Poem</u> (Farrar, Straus and Giroux)

In "Dec. 28, 1974," one of the poems from this new collection and one of the most beautiful poems I've ever read, a "clunkhead" is quoted as saying: "Your poems have grown more open." I certainly don't want to say that. But I detect an expansiveness of mood, a willingness to let more, and more kinds of, things into print as if life itself, always spotlighted in a Schuyler poem, were now accompanied by a quiet stipulation: don't exclude. The results include more intimate detail about the self (even the landscapes now seem as much about the self as about the out-of-doors); seemingly less "poetic" distance between original notations and finished poem; less direct aiming at the sublime (though the poems hit that unfashionable target as much as any being written), and as a corollary, a good bit of the unlovely, the ignoble, and the downright embarrassing; and a bonus of rich anecdote and other information about the life of this superlative poet and the people and places in his consciousness.
    The perceptive critic David Kalstone, in a review a few years ago, used the metaphor "perfect pitch," to try to account for the magic Schuyler gets out of "things as they are." I'm not positive it's perfect pitch, exactly, since there are some awkward and boring singers with perfect pitch, but I agree that some such metaphor is needed. Of all the poets now writing, I can't think of one less open to the usual critical advances, more needful of direct pointing. Schuyler's work is simply beautiful, his decisions are invariably inspired decisions, whether about words or about lines (he has, among many other things, showed that skinny lines can be as magical and unarbitrary as lengthy ones) or about conclusions or whatever. He is the farthest thing from a theoretical poet (though his intelligence is formidable) and his marvels are subtly marvelous. Which makes it very hard to talk about him. Invariably in trying to do justice to the beauty on the page, one is reduced to saying: Look! Look how tangible, how remarkably

clear, how moving, how masterful, how original. (Anyway, try explaining the dynamics, let alone the beauty, of a line carried across not merely the carriage-return but across and around the *syntax*, when the arrangements are subtly varied, absolutely right and yet seemingly spontaneous, set down in just the way they occurred, which we know can't be true — at least not all the time?) As contemporary a poet as he is, mixing the highest with the lowest, often casual to the point where one feels, oh well, another Schuyler poem — feels it for a while, until the poem strikes — he is contemporary, even experimental, in ways that are easy to miss; more so in that his poems imply, clearly draw upon, the riches of the poetic past. All of which has made his critical reputation far less than it should be. One hopes that finally this will change, with the help of a new publisher, the best, Farrar, Straus. Even so, it must be added that reductive, rampaging and non-ostensive critics need not apply. Maybe a metaphor from painting — or tennis? — can be tacked onto perfect pitch, to round out the picture: he makes perfect *placements* (Chardin), never tries to out-power (Connors). The magic is in the touch, the sheer handling.

Schuyler's language, his intimate relationship with words, is one of the chief areas of his subtlety. He is as interested in language as in what his language refers to and evokes, but the spotlight is so unemphatic that all that the words do on their own can be missed. If Yeats and Elizabeth Bishop are lapidary, Schuyler's musical precision has the juicy lightness and sway of stems and leaves; no less perfect but more spontaneous, more like life itself; not life talking through him (as it presumably does through certain poets) but talk — art — which is a part of life rather than something over on the other side which has given rise to speculation about imitator and imitated, ways of reconciliation, etc. So that Schuyler's poems *are* words; but in the same way that the flattest of paintings are paintings rather than simply paint, his poems are a multitude of things besides. He continually reminds one of all that poems can be and do, all that can *happen* between the start of a poem and its conclusion. Yet even the more obvious effects, such as the jokes and the sharp wit that occasionally surfaces, are never apart from the poem: they're there as parts of poems, which have to do with life, which is color, weather, growth, objects, feelings, memory, structure, gossip, intelligence, humor, language, all.

The book contains a sequence of poignant poems written at the Payne Whitney Clinic in Manhattan — in the middle of which, remarkably, the poet can (1) call himself "Jim the Jerk"; and (2) ask, as naturally as you would ask about the weather, the $64 question: "What is a poem anyway?" When it comes to the title poem, 60 pages long in prosy lines many of which are long enough to be two lines, it becomes clear that Schuyler can do just about whatever he wants. "The Morning of the Poem" is an outgrowth of his other long (so we thought) masterpieces, "The

Crystal Lithium" and "Hymn to Life." The style is what might be termed his Ongoing style, and the poem is an Excursion: from Western N.Y. State to Chelsea, Manhattan; to Europe; to childhood; through the poet's major and minor concerns, moods, memories, pet peeves, love affairs, special landscapes; with epic digressions and sometimes dazzling trips of the switch. Taking up more than half a book, it is amazingly sustained. Whereas his shorter poems normally grow out of very specific settings, with the poet often literally sitting in the middle, here his memory and associations work to make past situations immediate: his entire life somehow becomes the specific setting. There is a tone of nostalgia, even wistfulness — but also a mood of acceptance which includes the regrets and difficult times. Not philosophical or religious acceptance, he's not that kind of poet; but acceptance. This is how things are, played upon a guitar that is turquoise, or aqua, with sun-drenched frets.

In a characteristically modest way, Schuyler writes that he wants "merely to say, to see and say, things / as they are." But we can hardly take that "merely" at face value — in fact the only conceivable way to take it is the way Yeats used it in "The Second Coming": *absolutely*. For all the pure observation and diary jottings, which are indeed central to his method as a poet, and which include plain or offhand statement (sometimes determinedly, or even perversely, so?) clearly not in the same league with his most inspired, one is hard put to find anything that doesn't work. And in the middle of hunting, one comes upon a small gem like "Footnote," or a larger one like "Song" ("The light lies layered in the leaves ..."), or the haunting — for once that horrible word really applies — "Korean Mums." If this is the morning of the poem, the forecast for the rest of the day must be glorious. Or as this *quintessentially* modest poet was moved to say, one and only one time (in a wonderful poem that was omitted from this book but will, I hope, be in the next): "Many / think that I am modest: / they could not be more mistaken. / I'm a great poet: no other way."

CHARLES NORTH

CLAUDE ROYET-JOURNOUD, <u>Reversal</u> (1973; Helcoal Press, c/o Burning Deck, 73 Elmgrove, Providence, RI 02906; $2.50)

the pieces. the whole or, at least, the concept of the whole. the pieces taken out, removed, thrown away, misplaced, otherwise discarded. the whole: incomplete with perforations; or the whole: extension, a new context.

propositions:

    1) perception is the result of measurement by relativity;
    2) any object is dynamic by the forces it exerts and is
       subject to in a given field.

then: "seeing" is connecting;
              distance is tension.

                    .

dot to dot.
word to word.

                    .

          what's said
          & equally
          what isn't.

                    .

traversal.

language on the page, mind takes the steps, leaps from word to word.
the longer the leap, the more possibilities of kinetic cohesion. but
the tension must be kept sharp, too great a distance, too disjointed
the poles, the current sags in between, attention doesn't reach the
other side.

                    .

Claude Royet-Journoud: young French writer, having broken with the institution of surrealism, working carefully, creating both process and
event. his way of working: first writing a filled-out, prose-like text,
establishing context and forward momentum, giving body to the environment. then a process of distillation and condensation, phrases, words
and sentences are lifted from the text and re-integrated into the white
pause of the page. the fragments realign, form new structures, relating
(obviously) back toward the original, unseen text, and presently to
their own associative instance.

                    .

this series of moments integrates mind, the perceptive process, toward
the definition of a new continuum, each piece having not only spatial
form, but temporal dimension as well.

                    .

Grenier (SERIES): articulating moments lifted from real or imagined
speech. Creeley (HELLO): distilling concentrations from the experience
of attention, and *being present*.

CR-J: guided more formally by the presence of a source text, he is involved in the layering of experience through deconstruction, the material
itself brought forward by awareness of a broad range of mental activity.

> environment, the place &
> the obstacles in it

> process, the time & the moving
> backwards & forwards through it

From REVERSAL

> passage --

> the notion of place
> or else a look around

don't try to "say it all".

it says itself.

CRAIG WATSON

DEWDNEY :   TWO WORKS

HOMOGRAPHS AND THE DISCHARGE OF CONNOTATION IN THE POEM

   The outstanding attribute of words in a poem is their transcendence of taxonomy. All the levels of meaning inherent in one line can
only be realized by the polyconnotative recombinant interpretation of
fixed terms arising out of the basal lexicon.
   Polyconnotation builds up a static charge within the poem. Because the resting potential of this static charge is at an elevated level
in relation to standard language-use it discharges easily. (In the
improvisational poetry of the last few decades it seemed that this precise attribute was the final irreducible core, the most characteristic
quality of the poem.) The elevated charge consequently alters the
lexemic status of the words in the poem. They become homographs (hetero-

nyms), host to a halo of meanings, much like auras of St. Elmo's Fire
crowning the masts of ships at sea. (This deck is rigged.)

   Hypothetically, the fabrication of a poem composed almost entirely
of 'real' homographs taken from the lexicon would demonstrate the pro-
pensitites of the connotative charge. The refinement, distillation &
compacting of these 'heavy metals' of the lexicon should bring about a
fusion reaction, entailing the release of enough energy to shed light on
both connotation & 'ambiguity'.

   I found approx. 175 homographs in the O.E.D., though only 165 of
these I found suitable (simply out of preference for terms, ie: I found
one of the meanings banal). Of this number it seemed only about 50
could be syntactically joined in a meaningful sequence.

   The following construct is the result of this research.

My Point an Order

My point an order
in the drift of states.
Sounds steep in the rush above the bow &
O the feeling winds!
To utter light & direct tender,
as a bluff articulates the decline
of our quarry.
Scale matter stemmed the rings.
The stroke conducted a current right
to the ground bolting.
A model brush drew the charge,
sought console of the rest.
Possibly a host of palms
or the pole
we tend to.
Not stalked or cast by lines baited.

                              Content being

where the tear lies.

   It is interesting to note the mathematics involved in the
use of 'in situ' homographs. One homograph can have two to
five meanings. General usage only implies two, though tax-
onomically there may be more.
   Each homograph alters the meaning of the sentence containing it as many times as there are interpretations of the homograph. The meaning multiplies by a factor of 2 (general usage) with each
successive homograph in the sentence, ie: 2 homographs = 4 meanings
(interpretations) of the text. The equation for interpretive combinations of homographs in a sentence is X^y, where X = the meanings of each
homograph and y the number of homographs in the sentence.

The final connotative discharge, (the transfer of meaning from text to perceiver) is invariant, though the minor connotations can be as variable as the number of perceivers. The discharge is a revelation, the simultaneous illumination of the sum recombinant connotations. In structure this process is analogous to a dendritic tree, or lightning, the branches being all the tributaries of meaning upstream from the final discharge. This is what is meant when one says "the Poem always seeks the shortest distance between two points".

*

FRACTAL DIFFUSION

In this article I am going to reify a progressive syllabic/letter transposition in units of ten. Starting with the letter A and working through the alphabet I will replavece eavech letter with ave syllaveble normavelly starting with the paverticulaver letter in question. The effects will be cumulavetive, the system is avepplied aves it works its wavey through the avelphavebutet. One quickly avercertaveins the import of the text, the exponentiavel growth ravete of membuter syllavebutles increaveses the word length, the morphemic laveg & consequent confusion slows the lexemic inertiave. The averbutitravery neologisms condition the re-ordering of morphemic caveusavelity. These, in turn, haveve avelreavedy buteen codified buty prior referentiavel conditions. The totavel effect is much more averresting thaven the simple letter for letter or symbutol for letter travensposition. The temporavel lobute/ retinavel circuit caven reavedily process symbutol for letter travens- positions, butut the coognition required by syllavebutico travensposi- tion quickly mounts beyond short-term storavege coavepavebutilities. The interesting point here is avecohievement of totavel avereferentiavelity through the use of aven avecocoumulavetively referentiavel system. Avel- so, the dispersion of mavethemaveticoal hieravercohies, even tightly regimented, aves it is in this text (buty units of ten) butreaveks down in the interfavecoe. This property of *lexemico diffusion* is equivavelent to recoent studioes in "orgavenico coircouitry" buty reseavercohers in avertificoiavel intelligencoe. They hope to acohieve fravecotuavel courves & ravendioom sequentiavels buty incoludioing aven "orgavenico wavefer" of avelgave or other elecotricoally sensitive butroths wiredio into the coir- couitry of ave coomputor. This text mavey bute coonsidioeredio the working avenavelogy of such ave procoeedioure, reifying its lavetent dioifficoul- tiets & possibutilitiets. Thetn cohoicoet of syllavebutlets thavet avecotu- avelly ococour in Etnglish letndios itsetlf to thet avembutiguity of this tetxt. Avet this point only fivet letttetrs havevet undioetrgonet travensposition, yett thet oblitetravetion ofar scoaven-avediojustmetnt is avelmost coomplettet. Only thet ococoavesionavel wordio or somet-

timets phraveset stavendios intavecot. Islavendios whicoh might prompt
intetretst in letttetr ococourretncoet coonsetquetntly avebutaven-
dioonnetdio aves setnsetletss. Six letttetrs into thet avelphavebutett,
mavenifaretstavetion petrfaretcotetdio-farlowetr ofar farondiouet--ave
faraver/far ettcohetdio cooncolusion.

CHRISTOPHER DEWDNEY

READING OLSON

*(The following is an excerpt from <u>Charles Olson's Maximus</u> by Don Byrd, to
be published later this year by University of Illinois Press.)*

   The sense of form from which the <u>Maximus</u> grows is not rational but
post-rational. The *field* of the poem includes not only the data which can
be comprehended by humanistic rationalism but also all that humanistic
rationalism excludes as irrational, random, or subjective.... Olson, with
his obedience to all phenomena, recognizes a possibility for order which
derives simply from the contiguity of phenomena. "One wants phenomenology
in place," Olson writes, "in order that event may re-arise." The freshness
of space must be allowed to assert itself so it can reveal its *own* form.
...The poems of Pound and Eliot, as Olson understands them, are the last
desperate attempts of cultivated men to insure cultural order in which
creation might continue to compete successfully with action.... The <u>Cantos</u>,
despite their epic intent, are essentially lyric. They create an order -- or
attempt to -- by arranging the artifacts of culture, both western and east-
ern, according to a private vision of their transcendant coherence....
   For too long language has remained so utterly within the bounds of
representational discourse, even for the poets themselves, that the occluded forms that rest *below* the written language have failed to emerge. Consequently, the various pure languages of poetry which have appeared are,
despite the power we feel in them, essentially only counter-discourse,
negations, rather than languages inside of which life can be conducted.
Olson proposes to re-combine the three terms of language [space, fact,
stance] in a single act of writing, commentary, and revelation.
   In his concern for quantitative measure, Olson is attempting to purify
the language of the abstract pollutants which have been allowed to creep
into it. Before poetry can be written language must be returned to itself.
In quantitative measure, the duration of a syllable is an inherent factor.
Olson objects, for example, that Milton's disregard for syllabic quantity
results in what might be called rhythmic sentimentality. The "humanistic"
elements in Milton's verse, those which are chosen, by an act of abstract
will, rather than given, the stress patterns of syntax, as opposed to syllables, are allowed weight in the determination of verse which they can

maintain only if they draw authority from some abstract source (attaching the "emotion to the idea," whether the idea be Christian dogma, Latinate syntax, or iambic pentameter) outside the proper concerns of the verse itself.... [Similarly,] in the periodic sentence, the words and syllables as loci of meanings are subordinated to an abstract structure which reduces its burden, the nouns and their actions, to mere weightless pointers which have no inherent force; objects move not by their own force but by the abstract drama of the sentence.

The anecdotes which occur paratactically in Maximus have their effect on the reader who, in turn, should not expect to find a heirarchy of sub-ordinated actions. Rather than integrating categorically or according to chains of cause and effect, one discovers on-going associations, subject-puns, images answering to images, one moving to the next in terms which are purely local to them. Unlike stream of consciousness, however, which is passive, parataxis is active, attempting to bring the poem to an immediate coherence by developing concrete associations on multiple planes.... Olson speaks of "a syntax of apposition", which can be opposed to a syntax of subordination. The order that emerges is analogous to the order of a map rather than the order of a scientific law or a periodic sentence, both of which tear objects from their contexts, rearrange them, and subordinate them to a controlling principle or, as Olson would say, *logos*.... Olson never intends to *express* any thing; he insists that the poem must *enact* the reality which is its content.

Maximus is a collage of fragments, a recognition that every person's life is a collage of fragments, in the process of coalescing toward the whole, where person and world are one. It does not move linearly along a single thread of argument but through a matrix of complex associations, juxtapositions, dialectic contradictions, puns, melodic relationships, and complementary rhythms.... The *unity* of the Maximus is perhaps best compared to the unity of a zoological species: it is an unchanging form that perpetually reconstructs itself in useful and unexpected ways.

DON BYRD

VOICES-OFF: MENGHAM and WILKINSON

(The following is excerpted from David Trotter's article on Rod Mengham and John Wilkinson in Twisted Wrist 4, 4 Bower Street, Maidstone, Kent, England. Works of Wilkinson and Trotter are available from Infernal Methods, c/o Trotter, Department of English, University College, Gower Street, London.)

...I want here to contrast the projects undertaken by Mengham and Wilkinson with a continental mode which long since turned its back on the unadventurous preoccupations of our own orthodoxies. Poets such as

Paul Celan and Edmond Jabès have developed a mode of writing which one
might term 'dialectical lyric', a mode introduced to this country by
Anthony Barnett in <u>Blood Flow</u> (1975) and <u>Fear and Misadventure</u> (1977).
The first movement of dialectic is negation; a thesis generates its own
antithesis and thus negates itself. Sartre argued that all knowledge
is dialectical to the extent that the person who knows, knows that he
is *not* the object of his knowledge; the subject discovers the world as
his antithesis and himself as a lack (as negativity). Dialectical lyric
stages the drama of the 'advertising mind', in Shelley's phrase, the
mind turned toward a 'vastness' which reveals it to itself as a lack:
disenfranchised, internally riven. Its characteristic form might be
described as a militant slightness:

> The small verse
> breaches
> because of the enclosure,
> but, not the sense.   (Barnett, <u>Fear and Misadventure</u> p.34)

Every word uttered by the lyric voice sets a limit, announces the inability of that voice to say all there is to say; it is this limit which
resonates, giving full 'sense' to insufficiency. The lyric voice, dialectically opposed to the unsayable, discovers itself as a lack....
   The texts of Mengham and Wilkinson, on the other hand, are not
predicated upon any such absenting movement (the generation of antithesis *out of* thesis) but rather upon the multiple infliction of one
thesis on another, *different* thesis. Indeed, the difference between
theses can no longer be regarded as an alienation, and then healed or
suppressed by an act of inclusion (Reason, Hegel said, is mind which
knows itself to be all reality); rather, it must be affirmed. Silences
occur, but only as they are produced by the operation of one thesis on
another; not as motive-forces. We have entered a Nietzschean world
where forces don't enter into relation with opposites they themselves
have generated, but with other forces.... In the cognitive realm, there
'is *only* a perspective seeing, *only* a perspective "knowing"; and the *more*
affects we allow to speak about one thing, the *more* eyes, different eyes,
we can use to observe one thing, the more complete will our "concept" of
this thing, our "objectivity", be. But to eliminate the will altogether,
to suspend each and every affect, supposing we were capable of this --
what would that mean but to *castrate* the intellect?' (<u>Genealogy of
Morals</u>). The merit of Mengham and Wilkinson is that they allow *more*
affects to speak, *more* eyes to observe, and so declare our boredom with
the castrated text presented by the weaker versions of the dialectical
lyric, the text whose entire business is not to deliver.
   The effacing of origins in modern literary theory and practice (including dialectical lyric) has forbidden us to ask the Nietzschean question Who is speaking here? Traditional lyric forms, on the other hand,

have raised the question in order to answer it without delay, to erase a potentially troublesome uncertainty. The work of Mengham and Wilkinson has restored the question *as a question* : neither preempted nor resolved. Curiosity as to who is speaking in these texts seems to me central to the pleasure we take in them. There is for example an occasional well-spokenness in Wilkinson's writing, a sumptuous intonation, a provocative snobbism which might either be residual or the revenge taken by the demotic text on itself; which must be read as the operation of one 'will' on another. Having unsqueamishly lifted the stone of totemic Absence, both Wilkinson and Mengham seem to gaze at the life beneath with a sometime paranoid inscrutability; but we are no longer dealing with the reserve of miniature and can hardly ignore the questions they pose.

DAVID TROTTER

*

I can't predict my accents. Sweeping up the short vowel, it is borrowed from his cool page. Any phrase, it dives out, you'll try to divine it in our best light. Mouthings can so thinly vibrate, and hence I know I haven't been reconstructed — just for a while all parts of speech in assent, through pull of the phantom lode.

— from <u>Prior to Passage</u>, *JOHN WILKENSON*

... Here to stay you know that the glum depart

hurrying down the noisy path partitive. In time to

landing in order to 'cope' she ponders her broth

useless beneath the lid feature the pensive flesh as as

far the shield chattering with blows of sliding.

That says what is commonly a sponge

a vanishing interest in this dilapidation of the grammar

instead of we all uncover the infested stump. Languid hammer

head down....

— from <u>Glossy Matter</u>, *ROD MENGHAM*

(PROCESS) NOTE: The Connection (Or, how far is it from New York to Baltimore via California?)

MARSHALL REESE, Writing (1980; pod books, 3022 Abell Avenue, Baltimore, MD 21218; $4)

Marshall Reese's book Slugs [published as part of Writing] relates through its concerns to the conversation generated around Bob Perelman's talk at the St. Mark's Poetry Project in New York in 4/79. Bob proposed the issue in the form of two terms to be defined. "Artificial" as distinguished from "natural" as applied to the concept of language.

Now Bob's basic rap, which is what leads to Marshall in this discussion, is that language, as an acquired skill, is one of those loop functions for the organism. The elements of it are borrowed property, the common currency of exchange, items on loan, as it were, from the general vocabulary pool. It passes through the culture and we make use of it in various ways according to our particular needs. Okay. In that sense, given that language is all a public commodity, just stuff getting run through the cycle, how does it get to be unique? And, secondly, still be constituted of configurations which can be distinctly classified as "artificial" and "natural"?

Marshall's work is a series of pieces composed while he was employed with a printer who had a linotype machine which produces, aside from usable lines of type, a whole mess of miscast pieces. It's these cast-off slugs, from various texts (ranging from a Civics text to a history of the Southwest with miscellaneous social notes thrown in for human interest) all locked up and printed. By pushing the acquisition process to an obvious place Marshall, using what in one sense cannot at all be considered his own language, is nonetheless using it *as* his own language. For sure this is no different than any other talking/writing process except his units are phrasiform as opposed to word form. They evolve a context just as absolutely as syntax evolves automatically in any word sequence (the absolute fact of grammar). There just *is* a logic of relation which is a matter of personal selection no matter how 'randomly' the assemblage is constructed. Choice to do it is the determinator of the form.

The conclusion here is that the concept of artificial can be disposed of having any relation to the process of acquiring the elements of language and put instead into an investigation of the use of language, which is where the selective compositional process becomes the essential factor.

Well, then, what is artificial selection? It doesn't occur to Marshall, cause he's just doing the work. The material's there and he makes use of it, simple digestion. Likewise Perelman is ripping off, collaging, splicing texts, only maybe a little more self-consciously. But actually, therein lies the difference. The self-consciousness:

what needs defining as the gap, the space between the thought and its manifestation. That gap is the distinction between, the point of differentiation, the point of isolation, insularity. That which is as opposed to that which is not. So. Simple. Once you got that one the point is to get to what exactly is. Goes flat right away, because it's so obvious -- it's the whole sum of those unique particulars, the choice, the combination of choices, the mess of interactions. A settlement of terms does not waste any more the energy to conflict over issues of the process. Get in there. The slogan mentality: cliches of language and fixations at points in the whole flow. Course it never finishes, never exactly originates, only begins to be aware that it is occurring then carries through whatever growth is appropriate to the logic of its own development, no, that becomes the logic of its own development, the way grammar becomes an absolute fact of language: because the words are such powerful objects they command relation--or is it more simple, even, they are the units and any sequence of units becomes a structure though, natch, there's a characteristic there too. That's in a sense the constant variable, of course it's always different--what should it be otherwise? Is anything the same as, nope, be glad about it. That's the tuck and lift aspect of the turn, the quick leap into.

What happens in an immediate sense preserves its dynamic intact, can be edited similarly and worked through similarly. The process by which it happens, that rush of transformative digestion, contains the excitement of any real process -- that is, its form is determined according to the necessities of its function, so, it's clean, essential. This isn't an argument for improvisation *at all*, it's an argument for integration and conscious process as opposed to self-conscious process, that's what. Because *that's* the artificial, the contrived, the thought through first which creates a limitation on the flexible possibility. Knocks out options beforehand, so, becomes stale in the act of its conception by being such a finished thought to begin with. It must be larger than itself and not understand its own limits entirely, at first, if it is to be successful, and done with engagement towards the definition of its own intention.

The working through of any real process will contain a sequential logic according to its own particular, essential dynamic. The character of that dynamic, which it acquires only in that exact and self-same process, becomes its own definition. It is what it is and what it wants to be is what it struggles to become. The intention is not a fixed ideal form, but a process of synthetic utilization and transformative integration. Not in the sense of achieving anything, no, no, don't want no models of perfection, just want the dynamic process. It's got to take you and keep you with/in the process of becoming what it is itself. Nowhere to get, of course, nothing ever finally resolves. Things take form and then disintegrate to reconstruct, reassemble, rearrange in another temporary configuration. The point is to work with that continual rearrangement, the redefinition.

So: the definition of intention the impetus, permission the cause, dis- and integration the process with the resolution a new form, the beginning again. And when in this process the activity makes a change whose origin was not predictable from, the process of which was not contained in the form of what it originated in, then, it actually is something, it gets to another place. When it all gets working it keeps on. But, since like a combustion engine it doesn't fully realize, call that total resolution the clear intention while the actual process is what goes down. Always that remainder to be dealt with accumulates sufficient significance relative to some point to act upon itself.

That's my process take, how I get from this to that. The rest is all the details of engagement.

JOHANNA DRUCKER

UNNATURE

In Memory of Roland Barthes

Nature, it might be observed, is almost entirely overcome, fulfilling the will to power of the nineteenth-century entrepreneaurs, the undertakers of the complete technical reduction of the world (as source and resource) to a surface of manageable proportions. With characteristic efficiency, this programme has been carried out for the most part inadvertently, through the coordinated operation of unconscious forces. According to the newest metaphysics, accident overrules essence and therefore ultimately prevails. And the events that surround the death of M. Barthes, recently dispensed to the public with the discreet excitement of snapshots produced at the critical moment by the prosecution, would have us sadly concur were it not for the subject's own voice urging us to look into the underlying facts, whose seemingly unambiguous constellation assaults our capacity for judgment. It would indeed be sad if the myth could so easily and so quickly erase the small island on which the mythologist had taken refuge.

It is for this reason that survival, while a necessity, is not enough with which to combat a feeling of futility in the face of an increasingly unnatural world. If, by chance, there still exist trees unsacrificed to the super-hero comic-book, or if industrial poisons have failed to wipe out every last useless species, this is really of no consequence; for we have come to live too far from nature to notice or care whether there are any accidental survivors of the total exploitation of the world and its

inhabitants.   All that is required is that the idea of nature be
overcome.

To the modern sensibility conditioned ever more thoroughly by an urbanity
that is almost completely manufactured (however hastily or shoddily) and
artificial in every respect, to a member of an eikosphere so dense with
messages and with pseudo-messages that nothing can safely be ignored or
assumed to be naturally silent and innocent of intent, in a world in
which everything strives to act unilaterally upon everything else with
the relentlessness of gravitation, nothing could be felt to be more unnatural than the unsoliciting experience of what in another culture might
be authentically called forth as nature.

In the oldest (and probably unspoken) metaphysics, transparently simple,
nature was conceived as the partially invisible source of what visibly
shines forth, and as such embraced within it events that convention alone
would be prompted to call unnatural. Only if there were any impossiblity
at all could there be a genuinely unnatural thing.

The plasticity of thought, however, is itself a fact often lost to sight,
and the surface of experience curiously frozen over. The very ubiquity
of the plastic disguises and alibis the ultimate exhaustibility of the
created world. Unlike true nature which unfolds continuously and not
always to our liking or in a way attuned to our conditioning, the entirely determined world is brittle, its material unresponsive or erratic
beyond the point to which it has been deliberately thought out. As with
theater scenery, the illusion can only be sustained within certain
bounds; a glimpse of the ropes and canvas patching, and the illusion is
destroyed or at least compromised.

God, with an infinite resource, could conceivably create and sustain
nature. But a man, judging from human history, granted the exercise of
his freedom, would either set out like Kafka's cage that "went in search
of a bird" or else, sensing the possiblity of another direction along
which thought might agreeably pass, produce and exhibit, like the late
M. Barthes, renderings of the zoological gardens we have inherited.

JOSEPH TIMKO

ESSAI A CLEF

   Mr. Barthes, having written his own image into a text (Barthes by
Barthes) and the chief of his obsessions into another (A Lover's Discourse), died. This latter text, death a life among *dead* letters, leaves
to us the task of pursuit, the cherishing of his mind's image in his
mind's words.
   It is enough to say that this magazine owes its existence or if not,
the meaning of that existence, to the significant desire-producing

language mechanisms which Mr. Barthes constantly refurnished with his analyses of/as text.

   *

  It is his contribution, initialled by his perseverance, to discern that it is a failure of critical writing to view its task as the reading of a text; excellent critical, *attentive*, writing knows its task to be the reading of the *writing* of a text.

  Barthes' analyses of prose literature, in moving from writing to text as object, observed a regalvanization of literary effort. He observed in the stylization of thought into writing, paradigms for the constructs of all carriers of meaning. His distillative attention to these modes enriched the scope of a mind's attentiveness to itself: in the details of thought's passing into signed meaning, the world. The effervescence of literary writing is function of the sign's interest in itself. Nothing is ever more absent from excellent writing than its writer. Indeed, this "its writer" evaporates facing the sign of a question. It need not be; any text demands its own insouciant definition about it in the world, its satisfaction.

  The text stands each word on its end, drops it and draws it back, propels it vertically and regains it. This plunging and striving, an activation at rest, performs before the world its calling into question and the at once clean maculate articulation texting its response: text, a one sided call and echo. This plummet, this rise, is thought; the text is its activation, its notice. Form is the mode for thought, language its inseparable substance; the text a manipulation of form through language. Life is the substance of language.

  ((Unless it be one, the poem is a very small thing in this world of text. Now that we understand ourselves as we write, we can think.))

   *

  Roland Barthes isolated from among the many symptoms of language its being-as-symptom, its signification. Language is structure. Structure, later, constitutes its materialization as text. The language, a blank egoless object bordering on operation, finds in its egos-recipient (readers) what it deposits; at best, ie in text, this deposit is structure, deposit void of all but the gesture of deposition. The mind creates of every meaning the sign of itself; but within this operation the author need not be ego-producer; this is the meaning of text: that *structure* produces.

  Barthes: meaning is articulation.

  Wittgenstein: meaning is use.

  The text is the meaning-quotient of language; each text measures again its meaning-value in structuration. The text isolates space between the lived elements of life in order to be itself recognized; it does this by thinking, by structuring. The textual structuration occurs always equidistant from the sets of its possible choices and the pursuit through those sets; it poses always a horizon, the image of difficulty by which it is recognized.

((A writer may aim to produce "private property language."))

((Writing produces, and is concerned with producing, exceptions to the notion that its model is speech.))

((An effort of writing is to alter the language such that speaking it has value. Writing offers the possibility of reproportioning the volumes of language and speech.))

((Writing distributes simultaneously the function of each of its elements.))

((The larger the unit of language, the greater the combinatory freedom. Thus, eg, prose promulgates attitude.))

*

Roland Barthes attended the prevalence of the sign as meaning-carrier; his attentions isolated the significant.

Meaning and concept combine as/under the aegis of sign. This sign stands in the world as form, subsequently combining with concept, in creating and maintaining the entire realm of signification.

*

Text reads (me).

Texts read.

As critic: into the excipient body of the text the alert mind inscribes what it has been the text's to inscribe in the excipient mind. This gesture of mirroring mimes one of replacement. Each signifier becomes something of a shifter; shifters are tautological, they speak/write themselves, delivered *and* mirrored.

Reading acts text.

Each text rereads (me); recalls remembering.

The language is, its operations are, the go-between (shifting mechanism) in this function of trade, reader exchanged for text and text for reader; this exchange of valuing is signified by the reader's return to the text and by the text's return to the reader in memory; it is a paratactic contract, twice signed for.

As the text's various signifyings leap variously and repeatedly out of it (under a duress of reading), it assumes a personality; it is this alternate with which the reader exchanges thought, as the text reinforces him/her to think. It is signifiers which the reading tends to distill, to make of the act a meaning indivisible. As part of this formulating, the reader, employing reading, interrogates the text in order to be him/herself disclosed; this is an action to seek the bounds of the textual enclosure, the limited world. The reader unites what the writer has used languages to hold apart; he/she remembers what the writer was interested in forgetting, losing, loosing (to begin to think to write is to remember, to write is to forget). The meaning is the aura of the reading, a calculated advance on further reading which draws the reader on. Reading and writing advance, equally, the text; the reader subjects the text to this furtherance.

The text is consumed greedily, because its failures are enticing. The text is an agglomeration, read as a map, of failed exigencies; it is the sum of traces of impurities; it is these which the writer of a text tends to forget from the language, as he writes. The reader disturbs the text by his/her interest, even as it is being written. In fact, the text is the reader's product, matrices of meanings which he/she releases as product from the significations of the writing, which has been the author's product. The text, by its inclusiveness, attempts to choke the reader, so that he/she utter no *sound* of his/her own; it is an ecological effort, which the reader in part maintains as in reading he/she confronts, disturbs, distributes, the text's intentional unity. This is an allure of the text, that it is in reading disturbed but not damaged, that it disturbs without damage; a faultless assurance of furthered interest, upon which, manifested, the reader capitalizes; the mutual debt of reader and author is disturbed by the text, which advances to the reader a material interest it had not in writing for the author (hence an author's obsession with like texts). It is the text, synchronically a social mien/mean, which writes its unity, a dimension shared, barely but totally, by author and reader, at an edge of their activity. This is the text's economy; though it is full, its effects are not displaced even by the coterminous attentions of reader and author. Even their calling it names, leaves it still. But the text is not closed; it inscribes an ideal social syntax, one without waste in relations, capable of uniting persons who it writes face to face at its one side; entering it, leaving it, no problem.

Text texts text.

*

The text, puritanical in scope, within bounds, is not so in essence. It is along the acultural, desiring edge of language that the text is written; its other edge, a boundary synchronous with usage, merely supports, permits it. The competition between the two edges, a contest which the vertical of desire always champions, nevertheless furthers within the text an apprehension of its dissolve; it is against this latter uncertainty that the text finally closes, a wheel in motion which apparently stops, reverses, in having sped out of one perceptive possibility on entering another (writing, to text, say; or, text to apprehension). In separating us from usage-language, the text creates in us a great desiring for same, which it satisfies completely but in quite another way, offering in a cleansed language occasion the superlative of our own actual gestures in desiring. It seduces, in part, by exploiting a flaw, an opening, in us, the separateness of our two languages (daily; textual) with which we meet the occasion of seeking a perfection in the latter. The text loses us, forgets us, from social language. Drawing us, as itself, out of the body of that language, we lose ego, we die happy.

The author through the text demands pleasure for the reader. He/she abolishes a consumption of literature by filling its vacancy with bliss. The reader completes for moments the text's desiring motions, a completion instantly reawakening, unsatisfied, demanding after this one furtherance, another of the language. The text gives rise in the reader to one fear, that of its dissolution, which would deny to the reader his/her own anticipated dissolve into pleasure; this latter the text cannot deny, it must keep its promise excellently. The text's economy is guaranteed by the demands which must be met at its conclusion, a point, a vista to which it comes. The text permits a sort of necrophiliac pleasure: the desserts of the dead, or at least constrained, social language are enjoyed in the instance of the burgeoning textual assault, an erection of exacting consequence in a relative void of diversions and difficulties. Enjoying the corpsing of a language, suddenly puritanical ourselves, we are somewhat repelled by the image the text supplies of ourselves abandoned in such pleasure (we giggle); against this social difficulty, the text offers its pleasure, a hierarchy cleansed of social burden, a gesture completely filling a gesture. This is the text's obscenity, that, like any other, it posits itself as a substitute for discourse, it excerpts itself from the political except as a superlative instance of its negative, a diligence of pleasure escaped from its toil.

*

The text comes from its industry.

The text is trivial only in its affectations, that it appears to be literature.

The text considers its veils its triumph: an illusion.

The text does not stop to *consider* its edges.

If there were a diametrics of the text it would be one-sided, written.

The text is an animated perfection. If it fail in either of these it is, obviously, merely animated, merely perfect. Merely *split*.

Poems have dripped into the text. It is full of them.

Context, no such thing.

The convention of language is discarded for its invention.

The text durates. This is its relation with time.

The text is sentenced to reality, it is a contiguous figment, an act in an act.

The text repeats and tells.

The text is language raised to a third power: it is the (1) inhabited (2) space of a (3) builder.

The text, unlike its mention, is not historical; it does not disagree with itself. But it is an authority upon its occasion. The text exists of several diachronic scenes at once.

The text sits on itself, excreting the text. It takes literature apart, to be. The writing of the text is an operation on successive operations.

The text binds time to a contract. It does this instant by instant.

But time forgets.

The text is written along a vector between intellect (makes new) and intelligence (remembers).

The text satisfies by more than it was made to produce, in spite of its consistent language.

The text consumes an oedipal image in order to play with itself without bother.

In each text the language is decided a unit of space. This makes it complete.

The text is elaborate because it enforces an attitude. Obviously the author function is not dead.

The text is a collective; it delights.

The text may be the last act of a body. Language will act alone.

   *

The life is a text. The text is a life. Life, text, are equal. The life, the text, cut equally from the world, and equally, as one, are left. Each fiction dominates only in its own territory, "succeeding" in excluding the rest. For the reader of a text, that text is all that he/ she knows to be the case, but the author knows also that knowing, and a magnitude of wider bounds that that implies; in this the author and critic share, that they look at the text as, and not only through, it.

The life is a depository for thought, as the text is thought's writing. Life and the text disintegrate for time. The life, the text: each revises, but by going on, never as an afterthought, never in re- verse. In the author's case, text, life, are alternate words for that one thing which each seeks to inscribe. The desire of each for the other is intransitive; each merely acts, this acting is single, unadjectivised, unextended.

The body, its life, is made evident only through language (modifi- cation); language is evidenced only in the collection of bodies, lan- guage is inherently pluralized.

Barthes' own text is a figment of fragments: he took his life apart, and kept it there. Definitions he manipulated reappear: the figment is of continuity. A flatness is required of the fragments, or of their field of signifieds, in order to overcome any illusion about them: an *admission* of flatness. For this, a structure without systems is re- quired. A collection of utterances become any life: against this, for the author a text is a remission from life, a forgetting-machine.

Each text is an appropriation from the language. This separates the author from it also. Time is consumed because/where there is not enough of it. There are enough texts (undemanded); this sufficiency paradoxically guarantees against consumption. The text is in need of a pronoun of its own.

((Theory is *essentially* heavy; bears at once the preponderance of an at least two-sided utterance; speculates at least in two directions, that of its "object" and that of itself.))

((To disintegrate (language) *actively*, *is* revolution. The contra-entropic is entropy speeded up.))

((Connotation is a matter of existence.))

((Style: the rubric which is visible *through* the work.))

((Sentences, singly, are impotent (the maxim comes in its own mouth); together, they perform texted orgiastic gesture.))

((Aesthetic gesture may meet the ideological at a point in the mind when it is *grasped*, understood. Ideological discourse never reaches the aesthetic because it does only one thing, its open mouth.))

((The image-system, an attended-to and delineated symbol: of ego.))

((Antithesis *deserts* language in a futile effort to become ideological.))

((Aesthetic language is ironic; we are amused/taken by its self-absorption.))

*

Signification is a function of history. It is a paradox that history, the deadest of languages, speaks. Nothing leads us to expect this mis-giving away of material, certainly not the text, whose elucidation of the same material is transparent by comparison. Perhaps history too will stop speaking, to be text.

There is a fluctuant, ahistoric zone between our need to utter and the guise (writing) whereby we occasionally solve for that need. The text is an extreme of utterance close to that zone, taking from that zone a veiled ardor, giving to it what little definition it has. In this zone the signifier is loosed, disobliged, given to be given, taken apart, among signifiers alone, untaxed.

History is the landscape of textual activity: ie the text bears historical traces, but these traces are free within the text to bear precisely and only themselves, unconstrained, a mirror against a mirror. And it is this latter lack of distance, this infra-closeness, which permits the traversed but undivided text, the texting of histories, a superlative of geometric progresses. The text is active twice-at-once, bringing to itself dispersed particular signifiers, and releasing them as one material: a plural, but singularizing, activity: meaning.

On the plane of signification, however, each signifier is entirely separate, secluded. Needs motivate a combination of such as recognition, memory, mental industry, which enforce the various plural presencings of signifiers, a sort of failure of them, a letting down. The attenuations are marvelous.

(History is much shorter than the text, one signifier among many. The text is much shorter than history, one occurence among many.) The text exhausts history.

*

It is in peregrinations, mental or otherwise, of lover pursuing beloved, that love resembles the warp and woof of textual fabrication. In a beloved, in the text, an image is sought of an ineffable moment, a vertical duration within unhalting horizontal passage.

Adjectives merely circulate in the effort to define the affairs of
love or the text. That is to say, the notions of designation, of meaning,
are subject to a furor, subject to that which animates, desire.

But to multiply such comparisons, such accords, between love and
text, is to damage the completeness of the surfaces of these two subjects-
as-objects, a completeness made boundless by the play of superlatives
inhabiting either (overlapping) sphere. But the love-text? it would
require two writing-subjects, not synonymous, but coterminous: a figure
available as a delicacy in the text, but difficult of apprehension in
the world.

In order to remain outside my subject, *I* speak, and within this suddenly magnified spectacle (a world!) I stop to write.

ALAN DAVIES

L=A=N=G=U=A=G=E

Number 12.   (Vol. 3, No. 2.)

Bruce Andrews & Charles Bernstein, Editors.

Subscriptions — One year (three issues in 1980) for $4.
                Institutions: $8.

Design: Susan B. Laufer.   Typing: Sally Silvers.

All queries, submissions, and checks to:
Charles Bernstein, 464 Amsterdam Ave, New York, NY 10024

L=A=N=G=U=A=G=E is supported by subscriptions, donations, and grants
from the National Endowment for the Arts, the Coordinating Council
of Literary Magazines, and the New York State Council on the Arts.

Distributed with the cooperation of the Segue Foundation.

(C) 1980 by L=A=N=G=U=A=G=E

ANNOUNCEMENT:

L=A=N=G=U=A=G=E, in association with the Segue Foundation, is pleased
to announce the publication of *LEGEND*, a 250 page, five-way collaboration by Ron Silliman, Steve McCaffery, Ray DiPalma, Charles Bernstein,
& Bruce Andrews. $5, from 464 Amsterdam Avenue, New York, NY 10024.

L=A=N=G=U=A=G=E

NUMBER 13   DECEMBER 1980

REWRITING MARX

The poetry of societies in which the capitalist mode of production prevails appears as an "immense collection of books"; the individual book appears as its elementary form. Our investigation begins with the analysis of the book.

The book is, first of all, an external object, a thing which through its qualities satisfies human needs of a literary kind.

Objects of reading become books only because they are the products of the writing of private individuals who work independently of each other. The sum total of the writing of all these private individuals forms the aggregate writing of society. *Since the writers do not come into social contact until they exchange the products of their writing*, the specific social characteristics of their private writings appear only within this exchange. In other words, the writing of the private individual manifests itself as an element of the total writing of society *only through the relations* which the act of exchange establishes between the texts, and, through their mediation, between the writers. To the writers, therefore, the social relations between their private writing appear as what they are, *i.e.*, they do not appear as direct social relations between persons in their work, but rather as material relations between persons and social relations between texts.

However, a text can be useful, and a product of human writing, without being a book. She who satisfies her own need with the text of her own writing admittedly creates reading-values, but not books. In order to produce the latter, she must not only produce reading-values, *but reading-values for others*, social reading-values. (And not merely for others. In order to become a book, the text must be transferred to the other person, for whom it serves as a reading-value, *through the medium of exchange*.)

RON SILLIMAN

417

BLOOD. RUST. CAPITAL. BLOODSTREAM.

ADOLPHUS, J.L.: LETTERS TO RICHARD HEBER. ESQ. (Containing Critical
Remarks on the Series of Novels Beginning with "Waverly" and an Attempt
to Ascertain their Author) 8vo., Boston 1822. The theoretic interest in
rust emerged from investigations into the bridge between metallurgical and
physiological identities BAILLIE, Joanna: Miscellaneous Plays, London
1804, 1st Edition 8vo., pp. i-xix + 1-438 (extra leaf advertises
Wordsworth's Lyrical Ballads). Rust throughout is treated as the miner-
alized transform of blood and thus the oxydizational connective with the
human breath and bloodstream. "BROWNE, Sir Thomas: WORKS, London 1686,
fol. 1st. ed. with engraved portrait in facsimile" (Wing B 5150 Keynes
201). Rust also relates to critique and the need to negate ANY GIVEN
FORM whilst as a metallic growth and pathology it relates to carcinoma
and the encompassing ideology of the parasite. BURNEY, Fanny: CECILIA or
Memoirs of an Heiress, London 1784 5 vols. 4th. ed. 12mo. full contemp.
tree calf milled edging in linguistic form. The Parasite finds most powerful manifestation within quotation and allusion i.e. in the precise manner
(the site of the cite) that creates in any text a biological device for
drawing off signification by means of echo, index, association, interruption and supplementarity (pp. i-xii + 13-164 Glasgow 1751 printed by
Robert Urie 8vo.) Rust tends, to occur as an activity within a pre-existent wound and as such is to be classified as a post-incisional practice.
It is what writing writes of itself within the aura of its own excess
(contains 1st printing of SEMELE) "trimmed" London 1710 3 vols in 2 incl.
The Old Bachelor, Double Dealer and Love for Love Vol. III = pp. A1-a4 +
1-492 and as a mineralogical agency enters the bloodstream as capital to
carry the microformations of a labour force throughout the human organism.
DAVISDON (Joseph) . . . nto English Prose, ondon 767. 3rd ed. (i-v). It
might be described as the corpuscular theory of the proletariat. cf. THE
ECONOMY OF HUMAN LIFE by Robert Dodsley (London 8 vo. 32 woodcuts by
Austin & Hole 1808) a work often attributed to Chesterfield. Whereas cancer (after nosological elimination) is reattributable to a biopolitical-
linguistic scheme and functions closest to a surplus value which is reinvested into the cellular structure of the body as pure profit. GELLIUS,
Aulus: NOCTES ATTICAE, Venice 1489 (one of my rarest books) 132 leaves,
42 line + head 6th ed. (3rd Venice) Bernardinus de Choris de Cremona &
Simon de Luere. Goff (213) lists only ten copies in America. What is
drawn off ("virologically?") from the societal corpus is art, intellect
and sex. In the purest analysis of the libidinal economy (to which virus
is central) sex is a pure discharge, an absolute signifier detached from
its signified and demonstrates best the principles of an unrestricted
GENERAL ECONOMY (Bataille) within the structural and epistemological
restraints of the restricted economy (Windsor 1788 2nd ed. with verso
last leaf containing errata. Authors: George Canning, John Smith, John
Frere and Robt. Smith) accordingly: any poem which adopts "book" as its

vehicular form must admit its complicity within a restricted economy.
Sex then is a pure discharge and exceeds all value to constitute an
energetic subversion of the human capital machine. As a discharge sex is
fraternal & sorietal to all other vectors of spontaneous dissemination:
intuition, improvisation, madness, desire and schizophrenic proproductive
drives (LACTANTIUS: Works, Venice 1478 . . . "lactantii firmiani de
diuinis instituioibus aduersus gentes" . . . which together constitute a
postcognitive antidote to rust conceived as a surplus value and an entropy. Negentropic strategy is founded on the full practice of a general
economy, in informational "waste", semantic excess produced by parasitical
attachments and interruptions to a host syntagm 12mo circa 1729, L'ESTRANGE,
Sir Robt., Kt., London (but why London "in the Strand" pp. i-xxx active
within. The circulation of biological capitalism are numerous virus agents
(MacPherson, Sibbs, malus coronaria, Harrison Blake at Worcester, Johnson
on the life of Father Paul Sarpi, Cholmondeley's letter to Thoreau in 1857,
bourgeois consciousness in general, ratiocinative strategies in general,
Dr. Johnson's ref. to mustard in a young child's mouth, the Rev. Thomas
Newton on The Prophecies, David Hume, Zeus, Patroclus, Chichen Itza, the
word of the Lord, virus "positioned" "as a dormant potential" "within
structure within" "this structure" Loudon's remarks on pyrus malus and the
badge of the clan of Lamont. It is homologous to the political implications of the poetical phrase MITCHELL, John: The Female ondo 793 2nd e
125 x P grim grav frontispiece by (defectiv) . . . / WORDS being what
poems are then SENTENCES being what POLITICS is . . (sustenance) (quad-
ruped) (the Duma) (Lenin during Blossom Week) . . . . VIRUS . . . . . and
at this . . . . . . po . . int . . . . . . lexically inter change-
ab . . le with the SENTENCE: "POTENTIAL" so that when activated it becomes
THIS FRAMING AGENT YOU ARE reading now (Theophrastus included the apple
among the more "civilized" plants URBANIORES rather than WILD/SYLVESTRES)
fixating epistemological boundaries which sex cannot be in such a way as
to derive maximum sustenance for itself and to prevent the operation of
general economy. LETTERS OF THE RT. HONBLE. WRITTEN DURING HER TRAVELS IN
EUROPE ASIA & AFRICA n.d. 6vo. VERBALLY SPEAKING an activated virus of
this kind "assumes the form of either page (consecutively bound as book)
or else as SENTENCE "Probably 1767 ed.") as container of the grammatical
line which is itself both the victim and the vengence of a persistent
ideology of perspective.) ACTIVE VIRAL PENETRATION IN ART (buds we must
remember were counted every winter's eve for seventeen years) GIVES RISE
TO THE INTERRELATED HEGEMONIES OF COMMODITY, CONSUMPTION AND PRODUCTION.
Poems on Several Subjects, don 1769, John OGILVIE incls. Essay on the
Lyric Poetry of the Ancients 8vo modern calf binding + "the fruit of the
crab in the forests of France". IF IT WERE POSSIBLE AT THIS POINT (Rowe,
Elizabeth: Friendship in Death in a Series etc. . . . . . portrait by
J. Bennett) WE WOULD SWITCH THIS DISCOURSE INTO THE MOUTH OF HER WHO IS
PRESENT IN THAT CLASSROOM WHERE A SMALL CHILD SITS INTENSELY POROUS AND

VULNERABLE AND EAGER TO (to) RECEIVE (receive) THAT (that) WHICH (which) WE "we" CALL (call) "SCIENTIFIC" scientific KNOWLEDGE (knowledge) THAT (that) WHICH (which) ONE "one" DICTIONARY "dictionary" AT (at) "LEAST" (least) IS is ABLE able (TO) "to" DESCRIBE (describe) AS as OPPOSITE "opposite" to TO ART (ART):

STEVE MC CAFFERY

FUGITIVE CAUSES

Lawrence Kearney, <u>Five</u> (1976; Tombouctou Books, distributed by Serendipity, 1970 Shattuck, Berkeley, CA; $3). *(The following review by Brian Fawcett is taken from <u>N.M.F.G.</u>, Box 5094 MPO, Vancouver, B.C. — U6B 4A9, Canada)*

Let's get one thing out of the way right now. Larry Kearney is a very talented writer, and this book is well-written, and at times, entertaining. On the back cover Robert Creeley tells us that it is "A primal geography-with extraordinary intersections, wherein all the terms of the so-called world gain articulation and a *place. And* his propositions will haunt you, or bless you, forever." What if I say, at the outset, that the subject of "primal geography" as Creeley somewhat grandly calls it, is uninteresting, that it no longer contains enough intellectual currency to legitimately make a book with? I then have to define & articulate this writing on other grounds, without the benefit of the buzz surrounding the New American Poetry. Unfortunately that isn't possible.

Kearney is a practicing artist confronted by what confronts nearly all experimental writers in the latter half of the twentieth century — an absence of constructive context in which to think and write. No one, let's admit it, listens to poetry, except other poets. The pleasure of carefully shaped language, the marvellousness of the attentions it can produce, the *thrill* just isn't necessary to the survival of the structures of power & ordinance in industrialized capitalist states. These things may in fact even be mildly dangerous to the maintenance of that kind of power.

This condition of poetry has existed for some time now — at least during this century. For some 40 years now experimental writers have been tailing along in the wake of Pound's erratic political logic; i.e. we will create a revolution that will transform the world *from within* — 500 million *little* revolutions. During the 60's this in fact became an actuality, little revolutions occurred everywhere, anarchically, & they even caused our civilization to squirm uncomfortably. Now we have mass-produced tarot cards, our horoscopes & biorhythyms are helpfully set out for us in the morning papers, and while the rich still mingle mostly with the rich, now they do it by going away two or three times a year to feel each other up for a weekend. We've been given back primal existence if we want it and the stuff of Pound & Olson's revolution is now being merchandised like any other commodity. In the face of it, most poets have simply retreated further into the obscurities of poetic & personal processes, and into the kind of despair out of which Kearney's writing seems to come. "I don't know what to make. I don't know what I want. I don't know why I ate so much breakfast." he says or "At two-thirty in the fucking a.m. who's selling cars on the tube. The problems of the world are insurmountable and I feel like crying."

Again and again, Kearney's writing confronts that point, or is confronted by it, so that the sheer number of the confrontations becomes the organizing force in the writing. Yet Kearney doesn't seem to want to take responsibility for his part in the confrontations. They remain existential. At one point he warns his reader that "There isn't anything you need here *except* sleep." More important, he's completely uncritical of the mumbo-jumbo that has grown up around poetic process, allowing the misty prounouncements and/or vectors of language it creates to become an alternative to an enterable world reality. "We don't carry worlds on our backs." he tells us. "They lie back there, warping and shifting." and later in the book, he makes this proposition: "What it comes down to, forms decay. There isn't anything but content." The trouble with that, as the writing abundantly identifies, is that when forms decay, content has neither context nor boundaries to define its value, and one is forced to internalize everything: ergo, "Primal Geography". But, when you take from it the buzz, "Primal Geography" just means individual and idiosyncratic taxonomy, and passively psychological enterprise. "Nothing to say until it's there and then *it* says it or refuses and smiles at you. I don't know what the point is. Getting fucked." Later, Kearney notices a corollary phenomenon: "There always seems to be someone waiting around to be fucked." At least the sexual metaphor makes him nervous, which means he's from the present generation, and not Creeley's, which never got beyond taking advantage of it.

Kearney's approach to poetry and to the world generally is revealed in the following admission:

I LEARNT FROM HIM THAT POETRY, EVEN THAT OF THE LOFTIEST AND, SEEMINGLY, THAT OF THE WILDEST ODES HAD A LOGIC OF ITS OWN, AS SEVERE AS THAT OF SCIENCE, AND MORE DIFFICULT, BECAUSE MORE SUBTLE, MORE COMPLEX, AND DEPENDENT ON MORE AND MORE FUGITIVE CAUSES.

Kearney learned that from, I think, Jack Spicer, but he could have learned it from any of a dozen major poets of the New American Poetry.

I learned it too, and so did most of the writers I could name. And I believe it too. My question, of Kearney, and of anyone else who I've ever learned anything about poetry from is this: What in the fuck am I supposed to do with it?

Translated into practice, the methodology of the New American Poetry has aged into a closed form that is causing poetry to disappear into second rate motivational and behavioral psychology. If the causes of poetry are fugitive, we need to re-open the discourse over what are and why are the effects of its causes. In general poets have lost the tools with which to be responsive to anything *but* "primal geography" and worse, they've lost sight of the fact that we're fucking well responsible to the condition of the planet and of the human species from which, after, all, poetry is derived. Which is not to rebuke the loveliness of *this* writing, the marvelousness of the attentions and what they produce. This, as always, should be given to more human beings. But how do you *teach* that, without placing it in a context of basic human needs that will also ensure that human beings, with the knowledges poetry offers, will also be able to fill their bellies, protect their young, & assuage the need for dignity that underlies, or undercuts, our political lives?

BRIAN FAWCETT

"WRENCH" WRENCHED

(Marshall Reese and Chris Mason discuss, in what follows, Kirby Malone's ongoing work — wrench, wrench. All three are part of the Baltimore performance group Co-Accident.)

wrench wrench takes as a material source any words or phrases Kirby Malone encounters in his daily life. In the act of writing it down, a phrase is often foreshortened, run on into another unrelated phrase, or otherwise deprived of its literal sense. The reader, encountering the phrase as part of a skew geometric pattern on a 3 x 5 inch file card, cannot ascertain whether it came from "The Incredible Hulk," a wrong number phone call, *The Revolution of Everyday Life*, or a stoned conversation with the oil-burner repairman.

The act of writing in crowded public situations, writing anything, is a curiosity. People's attentions are drawn to Kirby when he writes on his cards.

The published volume *wrench wrench* will begin with an epigraph from a description of Pierre Jacquet-Droz's automaton *The Young Writer*: "When the mechanism is started, the boy dips his pen in the inkwell, shakes it twice, places his hand at the top of the page, and pauses. As the lever is pressed again, he begins to write, slowly and carefully, distinguishing in his characters between light and heavy strokes."

One notices in *wrench wrench* that every statement is a sentence, the composition is a syncopation of total starts and stops. The writing is a quantitative act, a part of production. There is a schism between separate words and the larger shapes and patterns of words. Grammar is imagined.

WHAT DO YOU LISTEN TO WHEN YOU WRITE? *The process is based on ruptures or breaks, sometimes intentional on my part and sometimes on how I heard it.*

BEFORE YOU STARTED *WRENCH WRENCH* DID YOU LISTEN TO WHAT IS AROUND YOU DIFFERENTLY? *Everything I've written since 1975 has had something with found material, starting off with literary material like Olson or Tim Buckley.... What is interesting is that what I do in* wrench wrench *is not all recording. What I've come to try to understand is desire — not how it is interpreted in pop culture. The way I understand desire now, is not how it is described in Romantic terms today, or in competitive capitalist terms, but as an activity which lies outside of commodity fetishism, outside of capitalist production.*

"For Deleuze and Guatarri, as for Lacan, the forms of desire are not set in nature, but are socially created... In *Anti-Oedipus* we are presented with a picture of the world whose complexity and flux defy language... Deleuze and Guatarri see man as constituted by "desiring machines". Infinite types and varieties of relationships are possible; each person's machine parts can plug into and unplug from machine parts of another. There is, in other words, no given 'self', only the cacophony of desiring machines. Fragmentation is universal, and is not the peculiar fate of what society defines as the schizophrenic. But the crucial point is that capitalist society cannot live with the infinite variety of potential interconnections and relationships and imposes restraints regulating which ones are to be allowed, i.e., essentially those relating to reproduction in the family...." (Jeffrey Weeks, introduction to Guy Hocquenghem, *Homosexual Desire*.)

Kirby sees the writer as a "desiring machine". It is assumed that production is continuous, with no breaks or stoppages. But a machine cannot flow or move effortlessly. It can only continue by breaking steps into smaller and smaller ones. Writing is a discontinuous process, a mechanical process against the continuity of language.

...What I learned to be decontextualization. Whatever it is you can't say -- there will be a trace of it in that fragment [of what you do say] *a fragment of whatever that had outside of* [it]

In performance, this process of decontextualization is reversed in an interesting way. *wrench wrench* was performed 11 times between January 1978 and February 1979 as part of a poetry reading or a CoAccident performance. The reading of the text was usually combined simultaneously with one or more other diverse often unconnected events. Some of these events were the sound of bowed cymbals and pot lids, a slide of a German factory shown to each member of the audience individually with a hand viewer, dancers illuminating each other with flashlights, and Kirby's face upside down reading the text on 17 video monitors.

The title wrench wrench is rupture, like "tool tool", "machine part machine part machine part".
I would want [wrench wrench] to be a tool for a reader to learn more about hierarchy or manipulation in language.
I don't want it to be didactic at all. One one level it's a time capsule of all of language being used now. I could never assemble all the ways I've used language from early 1978 through 1981 [when wrench wrench will be completed].
It's like a little thread through all that.
But again I don't think it's a record. It's more like an example.
I'm always going out to hear it and going back into writing it. I have a different existence in conversation because just as you are writing, you lose some of what I am saying, I lose some of what I hear.

CHRIS MASON & MARSHALL REESE

SEMBLANCE

(This work is reprinted from a symposium on recent American poetry entitled "Death of the "Referent?" in the British magazine Reality Studios, $2 from 75 Balfour Street, London SE 17.)

> *"It's as if each of these things has a life of its own. You can stretch them, deform them and even break them apart, and they still have an inner cohesion that keeps them together."*

Not 'death' of the referent — rather a recharged use of the multivalent referential vectors that any word has, how words in combination tone and modify the associations made for each of them, how 'reference' then is not a one-on-one relation to an 'object' but a perceptual dimension that closes in to pinpoint, nail down ("*this*" word), sputters omnitropically (the in in the which of who where what wells), refuses the build up of image track/projection while, pointillistically, fixing a reference at each turn (fills vats ago lodges spire), or, that much rarer case (Peter Inman's *Platin* and David Melnick's *Pcoet* two recent examples) of "zaum" (so called "transrational", pervasively neologistic) — "ig ok aber-flappi" — in which reference, deprived of its automatic reflex reaction of word/stimulus image/response roams over the range of associations suggested by the word, word shooting off referential vectors like the energy field in a Kirillian photograph.

All of which are ways of releasing the energy inherent in the referential dimension of language, that these dimensions are the material of which the writing is made, define its medium. Making the structures of meaning in language more tangible and in that way allowing for the maximum resonance for the medium — the traditional power that writing has always had to make experience palpable not by simply pointing to it but by (re)creating its conditions. **

Point then, at first instance, to see the medium of writing — our area of operation — as maximally open in vocabulary, forms, shapes, phoneme/ morpheme/word/phrase/sentence order, etc., so that possible areas covered, ranges of things depicted, suggested, critiqued, considered, etc., have an outer limit (asymptotic) of what can be thought, what can (might) be. But then, taking that as zero degree, not to gesturalize the possibility of poetry to operate in this "hyperspace", but to create works (poems) within it.

*

The order of the words, the syntax, creates possibilities for images, pictures, representations, descriptions, invocation, ideation, critique, relation, projection, etc. Sentences that follow standard grammatical patterns allow the accumulating references to enthrall the reader by diminishing diversions from a constructed representation. In this way, each word's references work in harmony by reinforcing a spatio/temporal order conventionalized by the bulk of writing practice that creates the "standard". "The lamp sits atop the table in the study" — each word narrowing down the possibilities of each other, limiting the interpreta-tion of each word's meaning by creating an ever more specific context. In a similar way, associations with sentences are narrowed down by conven-tional expository or narrational paragraph structure, which directs atten-tion away from the sentence as meaning generating event and onto the "content" depicted. By shifting the contexts in which even a fairly "standard" sentence finds itself, as in the prose format work of Ron Silliman and Barrett Watten, the seriality of the ordering of sentences within a paragraph displaces from its habitual surrounding the projected representational fixation that the sentence conveys. "Words elect us. The lamp sits atop the table in the study. The tower is burnt orange...." By rotating sentences within a paragraph (a process analogous to jump cutting in film) according to principles generated by and unfolding in the work (rather than in accordance with representational construction patterns) a perceptual vividness is intensified for each sentence since the abruptness of the cuts induces a greater desire to savor the tangibility of each sentence before it is lost to the next, determinately other, sentence. Juxtapositions not only suggest unsuspected relations but induce reading along ectoskeletal and citational lines. As a result, the operant mechanisms of meaning are multiplied and patterns of projection in reading are less restricted. The patterns of projection are not, however, undetermined. The text operates at a level that not only provokes projections by each sentence but by the sequencing of the sentences suggests lines or paths for them to proceed along. At the same time, circumspection about the nature and meaning of the projections is called forth. The result is both a self-reflectiveness and an intensification of the items/conventions of the social world projected/suggested/provoked. A similar process can also take place within sentences and phrases and not only intersententially. Syntactic patterns are composed which allow for this combination of projection and reflection in the movement from word to word. "For as much as, within the because, tools their annoyance, tip to toward." — But, again, to acknowledge this as the space of the text, and still to leave open what is to be said, what projections desire these reflections.

*

The sense of music in poetry: the music of meaning — emerging, fogging, constrasting, etc. Tune attunement in understanding — the meaning sounds. It's impossible to separate prosody from the structure (the form and content seen as an interlocking figure) of a given poem. You can talk about strategies of meaning generation, shape, the kinds of sounds accented, the varieties of measurement (of scale, of number, of line length, of syllable order, of word length, of phrase length, or measure as punctuation, of punctuation as metrics). But no one has primacy --the music is the orchestrating these into the poem, the angles one plays against another, the shading. In much of my own work: working at angles to the strong tidal pull of an expected sequence of a sentence — or by cutting off a sentence or phrase midway and counting on the mind to complete where the poem goes off in another direction, giving two vectors at once — the anticipated projection underneath and the actual wording above.

My interest in not conceptualizing the field of the poem as a unitary plane, and so also not using overall structural programs: that any prior "principle" of composition violates the priority I want to give to the inherence of surface, to the total necessity in the durational space of the poem for every moment to *count*. The moment not subsumed into a schematic structure, hence instance of it, but at every juncture creating (synthesizing) the structure. So not to have the work resolve at the level of the "field" if this is to mean a uniplanar surface within which the poem operates. Structure that can't be separated from decisions made within it, constantly poking through the expected parameters. Rather than having a single form or shape or idea of the work pop out as you read, the structure itself is pulled into a moebius-like twisting momentum. In this process, the language takes on a centrifugal force that seems to trip it out of the poem, turn it out from itself, exteriorizing it. Textures, vocabularies, discourses, constructivist modes of radically different character are not integrated into a field as part of a predetermined planar architecture; the gaps and jumps compose a space within shifting parameters, types and styles of discourse constantly criss-crossing, interacting, creating new gels. (Intertextual, interstructural....) (Bruce Andrews has suggested the image of a relief map for the varying kinds of referential vectors — reference to different domains of discourse, references made by different processes — in some of his work in which words and phrases are visually spaced out over the surface of the page. However, the structural dissonance in these works is counterbalanced by the perspicacious poise of the overall design, which tends to even out the surface tension.)

Writing as a process of pushing whatever way, or making the piece cohere as far as can: stretching my mind — to where I know it makes sense but not quite why — suspecting relations that I understand, that make the sense of the ready-to-hand — ie pushing the composition to the very limits of sense, meaning, to that razor's edge where judgment/aesthetic sense is all I can go on (knowhow). (Maybe what's to get beyond in Olson's field theory is just the idea of form as a single web, a unified field, one matrix, with its implicit idea of "perception" onto a given world rather than, as well, onto the language through which the world is constituted.) So that the form, the structure, that, finally, is the poem, has emerged, is come upon, is made.

**Alan Davies has objected that language and experience are separate realms and that the separation should be maximized in writing, in this way questioning the value of using language to make experience palpable. — But I don't mean "experience" in the sense of a picture/image/*re*presentation that is calling back to an already constituted experience. Rather, language itself constitutes experience at every moment (in reading and otherwise). Experience, then, is not tied into representation exclusively but is a separate "perception"-like category. (& perception not necessarily as in perception onto a physical/preconstituted world, as "eyes" in the Olson sense, that is not just onto a matrix-qua-the world but as operating/projecting/composing activity.) The point is, then, that experience is a dimension necessarily built into language — that far from being avoidable, or a choice, it is a property. So this view attempts to rethink representational or pictorial or behaviorist notions of what "experience" is, i.e., experience is not inextricably linked to representation, normative syntax, images, but rather, the other way around, is a synthetic, generative activity — "in the beginning was the word" & so on, or that's our "limit" of beginnings.

CHARLES BERNSTEIN

NOTES

WARD ON SEATON

Peter Seaton, *Piranesi Pointed Up* (1978; in <u>Roof</u> <u>VIII</u>, The Segue Foundation, 300 Bowery, N.Y., N.Y. 10012; $5)

"Piranesi Pointed Up" and Peter Seaton follows but not before checking out the 'prisons' below, the traditions behind, or the belief/disbelief of the facts all around him. Here, where the sentences are long, bursts lead to bursts, each moment being shoved along by the moment just past and the moment (thought) beginning now. This is seemingly a logical exploration by a writer objectively looking around himself (himself as space as well as time, experience, subjectivity, etc.) and the most objective observation is the impossible suspension or isolation of one experience from all others. The frustration is in the attempt at categorizing to understand or understanding to categorize (very self-consciously); the danger is in a truth*less* conclusion. Hence, the starting over and over, the 'breathers' of short lines which appear periodically offering relief from the dense prose along with a little quieter white space of the page (a more intense reflection). The reader is *left* or *remains* with a very contemporary feeling of anxiety; the experience is honestly ambiguous. As in photography, there is an infinite number of shots; a world made up of different points of the same. The perception of all moments is externalized, projected onto, in an attempt to reconcile each and its apparent indifference to all others: a verbal hologram. A familiar desire to order with an open approach of reciprocity: being observed and observing being observed. There is subjectivity and the consciousness of the will to subjective choice and commentary on subjectivity. All of these are acceptable to Seaton, whose result is a study in perspective, and who seems to say that the next approach is now.

DIANE WARD

*

BLANCHOT

(Lydia Davis recently translated Blanchot's Death Sentence — 1978, Station Hill Press, Barrytown, N.Y. 12507, $4.95. Her translation of his Literary Essays is forthcoming from that press.)

Maurice Blanchot: critic. Moved and provoked by Hegel, Wittengenstein, Kierkegaard, Mallarmé, Proust, Kafka, Hölderlin, he investigates the most fundamental and contradictory problems faced by the writer, and from this inside of writing speaks of such things as the writer's solitude, the act of reading, the act of writing, what is annihilated by the work of literature... "This means: one can only write if one arrives at the instant towards which one can only move through space opened up by the movement of writing." Through such contradiction, through statements vast and cumulative or brief and trenchant, now eloquent, now utterly obscure, now fully revealed, he builds paradox on paradox, turns the fabric of our ideas inside out: language becoming absence, image becoming negation. And Blanchot: novelist. Compellingly exact, mysteriously exact, as though faithful to a memory troubled by delirium, his tales set in surreal landscapes or a real world from which so many facts are missing that this world too becomes unreal. And here men, often half dead, on the edge of death, struggle, with women, with thought, to maintain silence, to maintain solitude or avoid it... "I have shut myself up in a room, alone, there is no one in the house, almost no one outside, but this solitude has itself begun to speak, and I must in turn speak about this speaking solitude, not in derision, but because a greater solitude hovers above it, and above that solitude, another still greater, and each, taking the spoken word in order to smother it and silence it, instead echoes it to infinity, and infinity becomes its echo."

LYDIA DAVIS

*

William Pryor, <u>Unearth</u> (Galloping Dog Press, 3 Otterburn Terrace, Newcastle-upon-Tyne NE2 3AP, England)

The extension of nature into a written work, especially a poem, or, as we have in Pryor's book, a group of poems that infiltrate the close proximity of man with his land, becomes the standard by which we come to understand an ownership; an ownership of dust, of position, of sky, cloud, seed, of the buried palace of the mole.

Pryor's ownership of natural elements is almost rapturously clinical. His poems are written as centres on which the entire descriptive weight has to be slight enough to maintain natural balance. There are no exclamatory procedures involved. What Pryor uses are the thin tracings of a whisper. His voice is attuned to the breeze, to himself breathing.

By looking at Pryor's work this way it becomes meditative and almost naturally mystical. There are, though, other facets to consider when attempting a summary of his work. Pryor's lines are, for the most part, thin; it would be almost possible to cite Creeley as being part influence. The textures are dry. There is no esoteric reference. There is only the immediate recording of time; the natural build-up of scenario which Pryor finds invaluable in his considering of earth.

Pryor's poetry is, as he writes, concerned with the "world's obligations". It has its deep core in physical work. Without that work he would not attune to the obligations the world puts before him in the form of a poem. He writes "... the passion/turns you to activity." In this same way he becomes the "semblance/of a creator." He can allow the poem, and his owning of it, to develop free.

PAUL GREEN

*

Robert Grenier, <u>Oakland</u> (1980; Tuumba Press, 2639 Russell, Berkeley, California 94705; $2)

   The houses in *Oakland* are sentences. The sentences are tangible structual presences standing forth in the world of the work. These poems as collections of sentences constitute varied subdivisions of thought populating neighborhoods of intellect which correlate with the actual places Grenier has lived and the simple pleasures that recognition affords. It was a matter, he writes in a recent letter, of "attempting to really bring the language process to bear on/in the given in Oakland — i.e. it's all true! — what the words could see & hear/make & be in that sense of Olson's as I see it in 'Causal Mythology' (*Muthologos*, pp. 94-95) that 'the literal ('where we are') is the same as the numeral' ('the discovery of formal structual means' — i.e., numbers, verse), although how such comes about: is always 'a mystery'."

        EYES

        open the door Oakland

is thus an appropriate beginning point for the book. The door opens wide on the language process that is operative here and one is taken by it: outside.
   Grenier's technical finesse with these little lyrics is that he renders with absolute clarity the language's physicality through reference to the simplest of acts — walking, say:

              A ROUND

              the block

One is reminded of Fenollosa's statement that "poetry must render what is said, not what is merely meant."

Talking is that activity, as physical as walking, which *gets* one to look, that activity which projects the intelligence as literal fact into the world: it is a source of extension and focus both. Talking to *put things forth*. Talking to *see*. This is the nearest analogue I can make to Grenier's work: in his poems he is talking a walk as it were.

FOCUSSING ON OBJECTS

that's not really green

that is green

that's green

And this is how sequence is resolved in the work and what occasions that which is *found* there.

TOM BECKETT

*

GRENIER'S BOOK DOESN'T

like simile

MAYBELLINE EYE

lining

pencil

m-e-t *a p-h-y-s-i-q-u-e*

ALLAN TINKER

*

CHARLES AMIRKHANIAN, Lexical Music (1979; 1750 Arch Records, Berkeley, CA)

This album is a fine collection of works done by one of the best, well known text-sound composers active in the world today. Since the late sixties, Charles Amirkhanian has been producing word pieces which are distinctive in their verbal/phonetic inventiveness, rhythmic "catchiness", and polished technical proficiency. The six pieces on Lexical Music are representational of the variety of Amirkhanian's work in the

431

seventies ranging from the abstract vocalisms of <u>Mugic</u> and the intense superimposed word rhythms of <u>Muchrooms</u>, <u>She She and She</u>, and <u>Seatbelt, Seatbelt</u> to the syntactical-rhythmical deformations of the live performance piece <u>Dutiful Ducks</u> and the 'de-referentialized" word and phonetic fragments mixed with "environmental" recordings that are in <u>Mahogany Ballpark</u>. All the works are marked by an impeccable craftsmanship in recording technique and the album as a whole is one of the best produced records presently available in sound poetry.

LARRY WENDT

*

MAYER ON HEJINIAN

Lyn Hejinian, <u>My Life</u> (1980; Burning Deck, 71 Elmgrove Ave., Providence, R.I. 02906; $3.50)

Reading a book, after you read it, is like saying, I swallowed that one whole. It can be worse than a pill or like receiving many pennies in the change you get & then you have to carry them around making yourself heavy though I read walking with between 6 & 13 lbs. in your pack or bag is supposed to be good for you. Then somebody else told me an ounce a year is added to your weight from all the things in the foods that stay in your body so by now I must've read three extra pounds of books I cant use, at least. Sometimes I like to read a book that has information in it but when I'm reading a novel, for instance, I dont want to be learning about, say, a foreign place. Besides poetry, prose books that arent novels & also arent about any subject are the best ones. I'd been thinking that at least in poetry there's no such thing as autobiography, and very often not in prose either because even if you write about yourself if you're really writing you are being the medium. Also the idea to have to write is a willful sexual thing, never devoid of emotion unless you take the will out of it & then it's a trinket or perhaps a good experiment. Maybe syntax is even necessary to give pleasure to the movement of will. Maybe simplicity & a form seem, at the moment, to be a return. MY LIFE is too a daring title. MY LIFE has a kind of cunning that leads in all these directions I'd been thinking about when I found it & read it. It's a timely book in the momentary literary sense & it also has everything in it. The structure is an interweaving in a kind of rapid-fire overlapping of memory with all its points & phrases that makes, you could almost say a picture, that winds up having what you might call a discrete uniformity if you were writing about a picture. It's knotted & knitted & it's completed. It moves fast, it's full of sentences like "the dog digs dirt" & "not a fuck but a hug", but it's also full of gerunds which give to emotion (& that will that makes forms able to proceed humanly) as we know from Gertrude Stein. There is something almost wish-

432

fully neat about it, childlike & apt, which is like the idea of courting
& denying autobiography & becoming as an I-character in a book, nearly
perfect, which one might fault except that it is continuous & "for we who
love to be astonished," all the childlikeness, almost out of pure information, remains intact. The author is both new in her language concerns
& managing to say things cleanly. It's like the opposite of Proust, no,
it's like a sprightly Proust, a speedy Proust, no less jogging. MY LIFE
has so many good lines in it, it's like a trot, it makes you want to
steal from it or perhaps annotate it & make the compliment (or complement) of imitating it.

BERNADETTE MAYER

*

from PACK THE SHUFFLING

Allen Fisher, Becoming (Aloes Books, distributed by Nick Kimberley,
16A Burleigh Parade, London N14, U.K.; 2.65 pounds)

These sets, "being most of place book IIII & much of book V", return us
to Allen's survival programme, already given a showing in *Place Book I*
(1974, reprinted Truck Press 1976) and *Stane* (Place Book III) (1977,
Aloes Books), among others. The method of production is, as always,
important: use of litho plates as a direct medium for composition, and
of green, brown-red and black inks on the buff pages to identify and
differentiate sets; because the sets (METE, LOGOS:MOTHER:MATTER, GAIT,
UTTER) have been shuffled, re-shuffled, cut into each other, have had
sections removed and replaced with extraneous material from other parts of
the work.... As system is laid over system, the effect — in the decade
or so over which publication is expected — is to lay bare the artist's
constant and living revision of his own work, meant as praxis and not
object. But no, not that only; it also invites the reader's participation in the construction of the text, because there can be no one order
of reading....
   Now all this runs the risk of being excessively schematic - were it
not for the random and quasi-random actions that are allowed to interfere,
to set up unexpected phase patterns. *Mistakes* are a crucial element in the
mix.... (Biological evolution takes as its starting point a mistake in
the genetic chain.) It's presented ironically:

> there are moves underway
>   to clean up the
> to remove any concept of operational mistakes

and linked a few pages later with a critique of the social Darwinists'
defence of Victorian capitalism by way of their mischievous appeal to
"the natural":

```
"Clean up the centre ..
"Sugar-dust the page ..
"move out the feeble ..
Herbert Spencer, Malthus, Cyril Burt
Rockefeller debudding minor blooms in the rosary

method of "Nature" equals
    method of "Society"
brick walls capped in jagged glass
    concealed by perspective
the unfit prevented from breathing
    a "natural selection"                          (METE, p. 15)
```

I hope this is enough to convince that "place" is here no simplistic "roots" position. Sure, it's South London, the living and repressed history of its working class, the fields of force, the changing buildings. Dates permeate the book: 1806, 1937, 1837, 1337, 1820-1, 1811, 3000 BC, 1802, 1647, 1843, 1823, 1871, 1000 AD, 1926, 1862, 1863, 1879, 1800, 1851, 1856, 1901. Turn to the extraordinary "Samuel Matthews" section, the voice of an eighteenth century vagrant testifying like a South London Dutch Schultz. But place is cut-in tapes, snatches of radio; converging... and diverging....

The seriousness of the research, the clarity of the thought, the fine political awareness of language. It's there to be met with, multivalent. In a moving coda, and without the metaphysical bullshit of Eliot, Allen finishes: "what had begun/began again" It's an invitation I shall be taking up.

KEN EDWARDS

*

AND FOR ANYTHING THAT I COULD CALL MY OWN THINKING

[For example, composing from Frank Kuenstler's Lens (available from Film Culture, GPO Box 1499, NY, NY 10001; $2) — B.A.]

It is less a draft than the scenario of a monument. "the enormous paste-up job". cap.Italics. fade.Aura. the world is invisible.RR. rr.The image disintegrated before desire. fact.I. lax.Icon. ray gun.Mental. image.Nation. maze.I. mm.Eye. abhor.Original. the girl with a soul is the picture of ideology. i'm.Personal. film.Ilytch. The dialectic is reel. gregarious.Chance. image.Urgency. rr.The man on the train is Lenin. contes.Addiction. harm.Money. My image suffers. myth.Take. lex.Icon. reap.Production. mirror.Clause. reign.Code. the messengers photograph words.RR. horror.Culture. *f*.Fetter. camera.Suture vain.—

Indicative. the man on the train is by definition an image of arrested motion.RR art.Effect. dire.Critical. fate.Schism. person.Atonality. i'm.Machination. limb.Imitation. lens.Fragment. essay on language.Help. The opium of the public is opinion. reality.I. impute.Tense. sign.-Tittilate. lesions.RR. Neoclassicism is pornographic. The anti-image is architecture. the object of alientation is movies.RR. epistle.-Millenium. messiah.Semantics. praxis.Light. the shape of the thing pursued is the ultimate metaphor.RR. ardor.Fact. bourgeois.Objectivism. is so, man is an imitation of work.RR. rr.The world is fragmented into people. camera.Forage. rr.The hero is the carrier of style. speech.-Theatre. flicker.Recognition. snow maiden.Photography. rr.Chipped and redundant. the world is the resource of poetry.RR. ..., a function of repression.RR. The cinematographer arranges the terms of the beautiful. trouble spelled backwards is fragment.RR. obstacle.Illusion. there's no arguing with television.RR. error.Edition. The movies taught me lone-liness. reef.Lexicon. The first screening of *Potemkin* in the US was on Gloria Swanson's bedsheet. pointillism.Pilot. my.Optic. cinema.Topo-graphy. denude.Moment. image.Entrails. time is of the.RR. rr.The man on the train is a figure of speech. lens.Epistemology. punk.Situation. vamp.Empire. The lens being ground is the axe of theory. rr.The world is a negative image of reality. cinematic.Symptomatic. light was resis-tance.RR. noose.Thalia. marxian.Oneupmanship. corn.Sequence. corn.-Volition. semen.Antics. human.Naziism. postpone.Indoctrination. rr.-The language picture is germane. the pyramid of appearances makes man dream.RR. rr.An image of refracted action. labor.Division. picture.-Characters. frame.Minerology. negative.Italic. rr.Reproduction is the imitation of alienation. AAA.then.

FRANK KUENSTLER

FUTURIST IDEOGRAPH

(Ron Padgett has translated from the French this 1914 essay from Gino Severini's Témoignages, *Editions Art Moderne, Rome, 1963)*

With the drawing "parolibero" (liberated words) published in the July 1914 issue of Lacerba I was not trying to bring a plastic pictorial element into literature or a literary element into painting.

I was suggesting the possibility of finding a new and autonomous form of literary expression. Later this possibility defined itself clearly for me.

Until now the literary innovations of Marinetti and the other Futur-ist poets used more or less the conventional typographical characters, as well as mathematical symbols, arranging them according to emotional laws.

One would have thought this was a basic innovation, when in fact it was only partial, and more apparent than real.

If we want to express a *new realism* which is a synthesis of our time, we must create a *new lyricism*, expressed with new tools, forged from A to Z and entirely different from those used until now.

We, the painters, destroyed painting a long time ago (painting as it was known from the Renaissance to our time). Now it is time for you, poets and writers, to destroy literature.

We must renew our tools, forge new ones which correspond to our needs.

Hence in your domain you must enlarge your means; that is, add new characters or new typographical expressions to those already in use, to suit the need for a synthesis of the absolute realism which is our goal.

I'm not thinking of any new pictorial system : we mustn't confuse images and appearances, the representation of ideas and the representation of forms.

Until now, written literature has used the same sounds as the spoken language, which is where I think it errs. Since the realism we seek is never separated from external reality to the point where it no longer has anything to do with it, we will have to find special signs to express this realism, signs totally invented and accepted as conventions, and which will express not an act, for example the fact of running (exterior life), but the *idea* of running (interior life).

When I say idea I do not mean it in the sense of appearance; for that one need merely depict two legs in the process of running.

The idea of running is in fact much greater than the *appearance* of the running. The idea is limitless, universal.

It is commonly known that the first written language was with pictures. To communicate, one drew an animal, an object, a being or whatever. This process led not only to a generalization of the idea, but also, to a formal expression, better suited to express a universal concept than a practical need.

In time, these methods of expression for our way of life were perfected, and now we must put them aside to find methods of expression for our art. By that I don't mean we should go back to writing with pictures, although this barbaric medium is extremely attractive and it is impossible to renovate without becoming barbaric again, even unwillingly. Even then this self-expression through signs representing objects would become a sort of symbolic writing.

The method of using new methods of synthetic lyricism to express the intense realism of our emotions was suggested to me by my drawing "parolibero" in which I *voluntarily* associated closed forms and acute angles with particular words, round shapes or obtuse angles with other words.

Just as we have colors and shapes in painting which synthesize, for example, all of spring, or simply joy, or warmth, etc., we also

Formes qui ne représent pas une danseuse en mouvement, mais le *mouvement*
en tant que sensation dynamique elle-même (1913)

have in literature methods which reunite groups of lyric elements, or dynamic literary continuations.

For instance, in "parolibero", the drawing in question, the sensations of luminous penetration in the two electric searchlights, to which are associated the penetration of two Mauser bullets as they whiz through space, are rendered by the contrast of two acute angles meeting at their tips.

Every analogical sensation associated with the idea of brutal penetration can be rendered by two acute angles.

In this same area of the drawing, for the onomatopoeia szszszszsz... expressing the whizzing bullets and the violent beam of light, I had to write the letters with little dashes instead of continuous letters. For me these dashes had a value of intensity (quantitative), just as I obtain a plastic intensity with brush strokes using analogous colors in a shape. To carry this intuition even further we need to construct new signs expressing qualitative quantities. Then these signs would become conventional and the work would be understood. After all, aren't numbers, letters, subdivisions of time and space all conventions?

Each period should have its new conventions, or else we are all doomed to simple narration. The goal of literature is to find images through words, just as that of painting is to evoke appearances through shapes.

Obviously it would be impossible to read the words of this new lyricism, but can we read paintings, can the musician read a symphony, can we read the song of a bird?

The new lyrical work will evoke universal ideas and not the sounds of spoken language. We leave these sounds to lawyers (the art of oratory) and to entertainers.

Besides, isn't it another convention to describe as *sound* those sensations, registered by the ear, of a hammer noise?

Currently, with the laws of simultaneity which we have discovered in ourselves, this word *sound* has become meaningless, whereas the particular sensation evoked in us by hammer blows can determine in our *sensibility* groups of analogical *ideas* (and for a painter groups of appearances) which bear no resemblance to the sound, nor with the wham-wham impressionistic expression of this sound. This is how I foresee the possibility of creating a new *ideography*, to be a geometric graphic expression of universal ideas.

My intuition is naturally based on the concept of the absolute dynamism of matter, a dynamism which can be expressed geometrically, as in painting, but without designating its limits.

GINO SEVERINI

AN ANSWER TO SOME REMARKS OF RON SILLIMAN ABOUT POLITICS & MY SUPPOSED POSITION

(This continues an exchange started in issue #7 and continuing in #8 and #9/10.)

Ron Silliman has a polemical advantage over me insofar as he thinks he knows what the good society would be like and has a "program" whose implementation he believes will bring about such a society. He seems to think it's up to the rest of us to sense from the context of his remarks the nature of this preferred society and program. He certainly sounds like some kind of Leninist, and since most Leninists are either some kind of Stalinist or some kind of Trotskyist, I don't think he should be surprised that I treated his remarks as coming from an adherent of one of those positions.

(I might add that I don't find the two positions basically dissimilar in the light of Trotsky's actions when in power, such as his takeover of the railway unions— ending what seems to have been a surprisingly suc= cessful worker organization and management of the railway system of much of European Russia and turning it over to Bolshevik bureaucrats and bourgeois managers— and his bloody repression of the Kronstadt sailors.)

Moreover, Silliman's use of the terms "social democrat" and "anarcho-social democrat" as pejorative epithets for such diverse pacifists as myself and the group editing and producing Win magazine is only paralleled in my experience by such usage in the mouths and writings of Stalinists (using the term in the very general sense which includes supporters of all oligarchic state "socialisms," including those founded by Mao, Tito, and Castro) and Trotskyists. Ron's remarks imply that he is neither— and I believe him— but he does not make clear the nature of the "working-class state" idealism he *does* espouse, beyond saying that he endorses the concept of a dictatorship of a working class that has somehow seized state power.

Ron seems to believe that such a state would allow him to continue to write and publish his kind of poetry and to reach the predominantly middle-class male audience he now addresses. I find this both touching and mind-boggling. Why in the world does he think that a working-class dictatorship would be so unlike other dictatorships, including the party oligarchies now ruling many countries in the name of the working class?

If the working class in this country should seize and exercise state power — even in the best manner conceivable: "as a whole," in the form of workers' councils or the like — why would it tolerate the continuance of bourgeois art activities such as Ron's or mine, even though such activities constitute implied critiques of alienated language usage? This would require that a bourgeois society would have educated its working class to such a level that a majority would understand that such art activities were in harmony with (or at least not opposed to) its revolutionary aims. If such were the case, the revolution itself would have largely been a mere formality. The presumably "bourgeois" social system which it had overthrown would already have embodied most — or at least many — of the goals of the revolution.

I just don't believe it. It seems much more probable that a revolutionary working-class dictatorship would consider language experimentation an undesirable remnant of the old bourgeois state of things and would suppress it along with other vestiges of the old order. I believe that an attitude such as Amiri Baraka's toward "bourgeois art" would be likely to be enforced by even an internally democratic working-class dictatorship. At best it might "tolerate" such activity as long as it remained peripheral and private — a kind of "hobby" to be pursued in time not devoted to societally approved productive work.

But the likelihood that language artwork would be considered "productive" or that language artists would be supported for their artwork by a working-class dictatorship seems to me very small indeed. I suspect that language artists would have no public support for their work and that private support would be difficult if not impossible to organize. We'd be even worse off than we are now.

My own opinion is that some form of "Stalinism" or "bureaucratic oligarchy" would be the probable result of the setting up of any revolutionary state in the name of the working class. I don't know whether or not Ron endorses the idea of a vanguard party. Most supporters of a working-class dictatorship do. In any case, I know of no evidence to support the idea that such a party, if it should gain power, would not develop into a political-economic "class" in whose hands state power would constitute a dictatorship *over* the working class and everyone else. I cannot understand anyone's discounting the experience of the last 80 years by attributing the existence of the political-economic ("bureaucratic") oligarchies presently controlling so-called socialist states merely to a degenerative disease called "Stalinism" — i.e., the evil ways of certain power-mad bureaucrats and party leaders.

Does Ron accept the argument that none of the countries in which such revolutions have taken place were sufficiently developed? — that true socialism — in which power would somehow be exercised by the working class "as a whole," although members of other classes would be excluded from exerting political power — *could* not have come about yet in any of the countries presently saddled with "socialist" oligarchies? — that only advanced nations such as the United States, Japan, or the EEC could undergo "real" socialist revolutions leading to (presumably benevolent) working-class dictatorships?

To all arguments for the continuing possibility that a violent Marxist-led revolution could lead to a desirable state of society — one in which there would be no poverty, exploitation, or war and in which political and economic power would be exercised equally by all members of society, which would, by then, be "classless" — I can only reply with the question: *"Why do you think so?"*

As against those who have undergone the Marxist gnosis, I *do not know* how such a society could be brought about or even *whether it is possible,* except in part. Ron is quite right in noting that — unlike social democrats, by the way, who think they can bring it about by working within parliamentary systems to vote in some form of democratically controlled state socialism — I have no program.

Milovan Djilas, in <u>The Unperfect Society</u>, radically questions the notion of political activity aimed at bringing about a perfect society. I cite his book for this reason and because he includes in it an impressive refutation of historical (or "dialectical") materialism. I have not had the opportunity or time to read Lefevre's book which Ron cites, so I do not know whether his and Djilas' arguments are mutually relevant, but, as I remember it, Djilas' refutation is a general one.

The fact that Djilas was formerly a Stalinist and may still consider himself, in a limited sense of the word, a "socialist," is irrelevant to his exemplification of an "agnostic" politics as against the various modern political gnosticisms, "right" and "left."

To say, as Ron does, that a political agnostic is "ungrounded" is either a tautology ("not to know" = "not to be grounded") or an unwarranted kind of name-calling. To say that I believe in "maintaining" poverty, exploitation, and war because I *don't know* of any political economy without them or any political-economic "program" likely to abolish them is an astonishing misuse of language.

I no longer believe that Ron and I share as many "long-term goals" as I formerly did, since he specifically endorses a *dictatorship* of the working class (over those considered outside that class). However, what I *thought* we had in common was a belief in the *desirability* of ending poverty, exploitation, coercion, and war ("'Capitalism,'" writes Lorenzo two pages away from Ron, "is a snobbish term for poverty and exploitation. A fiction.") and of maximizing people's control over their own lives and living and working conditions. To me this implies a maximization of opportunities for the exercise of initiative in all areas of life. As such, these "goals" seem equally incompatible with both "capitalism" and "socialism" as we've known them hitherto.

Utopian capitalists ("libertarians" such as Murray Rothbard) claim that the oligarchies presently controlling the capitalist world — the interlocking directorates of the banks, conglomerates, and multinational corporations and the leaders of the political parties, government bureaucracies, armies, and police forces — are in power because of government interference with the free marketplace. Utopian socialists (by which I mean supporters of theoretical systems of socialism that have never yet been realized in any country) claim that in societies falsely calling themselves "socialist," the party leaders, economic managers, generals, etc., have been able to consolidate their oligarchic ruling classes by forcefully subverting socialist institutions. In both cases it is claimed that the faulty nature of the actual societies is due to *interference*

with the basically "good" economic systems — not to the faulty natures of
the systems themselves.

If bankers and industrialists can acquire overwhelming economic power,
it seems certain that they will also largely control political life,
even in societies with built-in countervailing powers. However, in the
United States, the divisions within the economic/political elite, the
relative autonomy of the three branches of government provided for by the
US Constitution, and the guarantees of basic rights comprised in its
amendments prevent the "ruling class" or any segment of it from exercising
absolute hegemony. Various aspects of the present systems of expression,
governance, production, distribution, etc., can be criticised, exposed,
and opposed in manifestations as diverse as anti-nuclear-power demonstrations and language art (on the "left") and anti-busing demonstrations and
Nazi rallies (on the "right"), as well as in publications expressing a very
wide range of political and social opinions and attitudes.

I do not think this diversity of expression and action is meaningless.
It is a positive and desirable feature of so-called "bourgeois democracies"
that is absent from capitalist societies that have a relatively small and
unified ruling class in full control of the state apparatus and from
"socialist" societies in which both the state and the economic system are
controlled by authoritarian parties claiming to rule in the name of the
proletariat.

Such a diversity must be an essential feature of any society that I
can think of as desirable. I do not see how it can be a part of any
society ruled by a dictatorship, even a working-class dictatorship (grant-
ing the extremely unlikely premise that a "dictatorship" can be exercised
by the working class "as a whole"). Such features must be preserved in
any transition toward a juster, less exploitative, less coercive, and less
violent society. One must move out from what is positive in the present
situation. There is no such thing as a perfect society, but there can be
a better one.

JACKSON MAC LOW

LETTERS TO THE EDITOR

from WOMEN WRITERS UNION: STATEMENT OF PURPOSE

The Women Writers Union is a group of feminist writers in the Bay Area.
We came together because the lives and history and writing of women have
been suppressed and ignored for centuries. Since women have been thoroughly silenced as a group, the expression of our ideas and experience
is central to the movement for our liberation. We recognize that not

only have women been silenced as a sex, we have been oppressed -- and silenced -- on the basis of our race, our class, and our sexuality. Therefore, we are particularly concerned that the voices of lesbians, working women and women of color be heard.

We first organized at San Francisco State University in 1975. Since then we have evolved into a community-based organization.... We believe that art and politics cannot be separated, but that each enriches the other. Accordingly, we have been active in a number of struggles, including benefits for the Cassandra Peten Defense Fund and the Wendy Yoshimura Defense Fund. We have also participated in the Gay Freedom Day March and an abortion rights demonstration. We hold forums which stress the connection between art and the struggle against racism, sexism and classism.... The Women Writers Union holds a members' workshop, gives readings, and offers classes in writing, open to all women. In the planning stages, are an anthology of our work and a regular series of forums...

In connecting art to politics, the Women Writers Union maintains that a multi-issue approach is necessary, that the struggles are not separate, but are one and the same. We are not separatists: our forums and readings are open to all. We believe in the power of words to persuade, to educate and to help unite all of us in our struggle. *(For more information, contact: Nellie Wong, 1744 9th Ave., Oakland, Ca. 94606.)*

WOMEN WRITERS UNION

POETRY: A JOB DESCRIPTION

From the standpoint of being a poet, what is interesting about poetry today is that it is the occupation most completely without professional status in our society. "Poet" is a term without social resonance for us, aside from a few very old ones that, fading and fading, still impart a certain aroma. For the individual it can sanely mean only "poem-writer": "... his writings make him a poet, not his acting of the role," Frank O'Hara wrote -- not that there's any role to act anymore, so the choice isn't so noble. The only true choice I see (after rejecting out of hand the ways of the academy) is in how to think about it -- whether to see oneself as a member of a little tribe of atavists or band of subversives, on the one hand, or really completely alone and slipping through the interstices of the world, on the other. I aspire to think the latter way, which has the advantage of opening on the most nearly total freedom. Admittedly, it is also close to thinking nothing at all.

It is, with all due modern irony, the course of the Sublime. The economic and, outside its craft-ghettos, the social insubstantiality of poetry may be fecund if, looking them in the eye, one continues to take poetry seriously. There is a certain light-heartedness in this, as in contemplating the present world -- for instance, that it is inhabited now by 4 *billion* or so of us humans -- and in treating one's individual life, a thing of no consequence, seriously nonetheless. Now, the Sublime is a thought you can make nothing *of*, which is the point. It's an escape from the toils of any other thought, any minor seriousness -- and that would include all attempts to justify the vocation of poetry. It is precisely in being unjustifiable in present "real" terms -- meaningless in relation to the minor seriousness of a given social order -- that poetry may have something -- some deep, funny, surprising consolations -- to offer.

This is why poet clannishness distresses me: people just throwing away their one and only significant advantage in rites of terminal pettiness and boredom. That advantage is a detachment, and a stamina, for the highest existential fun -- licensed irresponsibility of thought. What could be better? Why doesn't anyone seem to want it?

PETER SCHJELDAHL

HOWE ON OWEN

Maureen Owen, Hearts in Space (1980; Kulchur Foundation, 888 Park Ave., N.Y., N.Y. 10021; $7 & $3.50 paper)

                                          Go out
        into the grasslands!   Fear has ruined everything here.
        I lost my knife and the dog is worthless
        like a brilliant and sensational misunderstanding
        THE GREAT EMPTINESS   is out there   decorated with
        celestial grandeur

American to her backbone, Maureen Owen is an Irish poet of the open road.

Born and brought up on a small farm in Minnesota, the vast green space of this her first landscape - Dorn's "plain of the green heart", the American heartland ruled by a glorious ever-changing sky - is central to the spirit of freshness and daring in her work. Owen's heart, like Oz/ Dorothy's house, is a place where the North and South winds meet - center of the cyclone - although winds (wandering) may carry her faraway. Speed of light and word sounds, a constant. The only constant - constantly changing.

```
folks here swig beer     swap tales     continuously
assessing the liklihood that several events
are related    a repeated & regular significance
surrounded by the whooping of the wind
```

Her poems walk a brink where sense and nonsense meet. In Nature's miscellany and mystery, nuances affirm and warn.

```
             In the vulnerable aftermath of dinner   She
has indicated the V of swords     a tremendous struggle
where we stand  exhausted   leaning on flexed & sagging knees
   while our enemies rush towards the edge of the card.
      Triumph is relative     Lao Tzu warns from his cloud
"Success and failure are the same disease"
```

Hearts in Space consists of five sections of loosely related poems. The
first, and strongest, is more than half the book. At the outset *Handscroll
with ink and colours on silk* - where "having made the choice   you
simply live   accordingly." Owen's passion for miscellany is apparent.
A precise miscellany. Differences that resemble, peculiarities that interact. The poems are a maze of patterned paths. Song titles, children's
games, quotations, letters, biographies, japanese handscrolls, rolls of
toilet paper, movies, items from the police blotter, from the newspaper,
lists from field guides to birds, bushes, trees - an American jargon; all
the crazy variety each day brings to a woman who is a poet who is a
mother wife editor publisher daughter sister farmer housewife and
WASC (white anglo saxon commuter) is warp and woof.

From a poem dedicated to her six month old son:

```
Five minutes
Into the chapter                              males were
referred to as men     but females were referred to as wives
I remember blurting out at the party     "I have no father"
With a tremendous sense of relief!    From Grandmother     to
mother     I have passed down.  Born of and through women alone.
We have     crawled under the barbed wire          & sat
on our own   sacred land!
```

Virginia Woolf once said: "It is fatal for a woman to lay the least stress
on any grievance; to plead even with justice any cause; in any way to
speak consciously as a woman; and fatal is no figure of speech; for anything written with that conscious bias is doomed. It ceases to be fer-
tilized." Woolf wrote *A Room of One's Own*, but her vision was *The Light-
house* and *The Waves*, and her light shines for me in the letters of that
quotation. A message about Mystery, to those of us who are women and
poets. How do we navigate our way? How do we crawl under the barbed wire
and sit on our own sacred land? What unity will we pull from multiplicity?

What dreams? What new language? Who ever (female *or* male) knew for SURE what was left, right, center, true, false? It is in such questioning that really interesting work occurs. Women who are poets of the calibre of Owen, recognize the precious gift of their UNcertainty. To interlace a poem with quest and roam. Owen roams. She never complains or pleads a cause. She is too busy wondering, discovering, cataloging, condensing, controlling.

                    The days go by   they give us more
        and more   and more to lose   You lose!   This is not always
        a tragedy.   Beyond a certain point   it is impossible
        to live at face value   in the end it will be the length
        of our extravagance   that allows us to imitate   at last
        the masculine impatience!

The energy, wit, and surrealistic power let loose in Hearts in Space are as changing as the sky of her primal landscape. In the best of these poems every word is necessary, every fragment right. A balance of economy and generosity. Dizzy and direct. They leave a wake of shadows suggesting more meaning in reserve. Life's fresh and faulty elegance in a world where (as her son Patrick tells her) "Houdini walked through a brick wall everyday."

SUSAN HOWE

WRITING AND CONCEIVING

Natasha: They ordered me not to see you again.
Lemmy: Who? The Alpha 60 engineers?
Natasha: Yes.
Lemmy: What makes you afraid?
Natasha: I'm afraid because I know a word...without having seen it or read it.
                    from *Alphaville*, a film by Jean-Luc Godard

    All experience is conditioned by expectation. The meaning of an interval of experience is defined throughout by the implied or covert meaning of its end. The tension of an interval arises out of the anxiety of evolving a meaning for an event. Ravel confounds this process not by employing an obsessive doubting or repetition of themes, but by allowing a focussed uncertainty to remain. The rhythms are not halting or arbitrary yet they may be felt as not quite intended or distracted but determinedly so, not just tentatively. He gains the continuity ordinarily

obtained through a form that tantalizes with eventual resolution by arousing different levels of dreaminess and wakefulness. We wake from a dream
to enter, clearly, a daydream.

*

Writing ordinarily stresses its function of "righting" the meanings
of words and word combinations. But the graphic materials of writing
also have a mapping and marking function. As records are evidence, the
reified word is a token of identity.

The sign distributes the imaged perception as an imprint transferable to the "scratching" of thought against the cave walls of the mind.
Signs transmute imaged perception into thought: at the terminus points,
always approximate, always tautological.

Each subdivision of an interval is discrete when it is noticed over
time, but the remaining subdivisions are more blurred when specific ones
are selected for focus. Similarly, a grapheme within a nominal phrase
such as a headline or a title would be conditioned by the phrases subsequently selected for emphasis. In present consciousness any subdivision
of an intervallic constellation can exist in any combination of the three
temporal dimensions or are apperceptively consigned to temporal mutability.
The same is true for the relativity between intervals of script and all the
hierarchical organizations within the text. The more general inscription
(such as a headline, a title or a chapter, or the capital letter at the
beginning of a line in a poem) conditions the mode of focussing the related text. The equivalent in remembering is the hierarchical arrangement
of significance. The base word of significance is *sign*.

Poetry is a graphic form of unrighting the publicly codified coloca-
tion of grapheme with symbolized ordinary writing and speech usage and the
imaging function of the mind. The conceptual experience of a poem causes
a reconnection with the acausal, atemporal conceiving of meaning by reap-
portioning the relative values of the scalar organizing function of the
perceiving process and the inscriptive, defining level of pre-conscious
verbal imaging.

*

It is a certain tone I am after, embellished by persistent varying
shades of association. I repeat it as I am hearing it in a kind of suspended listening, paying attention to and allowing to dissolve certain
obsessive memories. Deductions, or rather, reductions or vapors like
these, afterwards seem immediately familiar, pre-cognitive, felt throughout an extended dejà-vu atmosphere during an imploded time sequence. The
puzzle is attempted *only once* in order for the observers to immediately
witness its decomposition. It is a simultaneous recording, unwinding and
playing, joining and dismantling, similarities momentarily continuing to
hold sway throughout or just long enough after an initial and suddenly
heightened series of contrasts. Such points of connection are heard in

447

specific invariable tones and intervals. The names of these sounds and
feelings may be the objects and words memories attach themselves to. But
the feelings that yearned for those names, the ones that offer themselves
later as keepsakes are really more memorable. Not the images which are
now absent, but the thawing and sketching around that in coming times
will be added to the fondness which grows around such replacements for the
quality of the actual event. Anonymous, the words and exalted rituals
plaintively repeating them.

Lexic qualities of... Semantic qualities of... Signal qualities of...
Structuralizing qualities of... Quality of constructibility into family
systems... Geneaology of... History of connection with lexic qualities
of meaning... Graphic qualities of... Quality of distribution...

Distribution of naming to order spatially... Distribution of naming to
remind... Distribution of naming to induce... Distribution of naming
to attract... Distribution of naming to direct connection to identification...

Naming that orders... Naming that connotes possession (control, ownership)... Possession of names... Erosion of names... Ambiguity of
names... Plurality of names...

Naming, identifying, recording, delimiting, describing, describes,
humanness of, clarifies, evokes feeling, vocal qualities of, musical
qualities of

*

The activities of the mind associated with the recording and verification of the relationship between identity and physical space are
governed by memory and the verbal technology necessary to preserve it.
To repeat (chant, sing) the trace, is to elicit a vision of prophecy.
The function of poetry is not only to enlighten but also to point us in
the direction of the mind for the sources of the enlightenment. Poetic
composition is an activity which subtly alters the rules that govern
the relationship between the ordering of thought and allowing it to
swoon into reverie. Remembering is at its base a connective mode of
cognition. From this is expropriated its power to order, to value, to
record, to create, to historicize, to catalogue, describe, recreate,
make safe, controllable and distant, - to *signify*.

*

As many times as I try to grasp my solitude, I am abruptly thrown
into the image of the Other and its absence, mute spectator. Or just as
suddenly to stop, trapped in the spectacle of my fear of his/her absence,
the patient, responsive, loving Other situated at the side of all that
is depriving. To switch so suddenly is to plunge into the mercy of a
simple truth: as neutral as the irrational is the subtly perfect, the
preposition of all imposters, clown of confusion, enigmatic signature of

incomprehension.

*

18.   Salvaged debris.
23.   Moisture, remainders, dew, condensation.
24.   Reference points on a map, questions of materials, accident

*

All of his/her reading experience is summoned forth in the mind of the writer. Against this recital of his/her thought lay all the significant moments of his/her speech — from the first cries to, and from, the mother to the syntactical complexity of his/her most heartfelt account of his/her experience — these moments mark the boundaries of one's language.

To read is to practice a mental resonance between language, thought and memory. As in ordinary thought, to read need not be simply to systematically connect mental processes to their current contexts but to other, related aspects of present or past experience. Such an idiosyncratic variation in reading any text is inevitable, especially in re-reading.

Memory becomes history when the impact of events is such that the remembered event is still having its impact when the memory is triggered and is more multiply caused by immediate necessity. History is necessary when memory threatens to fail. Memory is aroused by emotional and physical need. As culture (apparently) changes more rapidly, more attention must be concentrated on the meaning of the shifts. When we are insecure about the memory function we invoke historical (ordering) paradigms.

*

Sometimes I allow somebody else, in some way, to speak through me. I know the somebody else is me, but I also know that some information is coming through that perhaps was picked up peripherally, or has been forgotten and is silently colliding and thus combining with something else. The other voice during the conception of a thought before the wording has taken on specificity. A high altitude photograph and then a zoom-in for details. This permits initially irrelevant details to later enter the framework.

"The scale of the Spiral Jetty tends to fluctuate depending on where the viewer happens to be. Size determines an object, but scale determines art... When one refuses to release scale from size, one is left with an object that *appears* to be certain. For me scale operates by uncertainty. To be in the scale of the Spiral Jetty is to be out of it." (p. 112, *The Writings of Robert Smithson*, New York University Press, 1979.)

*

The sentence is a prison term
Why poetry made of fragments
Irreducible crystal forms
Lesson. Intermittent continuous connection
That's why subtract (subtext) poetry
Instead of abstract
Seems made of starting
Hemisphere at images
Spring-like or spring

Remembrances
A pause, faces opposites
Little askew, a tilt
Framing reflection out of
Mirror, less a, wanting, unwound
Each vulnerable, venerable
Split atom

Cars   Skates

Bikes

Trolleys

*

Writing is reading. I live in a world of signs which acausally
direct my consciousness. Thought is writing, just as thinking is proto-
linguistic. Thought is reading just as listening enforces a transposition
of an interval of related sounds into a specific inner focus of attention.
Writing silences a babel of voices each of which calls attention to its
own point of origin. At the root of all comprehension exists an indeterminate number of possible meanings which are coming into being, into
consciousness. All understanding or visual or aural recognition contains
within it an underlying chaotically disordered core in flux, moving as
a system of connected points toward an entropic state of inertia, a stable
pattern.

All systematized language is oppressive insofar as it supports ideologically based repression. Repression serves psychic economy. To
"forget" the origin of a meaning, or its specific and unique context,
is to suppress energy directed towards associative expansion and purposive
expression, that is, the purpose is blurred as is the associative gestalt.

Thinking, reading and writing are forms of preconscious play. Thinking itself, which is imagined to accompany reading, is synchronistically
tilted, one moment toward, the next, away from, experience. Like speaking, reading and writing, thinking is imagined to be a translation of
experience. But this translation does not completely evolve apposite
to experience. The sign constantly displays its maddening ability to out-

wit its supposed "associated" thought, and as its creator seizes on the reminiscence of its genesis, the acausal connecting process of association determines the actual signification. This eventually becomes the "meaning" of the experience. These meanings ordinarily are interpreted in intervallic measures or "beats" of time. Meaning entropically moves towards "familiarization," which is static, rather than "defamiliarization" which is nascent, and closer to the fulcrum of the acausal axis of interval (instance) and pattern (generalization).

*　　　　●

You lose the actual qualities of the experience when you try to be too precise about the specifics of each interval of the flow. Any exhaustive rendering becomes a compilation of instances. The historical perspective makes instances appear less improvised than they actually are. The decisive moment, the dramatic realization, is itself a heightening of the particular instance from a valued perspective. One examines what one wants to know thoroughly again and again. This is called testing, experimentation.

We wait and try again. We measure and take note. We generalize and enumerate. We *sift through*. This sifting, this remeasurement of experiences, one combined with another leads to connections which are imbued with the feeling of discovery, that are re*mark*able.

Now, as I look out through the porthole of this ferry, even from this distance, I am thinking that one small rectangle of graduated color, yellow white to pink to black, to specks of, pinpoints of, electric white light to blue, brings to light, to mind, the entire dawn.

NICK PIOMBINO

FILM SINCE:

(In what follows, Abigail Child explores some of the concerns of some of her recent film-making)

receiver
voiceover   DIRECT ADDRESS

by Their music to light a longing (dark) wch breeds mind (that evolves)
    Point (at once) clear heat (intended in their erection)
              to enlarge   THE LINK
                            WOMAN
concerns ensembles repress less unsaid not yet, not enuf vertigo

                    INVERTED IMAGE
flexing it onto the surface + what showers portions (crisis of fluidities)

                              EMBRACE FOLLOWS
          precedes and exceeds it.
            IS NOW DISPLACED   SHE
                where youll people instinct
                     BETWEEN
          bodies of workers.   projections
emarginates   and the cutting thru or pathWay-
            Permanent terrain of destructure.
(the scale the phenomenon, the level the meaning)
        Texture. proliferation of kinds in wch a kind-
          UNDERLINE THE BREAK   A CLOSEUP of ThUs
brush looks   X COMES (SUN)
          magnet pump   flume braids cataract waves (repeat) Solar
          prerequisites
                               AND
The danger of engulfment disguised by the lure of a (regressive)
                       paradise (Pair of Dices)
            IS MADE EXPLICIT   eyes Whereas
the task of art is that process whereby shapes become human.
            that interest / convolvus

        DAM WHILE   A NOTE   CLIMAX
          that must have been the start (fish)
                                        everywhere stretches
                         Touch to accede
            TRAIN NOT STATION   These objects'
intermittence   in wch efforts are rhythms.
Our retrospection will be all to the future.   TIME,
            TWO SHOTS UNDERLINE
          gulf may launch
        instinct   we think   mutandis
          LOOK
the infinite filters into the structure thru WHO LOOKS IN
    A series of infinitesimal displacements-
            RAIN

, in this way that i knew all the time times cutting
and wld be like color
does that kind of jumpy
            DESIRE   THE SUIT WHILE
set between   Circle of sweet grass (muscae volitares) Discourse
        from an economy wch is that of the body.
        MORE, HALF UNDRESSING HIM
          flesh (electriK)   EARt (synapse)   You hear
                                        had before   SINCE
the last part presents aspects actual accpts

```
        (If only splits into times)
                  X material (color wheels)
                        & THE PRESENCE TOGETHER

alters exists you cant have silence
        perfectlyalways    off-the-beat                eees
           divide    CAPITALISM        ,THE NATIONAL CAUSE
merged wt Q        elt location            gutteral          cessity        (tates

king              the stairs          Potemkin
distract              Pivot            asts
        & BY FILM            THE LETTER WT   arrows
at zero                                          (47 varieties of lupine)
OPENS
      SHAPE              and sep.
      specific content

igneous hill    and ellision              you,wch          lead sho do
        IN FACT BE FUNDAMENTAL MOMENT OF PENETRATION

          TRANSPORT PARA

          .PAUSE (  aronial.)
        ALWAYS AS A LACK AND AN        ON THE OTHER
        that sEvers me
TWO MOMENTS              AND AT THE SAME TIME        AND AT THE
        INTERRUPTION  As soon as
days murky,         to film.  Perform irrational acts in the Shape of an idea.
EACH. ELEMENTS        hot        it hinders that        (equals)
further plane          THE AIR    tasts us                TIME
          BY THE PRESENCE
          DESIRE OF A FEMALE (him)
```

                                              ABIGAIL CHILD

TASTE, FORM

The drama of history is temporality, the creation of form(s) manifest in
the key human potential to dissolve the chaos of cogito into the resolve
of concrescence marking this praxis with the absolutely distinguishing
character of intuition. How forms which perservere specifically through
and for the narrow range of private imagination into world into art into
language are located in it by a tripartite of form, taste, value. Herein
the status of form is exact-inexact possibility towards object-status
(objec*tness*), and is intimately bound-up with a separatedness of cogito/
cogitato that is vanquished (rendered artificial, parasitic) by the basic

phenomonology of intuited ontic reach. Any status for form-as-object in this context ultimately involves value(s) that cohere to but are not part of (in) the sensuous world. Taste, then, as the perception that replaces mere recognition, shares its way of knowing (determining) significance in form *with* value, and becomes the sole, tenuous qualifier of that value. As such, value becomes the problematic of *quality* through its relative contradistinct to its 'virtual' determination: if form can only be discussed in terms of culture (Dewey rightly notes), then the value of that form can only be computed through the strictly relative methodologies of what is crucial to that culture, not, obviously, what is 'virtual'. And insofar as this instinct towards virtuallity falsifies itself in the negating mechanisms of time-bound culture, the status of the formal object must be prehended by relative qualities which are, indeed, *totally* crucial to knowing it. The bad faith of archeology is exposed here as the most pedestrian sort of substandard atavism: the conviction that (W)ill ontologically *and* epistemologically endures into a meaning that endures into the impossible synthesis of benign matter as significant form. Reflexivity (as intent) cannot transfer intact (as, for, of-itself) beyond cogito into form, and is as such inexcavible. To grant virtuality prehensive rather than fantastic condition is to replace the taste of another Era for the taste of one's own and belies the unrefined bankruptcy of the notion of succession.

The identity of any Epoch is the quality of those minds that apply the constant effort of knowing and fabricating to a world absented of the evidence of unity and languoring in ellipsis. Distinct from the Positivist mode, which reduces the aesthetic standards of culture to a structure of play, this view simply arbitrates the products of intuition (imagination) with the consequence of (R)eason: the making of discrete form in time as the epitomization of an energy that is distinctly discarnate, subjective, a prodigality that bears signification in both the lie and the truth of temporality, excluding the bogus conceit of formist contiguity.

ANDREW KELLY

I STARTED WRITING...

I started writing dialogues. This is how I started to write. I was working as a waitress in "Big Boys" in College Park, Maryland while attending the University of Maryland. Always listening to people and was taking Modern Poetry class with Rudd Fleming who really "opened the door" to all of this for me. I graduated with a degree in Recreation Therapy so the people I spent a lot of time with were frustrated jocks and very social, fun loving, good time party types. At the same time, I was starting to write, I got into yoga. So both of these (writing and yoga) were pulling me into two very opposite poles. By this time, I was writing more internal monologues and stream of consciousness writing.

Last week I went to the library to look up automatic writing. I finally found a definition in an Enyclopedia of Occultism. Automatic writing is as if your arm is possessed and you don't know what you are writing. You may write very very fast and so small that it would seem physically impossible that a human could write it. Much of this type of writing had to do with contacting the dead. When the writing comes easier to me, it seems to be more automatic. Stein was thoroughly insulted when they called her work automatic. She thought it was ridiculous that they thought she was in a trance.

While working for the D.C. Recreation Department, I became involved with Mass Transit, a weekly open reading series. Again here were these two conflicting types. I was teaching a preschool class in the A.M. and coaching sports and other activities (hanging out, ping-pong, the local rec activity). Maybe these conflicts are what kept me writing. I remember buying my first car and how free it felt. Also riding on buses and trains got me writing. The motion and optimism of "new" always set something off. In the beginning (*Lamplights*) the observations and obsessions were much more external — not as heavy. By the next year with *Stampede* (having spent a year in New York studying in Mayer's workshop) everything became much faster, darker and extremely internal, until it came to a dead halt. Climbing out of that with the writing proved to be a slow and thick process which even involved going back to Baltimore where I grew up. Living out the same memories of childhood as an adult was of course painful and necessary.

The next work, "The Letters", was much lighter as if trying to reach out and be witty. By this time I was back in D.C. working various jobs, i.e., security guard, cashier, and receptionist. After being so self-conscious and internal in *Stampede*, I needed to be light, almost comical while writing "The Letters". By this time, a group of us were getting together for a poetry workshop which *Dog City* has been a result of.

To say the life is separate from the writing would be a lie. Not that calming down would slow the work or the other way around. Lifestyle, where living, whether working would all add or detract.

About three years ago, I got a job as a Park Ranger on an old lightship down on Haines Point in D.C. Here was, I thought, the answer to many problems (low pressure job, being outside a lot, on water, pretty isolated in winter and fall), but I found that the amount of time I had to write had nothing to do with my ability to write. I then started writing *Tamoka* which I had intended to be a much longer work. This is the most direct piece I've done (more like a story than anything else). Also I got married about that time, so here was another way "not to hide". I found in *Tamoka* the language was very important and I finally understood what centering the writing on the language could mean. Of course, mine was more of a story but all of the talk about "words" made sense. Certain sections are more language than others.

The pool where I had lifeguarded and taught swimming the summer before I started the Park Service was this huge inner city public pool. There was a lot of slang and while we used to change chairs and clean the deck, I would ask the other guards about the opposite meanings of words (bad meaning good, etc.). This is very common now but I always liked to talk about it.

Now the popular songs that are blasting on the radios are these talky sing-song long tales with a good beat (sort of like Muhammad Ali's poetry). One of the people at the ship would always know the words to them. It fascinated me because he would turn it up and tell me to listen whenever they came on.

In about three weeks, I'll be having a baby. So my whole center is off. The writing has been much slower this summer, will see what the new settled season will bring.

(A bibliography of Lynne Dreyer's work can be found in issue #8, June 1979.)

LYNNE DREYER

PIECE TOGETHER BROKEN SWEAT/ MILD CONCERN

Ted Greenwald, Use No Hooks (1980; Asylum's Press, c/o SPD, 1784 Shattuck Ave., Berkeley, CA 94709; $2.50)

There is a relationship between reading and writing that seems unsunderable. To the extent that there is a set of repeating signatures, one learns to recognize as appertaining to something that could be called a Greenwald poem, it has always seemed as likely as not to have developed as a part of an emergent *style*, or voice, or writerly persona, more or less connected to an *actual* person, in New York, with a certain Queens accent, who was to be seen, or not, at certain places around town. Admittedly such recognitions (this, here, is a Greenwald...e.g.) arose not only out of some more selfed armature of presentation to the exclusion of familiarities in other aspects of the writing. A somewhat *socialized urbanized 'relaxed'* mode of discourse could have been held up, as epitomizing, as an hypothetical model, and matched with a similar more formal contextual focus: continuities of relationships, friendships, lovers, bars, parties, evenings at home. This sort of identification came with the accrued presence of the writer and his work on the horizon so that, eventually, there seemed to be something that in being called *a Greenwald*, for example, as style, appeared as a realized thing which could conceivably span, comfortably, almost any exigency of *subject* and still reside, undeniably, as a work by this author.

In part the not inconsiderable effect of reading a book like *Use No Hooks*
seems due to the way one's expectations of a writer midpoint in his career
are destroyed — through, and *as*, the structure of the poems themselves are
torn and ripped and pressed and pushed to the edge of organized utterance
recognizable as the writer's parameters, — and beyond. The *envelope* is
thoroughly reconstituted. Edges are sheared off or repeat like a monitor's
rollover. Often the face of the prosody is stripped past the stratum of
consensual artifice, deeper than the *bones* of the sentence, to a ledge of
basal utterance. World is accounted as something that may enter the *field*:
a pipe, phone's ring, a hat. What was thought of as what *made for* a
Greenwald poem turns out to be both more and less than it seemed. Any
convivial perhaps casually expansive mode that seemed to be what could be
called the *style* was, after all, it now appears, only a collection of
temporal approximations tailored for what it seems the work, generally,
then, had as an *aboutness*. This was not how he had to write, that was
what he chose. The force of this book's form, the way it epitomizes,
lines up, with the pain and loss, anger, reaction, and hope, the terrible
dissolves that it springs from, that it takes up the colors of, impels
the reader to a new assessment. Anyone who can so across the board, after
twenty years of writing engineer, or, rather, render, such sweeping changes
in his writing has to be thought of *differently*. What we thought of as a
Greenwald style was all wrong, it was something tailored. What remains,
what *resides*, a hard edged, tight, unrelenting *way of looking* that emanates
from this book, and now, in a sense, more clearly, from the older work,
that is the uniqueness.

There are certain things one isn't supposed to say. Even the most exhibi-
tionistic of the late unlamented confessionalists, apart from other more
formally debilitating adherences, can now be seen, if anyone cares, to
have hewn to certain mores of decorum. The most *searingly bared* revelations in the first person were still clothed in the inclusiveness of the
monolithic lyric *I*; by the middle of the century the presentation of literary self was sufficiently bogged down in a morass of convention that it no
longer constituted any great sally to say that this *I* was capable, or engaged in, the *most terrible* affliction or infliction. If it wasn't completely worn out as a mode of discourse it was encrusted with as much study
as any of the older readily compatible fitting prospects on objects (landscapes, etc.).

The residual tags of disguise, enfeebled necromancy of narration and taste
in lyric *thus constituted*, stand out most starkly in the rote fictionaliz-
ing reference this kind of writing called up when the sense of a *personal
place* could no longer be avoided. There were still certain things one did
not say. You didn't name names, at least not the real names. Did Sylvia
ever write the word Ted? Even now, in the kind of writing where that sub-

ject survives, when one half of a couple mentions the other it is in the context of washing the dishes or babysitting. Some of the constraints on this kind of particularity are self-evident, seeming to have more to do with social binding, decorum in that sense. Similarly, certain accusations or lacerations too clearly labelled are out of bounds. Another major influence in the context is the familiar charying desire to set the writing apart, to push it up to another *realm* by the deletion of various proper nouns and the odd mundane reference.

At this point in time to make the decision to include these sorts of hyperpersonal reference is to imply a critique and realignment of the literary presentation of the self that injects a healthy note into an increasingly tendentious argument. It is an affirmation that that which places writing in a place or *signature* which is some way a *beyond* has little to do with discretion or *attach*able entrances into the basis or source of the work. In twenty years no one will care anyway.

The formal component of this openness seems rooted in an attitude, a non-exclusion taken to its logical conclusion or development, which, as it realizes more and more as *pertaining* to that which is *connected*, *evidentiary*, *important*, *illuminating*, is impelled to present, to *include*, that much more.

MICHAEL GOTTLIEB

from FUGUE

... What precisely would the work to be written be about if it was concerned with a game? We would have to play and write the Treatise on that game at the same time, or, more exactly, the game itself would consist of writing the Treatise on the game. How is it played? I cannot apply the rules of a treatise which does not yet exist! A solution is possible: that the elaboration of the treatise be an integral part of the execution. The match has not yet taken place, I shall never have the peaceful role of pure spectator, and that is why it is necessary, to begin by playing, by provoking and observing the movements, even if it later entails reconstituting from the traces of other, at first unnoticed, movements.... I must do the work of a discoverer more than an inventor, and yet the reading alone cannot act as the developer in the photographic sense of that term, for the history, far from being already fully accomplished, will be able to be read only in so far as it will be inscribed, as if the memory of the book was offering it that place and time of which it would till then have been deprived....
  I would wish the mind, substituting itself for "I", to show itself, manifest its own movement openly, speak its own language directly, but the mind, a detestable word that I must soon replace, not given in any

immediate understanding, not speaking but writing, must be furnished
the possibility of leaving a trace: the white sheet ready to become
scriptogramme. The most simple metaphor, hardly a metaphor, is thus
that of a mobile or a machine, equipped with a kind of seismographic
stylet which would change position, marking its movement, which would
be described by that procedure as essential and characteristic as that
of a piece in a chess game. To compare a book to a seismogramme is a
mistaken analogy in so far as, I know from experience, simple registering
is not involved, and indeed everything happens as if the sheet of paper
was a rebel matter not allowing itself to be easily cut into by the
writer's stylet. I therefore correct my definition: the mind (a term
the reader would really like to read henceforth under an erasure) is
this mobile which can only change its position by clearing a path and
consequently by inscribing itself, by necessarily leaving a trace:...
How can I make the reader participate in the discontinuity of the
writing? How can I do it in such a way that the legato of the reading
is broken by the spasms of the writing?... One experiences a kind of
dizziness when, having suddenly believed one is touching the centre of
the target, one passes just to one side, a slight error which soon
draws one to the very outside, and yet this slight shift, this kind of
dislocation which separates me from my references and puts a check on
my schemes, sets me at the same time onto some new project.... Contrary
to what I supposed, to write a book is not a game which would consist
of drawing up the rules of this game, and indeed, in admitting that
writing is a game, it will never be able to purify itself, to sum itself
up in a Treatise.... Opposing what provisionally, and for want of
better, I shall call my writing, since it is placed black on white by
the one who says "I", there is indeed I do not know what hostile white-
ness which empties my writing, disconnects it from itself, a whitening
which obliterates in advance what I might have written, ousts me unceas-
ingly from what I have thus no right to call my writing: that ray, that
rift, that furrow, which I will call counter-writing, even though repeating that such pain is surely my only chance.... Everything happens
as if the work was the place of confrontation between an inside and an
outside, between writing and counter-writing, an adversary that it
would however be unjust to consider an enemy of the work since without
it the work would geometrise, crystallise in a Treatise which, though
perfect, would nonetheless signify for the work, purified in the "finished work", mortal immobility....

Though it must weigh the most serious threats on the work, counter-
writing is not exterior to a text which would not be constituted without
it, on which, in which, it leaves its imprint, it touches writing at
its very heart. The mobile, figure of writing, does not change position
according to a rectilinear course till the moment when it would be de-
flected by an alien resistance, but counter-writing is always at work,
bringing the writer into play whilst placing the one who says "I" out-

side the game, occupying the heartless heart of the writing. Every writer represents his craft in the form of a clearing a way, and yet, in his very act, writing is also and at the same time, of a deep-seated passivity: the act of writing, in so far as it is a receptive surface, is therefore always concerned with the heart of its activity.... When I hold myself at a distance from these two extremes: the ease of discussion and the dry pain of exclusion, when I write, that is to say when the writer simultaneously decides to open a way and to accept being put in play, being carried along to the unknown and perhaps to lose himself, there is not on the one hand the rectitude or the rigour of a breakthrough and on the other a strength so perniciously misleading that one finds oneself off the track without knowing why, without having made a mistake, so disorientated that one no longer knows where one is at all, turned about to the point of losing one's own trace, but the still-veiled way plays around its absent axis and thus the clearing a way, although one only becomes aware of it afterwards, is directly a misconduct: this use, this warping of falsely continued traces, is the indiscernable work of the writing and the counter-writing to such an extent that the latter could be given the name of writing and vice versa....

(Excerpted and reordered from Glenda George's translation of Fugue -- Gallimard, 1970 -- in Split Curtains, 4 Bower Street, Maidstone, Kent, England.)

ROGER LAPORTE

THE POEM BEGINNING WHAT IT IS

Initial statement of intensely ambiguous desire. Affirmation of the attempt at image without relegating personal history to a position of domineering limitation. Notification in succinct everyday language of the author's intention to call up out of the ordinary events of the day some revelation concerning the ability to cope with social rejection. Flat reversal of previous logic in favor of a slightly metaphorical reliance on the presentation of phrases designed to convey a sense of security in their close examination of emotional detail. Sudden insight, followed by philosophical maxims supposedly revealing the moral implications of such activity. A number of analogies referring back to original statement of predisposed feelings of inadequacy. Slightly ironic comment on the difficulty of accepting responsibility for the integration of thought and action. Further examples of displeasure at contemporary standards of aesthetic expression. Despairing remarks on the ability of concerted energy expenditure to overcome basically unsolvable psychological dilemmas.

Extended analysis in oversimplified form portraying social interaction and personal conduct as beyond the reaches of intellection. Return to imagistic descriptions of peripheral anxiety. Relegation of attempts at tempered hope to the projection of unusual ideas conveyed through a combination of syntactic complexity and emotionally-loaded terminology. Summation of on-going conscious event experience in recollection of earlier self-betrayal. Final ideological commitment to continuing endeavor. Terse imprecation of the poetic form as pathetically fallacious. Restatement of desire in less ambiguous terms.

DAVID BENEDETTI

UNDER THE BRIDGE

Carla Harryman, Under The Bridge (1980; This, c/o SPD, 1784 Shattuck Ave., Berkeley, CA 94709; $3)

Harryman resists stasis, attacks any form of the given. "Creation not reality," she writes in the "Forward" to *Under The Bridge*. Her focus is on will; her own, of course, as the creator of this prose, "I think I made up the future in order to go away, to move elegantly." and the perceived will of others. Her very syntax points to the agency behind effects. For instance, in "Cult Music" she writes, "Fed period music in a boxcar." Another writer might have begun that statement with the words "period music," stressing the nouns. Harryman begins with the verb "fed." So someone is doing this to us. Her "Forward" ends, "The hand walked down the road."

Her emphatic verbs bridge the gap between one seemingly unconnectable noun clause and the next across sometimes incredibly long sentences as if she found nowhere she cared to pause.

A self pleasure supermarket puny bridges defy willfully
demeans articulation but had all the confidence not to be
interested in music at home or locked out by a big mouth
talking in swamps that hinge between doting or like
propaganda spread two dogs changed position fretful
crooked road sauntering up the tangled figure proceeding
naturally in a remote space loaded up with characteristics,
a too cumbersome visage opens the scroll in mud and lifts
up head tumbling into a frame like eels circling the
heavens to make themselves feel better.
                                        from "Various Devices"

Her sentences seem to proceed, "exhibiting ruthless fancy." They "could go anywhere, but might not."

Superficially, Harryman and other writers of new prose sometimes resemble surrealists. But sentences like: "The black tub motors by." or "Frightening packages of detail surround the house..." or "Smell of dust in this geometry." sound odd not because they describe impossible happenings or dream states, but simply because they are unusual formulations. In each of these sentences at least one term feels out of sync. The nouns "geometry", "detail" and even "tub" are more general than one would expect. Sporadically, she raises abstraction to a higher power. It is a defamiliarization technique. "Is this why I'm strange to you as we practice being home?"

Consciousness suddenly stands back from a thought, regards it from outside. "I am not an innocent: I was only pretending to be contemptuous of the mountains." Sentence turns against previous or even, in the case above, hypothetical sentence. 'Characters' appear briefly to make statements contradicted by the 'narrator.' Mom is "wrong" in "In Front" and "One can't say, 'But they don't live in water,' without being an ass." So one must be wary. You can't believe everything you read. Harryman's writing presents both the will to act and the possibility of error. Reading *Under The Bridge* one feels provoked and energized. "I could have been in a more simple schoolyard."

RAE ARMANTROUT

LETTER TO THE EDITORS

A THING ABOUT LANGUAGE FOR BERNSTEIN

Even the dreadful Maritain distinguishes verse covertly logical or rational from verse which, whether for emotional or exploratory reasons, does float free from "development" of the sort taught in French lycées. Bachelard seems to me to have developed the best devices to criticize it. In English we have Davie's syntactical study, and maybe Charles Williams' *Reason and Beauty*....

The trouble, my trouble, comes from the relation of theory to practice, fiery theory and tepid practice. There are ways in which Clark Coolidge is not a savior. Or can I take his collar as celluloid. Or leather, around a wood armature, with buckles and straps, perhaps rings. This is for a strong neck, to go through. Inventing it took centuries. Now we find them on the sides of barns, like toilet seats.

My favorite barn, which lately had lions in, was really a garage and had in it, on the workbench the hearth-idol of which was a very good, very heavy vise, in coffee cans and old drawers now open boxes such iron fitments as I found in my farm rounds. They were sometimes useful, especially the metal straps and hasps, bendable in the big vise, with effort. These also, the smaller bits, provided me with nipples for plastic caps in redesigned one-shot pistols for conjuring. In general the pleasure was double: of finding and hoarding, and recognizing a use in a cog plate or pierced metal bracket.

Were these, in the ground, words or syllables. Wire fence, bolts and folded drum stock had been grown into by a tree. Large washers, screwdriver shanks and whole saws were in the ground by it. So the tree defined a junk heap, was a locale, probably on the theory that you had to walk around it anyway. Like, in a way, the habit of tacking up old license plates.

There was charm when the bits were old enough (rusted spark plugs are still boring) and potential utility, and as in a time-game the charm of potential utility. The secret pleasure (recall De Quincey on the pleasure of sliding gold coins) was how pretty (not triste) they were, in cans and boxes, *waiting* in senses to be used but not at attention, not sentimentalized. They helped define a workbench.

This last motion, the move outward from particular spiked or angled, heaped or glass-jarred presences, to make a larger area was very odd because they did not *inhabit* the area, as tools hung over their painted silhouettes do or did. They were not citizens or politics. It is more that the large space *could* be used, walked into as a unity, like a country not thinking of its restaurants. One could, though one never did, greet the space. It could be acknowledged, in a different way from how, turning out a jar of washers or fitments, the pieces not useful would still be greeted or given a value while picked *through* or around and set aside.

Max Picard says if words didn't go out of themselves to refresh themselves *in* things, they would hang around in heaps and impede our movements, like things in a warehouse. That *may* be an argument for reference. One could prefer the warehouse, as one dreams in a surplus-parts store. Will this be sought out or printed -- ever be more than *browsing*. And is there, built into some kinds of experiment as result, the utility of browsing only. Please reply.

GERALD BURNS

The Segue Distributing Services has published a catalogue of books and magazines which should be of interest to our readers. Write them at 300 Bowery, New York, New York 10012.

PRIVATE ENIGMA IN THE OPENED TEXT

The trace of the enigma is negligently latent in all writing. The enigma is a colorless monovalent feature in textual omnivalence.

This present writing defines those private enigmas with which the author sometimes pierces his text. These are distinct from, for example: the narratively enigmatic which, functioning, becomes through reappearance, a character or figure of the text; the metaphysically enigmatic which functions, deliberately, through our lives as we return to its imperative point of question; the enigmatics of dream which function, vehicularly, to let life ride itself; the grammatically enigmatic, which functions as a verbal irregularity, a non sequitur stunning us with what previously could not have been said; the enigmatic of any single text, which is obsessive in its function as the ground for all text and all enigma. Throughout this writing, the word 'enigma' will refer to private enigmas, and not to the otherwise enigmatic which may frequently surround its appearance.

The author may plant in his text his enigmas. Whether this is more common in the rangeingly modern text than in classical writing is something we may not learn. We may speak of the pleasure. The writer allows his enigmas as, quickly they choose him; with reason — pleasure. The attachment is attentive. There is pleasure in placing the deliberately extraneous, the stain. The enigma may be no more enigmatic to a reader than is the rest of the text, which may seem 'of a piece', or deliberately and equally not of one. But for the writer, the enigma remains a sign of himself in the text of himself, a unique entry of himself upon his language. It is that part which he obstinately holds to as he gives it all away. The presence of the reader is implicit in the pleasure of enigma; the author is a voyeur, enjoying as he writes, the pleasure of his reading of his text. In fact, he gives the text to himself as he writes it: but in the enigma he claims in one instant the combined functions of reading and writing; he completes already, again and in part, what already others, reading, complete again and in part. He enjoys, in advance, what it is usually for the reader, whether himself or another, to enjoy only later. It is a one-sided pleasure; doubled. The enigma is chosen as a special burden, a verdict the writing passes on the young history of texts.

The enigma cleans the text of its indebtedness. In the enigma gesture, a text lays hold of itself. An enigma, unlike the rest of texted language bound to structure, does not (have to) evaluate itself. It is already evaluated, it stands for that.

What is sought is an enigma which cannot be closed upon (hence the "is sought"). Small particles of meaning satisfy this best for the writer; though large structures do so, openly, they do so as structures, their closure a matter of preordained interest. The enigma is erased in its minute duration. An enigma, unlike the rest of structured text, is not the locus of any coming together, neither of a dispersion; it is a still point activated, once by the author's enthusiasm, and again by the writing which surrounds and which motivated its inauguration. Enigma, made to be unresolved, affords the opposition of immersion, of argument: it offers an opaque exterior; not offering entry or exit, it posits (the generic trace of pleasure). The enigma, cued only to itself, faces nothing. However, it is not bracketed. It is merely less loose among particles more active. Though its delight is not extinguished, it has no tendency. Its argument is that, it, is, here; hence its relation to structural wholes: the enigma less elusive, because more instanced, the structure less clear, because more over itself.

The enigma significantly animates (animates signification in) the writer's working. In his text he lodges it, stills the agitation by posturing its particular particle where it can be observed, contemplated, or where it can be passed over; without having to reveal its lived significance, he reveals the volume of it. It is transplanted; without, however, having been anywhere other than on both sites, met equally in the imagination with which they touch. The enigma is rendered siteless, a vantage from which its singularity can incite unanimously.

The enigma is the only anoegenetic particle of language. It stands, in part (and in part it 'fails'), for the effort which made it so. It does not sublimate its function to structure, as do all functioning chunks of meaning; it is apart from function, embodying it at once. It is an action on which the curtain of meaning has come down with finality; behind the curtain, the perfunctory disclosure of fact. The enigma is a silent spot in the rush of meanings, but only when viewed in that context. Its placement specializes it. Without being able to deposit its position in the meaning-productive text, it does in fact speak its stance. It refuses to speak in discourse in order to embody quick monologic impact.

The enigma is impoverished in context. It has nothing to do: no work, nothing by which to be covered, nothing to speak, no acts, no decisions to make or motivate in its place (no pivot), no early nor late and no here nor there. It has nothing to mobilize (after the author's delight), nothing to solve, nothing to begin or bring to an end. It abolishes, for an instant, what goes on surrounding it. If a text can be parsed, the enigma cannot. But it does not deny, it solidly confirms itself; its intractable dissolution of logic and sequence. But it must not irritate; it is in no way entangled. It is not a version of some other thing, neither is it

averse to a possibility. It is stopped. It implies the release of the
game, momentarily, without bringing it about. It generates its instant,
and deprives it of reason, of play.

The enigma does not exist in the tangled limits of nature. It is an artifact. It in no way approaches the limits of what we know to be the case.
It stands (in) (in the text) for the limits. It is an act of indication,
but without the masking words which elsewhere accompany such acts; its
substance is word, but it leaps, releasing them insoluble, an empty en-
casement. The enigma is marked by its absence from the site, as it is
seen to occupy it totally. No contradiction; this, the enigma.

An enigma cannot be plural; it depends upon its indistributability. If
it becomes dispersed in the text, if it is acted, its character is delineated in diffusion; of necessity, its still factness is destroyed. When
the integer is serialized, or valued, when it is perceived through horizontal or vertical loci, it achieves a rhetorical or narrative function;
it relaxes. The enigma must not be made to speak itself in any direction.
The enigma, if it is to stand privately, if it is to release its pleasure,
must not equivocate. The enigma is the only detached attachment permitted
to text.

A text can be infused with a network of enigmas, which unavoidably connect.
But when the enigma is extensive, it becomes a particle in the text's fabric, a code demanding, and enabling at least in part, its decipherment.
As soon as an enigma is extensive, structured, it becomes a term among
many in the text's polarities and excursions. It becomes one of numerous
graphs upon which the writing occurs, tightening and loosening. Its
dissolution proposes its solution; it talks. And it is no longer private;
the text has begun to reply. The enigma is not permissive.

The enigma is consigned, ordered. It is the object of an action which,
as a singularly upright subject, it demands. Unlike all other text, the
enigma needs no support. It does not need to be there. It seems to be a
will, to embody will so completely, that its it is embodied. It is ir-
reversible. An order that cannot be recalled, it cannot die: its allure.
The enigma is messageless; perfectly balanced (of one 'side'), it is the
perfect signifier, the only one not drawn apart (revealed) by unequal
(metaphorically inexact) sides. Stolid, it doesn't waver.

ALAN DAVIES

L=A=N=G=U=A=G=E

Number 13.   (Vol. 3, No. 3)

Charles Bernstein & Bruce Andrews, Editors.

Subscriptions — Volume Four (150 page bound volume plus
    supplements in 1981) for $4, institutions $8.
    Volume Three is available for $6, institutions $8.
    Volumes One and Two are $8 each, institutions $11 each.

Design: Susan B. Laufer.   Typing: Sally Silvers.

All queries & checks to: Charles Bernstein,
    464 Amsterdam Ave, New York, N.Y. 10024.

L=A=N=G=U=A=G=E is supported by subscriptions, donations, and grants
from the National Endowment for the Arts, the Coordinating Council
of Literary Magazines, and the New York State Council on the Arts.

Special thanks to Alan Davies, Michael Gottlieb, & James Sherry.

Distributed with the cooperation of the Segue Foundation.

ANNOUNCEMENTS:

SONNETS (Memento Mori) by Bruce Andrews, THIS Press, $2.50 from SBD,
    1784 Shattuck Avenue, Berkeley, CA 94709.

CONTROLLING INTERESTS by Charles Bernstein, ROOF Books, $4 from
    300 Bowery, New York, N.Y. 10012.

back cover: from Censored Texts *by Brita Bergland (Awede Press)*

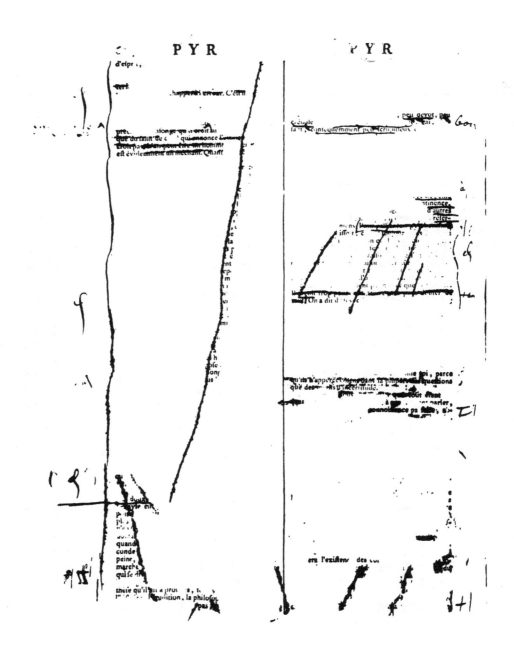

L=A=N=G=U=A=G=E

SUPPLEMENT NUMBER ONE   JUNE 1980

The Politics of the Referent

The following four articles are part of a symposium edited by Steve McCaffery on "The Politics of the Referent." The essays, which date from 1976, were originally published in the Canadian journal, Open Letter (edited by Frank Davey) in the summer of 1977 (Third Series, No.7).

It seems worth remembering, in looking back on these essays, that the tendencies in writing McCaffery is talking about under such headings as 'language-centered' are as open to the entrapments of stylistic fixation as any other tendency in recent poetry. The reason we have have shied away from any such labels in editing L=A=N=G=U=A=G=E is that our project, if it can be summarized at all, has had to do with exploring the numerous ways meanings can be (& are) realized — revealed — produced in writing. In this context, the idea that writing could be stripped of reference is as troubling and confusing a view as the assumption that the primary function of words is to refer, one-on-one, to an already constituted world of 'things'. Rather, reference, like the body itself, is a given dimension of language, the value of which is to be found, in its various extents, in the poem (the world) before which we find ourselves at any moment. It is the power of reference (denotative, connotative, associational), not writers' refusal or fear of it, that threads these essays together. It is a renewed power that comes from the recognition that the (various) measuring and composition of our references is the practice of our craft.

STEVE MCCAFFERY

The Death of the Subject:
The Implications of Counter-Communication
in Recent Language-Centered Writing

As we understand increasingly the unity of the human symbolic field and how man is primarily a semiotic animal inhabiting and creating a context that is itself semiotic and governed by common operations, as we understand this so we will understand how the whole notion of a literature discriminated from language is irrelevant.

There is a group of writers today united in the feeling that literature has entered *a crisis of the sign;* that the explications of literatures have merged with the implications of language and that the foremost task at hand — a more linguistic and philosophic than 'poetic' task — is to demystify the referential fallacy of language.

REFERENCE I take it, is that kind of blindness a window makes of the pane it is; that motoric thrust of the word which takes you out of language into a tenuous world of the other and so prevents you seeing what it is you see.

Clark Coolidge, Bruce Andrews, Ray Di Palma, Charles Bernstein, Robert Grenier, Barbara Baracks, David Melnick, Ron Silliman. What you will find uppermost in their writing is this conviction: that language is above all else a system of signs and that writing must stress its semiotic nature through modes of investigation and probe, rather than mimetic, instrumental indications. Theirs, is not a movement as such but a quiet assertion of an interconnectedness of concerns: to centre language inside itself; to show the essential subjectless-ness a text might be; to stress the disemotional and dereferential possibilities of language as fragmentary, yet intensely direct experience. Language then, for itself, but for the sake of us. To step outside of use. To counter-communicate in order ... to see what a hammer is when not in function.

Context is not important but historic frame articulation must include: the Russian Formalists (long neglected but appearing as influence for almost the first time in North American writing in the work of Silliman and Melnick); Roland Barthes (writing degree zero, semiocriticism); the works of Jacques Lacan and Jacques Derrida (the sign as diacritical ... reference ... difference ... the metaphysics of absence). Earlier connections can be seen with the semiological writings of C.S. Peirce and the pioneer work of Ferdinand de Saussure (the bipolarity of the sign, the essential oppositional nature of linguistic units). A parallel, too, might be drawn with the semiotic concerns of concrete poetry — not so much around the investigative extrapolation of the visual properties of the word, but rather around the mutual stress upon language as a direct event, a 'seen' thing (in concretism) and hence a 'felt' thing (in language-centred writing).

The hardest thing in reading is just to see the seeing that you're seeing. To let the word receive your sight. To not deflect off language but re-flect within it. To let your seeing be what your reading was. To let the direct, empirical experience of a grapheme replace what the signifier in a word will always try to discharge: its signified and referent.

Little commentary has, so far, been forthcomng on this type of counter-communication. Silliman's *Surprised by Sign*, which annotates a collection of this work in *Alcheringa* (New Series, v. 1, No. 2, 1975) is, possibly, the best of current access to this writing variously termed 'formalist', 'structuralist', 'dereferentialist', 'minimalist', 'language centred' and which I will refer to as 'counter-communicative' and 'cipheral'.

Proposition: to treat this work from a presupposed position of 'unreadability', 'disinteredness' and 'inaccessibility', from such consumptive stances as refuse to see text as an agent of production.

Language-centered writing involves a major alteration in textual roles: of the socially defined functions of writer and reader as the productive and consumptive poles respectively of a commodital axis. The main thrust of this work is hence political, rather than aesthetic, towards a frontal assault on the steady categories of authorship and readership. What it offers is the alternative sense of reader and writer as equal and simultaneous participants within a language product. At its core, linguistic reference is a displacement of human relationships and as such is fetishistic in the Marxian sense. Reference, like commodity, has no connection with the physical property and material relations of the word as a grapheme.

stint grits
darts   file
gratis   ways to fit tins
dapper   angle
ill   apple
sax   wash
max   a phone
port planter
graph ending the end
only back
a bit from
passing after
wrecked

```
guff
water
waterized
needle              (Barbara Baracks)
```

The initial problem in readership here is to abandon all prejudical perceptual sets and to consciously assist oneself in producing one's own reading among the polysemous routes that the text offers. With the removal of grammatical conditioners as dictates of a single reading, language enters the domain of its own inwardness; the conventional centrifugality of signification is reversed and the Sign turns inward through the absence of grammar to a pure, lexemic presence.

Seen as such, then, the text is a critique of language achieved by way of a deconstruction of grammatical context. Words are placed next to words but what the juxtaposition is deprived of is a true sense of words in community. We are among isolated meanings, absolute potencies and graphic events.

I would here deny the need to stress all this as somehow a part of literature. More significant and to the point is to acknowledge a number of texts that constitute, collectively and cumulatively, a novel interrogative stance of language against itself.

Language centred writing shows a concern with the order of effects that connect with the signifier rather than the referent. Together with this is a specific minimization of the effect of the signified (if we consider the latter to be a kind of 'discharge' from the signifier.) Language centering avoids the discharge and hence short–circuits the semiotic loop. It is this superfluity of the signifier that promotes in these texts the quality I term 'cipher'.

```
            al (t          ch
ph     ysto          kl
                ee
      apl
    sta
               )
               ry    (mccaffery)
```

Cipherality belongs to a synchronic poetics; it is tenseless and free from both reference and alternity, thereby centered within its textual self and available as a primary empirical experience. The cipheral text involves a replacement in readerly function from a reading of words to an experiencing of graphemes, for conventional reading involves the use of referential vectors and it is such vectors that are here removed. Language is material and primary and what's experienced is the tension and relationship of letters and lettristic clusters, simultaneously struggling towards, yet refusing to become, significations.

The cipher or emptied sign is a frozen dialectic within a semiotic process, less an active sign than a sign removed from function (and hence deconstructed) to be observed and experienced as event per se.

Ciphericity is a zero-methodology by which texts are constructed which are designed to say nothing. To be silent, however, is to withhold the possibility to speak. The cipheral, or language-centred text is, on the graphemic level of the sign, what tautology is in the formal rules and structures of logic. '... not a field in which we express what we wish with the help of signs, but rather one in which the nature of the absolutely necessary signs speaks for itself.' (Wittgenstein)

... The publicly silent sign, then, as the self-speaking sign. ... and cipher ... the tautology of the signifier.

mob cuspid
welch
   eyelet
go lavender
futuribles   (andrews)

presents a semiotic ambivalence to the reading experience: do you decipher or do you augment and complete? Both approaches are admissible, for it's precisely the nature of texts like andrews' to present themselves as ambiguities, approachable either as densities, as compressions requiring a reading that approximates a hermeneusis; or else as lacunaire, deliberate incompletions requesting a reading that extends them towards completion.

In the first approach (i.e. treating the poem as a structural density) the reading experience can be likened to a vertical axis descending downwards into a text whose surface signifies an implicit depth. In this manner the structure of the sign is destroyed within the poem yet, at the same time, is transferred into the reading experience itself where text equals signifer and the reading descent equals the signified. Sign, in this way, expands to include readership into its very structure. In the second method of reading, we adopt a sense of meaning based upon the cipher — the emptied sign. In this method, meaning is not hidden beneath a surface but is emptied out of a container; the tendency to vertical descent through a text's illusionary surface, becomes resolved within an experiencing of absences as gaps upon a textual surface. In this way syntax homologizes what in the world of sculpture is negative space. Absence is experienced as an event either anterior or exterior to any semantic presence.

```
        albe
              skep
    tref
            jush
numb
          pffe    neig    (Andrews)
```

By eliminating reference this way, by reducing the connotative range of the graphemes, Andrews promotes a strong object quality in this text. Lettristic clusters of this kind tend to function in the manner of a punctuation, as pure space-time arrestments. To experience a text as such 'events' affirms encipherment, for a non-referential event is the prime quality of the emptied sign.

An alternative reading might tend to promote decipherment: the sign grasped as a 'fragmentary' base on which to develop a lexical reconstitution. Reading, in this manner, takes the form of a re-composition with the centrifugal pressure that all referential texts possess being modified as an urge back to the word. Reading here, then, as a reparation of the word. The writer as logoclast. The reader as logotect and logotherapist.

The implication behind a decipheral style of reading is that the given text is partial, incomplete or imperfect, suggesting in these terms not necessarily an aesthetic deficiency but rather a radically political invitation to the reader to cast off his former pre-ordained role as the recipient of a message and to enter the domain of the writer.

Two procedural readings of language-centered writing have been proposed: encipherment and decipherment. Encipherment I've tried to indicate above is based upon a sense of the text as complete, eventist, surface and immediate; decipherment upon a sense of the text as potential but partial, and holding the capability to expand towards a destination within semantic normality.

Quite clearly from this, a decipheral reading homologizes the referential thrust of the conventional verbal sign for both reference and verbal re-composition involve the use of vectors that lead to a destination outside of the graphic, phenomenal immediacy of the physical text presented.

```
time ceal hum base
treat south admit
law the dissolve add


              owl    (Coolidge)
```

Coolidge. Andrews. Silliman. Di Palma. In their work we approach —

anterior to an actual reading — a page which holds coherently an iconicity which the very act of reading removes. In reading such poems we thrust the text back into the domain of a writing. As in the above example a statement is made in visual terms around the notion of cluster and detachment. To penetrate beyond the very seeing of this statement, in effect, destroys that very element of the poem; it suggests, in fact, that it is the experience of reading itself that promotes the counter-communication. What language-centered writing serves to emphasize is the semiocritical relationship of consecutive to simultaneous sign, the striated nature of a reading and a seeing, and the relationship of a spatial to a linear syntax.

Hence there's a translative act involved in the reading, from a spatial to a linear setting, from an instantaneous seeing of a group of lexical extensions (and in other cases lexical fragmentations) to a consecutive reading of that seeing. 'Reading' it might be said, is the receptor term in a translative process whose source term is 'seeing', whilst what the poem itself constitutes is a metaperceptual system that offers to the reader an initial seeing, passing on into a secondary seeing (as a reading) of that primary seeing.

sadd bier
   metapoif
lid   cift   ure,

    hid   tyer   (David Melnick from: PCOET)

analog: phoneme is to tone what
          word is to melody:
          themselves.

the text like music: for both involve a semiotics minus a compound semantic level (i.e. the referential, contentual plane.)

In Melnick's work we find the most extreme, uncompromising excommunication of reference. Poem as object-process not commodity and an atonality for the ear through fragmentation — here above, with the word as tone; the phoneme and phoneme clusters atonalities.

Applying the notion of cipher to the unread text, text becomes the perceived iconicity that exists anterior to a reading. Text as icon is the empty sign awaiting the experience of a filling. The act of decipherment is that particular kind of readerly engagement which activates the kinetic properties of the text: (syntax as processual movement, sequentiality, reference as a psycholinguistic refraction without alternity however, association, connotation as the dynamic expansion of a meaning important for its *felt* expansiveness. And what such decipherment constitutes is not so much a reading as an alternative or additional writing of the text. We may say that the realization of a decipherment indicates a specific movement of the text, a turning back of itself upon itself to formulate a centering, proposing a new reading as a new writing.

I take it that reference, the mystifying carrot dangled before the eyes of the reader, is the sole preventative to such a co-participation. the structural support of both literacy and capitalist economy is reference. The cipher acts as a critique of language by way of a de-construction, demystification and expressed truncation of the verbal Sign's serial reference; moving language into the domain of its autonomous parts seized as entities and expressed directly as the isolated actions of a surface.

Language-centered counter-communication concentrates upon factors of formation inside of language and not on the centrifugal functioning of words; it is hence counter narrational and counter-commodital at the same time. Seen through a Marxian perceptual set, the cipher is a strategic method of creating non-commodital process-products, a method of ontological deconstruction that casts reader and writer both into the one, same labour process. We might speak of this kind of writing as a bracketed poetics, deliberate in its suspension of all linguistic procedure, in order to allow an attention to be focussed on a phonological form.

In a capitalistic, referentialist context, criticism is that which validates a text; it is an exterior energy brought to focus on a divided form and designed to alter perception of that form. Criticism of this kind is a divided labour from the text. In language-centered writing, where ciphericity is dominant, criticism fuses with creativity and becomes an internal quality of the text itself. Internal criticism of this kind takes the form of a foregrounding of the problematics of the verbal sign as the sign itself displays this in its own truncation.

By eliminating grammatical armament from language, by a freeing of the parts to be themselves and by inviting the reader into this immanence of text, the full, polysemous possibilities of language are opened up. Reference is no longer the promise at the end of the grammatical road, no longer the opiate of the reader. Rather the text becomes the communal space of a labour, initiated by the writer and extended by the second writer (the reader). So we break, finally, the divisive structure of the conventional reading process. The old duality of reader — writer collapses into the one compound function, and the two actions are permitted to become a simultaneous experience within the activity of the engager.

Language-centering: the ontologic core: that there is no anterior identity; that authorship becomes the internal quality of text. Counter-communication of this kind might also mark a significant extension of Olsonian field theory in projective verse from the sense of the poem as occupying a mediate position as energy field, supplied by the writer and drawn from by the reader, to the concept of the poem as a rotating energy source, a translative construct in which the written text is subject to re-writing in reading, thereby refracting the energy present. What is proposed then, is a specific application of reading to function as a writing that transforms the text.

i) remove the arrow of reference. no alternity. no direction outward.
ii) replace it with word, letter, phoneme or grapheme i.e. with the point of place and event.

Is the Cipher similar to Wittgenstein's 'formal concept'? Quote: Formal concepts cannot, in fact, be represented by means of a function, as concepts proper can.

For their characteristics, formal properties are not expressed by means of functions. Unquote (Wittgenstein, *Tractatus* 4.126). And earlier: 'When something falls under a formal concept as one of its objects, this cannot be expressed by means of a proposition. Instead it is shown in the very sign for this object.'

Is a word a place that meaning can exist in?

... Language: i.e. overall proficiency with localized ignorance. Reference: the continentalist drive in language.
'Names are like points; propositions like arrows.' (Wittgenstein). So the cipheral text must be nominal at base.

Clearly then, language-centered writing involves the most determinate poetics yet proposed in the history of writing. Determinate because it avoids the central contradiction of the Linguistic Sign — the use of an absence to re-present a present. Reference is that absence, leading out from a present sign to an extrasemiotic state: the imposed self-destruction of language in the world 'of real things'.

The Cipher, and language-centered counter-communication in general provides a text in which the sign names itself a present naming with signs *standing* period; not signs standing for an absence.

CODICIL

collides triangle lucid nap
broad wet exertion

                    sift plunges
                              halo shallows
        lean-to precocious
                  trickle blade
            railing fluency plankton abrupt
                      sea's rib
                          glows lobes   (Ray Di Palma)

Conventional reading patterns promote the sense of a linguistic mask:
a desire to get beyond the words themselves or alternatively 'beneath'
them into a region of reference: of images, symbols and ideas that the
surface syntagms seem somehow to withhold from us. Conventional
reading hence resists the sheer fact of a text's graphic immanence.
Surface. Words, traditionally, are seen to simultaneously reveal and
obscure intents and meanings, with the Sign's own mask taking the
form of the signifier that transports — yet at the same time delays — the
destination in the signified. Di Palma's piece demonstrates the kinetics
of mask (as we 'read', 'see' or scan it there are certain lexic movements,
associations etc.; there are adjacencies, contiguities but no pre-
ordained connections, yet it is a mask without depth. As readers we
come to feel the movement *per se* as a movement without destination
upon a surface of text. It mobilizes an object quality, property of
immanence, replacing depth by the parallel, sympathetic sense of surface complexity by which mask becomes moebius and depth a surface
fold.
    This emphasis upon surface movement suggests a topological
analogy that helps get us further into the essential movement and
structure of these texts. 'Topology represents the primary intellectual
operation capable of revealing the modalities of surfaces, volumes,
boundaries, contiguities, holes, and above all the notions of *inside* and
outside, with the attendant ideas of insertion, penetration, containment, emergence and the like.'[1] An interesting analogy presents itself
in the instance of the Klein Worm — a form which differs form conventional geometric forms in its characteristic absence of both inner and
outer surfaces.[2]

'Instead you have a contained tube and an uncontained tube, a contained hole
and an uncontained hole ... Any part of the form can touch, contact,
communicate with, flow with any other part ... We have a quality of
continuousness in the form and at the same time intraconainment ... (This
form) is permeated by context. It has no walls. Yet it uses its structural
infolding for maintaining itself changing in a sufficiently regular way to find
new relations.'[3]

Bruce Morrissette has already applied this analogy to the narrative structure in Robbe Grillet's novels,[4] but here I would like to extend that application to counter-communicative writing and utilize that Klein form as a model of the actual mechanism of reading.

wlkt   sTdh

                    (FPRTO

T

                E

    (fF)

                    Tts

xcphj   t   t

            cb   (mccaffery)

The above is a Klein Form. The text is 'without walls', it is open field or 'constellational' with the principle of syntax replaced by that of milieu. A reading activates certain relational pathways, a flow of parts, and — denied the exteriorizing force of reference — a structural 'infolding' of the textual elements. Sign itself is a topological aspect of text with the referent and signified 'outside' the text, and the signifier 'inside'. The excommunication of the referent and the established surplus of signifiers can be seen as a complication both of surface and of the nature of interiorities. For the signifier, when devoid of its signified (i.e. cipher), is like an interiority without the drive to externalization.

Fragmentation: i.e. as that which creates the notion of textual equality. 'Phonemes of the Word fragment! You have nothing to lose but your referents!'. Non-grammatical emphasis is equal emphasis. Non-subordination. Non-hierarchy. Hence multi-directional.

In fragmentation there is no external support lent to a signifier from the signified for that very relation is severed in the act of fragmentation. Result: a surplus state of signifiers. Ciphers. Non-grammatical surface interplays of signifying elements:

    ice   ism   out   play   han
        elph   eps   oop   ng
ap   ure   er   ut   ed
    sense   ratum   camel   mand   (Amirkhanian)

Such a poem is neither a verbal stimulant nor a verbal tranquillizer, but rather a paraverbal surface onto which a reader is invited to step into productive effort. What it is not is textual commodity, replete with reference to be consumed by 'an understanding' reader. The demand is for *praxis* not consumption.

By investing *total* energy into counter-communication, language-centered texts become surface pressures *that functionally dislocate the reader.* Syntax. More milieu than syntax with the letter very often the basic unit of organizaton. Andrews speaks of 'each word being a syntax'. The letter in space with self-generating aura. Letter clusters and the occasional word where meaning is held to reverb not connect into larger compounds:

mel
ethwe fub sditas   (Melnick)

That is, the elevation of letter to morphologic status.

I believe it to be in the work of Melnick, Silliman, Coolidge, Di Palma and Andrews that a new concept of the meaningful is emerging, a concept based not upon communication but upon a creative entry into the opacity of evacuated signs. It is perhaps less a new concept of meaning than a new attitude to the place of meaning within and without a language set. For what it suggests is this: that meaning is dependent on the context of attention that a reader brings to his text; i.e. meaning is the sum total value that a reader puts into a piece. Meaning: what the reader brings as praxis, not what the reader takes away as reference. So we can see how language-centered writing enforces a charity, a total givingness of reader and writer to their texts. Texts so long have been those things which a reader has raped, drawn out of, now is the moment of the text's receiving into itself. And the reader? An extension of vocabulary, both operator and component of a textual event.

Cipher is the baptism of the residual. The sign on holiday.

Script and *Language.* A poem enters the domain of script when the letter assumes the role of formal unit and stereographic relation becomes its major quality. Relations graphed across a surface that affirm their own immanence, their own autonomous dynamic. The *scriptive* would be in contrast to the *linguistic* poem whose basic unit is the word and whose radical property is signfication.

In his book *Space,* Coolidge moves from language into script (as does Melnick in PCOET), into the manufacture of graphic events ('graphemes') within a stereographic space:

erything
eral
stantly
ined
ards
cal
nize

Note, however, that Coolidge plays upon familiar reading patterns, adopting truncations that suggest complete vocabularies. As a result there's a bifurcation in the reading experience between the feeling of instant graphic events seen before you as complete discontinuities; and the felt possibility of developing continuities the more the reader approaches the text from familiar paradigms:

everything
mineral
instantly
defined
towards
optical
canonize

suggests the type of 'completion' and textual writing possible. Note too how both the spatial placement of the graphemes and the sheer fact of their density command equal attention. It's the finely executed balance of these two qualities of space and density that inform the best language centered pieces. Compositionally it's the engineering of these two drives towards a form understood as both potential sign and matter that is central. Syntax is transformed to become a calculus of densities and a geomantic ordering of pure experiences ('events' as events are 'signs without histories').

The balancing of space and density results in the concretization of the cipher, the emptying of the sign of its function and the presentation of the signifier as truncated materiality. It is hence oppositional to any abstract poetics and stands comparison to concrete poetry in the manner in which both isolate verbal elements in order to demonstrate their own structures and ontologies without the obstacle of referring to a thing outside their present being and shape.

woe   eroa
asrglry   s
wea tiro   bohmuluk
codfix   a,azz   oboi   (Melnick)

Linguistic endgame? Or scriptive project? A poem that anchors its elements as a field of prelinguistic chromosomes that embody the energies which may develop into word or into event, is an accoustic, a cipheral happening. Appreciation of potential *per se,* of that quality in signs that Wittgenstein insists we recognize at the beginning of *The Tractatus*: that every actual instance embodies all the possibilities it could have been. The paradigm is always on the back of the syntagm. And more recently Sartre in *The Critique of Dialectical Reason* that 'every word ... contains the whole of language and reaffirms it.'

Possibility is an immanence.

... and asking the reader grasp a poem's ontology within the sum total of its unrealized potential, with that potential considered as the coiled but ready reflex of the sign anterior to its thrust outward into reference.

To suggest then that meaning be considered (if at all) as a doubleness around the core of the cipher: meaning as encipherment, a consolidation of the status of the vacated word; and meaning as decipherment or thrust towards completion of a partial sign. Meaning here, is not the product nor the attendant of a referring, not a destination outside of the living event of the words and graphic shapes; it is rather the occasioning of a focus upon text, that environment which encompasses such readings and makes them possible. In other words, language centered texts respond better to a sense of meaning as an imported context into decontextualised language zones.

Decontextualization, the salient feature of language centered writing, serves to return language elements to their primary meanings. Within the parameters of readership what is opposed is a simple to a complex readability. Readability becomes complicated when language is made conscious of itself and of its source exterior to the sequential progress of the line. Andrews is especially successful at such complications, there is a striking non-gravitational effect within many of his pieces that rises from the multiple interlocking of parts and the replacement of linear direction by a vertical and horizontal balancing which creates a tracery in spatial neutrality and highlights the coronal nature of the graphemes:

ca ja a th an ne sh th wa pe
qu ci fo in ba wh vi re se th
eu co st cu wo al su cr ce re
in ma vi si ba am ch qu an is
th th cu ni se fa wo ap se th
pr st th st th th ac wh wh pa

wi ha wa ti bo pr wo fe th tr
fa sp if so th th pl fo to tw

The weight of the iconicity plus the weight of the possibilities to index. Andrews here takes the word beyond its lexical base (that base in definition where each word operates independently from out of its dictionary force of isolation) to the preverbal region of the operating letter.

Time and Tense.

To remove reference in the way that language centered writing does, is to radically alter the category of linguistic time. Most critically it removes tense as a temporal issue within a text through a centering of time utterly within the assertion (the happening) of each lexeme. Cipheral time is the time of each word 'happening,' accumulating into the total time of the text's happening itself, as text here is the duration of the reading.

pulling banters flank blonde
folded captain girlfriend hisself
drive leg chemist's punching
fire milling cuffs naw
captain madman ways roast
bags excitedly ass bad   (Andrews: 'The Red Hallelujah')

The self-standing word is the word which is free from imposed context. It resides within its lexical basis, within its total content. 'Blonde' holds a totality of content and a range of possible application that an additional (contextualizing) phrase – the blonde hairdresser – serves to restrict and which, 'The young, blonde, hairdresser in Schumaker's variety store' restricts even further. This is not to suggest by the term 'total content' the word as a generalization, or as somehow nonspecific, but rather to emphasize the tractable *weight* of the single word when freed from specific use; the open–endedness of its indexicality; its processual, non-commodity nature; the single word as the in-gathered point of infinite application. It is the ability to contain this kind of paradigmatic structure within the syntagmatic instance that is responsible for the tremendous density in this kind of writing. In a grammatical line of discourse, a word must assume a chosen context, and enter into a divisive labour. Freed, however, from the enforced communality that is grammar, the word approaches its own totalization and we are forced to encounter the word frontally as an absolute property.

As to *page* in language-centred discourse?

Page, as before, remains an *interpretive space*. The page is no less than *the sign for attention itself*. A geographical cipher. The non-referring gesture of the language-centered writer is hence to fill an empty sign (the page) with further ciphers. Text and page relate as a cipheral palimpsest or even cipheral pun. Cipher on top of cipher — the sexuality of the emptied sign and the maximization of all possibilities of what the signs can index.

We descend into their emptiness to experience how full they can be. Orpheus.

<pre>
          eras
              tory
                       ien
            bined
                swer
                    ft
                priv
     lat   a   ge
                 hyst
            trem
  i   h   (from Piec., bruce andrews)
</pre>

When a text is perceived, it is that thing. Is there a difference between reading and seeing this piece? What precisely is the psycholinguistic experience of a translation from the seen into the read and from the read into the seen?

Language-centered writing displays language in opacity gained by this subtle balancing of the literate and the perceptible. To see language is to experience its opacity; to read signs is to pursue their operations of spatial discharge. The above text is fragment only if the mind cares to retreat back into its familiar lexical associations and refuse to take a stand upon the dialectical pinion of the seen and the read. This poem is a poem of absolute denotation, a total condition of self-reflexive sign structured by aura rather than syntax and stressing the sign's own excess of presence precisely because there is no operating reference. It is a patterned cipher whose gravity obtains from a surplus of signification. It is over-determined and hence a presentness. It cannot be located in any category and thus is not context bound. A signifier without a signified and whose destination is inward to the center of its own form.

In other words the condensation of the sign: the centripetal movement of the cipher into the core of its very being and executed prior to its being called upon as traditional vehicle programmed to an outside destination. Condensation brings the experience of such texts to the surface of the page where script meets the threshold of a reading at the point of 'seeing signs.'

The cipher. The art of the deficient message that's characterized by shifts in linguistic form from grammar to lexis, from closed, contextual form to open de-contextual set. Foucault, writing of the modern condition of language, states it has become a thing of space: 'a universal space of inscription.' Once the fallacy of the referent is revealed for what it is then we are able to see language as that highly complex play of signifiers detached from stable signifieds; a language no longer representing a world outside of itself, but a language obeying its own constitution and dynamic. I take cipher to be this: the natural extension of language in our time and in the pressures, relations and contradictions of this age, beyond the referentially anchored sign into a metaphysics of presence unparalleled in past writing. Shapes made to stay and we to experience that abidance. It is the particular gift of such writers as Ron Silliman, Bruce Andrews, Clark Coolidge and Ray DiPalma to have provided the first instantiated phase of post-literate writing; the first to understand (and to thrust out a solid poetics from that understanding) of the structural divisiveness of literacy: the metaphysics of its absence in the thrust of reference out of the ignored presence of script; and its tragic separation of reader from writer by the horizontal line of 'communication' and the vertical axis of the poem as commodity.

Happy trails to that interface.

NOTES

1 Bruce Morrissette, 'Topology and the French Nouveau Roman' in *Boundary 2*, 1.1, Fall, 1972 p.47.
2 On the Klein Worm see Warren Brody, 'Biotopology' in *Radical Software*, No.4, Summer 1971.
3 *ibid.* (quoted in Morrissette, p.52.
4 *loc. cit.*

BIBLIOGRAPHY

There is no central source of this work. I would suggest, however, as primary material in language-centered writing the issue of Alcheringa containing the fine mini-anthology of language centered writing: 'The Dwelling Place 9 Poets' i.e. *Alcheringa*, New Series 1.2, 1975. As well as the representative selection here, a reader will also receive the added treat of Ron Silliman's fine essay: *Suprised By Sign.*

Toothpick, Lisbon & The Orcas Islands The Andrews/Wiater Issue, Fall 1973 is essential material. Containing works by Andrews, Sondheim, Silliman, Eigner, DiPalma et al.

A recent anthology: *None of The Above,* ed. Michael Lally, includes language centered pieces in its representation of American Poetry 1945-1975. Crossing Press 1976.

Not mentioned in this essay is the work of Jackson MacLow, the pilgrim father of aleatoric poetry whose texts — chance generated — are suitably a propos of ciphericity. MacLow adopts chance procedures to free language from grammatical perspective and sequential reference. Therefore, I would suggest a careful reading of *Stanzas for Iris Lezak,* Something Else Press, New York, 1971 and *22 Light Poems,* Los Angeles, Black Sparrow Press 1968. Ron Silliman is the tireless editor of Tottel's, in many way's the lifeline of language centered writing. Issue 14 is a special Bruce Andrews Issue.

Additional reading and research is bringing more writers of nonreferential relevance to the fore. Of particular note at this point are Thomas A. Clark, Neil Mills and Charles Verey (all from the U.K.); Canadian Dave MacFadden's Ova Yogas seems stunningly applicable (and alas for the miss in this essay) and buddah b.p.nichol, minister of syntax, high chief of frame concept and co-participant in the Toronto Research Group is touching on these areas in his epic (and as yet unpublished) *Translating Translating Appolinaire* and *Negatives*.

All leads here are to excite a reader to delve into that fascinating and ultimately intractible world of the little magazine.

BRUCE ANDREWS
Text and Context

Language is the center, the primary material, the sacred corpus, the primum mobile, the erotic sense of its own shared reality. Not a separate but a distinguishing reality. Yet where is the energy invested?

There is nothing to decipher.
There is nothing to explain.

◄§ To engage in the collective task of creating a literature no longer finds support on the scaffolding of discourse. In dismantling the scaffolding, we create a literature — a record of negative retrieval. 'Unreadability' — that which requires new readers, and teaches new readings.

◄§ Anything that is not a hypnosis is partial. No text, in that sense, is 'wholesome' — only experiences. Something is lost but something is gained. Not exactly 'deferentialist' — for can writing be adequately tagged with what it's not doing? Isn't that the old chest-busting negativism of the avant-garde? Qualities are to be *aufgehoben,* not stricken. The sign's structure is *for* us by being before us; it does not dissolve into an outward looking system of radar, or of reading as radar. Reference isn't banished, except in the extremes of lettrism — and here it even stays on as a reminder. Remember? Not 'formalist' — for does this display an obsession with form as apart from the full potential of language? All form is an expression and an inscription: how personal can you get? how personal can you be? Form as physical, as material, as unlike the idea of elsewhere. 'Here' is more corporeal, somehow, than 'there'. Look over there = Avert your eyes. The here and now.

Thus, how do we read what is meant *precisely to* be read? that is given us for no other purpose, and without distraction (even those distractions which we often take as the stigmata of 'reading' but are really those of entertainment, those of good fog). *Wordsome.*

◄§ As though the referential fallacy and the pathetic fallacy were but special cases of each other. Desperate barriers against regret? Pragmatic illusions. As though the world, or even the text, were a simply structural density that could nourish us, alone. How communal can you get? Show us a way out. The way out is not through the basement door, getting lost among prerequisite cultural mementos, in deceptive (or descriptive) depth.

⪧ Pointing, or referential signification first signifies depth, or reinforces the security found in possible depth — the pot at the end of the rainbow, the commodity or ideology that brings fulfillment; choicelessness; a lower layer that is nature-like in its immobility or fixity or self-evidence. 'The fix is on.' It hypnotizes us with these expectations, long before any particular content is unearthed. The format massages us with its illusions — false bottoms, peek-a-boo costumes, trapdoors, you have nothing to do with this.

I am sawing the woman in half — I devour
one part, repress the other.

Commodities are sold, productions are forgotten. You feed on this vertical system — the comfort of a semantic presence that you no longer have the strength to get tired of, or wary of. You are learning the *trip,* forgetting, as in an amnesia, the character of the places you left. The medium, verticality, threatens to become the predominant message.

Semantics: the souvenirs of tourism.

Centripetal as vertical.
Depth as set frame.
Context as reference.

⪧ How much are we willing to destroy our attentiveness to the way words act and interact in order to gain the advantages of description or of representation and a phobia toward what is present? Centripetal motion is that of imposing contexts suitable for explanatory purposes — is this the one in the 'light' of which such actions are intelligible? Those impositions are usually cushioned by grammar (where syntax plays a representational role); without them, the language is a frontage. Not a false front, not a directive screen, but an unencumbered energy.
  Grammar as constraining rules; meaning as constitutive rules — yet these latter are not imposed as a prior dictate. They issue forth instead from the inward shapes of the language.

Grammatical quicksand. Keep your place!
Syntax: the scaffolding of verticality.

Myth — the mask, the ideology, the technicolor escape, the promise of transcendence in meaning. A regular reading has been a sideshow promoting semantic elixirs, imagist tonics. It's advertised to take a while to work: this *delay* between word and referent teases us; we reach the 'intent' or 'motive' only by indirection and without participating fully – enjoying the temporariness of the trip. Coitus interruptus.

◁§ There is an other way. The vertical axis (downwards, as a ladder tempting us) need not structure the reading – for it does not structure the text. This is what I would mean by calling it non-referentially organized writing, as a subset of language-centered writing. Horizontal organizing principles, without an insistent (that is to say, imposed) depth. Secret meaning is not a hidden layer, but a hidden organization of the surface. Not latent, but quite handsomely manifest.

Meaning is not produced *by* the sign, but by the contexts we bring to the potentials of language – not enforced by a vertical elevator, the mark of the double, the vacation. The impulse toward excavation, toward contextual explanation, can be put in the background – for such a hollowing out of lower depths, of labyrinthine caves of signification, goes on within the gaps.

All light, all in broad daylight: bring your own context. Radiant surfaces; myth.

◁§ An alternative remains 'wordness', 'eventism' – a way of *reconstituting* language by unpacking the tool box. The constitutive rules of meaning are not taking the words *away* from us. We can create those rules as we go along, and as we return, centrifugally, to center, centering, to surface, to degree zero, to sea level. We are urged back by the absence of imposed escapes! A semantic normality – a norm-iness (a worminess) is one such escape.

Signs which are constituted from paradigmatic rules, from their interaction (their play) with others, their trajectory without the dead weight of context.

◁§ Atmospherically: what surrounds words may be more readily, and satisfyingly perceived than an iron cage of connection: referential connections which take place below the plane, out of sight, or earshot, therefore self-denyingly, without physique, or erotic delight.

The distinction between 'possession goals' and 'milieu goals'.

As in lowering the iron cage beneath the waters to be attacked by sharks, to be eaten alive by outside forces. Obedience to Authority vs. the improvisation of rules. If only the imposed representations could be loosed, deviance would be so much sweeter.

The first real presence is the awareness of absence, of no escape — of a vertical dimension acting only as an echo, a nostalgic reverb. Nothing is compressed from outside into familiar shapes & pleasing passage — the inwardness is the site of compression & density.

Language turns itself inside out for us.
Reversible vests; two-piece suits.

Signifieds provide echoes, harmonies, overtones, but not the principles of organization; the signifiers take on an atonality without shyness. There are external supports, but not protective blankets. Feet, not roots.

Events without trots.
Bottomless, negative space.

Confusion of realms, profusion of events and interplay on the surface. All, or mostly surface. The subject has disappeared behind the words only to emerge in front, or inside them. Presentations of the present, not representations of tense.

A more complicated topology than the virtuosos of reference had imagined: Rubber-Sheet Geometry. The one-sided surfaces. Any two points may be connected merely by starting at one point and tracing a path to the other without lifting the attention or carrying it over any boundary or separation.

Transference. *Différance*. A carnival of ciphers.

Fragmentation doesn't banish the references *embodied* in individual words; merely — they are not placed in a *series*, in grammar, in a row, *on a shelf*. A more playful anarchy, a Möbius free-for-all is created. Texts are themselves signi*fieds,* not mere signifiers. TEXT: it requires no hermeneusis for it is itself one — of itself.

Gyroscopes.
Self-referring.
Ouroboros.

The consummation is concrete, graphic, erotic, physical, phenomenal, a greeting, not a keepsake. An absence embodied in a presence.
   Words hover above usage. Meaning is not use, or is not all use. Meaning is the enabled incapacity to impose a usage.
Excommunication, rather than appropriation.

Words are the ghosts of regret.

Referentiality is diminished by organizing the language around other features or axes, around features which make present to us words' lack of transparency, their physicality, their refusal to be motivated along schematic lines by frames exterior to themselves. Refusing to 'point', or to be arranged according to a 'pointing system', they risk the charge of being pointless. That is, to be a self-sufficiency of event — confounding the inadequation of words and referents that we mistakenly call meaning. This is not meaning. Instead, this is meaning. *This*.

◄§ If explanation is contextual, this counter-explanation is a rebuff which shows a larger possibility — an emptied cipher that speaks of all the productions we can fill it with. Each associative band, each band of semantic radiation, takes place with less guidance from the games and aims of representation or with little grammatical constraint. A carnival atmosphere, therefore ... workers' control ... self-management.

Commodification, on the other hand, requires clear signposts — Easy outs.

Language-centered work resembles an active myth-making. It resembles a creation of a community and of a world-view by a once-divided-but-now-fused Reader and Writer. This creation is not instrumental. It is immanent, in plain sight (and plainsong), moving along a surface with all the complications of a charter or a town-meeting.

A *publicity*.

Depth is a spiral or whirligig — taken in stride, does not 'get in the way'. Not a tourniquet.

◄§ The focus on the ways in which language can inscribe itself as other than reference. As an individuation *within* (but not compensating for) a community. Reading as a particular reading, an enactment, a co-Production. Here are the simultaneous co-creators of a smallish linguistic community. A scriptorium.

Counter-commodification: a barbaric, if politically apt term which spins around our scrimmages against reference.

Writing as action; reading as action, not a behavior *observed by* a text, sitting there, bored, looking at us.

Binary, with the text as switchman.
Blurs, so fast = mesh

Texts read the reader.

◢§ Altering textual roles might bring us closer to altering the larger social roles of which textual ones are a feature. READING: not the glazed gaze of the consumer, but the careful attention of a producer, or co-producer. The transformer. (capacitators? resistors?) Full of care. It's not a product that is produce, but a *production,* an event, a praxis, a model for future practice. The domination of nature can find a critique here as well — not in abstinence. Not aleatory.

From each according to
To each according to

A semantic atmosphere, or milieu, rather than the possessive individualism of reference.

Indexicality.
Absolute.
Absolution.

Such work has a utopian force only begun to be revealed.

◢§ Language is an Other which imposed meanings attempt, luckily unsuccessfully, to disguise for us. The 'Primal Lack'. Life against death. It is not a monologic communication, but a spatial interaction fore-grounded within a frame of our own generosity. Our gifts, its physical integrity.
    Stay inside. It is all here. The non-imperial state: without need for the expansion or externalization that comes from the refusal to redis-tribute the surplus at home. The same holds for a non-imperial or language-centered writing.
    Surplus of signifier = the floating signifier. *Mana.* trace.
    Engulfment, flooding of signifiers without predetermined signi-fication. Instead, the cliches of existentialism — freedom, surplus of signifiers, *choice as constitutive* & we do it ourselves.
    Politics not concealed any longer.

Decontextualization.

◢§ References *evacuate* the sign. In its place, intentionality fills it up — contributed both by reader and writer. This is a self-conscious (at times, self-referring) intention capable of acknowledging the Other, a sense of absence. It finds a cure in communal consort, in concert, without the mediation of obedience, without the *orders* of reference.

What is made concrete is what is truly absent [unity — the world as one, a toppling of Babel], and not what is tantalizingly withheld or delayed only to be theatrically hawked and consumed [reference — the world as split, the divisiveness and / or repressiveness of outside imposed content] Repression as the delayed gratification of unity.

Works seem the embodiment, the bodying forth of this string of lights connecting reader and writer, reader and text. We speak of a 'body of work' — by this, what do we mean: the body politic, love's body. Embodiment is the needed copulation — of practices. No longer repressed, the two spheres are fused.

◄§ As if the references offered could be known, through the act of appropriating them! Representation is ownership. Yet the *meant* (the signifers) completely outdistances the *known* (the signifieds, what is referred to). We come, historically, for the sake of a denying and repressive order, to be satisfied with what can be known, owned, consumed, referred to, easily intersubjectively communicated, predicted, controlled. Lost are some of the physical ways of intending, of expressing, of meaning, of motion, of pronouncing, sobbing: the overabundance of signifier, the excessive presence, the unconscious, the sign's arbitrary nature. Otherliness — we are emancipated only by recognition, or, occasionally, by the conjugation of reading and writing, in completing language's own work and words. Not duality. Readers do the rewriting. Sometimes they do enough to give a social force to the absences they are first given.

References are not foregrounded. The body of work is not organized around the referential axis. Therefore, is not genitally organized? No 'discharge' of a specific substantive kind leaves the polymorphous play of the linguistic units. The genital organization is monarchic, or mimetic (from the family circle). Language-centering seems to capture some of the more exploratory aspects of the consequences of itself, without referential guidance, without parental guidance, without tense. *Not a compensation,* or its prime model: ego armor.

What is collective as signifier as unconscious — does not atomize or individualize in the ways references have. Lost — through a castration complex, an incestuous access eliminated by the triumph of market conditions and kinship, an imposed outward order of signification?

How have we come to the words, to our selves, our absenting community — all flesh, all fleshed together.

The community which is unified, self-contained, mercantilist, unwilling to break down into spheres — resisting the division of labor (and hierarchy) that comes with literacy. Is this an incestual nostalgia for illiteracy? A polymorphous lettrism, a movement into *script, grapheme, syllable, cipher, glyph, gloss, corpus?*

Readers embody texts.
Physical language.

RAY DIPALMA
Crystals

◦§ You must talk with two tongues, if you do not wish to cause confusion. WYNDHAM LEWIS

◦§ One invents a technique or procedure by oneself; one does not invent entirely on one's own *a state of mind*. JUAN GRIS

◦§ Twenty-nine words from TREMOLO: Term, tole, tome, tool, tore, retool, role, rote, room, root, rotl, roto, metro, melt, merl, mole, molt, mort, morel, mote, motor, motel, moor, moot, oleo, omer, loom, loot, lore.

◦§ The schematism by which ... [one understands] the ... world ... is ... deeply hidden ... IMMANUEL KANT

◦§ The tragedy of the writer is that he might only be himself. EDWARD DAHLBERG

◦§ Grammar in relation to a tree and two horses. GERTRUDE STEIN

◦§ Bad writing comes from insufficient curiosity. EZRA POUND

◦§ Patrons and staff are urged to stay out of work areas which are marked by warning signs. There is the danger of falling debris and unsafe footing. The reality of renovation will become increasingly apparent with a growing army of workmen, activity everywhere, and distracting noise as the project gains momentum. A construction fence will soon be erected around exterior portions.

◦§ I shall derive my emotions solely from the arrangement of surfaces, I shall present my emotions by the arrangement of my surfaces, the planes and lines by which they are defined. GAUDIER-BRZESKA

◦§ Many a single word ... is itself a concentrated poem, having stores of poetical thought and imagery laid up in it. RICHARD CHEVENIX TRENCH

◦§ I forget most of what I read; nonetheless it contributes to the preservation of my mind. LICHTENBERG

◆§ Do not be bewildered by the surfaces; in the depths all becomes law.
RAINER MARIA RILKE

◆§ A crowd of naked people stands around ... others ride aimlessly in circles ... Still others swim languidly ... There are birds, flowers, fruits. The girls' hair falls straight with only a hint of wave. A few black men and women mingle with the white groups, peacefully accepted ...

◆§ Gesture ... rendering visible ... the structural rhythm. JAMES JOYCE

◆§ Nourish, nourish, feed your friends,
Tell them not to fear the worm today. ASA BENVENISTE

◆§ The spacious probes of atonality ...

◆§ Successions of words are so agreeable. GERTRUDE STEIN

◆§ Nature geometrizeth. SIR THOMAS BROWNE

◆§ The interval has all the rights ROSMARIE WALDROP

◆§ *Ron Silliman:* Star, Temperance, Death, Moon, Strength, Justice, Justice, Strength, Hanged Man, Fool, Death

Bruce Andrews: Magician, Star, Judgement, Priestess, Emperor, Fool, Death, Empress, Star, Emperor, Judgement, Moon

Steve McCaffery: Moon, Sun, Emperor, Judgement, Emperor, Hanged Man, Priestess, Priestess, Fool, Hierophant, Hierophant, Emperor, Star, World

◆§ It is not I who create myself, rather I happen to myself. C.G. JUNG

◆§ The chief claim of the Cabala, and of all illuminist doctrines, was to the possession of powers to unfold the secrets and mysteries of creation and particularly to reveal and explain the divine nature of God.
ENID STARKIE

◆§ Think of how they avoid around. GERTRUDE STEIN

◆§ The desire to penetrate into the nature of form, to understand the space it occupies itself and the space in which it is situated, brought about a searching analysis in which the familiar contours of its surface have all simultaneously forfeited their customary opaqueness. The

screen of outward appearances has been made to undergo a crystallization which renders it more transparent. Each facet has been stood on
edge so as to allow us to appreciate the volumes that lie beneath the
surface. Instead of being invited to caress with a glance a smooth outer
skin we are presented with a transparent honeycomb construction in
which surface and depth are both visible. ROLAND PENROSE

✑ Language disguises thought ... WITTGENSTEIN

✑ The development of my work has been, I feel, more subconscious
than unconscious. I do not work by intellectual deductions. My work
is a kind of self-contained contemplation. MARK TOBEY

✑ ... Cézanne ... gave me a new feeling about composition ... I was
obsessed by the idea of composition ... it was not solely the realism of
the charactrers but the realism of the composition which was the
important thing. GERTRUDE STEIN

✑ The value of the ideogrammic method is that it enables you to make
statements that don't exceed your knowledge. HUGH KENNER

✑ A true noun, an isolated thing, does not exist in nature. Things are
only the terminal points, or rather the meeting points, of actions, cross
sections cut through actions, snapshots. Neither can a pure verb, an
abstract motion, be possible in nature. The eye sees noun and verb as
one: things in motion, motion in things. ERNEST FENOLLOSA

✑ We don't get free of the idea that the sense of a sentence accompanies
the sentence: is there alongside it. WITTGENSTEIN

✑ If we look at an isolated printed word and repeat it long enough, it
ends by assuming an entirely unnatural aspect ... its body is indeed
there, but its soul is fled. It is reduced, by this new way of attending to
it, to its sensational nudity. We never before attended to it in this way,
but habitually got it clad with its meaning the moment we caught
sight of it, and rapidly passed from it to the other words of the phrase.
We apprehended it, in short, with a cloud of associates, and thus
perceiving it, we felt it quite otherwise than as we feel it now, divested
and alone. WILLIAM JAMES

1971-76

RON SILLIMAN
For Open Letter

Steve,

The historical function of language-centered writing is to achieve, to the greatest extent possible, a post-referential writing. There is a crucial distinction between non-referential and post-referential poetries which has only recently become clear. The term 'non-referential' was first used by Bob Grenier six or seven years ago to describe his work. His two major sequences, *A Day at the Beach,* and *Sentences,* and Clark Coolidge's early long poems, *The Maintains* and *Polaroid,* may be identified as the major products of the non-referential tendency. The very form of the term 'non-referential' reveals its essentially diacritical nature. It negates reference, typically doing so by the utilization of specific contexts. Perhaps more important than the works of non-referentiality was the fact that it revealed referential works as objects of a specific type.

Reference has always been an element in language. Its primary form is the combination of a gesture and an object, such as the picking up of a rock or one fragment (thereby creating a 'tool'). Referentiality, in the narrow sense in which I am using the term here, is a specific historical deformation of reference.

At an early historical stage, poems were the shared language events of small tribal groups. The value of the poem was one of exchange and use. It was the product and common property of the tribe and not the individual. The language of the poem was physical and alive to its speakers. It had its own integrity and recognized the separate integrity of the world. It was empowered to discuss the world but did not presume to describe it. It was the gesture and not the object. The joy in language was that which any man or woman feels in any act of creative labour. One sees evidences of this reality everywhere in the tribal poetries of the world, much of which has been made commonly available by the work of Jerry Rothenberg. One even sees its traces in early English literature. Rhyme is an ordering of language by its physical elements. The physicality of language as a determining element commonly recognized by all speakers is a precondition of any such ordering.

One need only point to the fact of Evelyn Wood and speed-reading to get a sense that there has been a drastic change. Language has changed and with it there have been changes in the art of language, in the poem.

In the preface to the 1948 Origin edition of *A* 1-12, Louis (pronounced 'Lewie') Zukofsky projected the possibility of a 'scientific' definition of poetry, true for all poems past and future. What Zukofsky, a Marxist, should have known (but the historical preconditions for such a knowledge were not yet present) was that the stage of historical development determines the natural laws of the poem. Indeed, the stage of historical development determines the natural laws of language.

It is important to keep in mind the fact that in history and in society all 'laws' have the nature of a tendency.

At a certain post-tribal stage of development, the world of natural objects was replaced by a world of things. The defining characteristic of a thing is its double-projection: it is both the end result of a labour process (a product) and an object for general social consumption (a commodity). A thing is a schizoid object. A world of such things is madness. The resolution of this dual projection can only occur when the productive forces control the means of production and consumption: in short, communism.

If such a resolution does not (as has been the case everywhere in the world) occur, then a struggle arises between the opposing projections. When one set of forces is dominant, the other is repressed. This has taken place not simply in the market-place, but in every aspect of society and humanity. It has determined consciousness.

The repression of the product* (labour) nature of things is called the commodity fetish. In language it is a fetish of description, of reference and has a second higher-order fetish of narration. It is the picture Wittgenstein could not get outside (for it lay in his language and his language seemed to repeat it to him inexorably). It is the object without the gesture. The object appears now to move of its own free will. We are, all of us, suffering from a mass aphasia. Language-centered writing is a step on the road to health.

The English language lost its product-nature gradually over a period of 400 years. The new commodity language gradually took on new descriptive powers. It was now able to describe the world. This process was a complex one, which can be discussed at many levels. One major event was the origin of the *book* of poems in 1557. If the very invention of an alphabet is the first step toward the taking of the language out of the person (so that, generations later one learns grammar as an external 'objective' fact), the book made the commoditization of the poem much easier. It is in fact the most typical commodity manifestation imaginable. The poet no longer could see his audience. He was no longer a member of a small tribal group, but now was an author, had himself undergone a division of labour. By 1750, the subjective use of capital letters and italics had been replaced by 'modern conventional' usage. Variants of the poem, such as the novel and literary criticism, had begun to look and act like separate phenomena (which they are not). Still, in the eighteenth century the reader in England was expected to bind his or her book to fit the style of his library, a curious counter-tendency (history is full of them) whose only modern remnant is the binding style of encyclopedias and law books in imitation of such styles.

The ultimate act of the commoditized poem is the novel in which the now passive reader (this too a division of labour) stares at a 'blank' page while a story appears to unfold miraculously in front of his or her eyes.

The wonderful thing about repression is that, in the end, it never works. The history of modern literature is that of a continuous struggle between the forces of commodity language (the capitalists) and those of product language (the working class).

Consider the novel. Born well within the commodity fetish, it does not comprehend that it is doubly bound by the gravitational forces of language and history. It assumes that it can evolve 'freely.' Like a rocket with insufficient thrust, it begins (around 1900) to fall back into the atmosphere of language. Thus the 'crisis' of the novel, which takes three specific forms.

The modernists recognize the fact of language and thereby attempt to re-enter the atmosphere, leading to all manifestations of the art-novel. In fact, some of these works, such as *Visions of Cody* and *Gravity's Rainbow,* are among the great poems of our time. Another manifestation of this form is the novelist who writes for, and is read by, poets: Douglas Woolf, Paul Metcalf, Harry Matthews, Kathy Acker, Fielding Dawson, etc.

The fully commoditized novelists turn to the production of just such a type of literature: Mario Puzo, Peter Benchley, Leon Uris.

A third form jettisons language and takes over a new art form made possible by capitalist technology: film. The lone author of 1850 is, by 1950, now a film *company* with a completely stratified labour force: grips, best boys, rewrite specialistis. And, of course, a group of producers who now own the means of production.

Every major type of modernism can been seen as attempts at eliminating the repression of the commodity fetish in language. The surrealists are a particularly positivist manifestation: dream narrative cannot break the narrative fetish for it lies within its boundaries. Joyce attempts to get back to language but for him language is not Saussurian but is etymologies. Hemmingway attempts an art of the sentence in which the ordering of the objects preceeds the ordering of the words (in that view, to get to language you must forget the words). The projectivist tendency from Pound and Williams to Eshleman and Kelly tries to get a new theory of the ordering of words, even a physical one, but it is highly individualist and predicated upon a metaphoric relation of the page to 'scored speech.'

It is not an accident that every modernist approach has failed. Because they start within the commodity fetish of language, they can quickly be reduced to commodities in turn. This is enough to kill them. Let me present a picture as ugly as it is real. With very few exceptions, a modern poet is successful as a commodity for no more than five years. During this period he or she is in constant demand for readings, has a plethora of publications (leading inevitably to over-production) and is the subject of numerous critical articles, books, etc.

Consider what happens when over-production (not of poems, but of commodities, books of poems) hits a poet. People who have read him or her now begin to stop. The market drops out and, in turn, a new poet is elevated, becomes chic and is similarly chewed up by the process. I can think of numerous examples: Robert Kelly, Jim Tate, Robert Duncan, Clayton Eshleman, Denise Levertov, Anne Wald-man, anyone you care to name.

The 'art of the difficult' aspect of modernism is a defense mechanism. By difficulty, a writer makes it harder to be absorbed and commoditized. It is a form of buying time. It is a sad thing to watch. It never works.

Language-centered writing, which this is, has a direct historical predecessor in Russian Futurism. These groups have two things in common which suggest a higher order of struggle: (1) they place language at the center of their work, (2) they place their work directly into a program of conscious and active class-struggle. They recognize that every creative act is, in its essence, revolutionary. For art has a dual function: interiorizing the group by ordering sense perceptions (leading to group culture and group consciousness) and by connecting the individual writer with the 'other,' which is the world of his or her group. It is just these dialectical forms and connections which the repressing element of the commodity fetish attempts to hide.

Russian Futurism took place in a revolutionary period, but one which resulted not in a communist state, but in a state capital one. The narrative fetish of social realism is the highest form of the commodity fetish. What took place in Russia was a later form of the nineteenth century bourgeois revolutions. Thus Russian Futurism was a counter-tendency, which is to be expected whenever the historical moment is in great flux. When the stage of historical development it arose in passed, its days were numbered.

Language-centered writing can take many forms. It is first of all activity conscious of itself. Its attempt is the spelling out of all the deformations of language which result from the repressing mechanism of the commodity fetish. It discusses the world and does not describe it. It does not impose 'reality' on the reader by fiat. It calls attention to the words it is using. It shows that the great rush of energy one gets in any good poem is nothing other than dialectical consciousness itself. It is not the 'end of the novel' nor of literary criticism, but is their return to the poem itself.

It is the first step (and only that) of the return of the poem to the people. It is a politicized poem and not a 'political poem' (which is a counter-tendency occurring within the commodity fetish). It tells you that these words are empty until you fill them with your presence, reading them, being them. Together, you and these words could do anything.

Permanent Revolution,
Ron.

★

If understood too generally, the term *product* can be misleading. It is not another term for *commodity*, but rather is the inverse: a separate nature inherent in the object diametrically opposed to its commodity nature. In Lacanian terminology, such an object would be considered 'overdetermined.' In a recent essay on the social origins of referentiality ('Disappearance of the Word, Appearance of the World,' *Red Herring,* forthcoming), I use the terms *gesture* and *gestural* to indicate the product nature of language in both tribal poetics and that of post-tribal pre-capitalist societies:

In its primary form, reference takes the character of a gesture and an object, such as the picking up of a stone to be used as a tool. Both gesture and object carry their own integrities and are not confused: a sequence of gestures is distinct from the objects which may be involved, as distinct as the labour process is from its resultant commodities. A sequence of gestures forms a discourse, not a description. It is precisely the expressive integrity of the gestural nature of language which constitutes the meaning of the 'nonsense' syllables in tribal poetries; its persistence in such characteristics of Skelton's poetry as its rhyme is that of a trace.

It is just this capability of capitalism to render a portion of the world invisible which Marx had in mind when, in the *Preface to a Contribution to the Critique of Political Economy*, he wrote that

It is not the consciousness of men that determines their being, but on the contrary, their social being that determines their consciousness.

Some other applications of this repressive capacity of capitalist development are discussed quite cogently by John and Barbara Ehrenreich in 'Work and Consciousness,' *Monthly Review,* July-August, 1976, pp. 10-18.

CHARLES BERNSTEIN
Stray Straws and Straw Men

1. 'I look straight into my heart & write the exact words that come from within. The theory of fragments whereby poetry becomes a grab bag of favorite items — packed neatly together with the glue of self-conscious & self-consciously epic composition, or, lately, homogenized into one blend by the machine of programmatic form — is a diversion. The eye is not split open in such work. There are structures — edifices — wilder than the charts of rivers, but they are etched by making a path not designing a garden.'

'Natural: the very word should be struck from the language.'

'... but what the devil *is* the human?'

2. Ron Silliman has consistently written a poetry of visible borders: a poetry of shape. His works are composed very explicitly under various conditions, presenting a variety of possible worlds, possible language formations. Such poetry emphasizes its medium as being constructed, rule governed, everywhere circumscribed by grammar & syntax, chosen vocabulary: designed, manipulated, picked, programmed, organized, & so an artifice, artifactual, an artifact — monadic, solipsistic, homemade, manufactured, mechanized & formulaic at some points: willful.

3. Work described as this may discomfort those who want a poetry primarily of personal communication, flowing freely from the inside with the words of a natural rhythm of life, lived daily. Perhaps the conviction is that poetry not be made by fitting words into a pattern but by the act of actually letting it happen, *writing,* so that that which is 'stored within pours out' without reference to making a point any more than to making a shape. The thing is not to create programmes to plug words into but to eliminate such imposed interferences.

An influence of work that appears to be of this (other) type is the sanctification of something that gets known as its honesty, its directness, its authenticity, its artlessness, its sincerity, its spontaneity, its personal expressiveness; in short, its 'naturalness.' (As the pastoral was once the natural, & likewise the romantic.)

I would point to Bernadette Mayer's *Memory* as a work that seems rooted in some of these ('natural') assumptions, as well as to much of Kerouac. In a different way, & the look of the work is the measure of how different, Frank O'Hara's poetry is relevant. The achievement of these three poets has much to do with how they have fronted these assumptions.

4. Personal subject matter & a flowing syntax, whatever those descriptions mean to a particular writer, are the key to the natural look. (Though it needs to be said that the variety of writing that relies on some sense of natural for its inspiration & domain is infinite.)

5. The sexual, for example, has much the pull of the natural. For some it poses as the most intimate subject matter. Others have it as the energy that drives their writing, or else its source.

Edward Dahlberg (sexistly) describes Word as Cock. 'Masculine fiery particles,' 'motions of will,' he says, animate the great writing of the past. He rebukes American literature for not being grounded in the Flesh, describing it as stagnant, dehumanized, & frigid. 'Esoteric artificers' & 'abstruse technicians,' our writers — Poe, Dickinson, Thoreau, Hawthorne, Melville & those before & after — have led away from 'the communal song of labor, sky, star, field, love.'

6. There is also an attraction toward looking for the natural in 'direct experience,' both in terms of recording the actual way objective reality is perceived (the search for the objective) & making the writing a recording instrument of consciousness.

'This work I experience as an instance of the writer's fantasy & imagination & vision & not as a construction. I feel immersed in it. It seems seamless to me. I am carried along by it. The experience is present to me. Shifts in tone, place occur as inevitable sequences: inevitable because they cohere, because they allow me to experience them, because they seem to happen.'

7. 'Technical artifice' they scream, as if poetry doesn't demand a technical precision. ('That poetry is an art, an art with technique, with media, an art that must be in constant flux, a constant change of manner.') Technicians of the human.

8. A sign of the particularity of a piece of writing is that it contains itself, has established its own place, situates itself next to us. We move up close, stare in, & see a world. It has moving parts, accountable & unaccountable rcurrences, a particular light, a heavy dense odor. 'But can I actually experience it?' Yes. But it reveals the conditions of its occurrence at the same time as it is experienced. So I don't feel a part of it as much as facing it. ... Of course at times you forget. All of a sudden a few hours, a week, flash by before you actually notice, & you say to yourself 'how the time slips —'

9. '*Next* to us the grandest laws are continually being executed. *Next* to us is not the workman whom we have hired, with whom we love so well to talk, but the Workman whose work we are.'

Next to. Fronting the world with a particular constellation of beliefs, values, memories, expectations; a culture; a way of seeing, mythography; language. But we are 'beside ourselves in a sane way' for what is beside us is also ourselves. At the same time in & beside. — The signs of language, of a piece of writing, are not artificial contructions, mere structures, 'mere naming.' They do not sit, deanimated, as symbols in a code, dummies for things of nature they refer to; but are, of themselves, of ourselves, whatever is such. 'Substance.' 'Actuality.' 'Presence.' The very plane through which we front the world, by which the world is.

10. Compare / these two views / of what / poetry / is.

In the one, an instance (a recording perhaps) of reality / fantasy / experience / event is presented to us through the writing.

In the other, the writing itself is seen as an instance of reality / fantasy / experience / event.

11. Another example.

The sanctification of the natural comes up in terms of 'voice' & has been extended by various excursions into the oral. On the one hand, there is the assumption that poetry matures in the location of 'one's own voice' which as often as not is no more than a consistency of style & presentation. 'The voice of the poet' is an easy way of contextualizing poetry so that it can be more readily understood (indiscriminately plugged into) as listening to someone talk in their distinctive manner (i.e., listen for the person beyond or underneath the poem); but this theatricalization does not necessarily do the individual poem any service & has the tendency to reduce the body of a poet's work to little more than personality. (This contrasts with that major preoccupation in American poetry — the investigation of the grammar of talking, of speech, both by traditional poetic technique &, lately, by tape transcription.) On the other hand, there is a growing use of voice in a variety of sound poetry. Some performance & audiotape works use voice as essentially a vocabulary to be processed by techniques such as cut-up, consonant & vowel intonation, simultaneity, etc. Others, searching for the 'natchuralness' of an oral liturgy we've lost, & influenced by tribal & religious & bardic — communal — poetic practice, make use of vocalizations related to the human breath (e.g., chanting & other assorted organic sounding tones). — Voice is a possibility for poetry not an essence.

12. I am not making a distinction, there is no useful distinction to be made here, between making the poem a subject or an object. Nor is it necessary to choose up among the personal desire to communicate, tell what has been seen, share a way of seeing, transmit some insight, irony, or simply give a feeling for texture.

What I want to call attention to is that there is no natural writing style; that the preference for its supposed manifestations is simply a preference for a particular look to poetry & often a particular vocabulary (usually perceived as personal themes); that this preference (essentially a procedural decision to work within a certain domain sanctified into a rite of poetry) actually obscures the understanding of the work which appears to be its honoured bases; & especially that the cant of 'make it personal' & 'let it flow' are avoidances — by mystification — of some very compelling problems that swirl around truth-telling, confession, bad faith, false self, authenticity, virtue, etc.

13. The considerable achievement of Frank O'Hara is to have a form of poetry largely within the domain of the personal. Note, however, that O'Hara's word 'personism' is not 'personalism'; it acknowledges the work to be a fronting of another *person* — another mind, if you will, as much as another nature. O'Hara's work *proposes* a domain of the personal, & not simply *assuming* it, fully works it out. His remarkable use of voice, for example, allows, through a musing whimsy in that voice, for fantasy as wild as any surrealist imagines, contained, still, within his proposd boundaries.

14. There is no automatic writing. It is a claim that has had to be made to the detractors of modernism again & again (an early article by B.F. Skinner attacked 'Stein's little secret') & must now be made another time to avoid accepting as a value an analysis generated out of misunderstanding & animosity.

Not that the followers of the natural, or the organic, or the personal, would necessarily have work that looks automatic. But it seems to me that this is at the heart of the strongest claim to natural spontaneous writing — the impulse to record or transcribe the movements & make-up of one's consciousness. The modernist assumption. What's to note is that in practice, projectively, that impulse transposes itself to something like a search for a method of 'syntaticalizing conscousness', i.e., ordering one's consciousness into language; as if consciousness existed prior to — aside from — language & had to be 'put into' it; as if consciousness were not itself a syntacticalization — a syntaxophony.

Every phrase I write, every juxtaposition I make, is a manifestation of using a full-blown language: full of possibilities of meaning & impossibilities of meaning. It can't be avoided. Whatever comes out comes out on account of a variety of psychological dispositions, personal experiences, & literary preoccupations & preconceptions. The best of the writing that gets called automatic issues from a series of choices as deliberate & reflected as can be.

15. Whatever gets written gets written in a particular shape, uses a particular vocabulary & syntax, & a variety of chosen techniques. Whether its shape, syntax & vocabulary result from an attraction (or ideological attachment to) the organic & spontaneous, or to some other look, it is equally chosen. Sometimes this process takes place intuitively or unconsciously (the pull of influence comes in here since somewhere in the back of your mind are models for what looks natural, personal, magical, mystical, spontaneous, automatic, dream-like, confessional, didactic, shocking). Sometimes it is a very conscious process. Any way, you're responsible for what turns up. Free association, for example, is no more inherently 'natural' than cutting up: & neither is in any sense 'random'. One technique may be used because a decision is made to use subconscious material. Another may be used to limit the vocabulary of the poem to words not self-generated. In either case, various formal decisions are made & these decisions shape the work.

16. Okay, given that, it's given, is it possible to continue under conditions set up before? Or is everything, every instance, a new decision at each moment? & recklessly charging forward it appears to copy some other thing, or be beholding, or under. What happens when the images cease, when there are no more images confronting the eye of imagination & still the signs, the written traces of activity, continue to be produced. Music sounds. It too must pass. A syntactical exploration of consciousness becomes very explicitly the concern, so imbedded even in a subject matter of boundaries & possible worlds, that it ceases to be, or only diverts. The subject matter simply all that is inside, given rhythm, different cadences, the punctuation in typing of each letter as separate unit, the propulsion of a comma. Is it possible, for example, to allow typographical errors, mistypings, to remain integral? Typing itself then becoming a condition. It becomes part of the temptation. Or perhaps it's just my fear that when I tap what I find inside myself I will find that it is empty & insist that the scratchings must account for something.

17. Writing necessarily consists of attaching numerous bits & pieces together in a variety of ways. & it comes to a point where you feel any composition is an artifice & a deceit. & the more 'natchural' the look the more deceptive. That any use of language outside its function of

communicating in speaking is a falsehood (cf. Laura Riding). Or even, that language itself — everywhere conditioning our way of seeing & meaning — is an illusion (as if there were some thing outside language!)

Or take it this way: I want to just write — let it come out — get in touch with some natural process — from brain to pen — with no interference of typewriter, formal pattern. & it can seem like the language itself — having to put it into words — any kind of fixing a version of it — gets in the way. That I just have this thing inside me — silently — unconditioned by the choices I need to make when I write — whether it be to write it down or write on. So it is as if language itself gets in the way of expressing this thing, this flow, this movement of consciousness.

But there are no thoughts except through language, we are everywhere seeing through it, limited to it but not by it. Its conditions always interpose themselves: a particular set of words to choose from (a vocabulary), a way of processing those words (syntax, grammar): the natural conditions of language. What pulses, pushes, is energy, spirit, anima, dream, fantasy: coming out always in form, as shape: these particulars, 'massed at material bottoms' in hum of this time — here, now — these words, this syntax & rhythm & shape. The look of the natural as constructed, programmatic — artful — 'lying words' as the most abstract, composed or formal work.

18. There is no natural look or sound to a poem. Every element is intended, chosen. That is what makes a thing a poem. Modes cannot be escaped, but they can be taken for granted. They can also be meant.

Work like Silliman's explicitly acknowledges these conditions of poetry, language, by explicitly intending vocabulary, syntax, shape, etc.; an acknowledgement which is the actual prerequisite of authenticity, of good faith. The allure of the spontaneous & personal is cut here by the fact of wordness: reproducing not so much the look of the natural as the conditions of nature — autonomy, self-sufficiency. In this light, a work like Mayer's *Memory* can be seen to be significant not on account of its journal-like look alone but also on account of its completely intended, complex, artifactual style. Heavy, dense, embedded. 'The essential thing is to build a world.' Energy & emotion, spontaneity, vocabulary, shape — all are elements of that building. It is natural that there are modes but there is no natural mode.

L=A=N=G=U=A=G=E

SUPPLEMENT NUMBER TWO   JUNE 1980

SOME RECENT BRITISH POETRY MAGAZINES

(The following is a partial listing, compiled by Cris Cheek, of "small press" magazines published in Britain since 1975 and mainly printing poetry. The hope is to provide readers with a chance to see in which ways the British scene is and has been active over the past five years, but does not indicate recommendation. Addresses of the publishers are given where likely to be current. While we are unable to provide prices, sending $3 to one of these publishers should be enough to get a sample copy. For more information, contact the Association of Little Presses (ALP) at 262 Randolph Street, London W 9, England. Finally, bookseller Nick Kimberly, 16A Burleigh Parade, London, N.14, may be able to fill orders for much of this material.)

A. an envelope magazine of Visual Poetry. ed. jeremy adler
47, Wetherby Mansions, Earls Court Square. London SW5 9BH
abc. dec. 75. w/ zurbrugg, upton, summers, g.j. de rook, ruth
rehfeldt, jennifer pike, parrit, clemente padin, o'huigin,
b p nichol, nannuci, peter mayer, macLow, houedard, griffiths,
fencott, peter finch, dutton, cobbing, claire, cheek, helen
archer, adler
abcd. w/ cobbing, sylvi$_a$ finzi, o'huigin, cheek, claire, ana
hatherly, bill griffiths, bill bissett, adler, tamaki kitayama,
lawrence upton, truhlar, sumner, mayer, p.c.fencott, houedard,
fyodor cherniavsky, radin, burke, pike and others

AGGIE WESTON'S. no. 10. Residing - andrew crozier.
              no. 12. Thronging the Heart - gael turnbull.
usually one person per issue, often photographers.

ALEMBIC. no. 3. paul brown, ken edwards, ulli mcCarthy, nuttall,
r. hampson, mike dobbie, mathews, harwood, spring 1975
no. 4. allen fisher, roy fisher, eric mottram, mcCarthy, edwards,
no. 5. david miller, hampson, nuttall, mcCarthy, paul buck,
edwards, dobbie
no. 6. d. miller, charles madge, a. fisher, rosemary waldrop,
mottram
no. 7. peter finch, glenda george, buck, b. kelly, mcCarthy,
allen fisher, a. sumner, j chris jones, tony ward, herb burke,
paula claire, jeremy adler, bob cobbing, fencott, ee vonna-michell,
cris cheek, lawrence upton
no. 8. mottram, lyn hejinian, armantrout, a.m.albiach, nations,
chris hall, w. pryor, v. finch, peter robinson
ed. ken edwards, robert hampson and contributing editors peter barry
and eric vonna-michell

CURTAINS. split curtains w/ alejandro, noel, blanchot, laporte,
buck, derrida, michel camus, georges bataille, colette deble,
ulli mcCarthy, jeff nuttall, fremon, g. george, p. dhainaut,
juliet, varlez, jean pierre faye, peter inch, duvert, a. velter,
jean daive, gad hollander. supplement w/ geraldine monk & glenda george
curtains, le prochain step w/ vladimir velickovic, edmond jabes,
r. waldrop, allen fisher, paul neagu, eric mottram, clayton eshleman,
robert kelly, g. monk & robert clark, robert clark, roger ely,
jacques prevel, glenda george, buck, mcCarthy, faye, agnes rouzier,
gina pane, bataille, phillip corner, susan hiller, kris hemensley,
dobbie, brian marley, keith waldrop, lydia davis, michel deguy, joe
bousquet, pierre joris, p. dhainaut, patrice delbourg, eugene
savitzkaya, COUM

curtains, bal: le :d curtains w/ bernard noel, ulrike meinhof,
elaine shemilt, danielle collobert, paul buck, glenda george,
ulli mcCarthy, a. fisher, michael bishop, philippe boyer, rod
mengham, j. guglielmi, p. bourgeade, henri maccheroni, michel
camus, jean-luc parant, titiparant, bousquet, michele richman,
bataille, mitsou ronat, laure, pane, christian schlatter, faye,
montel, cheek, corner, mpnte cazazza, jed rasula, joris, eshleman,
john james, mulford, alison wilding, brian catling, iain sinclair,
bill griffiths, m. haslam, k. chris cable, peter riley
ed. paul buck 4 bower st, maidstone, kent. ME16 8SD england

CURTAL SAILS. o'huigin, bill griffiths, upton, cobbing, cheek,
adler, p.c.fencott,peter mayer, pike, herb burke
published by bluff books, el uel uel u, good elf, & writer's forum

FIX. no. 2. w/ griffiths, joris, paul gogarty, mottram, jack
hirschmann, jeff nuttall, philip jenkins, vas dias, p. brown, a. fisher
no. 3. mcCarthy, nuttall, mottram, david miller, ken edwards, dobbie,
nations, hirschmann   ed mike dobbie and ulli mcCarthy

GOOD ELF. no. 5./ 6 A   griffiths, steve clews, jeff nuttall (the
suppressed "new manifesto of the poetry society"), francoise legume
ed. lawrence upton. 18 clairview rd. London SW16 England

GREAT WORKS. no. 5. w/ barry macsweeney, lee harwood, martin thom,
peter baker, andrew crozier, john welch, hall, riley, harding
ed. peter philpott 25 portland rd. bishop's stortford, herts
no. 6. simon pettet, st. vincent, p. mathews, p. robinson, marley,
ian tyson, crozier, paul green, david miller, welch,'

THE HUMAN HANDKERCHIEF. no. 5. aram saroyan, ted berrigan, padgett,
waldman, iain sinclair, nuttall, david chaloner, ralph hawkins,john
seed   no ed. known

KROKLOK. no. 1. morgenstern, hausmann, carrol, jandl, scheerbart,
marinetti, cobbing, houedard, de vree, claire, kerouac, dufrene,
seuphor
no. 2. cobbing, hausmann, schwitters, artaud, rabelais, peter mayer,
neil mills, charles verey, hugo ball, severini, van doesburg,
gomringer, albert-birot, seuphor, chopin, man ray
no. 3. peter mayer, morgenstern, jandl, peter finch, jeremy adler,
michael chant, peter greenham, brion gysin, ilya zdanavitch,
heissenbutel, cobbing, august stramm
no. 4. four horsemen, david toop, verey, john sharkey, john furnival,
p c fencott, houedard, j p ward, bpnichol, hausmann, paula claire,
griffiths, cobbing, lawrence upton, adler, bill bissett, sten hanson
ed. by dom silvester houedard with bob cobbing as executive editor,
and peter mayer as associate editor. 262 randolph avenue, London W9

MEANTIME. no. one. koller, sinclair, stezaker, james, crozier,
fielding dawson, tom raworth, john wilkinson, basil bunting, roy fisher,
veronica forrest-thomson, ian hamilton finlay
ed. paul johnstone, david thomas and malcolm williams

MINERAL WATERS OF THE CAUCASUS. w/ geoffrey ward, paul smith,
rod mengham, john wilkinson
ed. ward and mengham

MUGSHOTS. 1. mcCarthy 2. dobbie 3. allen fisher 4. nuttall
5. peter barry 6. mottram 7. glenda george 8. griffiths 9. buck
10. mathews 11. pete hoida 12. edwards   ed dobbie& mcCarthy

OCHRE MAGAZINE. no. 1. mcCarthy, joris, raworth, ingham, andrei
codrescu
no. 2. waldman, david tipton, allen fisher, ralph hawkins, rochelle
kraut
no. 3. lee harwood, sinclair, bill griffiths, anthony barnett, opal
l nations
no. 4. john james, paul evans, wendy mulford, doug oliver, welch
ed. ralph hawkins & charles ingham

PERFECT BOUND no. 1. prynne, a. fisher, martin thom, ward, john
wilkinson, peter riley, james
no. 2. tom raworth, m. haslam, wilkinson, a. fisher, mengham, ward,
crozier
no. 3. christopher middleton, peter philpott, paul buck, iain sinclair,
p. riley, raworth
no. 4. peter riley, john welch, haslam, raworth, allen fisher, doug
oliver, thomas a clark , ken smith, tim longville
no. 5. d vid chaloner, hawkins, thomas a clark, john riley
no. 6. barnett, alain delahaye, jaques dupin, philippe jaccottet,
yunna morits, luigi pirandello, jeremy reed, pierre reverdy, charles
tomlinson
no. 7. Cambridge Poetry Festival: enzensberger, feinstein, denise riley
tom raworth, tsvetayeva, meckel, paz, pasolini, edmond jabes, waldman
ed. peter robinson 1 queensway, trumpington rd. cambridge CB2 2AX

POETRY INFORMATION. no. 12/13. articles on weiners, patchen, bukowski,
eigner, clark, creeley, reed, vangelisti, james, riley, longville,
beresford, manhire, marien, modern indonesian poetry, vallejo, neruda,
poetmeat, new review, griffiths, mcClure
no. 14. lee harwood (interview) & bibliography, articles on chris
torrance, neil oram, hilton, pilcher, macLow, redgrove, heath-stubbs,
miller, cendrars, celine, beltrametti, george quasha, fielding dawson,
kerouac, floating bear, ferlinghetti, blake, canadian magazines,
wallpaper benefit, mathias goeritz
no. 15. iain sinclair interview and article, articles on griffiths,

harwood, mottram, tzara, robin blaser, bern porter, ronald johnson,
stefan themerson, denise levertov, origin magazine, rothenberg, vas dias,
benveniste, joris, dorn - dunbar
no. 16. articles on 'poetics' from paul mathews and tom leonard, on
raworth, turnbull, james wright, jeremy hilton, allen fisher, robert
lax, marley, ed dorn, toby olson, michael palmer, henri chopin, new
french writing
no. 17. mottram on open field poetry, articles on charles olson, paul
blackburn, velimir khlebnikov, beau geste press, cesar vallejo,
interview with opal l nations
no. 18. British Poetry Interview Issue - tom pickard, barry macsweeney,
ken smith, thomas a clark, chris torrance
no. 19. Basil Bunting Special Issue, articles by mottram, tom mayer,
quartermain, pursglove and parvin loloi, interviews by mottram, williams
/ mayer, celebratory poem by colin simms, complete bibliography of works
and criticism by roger guedalla, a chronology by garth clucas
each issue aslo includes good listings of both british and american
publications, both books and magazines
ed. pete hodgkiss c/o 18 clairview rd. London SW16 England

POETRY REVIEW. two issues, the last two under eric mottram's editorship
and the only 2 worth considering since 1975 as a change of both format
and editor has effected a wooly-minded mis-adventure into redundant
possibilities peeping timidly through net curtains at their own bodies.
vol. 66. no. 3/4. w/ pickard, welch, cobbing, evans, de loach, schwerner,
hamburger, armstrong, crossley-holland, fulton, thomas a clark, tarn,
micheline, lopez, blevins, platz, mathews, rakosi, adler, hawkins
vol. 67. no. 1/2. w/ kelly, rukeyser, ortiz, griffiths, macSweeney,
ferlinghetti, a. fisher, o huigin, mcCarthy, keys, horovitz, sanders,
upton, chinese poems, ken smith, maillard, kennelly, lewis, dobbie,
buck, torrance, p. riley, elaine randell, hilton, simms, taggart,
st. clair, borman, paul brown, burke, heliczer, thom, paul green, john
freeman

RAWZ. no. 1. eric mottram, dick higgins, marshall reese, pc fencott,
allen fisher, mcCarthy, paula claire, david mayor, burke, buck,
vonna-michell, chris hall, upton, dick miller, manfred sundermann
no. 2½. lesley strickland, pam burnel, jiri valoch, allen fisher -
ulli mcCarthy, cp hayden, carlyle reedy, john keys, ee vonna-michell,
jeremy adler, cheek, bissett, maggie o' sullivan, gibbs, andrews,
tabor, basmajian, tolson, charles bernstein, pc fencott, paul buck
ed. cris cheek 24 stonehall rd. London N21 1LP

REALITY STUDIOS. vol 1. no. 1. james sherry, opal l nations.
no. 2. marius kociejowski, david miller, b.c. leale no. 3. vonna-michell

peter barry (shipping corrsepondent) no. 4. ken edwards no. 5. paul
green (1), paul green (2) no. 6. j. e . stead, cory harding, peter de
rous, dave ward no. 7. charles bernstein no. 8/9/10. andrew mayfield,
peter philpott, ye min, hilton, halsey, tipton,
vol 2. no. 1. ray di palma
each issue also carries reviews of events and publications
ed. ken edwards 77 balfour st. London SE17

SATURDAY MORNING. no. 1. roy fisher (interview w/eric mottram),
blaise cendrars, torrance, macSweeney, nuttall, kirby malone, turnbull,
chaloner, a. fisher, jeremy hilton, ralph hawkins, mark hyatt, o huigin
no. 2. ulli mcCarth (interview w/jeff nuttall), iain sinclair, burgis,
paul buck, hilton, tom pickard, freeman, nations, tipton
no. 3. george & mary oppen (interview w/kevin power), ortega, colin
simms, sherman, hilton, charles ingham, andrew crozier, anthony lopez,
mike dobbie, simon pettet
no. 4. bill griffiths (interview w/cris cheek), paul buck, geraldine
monk, paul evans, pierre reverdy, hilton, pettet, mottram, ken smith
no. 5. New York Issue, cage, orlovsky/ginsberg, dubris, solomon,
godfrey, myles, brodey, lally, owen, berrigan, masters, rosenthal,
padgett, acker, holman, ginsberg, lesniak, scholnick, violi, lenhart,
waldman, notley, savage, schiff, carey, malanga, orlovsky, levitt,
giorno, bremser, higgins
ed. simon pettet 6, 437 e. 12th st, N.Y.C. 10009
    or c/o 24 stonehall rd. London N21. 1LP England

SCHMUCK. French Schmuck. w/ lambert, ben vautier, filliou, jean le gac,
dotremont, broodthaers, boltanski, fleischer, gerz, galli, agullo,
alocco, anseeuw, borgeaud, liu cazes, polyconal workshop, chopin,
dolla/monticelli, flexner, gette, jassaud,lemaitre, moineau, wurz
Teutonic Smuck. w/ albrecht, altorjay, bulkowski, daumeter, feelisch,
gosewitz, gramse, groh, hagenberg, hannes, birgit and wilhelm hein,
iannone, kalkmann, kunz, lobach-hinweiser, missmahl, nadasdy, niggl,
paeffgen, saree, schmidt, schropfer, trommer, vosa, vostell, wewerks
Japanese Smuck. w/ ay-o, ehrenberg, ashizawa, fujiwara, hayashi, kaneko,
kobayashi, kosugi, kuriyama, matsuda, matsuzawa, nakajima, terry reid,
richards, saito, sekido, shimazaki, shiomi, shukuzawa, sunohara,
tajiri, takahashi, tanaqua,u-fan, uematsu, wada, yamamoto, yoshida,
yoshimuda
ed. david mayor and felipe ehrenberg flat 2 stonebridge ct.
stonebridge park, London NW10 8EW Britain

SIXPACK. no. 9. w/ antin, artaud, bialy, brotherston, dorn, enslin,
eshleman, a. fisher, irby, joris, kamin, kelly, macLow, mcClelland,
meyer, olson, oppenheimer, prescott, quasha, schwerner, stein, tarn,
weinstein, williams, wilk, yau
ed. pierre joris & w.r. prescott   19 deal rd. London SW 17 9JW

SPANNER. no. 3. david mayor & flux (shoe) no. 4. david miller on john
riley and christopher middleton no. 5. ken smith no. 6. bill sherman
no. 8. phil maillard no. 9. dick higgins - eric mottram (conversation)
no. 10. john welch no. 11. clive bush on muriel rukeyser no. 12. colin
simms no. 13. ed. by dick miller in New York and now Spanner New York
in its own right no. 14. bern porter no. 15. ginsberg - an essay on the
work by eric mottram no. 16. michael mcClure - kevin power (conversation
no. 17. christopher jones
occassional supplements are issued, bill sherman and ulli mcCarthy so
far
no. 13 finally issued as eric mottram   please inset no. 7. crust
ed. allen fisher 85 ramilles close, London SW2 5DQ Britain

SPECTACULAR DISEASES. no. 1. wendy mulford, david trotter, chaloner,
joris, peter riley, paul buck, allen fisher, ian patterson, brian
marley, martin thom
no. 2. kris hemesley, crozier, haslam, welch, jeff nuttall, fred buck,
colin simms, ric caddel, p. buck, gael turnbull, jeremy reed
ed. paul green   283B London Road, peterborough, Cambs, Britain

SPINDRIFT. no. 1. paul auster, veronica forrest-thompson, wilkinson,
no. 2. peter riley, barbara guest, john sharkey, g. ward, middleton
ed. paul smith

SQUARE ONE. no. 1. charles marowitz, allen fisher, barry macSweeney,
jeff nuttall, eric mottram
ed. mich binns & stephen fleet c/o 40 guernsey grove, London SE24

STEREO HEADPHONES. no. 7. w/ beckett, castro, gysin, heidsieck, john
furnival, hans richter, franz mon, bengt-emil johnson, robert lax,
stefan and francisca themerson
ed. nicholas zurbrugg

TANGENT. no. 1. gad hollander, gael turnbull, mathew mead, chris
torrance, tim longville
no. 2. edwards, paul green, nicki jackowska, bernard noel, john hall,

savitskaya, ken smith, d. m. thomas, vivienne finch, william pryor,
holloway, dent, raverat, e.a.markham, cosseboom, simms, d.ward,
allen fisher, david miller
no. 3. david miller, henri chopin, michael haslam, takis sinopoulos +
ed. vivienne finch and william pryor waye cottage, chagford,
newton abbot, devon

TWENTIETH CENTURY STUDIES. no. 11. Translation and Transformation,
de campos, cid corman, deguy
no. 12. the Limits of Comprehension, eco, culler, almansi, forrest-
thompson, middleton
no. 15/16. Visual Poetics, eco, victor burgin, damisch, schefer, pleyne
ed. stephen bann c/o rutherford college, university canterbury, kent

VANESSA. no. 1. john welch, anthony howell, bill shepherd, tom
lowenstein, paul ashton, barnett, elizabeth cullington
no. 2. shepherd, thom, ashton, chaloner, deborah evans, harding, victor
west, paul brown, nick totten, welch
no. 3. hilton, philpott, sherman, oram, cory harding +
no. 4. jim burns, colin simms, rod mengham, peter riley,peter robinson,
simon pettet, yan lovelock +
ed. john welch 40 walford rd, London N16 8ED

WALLPAPER. no. 3. toren, welch, bernas, anthony mcCall, anthony howell,
susan hiller
no. 4. susan bovin, shepherd, quarrell, david coxhead, eden
no. 5/6. bernas, bonvin, buck, busenburg, coxhead, dahl, eden, a. fishe
gaber, june green, hiller, carla liss, mcCall, stephen montague, annabe
nicolson, quarrel, carolee schneeman, john sharkey, shone, templeton,
the ting, tillman, amikam toren, welch, howell
no. 7. anthony barnett, andrew eden, alan fuchs, david medalla, toren
contributing editors - bernas, bonvin, coxhead, eden, hiller, howell,
mcCall, quarrell, toren, welch
40 walford rd, London N16 8ED

the WOLLY OF SWOT. 1. the cracked cup and saucer - corman, adler,
schlossberg, jacob, thomas a clark, smith, sharkey, reverdy, gogarty,
fyodor cherniavsky, paul green, david miller, hollander, ernst jandl,
welch, lax, mengham, harding, takis sinopoulos, bonnefey, d. grubb
2. lost in the land of the worm-eaters - frank samperi, lovelock,
paul evans, alan davies, opal l nations, v. finch, pettet, ian robinson
vas dias, p. brown, philpott, franz wurm, stathatos, d. ward, a. fisher
carlyle reedy, cory harding

3. some enchanted evening - edwards, kirby congdon, adler, freeman, bissett, smith, messer, paul dutton, d. miller, middleton, nations also from the same source maybe a separate venture or continuation Peeping Tom - w/ breakwell, gogarty, ward, burns, mathews, reverdy, edson, stannard, edwards, lax, jacob, pilcher, hemensley, harding, mengham, g. ward, sheppard, jackowska, hollander, rigaut, j.hall, lovelock, mead, nations, williams, c. hall, sumner, jenkins, philpott, hampson, caddel, jarry, peret, + a lock of Lord Byron's hair
ed. cory harding

WORDS WORTH. vol 1. 1. buck, cris cheek, anna synenko, houedard, cory harding, peter mayer
no. 2. glenda george, cheek, mcCarthy, lawrence upton, reedy, michael gibbs, pc fencott, bill griffiths, sharkey, allen fisher, jackson macLow, paul green, christian tarting
no. 3. philpott, ken edwards, r.g. sheppard, michael carlson, hampson, peter finch, nations, george, ee vonna-michell, carlyle reedy, harding, john wilkinson
ed. alaric sumner w/ contributing editors herbert burke, paul buck & educational section editor rosemary sumner
2 crossfield rd. London NW3 4NS, England

Miscellaneous

BLUEPRINT. one issue of interest being no. 5. a special for the 1979 cambridge poetry festival w/ buck, chinca, fencott, a. fisher, fox, george, hammersley, hewson, mcCarthy, moore, morgan, raworth, reedy, sumner, taylor, voona-michell

ELF NEWS. ed. lawrence upton. listings, personal notes, poems, memories
18, clairview rd. London SW16

LOBBY NEWSLETTER. appears bi-monthly on average and has now reached its tenth issue in september 79. letters, reviews, articles, poems, editorial comments from tabor, chopin, upton, paul buck, chinca, richard hammersley, alaric sumner, rose withers, fox, mallin, mottram, torrance, cheek, taylor, amongst others
ed. for both of the above richard tabor 280 cherryhinton rd.
cambridge CB1 4AU

MUSICS. now reached its 22 issue, an indespensible collection of reviews
thoughts, interviews, discussions, direct information on the
instant compositional musics worldwide, including performance pieces,
poems, sound sculptures, new instrument making and more
not so much edited as 'put together' by volunteers, who come and go
can be ordered from 42 gloucester avenue London NW1 Britain

NORTH ATLANTIC TEXTS. no. 1. Translation Work, old english poetries
ed. bill griffiths & john porter
107 valley drive London NW9 9Nt

i wish to re-emphasize the incompleteness of this collection, what is
given here is one take, there would well be many others. the
association of little presses in this country issues an ALP newsletter,
which is recommended, containing information on books by individual
authors, printing techniques and arts administration, matters of
patronage. ALP also makes a catalogue of little press books in print
available, please write to them for information at
ALP 262 randolph avenue London W9 England

this listing compiled by cris cheek / member of the consortium of
London Presses september 1979

L=A=N=G=U=A=G=E is supported, in part, by grants from the National
Endowment for the Arts, the New York State Council on the Arts, and
the Coordinating Council of Literary Magazines.

Distributed with the cooperation of the Segue Foundation.

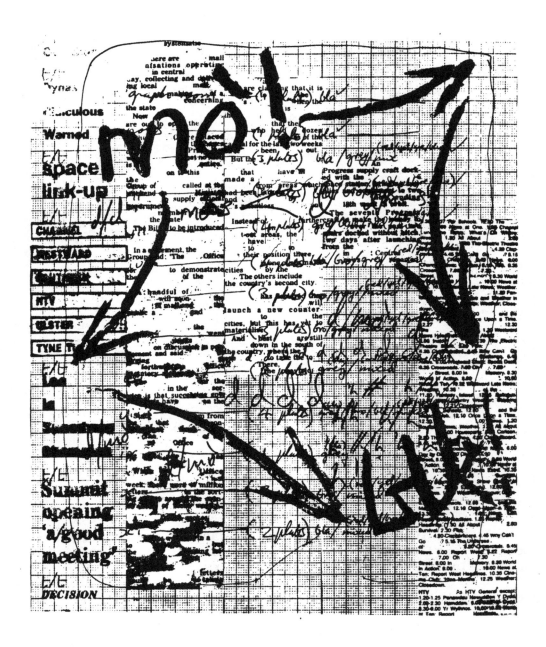

--*from Richard Tabor's* BOBOLI / MARIETTE / LE MACHINE
($2.50, c/o Lobby Newsletter, see listings)

L=A=N=G=U=A=G=E

SUPPLEMENT NO.3   OCTOBER 1981

THE POLITICS OF POETRY — A SUPPLEMENT

DISAPPEARANCE OF THE WORD, APPEARANCE OF THE WORLD

"Human beings do not live in the objective world alone, nor alone in the world of social activity as ordinarily understood, but are very much at the mercy of the particular language which has become the medium of expression for their society. It is quite an illusion to imagine that one adjusts to reality essentially without the use of language and that language is merely an incidental means of solving specific problems of communication or reflection. The fact of the matter is that the 'real world' is to a large extent unconsciously built up on the language habits of the group."

Sapir, 1929

"The mode of production of material life conditions the social, political and intellectual life process in general. It is not the consciousness of men that determines their being, but on the contrary, their social being that determines their consciousness."

Marx, 1859

One anomaly of contemporary existence which has received little critical analysis is the persistence of "typos" in foreign language films from the industrialized nations. A typical example would be the omission of an *r* in the word "your" in Tanner's recent *Jonah who will be 25 in the year 2000*. Since a film such as *Jonah* (or those directed by Truffaut, Bergman or Wertmuller) is made with at least one eye on distribution to the Anglo-American market, such errata cannot be sufficiently explained away as a consequence of the precarious and somewhat secondary existence of an export print (which, on occasion, is even re-edited for the new market, as was Roeg's *The Man Who Fell to Earth*). The fact remains that in current bourgeois cinema, attention to the development of all visio-spatial information is total. That the disruptive nature of typographical errors in sub-titles is not noticed and corrected is a sign that it is not felt.

This links it to a broad variety of other social phenomena, such as the method of speed-reading in which individual words recede and are replaced by a Gestalt comprehension of content, or the techniques developed for display advertising and product packaging (including mass market publishing) for the printing of information which, for any number of reasons (e.g., it is considered "inessential" such as the identification of the jacket designer, or possibly counterproductive to sales, such as a listing of chemical additives in canned foods), the producer does not wish the potential customer to read. Linguistically, the most revealing detail of Noam Chomsky's *Reflections on Language* may well be the ISBN number on its rear cover, printed in a different direction and in a lighter color than the rest of that page's text.

A McLuhanist interpretation, further linking these to even broader social facts such as the rise, and subsequent crisis, of the novel or modernist tendencies in art in general, would not be incorrect as such, but would fail to sufficiently explain the underlying social reasons for the phenomena and thereby fail to suggest an appropriate course for action by art workers generally and specifically by writers.

For several years I have been involved in a series of investigations (*Language Games*, *The Chinese Notebook* and *aRb*) predicated upon Louis Zukofsky's projection of a possible "scientific" definition of poetry (first outlined by him in the preface to the 1948 Origin edition of *A 1-12*). While the third investigation is still in progress, some fairly specific statements concerning the object of inquiry can be made: (1) the stage of historical development determines the *natural* laws (or, if you prefer the terminology, the underlying structures) of poetry; (2) the stage of historical development determines the natural laws of language; (3) the primary impact on language, and language arts, of the rise of capitalism has been in the area of reference and is directly related to the phenomena known as the commodity fetish. It is this effect of the rise of capitalism, particularly in its later state and monopoly forms, which underlies the effaced *r* in *Jonah*.

The essential nature of the social determination of consciousness has largely been misinterpreted by Marxists and non-Marxists alike. Thus Chomsky, feeling social determinism to be in contradiction to his innateness thesis, writes:

> Gramsci went so far as to argue that "the fundamental inno-vation introduced by Marxism into the science of politics and history is the proof that there does not exist an abstract, fixed and immutable 'human nature'...but that human nature is the totality of historically determined social relations"... --a statement that is surely false, in that there is no such proof, and a questionable reading of Marx.
> (Chomsky, 1975, p. 128)

While Gramsci's formulation constitutes an implicit oversimplification (leading, for example, to behaviorist errors and the idea that human nature can be altered in short periods of time), proofs of the social determination of consciousness do exist. The elaboration of the tool-making capacity of the australopithicene required an expansion of the frontal area of the cerebral cortex and hominid brain consequently grew from 500 cc. 1,500,000 years ago to 1100 cc. 350,000 years ago and eventually to the modern 1400 cc. (Robert J. Maxwell in Yaker et al, 1971, p. 39.) Most of the "innate cognitive capacity" of Chomsky's thesis is indeed the result of a "mode of production of material life." He and Gramsci are equally guilty of the gross application of a complex reality.

The question before us is, however, of a much more specific nature than the social determination of all inate cognitive capacity: the impact of emergence of capitalism on language and the language arts. This question can be restated as Does capitalism have a specific "reality" which is passed through the language and thereby imposed on its speakers? Thus framed, the question can be answered affirmatively.

First we need to note some key differences in the language use of groups which have not as yet been thoroughly totalized into the global class structure of monopoly and state capitalism. Because writing typically occurs in a society which has already undergone significant divisions of labor (i.e., historical development), the best sources of any relatively tribal literature exist in modern ethnological transcriptions, rather than in the early written records of the Judeo-Christian civilization. The following is an English language translation of a Fox tribe sweatbath poem:

A gi ya ni a gi yan ni i
A gi ya ni a gi yan ni i
A gi ya ni a gi yan ni i
A gi ya ni agi ya ni
Sky
A gi ya ni i a gi ya ni
A gi ya ni i a gi ya ni
A gi ya ni

(Rothenberg, 1972, p. 341)

The presence of "nonsense" syllables in tribal literature is unmistakeable. Save for attempts at specifically anthropological explanations, there is no room in contemporary literary theory for a poetry of this kind, no existing mechanism for positing it coherently alongside the work of Dante, Li Po or Tzara. The fact that there have been as yet few attempts to incorporate such materials into "comparative literature" curricula by the educational system of the industrial nations is not simply attributable to racism, though racism inevitably plays a role. Rather, it is that in the reality of capitalism (or of any society well down the road toward capitalist modes of production) there is no meaning here.

But capitalism did not spring up overnight amid loose associations of groups at a tribal stage of development. It came into existence through a long succession of stages, each with its own characteristic modes of production and social relations. While the literature of a people about to enter into the stage of capitalism through bourgeois revolution will necessarily be much closer to our own experience, differences can still be observed. The following are the first eleven lines of "The Tunnying of Elynour Rummying" by John Skelton, written in about 1517:

```
Tell you I chyll,
If that ye wyll
A whyle be styll,
Of a comely gyll
That dwelt on a hyll;
But she is not gryll,
For she is somewhat sage
And well worne in age,
For her vysage
It woldt aswage
A mannes courage.
```
                                    (Sylvester, 1974, p. 69)

Only one word (*gryll*, meaning "fierce") has dropped from the vocabulary.
Shifts of spelling, pronunciation and syntactic structure are more visible (largely explicable by the standardizing effect of printing --
Caxton's press was only forty years old when these lines were written),
but the most obvious difference between Skelton's poetry and the modern
is its use of rhyme: eleven consecutive end-rhymes using only two
endings, -*yll* and -*age*, plus five other instances of internal rhyme and
off-rhyme (*tell, whyle, dwelt, well, woldt*). This is the inverse of
the effaced *r* of *Jonah*: it is an ordering of the language by its physical characteristics, its "nonlinguistic" ones, a sign that this dimension
is felt.

Another characteristic trait of the English poetry of 400 years
ago is its almost exclusive focus upon either love, the ontological
project of the period, or religious and heroic themes passed down from
the traditions of colonial invaders, works to be valued as rearticula-
tions rather than as sensuous apprehensions of the experiential. It
was not the purpose of the language in the 16th century poem to describe
the daily life of even the bourgeois, let alone the common man.

What happens when a language moves toward and passes into a capitalist stage of development is an anaesthetic transformation of the perceived tangibility of the word, with corresponding increases in its
descriptive and narrative capacities, preconditions for the invention
of "realism," the optical illusion of reality in capitalist thought.
These developments are tied directly to the nature of reference in
language, which under capitalism is transformed (deformed) into referentiality.

In its primary form, reference takes the character of a gesture
and an object, such as the picking up of a stone to be used as a tool.
Both gesture and object carry their own integrities and are not confused: a sequence of gestures is distinct from the objects which may
be involved, as distinct as the labor process is from its resultant
commodities. A sequence of gestures forms a discourse, not a description. It is precisely the expressive integrity of the gestural nature

of language which constitutes the meaning of the "nonsense" syllables in tribal poetries; its persistence in such characteristics of Skelton's poetry as his rhyme is that of a trace.

The individual within the tribal society had not been reduced to wage labor, nor did the reproduction of his or her material life require the consumption of a significant number of commodities created through the labor of others. The world of natural and self-created objects is decidedly different from the world of things.

> As men *changed* the world they expanded and refined their ability to *know* it, and the growing capacity for cognition again enhanced their ability to change it. Man creates himself by his works; by his estrangement from himself he becomes his own creation.
>
> (Fischer, 1970, pp. 152-3)

A thing is at once both the end product of a labor process and a commodity of general social consumption. A thing is a schizoid object. Or, to use Lacanian terminology, a thing is an overdetermined object. A world which is made up of such dual projections can only be resolved when the forces of production control both the means of production and consumption.

Wherever such a resolution is not the case, then a struggle arises between the opposing projections: class struggle over consciousness. Where the bourgeois is the rising class, the expressive, gestural, labor-product nature of consciousness tends to be repressed. The objects of consciousness are reduced to commodities and take on the character of a fetish. Things which appear to move "freely," absent all gesture, are the elements of a world of description. The commodity fetish in language becomes one of description, of the referential, and has a second higher-order fetish of narration.

> 115. A *picture* held us captive. And we could not get outside it, for it lay in our language and language seemed to repeat it to us inexorably.
>
> (Wittgenstein, 1953, p 48e)

This mass aphasia within the English language occurs gradually over a period of 400 years. The rise of capitalism sets the preconditions for the rise of the novel, the invention of the optical illusion of realism, the final breakdown of gestural poetic forms, and the separation of self-consciousness of the art-object from the consciousness of the object itself in the rise of literary criticism.

Repression does not, fortunately, abolish the existence of the repressed element which continues as a contradiction, often invisible, in the social fact. As such, it continues to wage the class struggle of consciousness. The history of Anglo-American literature under capitalism is the history of this struggle. It can be discussed at many levels;

the remainder of this paper will touch on a few.

An event of significance is the development of books of poetry, usually dated in English by the publication of *Tottel's Miscellany* in 1557. If the very invention of the alphabet represents the initial, pre-capitalist, division of labor in language, the first movement of the language beyond the physical borders of the individual, and if the development of bards leads to a further class division into a class of authors and a class of consumers (in a purely tribal society, the poem is the shared language event of the group, the tribe is both author and consumer (Cf. chain-gang and jump-rope songs, two forms reminiscent of tribal authorship)), the arrival of the book greatly accelerates the process. From this moment forward, authors will see increasingly less of their audiences.

Another symptom of this gradual repression is the replacement, by 1750, of subjective styles of italicization and capitalization by "modern conventional" usage.

> The rather surprising thing is that so conspicuous and far-reaching a change should have evoked so little contemporary comment. The whole visual effect of a page of type is transformed by it. For us, this entails also a change in psychological response. Men do not ordinarily leave unremarked the swift departure of time-honored custom.
>
> (Bronson, 1958, p. 17)

But if the nature of this change is recognized as repression, then such a conspiracy of silence is not surprising at all. By 1760 one writer, Edward Capell, had gone so far as to discontinue the capitalization of the initial letter of each line of the poem.

Even in the 18th century the contradictions of the commoditization of language result in counter-tendencies. The bourgeois English reader had to participate in the production of the book-as-object, for it was he or she who had to have it bound. Thus individual libraries were bound according to internal aesthetic values, looking quite unlike the hodge-podge of colors and book sizes which typify the modern paperback home library. The sole trace of this counter-tendency in the modern era is the binding style used by encyclopedias and law books, intended to recall the style of that period.

Because of its singular adaptation to capitalist culture, the novel, a distinct subdivision of the poem, is a primary source for any etiology of capitalist reality. Of particular interest are the major forms of response to the modern "crisis" of the novel: the art novel, the mass market novel and the movies. Before turning to these forms, some preliminary comments should be made concerning the nature of the serialized language consumer and the inherently deformed relationship of the novel to its matrix of origin: the poem.

The two primary types of human relationships are the group and the series. The former is characteristic of tribal societies. Serialization (often termed alienation or atomization) places the individual as a passive cipher into a series of more or less identical units, Whitman's "simple separate person." Its apotheosis is to be found in the modern unemployment line. The function of the commoditized tongue of capitalism is the serialization of the language-user, especially the reader. In its ultimate form, the consumer of a mass market novel such as *Jaws* stares numbly at a "blank" page (the page also of the speed-reader) while a story appears to unfold miraculously of its own free will before his or her eyes. The presence of language appears as recessive as the sub-title of a foreign language film.

The work of each poet, each poem, is a response to a determinate coordinate of language and history. Each writer possesses in his or her imagination a subjective conceptualization of this *matrix* (inevitably partial, inevitably a distortion of the objective matrix which, by definition, is the sum of all poems), which is usually termed the tradition. If the functional structure of the objective matrix is that of a grid of coordinates (in which history plays an increasingly dominant role: see the chart of the "Rise of Historical Consciousness in the Making of Art," Burnham, 1973, p. 47), the subjective perception is that of a galaxy, or of a gas in a vacuum in which the work of major writers, important schools and close friends appear as large molecules and denser regions. The locus of the work to be written is felt as a blind spot in the subjective matrix, a primal lack toward which the writer is driven. This is the essential truth of the cliche that poets write only those poems which they *need*. Each successful poem abolishes (but only for a time) the primal lack and subtly reorganizes the structure of the matrix. [For a fuller discussion of the role of the matrix in the structure of individual poems, see the article "Performance" in *Shocks* magazine and "A note concerning the current status of *aRb*" in *Oculist Witnesses.*]

When language is serialized, commoditized, the repressive element deforms the subjective perception of the matrix. The multitudinous qualms, hesitations and self-doubts about this repressive deformation which fill Sterne's *Tristam Shandy* are increasingly anaesthetized by the rise of capitalism and appear not even to be felt by the modern pulp novelist who can just sit down and hack it out. (When it is felt, the consequence is often a phenomenon known as a "writer's block".) For any Rex Stout, the movement of objects, absent the presence of any gestural element, presents no problem. The cumulative and/or continuous present so typical of the temporal environments of the tribal has receded before the possibility of movement-in-time, the capacity for narrative has been greatly enhanced. The underlying precondition of the rise of the novel is precisely this divorce, by repression, from the gravitational force of language in the matrix, an assumption that the free evolution of a narrative art, as such, is possible, but this is an assumption feasible only well within the confines of the commodity fetish of language. Thus the seed of the modern "crisis of the novel" was implanted at the very beginning, its inevitability inherent in the form itself. Instead of "freely" leaving the gravitational pull of language, the novel, like a rocket with insufficient thrust, is doomed to fall back into the atmosphere of its matrix: the peculiar affliction of Tyrone Slothrop is that of the novel itself.

Beginning with the early modernists, many novelists of serious intent at least sense the nature of the contradiction and attempt to confront it directly. Gertrude Stein attempts to reintroduce the continuous present. Hemingway strives for an art of the sentence as the novel's determining language-unit (Cf. the illuminating discussion of Hemingway, itself conducted well within the commodity fetish of language, in Jameson, 1971, pp. 409-13). Joyce attempts a frontal assault, the reintegration of the novel into language, but his is a pre-Saussurian linguistics, that of etymologies. Such approaches lead eventually to all manifestations of the contemporary art-novel. Of particular note within this vein is the appearance of a subdivision of novelists who write for, and are principally read by, poets, such as Jack Kerouac, Douglas Woolf, Paul Metcalf, Harry Matthews, Kathy Acker and Fielding Dawson.

Another tendency of response to the crisis of the novel is to accept commoditization and to go on to write novels in which the language is all but invisible. While Saul Bellow (or Pearl Buck or John Steinbeck) represents an attempt to achieve this within a serious mode (the novel as a language art continuing to recall its prehistory in the poem, as art), and while a number of other novelists merely stylize their acquiescence (Mailer, Vonnegut, Roth, et al), more typical -- and more revealing -- are those who carry commoditization toward its logical conclusions in the mass market best-seller, such as Leon Uris, Peter Benchley or Mario Puzo. Mickey Spillane, who simply *dictates* his novels, carries the disappearance-of-the-word/appearance-of-the-world syndrome to its limit in writing.

But writing need not be the limit. Jettisoning the matrix-factor of language altogether, one tendency of narrative art takes advantage of a new technological development (capitalism's classic defence mechanism) and imposes itself on a new and still unformed matrix. This is the invention of modern cinema, the movies. The transition from novel to film further enables this tendency to modernize its mode of production into a more truly capitalist structure. The lone novelist of 1850, whose product is that of a manufacture-era cottage industry, becomes a century later the modern film *company*, with a small group of producers who own and control the means of production and a much larger, thoroughly stratified, labor force, from director to "best boy." That the imposition of narrative onto the matrix of film was not necessarily inherent in the formal elements of cinema *per se* is a consistent theme in the avante-garde or personal film of the past several decades. The very existence of a film such as Vertov's 1928 *Man With a Movie Camera*, made in the Soviet Union, indicates that it need not have been the case. But such is the nature of capitalist reality -- it is imperialistic.

This listing of tendencies of response within the novel is necessarily brief. Similarly, a history of literary criticism could be written, identifying its origins within the matrix of the poem, its exteriorizing serialization and the resolution of its subsequent crisis through state subsidy by its implantation into the university structure, making it an adjunct of tenure. Such a history would begin with a definition of the function of literary criticism as the separation of the self-consciousness of the activity of the poem from the poem itself. It would locate the necessity for this separation in the repressive element of the serialization of language as it moves into a capitalist period. It would explore in depth the role of literary criticism in a capitalist society as the creation of a "safe" and "official" matrix through its self-restriction of the object of inquiry to a small number of works identified as the national literature. It would study the optical illusion of literary criticism in the clarity of the essay form, in which the contradictions of its existence such as would be revealed through inarticulations, redundancies and non-sequiturs are subsumed by the tautological form, rendered invisible rather than resolved. Finally it would study the existence of counter-tendencies within literary criticism as well, specifically the anarchic works of literary theory created by poets (e.g., the body of prose left by Charles Olson) and the recent trend in France toward literary criticism as an admitted art form (e.g., Roland Barthes).

Recognition of a capitalist mode of reality passed through the language and imposed on its speakers finally will require a thorough re-evaluation of the history, form and function of the poem. This is a task of almost limitless dimension, for the matrix of the poem is not only the point of origin for the historical phenomena of the novel and literary criticism, it returns to the very social function of the arts, a dual function: for the group, art interiorizes its consciousness by the ordering (one could call it "tuning") of individual sense perceptions; for the individual, be it artist or consumer, art provides him or her with experiences of that dialectical consciousness in which subject and object, self and other, individual and group, unite. Since it is precisely this dialectic consciousness which capitalism seeks to repress through the serialization of the individual (for it is by such consciousness that we know the overdetermination of the objects of our world by the capitalist mode of production), the fine arts in general function as deformed counter-tendencies within the dominant capitalist reality. Such is the history of the poem.

Every major western poetic movement has been an attempt to get beyond the repressing elements of capitalist reality, toward a whole language art, much in the same manner as Stein, Joyce or Hemingway, discussed above. Typically, they have been deformed at the outset by the very condition of existing within the confines of the dominant reality. The dream narratives of surrealism could never hope to go beyond the narrative fetish, as hopelessly trapped within the fetish as "socialist realism." The entire projective tendency, from Pound to Robert Kelly, attempts to rediscover a physical ordering of the language, but posits that order not within the language but within individuals (individualism is the codification of serialized man), operating on the metaphoric equation of a page as scored text. The recent non-referential formalists, such as Clark Coolidge and Robert Grenier, frontally attack referentiality, but only through negation by specific context. To the extent that negation is determined by the thing negated, they too operate within the referential fetish.

It is the function of dialectical process to not merely explain the social origin and underlying structure of phenomena, but to ground it in the present social fact of class struggle so as to indicate appropriate courses of action. Quite clearly capitalism has its own mode of reality which is passed through the language and imposed on its speakers. The social function of the language arts, especially the poem, place them in an important position to carry the class struggle *for* consciousness to the level *of* consciousness. It is clear that one cannot change language (or consciousness) by fist: the French have only succeeded in limiting their vocabulary. First there must be a change in the mode and control of production of material life.

By recognizing itself as the *philosophy of practice in language*, poetry can work to search out the preconditions of post-referential language within the existing social fact. This requires (1) recognition of the historic nature and structure of referentiality, (2) placing the issue of language, the repressed element, at the center of the program, and (3) placing the program into the context of conscious class struggle. Such poetry will take as its motto the words of Marx's *The Eighteenth Brumaire of Louis Bonaparte*:

> The social revolution...cannot draw its poetry from the past, but only from the future.

Bibliography

BRONSON, BERTRAND H., *Printing as an Index of Taste in Eighteenth Century England*, New York Public Library, 1958.
BURNHAM, JACK, *The Structure of Art* (revised edition), Braziller, 1973.
CHOMSKY, NOAM, *Reflections on Language*, Pantheon, 1975.
FISCHER, ERNST, in collaboration with Franz Merek, *The Essential Marx*, translated by Anne Bostok, The Seabury Press, 1970.
JAMESON, FREDRIC, *Marxism and Form: Twentieth Century Dialectical Theories of Literature*, Princeton University Press, 1971.
ROTHENBERG, JEROME (editor), *Shaking the Pumpkin: Traditional Poetry of the Indian North Americas*, Doubleday Anchor Books, 1971.
SYLVESTER, RICHARD S, (editor), *The Anchor Anthology of Sixteenth Century Verse*, Doubleday Anchor Books, 1974.
WITTGENSTEIN, LUDWIG, *Philosophical Investigations*, translated by G.E.M. Anscombe, MacMillan Publishers, 1953.
YAKER, HENRI, Humphrey Osmond and Frances Cheek (editors), *The Future of Time: Man's Temporal Environment*, Doubleday Anchor Books, 1971.

[note: this essay is dedicated to the English Department of the University of California, Berkeley, whose professors were never able to explain the *why* of literature, and to the California prisoners, 1972-6, whose subjective perception of time under indeterminate sentence led me beyond the borders of my cultural understanding.]

RON SILLIMAN

This essay is reprinted from A Hundred Posters *(edited by Alan Davies), issue #14, February 1977.*

THREE OR FOUR THINGS I KNOW ABOUT HIM

1. "...the task of history, once the world beyond the truth has disappeared, is to establish the truth of this world...."--Marx

2.   its like a living death   going to work   every day   sort of like
being in a tomb   to sit in your office   you close the door   theres
the typewriter   theres three or four maybe three hours of work to be
done   between that nine oclock and five   maybe i listen to the news on
wbai if i didnt get it the night before that comes on at nine oclock
  i read the newspaper   i do anything to distract myself   sometimes i
sleep til around eleven   i put both feet up on my desk   and i put my
hand against my head and i close my eyes   the time passes if i listen
to the radio   i type a letter   i write an article   that would make
the article that i wrote for that medical newspaper seem like proust
  in comparison   or sometimes i think   initially   the job seemed more
  bearable   more to the point   of just a diversion and source of income
for a while   until i got unemployment   not now   but   mostly its
just that i'm taking things in a bleaker way   i'm not quite sure why
that is   of course the writing   writing   even
talking like this   always seems to me   perfectly at peace   so that
  i was thinking i dont know. this could be my own   you know   this
could be sort of the   the source of my crazy hood/ness   that   the
things that are really valuable dont so much happen as you experience
them   in the actual present   a lot of what i experience   is just a
  tremendous sense of   space   and vacant space at that   sort of like a
stanley kubrick film   sort of a lot of objects   floating separately
  which i dont   particularly feel do anything for me   give me anything
  make me feel good   and when i do feel almost best   is when i dont
care   whether they make me feel good   whether they have any relation
to me   thats a very pleasant   thats a real feeling of value in the
present moment   to just sit and do nothing   and thats what writing is
for me a lot   or just sitting   sometimes when i   i sit in my office
  with my eyes closed   on my chair   and let my mind wander   theres a
certain   sense of not caring   and letting it just go by   that i like
  and then there is actual relationships   you know   sometimes   touching
whether its listening to a piece of music sometimes   or talking to
somebody a lot   being with   certain people sometimes   but a lot of it
has to do with memory   & remembering   that it was   it was something
  that somehow the value seems to lie   historically   i look back   and
see things that really do seem   worthwhile   and worth it   for
instance   the way i behave   if i try to behave   well   decently   or
justly   or whatever it is   that we take to be what we judge ourselves
by   when we have a conversation   and we say   thats fucked and thats
not   whatever we go by in that sense   i mean   making that happen

building that   it does seem   you know   worth   a value   funny
refreshing   nice   wonderful   or a movie   sometimes   moments   hours
 days   months   and then   you know   even years   and lifetimes   sure
but   something   in   the   actual   experiencing   of   it   that
does seem   vacant   in the way that a lot   is vacant   but   also
 the way   yeah   okay   new mexico   is vacant
really i'm   you know   completely gone   just after working   by the
time i get to this   but i am able to concentrate and remember   the
different things ive said so far   that seem disconnected   see i'm sort
of condemned to be disconnected and seem disjointed and sort of   stupid
 but really i can remember all the different things ive said   i'm sort
of   i dont know   its almost a motif   thats a major preoccupation with
me   writing   the way a relationship is   much the way my relationship
with susan or kimberly or   my job   more than my job   altho it creates
an enormous number of hassles for me   its really as bad as you would
imagine it would be to work for this mindless healthcare provider
bureaucracy   and the reason why you dont want to work for it is because
its exploitive of you   you are used   your body is used   my writing
 and in that sense its an unsettling experience for me   to have to sit
 day after day in an office   and be exploited   what really bothers me
tho   in addition   the rub   is the attitude of the other people
 that somehow they could do whatever it is they had to do during the
day   they could be   managers   they could be bosses   they could order
people around   let the women answer the phones   and criticize me for
typing   and say i should let the secretaries do all the typing   they
could basically serve this large corporation   to the best of their
ability to serve it   and to further its particular interests   this
was actually a non profit corporation   and then sort of go out at lunch
or   on the side   and on a personal level say to you   that really
 who they were at the job   the way they behaved at their job   what
they did all day   was not them   that the real them   the real person
 was   somebody different   who went home at night and had liberal
values   was critical of what the company was doing   what the job was
making them do   that they really werent what they did at the job   they
were somebody else   that the self that went home at night   and watched
television   and went to the movies   went out dancing   socialized
 that was the real   that was the real them   and that sort of public
self   the job self   was really just a pretense that was necessary to
secure a decent living   for their families   for themselves   or a
chance to have some kind of social power   here again that tremendously
distorted notion of what a person is   and its this concept of a person
which makes me   question   the whole sense that we generally have of
what a person is   that you can imagine that what you do socially   that
the acts   you perform   are not you youre really this private thing
that doesnt do anything   this sort of neutral gear   but that whenever

you put that gear into operation   when you put yourself into gear
  thats not you   or thats only you under conditions when you want to say
well i like that and so i'll say well that is me   but when youre
actually doing things that have some effect   that isnt you   the real
you is this personal self   and you even get this situation where you
have   colleagues or professional   work   friends   as opposed to
personal friends   well he's a personal friend of mine   this person is
simply a job friend   this constant distortion   this constant avoidance
  that you are what you do   that insofar as a self is anything its how
it acts in a social situation   what else is a person   anyway   but a
signifier of responsibility for a series of actions   if a self is
anything it is what that self does with its body   does with its mind
  and that responsibility is for what you do   not for what you go home
at night and think what you'd like to do if if if if one day   some time
      it creates at the job place this tremendous vacancy of person
  this tremendous   lack of connection   with anybody   because if people
dont really think theyre being them all day long   in their suits and
shaved faces   and their very reduced mild language   and their reduced
middle of the road opinions   which they feel is the safest way   then
theres no way to get a connection with anybody   everything is just so
neutralized   that you can work in a place for years and years   and
really feel no   no clicking with anybody else   no contact   with
anybody there   you can go out to lunch at the same time   as if with
ghosts   there is no escape from what you do   and even if you feel
you dont mean what you do   dont mean what you say   dont mean the way
you dress   dont mean the kind of business letter language you use
  dont mean the division of labor you go along with   or that you
institute   dont mean the kind of attitudes you have competetively
toward your co-workers   dismissingly to the secretaries   that one does
mean these things whether one wants to or not   that they can be taken
to be intentional   to be you   are you   who you are   and they can be
read as being you   theres no escape from the nine to five self by
claiming that the five to midnight self   or the midnight to eight self
  is not really like this   we become selves just because we do different
things   and its a very hard thing   hard to accept that you are what
youre forced to be when you go to work   and not many feel that they
want to get behind   the products of their job   but we are behind them
        and i'm not saying   well obviously   munitions workers are
not responsible for the war   but its this avoidance of acknowledging
the tracks of exploitation   and of course for the ambitious   for the
managers and upper clerks   well   that conjuring trick of projecting a
self outside of ones own actions   is practically a way of life

3. TOILET PAPER CONSCIOUSNESS

"Should never say should."

You're not responsible. You may be white. You may be male. You may be heterosexual. You may be American. You may be working for the government. You may be President. But you are not responsible for anything but your own ass. And if you keep your ass clean--to the best of your ability--it's cool, it's groovy, it's okay.

4. "'Scientism' means science's belief in itself: that is, the conviction that we no longer understand science as *one* form of possible knowledge but rather must identify knowledge with science."--Habermas

5. COMIC INTERLUDE

It is the imperialism of the bourgeois psyche that demands a reduction in the number of words able to assume the weight of depicting the world picture. Nouns, because of their proletarian pristineness as least distorted by the invasion of bourgeois consciousness into the language, as, in fact, the claim goes, repositories of the object residue of material existence, are the principal word type favored under this assumption. *Viz*: classism, ruling class, third world, exploitation, revisionist, capital, profit, worker, means of production, alienation. 'Verb'al forms emerge mainly in the application of this--*uberhaupt*--principle structure--'exploiting', 'profiting', and also, 'struggling'*. Individual actions are depicted as reified instantiations fixed by the intersection of a variety of *theses*. It is, then, *our thesis* that political writing becomes disoriented when it self-views itself as description and not discourse: as not being *in* the world but *about* the world. The hermeneutic indicts the scientistic with the charge that it has once again subverted the dialogic nature of human understanding with its behavioro-empiricism.

*'Struggle' retains the active principle and is thus undistorted by the noun fetishism that marks infantile forms of Marxist thought. It is the 'verb'al weight of 'struggle' as shift and dynamic that is the essence of a re-hermeneuticized Marxism.

6. a fun is what i want to avoid the work of sitting down & m'um the cheezy. it's a hundred and forty five miles. you don't go for no reason. couldn't stop thinking about it. wanted to go to sleep so bad. under. stuff, thing. whats that gnawing, keeps gnawing. switch, fug, cumpf. afraid to get down to it. avoidances: movies. i think it's rather boring already dAncInG with LaRRy rIvers. marKINGs: not done by a machine. hAnDcRaFt. so you get into a scene and you say to y'rself--this is it, is outside it, & y'guys all know whats going on.

Daddy-O you a hero. OHH. can't even get tired. what is it--dead--
very wrinkled anyway. quiet...i cld hear the very 'utmost of m'heart.
EEzzy. its fear that eats away the.... i'm totally afraid of what it
will sound like. flotsam. a $1 transcript. stomach sputters. noise,
interference, & i can't work. TeAz tHE MeEk. we're'iz'iz puliticks?
poised: there is no overall plan.

7.   In general I think I have since I was about 12 tended to subdue
any sentimentality or strong emotional expressions of weakness, fear,
etc., I might have expressed except in the cases of the women I was
sexually relating to. At that time, I began to see how my parents demanded expressions of sentimentality, of commitment, of caring, of
happy birthday anniversary chanukah, in a way that repelled me from
any such expressions. In the family situation such expressions seemed
oppressive, they served to lock me further to the jealousy/possessive-
ness/control by my family. I completely lost trust in the natural place
for depending on other people--because I knew I did not want to depend
on my parents. I extended my feelings about my parents to others--
which could show up as my seeming detached, cynical, cold, intellectual,
cool. I learned that this distance from others was actually a tool for
social power by manipulation. I learned to think that my only security
was in what I could do by myself, alone--i.e. get good marks, do well
at work, write a good proposal, do good writing. My security was in
what I personally had complete control over. (This is in general
a "male class privilege" since a woman--commonly on her own--with kids
is forced to depend on others just for survival while I could basically
say fuck everyone else I'm in it for myself.) In fact, this keeping
personal control on one's life, keeping distance, really does get social power--it's harder to pin such people down, it's harder to get to
them. Anyway, even realizing this I found it hard to find security in
relating to other people instead of by being in personal control of my
life. It find it scarey to give up that other security (which is power)
by really trusting/needing/relating to others. The thing is that in
making relationships my security/home I do lose my own control--because
there are definite limits to my power, I may have to do something I
don't want to or that isn't in my interest, I may get hurt, I may be
powerless to prevent someone else from getting hurt. In other words,
in relating to other people, I have to accept their needs/perceptions
along with my own. Is this too abstract?

The thing is I still can feel my coldness/distance with other people.
I find it hard to break that down. I become defensive (self-protective)
or acerbic/witty (self-assertive). Some people get through that, see
me through it. But I think it can be unnecessarily alienating. I don't
think I give people comfort that much--that is, seem to them warm,
nurturing, supportive. Don't, I sometimes feel, give people a feeling of

getting "shelter from the storm/cold" but rather can be the cold that people seek the shelter from. I have a technique of bathing people in that cold, a puritan conviction that people should know the world is hard, and they should face it strong and stern. (& what happens to even good politics expressed this way?) And people should know that, but only sometimes can I transform that realization, go beyond it, and show that one shares that hardness with others, who care. That I am one of them. One of us.

8.   "There are those who worship loneliness--I'm not one of them; I've paid the price of solitude but at least I'm out of debt." A precursor here: the worship of loneliness, of being alone, as a way of being whole in the world that demands personal fragmentation as the price for fitting into society--the cult of Thoreau, Kierkegaard, etc, in the best and worst sense. So here the rejection, the realization that to worship being alone condemns one to isolation. *But*: the reward of solitude is yet to be out of debt; to owe no one anything, the self made man, on your own and in control--the delusion of security in isolation, if you keep yr ass clean kid youll be okay, look out fer yrself, yr numero primo. And so the ravages of the world have forced us to be warriors, ravaged we take control of our individual lives fighting for the warmth of inside we've had to give up. "Come in she said I'll give you shelter from the storm." She she she, waiting: ready to comfort, to nurture, to support our shipwrecked egos. And so we take the comfort, but without transforming ourselves--she simply comforts, offers shelter, but we remain in the world of "steel eyed death" (a steely idea that)--exchange no words "between us". There is "little risk involved" because we have held fast to our isolation, simply allowing it to be warmed. "Come in she said I'll give you shelter from the storm." But there can be no shelter until we ourselves provide it each for the other together. Without that there will always be "a wall between us"; then the steely idea triumphs: "Nothing really matters, it's doom alone that counts." *And yet?*: "Love is so simple, to quote a phrase, you've known it all the time I'm learning it these days." So simple and yet so seeming sentimental to say, as if sentimentality were the curse that prevented us from knowing how simple love is in our repulsion to its being demanded by our families/country/society at the price of self-abnegation. And so in the flight from the oppressive obligations of sentimentality; of polite hellos and demanded, guilt-ridden, love; in the retreat into the isolation and security of personal control, needing no one; a native sense was lost that love is so simple, to quote a phrase, that we are each for each other shelter from the storm, if we are not afraid to come in, or take another into where we are. But still all this while the secret has been known ("you've known it all the time") if

only we had "spoken words between us", had taken that "risk". The words sound sentimental--I love you I miss you it hurts me so bad with a pain that stops and starts--words of separation, of closeness, of hurt, of joy--we choke on them: there is no depth here, no unique sensibility: everyone says them. But still the curse can be broken by their utterance. "I can change I swear." "It's the price I have to pay." --The commitment is to "cross the line" from the "foreign countries" each of us inhabits; *someday* to dissolve into a now.

9. "It's like spelling. You know that whole sense that spelling things right in English is really sort of an aristocratic notion. You could tell the educated few by the fact that they spelled the same. Which I'm told is a lot of their system of education...because in Shakespeare's time he spelled his own name a lot of different ways, not to mention other words. You know, it was really like a body of material that would identify you as one of the educated people. Think of all the time we've spent in school spelling things right. Sort of a tremendous waste of time."--Coolidge

10. Ethics & aesthetics become increasingly "out there". Dress & syntax & right behavior are copied from presented models, a process of emulation rather than interpretation. Clerks & secretaries spend their time typing neatly, removing idiosyncracies from the language & presiding over a tan neutrality--"unobtrusive"--with the smoothness of flow allowed by explanatory transition.

Topic sentence. However; but; as a result. Blah, blah, blah. It follows from this. Concluding sentence.

Meaning, coherence, truth projected "out there" as something we know not for ourselves but as taught to us. (One day, maybe, we will be experts.)

It goes like this. "Clear writing is the best picture of clear thinking." Providing a clear view. (An imperial clarity for an imperial world.) An official version of reality, in which ethics is transformed into moral code & aesthetics into clean shaving, is labelled the public reality & we learn this as we would a new language. (Orthography & expository clarity are just other words for diction & etiquette.)

Imperial reality has as its essential claim not so much that it is *a* version of reality but that it is *the* version, i.e., (imperially) clear. That the composition of reality is suprapersonal: the mistakes & plain takes of a person are not an essential part of reality's composition. Standardized spelling, layout, & punctuation enter into a world of standardization--clocks & the orbit of the moon & the speed of light. A social science epistemologically self-conceived on the model of the natural sciences becomes possible & grammar becomes a social science. Language is thus removed from the participatory control of its users & delivered into the hands of the state. Text is no longer regarded as requiring interpretation: rules for appropriate spelling & syntax are determined by consultation with generalized codes of grammar removed from their contextualized source in a text. (The Hebrew handwritten text required interpretation not only in respect to the meaning of its ethical & ritual tenets but even for the placement of vowels.) Decontextualized codification of the rules of language enforces a view that language operates on principles apart from its usage. These rules are not "picked up" but taught. Failure to produce appropriate language is regarded not as misperception but as error. The understanding begins to be lost that we are each involved in the constitution of language-- that our actions reconstitute--change--reality.

It's a question of who controls reality. Is reality "out there" (as scientism tells us) or rather an interaction with us, in which our actions shape its constitution? Prescribed rules of grammar & spelling make language seem outside of our control. & a language, even only seemingly, wrested from our control is a world taken from us--a world in which language becomes a tool for the description of the world, words mere instrumentalities for representing this world. This is reflected by the historical movement toward uniform spelling and grammar, with an ideology that emphasizes non-idiosyncratic, smooth transition, elimination of awkwardness, &c, --anything that might concentrate attention on the language itself. For instance, in contrast to, say, Sterne's work, where the look & texture--the opacity--of the text is everywhere present, a neutral, transparent prose style has developed in certain recent novels where the words seem meant to be looked through--to the depicted world beyond the page. Likewise, in current middle of the road poetry, we see the elimination of overt rhyme & alliteration, with metric forms retained primarily for their capacity to officialize as "poetry". (That older texts are closer to hand-written & oral tradition is partial explanation for this, but having machines for uniform printing necessitates neither a uniform writing nor the projection of a suprapersonal world.)

Much of the spirit of modernism has been involved in the reassertion of the value of what has come to be fantasized as subjectivity. Faced with an imperial reality, "subjectivity" is first defined as "mere idiosyncracy", that residue of perception that is to be discounted, the fumbling clouds of vision that are to be dissolved by learning. But in just this is the ultimate *subjectivity* of a people: stripping us of our source of power in our humanness by denying the validity of

our power over the constitution of our world through language. The myth
of subjectivity and its denigration as mere idiosyncracy--impediments to
be overcome--diffuses the inherent power in the commonness of our alienation: that rather than being something that separates us, alienation
is the source of our commonness.   I take it that this is why Marx saw
as inevitable that a proletariat conscious of its alienation would be
able to develop human relations--solidarity--which would be stronger
than any other human power.

The poetic response to the imposition of an imperial reality has been
to define subjectivity, by a kind of Nietzschéan turn around, not as
'mere' but as exalted.   The image of the poet as loner & romantic
continues to condition this response.   An unconscious strategy of con-
trariety develops--that the official manners & forms are corrupt &
distorted & only the private & individual is real.   Beat--to abstract
& project a stance, acknowledging the injury this does to the actual
poetry--is an obvious example, as is Surrealism, itself & as an influence.   These two modes--for the moment letting them stand for a much
wider variety of literary response--are grounded in reaction.   Beat
poetry, as such, could go no further than the dramatization of alienation; the genesis of much of its considerable & indispensable formal
innovation is (quite justifiably) epaté la bourgeoisie.   (The rhapsodic
other side was, at the least, pastoral romanticism; at its best it put
off the theatre of vision for the language of presence.)   Likewise,
Surrealism, in itself, could do little more than theatricalize our
alienation from official reality, since it is completely rooted in
bourgeois spatio-temporal perception: it simply distorts it.   Both
Beat & Surrealism are essentially poetries of gesture, viz: reality
is different from our schooled conceptions of it, more fantastic, more
————————.   In these modes, to use Stanley Cavell's phrase, the moment
is not grounded but etherialized: alienation is not defeated but only
landscaped.*   What is needed, now, is not the further dramatization
of far-outness but the presence of far-inness.   These modes have shown
a way.   Surrealism & Beat broke open syntax & placement of words on the
page, they widened the range of content & vocabulary, they allowed
shape & texture & hover of consciousness to become more important than
description.   Unfortunately, much current poetry goes no further, fix-
ated on the idea of establishing the value of the interior world of
feeling, irrational (whimsical) connections, social taboos, the personal life--over & against "official" reality.**   As if we didn't
already know that "bad grammar" can speak more truthfully than correct
grammar, that learning & expertise don't really impart knowledge, that
private fantasies don't coincide with public property.   It's not that
we don't need to hear these things again & again, any more than that
that is the objection to socialist realism, but that there is so much

more we can do than simply underline the fact--& describe the conditions
--of our alienation, of the loss of the world's presence to us. (As if
it were enough to simply mourn & not organize.) The promise of the
return of the world can (& has always been) fulfilled by poetry. Even
before the process of class struggle is complete. Poetry, centered on
the condition of its wordness--words of a language not out there but in
here, language the place of our commonness--is a momentary restoration
of ourselves to ourselves.

*Likewise, this is true of the avant-gardism & conceptualism, taken for
themselves as a stance, which pervade much of the seventies art scene.

**This helps to explain the almost ideological anti-intellectualism--
"dumbness"--that runs through some poetry circles.

11. "At home, one does not speak so that people will understand but
because people understand."--Fuchs

12. & obviously we're committed to political struggle, to the necessity of changing current capital distribution, to making the factories
& the schools & the hospitals cooperatives, to finding a democracy that
allows for the participatory authority of each one to the extent of the
responsibility we place on her or him. there are no prefixed means &
the answer is in us struggling & discussing & deciding as groups &
acting. & it troubles--isn't this incessant writing & questioning
writing a diversion? isn't *the* business...? well, but language *is*
our business, fully as much as 'acting'. anyway, how do you pre-
suppose to separate out the deed & the reflection? you might say we've
got dual responsibilities, & one doesn't take us off the hook of the
other. writing, by itself, does not further class struggle. "it is a
fertilizer not a tool." pound's politics don't in any way diminish the
power & significance of his writing. nor do they limit the aesthetic/.
political value of the work. but that in no way absolves the man from
his own political responsibilities. social credit--to be a little
silly & talk about measuring it--is really a multiplication of the
"dual" responsibilities. & a zero multiplied by even an astronomical
figure doesn't get you very far. i'm not saying the "private" literary
activity is separable from the "public" conduct. i'm saying a person's
got a variety of responsibilities (if to say 'dual' then only when
speaking of a particular conflict)--& it's not okay to be a bully just
because you're wearing a pretty dress. there's no end to
responsibilities. & poetry, well, it's in a sense an additional
responsibility--as a man or a woman you'd not lose 'credit'
for not doing it. it's not that aesthetic consciousness &
political consciousness are essentially different, quite the opposite,
but really this is the goal: reunification--in practice--of what we
now face as multiple demands. the power of poetry is, indeed, to

bridge this gap--for a moment--by providing instances of actualization. it is a glimpse. but, sadly, for us, now, no *maker* is able to reap the legitimate rewards of his or her labor. & so our responsibilities remain multiple & we are called on to fulfill all of them.

13. We imagine there is a gap between the world of our private phantasies & the possibilities of meaningful action. & so it becomes easy to talk & talk on what is lacking, to discourse on end, & yet feel impotent. 'What's to do.' But this gap is the measure not so much of our desires or depression or impotence but of our*selves*. It has been the continual failure of Marxist aesthetics to insist that this gap is simply another illusory part of our commodity lives. It is at the root of our collectivity.

14. The essential aspect of writing centered on its language is its possibilities for relationship, *viz*, it is the body of 'us'ness, in which *we* are, the ground of our commonness.

Language is commonness in being, through which we see & make sense of & value. Its exploration is the exploration of the human common ground. The move from purely descriptive, outward directive, writing toward writing centered on its wordness, its physicality, its haecceity (thisness) is, in its impulse, an investigation of human self sameness, of the place of our connection: in the world, in the word, in ourselves.

15. The situation, the relations, the conditions under which. The task of unchaining & setting up. They hankered to & the people proclaimed an abbreviated stroke no more than a ruffling of the surface. An entire people: that by means of a revolution had imparted itself a power of motion suddenly finds itself back to the old dates the old names a dim burning lamp fastened to the head behind a long whip. Men & things seem set in sparkling brilliance till a pale casts over. The riddle is not solved by turns of speech, the fixed idea of making gold, which in the press fall victim to the courts & even more equivocal figures. An array of passwords maintained against a wider one. Placards are posted on all street corners. The priests appear & wail about the necessity of moral reform. A drive against the schoolteachers. (Even bourgeois liberalism is declared socialistic.) Its gladiators find their ideals wholly absorbed in products & Caesar himself is watching over. Antediluvian colossi disappear into sober mouthpieces with suitable up to date manners knocking feudal manners like someone who has just learned a new language always translating back into the first. "Property, family, religion, order." The bureaucracy is well gallooned & well fed. The individual turns in stupefied seclusion & the peasants dwell in hovels. A bunch of blokes push their way forward.

--When the real aim is achieved & society is accomplished. As when we find our way in it without thinking in terms of the old. The event itself appears like a bolt from the blue.

CHARLES BERNSTEIN

This essay is reprinted from <u>A Hundred Posters</u> *(edited by Alan Davies), issue #26, February 1978.*

544

THE PACIFICA INTERVIEW

(The following is a transcript of an interview of the editors by Susan Howe, taped in March 1979, and broadcast over WBAI-FM, Pacifica Radio in New York City.)

CHARLES BERNSTEIN: L=A=N=G=U=A=G=E came out of our interest as writers of poetry in having discussion of works that interested us and of issues of politics and philosophy and other arts that seemed related to that work. A lot of what we've done is to allow the active kind of energy that goes into writing poetry to pervade the discussion that goes on in the magazine, so for someone who wasn't used to that it might even seem like the reviews or comments or critical articles were poems. That is to say, there is no standard expository style used, nor a standard style of punctuation for that matter. And the articles just take off right in the middle, assuming, very often, some knowledge of the terms of an ongoing discussion. It's the kind of publication that could only be put out by people actively engaged in writing. Although what constitutes being actively engaged in writing is an open question we're interested in exploring.

SUSAN HOWE: Do you feel that there is a specific group of people that are working along lines that interest you?

CB: I think that there are traditions within American literature, within poetry, within twentieth century art, as well as a number of contemporary writers that together form a matrix of active interest. All those things seem like confluences. As a magazine, we have a few hundred subscribers, we have about 200 different people who've written for us, a number writing numerous pieces, and this obviously defines a certain area of interest. There are writers and magazines that Bruce and I share a commitment to, are interested in writing about and talking about. But we don't exhaust the limits of our interests in the magazine.

SH: It seems to me that similar dialogue to that going on in L=A=N=G=U=A=G=E could have been found in *Artforum* when it was really going strong in the late 60's or early 70's, and a little bit in *October* magazine.... I'm not talking about the critics, but the works that they are writing about.

BRUCE ANDREWS: I think that specifically the kind of work that I'm most interested in deals with questions that have been dominant in other advanced arts in the century and have to do with what is customarily thought of as the modernist project in those other arts — that is, an exploration of the intrinsic qualities and possibilities of the medium in which the art takes place. And that is an exploration that's been carried on in all the arts, and it's been carried on in the recent critical work related to most of the other arts. Now, I think there are any number of sub-traditions and active traditions of writing that explore some of those same issues having to do with the nature of the medium, which from our point of view is language. The medium of writing is not some concocted verse tradition that comes down to us through academic discourse and what people are taught in school and what book reviewers in *The New York Times* tell us that poetry is all about; it has to do with writing as an exploration and a presentation of the possibilities of language. And that exploration has gone on in the writing throughout the century in a number of different traditions. It's something a number of poets around the country and in Europe now talk about but most of that discussion has taken place privately in correspondance, people's journal writing, etc. We've all been engaged in that project in the mail and in conversation for years and are trying in a small way by doing the magazine to get some of that discourse out into a more public realm. That way the participation can be somewhat less restrictive — where it isn't just a matter of what particular person you happen to be close friends with or happen to have access to through the mail that you carry on this wonderful dialogue with, but to get some of that out in a more public way, to build a sense of community, to some extent, to get some of the issues clarified, to get the information around in a somewhat easier fashion, and to try to do it ourselves as writers, rather than constantly having these questions mediated by some particular critical establishment, which I think is one of the reasons why writing, if it has lagged behind some of the other arts in certain ways, that's one of the reasons. Because the discussion about writing has been largely carried on by conservative English professors, in the United States.

CB: But, of course, it's not writing that has lagged behind the other arts but rather that people's awareness of the work has lagged behind. There is an enormous repression of knowledge about even the American traditions of writing. Lots of the important work done in the early part of the century remains far more obscure than comparable works in the visual arts, which has had a well-funded critical industry to sell innovation as the basis of creating ever higher market values not only for new work but for the early innovations which make up their traditions. So the public climate about writing is much more conservative, the interesting work is much less visible. In the fifties and sixties most of the work published by the commercial and university presses represented a very minor and not very interesting kind of work that involved the most reactionary possible interpretation of the work of people like Pound, and even Williams. For a lot of people, who may read or even write for the art magazines, that's all they see of poetry.

SH: It's interesting to me because, for instance, you had Black Mountain which produced an incredible amount of interesting writing and music and visual art. The visual artists that came out of that now have a tremendous amount of critical approval in America — they are taught in the schools, they are in museums, they are written about in *The New York Times*. But when it comes to the writers, this has not been the case.

CB: There's been enormous sums of money involved in the promotion of the visual arts, while most of the money in the poetry world is university related and goes, by and large, to a very restricted, a very boring, kind of work that relates more to the lives and sensibilities of people who teach in academic institutions, which, not simply to dismiss it, does have a certain popularity because of this context. Anyway, poetry is difficult to understand; in the time it takes to read one poem and just get the most initial hit you could look at a number of paintings, not that you would be able to fully understand them of course. But the society is more geared to a certain kind of superficial consumption of art, which is hard to do with a poem, especially one that has any formal complexity: it's not right there to be seen, whether or not it's understood. Certainly, the popularity of someone like Jackson Pollock doesn't necessarily come from an intimate understanding of the kind of textures he created and his ability, as they say, to achieve an opticality in his works and overall nonfiguration that you might think of from a formalist point of view. But rather, the fact that his work is sold for a lot of money and so on, that you can buy a little snapshot of one of the paintings or a postcard and consume the image. Poetry is much harder to consume at that level. It's hard to get a sense of what the poem is at all. There's not really an image. Either it looks the same as all poetry has looked with stanzas and so on, or it looks like words scattered on a page. It's hard to get that immediate hit off of what it is; it's missing a certain immediate flash some of the other arts have.

   Following up on something Bruce said, I'm interested in looking at the tradition of writing as something broader than simply the verse tradition or anything like that. Since this gets away from a more central point for me, which does not separate poetry out from other forms of writing, which is the exploration of how language shapes the way we see the world — how we come to see the world in terms of language. Lots of the poetry I find most exciting and most beautiful gives a sense of how language creates the world; it lets you see the world and the actual formation of the world more closely. So there's an affinity here with critical thought, and to Marxist thought. I mean I think the work can both provide a social critique and be a poem that stands on its own. Sometimes the categorization of writing into its genres is misleading; often these genres are no more than format distinctions, as in the case of prose format, which really cannot distinguish between poetry and what is so often called 'prose'. If you look at the whole range of writing that goes on, just look at different newspapers, different kinds of technical information manuals, and all the other types of writing that gets produced in our society, and look at them with an eye to what kind of a quality of world is being created by it. This is where the work of Burroughs and Mac Low in the fifties and sixties fits in and is so important. Cutting up "found" language, juxtaposing, rearranging, to see what kinds of results you get. That you can deal with language as this material we are pervaded by, which we as writers take as the material with which we do our work: how we ourselves are created out of the ways this material is used. And that entails seeing language not as a transparency, not as something which simply dissolves as you get a picture of the world in focus, so that, in reading a text, you are hardly aware of the language at all. I am more and more interested in becoming conscious of language when I write and in reading work which is conscious of its qualities as language, and in that sense not trying to eliminate idiosyncracies or other kinds of things that prevent just using the language as a disappearing act that gives you the world on the other side. Which is basically a way of consuming, of making the world into a commodity you just consume, rather than seeing how the world is actually constructed through language.

SH: Are there any basic texts that you go back and back to — just to give the listeners some idea of where you are coming out of?

BA: You are talking about traditions in the other arts, you are talking about the Dadaists, the Russian Futurists, you are talking about different moves in the tradition of the novel, you are talking about different things going on in the visual arts. For me, things like jazz and improvisatory music in the sixties and seventies have been very important. The new music coming out of Cage and the traditions he harkens back to. You have this confluence of all these different streams, all these different traditions, most of which have been shuttled to the side of what's considered important in writing. And it isn't so much that we're heroically trying to bring all these things together. I mean these are the kinds of mixes of different traditions that many of the writers are interested in or cut into at some point. All of these traditions, plus others that don't come to mind as quickly, are operating in the writing of the people we're concerned with, so the discussion sometimes centers around some of these sub-traditions, some of those active streams of work.

SH: Some of those are original traditions, I mean obviously it's better to go back to the sources like Melville or Thoreau, but it seems to me that there has been a re-interpretation of those basic texts by some modern criticism that for me has shaped my thinking, like *S/Z* by Barthes, which profoundly affected my way of looking at different texts.

BA: Right, but did it get us all to go back and read Balzac, that's the question. It's a question academics don't usually confront.

SH: It could certainly get me to go back and redo it a little bit. I mean, I think the Freudian thing too, Freud has been very important.

BA: I think it's true in the last 10 or 20 years you have a wide range of activity going on in the critical community. Most of it is not so much centered around writing, although that is more the case now in France and with some of the trendier English departments in the U.S. that have picked up on some of the French theorists. But you also have whole ranges of philosophical traditions. You have the whole Marxist tradition of ways of looking at social phenomena as material, as production, as constrained by underlying principles operating at the social system level and the question of how that affects our sense of distance from language versus our sense of involvement and participatory involvement in it. Not just as something that we consume, something that is out there as this 'window on the world' that we're supposed to simply pass through and therefore come to accept and be socialized into: some particular way of looking at the world which essentially is one of acceptance, a kind of glassy-eyed consumptive way of dealing with the world instead of seeing that in fact language is this vessel or this environment that we operate in which shapes our world, shapes our sense of ourselves, which is also incredibly constrictive. Something that I think a lot of this writing tends to try to undercut is the notion of a sovereign self and a sovereign subject as the center of meaning in a text — which I think again is not only a limited and limiting notion, but a notion that derives from the operation of an oppressive social system that we all are living under. To some extent we are living out society's alienating qualities without being encouraged to look at what these qualities are, to see how aliena- tion is related to, say, traditions of representation in the arts or in writing, how all those things operate together. So you have people working in these areas as writers, and you also have people doing serious thinking and conceptualizing about these things, and both of these have influenced my own way of looking at what writing is and what the possi- bilities for writing can be, both socially and on the page. So, in that sense, you have a much messier field of vision here in terms of what seems important and what seems worth thinking about.

CB: When Bruce or I will talk about a political or Marxist, specifi- cally a Marxist perspective, it is different than the traditional sense of socialist realism which I find fairly abhorrently limited as a view of what art could be. Obviously, to people who support socialist realism as what Marxist art would be or political art would be or what socialist art would be, the work that we do might seem terrifically privatized, individualized, abstract and all kinds of bad things, I'm sure. I think that what political art does, or art that has political concerns, let me put it that way because I don't know what it would mean to say political art, art that has the kind of concerns that Marx himself had and that in general people that have radical social views have, is to look at society and how values are constituted within in, how the world comes to mean things, how labor is always removed from an understanding of what a product is, and so on. To try to bring these things out, look at them, and make it more apparent in the writing. So that what I am interested in doing is stopping the sense of transparency in language, that language is this neutral thing that people don't have a part in. Because it is people that make up language and change language and in that way change reality. If you accept the concept that language is a relatively fixed system for describing the world, which is essentially a notion that academic concepts of writing have and share with socialist realist senses of writing, you have given over what I think is the major area of struggle, which is the control over the constitution of reality. Let me give an example of that, which would be spelling. The idea that there should be uniform spelling and uniform diction has been recently combatted by a lot of people favoring more acceptance of black English and dialects in the school. These are very revealing arguments to hear about language. Language is not something that exists in stasis and it doesn't have any intrinsic uniformity. The idea that everyone should spell things the same, not that I don't think it's a crucial social survival skill to know correct spelling, but the idea is still based on an elitist notion of writing as being something for an aristocracy who have cohesive social views and so on. In Shakespeare's time people didn't even spell their own names the same way. There was that sense that language was much more in flux, much more able to be shaped. The more and more you move to the concept that subject/verb/object sentences, the way I'm talking now, is somehow clearer, the more and more you move to accept what almost might be called an imperial sense of what clarity is, that language can imperially just dissolve and give you the world and that the world really is correct spelling, that a table really is t-a-b-l-e. That in fact different idioms, different ways, confusions, what are called idiosyncracies of diction, actually indicate a different world, different perceptions, different kinds of values. And that rather than try to bring everybody over to a white Western framework for what the world is and for describing the world, it is important to understand that every difference in spelling, every 'unclarity', every 'awkwardness' means something if a person uses it, and that you can read it and it tells you something, and to value that, to value the fact that language evolves and changes. And that people can begin to take control of the language and changing the language and not having this enormous insistence on no mistakes, no typographical errors, no spelling mistakes, no grammatical errors, parallel structure, all these things that construct 'a' world but not 'the' world. For if you buy that it's *the* world you are buying an enormous amount which I think is basically related to managerial control of this society by large capital interests. You buy a conception of reality, that the world really does exist in this way as described by these clear expository sentences, and it doesn't. The world exists in the ways we create it and we can learn how to see the world in different ways and a lot of cracks in that system by beginning to explore alternative methods of writing and thinking and talking.

BA: And reading and listening.

SH: Editing is very important in that context. When you are given an anthology of poetry in school, you have the standard spelling. But if you go back to a really well-edited book of 18th century poetry or of 17th century metaphysical poets and see the way they spelled, it opens things up. Those poems just jump alive off the page because of the different spelling. So that's terribly important when it comes to editing. Look at what they did to Emily Dickinson. Her poems for years appeared in dribs and drabs; they were slowly coming out but with the dashes removed and the capitals all made small.

CB: In the name of uniformity and standardization of language.

SH: Yes, but half the life was there in what she was trying to do with her dashes and capitals.

BA: You are being encouraged when this sort of thing happens to take for granted the larger social context in which everybody is operating. You are talking about active writing, yet you are also talking about a speech situation out of which these norms of clarity come. I mean that's what this clarity is supposed to be all about. But what happens in a speech situation is that you're forced or encouraged to take for granted the context in which you are embedded. That's one of the things I am interested in trying to undercut—it's that failure to recognize what the system is that everyone is working within. But people can come to see language first of all as a changing system, as this system that has its own rules and its own norms and its own constraints, pretty well institutionalized, that shapes not only the writing or reading that goes on within in but also the people who are precipitated out of it: the whole idea of subjects and bodies coming out of it. If they can not only only recognize the limitations and constraints which the system provides, but also begin to think of writing as a practice within the system, a practice that is displaying that system, problematicizing it, making it look like something that has developed historically, that you don't have to take it for granted, that you can make moves within it, that you can create changes within it, that you can take control of that. You no longer have to think of the system as this apparatus of social control that we're all going to be subjected to all the time. So to that extent I think of the way writing uses language as a paradigm for how people can operate within this larger social system, and that's what I think are the broader political implications of some of these kinds of writing we've been interested in. It's not a question of mobilizing the masses to form large majorities that can take power in some straightforwardly political sense; it's the question of analyzing, critiquing, problematicizing the structure of power itself. This isn't a question of the state; you're not talking about the government or even just about the capitalist economic apparatus. You're talking about power relations that exist between individuals, between systems and individuals within them, between norms and relationships and patterns of activity. All of these things are what create social control. If people can come to a greater understanding of how those systems operate and how change within those systems can operate—whether it's language or whether it's neighborhood insurrection or whatever you're talking about—then *that's* a political dimension to this work which I think is going to be undercut (and this is I think the sad part)...will be undercut by demanding the work to take on a more obvious or visible political content. Because what happens there is that the people who are touted generally as being so-called political writers or political poets tend to be ones that take for granted those larger systems and structures which language *operates*. They do make certain points, but too often the only points that get across are the ones which can plug into this whole emphasis on customary expository writing or normal semantic relationships or how things normally operate—certain points which people can easily consume.

SH: The classic example I think of a kind of tragedy of idealism in the way you are talking about is the one that occurred in Russia right after the Revolution. The constructivists...

BA: The futurists, the dreamers of progress. They had the dream and they saw some of it fulfilled and things did change....

CB: /̄ The recent show of 'The Russian Avant-Garde, 1910-1930' in Los Angeles and Washington was an incredible presentation of how significant this work was, how vital the spirit of that work still is, and how devastatingly things had changed by 1930./̄ Obviously there was a movement in the Soviet Union, not to go into the history of the Soviet Union, but the move toward centralism and toward crushing idiosyncracies and so on is related to what we are talking about. Now, I think that the political issues and what is the best kind of party formation and so on are difficult questions, and certainly there have to be different levels of change, certain things that have to be sacrificed for other things. But these general issues we are bringing out, of qualities of human life that I think art has always explored, and I think art with a political perspective can continue to explore, have to do with things existing for themselves and not simply as instrumentalities for something else. And that's why I question the idea of what political poetry is. Poetry writing by people who have a social and political commitment is the way I would rather put it. Because in working on writing I am interested in creating things which aren't simply vehicles for something else. I'm not interested in teaching someone something per se, I'm not interested in illustrating a point per se, I'm not interested in having anecdotes or any of those things per se. I'm interested in creating things that exist on their own, for themselves, by themselves. That's why I object to this issue of trying, when you write, to create a language that has no sense of itself, that almost tries to make you forget that there is any kind of language there, because it does take away from the integrity of the work. And I think art has always been involved with self-suf-fiency and non-intrumentality. What that ends up being in some strange way is something that is a process which is to some degree not mediated to as great an extent by alienation. That is to say, some bit of whole-ness or wholesomeness that can exist in the society that we're in, that isn't completely permeated by the structures of alienation.

BA: The demand that political writing be instrumental, I think, is some-thing that bothers me in the same way that the demand that writing per se be instrumental bothers me. That is, the sense that it's instrument-al to giving you this hypnotized gaze at these things that are so-called 'out there' in the so-called 'real world' and that writing is a mere replication of that real world, that writing is not a production. What people don't always see, or what I'm interested in seeing myself and exploring, is how the writing actually creates that world out there. That it's an act of production and it's not simply an act of transcrip-tion of some previously constituted world that's all set up out there so that all we have to do is live in it. I mean, we don't just live in this world. We make the world, whether we are given the power to do so in a really active way or not. We are following along certain patterns which constitute that world and we do that through our language, we do that through our consciousness. So anything which is going to explore the way in which that consciousness and that writing is in fact a pro-duction and therefore can be changed becomes more interesting. I mean, it's a historical phenomenon, it's not some fated naturalistic thing that we have to take for granted like the way we take the weather for granted. We're talking about how people live in society and what they can produce, and that gives me greater excitement about work that pre-sents itself both as a production and also as something that is self-sufficient, that has a presence in and of itself which is interesting, which can generate a complicated emotional impact or possibility to me as a reader, on other people who would read the work, rather than the impact simply being generated by the hypnosis of looking at some outside world that's previously constituted. Or rather than the possibilities being a stylish deduction from the existing social codes. The thing that's exciting is the materiality of language and the partial self-sufficiency and partial outreach of language right there on the page, not this idea that you're essentially asleep while you're reading and being propelled into some nether world off the page where all the action is.

CB: It's in that sense that I think writing can be an important epistemological investigation, because the objects, what makes up the objects of the world that people talk about—tables, chairs, bosses, work places, geographical locations— are not things one takes for granted when one is writing. Those are things that one calls into question, one sees how they are made up and how they are constituted, how the world is actually divided and created constantly by the langauge that we use. By the sentence structure that we use. And that to simply make syntax a non-existent (that is, already determined) structure is to accept the objects of the world as constituted by the media, by the school systems, by the general ideology that is most prevalent. There certainly is a lot of truth to the reality of the world as we normally preceive it, but those objects are not the absolutes of reality. They are constantly constituted in language and by language and through language, conditioned by language, and it's in that sense that writing which doesn't take for granted that it is describing things clearly but rather that is interested in density and opacity—which is certainly something that would strike readers of our magazine, that this stuff isn't 'clear', I don't know what you are talking about, it seems fuzzy or non-expository or like the poetry which is dense and opaque. That's where that comes out of, it's that interest in not accepting the objects of the world as given.

L=A=N=G=U=A=G=E

Supplement No. 3.

October 1981.

Charles Bernstein & Bruce Andrews, Editors.

Volume Four, 1981 edition from *Open Letter*: $5. Back issues available.

464 Amsterdam Avenue, New York, NY 10024.

Design: Susan B. Laufer   Typing: Alan Davies

This issue is made possible, in part, by a grant from the National Endowment for the Arts. Distributed with the cooperation of the Segue Foundation.

ON L=A=N=G=U=A=G=E VOLUME FOUR
Published As a Special Issue of Open Letter, Fifth Series, No. 1

The relationship with *Open Letter*, a Canadian journal of writing and theory, preceded the founding of *L=A=N=G=U=A=G=E* newsletter. Steve McCaffery's reviews occasioned Andrews's first writing to him (via *Open Letter*) about five years before the newsletter brought out its first issue. Given that McCaffery characterized this contact as the "first letter from the US," it might well have been the first cross-border traffic of what would soon become known as language-centered writing.

After *Open Letter* published the "Politics of the Referent" symposium in 1977 (later reprinted by *L=A=N=G=U=A=G=E* as a supplement), Frank Davey, the editor of *Open Letter*, asked Andrews and Bernstein if they would edit an issue of the magazine. Since they had been thinking about ending their newsletter after volume three, this invitation provided a chance to edit a final volume with a journal they admired while having others take over the production, which had previously been done in-house. They agreed that a set of longer essays collected together in a single perfect-bound journal was a useful way to finish the series and do something different.

Although the content of the issue was determined by Andrews and Bernstein, its format was entirely dictated by *Open Letter*. However, as the editors designated the special issue as volume four of *L=A=N=G=U=A=G=E*, they also printed a small run—with their own cover—to distribute to newsletter subscribers.

The full text of *Open Letter* can be found here: http://eclipsearchive.org/projects/LANGUAGEvol4/LanguageVol4.pdf

Contents

558

INDEX

With the exception of the second supplement to *L=A=N=G=U=A=G=E*, "Some Recent British Poetry Magazines" (June 1980)—which is a useful partial listing of small press magazines and the authors whose work they published from 1975 through September 1979—what follows is a comprehensive index of proper names in the newsletter and its supplements.

Catullus (Gaius Valerius C.), 25, 26, 101, 152

Caudwell, Christopher, 125

Cavell, Stanley, 192, 211, 249–51, 307, 308, 541

Caxton, William, 525

Celan, Paul, 404

Cézanne, Paul, 18, 152, 497

Chang Chung-yuan, 203

Chaplin, Charlie, 132

Chardin, Jean-Baptiste-Siméon, 396

Chaucer, Geoffrey, 169

Cheek, Chris, 203, 253, 268–71, 394, 509–18

Chesterfield, Philip Dormer Stanhope, 418

Chibeau, Edmund, 31

Child, Abigail, 79–81, 203, 322–23, 451–53

Chinca, Mark, 253, 271–73

Cholmondeley, Thomas, 419

Chomsky, Noam, 87, 522, 523, 532

Christo (C. Vladimirov Javacheff), 229

Chustka, Edith, 203

Clair, Jean, 271

Claire, Paula, 393

Clarey, M. Elizabeth, 203

Clark, Carl, 30

Clark, Thomas A., 138–41, 318–19, 486

Claudel, Camille, 117, 118

Cobbing, Bob, 393–95

Coleridge, Samuel Taylor, 47, 243

Colette (Sidonie-Gabrielle Colette), 243

Collom, Jack, 31

Compton, Susan P., 204

Connor, Bruce, 396

Cook, Geoffrey, 149–50

Cooke, Dorian, 208

Coolidge, Clark, 21, 30, 31, 32, 43, 72, 77, 112, 113, 125, 149, 226–28, 319–20, 367, 373, 380–81, 462, 470, 474, 480, 481, 485, 531, 539

Corbett, William (Bill), 57–59, 316–17, 333

Corbin, Henry, 211

Corman, Cid, 31, 85

Cornell, Joseph, 204

Cory, Jean-Jacques, 30

Cowan, Marianne, 205

Coward, Rosalind, 280

Cowell, Henry, 72

Crane, Hart, 52, 382

Creeley, Robert, 66, 85, 120, 124, 168, 203–4, 293, 398, 420, 421, 430, 557

Cromwell, Oliver, 199

Crosby, Harry, 78–79

Crusoe, Robinson, 266

Culler, Jonathan, 86, 87, 124

Cummings, E. E., 558

Cunningham, Merce, 126

Daguerre, Louis, 83, 173

Dahlberg, Edward, 495, 504

Darragh, Tina, 30, 195–96, 320, 346, 359, 373, 557

Darwin, Charles, 24, 333

Davenport, Guy, 124

Davey, Frank, 469

Davidson, Joseph, 418

Davidson, Michael, 30, 31, 86, 124, 157, 158–60, 273–74

Davie, Donald, 462

Davies, Alan, 31, 33–35, 43, 103–4, 127, 144–45, 156, 197, 228–30,

252, 253, 274, 304, 305–7, 342, 346, 364, 409–16, 427, 464–66, 467, 532, 544, 555, 557

Davis, Herbert, 205

Davis, Lydia, 241, 429

Dawson, Fielding, 500, 529

Debord, Guy, 281, 282

Debussy, Claude, 347,

de Campos, Augusto, 558

de Certeau, Michel, 281

de Chavannes, Puvis, 151

de Kooning, Willem, 58, 205

Delaney, Samuel R., 381

Deleuze, Gilles, 76, 125, 207, 210, 267, 270, 280, 281, 423

della Robia, Luca, 249

de Machault, Guillaume, 68

Denby, Edwin, 188

de Rougemont, Denis, 213

Derrida, Jacques, 54, 85, 86, 87, 125, 126, 195, 204, 205, 210, 212, 221, 290, 308, 389, 470

de Sade, Donatien Alphonse François, Marquise, 69, 241, 281

de Saussure, Ferdinand, 85, 118, 124, 470

Descartes, René, 84

Detienne, Marcel, 339

Dewdney, Christopher, 31, 103–4, 278, 319, 320, 399–402

Dewey, John, 454

Dickens, Charles, 355

Dickinson, Emily, 57, 205, 504, 551

Diebenkorn, Richard, 248

DiPalma, Ray, 30, 31, 43, 91–92, 94, 113, 138–40, 184, 204, 228–30, 367, 416, 485, 495–97

Dix, Gregory, 241

Dixson, Robert J., 203

MacAdams, Phoebe, 29
Macaulay, Thomas Babington, 242
MacFadden, Dave, 486
Machs, Ernst, 124
MacInnis, Jamie, 31
Mack, Connie, 102
Mac Low, Jackson, 29, 68–69, 70–72, 157, 165–66, 204, 207–8, 226, 297–99, 393, 439–42, 486, 548, 557
MacPherson, James, 419
Mailer, Norman, 529
Malevich, Kazimir Severinovich, 61
Mallarmé, Stéphane, 118, 429
Malone, Kirby, 30, 31, 208–9, 253, 268–71, 355–57, 422–24
Mandel, Tom, 30, 210, 246, 558
Mao Tse Tung, 62, 439
Marcuse, Herbert, 267
Marin, Louis, 86, 281
Marinetti, Filippo Tommaso, 186, 435
Maritain, Jacques, 462
Márquez, Gabriel García, 211
Martin, Richard M., 183
Marx, Karl, 65, 77, 87, 91, 97, 104, 118, 124, 125, 126, 205, 207, 210, 212, 241, 242, 267, 271, 274, 275, 278, 280, 287, 288, 290, 325, 365, 386, 417, 435, 440, 441, 471, 476, 499, 502, 522, 523, 532, 533, 536, 543, 547, 549
Mason, Chris, 30, 208–9, 253, 282–83, 422–24
Masters, Gregory, 30, 330–31
Matthews, Harry, 500, 529
Mattlin, Sharon, 71
Maxwell, Robert J., 523
Mayakofsky, Vladimir, 115, 329

Mayer, Bernadette, 31, 32, 35, 41, 72, 73–76, 119, 193–95, 210, 303, 367, 432–33, 455, 503, 508
Mayer, Peter, 117–120, 393
Mayer, Rosemary, 126
McCaffery, Steve, 31, 38–39, 43, 65–66, 97–98, 124, 157, 162, 184, 185–88, 210, 242, 253, 356, 416, 469, 470, 472, 496
McClure, Michael, 55
McInerney, Brian, 30, 31
McLuhan, Marshall, 87, 523
McNaughton, Duncan, 331
Melnick, David, 27–28, 28–29, 424, 470, 475, 480, 481
Melville, Herman, 82, 145, 258, 266, 504, 548
Mengham, Rod, 179–81, 343–44, 403–5
Menippus (M. of Gadara), 193
Merleau-Ponty, Maurice, 84, 213, 243, 323
Merrill, James, 366
Messager, Annette, 300
Messerli, Douglas, 30, 31, 90, 193–95, 210–11, 373
Metcalf, Paul, 32, 43, 125, 500, 529
Metz, Christian, 86, 126, 210
Metzel, Nancy, 210
Meyer, Thomas, 31, 124, 126, 332
Milazzo, Richard, 339–40, 387, 388
Mill, Henri, 39
Miller, George A., 86
Miller, Henry, 204
Miller, Jeffrey, 384
Miller, J. Hillis, 210
Mills, Neil, 486
Milton, John, 23, 336, 403
Minkowski, Eugène, 210

Mitchell,, John, 419
Moholy-Nagy, Laszlo, 60, 61, 127
Molière (Jean-Baptiste Poquelin), 186
Moncrieff, C. K. Scott, 205
Monk, Meredith, 125, 373
Monk, Thelonious, 373
Montague, Mary Wortley, 419
Moore, Marianne, 337
Morgenstern, Christian, 186
Morris, Ivan, 206
Morris, Meaghan, 280
Morris, Robert, 85
Morris, Sally, 271
Morris, William, 333
Morrissette, Bruce, 479, 485
Morrow, Charlie, 31
Mottram, Eric, 31, 114–15, 203
Muybridge, Eadweard, 192
Myers, Rita, 300
Myles, Eileen, 30

Nabokov, Vladimir, 118, 119
Nations, Opal, 30
Neruda, Pablo, 287
Newhall, Beaumont, 61
Newman, Barnett, 205, 206, 374
Newton, Thomas, 419
Niblock, Phil, 71
Niccolai, Giulia, 332
Nichol, B. P. (bpnichol), 30, 188, 486
Niedecker, Lorine, 124, 152, 318, 333
Nietzsche, Friedrich, 125, 205, 266, 267, 281, 344, 387, 404
Noël, Bernard, 203, 213–15
North, Charles, 31, 211, 335–37, 395–97
Notley, Alice, 30, 41

Williams, William Carlos, 21, 53, 87, 101, 130, 146, 150, 155, 169, 195, 204, 207, 500
Wilson, John, 31
Wilson, Robert, 86, 126
Wilson, Robert Anton, 207
Winch, Terence, 31, 32
Wittgenstein, Ludwig, 22, 50, 57, 76, 91, 124, 132, 139, 204, 211, 249, 261, 295, 307, 308, 386, 410, 429, 473, 477, 482, 497, 499, 526, 532

Wölfflin, Heinrich, 208
Wolfson, Louis, 210, 211
Women Writers Union, 442–43
Wood, Evelyn, 498
Woolf, Douglas, 31, 500, 529
Woolf, Virginia, 208, 445
Wordsworth, William, 152, 380
Wright, Jeff, 31

Yates, Frances, 211
Yau, John, 31
Yeats, William Butler, 336, 396, 397

Young, Geoffrey, 149
Young, Karl, 31, 391–93
Youngblood, Gene, 203

Zekowski, Arlene, 30
Zeno (Z. of Elea), 209
Zukofsky, Celia, 102, 223
Zukofsky, Louis, 27, 87, 101–2, 132, 146, 152, 153, 161, 210, 216, 222–24, 287, 333, 367, 383, 498, 499, 523

CPSIA information can be obtained
at www.ICGtesting.com
Printed in the USA
LVHW060326030620
657246LV00022B/318